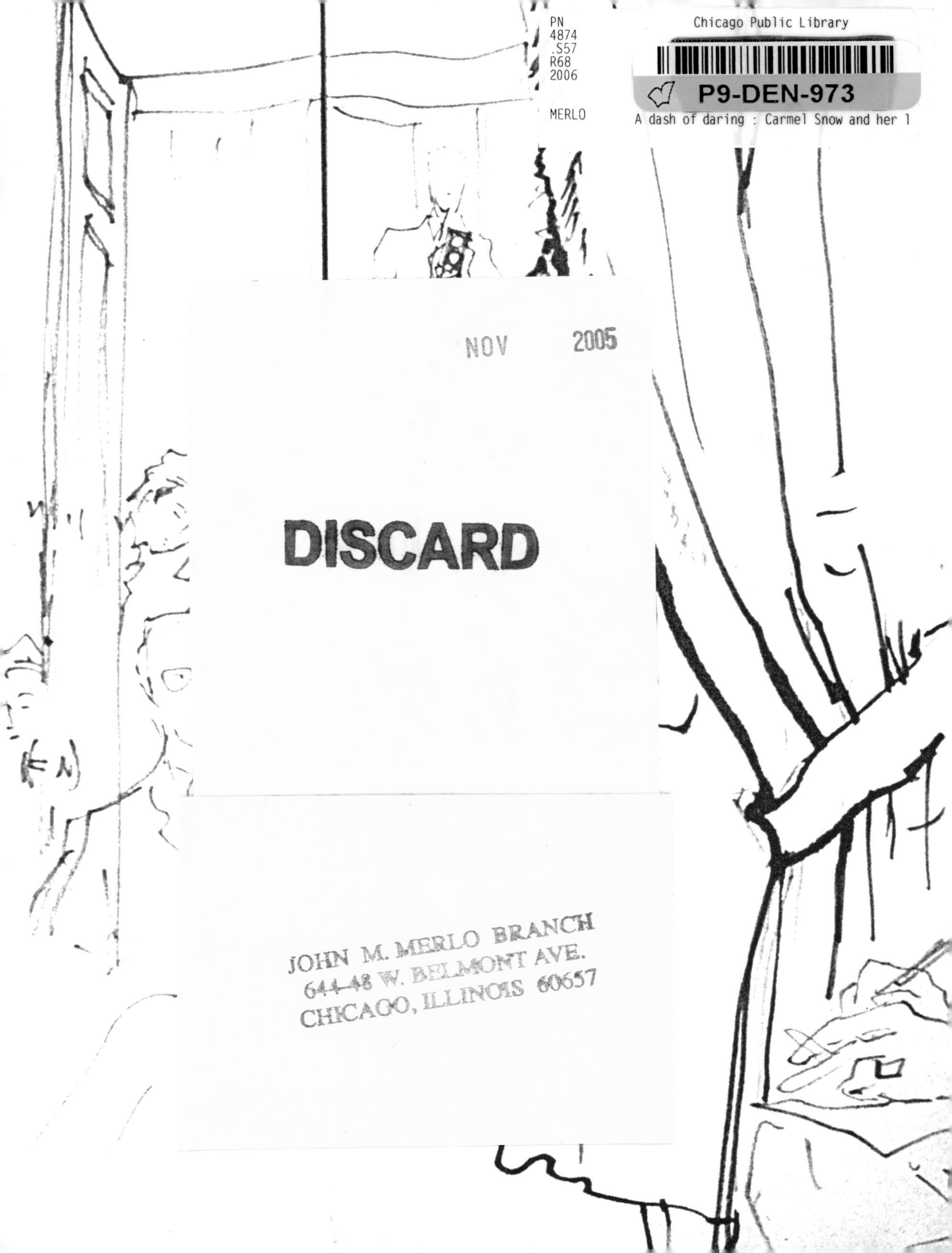

A Dash *of* Daring

à Mrs. Snow de mon ♥
N.Y. 1937
Vertès

A DASH *of* DARING

Carmel Snow and Her Life in Fashion, Art, and Letters

PENELOPE ROWLANDS

ATRIA BOOKS
NEW YORK LONDON TORONTO SYDNEY

TITLE PAGE: Watercolor of Carmel Snow by Marcel Vertès, inscribed "To Mrs Snow of my heart," 1937
Courtesy of Gillette Piper

PAGE VIII: Carmel Snow with Louise Dahl-Wolfe and model Dorian Leigh at the Paris studio of *Harper's Bazaar*, 1953

ATRIA BOOKS
1230 Avenue of the Americas
New York, NY 10020

Library of Congress Cataloging-in-Publication Data
Rowlands, Penelope.
A dash of daring : Carmel Snow and her life in fashion, art, and letters / Penelope Rowlands.
p. cm.
Includes bibliographical references and index.
1. Snow, Carmel, 1890–1961. Periodical editors—United States—Biography. 3. Harper's bazaar. I. Title.
PN4874.S57 R68 2006
070.5'1 [B]—dc22 2005053637

ISBN-13: 978-0-7434-8045-1
ISBN-10: 0-7434-8045-7

First Atria Books hardcover edition November 2005

10 9 8 7 6 5 4 3 2 1

Designed by Joel Avirom, Jason Snyder, and Meghan Day Healey

Printed in the United States of America

Permissions appear on page 561.

For my mother,
Arden James White,
and for
Julian

Elegance is good taste,
plus *a dash of daring.*

—CARMEL SNOW

contents

preface

I was on one of my first jobs on Seventh Avenue. The company was called Harmay. It was very inexpensive: dresses cost a couple of hundred dollars or so. Every designer was put in the back room, not brought out to the showroom.

I was a great fan of Mrs. Snow's and I'd invited her to the collection. She was my first idol. She made up her own mind about everything; she was a woman of her own beliefs. I had nothing but admiration for that.

Surprisingly enough, she came. I wasn't allowed in the showroom; I had to watch from a peephole in the back. When she arrived, I was overwhelmed. I was so flattered that a woman so knowledgeable would come to my show. I was thrilled to death.

She had a way of having a couple of martinis with lunch, then falling asleep halfway through the show. I saw she was snoozing. I thought she was bored, but then in the September 1955 issue of Harper's Bazaar, *a belted jersey suit of mine opened the magazine. It was one of the most thrilling moments of my life.*

They didn't give me credit, but they didn't give anyone credit then. It was a simple suit with a jersey Peter Pan collar, buttons down the front, and two big pockets. It was neat and simple and she chose it. It was the catalyst that lit the fire of better things.

I don't know if she'd heard that there was a new designer at Harmay who was worth watching. My clothes were not in the best stores.

I don't know how she got wind of it, but I'm so grateful for it. I never question good things. I was so in the background then that I never questioned anything, but I was thrilled to death. It helped create the fever; that's all I can say. Otherwise, I might never have become known.

People began to make something mythical of Mrs. Snow and that myth remains. She was a goddess to me.

My life has changed since that first encounter. I can now go into the showroom.

—GEOFFREY BEENE

IN FACT, THE SUIT COST ninety dollars and, thanks to the keen eye of magazine editor Carmel Snow, who saw a gem glinting among the offerings of a lackluster fashion house, it did end up in one of New York's finer stores, Henri Bendel. Its publication in *Harper's Bazaar* gave its twenty-seven-year-old designer, Geoffrey Beene, the jolt of confidence—not to mention the impressive tear sheet—he needed to jump-start his career. Before long, in the way things tended to happen when Carmel was around, the young man who had been forbidden to leave Harmay's back room was on his way to becoming one of the most revered names in American fashion.

163

The American Openings: Autumn, 1955

• The change, in America, is right on the surface—and under it. New, beautiful materials and a new "invisible" way of tailoring them: a tailoring so subtle and perfected you hardly know it's there. • This year's suit is a little eased, shaped by an adroit, marvelous cut to barely clasp the figure. • It's wearing a small fur collar, astrakhan or beaver, laid flat to the neck like a man's collar. • It's probably wearing a polished-up leather belt. • It's made of one of the new, thick, mat-finish wools—Loden cloth, maybe—and if it isn't brown, it's olive. Or, quite possibly, white. • The suit after dark is lighting up the scene in the furry, deep-piled glossiness of broadcloth, or in satin. There's a little snowfall of mink at the neck, emerald satin pumps below the hemline. (And day *or* evening, there's likely to be a slender slip of a dress beneath the jacket.) • This year's coat might be a shaggy, steamer-blanket plaid. Or: glittering metallic brocade, small-sleeved and cut up high under the bosom in the style of the Directoire. Lengths of both coats and jackets are the new unpredictables—anything goes, from really short to seven-eighths to just shorter-than-long. • This year's skirt is easy to know: it's slightly belled to hang round, not straight, not bouffant. • This year's dress is the little black dress—an important aspect of the new sense of balance, of composure, of dressing with discretion and chic. • Hats? Either they're hattier by far—big, puffy fur berets—or they're modest little nothings, perched like miniature fezzes on the top of the head. • Gloves? Bags? Shoes? Their news is in the tailoring, too, and in a glittering new *luxe* after dark. The longer, more delicate glove; the deep-plunging bag; the day-and-evening pump that's cut like a jewel and colored to match—watch for all of these in the pages of this new autumn issue. • Above left: The belted suit in black wool jersey, the jacket longer and carrying its pockets right on the hip—right were they belong, this year. By Harmay; Jasco jersey. About $90. Henri Bendel; Strawbridge and Clothier. • Above right: The belled skirt, shaped out below a low-belted overblouse in salt-and-pepper tweed. By Harvey Berin. About $95. Lord and Taylor; Bramson's. The "hattier" hat: a shallow-brimmed beret by Hattie Carnegie. • Pointing up the new directions in fashion: Early American weathervanes from the Downtown Gallery, New York.

Many lives were similarly transformed by encounters with the slight, impeccably dressed Irishwoman—a revolutionary in a pillbox hat—who edited *Harper's Bazaar* for a quarter of a century, from the early 1930s to the mid-1950s. Some of these encounters were glancing, such as the life-changing moment recounted above; others took the form of deep, unswerving friendship. Many people Carmel helped along have become so well known that their last names alone suffice—Vreeland, Avedon, Capote, Steichen, Warhol, Bacall, Cartier-Bresson, and more. And such golden fashion names as Dior and, most crucially, Balenciaga—both houses that are still reinventing themselves, with great success today—owe some of their staying power to the passionate patronage of the woman whom just about everyone knew as Mrs. Snow.

"She was a genius at picking other people of genius," as one of her nieces, Kate White, puts it. She was tiny and alert, almost frighteningly observant. If she thought you had talent—and she could sniff it out as quickly and unerringly as a trained dog routs out a truffle—she would open the world to you. The famous fashion photographer Louise Dahl-Wolfe, who called her "the magic Carmel Snow" and "the greatest magazine editor ever," credited the preeminence of *Harper's Bazaar* in her time to the way Snow had of keeping her contributors on a very long leash. No leash, actually. "She trusted her editors and artists completely, and fought commercial interests to produce a magazine of quality."

Even today, people in fashion all over the world speak of her with reverence. They may laugh at her foibles now; they may have fallen victim to her legendary toughness then; but they can't deny the extraordinary scope of her influence. And, besides, she was *fun,* with a wicked sense of humor.

Her mandate went way beyond fashion. As she so famously said, it was to produce a magazine "for well-dressed women *with well-dressed minds.*" Decades after her death, Carmel Snow's fingerprints are everywhere: on photography, literature, art, design. She worshipped "top quality"—words she repeated like a mantra all her life—in whatever form she found it, and she brought it to her pages in many guises, month after month. She cased the world constantly, as fashion editors do, looking

OPPOSITE: **The suit (*left*) that launched a career: Geoffrey Beene for Harmay, *Harper's Bazaar,* September 1955**

for the new, the next, the best. But she netted more than just amazing clothes (while, of course, doing that, too). Her *Harper's Bazaar* fearlessly tossed together the ingredients of its time, among them fashion, of course, but also distant cultures, surrealism and other art movements, social reform, even war.

Readers might have come to the magazine from deep in America; they might have retrieved their copies from mailboxes at the end of long, rural driveways or from newsstands in far-flung cities, but what they found within it—fashions by Elsa Schiaparelli, drawings by Jean Cocteau, interiors by Jean-Michel Frank—was always provocative and new. Can the editor of a fashion magazine be said to have brought the best of modern art and design to our shores? I'll dare that statement here. And eye-opening fiction, as well. As Jessica Daves, a long-ago editor of *Vogue*—*Harper's Bazaar*'s greatest rival—put it:

> *Towards the end of the 1930s the* Bazaar *began also to publish fiction from some of the most noticed writers of the day, and developed as a magazine for young intellectuals looking for the next step in writing, as well as for ladies knowledgeable about fashion.*

And, crucially, this vision wasn't just wrapped up and delivered to New York and Los Angeles; it went inland to the harder markets: Cheyenne, Omaha, St. Paul.

In the decades since her death, Carmel Snow's reputation has remained undiminished in the fashion world. But for the general public, she's fanned out toward the horizon, almost vanishing from view. Years have gone by, but she needs to be brought back for our consideration once more. For, working steadily behind the scenes, with great joy and humor, she played a part—an essential one—in shaping our world.

A Dash *of* Daring

chippendale and cottage

Out of Ireland we came . . .
—W. B. Yeats

"IT COULD BE HAPPENING" is the time-honored way that the Irish stories begin, and the story of Carmel Snow, who just may have been the greatest fashion editor ever, begins in a way that is about as Irish as any story could possibly get—at least one that played out in New York and, crucially, in Paris, far more extensively than in Ireland. It could be happening that in Dalkey, a coastal village eight miles southeast of Dublin, one evening in 1887—August 27, to be exact—labor pains caused a respectable matron named Annie White to rise up, as majestic as an ocean liner, from the table where a convivial, family-packed dinner party was taking place.

OPPOSITE: Annie Mayne White

ABOVE: Peter White with his son Tom, c. 1885

Dressed in one of the tentlike, floor-length gowns of the day, her habitual train sweeping behind her, this huge-breasted, amply built woman climbed into a waiting carriage, her youthful-looking husband, Peter White, in tow, and headed home to Saint Justin's, their large house overlooking the slate-blue Dublin Bay, where she gave birth to a spritelike creature, their third child and younger daughter, whom the couple piously named for Our Lady of Mount Carmel. The infant was baptized a week later at the Church of the Assumption of the Blessed Virgin Mary in Dalkey, a tiny, picturesque town that would be later known for its artistic inhabitants, James Joyce and George Bernard Shaw among them, but was then a fairly sleepy place, ancient in origin, and home to not just one castle but two.

The child's earliest years were spent in a constellation of six children in an atmosphere that a relative described as "both Chippendale and cottage." Carmel's parents had married in September 1883, in yet another Dublin suburb, Rathmines. Their union had been quickly blessed with a child—Tom was born just over a year later—and from then on others arrived in quick succession. Christine Mary came next, in July 1886, and then Carmel, whose middle name was also Mary, the following summer. Three other children—Peter Desmond (known as Desmond), Victor Gerald, and James—followed, all of them male and spaced about a year apart. The last was born in 1892.

Annie White's branch of the family was the more prominent one—"Chippendale," if you will; her father was a prosperous merchant named Thomas Mayne who later served as a member of Parliament for eighteen years. Peter White's side, the "cottage" one, was literally more down to earth: his late father, also named Thomas, had been a farmer. From both directions, the children were inescapably Irish—never an uncomplicated thing to be.

Ireland had been a "lordship" of the English crown since it was conquered by that country in the 1100s. Over the centuries, the extent of its Englishness had waxed and waned. By the time the young Whites were born, Irish nationalist feelings were running

Christine (*left*), Carmel, and Tom White in the 1880s

strong. Charles Stuart Parnell and other leaders were campaigning for home rule, which called for increased autonomy from Britain. It was a cause that Thomas Mayne, Annie White's father, whom an American newspaper described as belonging "to the old guard of Irish patriots," vehemently supported. His son-in-law, Peter White, born of the soil, was also a Parnellite, And he counted a prominent activist of the era, Michael Davitt, among his friends. (Davitt was, in fact, the Whites' landlord in Dalkey.)

A photograph, probably taken in the early 1890s, shows Peter White to be a handsome, solidly built fellow with light eyes, a long mustache—almost a requirement of the era—and a deep cleft in his chin, something he seems to have bequeathed to many of his male descendants. He was Irish to the core. In his work for the Irish Woolen Manufacturing and Export Company in Dublin, he aimed to resurrect a once-thriving national industry that, thanks to stiff tariffs and competition, notably from Scotland, had been in danger of dying out. Harris tweed had long eclipsed Donegal.

Ironically, by building a reputation for reviving dying industries in a country that seemed full of them, White ensured that his children's lives would unfold outside of Ireland. But none of that was clear, of course, when he was asked by the viceroy of Ireland, Lord Aberdeen, and his wife, the former Ishbel (the Gaelic variation of Isabel) Maria Marjoribanks, to be honorary secretary of the Irish Industries Association. (Lady Aberdeen was its president.)

It was once again, as it had so often been, a desperate time for Ireland, and the Aberdeens were determined to help. Together, they came up with a plan to use the small, craftsy things—from lacework to bog wood ornaments—that had been produced forever in Ireland's far-flung cottages and convents to turn the country's fortunes around. Besides reviving the country's traditional crafts, they wanted also to provide training in their production, thereby ensuring that some of its desperate citizenry had at least piecemeal work. Along the way, it was hoped, Ireland's image would be enhanced. "Irish goods were not sought after by the people who wanted the best things" is the delicate way the *New York Times* phrased the matter (in a 1911 article), "but in 1886, with the coming to Dublin of the Earl of Aberdeen, a movement for improving and extending the sale of Irish products began to take hold."

A Scotsman, Lord Aberdeen had recently been appointed to his post by the English Liberal prime minister William Ewart Gladstone. Newly in love with Ireland, he and his wife went straight to work on the seemingly intractable problems of their new country. For Ishbel, it was second nature to throw herself into a cause. Like her husband, she was the product of an aristocratic Scottish family. Born in 1857, she possessed a first-class intellect (she was said to have taught herself to read at the age of three) that, sadly, can't quite be described as irrepressible. While she longed to go to Girton College, Cambridge University's only school for women—in truth, the perfect place for her—she was prevented from doing so by her very traditional father. After her marriage, in 1877, Ishbel began what would become her life's work, aiding the poor. There seemed to be no limit to her charity.

The Emerald Isle was "still in the grip of poverty such as America has never known, not even in a depression," as Carmel later described it. It was rife with struggle of one sort or another. While the great famines of earlier in the century had subsided, the country was still reeling from an agricultural crisis that had climaxed in the 1870s. Much of its population was desperately poor. And the home rule struggle seemed perpetual; anarchy, or at least violence, flared up intermittently, notably after the Land League was banned in 1881. "Ireland is laid on us to do all in our power for her forever," Ishbel wrote in her diary. Before long, she and Peter White were putting in time on the country's unpaved, back-country roads, tirelessly scouting out both crafts and workers.

Peter White was perfect for the job. He was charismatic and hardworking, and he didn't hesitate to deploy his considerable charm in the service of the mission at hand. Before too long, he was making frequent trips to the United States, something he'd first done in the name of Irish wool. An article in the *Citizen,* a Chicago newspaper, gives an indication of how breathlessly this dashing Irishman—still in his thirties—was received in the New World. "Ireland never selected a more fortunate representative than Mr. Peter White," it reads. "His amiable and sensitive manner wins confidence everywhere."

For all their love of the place, the Aberdeens didn't last long in Ireland. They were just one domino in a row of them, and they all toppled over, one after another, in a long, jagged line. First, home rule lost in the House of Commons. Then Gladstone's Liberal Party collapsed. Its prime minister was out. And so, of course, were the Aberdeens. But in their time across the Irish Sea, they'd won over the desperate populace. As they headed back to England, people lined the streets, some weeping extravagantly; at one point, the couple's horses were unhitched and their carriage pulled along, ecstatically, by the crowd. "The scene in Dublin on his leavetaking after the fall of the Gladstone cabinet is said to have been such as never before witnessed since the days of O'Connel," the *Chicago Times* reported. The Aberdeens returned this loyalty by continuing their various pro-Irish endeavors after they'd returned home.

In 1888, when announcement was made that the World's Columbian Exposition of 1893—soon to be known universally, if not correctly, as the Chicago World's Fair—was being put together, the Aberdeens seized the moment, heading to the United States with both Whites in tow to raise money to finance an exhibit of Irish exports at the fair, which Peter White would organize and oversee. For the next few years, he and Lady Aberdeen traveled all over Ireland, visiting workers and meeting with officials, including the lord mayor of Dublin, to build support for the project. White made several visits to Chicago, and by 1892 had acquired the fairly grand title of Irish commissioner to the World's Fair.

The Aberdeens hoped to return to Ireland if Gladstone returned to power. But when he did, in 1892, some last-minute political maneuvering resulted in someone else being named Ireland's viceroy instead. As a consolation prize, the prime minister awarded Aberdeen the post of governor general of Canada. The Irish Pavilion would go forward, but with much less involvement from the Aberdeens.

In February 1893, just a few months before the fair was to open, White and Lady Aberdeen set out for one last tour, this time to the South "to pick the 'colleens' who would represent the Irish industries," as Carmel wrote. But then, as it so often does in Irish tales, death played its hand. White had already had lung trouble—the whole family tended toward the tubercular, as his oldest child, Thomas White, later recalled—and the travel, by rail and carriage, including an open-air version called an "outside-car," was grueling. As they were finishing their trip, "Mr. White felt himself seriously ill, but his love for the cause he had espoused and his indomitable spunk prevented him from giving in," an Irish paper wrote. On March 15, the *Chicago New World* announced that Mr. White would be late arriving at the fair. And then, quite suddenly, word came that he wouldn't be coming at all. "He caught pneumonia," Carmel wrote, "in those days a desperately serious illness, and a few weeks later he was dead."

His death, at the age of forty-three, on April 7, 1893, was reported in papers in both Ireland and the United States. "In the township of Dalkey there was universal evidence of the sorrow of the people," one Irish paper reported. Telegrams and letters flooded into Saint Justin's, and hundreds turned up for his funeral and burial in Dublin's Glasnevin Cemetery. It was a fitting place for a nationalist, having been founded earlier in the century in response to England's repressive penal laws, which had sharply curtailed the practice of numerous Catholic rites, even those involving the burial of the dead.

White left six children. His third born, Carmel, was only five. For the rest of her life, this toughest of magazine editors would attribute her own thick hide to the sight of her father "laid out like a waxen image" on the drawing room table. It was a vision that would haunt her for years: "The very thought of death was something I had to put out of my mind, and it may be that my ability to concentrate, to turn my mind, quickly and entirely, from one subject to the next, is the earliest lesson I learned."

She learned a thing or two, too, about strength from her mother, who, upon finding herself a widow with six children, made a daring decision. In a letter written on April 11, 1893, Ishbel wrote to Annie White on crested notepaper, acknowledging a suggestion from this very recent widow that she take her late husband's place at the world's fair. (He'd died only a few days before.) Lady Aberdeen responded with enthusiasm: "I believe this may prove best for you, as well as best for the enterprise. But you must not hurry yourself to settle anything—just lie fallow while you can. But if you do decide on going, please believe how I shall personally rejoice. . . ."

No "lying fallow" took place. Instead, the new widow moved with lightning speed, taking Saint Justin's apart, storing its contents among friends and family. She first sent her daughters to live at Loretto Abbey, a girls' school run by the Loretto order of nuns, whose convent, built in 1842, was just next door to the White home. The girls were too young for school, in their mother's estimation (Carmel was not yet six, Christine just a year older), so the convent functioned as a kind of holding pen. Even so, Carmel learned to read there and always remembered writing out her first words, "Loretto Abbey," in a tentative scrawl. Her other siblings were billeted among other relatives in and around Dublin.

Whether Annie White agonized over her decision to cross the Atlantic without her family can only be guessed; there's no evidence that she worried unduly over anything. Instead—"a feminist before feminism" in one granddaughter's words—she tended to plow assuredly ahead. The girls and their youngest brother, James Mayne White (later known as Jim), were next sent to live with their grandfather, Thomas Mayne, and their "darling grandmother," as Carmel called her, Susannah, at the couple's stately home, Cremorne, in the Dublin suburb of Terenure.

Reached by a long tree-lined driveway, Cremorne was a Georgian house with a limestone facade and a regal, stepped entranceway. Set on acres of land, it had an unmistakable grandeur and was as hivelike and full of intrigue as a dacha in a Chekhov play. Its shifting population included cousins, endless aunts and uncles of varying degrees of benevolence, and "the terrifying, Jove-like figure" that was grandfather Mayne himself. As for Carmel's three other siblings, Tom, Desmond, and Victor, they were sent to stay with Peter White's sister, Lizzie, who owned a shop in Clonalvy, and was forever complaining that the Maynes were grander than the Whites. To the horror of her nephews, this manifested itself in an almost obsessive attention to comportment. "She pounded 'good manners' into my brothers until they were sick of the thought of them," Carmel recalled.

With her children squared away, their tough, fearless mother set forth. She had work to do, a figure to cut, and she was certainly not going to resign herself to an Irish widow's fate, living under the wing of her domineering father, or any other man for that matter. A photograph of her taken at about this time shows her to be tight-lipped and determined. While she looks severe, even plain, by anecdotal accounts she was lovely—otherwise sensible American journalists seemed to swoon, at least verbally, in her presence. "And a mighty pretty woman is she," one reporter wrote (quite unnecessarily, I might add) as the fair began. The *Chicago Herald* commented rapturously on that "sweet-faced woman with her dimples and her Irish bloom."

Carmel's more sober description was of

> *a very magnetic woman, with hazel gray eyes, a dimpled smile, and auburn hair braided around her head like a crown. She was vain of figure (in my childhood she always had a train sweeping behind her) but it was her wit, which lost nothing in the telling, that made her all her life the center of an unusual group of friends.*

From her first weeks in the United States, when Annie befriended the great Canadian stage actress Margaret Anglin, then on a national tour, she attracted people who mattered.

"The Maynes were all beautiful," one relative, David Sheehy, reports. "They were tall and dark and very good looking." Both Carmel and Christine felt their looks compared unfavorably with their mother's. Their hair was limp, by comparison, and Carmel recalled her mother cutting the eyelashes of both girls in the hope that they might grow back thicker. (They didn't.) By contrast, White's hair, piled on top of her head in one photograph, is indeed luxuriant, as is her almost unbelievably complicated-looking lace-and-silk gown. (At some point, she began

Carmel's grandparents Thomas Mayne, M.P., and Susannah Mayne

wearing a wig; Irish relatives recall her visiting the Old Country with a whole trunk of them.) But mostly it's the extraordinary hourglass figure one notices—the waist not tiny, exactly, but trim enough, especially relative to the enormous bustline straining above. White looks centered, hardly a concept floating around in her day. You sense that she could take on anything. She came, as Sheehy reports, "from very determined stock."

The voyage she made was simple enough, traveling by boat westward across the Atlantic, but in fact it was a radical act "in that period when women, particularly upper-class Irishwomen, seldom ventured beyond the protection of their families." The odds against her were daunting, yet she bulldozed ahead, gathering so much momentum that failure scarcely seemed possible. Accompanied by her sister Agnes, White sailed on May 4, 1893, from Queenstown (now more commonly known by its Celtic name, Cobh) in County Cork. Given the era, it was only natural that her father, the family patriarch, would keep an eye on his widowed daughter by sending one of his four then-unmarried daughters along. The wonder is that she was allowed to go at all.

By the time the sisters sailed into New York Harbor, then caught a train to Chicago, Lady Aberdeen was already at the Irish Industrial Village, also known as the Irish Village, readying things for the grand opening less than a week away. Situated off a long boulevard grandly called the Midway Plaisance—a hugely popular feature that seemed to contain all the known world in the form of African towns, mosques, medieval villages, Polynesian huts, pagodas, and more—the Village had "the best and most prominent position in the fair," in Countess Aberdeen's estimation.

It, too, was exotic. Lady Aberdeen had loaded on the Irishness. To enter it, you passed through a reproduction of the doorway of a chapel that had been built on the Rock of Cashel by Cormac, a twelfth-century Irish king, then through a copy of the ancient cloisters of Muckross Abbey in Killarney. And that was just the beginning. Beyond, there lay a vast, circular lawn with a Celtic cross at its center that was surrounded by a ring of cottages—some transplanted from Ireland, others just copied, most of them thatched. In the distance lay the showstopper: Blarney Castle, or rather a copy of it on a two-thirds scale. It was Ireland in miniature, and "visitors were enchanted with it," Carmel reported.

Lady Aberdeen had moved into the first cottage near the entrance, a replica of Roseneath Cottage in Queenstown, which she and Peter White had visited on one of their last trips together. It had a deep thatch and latticed pillars and a sign over the front door reading "Cead Mile Failte," Gaelic for "a thousand welcomes." Inside, its walls were as green as the Old Country itself, and it was full to the brim with Irish antiques. The other dwellings around it, similarly charming, contained examples of traditional Celtic crafts. One was devoted to lacework, another to jewelry, yet another formed a concert area where Irish music was played.

According to the *Chicago Post,* a fourth structure was filled "with Irish rich bog turf which looks, as our Irish Americans put it, fit to eat." (To each his own.) This dirt, to name it for what it is, was actually for sale—for a princely dollar per square—along with such other native Irishisms as blackthorns and shamrocks.

There's something unique about the Irish love of their country's earth, the "ould sod," as they fondly call it. The rest of us may not understand it, but customers with cash, mainly nostalgic immigrants, certainly did. And business was brisk. Yet another cottage took the bog further; here, young men whittled ornaments out of its famous oak trees, offering them for sale along with Galway marble and, endlessly, more lace.

The Irish Village was formally dedicated on May 11 in what the *Irish Times* described as "a brilliant scene." A few weeks later, Countess Aberdeen transferred its management over to Annie White, before crossing the Atlantic to join her husband, who was soon to assume his Canadian post. From then on, the village was hers. Peter White may have been "the guardian angel of the Village," as one paper called him, but his widow was the one who "made it the hit of the fair," as Carmel wrote. Annie had a hand in everything, revising things constantly, restlessly seeking perfection when others might have given up. No detail was too small. When it occurred to her that she'd forgotten to include wonderfully intricate Carrickmacross lace in the exhibit, she telegraphed back to Ireland "to get all the cottages of County Monaghan to work making lace," a relative, Helen Sheehy, recalled.

White's first home in America was a comely thatched-roof cottage that she and Agnes shared. It was full of antiques, shipped by the elder Maynes from Ireland so that their daughters might feel at home. The stories Agnes brought back from the fair delighted her Irish relatives for years. She recalled meeting Buffalo Bill, giving rise to an oft-repeated rumor within the family that Annie and the American frontier scout and showman, whose real name was William F. Cody, had had a romance. (Curiously, Buffalo Bill allegedly also crossed paths with another larger-than-life female—Diana Vreeland—many years later. "What chic old Bill had! With his beard he looked like Edward VII. . . .")

Stories about the Irish Village took up a disproportionate amount of space in the press. White was mediagenic, as were many of the hundreds who worked for her, most imported from Ireland to dance jigs, spin yarn, and more. The young girls, in particular, were notoriously fun loving, and their pranks—pouring water on sleeping tramps, imitating roosters so that most of the fair reported early to work—were covered, with scant amusement, by the local papers.

And then there was the little matter of the big rock. The Blarney Stone has long been reputed to make "anyone who kisses it a great talker," according to Carmel, "so no Irishman is going to miss an opportunity like that if he can help it." When it arrived, the stone provoked enormous excitement in Chicago. "Blarney Stone Here," a headline in the *Chicago Post* blared on June 16, adding that the rock measured one foot square and was being kept in a safe. Carter H. Harrison, the city's distinctly non-Irish mayor, duly kissed it—how could he not, if he ever hoped to be reelected?—which was solemnly reported in the press. ("Mayor on His Knees" was the *Toledo News*'s mischievous headline.)

But there was increasing evidence that the so-called Blarney Stone was exactly that, a bit of blarney. In mid-June, the *New York World* referred to "an alleged piece of the Blarney Stone." A month later, on July 15, the heat was turned up: the *St. Paul Dispatch* reported that Sir George Colthurst, owner of the original Blarney Castle, as well as its namesake stone, was considering a trip to Chicago to out the impostor stone. Before long, the *Boston Globe* was reporting that in fact the original rock hadn't budged an inch from Ireland, no less made it to the Midwest. Some papers reported that the Chicago stone was there in part—a chip off the old block, you might say. Rumors swirled, every article in the press seemed to contradict the next, yet no one from the Irish Village quite clarified the matter, not even the saintlike Lady Aberdeen.

Whatever its origin, the thing was referred to as the Blarney Stone, and, mainly, people wanted to believe it. Hordes came to kiss it, paying ten cents each for the privilege, so many that it turned greenish from tobacco juice. One commentator put the whole thing in perspective by pointing out that wasn't the original Blarney Stone itself unrepentant nonsense? (Not, I conjecture, to a certain kind of Irish.) There is no record on whether he was run out of town....

What is recorded is that Lady Aberdeen's village, so recently at risk after the death of Peter White, was a "wild success," in Carmel's words. Ireland could be found there, distilled, and that was enough for Chicago's vast immigrant population, Hibernian or not. The cozy thatched dwellings, the lace-making demos, the turf fires burning beneath pots of boiling potatoes, all evoked something so powerful that nothing as tacky as a faux Blarney Stone could threaten it at all. Later in life, Annie White, never modest, sounded positively coy as she described her unexpected success. "Well," she told her family, "there I was in my widow's bonnet, and the newspaper gentlemen were very kind to me." One of her most slavish fans was the Irishman Peter Finley Dunne, who, writing as Mr. Dooley, was one of the most famous—and opinionated—Chicago journalists of his day.

After the fair closed, and with the backing of the Aberdeens, White took on a new project—a Chicago shop dedicated to bringing Irish crafts to the public. But first White had to sail back to Ireland to face her father, without whose permission she could never manage to stay. Their argument was long and protracted. Thomas Mayne, who had visited Chicago for the fair—"where every cab driver did him," as Carmel put it—knew firsthand that the United States was a terrible place. And besides, a woman's place was in the home. But White was a steamroller, if not a Mack truck, and in the long run she prevailed, although not after agreeing to leave all six of her children in Ireland, at least for a time. The boys would receive an Irish education and the girls at least a partial one; they'd join their mother once it became clear that the shop was a going concern.

So White returned to America alone. For the three of her children who lived there, life at Cremorne was crowded, but always entertaining. Ireland is full of "sons and daughters waiting to marry until their mothers release them by dying peacefully in their arms," as Carmel wickedly described the phenomenon, and the Mayne family home was no different: a full six unmarried aunts and uncles, of Annie White's thirteen siblings, still lived at home. The White children scampered about the house and grounds, puncturing the tires of their grandfather's "high bicycle"—an old-fashioned penny farthing—and stopping the pendulum on the elaborate dining room clock. For young Carmel, it sounds like a nice enough childhood, particularly since "like many girls it was my grandmother I loved. Her temperament, like her birth, was gentle (she was born a Verscoyle, which means something in Ireland), and since I have much of my mother's determination in my character, it was far easier to get on with someone who never wanted to dominate me." And perhaps, given her mother's "determination," as she discreetly calls it, it was a blessing to have been raised, at least for a time, beyond her sphere of influence.

To her relatives, White's decision to run a shop was a scandal. But it turned out to be a canny move. She hit the deck running, socially and in every other way, hosting tea parties at her Michigan Avenue apartment and attracting the artistic crowd she always favored. And the store was a triumph. The *Chicago Evening Post* heralded what they called "a first class shop" in a story entitled "Beautiful Things on Sale in the Irish Industrial Store." The store burst with Irishness in the form of linens, handkerchiefs, silk and wool underwear, hosiery, pottery, and the inevitable carvings of bog oak. The sales staff included some of the same lovely, mischievous colleens who had caused such a sensation at the fair. "Our object in establishing this depot is to help the thousands of poor women in Ireland who have nothing to do and know not what to do with themselves," White said. "We desire to help them to an opportunity of employing themselves in a work that will give them a living and will at the same time give the world something that is worth having."

Within the year the store had expanded, moving to newer, larger quarters just down Wabash Avenue, from number 268 to 179. By now almost a year had gone by since Peter White's death. On the anniversary, Ishbel Aberdeen cabled his widow from Ottawa, saying: "How glad he must be if he has been permitted to watch your noble life this year." If he was thinking at all, he was no doubt astonished at how much his wife had pulled off in his absence.

As the business prospered, White began to send for her children. Carmel and Christine came first, sailing together, each with one piece of luggage, from Queenstown on the *Lucania,* a large Cunard Line ship that had been built the year before, and arriving in New York on October 27, 1894. In making this trip, they followed a well-worn trajectory: by 1890, a full 39 percent of Irish-born people—

about three million in all—lived overseas, according to historian Roy Foster. And 84 percent of Irish emigrating at the time headed for the United States.

They were young to make the voyage, very young. The ship's manifest lists Carmel as being only six at the time, although in fact she was seven, while Christine—recorded here as "Christina"—was eight. They were just thirteen months apart, near enough to qualify as "Irish twins," as the old joke goes, and about as close as two sisters could possibly be. Even so, Carmel recalled the experience as daunting. "It was two frightened children who traveled alone on the big boat to New York. People were kind to us—I remember playing round games with an elderly man who took pity on us—but our arrival in America was too overwhelming to be remembered." After their boat pulled into New York Harbor, they were met by a friend of their mother's who placed them on a Pullman train headed for their new home in the Midwest.

Carmel recalled the train's arrival in rapturous terms:

> *Then Chicago at last and our mother meeting us. As we drove through the streets she felt she must prepare us for our new life. "Now you won't be living in a big house like Cremorne," she warned us. "It'll seem to you tiny after what you're accustomed to." We drew up before the apartment house where she lived, got out, and* gaped. *This was a bigger house than we'd seen in all our lives! Even when we were shown our small part of it, it still seemed tremendous—drawing room, dining room, bedrooms only for* us!

By then, the Wabash Avenue shop had evolved. Since much of its business involved the sale of Irish fabrics, handspun linens and the like, it seemed only natural to offer dressmaking services, too. From the start, the White girls had custom-made clothes—their mother dressed them alike in garments that, designed to last for two years, were invariably huge. "We felt too small for our clothes, and this huge building, and this strange new world."

When White went off to work each morning, she left her daughters behind in the apartment building on Michigan Avenue, considering them too young for school. Forbidden to play with the janitor's children—the only potential playmates around—the girls were desperately lonely. So education, at last, was allowed. Their first school was a convent in Davenport, Iowa, where they settled in nicely, adoring the nuns. Carmel spent Sundays, their one day away from classes, buried in one book or another. "We were still shy, different, *foreign* children," she recalled. And there they might have stayed, quite happily, had their mother not learned, to her infinite horror, that the father of one of Carmel's classmates was in law enforcement.

"Descendants of the McGuillicuddy of the Reeks would never associate with a policeman!" she's said to have huffed at the time. (If such a claim were true—and it's scarcely possible to confirm—it would position Carmel as one of the descendants of the original kings of Ireland, true Celtic royalty and more impressive, in its way, than the watered-down, largely Teutonic lineage of those monarchs across the Irish Sea.) It was made abundantly clear to all within earshot at her daughters' school that, while White might have lowered herself to the point of being in trade, she had no intention of loosening her standards any further. So the girls were shipped off to Dearborn Seminary in Chicago, which catered to the Windy City's genteel classes and was presumably unpolluted by the presence of children of blue-collar workers. It was here that Carmel learned for the first time that there were non-Catholics in the world, when one of her teachers shocked her by saying she'd never heard of Our Lady of Mount Carmel.

The girls spent three years at Dearborn, returning home for holidays, where life was always exciting. Mrs. White entertained all sorts of people, including Margaret Anglin, who stayed with the family when she was starring in a play in Chicago. "With her beautiful carriage, eyes lifted to heaven when she spoke in a pose copied by a generation of schoolgirls, she lit up our house when she entered it," a starstruck Carmel recalled.

She dated her visit to this unnamed play as

the beginning of my delicious involvement *with what I see in the theatre, just as my devouring of Dickens at this time was the beginning of my emotional engagement when I'm absorbed in a story . . . together with my lifelong involvement in the personal affairs of everyone around me, it planted in me the seed of romance.*

She was so wrung out by the play's tragic end that she crawled over to the great thespian's bed (to Carmel's rapture, the actress was sleeping in her room) and whispered, "Margaret, if *I'd* been that man, *I'd* have married you, dear." A diva who cheerfully agrees to share a child's room? It's hard to imagine a modern star taking such accommodations in stride. But Anglin was a family friend, and besides, actresses—those wanton creatures—were held in about as low social esteem as possible at the time. Grand hotels were for grander divas.

Other visitors to the White household included Josephine Sullivan, a celebrated harpist whose performances had been one of the highlights of the Irish Village. Stagestruck as she was, young Carmel could scarcely tolerate the presence of Miss Sullivan, who was the daughter of A. M. Sullivan, an opponent of Parnell's. "Our family was passionate Parnellites," she explained, admitting that even the presence of the young woman's gilded harp (a "coffin-like object when traveling that required a cab to itself, and that stood in our drawing room like a baleful presence") was a "nightmare" to her for this reason. As such comments indicate, Carmel was an intense child, funny, observant, sheltered in a wide-eyed way. Her slightly detached way of seeing things seems decidedly foreign: this world was new to her, and she wasn't going to miss a thing.

Chicago felt even more like home after another sibling, Tom, graduated from Clongowes Wood College, in the southeastern Irish town of Naas (where one of his older schoolmates was James Joyce). Annie brought him over first, "because he was the oldest," his daughter, another Carmel, recalls. He arrived in the Midwest in 1900, at the age of sixteen, ready, in the time-honored way, to seek his fortune in the United States, happy to find himself in the company of his mother and long-absent sisters.

Tom was an impressive young man, bright and hardworking, and his career in the States—most of it spent in the publishing empire of William Randolph Hearst—would truly be meteoric. But, for now, he was also just a kid, a funny one, who had a wicked verbal wit, in the Irish manner, and delighted in tormenting his young sisters. He loved shooting pats of butter up on the dining room ceiling then waiting until they, inevitably, rained down on a sibling's head—"preferably mine," according to Carmel, who, of all her brothers, was exceptionally close to Tom. "We spatted like Kilkenny cats (I've always had a touch of 'the Irish' in me), but we adored each other, and at home we were always clowning." When things got too wild, she'd pack a suitcase and announce that she was going to Bloomingdale's (then a lunatic asylum in New York, first in Manhattan, then in Westchester County—not the clothes emporium).

After a few years, White declared formal education to be over for her daughters—in truth, it had hardly begun—and they were moved into the next phase, that of being finished, like furniture. It was time to be transformed into ladies. Their first stop was a boarding school in Winnetka, Illinois, of all places—"our happiest school years," Carmel reports, although the two exceptionally close sisters scarcely made other friends. The center of their lives remained their Chicago home: "our mother's circle of theatrical and artistic friends was fascinating to us."

Then, at some point in 1903, it was on to another finishing school, this one in Brussels, which, Carmel quipped, "compared to Paris is like the sister of the girl you're in love with." Although she would be admired all her life for her "eye"—her sense of exactly how things should look—her ear was another story. Blame it on the convent in Brussels, the Soeurs de Sainte-Marie, where Carmel mastered her famously idiosyncratic French, which she spoke with a pronounced, almost comic Irish accent. She learned the language "on the pillow," as the French say, but not in the sexy way that expression implies. Instead, she absorbed it involuntarily after her bed was placed between those of two Belgian girls—best friends who had been separated for quietness's sake—who chatted to each other as she tried to sleep. "They talked to each other continuously over my head and I remember the sensation of distinguishing first words, then sentences, then this strange language was suddenly comprehensible to me." Although some in later life made merry with Snow's French, it would serve her for the rest of her life. "I could always make a compliment or have a row," as she put it. What else would one need?

It was also in Belgium that Snow experienced the first of many defiant fashion moments. Told to wear an underslip in the bath (a standard antisin ritual), she demurred, bathing naked instead, then swishing the undergarment around in the water to make it seem she'd obeyed. It was a small rebellion but a telling one, and one that she would always remember. "For all my shyness then, modesty has never been one of my afflictions," she noted. Later, Carmel and Christine, still teenagers, were allowed to leave the convent for a week to accompany their mother to the Paris fashion shows, which then mainly featured floor-length dresses, some with bustles, and all requiring enormous swaths of cloth. White put her daughters to work memorizing the fashions they saw—Carmel was assigned the top of each outfit, her sister the bottom—so that she could copy them later in her shop. "I found that I could remember the details exactly, that I actually had a photographic eye for fashion when I focussed it," Carmel wrote. It was an ability that would serve her all her professional life.

Back in the United States, White was going from strength to strength, her business booming, her social circle expanding. If there was a stigma to being Irish—and there certainly was—it was one she chose to ignore. Hers is an immigrant's story without pain: there was no loneliness or poverty in even her earliest weeks in the New World. And if you factor out her childlessness in those first years, a temporary condition, her new life was an immediate improvement over the old. She'd left a domineering father behind, not to mention a society that would have kept her in widow's weeds—with all the isolation that that implies—for many years to come.

Success came almost as soon as she touched down on American soil. For a time, everything was put in service to her shop. And then, suddenly, it wasn't. Or at least not that one. In about 1903, White attended the Paris openings with the four sisters who were the proprietors of T.M. & J.M. Fox, Inc., a custom dressmaking establishment in New York. Founded in 1885, their firm was—"One of the oldest and most exclusive dressmaking establishments in the United States," according to the *New York Times.* By now, the Foxes "had all become wealthy out of it and were ready to retire," the paper added. After watching White in action in Paris, scouting out fashions to reinterpret (some might say steal) in her Chicago boutique, it was clear to them that their business would be safe in her hands. Before long, they'd offered it to her for sale.

Manhattan can be notoriously charmless and cruel to newcomers. And White was just about as much of an outsider—an Irishwoman, of all unmentionable sins!—as you could get. But she was also unafraid. Her Chicago life, clearly, had run its course. She decided to close the Irish Industrial Store "for good and always," as the *Times* recounted in 1911, in a breathless-sounding article about White's life in the unforgiving canyons of Manhattan. "She did not care to have any one [sic] else in charge of what had been so intimate and personal a venture." Instead, she opted to move to a new, vast city, where such adjectives scarcely applied. "Anonymous" and "impersonal" would be more apt.

2 the steamer trunk

I am learning so much of life.
—Carmel White

BY THE TIME CARMEL AND CHRISTINE returned from their convent year, in the fall of 1904, their home was in Manhattan. They crossed the Atlantic with their mother, arriving in New York Harbor on September 12 and settling in at 326 West End Avenue, a remodeled brownstone building near West Seventy-fifth Street that had once belonged to Nat Goodwin, a famously dry-humored actor, and his wife, the noted dramatic actress Maxine Elliott. Drama reigned in the house's decor, too: the living room had been painted bright red to serve as a backdrop for Elliott's striking tawny looks.

To Carmel and Christine, everything about New York was brand new—down to and including their mother's fiancé, Edward Van Pelt Douglass, known as "Ned," whom Mrs. White had met and become engaged to while her daughters were abroad. When, on a visit to the convent, she told them about their impending stepfather "a shiver ran down my shoulders," Carmel recalled. "But I needn't have worried, he never entered into our lives tremendously." Nor, apparently, did he enter too profoundly into Annie White's. Little is known of him, beyond that, having been born in Greenfield, Ohio, in 1875, he was four years younger than his wife and that he was a New York retailer who

Carmel White and her stepfather, Edward V. Douglass, in front of their West End Avenue home, c. 1905

was said to sell mirrors. After he married White, probably in about 1905, he was at least on the periphery of her family during some crucial years, including the arrival of the three youngest boys—Desmond, Victor, and James—from Ireland, each of whom arrived separately in 1908.

Carmel went down to the New York docks to meet the boat when her youngest brother, James, then fifteen and just sprung from the same school that Tom had attended, arrived. She took one look at this callow, long-lost sibling, who was barely adjusted to being back on dry land, and . . . promptly took him shopping. "You can't be dressed like that," she said. It was clear to her immediately that his Jesuit school wardrobe (weedy tie, pants high above the ankles) could never cut it in New York. From the time he arrived, Carmel acted as a surrogate mother, his daughter says. It was lucky she did, since his own mother, whom he hadn't seen for years, scarcely seemed to care. "She just greeted him and said, 'We dress for dinner and if you're late don't bother to come.'"

With Jim's arrival, the family was complete. At the time of the 1910 census, both Douglasses and all six White children were living together on West End Avenue. Carmel recalled dragooning poor "Uncle Ned," as the White children called him, into playing Parcheesi with her and her siblings, joking that the couple's eventual separation couldn't entirely be blamed on that. The Douglasses were still married in 1911, or so the *Times* reported. At some point they separated—amicably, discreetly, and for good. Given Annie Douglass's Catholicism, there

"The White Boys" c. 1910:
Tom, Desmond, Victor, James

was no question of a divorce. The separation was "never discussed," says a granddaughter, Carmel White Eitt. "It was quite simply never discussed. It was a very different era. But they remained friends. They'd have lunch together."

The White sons would always be more Irish than their sisters; even so, the continued Irishness of all of them, girls and boys alike, was ensured by Douglass's decision to have them spend their summers in Ireland. Immigration records show them migrating seasonally back and forth across the Atlantic; as late as 1909, Carmel still listed her address on official documents as Cremorne. Four years later she was described on shipping documents as being a U.S. citizen "on father's papers." The American citizenship that had become Douglass's when she married had apparently filtered down to her children. From this point on, all the Whites were listed on passenger lists as American citizens, rather than under the dreaded heading "Aliens," as they had been before.

The six siblings plunged into American life, quickly finding their disparate niches. Carmel began attending classes at the Art Students League, the noted New York art school, which offered membership to "any candidate with acceptable moral character and the means to pay his dues." Luckily, no talent or artistic ability was required since, as Carmel breezily noted, she "hadn't a vestige" of it. Still, it was a pleasant distraction for as long as it lasted. She and Christine, who was also studying there, attended classes in its famous neoclassical building on West Fifty-seventh Street, designed by architect Henry J. Hardenbergh (who had already created one of New York's most famous structures, the Dakota apartment building on Central Park West, and would soon design the Plaza Hotel). Both girls studied with Robert Henri, a legendarily inspiring teacher whose former students included George Bellows, Rockwell Kent, and Edward Hopper. "He had the priceless pedagogical gift of stirring our imaginations and of making us excited about our work," one former student, Helen Appleton Reed, later wrote.

Henri was clearly inspired by Carmel, in turn: she soon began posing for a portrait by him in his studio on Gramercy Park. The striking results show an auburn-haired colleen with a slender figure and expressive blue eyes. While not quite a beauty, her nose was too dramatically sloped, her lips too thin for that, she came close, with wonderful high cheekbones and wide-set, expressive blue eyes. Her youth itself, along with her character—she looked energetic, ready to laugh—made her seem dazzling. People were drawn to her, at the league and elsewhere, and the evenings she spent socializing with its students and faculty, including Henri, his wife, and various members of the Ashcan School, Bellows among them, taught her almost as much as her classes. One way or the other, as she wrote, "Without knowing it, I began to absorb a good deal of knowledge about art." Given the talent problem, it wasn't going to become a career. Almost inevitably, she drifted into working part-time in her mother's shop.

Her siblings were all over the map. Victor had also been a student at the league; later, he moved on to Cornell University and Paris's Ecole des Beaux-Arts. Both Desmond and Jim were enrolled at the Massachusetts Institute of Technology. As the oldest, Tom, who had attended business college in Chicago, was the first to go to work; by the age of sixteen he was employed by a construction company in New Mexico. Later, he went to work for Mead, Patton & Co., a company that supplied newsprint to Hearst Publishing, then moved on to a clerk's job at Hearst's New York headquarters, the firm that would employ him for the rest of his life.

And Annie Douglass, with her sure hand and to the surprise of no one, was turning out to be a huge success at the helm of T.M. & J.M. Fox. Since its inception, the founding sisters had run this very special firm in an atmosphere of hushed discretion, almost secrecy. Their snobbishness was finely calibrated. They never advertised their wares—a stricture that Douglass would later breach. But she continued their tradition of not allowing anyone deemed to be vulgar to cross its threshold, a fact that was particularly ironic since, given the anti-Irish snobbism of the era, Douglass herself might never have been allowed to shop at the firm. Actresses were also not allowed. "They confined their dealings to the fashionable set, and not even a theatrical star of the first magnitude could get a gown at their shop," the *Times* reported (so much the opposite of today's approach, where designers send trunks of clothes, gratis, to even the most obscure celebrity).

ABOVE: **A class at the Art Students League, New York City, c. 1907, around the time Carmel studied there**

RIGHT: ***Girl in Rose and Gray: Miss Carmel White*** **by Robert Henri, 1911**

"When a stranger came whose introductions were not precisely correct," the paper continued, "word was sent down that there was nothing to show. This policy was immensely successful. The Fox sisters became rich."

The same article also noted—not quite correctly—that when Douglass bought the concern, which was located at 33 East Thirty-fourth Street, "she entered upon the management without knowledge of design or dress goods, New York women, or Paris fashions." Although her first two years were difficult, she soon found her footing, managing to

A newspaper advertisement for T.M. & J.M. Fox from the 1920s

retain the firm's blue-blooded customer base, while bringing others in. Given her lifelong love affair with the theater, it seems likely that she loosened the taboo on allowing actresses into the shop. But mainly she was shrewd enough to keep a thriving business running exactly as it had always been, right down to the position of its furniture and, even, its flower vases. Eight years after she took over, the *Times* noted, the same 225 employees (including the staff of the Fox workshop, sewers, embroiderers, and the like, who worked across Thirty-fourth Street at number 53) were still on the job, with the exception of two who had left to marry.

New York then wasn't what it's since become—a fashion capital in its own right. Sartorial taste was almost entirely dictated by Paris, even more than today, when Milan, London, and New York dilute, at least marginally, the influence of the French capital. Why there? It's an interesting question that *Time* magazine, of all publications, answered in a fashion cover story in 1957.

> *The plain fact is that Paris has a reservoir of skilled needleworkers and a tradition of craftsmanship that no other nation can match—a tradition established largely by the simple fact that no other people have been willing to devote so much time and thought to their clothes. . . . An elegant Frenchwoman will spend hours searching for the exact shade of stocking to go with a certain dress, spend days debating the choice of a dress or a hat.*

The obsession with elegance dated back to Louis XIV, the Sun King, and his court at Versailles. He bolstered the fashion industry, created it, really, by organizing the Paris dressmakers and tailors, elevating their stature at home and in the world. Before long, the most fashionable foreign women went ritually to Paris to shop and brides sent to France for their wedding trousseaux.

Like most American buyers, Douglass would head to France's twice-yearly couture collections, called "openings" and then held in November and May, as if on a kind of safari, hoping to bag the best specimens she could find, as quickly as she could. In those days, "foreign buyers were permitted to purchase single models from the French couturiers, which they could then have copied," according to the fashion curator Dilys E. Blum. Upon their return to the United States, the designs would be disseminated far and wide, without further compensation, and often without credit, to the couturier who created them in the first place. "After Paris explains the mode, New York offers it," *Vogue* told its readers in the 1920s—a statement that was literally true. As Edna Woolman Chase, the magazine's editor in chief, said in a lecture years later,

> *You all know how quickly we rush to Paris to see the openings and how eagerly we await the boat bringing in the new models, and we almost bribe the Customs to get these models off the boat just as quickly as possible. And then we rush to have them copied at all prices. We have good copies and bad copies and costly copies and cheap copies. . . .*

Many of the styles that originated from T.M. & J.M. Fox didn't pretend to be original; in every other way, though, including workmanship and price, they qualified as haute couture. "Her customers came from all over the country," Carmel wrote of her mother, "always by appointment, and they paid prices that began at three hundred and fifty dollars and went up and up. Moreover, they ordered twenty to forty dresses a season." They could find Paris originals at Fox, too, as well as a kind of hybrid. Douglass's youngest child, Jim White, used to say, mischievously, that his mother "would buy a dress in Paris, add a rose and some embroidery to it, and charge $500 more, and dress a Rockefeller in it."

Fashions of the first decade of the twentieth century tended to pack women in, padding them generously, like Victorian furniture. Their wearers looked upholstered, with ample hips and busts and impossibly cinched-in waists—the result of ritual torture. Women really did cling desperately to their bedposts, puffing and exclaiming, while their ladies' maids tugged on their corset strings, strapping them in for the day. "A carefree smile, a laced-up waist, and a heavy bosom were considered irresistible," according to fashion historian Charlotte Seeling. Physiologically, it must have been a challenge, looking radiant while scarcely being able to breathe.

To emphasize their hips and bustlines, women were encased in layer upon layer of cloth, creating the densely packed figure that was then the ideal. Seen in profile, the well-dressed woman of 1910 was S-shaped: her corset pushed her breasts up and out so that she resembled a ship's figurehead, angling into the wind. From her waist down, she jutted out in another direction altogether, thanks to the bustle that floated behind her like an abbreviated spinnaker, exaggerating her derriere to an almost comic degree. Except for the tiny waist, an ideal that—as Barbie demonstrates—never seems to go out of style, the look was the opposite of what prevails today, with its wispy supermodels and gaunt-figured aesthetic.

And clothes then were opulent almost beyond credulity. The designers who reigned before World War I, Frederick Worth, Jeanne Lanvin, Callot Soeurs, Paul Poiret, Jeanne Paquin, Jacques Doucet, and others, created extraordinary concoctions, tossing in the kitchen sink, metaphorically speaking, in the form of opulent fabrics—tulle, say, or silk duchesse—piling on ostrich feathers, painstaking embroidery, ruches. The legendary Poiret was just one of a number of reigning geniuses.

> *Year in, year out, his clientele looked like Asiatic princesses or Tartar priests in scarlet, black, tassels, and magnificent gold. (For his purposes*

the entire East was Poiret's oyster.) A Poiret dress could be identified as far as it could be seen, like the brilliant uniform of a prewar hussar,

as Janet Flanner, for decades the Paris correspondent for *The New Yorker,* writing under the pseudonym Genêt, once wrote.

In general, the earlier in the century, the more complicated the clothes; after the first decade, things became more streamlined. But until then, they were assertively baroque: some of the era's dresses look as if, once removed from their hangers, they could stand up on their own. And then there were the hats, which, by 1910, were often wide brimmed and ungainly: the well-dressed girl secured hers with up to half a dozen rhinestone hatpins. And for a brief, unappealing moment, hats were festooned with something the fashion writer Anne Rittenhouse (a friend of Douglass's whose real name, poor thing, was Harry-dele Hallmark), who freelanced for magazines and newspapers, described as "queer feathers," some of them downright unappetizing, as it turned out. Rittenhouse reported in the *New York Times* in 1910 that "one of these odd creations of the milliner's workroom when subjected to close observation proved to be a quill—common or barnyard variety—on which had been glued long hairs of monkey fur."

If Carmel was interested in hats or clothes, she didn't know it yet; she drifted into working at T.M. & J.M. Fox with dread. She hated being under her mother's thumb. "She was absolutely indomitable," she wrote, seeming to shudder as she did so. But then again, so was her daughter.... The sparks between them were forever threatening to burst into flame. Still, it was in the crucible of her mother's shop—and who knows, perhaps because of it?—that, over the next few years, Carmel developed the confidence and decisiveness about fashion that would make her career. "It was from our mother that all her children learned to make quick, accurate and imaginative decisions," she acknowledged.

At Fox, Carmel came face-to-face with glamour, both its appealing, illusory surface and the hard work that inevitably lies behind it. The women who shopped there were the very definition of the carriage trade. When they came for fittings, their horse-drawn vehicles would wait outside on Thirty-fourth Street, often with both a coachman and a footman in attendance. These customers came frequently, and paid exorbitantly, and Douglass's fortunes rose accordingly. They came for the personal touch, as well as for outstanding workmanship: Douglass's genius lay, in part, in her ability to discern each woman's style and to divine, each season, which Paris creations should be hers. Her client's names ring out like cash registers, even now. Mrs. Charles Schwab, whose rich industrialist husband was known across the States (as his son would be in our time), and such sought-after socialites as Mrs. E. Gary all had their carriages stop outside T.M. & J.M. Fox. Many of the shop's concoctions lived on in Carmel's memory, including such standouts as "Mrs. McCormick's gay velvet dress banded with chinchilla, her moleskin suit that we had to repair when she carelessly leaned against a radiator, her green velvet and ermine evening gown."

In early October 1911, Mrs. Douglass took a dramatic step when she purchased a mansion at 10 East Fifty-seventh Street from William Frederick Havemeyer for $220,000—a staggering sum. That she made a move at this point isn't surprising—Thirty-fourth Street was in decline. Once residential, it was being transformed into a thoroughfare of shops and hotels, commercial enterprises that would inevitably doom a business like Fox's, where walk-in customers were unknown and the clientele would much rather not mingle with the masses—or even catch a glimpse of them—while picking up their velvet-and-ermine gowns. As the *Times* put it so delicately: "The atmosphere of a great dressmaking establishment began to pass away, and this prompted Mrs. Douglas [sic] to look for a new location. She determined that this should be in a fine residential section."

Fine is putting it mildly. "The homes of a dozen well-known New York families are in the same block," the paper noted. Harry Payne Whitney had the mansion on the southwest corner of Fifth Avenue and Fifty-seventh and the redoubtable Mrs. Hermann Oelrichs, heiress to a silver fortune and a noted Newport hostess, was next door, at 1 East, while Mrs. Cornelius Vanderbilt was just across Fifth Avenue, at 1 West, in a beaux arts mansion designed by Richard Morris Hunt. White bought the property from Havemeyer, of the noted sugar-refining family, whose father had been a three-time mayor of New York. (He was a cousin of Henry Osborne Havemeyer, who, with his wife, Louisine, amassed a legendary collection of old master and impressionist art, which they later bequeathed to the Metropolitan Museum of Art.)

In the mid-nineteenth century, East Fifty-seventh Street, a critical east-west thoroughfare in the still-developing city of New York, had been lined with modest brownstones. But in about 1870, one grand edifice after another began taking their place; soon the street was full of French chateau-style structures, which together became known as Marble Row. The street was a broad thoroughfare, where horse-drawn conveyances, and even—the newest thing—motor carriages, as they were then known, could stop, two and even more abreast, as their well-heeled owners made their social rounds. At the time of Douglass's purchase, residents of Fifty-seventh Street were increasingly worried by the prospect of commercial development. Even so, there's no record of opposition to the appearance of a dressmaking establishment in their midst. Just down the street, a nine-story building belonging to the milliner Henri Bendel was going up; at the time, "his shop was the smartest in New York and his clientele was a Social Register of fashion," *Vogue*'s Edna Chase noted. Designed by H. O. Chapman, this edifice would also contain a branch of the famous Paris gallery Durand-Ruel, which had long been associated with impressionist art and was largely responsible for bringing it the American market. (Henry Havemeyer was one of Durand-Ruel's most active American clients.)

Douglass's purchase was an astonishingly bold move, particularly for a woman. The *New York Times*'s story about her appeared on page 7 under the headline: "Dressmaker Now in Exclusive Block"; and it gushed, rather more than was usual for this once-august paper of record (this was long before such frivolities as "Styles of the Times"). One subheading blared: "A Woman's Own Enterprise"; another described the article as one "Involving the Story of What a Resourceful Business Woman Has Accomplished in Eight Years in New York."

Douglass had eyed the Havemeyer property for two years before buying it, according to the report. She'd already hired decorators and architects and had shopped for furnishings in the "capitals of Europe." If Fox's location was about to change, its discreet way of doing things would not. The *Times* reporter, writing without a byline, might have been speaking straight to its customers when he or she wrote, reassuringly: "People will pass the house and never know that the gowns of the richly dressed women they pass in Fifth Avenue are being made inside." By now Douglass had become a public figure. When the *Times* story appeared, an unnamed person in the Hearst organization wrote a note to Tom White, then twenty-three and clearly a rising star, that read in its entirety: "White—Surely your mother is a woman of ability—It must require some acumen to manage an establishment of that size—RPH."

Fox's move had great symbolism since American fashion, too, was about to move to a better neighborhood. At the turn of the century it had scarcely existed. But, increasingly, there was a call to offer more than the watered-down copies of French styles that had so long passed for fashion in the United States. In a 1912 story, the *Times* writer Anne Rittenhouse noted that "big wholesale houses have been modifying French fashions to suit American tastes for years and calling the output American." Some in the fashion industry, she added, including Edna Chase, had "taken up the cudgel in defense of American fashions only for women." Soon Douglass was one of them. In December 1912, the *Times* noted that she "came out quite unexpectedly yesterday in favor of the American fashion movement which is causing such widespread discussion up and down Fifth Avenue." And the newspaper itself joined in, announcing its sponsorship of a competition for the best American-designed hats and gowns. T.M. & J.M. Fox had impeccable credentials in this department: "It is perhaps significant that at present all the designers employed by the Fox house are Americans," the paper reported, not mentioning that its "designs" were almost purely French. In her extended comment, Mrs. Douglass made clear that she considered American custom-made clothes—such as those being made in her shop—to be superior to their Gallic equivalents.

On its face, such a remark is preposterous. The workmanship behind haute couture has always been above reproach. Clearly, Douglass was motivated by political correctness, or whatever its equivalent was called a century ago. Even so, her respect for France and its culture comes through. "I was once told by one of the most famous couturiers in Paris," she wrote, "that much of her spare time, her Sundays and her holidays, was spent in the Louvre and other museums seeking ideas as to form, combination of colors and beauty of line." The problem on these shores, she pointed out, was the paucity of such resources; despite its great wealth, the United States was only just beginning to build its great art collections. Still, American craftsmanship was improving, she allowed, adding, "If a thing is good, we no longer care where it is made, whether in Paris or in New York."

By 1913, Douglass was prospering to such a degree that she and her assorted offspring moved from the West Side to 970 Park Avenue, just off Eighty-second Street, and she released her interest in her late husband Peter White's trusts in favor of her children. Each one received 142 Irish pounds—a nice bonus for a young person in New York, and one that must have come in handy. All the young Whites took full advantage of the city's social life, hitting the town routinely. "I *adored* dancing," Carmel recalled. So did much of America, as the century moved into its teens. The tango was undergoing one of its recurring bursts of popularity, as was a tortured-seeming new step, championed by the popular professional dancers Irene and Vernon Castle, who described it as "the sliding and poetical Castle Walk." It was actually more of a slide, with dancers never lifting their feet off the floor; done well, it took place with military precision. The couple had opened Castle House, where socialites, including Mrs. Stuyvesant Fish and Mrs. William Rockefeller, spent their afternoons "castleing," or whatever the verb might be. For those who actually had to work, night was the time to move to music, and Carmel and her siblings did exactly that.

Through friends of the Aberdeens, Carmel found a new dance partner, an attractive young Canadian, and the couple soon became engaged. "His name was Arthur Fitzpatrick and he belonged to a family who thought themselves grander than grand, though I didn't know that then," she wrote of the only son of the Right

Honorable Sir Charles Fitzpatrick, then the lieutenant governor of Quebec. "I knew only that I loved him, and he loved me, and that when his family invited me for a cruise on their yacht I was determined to do him proud." She headed up to Canada's Murray Bay for the trip, bringing along a wardrobe of too-girlish-looking Peter Thompson sailor suits that she discovered almost instantly were altogether wrong. A photograph of her shipboard with the suitor in question, himself looking rather weaselly in a mustache and cocked fedora, reveal her to be charming, fashionable or not, impossibly slender, and radiating a very becoming happiness. But her moment of bliss was brief. Chatting with her snobbish prospective mother-in-law, the imposing Lady Fitzpatrick, young Carmel let drop, proudly, the crucial fact of her mother's career. In so doing, she sealed her fate.

Married to an Irishman, Lady Fitzpatrick must have experienced her share of snobbery by others. But a daughter-in-law whose family was in trade? It was inconceivable. Before long, alas, her son began to see things his mother's way. "I couldn't believe my eyes or ears," Carmel writes. "That he would be *able* not to be in love with me!" But apparently he was. He paid a final visit to her family's Park Avenue apartment, where the couple closeted themselves in the drawing room for an entire day, presumably winding down their engagement. "*Nobody* knew what was going on," her mother later said. But not for long. Within a few years Fitzpatrick moved on to another young woman of Irish descent, Blanche Preston, who was only sixteen at the time of their marriage, in 1916, and presumably more palatable to his parents. The whole experience marked Carmel for life; in the words of one of her nieces, Julie Groupp, "she became bitter."

So rather than moving on to a new, glamorous life, Carmel found herself still at work with Mama. The future must have looked bleak. By now she was in love with clothes, so that must have offered some consolation. But her mother dominated, and any of Carmel's attempts to contribute her thoughts, about fashion or, indeed, anything else, fell on willfully deaf ears. Yet there were occasional consolations. In the summer of 1914, Carmel joined her siblings Victor and Christine, both still art students, in Florence, where both had gone to study with the artist William Merritt

Chase. Here, Carmel took up with a young friend, Walter Pach, who had studied with both Henri and Chase, and was then living in Paris. (He'd soon return to the United States where he would make his name as an art historian, artist, and critic.)

Carmel White c. 1915

Later in the summer, Pach and the three White siblings migrated to Paris to meet up with Douglass, in town for the openings. For Carmel the trip was a visual feast. She visited gallery after gallery in Pach's presence, even making a pilgrimage to what was then a holy site for impressionist art: the rambling apartment at 35, rue de Rome of Fox's New York neighbor, the famous art dealer and collector Paul Durand-Ruel, then in his mid-eighties. The place had been given over to impressionism: Monet had decorated the dining room and his canvases, as well as ones by Pissarro, Renoir, and the like, were clustered together, seemingly as plentiful as air. As she eyed one painting after another, Carmel had the satisfaction of discerning which ones were masterpieces before Pach uttered a word. "My apprenticeship as an editor had begun," she later wrote. Her eye was honed in other ways, too, notably at the couture collections, which she attended once again with her mother. Also in the French capital, she visited a fortune-teller for the first time, again with her mother, with whom she shared a lifelong fondness for seers. From this point on, Carmel would keep tabs more or less constantly on the unseen world, a passion that would never wane.

As exciting as her trip had been, everything faded after she returned to New York in mid-August and found herself back within the walls of T.M. & J.M. Fox, sometimes modeling, sometimes selling, sometimes picking up pins. She worried that she'd never escape. She dreamed of a job in journalism and asked one of her mother's friends, Frank Simonds, a New England newspaperman and political commentator, to read some sketches she had written about Ireland. But things never went much further than that. Simonds commended her, not on her writing exactly, but on the fact that she had something to say—a not insignificant achievement for any author. It was clear that writing wasn't her forte; his comments "pointed, I like to believe, toward my future career as an editor," Carmel remarked.

War had broken out in Europe in August 1914, but for a while, far away in New York, it scarcely seemed to change things at all. But those in the fashion world knew that, with Germany declaring war on France, that country's entire fashion industry would probably come to a halt. Sitting on the top level of a double-decker Fifth Avenue bus one day, Edna Chase, *Vogue*'s formidable editor, came up with the idea of creating a Fashion Fête in Manhattan to bolster the local fashion industry. "And suddenly, as if a little bird had flown into my brain with a full-fledged scene I had the vision of organizing a great show that would give the American designers a chance to see what they could do . . ." (Amazingly, Chase's fears went unrealized: the French fashion industry actually resumed production a short time after war was declared.)

The fair, which was held in November 1914, presenting homegrown couture—gowns by O'Hara, furs by Revillon Frères—to the matrons of New York, was a milestone in the history of American fashion. Over a hundred outfits were on display from the city's most prominent dressmakers, among them T.M. & J.M. Fox. Fox had even, as would become richly ironic later on, designed the gown that Chase—the indisputable star of the evening—wore to the fête, a concoction that Douglass had entitled Golden Dream. Chase was quick to assure this country's fashion allies that her advocacy of American modes didn't mean the rejection of French ones. "A break from Paris was not intended," she remarked afterward. "Rather, it was to uphold the tradition of smart dress, endangered by conditions abroad."

And those conditions were increasingly being felt back home. In 1915, Carmel's brother Victor White headed off to France to work with what would eventually be called the American Field Service (AFS); their brother, James, would follow him into the same service in the following year. And Christine, too, headed overseas, in her case to work for the American Fund for French Wounded, an organization that raised funds for the support of military hospitals in France. Christine's departure filled Carmel with envy: "From that moment I wanted above all things to go, too," she wrote. "I needed to get away where I would be useful, as I felt I wasn't in the shop. But there were difficulties about my passport, so the next summer I got no farther than Hyannis Port, where my mother had taken a cottage for the summer."

Talk about an anticlimax—Carmel, who longed to be in or near a theater of war, found herself summering on a sandy promontory instead. Still, it was an eventful season. Douglass bought a car, "in those days a very complicated machine." On the day it was delivered, she hired a mechanic to give her daughter an hour's lesson, then ordered her distinctly uncomfortable progeny to take her place behind the wheel. "Naturally I wasn't fit to drive, but I did," Carmel cheerfully recalled. "I had to!" She reports that their neighbors, the Hulls (probably Margaret Anglin and her new husband, Howard Hull) were terrified at the sight of her loose on the road. Still, "once my shyness wore off, the fearlessness I inherited from my mother took over."

By now Carmel's brother Tom had become engaged to Virginia Gillette, a young woman from an old American family. They knew each other through their siblings—Carmel and Virginia's sister had been friends in New York. This was a rare trajectory in those days, to be launched from Ireland into the heart of the WASP establishment, and one that Carmel would later follow as well. Their mother's New World marriage, though, wasn't faring as well. In a letter she wrote to Tom during his engagement, which had taken place on February 22, 1915,

Carmel indicated that her stepfather was still in the picture. Still, her description was guarded, to say the least. "Uncle Ned and she are on only rather good terms," she wrote on 10 East Fifty-seventh Street stationery, implying in the next line that she made a point of never discussing her mother with her stepfather. Clearly, the union was strained.

Two weddings took place, perhaps uncomfortably for Carmel, whose own engagement had ended so anticlimactically not long before. One was Tom and Virginia's in August 1915, in a vast, eight-bedroom Victorian summer house on Lake George that had long been in the Gillette family. In marrying Tom, the pedigreed Virginia was almost certainly ensuring a secure future: it was apparent to all around him that this young man would be a success. In a letter written a month or so before the wedding, Douglass described for her future daughter-in-law a typical day in her son's hardworking life. "You probably know that Tom leaves here at eight o'clock every morning and doesn't return until after eleven o'clock at night. As well as that, he has worked every Sunday with the exception of Sunday and Monday last week." She added that "it is hopeless to either worry or try to do anything for him, because as he says the work is to be done and if the day was ten hours longer they could still find plenty to do to fill it in."

Here and in other correspondence Douglass was welcoming to her new daughter-in-law—clearly she approved. Yet for all her apparent joy at the union of Tom and Virginia, just after the wedding, also in August, she underwent a mysterious collapse. She wrote to Virginia from a sanatorium in New Jersey saying that she was dangerously exhausted and in a doctor's care, citing the "extra strain of modernizing in 57th Street" as the cause. Presumably, the condition of her own marriage didn't help. And she might have been under financial pressure, too. The United States had entered an "acute business depression," as Tom White told his aunt Suie, one of his mother's sisters, in Ireland in a March 1915 letter, adding that T.M. & J.M. Fox had lost money in the two earlier years. "She has made such a loss that her working capital is seriously diminished." Whether the family finances were really in trouble, or whether Tom was just trying to forestall a handout to family back in Ireland, can only be guessed. Nothing else about Douglass's circumstances, including the fact that her family now traveled first class when heading to and from Europe, implies much of a financial strain.

Christine and Victor cabled their congratulations to Tom and Virginia from Paris, where both were fully occupied with the war effort. Victor, who had been one of the founders of the AFS's Ambulance Corps, served for more than a year and a half as part of the Second French Army in Baisieux, in the Somme, under harrowing circumstances, bringing wounded to field hospitals from the trenches or from shell-proof dugouts. He, along with his entire ambulance section, was awarded the Croix de Guerre for bravery after they endured a fierce and prolonged bombardment, and he made another contribution, too, by immortalizing the AFSAC's work with brush and color. (He memorialized his corner of the war by painting a scene of the Argonne Forest during intense fighting. And a painting of his from this period is perhaps the most impressionistic, romanticized image of an ambulance ever put to canvas.) White would later receive a second Croix de Guerre for his service, too.

Carmel (*right of groom*) at the wedding of Tom and Virginia White, Hulett's Landing, New York, 1915

After he left the AFSAC, his brother James, fresh out of MIT, took his place, serving for six months and sharing in the same award when it was given to his own section.

The second wedding took place after Christine returned from Paris to marry a physician, Francis Holbrook, whom she'd met in France. She'd wired the news of her engagement to her mother, who promptly offered to finance a Paris trousseau. After Christine arrived at the family's Park Avenue apartment, in December 1916, with her precious cargo, "we watched her unpack her trunk with eager curiosity to see what the French couture was doing," Carmel writes. Many Parisian fashion houses had closed during the war. Madeleine Vionnet's had shut down, as had that of Paul Poiret, who, to a chorus of tears from his assistants, had announced that "an artist is nothing when a soldier is wanted" and gone off to fight, wearing the blue-and-red uniform of the French infantry.

Even so, exquisite things were still being made. The French government, beleaguered as it was, had taken steps to bolster one of its important industries. As Anne Rittenhouse reported,

> *France, in her time of stress, has brought home her tailors and cutters and fitters from the front in order that the making of clothes should go on, so that the women and children would be fed. . . . France has urged and commended her great designers to keep their houses open and create new gowns for the trade.*

One designer, Madeleine Chéruit, who was best known for her afternoon dresses, sounded the battle cry: "Women must have clothes, war or no war. And those who make them must have a way to earn their living. We shall keep open and make what we can."

The clothes that emerged from Christine's trunk, including a wedding gown by Madame Chéruit herself, were of beautiful quality and very much in the latest style. Although dresses had become less structured, there was still a stiffness to them, from Lanvin's embroidered daywear to the more tailored creations of Vionnet. When Christine took out a dress of almost subversive simplicity, it made all the others pale, instantly, in Carmel's mind. The showstopper was a straightforward wool jersey shift with a collar of something Carmel described as "dubious fur." (It was probably rabbit, which the dress's creator favored at the time.)

Its designer, a young woman named Coco Chanel, was, in America at least, a complete unknown. She'd started her career by wearing a striped Breton sailor shirt—the kind French sailors wore—and a pleated skirt of her own design to the races in the fashionable resort of Deauville, accessorizing the outfit with ropes of false pearls. The look was an immediate hit, so much so that Chanel soon opened boutiques in that town and in Biarritz, where she sold her own startlingly unadorned creations—jersey tunics, flannel blazers, long linen dresses. There wasn't a corset, not to mention a bustle, in sight.

Chanel had been influenced by Chéruit, wearing the "walking suits" this designer had popularized before the war. She soon appropriated the concept herself, making her own signature simple suits for strolling and playing golf. But then a rich admirer—Chanel seemed to have legions of them—had come forward as a backer, and this sexy couturier's career was born. But it wasn't until after World War I that Chanel, after shortening hems and dropping waistlines, would, with consummate ease, singlehandedly topple the fashion world. "In 1919, I woke up famous," as she has said.

That Christine was able to score such a specimen so early in this young, soon-to-be-legendary couturier's career must have owed everything to her mother's Paris connections. Even so, Douglass was appalled. "My mother declared flatly that her good money might as well have been thrown away," Carmel recalled. Worse still, Christine accessorized the dress

Christine White

as the designer herself did, with strand after strand of artificial pearls. The look was pure Chanel, as fashionable then as it remains today, and it was indeed revolutionary. Since the designer counted the Duke of Westminster among her numerous, jewelry-bestowing admirers, her own pearls were real. But few mere mortals could compete. Undaunted, the women of Paris had, like Christine, begun draping themselves in fakes.

Soon, New Yorkers would, too, but that possibility must have seemed remote to at least two of the women gathered that day around the fashion-filled trunk. Chic American women were, after all, still tightly wrapped and bound. But Carmel knew immediately that the almost impertinently elegant dress before her implied radical changes ahead. "As happens once in a generation, perhaps," she wrote, "we were in at the birth of a revolution in fashion. I was delighted with the freedom of this new, easy, one-piece style—it took ten years off your age." Years later, another legendary designer would sum up Chanel's influence: "With a black pullover and ten rows of pearls she revolutionized the world of fashion," wrote Christian Dior. The fashion historian Valerie Steele parsed it further: "The real secret of Chanel's success was not that her clothes were simple or even comfortable, but that they made the rich look young and casual," she pointed out. "... [T]o wear one's clothes *'avec désinvolture,'* in a free and easy manner, was the look of modernity."

We'll never know if Christine actually wore the dress in New York, and how it might have been received in that city—so much more conservative than Paris! But we do know that she wore something tamer, the ivory Chéruit, when she celebrated her wedding mass, just down Park Avenue from the Douglass home, at the Church of St. Ignatius Loyola in New York. Not long afterward, in April 1917, America entered the war.

Within weeks, Carmel was on her way to Europe, following eagerly in her siblings' wake. She joined the American Red Cross in France, serving coffee and food to the "doughboys," as American infantrymen had been called for the past century (probably because their long-ago counterparts favored the pastry—an ancestor of the doughnut—of the same name). Although the other American girls elected to work in the Red Cross's officers clubs, Carmel chose a canteen in Paris's Gare Saint Lazare, where she'd determined that the need was greater. Her days were mundane and inspiring by turns:

> *It was no bed of roses. You stood on your feet for untold hours, doling out food and supplies to millions of troops and refugees, and then valiantly one-stepped them off at night to "Smiles." Your life fluctuated between grueling stretches of superhuman work, and brief oases of gaiety on leave in Paris, where every officer treated you as the queen and confidant of all time, regaled you with Champagne. . . .*

Carmel was thirty and, like her brother Tom—"a compulsive worker," in the words of one of his daughters—had superhuman stamina on the job; their mother's tireless example had served them well. "Mummy learned to survive and really work," Carmel's daughter Brigid recalled. "It was instilled in Mummy from her mother that work mattered." One day, when the girl on the night shift failed to turn up, Carmel took her place, then continued on through her previously scheduled shift the following day. A major happened by on an inspection tour after she'd spent thirty-six hours on her feet; he was impressed, but concerned, and offered to place her in another canteen if Saint-Lazare proved too much. Carmel declined, which only impressed him further. Soon he contacted her again, with another offer, this time to head all female Red Cross personnel in Paris. She accepted with alacrity.

Her situation improved overnight. She moved from spending her days in a cold, drafty railroad station into an office at the august Hôtel Regina on the place des Pyramides, deep in the heart of the fashion district that would one day, symbolically at least, be hers. The place Vendôme—even then full of couture houses—was only meters away; the chic rue du Faubourg Saint-Honoré not much farther. But that wasn't Carmel's geography during this particular sojourn. What mattered then was that the Regina was a mile from Saint-Lazare, and not too far from other Red Cross centers that she'd been called upon to supervise. She probably rode from one to the other on a bicycle—the streets were full of them during the war. The Red Cross girls could be recognized by their pale blue or violet riding costumes, complete with the divided skirts Americans call culottes, and perky small hats to match.

Carmel moved into the stately Hôtel Westminster, just beyond the place Vendôme on the ironically named rue de la Paix, where she'd stayed with her mother on buying trips for years (and which she would favor for decades to come). She pronounced it in the French manner—Vest-min-stair—and fondly described its "old-fashioned rooms" as looking "like a stage set for *Traviata* and something about that romantic period epitomized for me the romance and glamour of Paris, already the city of my heart." She wrote to her mother asking her to pay for uniforms, which she'd already decided to have made at Creed, a fashion house founded by the British tailor Henry Creed in the 1850s, and known for its crisp, elegant tailoring *à l'anglais* and its use of beautiful fabrics, including

Carmel White on the job for the American Red Cross, Paris, World War I

supple Rodier wool. The result was about as elegant as a uniform could possibly get. A photograph taken that summer at her Red Cross post in Paris shows it to be snug-fitting, crisply cut. Carmel looks radiant, war or no war, wearing a regulation necktie, like an English schoolgirl, and a flattering, wide-brimmed straw hat, which she acquired from Reboux, spurning the black straw numbers the other Red Cross girls bought at Motsch on the avenue de l'Alma (later Avenue George V). "My fashion sense was improving."

So was the political situation in Europe. After the armistice was signed on November 11, 1918, Carmel and others stayed on to help. American troops were still stationed in France, and they needed to be cared for. Much remained to be done, but the sheer relief at having the conflict resolved—and in the right way—must have tempered the postwar shortages and inconveniences. Carmel sounded distinctly playful in a letter written to her mother on April 2, 1919, on American Red Cross/Croix-Rouge Américaine letterhead. Writing in a breathless, endearingly girlish flutter, she gushed about having met a certain General Andrews. "But wait till you hear the *news,*" she added, "which is that although he leaves Paris tomorrow he is having Colonel Kerrigan put at my disposal a 5-passenger open Cadillac car. Can you imagine what that means today in Paris. . . . Isn't it wonderful? Could you believe it to happen to me?"

Although Carmel later spoke of having dated a general in France during the war, her relationship with this particular one was only one of friendship, she averred. In a punctuation-free rush, she assured her mother that

> *Andrews is just charming—married and not one iota flirtatious or cheap—on the contrary, I think the nicest man I've met since I came to France and he likes me I think too that is he just enjoys my company and he knows I'll give lots of the girls happiness with the car.*

The Paris Carmel describes is frivolous and fun, as if the armistice had been an excuse for one big party. She socialized madly, apparently, particularly among the French capital's Anglo-American community, going to dinner parties, dances, the opening of the Folies Bergère. She was taken by friends to meet Mildred Aldrich, an American expatriate who had become famous in the United States when the letters she wrote to friends during the first months of World War I, some of which literally took place before her eyes, were serialized in the *Atlantic Monthly* in 1914. (They were later published in the bestselling *A Hilltop on the Marne*—it went through seventeen printings—and three subsequent books.) Aldrich's cottage, called La Creste, was in the village of Huiry, just on the outskirts of Paris. Carmel described it, and its occupant, in rapturous terms.

> *Meaux is enchanting as old and quaint a little spot as there is in the world and Miss Aldrich's house a nice perfect little dot of a place that enchants you. No money spent but taste and brains and all the atmosphere that old age gives. Miss Aldrich is so much more interesting than her books. She is as plain looking as can be, but is beautiful with a radiant personality—a strong vigorous one—like a Roosevelt in Petticoats.*

Carmel and Aldrich were mutually impressed. The writer read the soppy James Stephens poem "Spring in Ireland" to her young visitor and, as if on cue, the Americanized-yet-deeply-Irish Carmel dissolved into tears. Aldrich seemed to know everyone: she was a close friend of Gertrude Stein and Alice B. Toklas, as well as many others, and she knew the poet, too, a fact that impressed Carmel deeply. ("She says Stephens is hideous to look at . . . ," she reported). Aldrich, in turn, was impressed by one of her young guest's acquaintances. "She adores Margaret Anglin and when she heard I knew her she took me just to her heart."

Carmel was thriving in her personnel duties, finding positions for the young American volunteers in her care and agonizing over their welfare. When a superior complimented her performance, she took it as a compliment since she was "the kind of person who never says even a wee bit of praise to your face." And the feedback from her charges was endlessly rewarding.

I do think the girls think I am just and I try to make them happy. You should see the flowers they bring me some days. It makes me very grateful you know mother darling. I can't be grateful enough to you for letting me have this experience. I'll never be the same again. I have about 175 people all of whom tell me stories, some tragic, some funny, and I am learning so much of life.

Christine had given birth to a son named John, known to all as Jack, and his photo adorned Carmel's desk. ("Her wee one looks at me every day and I love to think of her happiness.") Tom and his wife, curiously nicknamed "Virgin" here, had settled in Jamestown, Long Island, and were trying to have a child; Carmel asked her mother if there was any news on this front, adding, in the witchy way that would always be hers: "Things will soon be materializing I suppose with her. I will burn a candle for her and I think she wants a boy I will make that intention and tell her she can be calmly positive of the result as I have never asked for anything yet that wasn't granted." (For all of Carmel's psychic maneuverings, Tom's first child was a girl, Nancy, whose actual name at birth was Ann.) The rest of the letter is breathless, familial, appealingly Irish. "I don't know why am so happy," she wrote at the end. "The work is hard of course but you know I never mind that. Your very very own, Cara."

Toward the end of her tour of duty, her brother Tom, then thirty-five, turned up in Europe in what Carmel, in her memoir, describes as "a financial mission with a Morgan partner." The timing was perfect, since his sister was just winding up her Red Cross work. She took some time to linger in Europe. Tom introduced her to the partner in question, Edward R. Stettinius, and his family, and she became fast friends with young Ed Stettinius Jr., then seventeen. (He would later become secretary of state under Franklin D. Roosevelt.) She joined this extremely wealthy family, who had residences at 1021 Park Avenue and in Locust Valley, Long Island, as they sojourned through Europe.

In spite of the difference in age between them, Carmel and Ed fell in with each other like teenaged siblings; it must have been a relief to move from a position of awesome responsibility to that of being, effectively, a well-cared-for child. In France, the two spent their days bicycling, moving with the family from one hotel to another. Arriving in Brussels, Carmel took young Ed—"an idealistic, religious boy," in her description—off on a tour of her own. They visited her old convent, the Soeurs de Sainte-Marie, then, in a state of mutual rapture, apparently, moved on to the city's magnificent Gothic house of worship, the Catholic Cathedral of Saints Michael and Gudula, "that had made an impression on me when I was his age." If young Ed's parents approved of Carmel's influence on their boy, all of that may have changed when, toward the end of the trip, she cheerfully offered to spirit a Stettinius daughter's wedding veil into the United States, along with her own, newly acquired French lingerie. Carmel adored smuggling, something she would do with enthusiasm for the rest of her life, passing through Customs with suitcases full of label-free French couture clothes, but the Stettinius père was appalled and refused her offer. "He was far too law-abiding for that," Carmel wrote. In early August, when the Stettiniuses and she crossed the Atlantic together on the S.S. *France* from Le Havre, she was undoubtedly the only smuggler in their group.

For the third time, Carmel returned from Europe to a home she'd never set eyes on before: Mrs. Douglass had taken on a huge flat in the Navarro Apartments at 145 West Fifty-eighth Street. Built in the 1880s as one of the city's first cooperative apartment ventures, the Navarro was the "first elegant apartment building in New York," as Carmel pointed out. With most of her siblings still living at home, life there was anything but dull. But the experience of working at Fox, under her mother's supervision, was numbingly the same. Returning to it was an anticlimax of spectacular proportions. "Back in my mother's shop my old inferiority complex took over," she wrote. "Though I had proved my executive ability when I was on my own, under my mother I felt I was nobody. I didn't like not knowing anything and pretending I did."

The firm was prospering, at least in real estate terms. Douglass rode the postwar business boom in triumph. According to a *New York Times* story that ran in January 1920, she signed a twenty-one-year lease that month at 23 East Fifty-sixth Street, while her firm continued to occupy 10 East Fifty-seventh Street. (They had also recently bought 11 East Fifty-sixth Street, probably as an investment, which they, in turn, rented out, also on a twenty-one-year lease.) Her mother's empire was expanding—and Carmel was stuck.

The 1920s indeed began with a roar: for the first half of the decade, Prohibition's early years, frivolity, money, excess seemed to be at an all-time high. Manhattan's social distractions, its swank parties and speakeasies, seemed endless. From this point on, Carmel assumed a Cinderella-like existence where, no matter how depressing things might seem for her during the working day, her youth, vivacity, and beauty paid off handsomely in her off hours. They even, apparently, overcame her Irishness—which was death in New York's high society, rather more acceptable in the more artistic circles she favored. The legendary "No Irish Need Apply" signs that popped up in that era give a clear indication of what an ambitious young person from the Other Side would face in New York. Prejudice was everywhere—except for those rare young Irish who broke the mold. And the White siblings, including, particularly, Desmond, whom Carmel described as "an Irish charmer," certainly did that. Carmel, too, was an appealing combination—spirited, funny, naive. As it turned out, she could apply after all.

Her war work in Europe had given her newfound confidence, at least when she was away from her mother. Her social successes seemed to multiply. She didn't keep a diary—or at least none that survives her—but a close friend of hers, Ruby Ross Goodnow née Pope, did. Goodnow (who would become Ruby Ross Wood upon her marriage to Chalmers Benedict Wood Jr. in 1924) was one of the era's most promising young New York decorators, and she and Carmel formed part of a floating tribe, nomads who joined together night after night, decamping from parties to restaurants and openings. The designer's diary from the early 1920s lists the seemingly endless gatherings of this ever-shifting, fun-loving crowd. Inevitably, some took place at Douglass's home, with plenty of Whites in attendance. At one 1921 party, Carmel looked "lovely in a red gown," Goodnow reported, and she stopped the show by reciting her beloved "Spring" poem by Stephens—that Irish schmaltz—aloud. At another, Gilda Varesi, an actress then starring on Broadway, told Ruby Goodnow's fortune with cards. The cast was ever shifting: Carmel introduced Goodnow to Margaret Anglin, and they socialized a lot with Brock Pemberton, a leading theatrical producer of the day, and his costume-designing wife, Margaret McCoy Pemberton.

Goodnow had distinguished herself as a design writer before becoming a decorator, set designer, and proprietor of Au Quatrième, the decorating department of the John Wanamaker department store in downtown Manhattan, which she opened in 1918. Many of her artist friends, including Carmel's brother Victor, contributed decorative items—panels, screens, and the like—to Belmaison, the gallery she opened at Wanamaker's to provide art for the home. Among the artists she and Carmel frequented were Eugene Speicher, whom Carmel told Goodnow was "more like Renoir than any American painter" (and who was then painting Carmel's portrait); Bellows; and her old teacher, Henri. And she knew plenty of writers, too, including a shifting population of the group known as the Algonquin Round Table, among them the political writer Heywood Broun and the famously vicious, yet legendarily charming (to some) critic Alexander Woollcott, both then on the staff of a morning paper, the *New York World.*

Night after night, Carmel would bask in the glow of her admiring suitors from this artistic beau monde, only to be cut back to size at work the next morning, like wheat under a scythe, by her mother's cutting, and quite obviously jealous, remarks. And so it went, like something out of ancient mythology, until she was well into her thirties. Sometimes the bright spots burned brighter. In the early 1920s, Carmel made several trips to her beloved Paris with her mother—attending the collections, staying at the Westminster—but such reprieves never lasted for long. And then this dreary cycle came to a sudden, and triumphant, end. One day, Harry-dele Hallmark fell ill just before the Paris collections and asked

Carmel, who was to attend them with her mother, to take notes for "What the Well-Dressed Women Are Wearing," the witty, informative fashion column Hallmark wrote each week under the name Anne Rittenhouse for the *New York Times.* "Here at last was something I felt I could do," Carmel wrote. "I slaved over those notes night after night. For the first time I looked at clothes with a *knowing* eye, with the result that Harrydel [sic] was delighted with her report.

"I said to her: 'I'd rather be doing the work you're doing than anything in the world.' She said, 'I'll give you a letter to Mrs. Chase, the editor of *Vogue.*' And with that I was launched on my career." After meeting with Edna Chase—an intimidating force of nature who was at the helm of *Vogue* for a staggeringly long run, sixty years—the latter sent her on to meet with Condé Nast, the courtly magazine publisher, who had an eye for talent as well as for appealing young women. Delighted to find both in the form of Carmel, he asked her to contribute articles to the magazine. It was a euphoric moment—she'd long wanted to write. She submitted some pieces, apparently, but we'll never know if they ran. Like many magazines, *Vogue* in those days was written almost entirely anonymously: there was no masthead and almost none of its articles were bylined. Still, for Carmel, any connection with *Vogue,* the preeminent fashion publication in both the United States and Europe, was bliss.

But it wasn't to last. Soon, like Persephone, she was drawn back into the underworld of T.M. & J.M. Fox. With exquisite ill timing, Douglass fell sick with some since-forgotten malady, and her reluctant daughter was dragooned back into full-time service, overseeing both the shop and the Fox workrooms on Thirty-fourth Street. Yet even this depressing turn of events offered something for a future fashion editor to learn: called upon to supervise 250 fitters and seamstresses, she wrote, "I began to learn the architecture of clothes."

By the time her mother had recovered, Nast's offer must have seemed like a distant, ever-receding mirage. Carmel had put down her pen to run Fox and, given the silence emanating from his direction, assumed Nast had forgotten her entirely. Depressed, she thought of contacting the publisher but never quite did.

And then, one crisp morning toward the end of 1920, Nast himself turned up at the shop and, as in a dream, said exactly the words she'd been longing to hear. He had only a minute, the publisher explained, wearing, as always, a stiff collar and a pince-nez, and creaking forward in a half bow. He was on his way to Europe, a taxi was outside waiting to take him to the docks, but before he went, would she, could she, consider coming to work for him at *Vogue*?

Carmel could barely answer, scarcely needed to. As for asking the permission of her mother, who was fortuitously absent from the shop on an errand, there was no way she'd take the risk.... Years later she recalled watching in stupefaction as this messenger from the gods vanished again, leaving her to wonder if their brief encounter had been a dream. (His visit had lasted less than five minutes.) "Goodbye—so it's settled right now, Miss White!" he called out, almost shouting, as he sprinted out the door to his cab, which lurched away into the roar of noontime traffic. And from that moment, it all began.

3 *miss white of* vogue

Fashion to me is like a long serial story.
By the uninitiated, the next installment can't be guessed.

—Carmel Snow

VOGUE WAS THE SUMMIT, the apex, the ne plus ultra of the fashion world. It was, quite simply, It. By the time Carmel joined its staff as an assistant fashion editor, in 1921, the magazine, which came out every other Thursday, had long been required reading for anyone in America who wanted to live a fashionable life. It had the highest circulation of all the American fashion magazines. No other one could compete.

Needless to say, one of the overriding pressures of working at such an institution was a sartorial one. The *Vogue* offices, then on Twenty-fourth Street, were "ladylike (not to say la-di-da) to a fare-thee-well," as Carmel described it, so a first-day outfit there required careful planning. "I got myself up to kill," she recalled. She was wise enough to do so in an outfit by one of Paris's most exciting new designers, Madeleine Vionnet, who was credited with inventing the bias cut and known for her considerable talent as a draper. "I was proud of myself (I still am) for recognizing that here was an artist in fabric," Carmel wrote.

Madame Vionnet, who had a shop on the rue de Rivoli, was eternally ahead of the curve, dropping corsets as early as 1912. Some of her clothes were so complex that they required written operating instructions. Yet once on the body, if and when it finally got there, a Vionnet dress, with its gentle drapes and folds, had a majestic simplicity. Years later, no less a designer than Christian Dior would say of Vionnet: "Never has the art of the dress designer reached greater heights."

Even so, Carmel's carefully planned outfit was all wrong. She knew nothing of the magazine's dress code, which required hats, white gloves, and silk stockings at all times. But that was the least of it. For her first day on the job, she selected a dress and a matching jacket of dead black crêpe de chine—Vionnet never cared for color—a fabric more suitable for a recent widow than an ambitious young assistant editor. Worse still, her mother having impressed upon her the value of matching accessories, Carmel sank her fashion ship by doing exactly that. She covered her flowing auburn hair with a black hat by "Miss Jessica" (then of Bendel's), and adding ebony-colored gloves, stockings, and shoes. Douglass had opposed her daughter's journalistic career from the outset; it's tempting, in our post-Freudian age, to wonder if she hadn't, unconsciously or not, hoped to scuttle her daughter's maiden voyage by arranging such an inauspicious fashion debut. But such conjecture, however delicious, must remain only that.

In any case, and thus attired, Carmel entered the world of *Vogue.* Founded in December 1892 by a Princeton graduate named Arthur Baldwin Turnure, it was backed by a consortium of the New York rich, among them Peter Cooper Hewitt and Cornelius Vanderbilt Jr. The magazine aimed, as Turnure wrote in the first issue, to create "a dignified, authentic journal of society, fashion and the ceremonial side of life, that is to be for the present, mainly pictorial." The consortium included some Old Money names, but others that were not, and the magazine was envisioned as a place where the lives of both could be documented. In the nineteenth century, social climbers were fair game: with casual viciousness, an 1887 article in the society rag *Town Topics* had pondered the question: "Where were the Vanderbilts, socially, even five years ago?" By establishing a journal about society, Vanderbilt and other nouveaux riches aimed to secure a place in it. Which, of course, they did.

Carmel was right to describe the magazine as la-di-da. Its office resembled a hushed, well-run Fifth Avenue apartment, complete with antique furnishings and its own servant class. Even its reception area, Snow recalled, "was bound with leather-bound books (fakes) where the most beautiful girl in the world greeted vis-

Four young women at *Vogue* in about 1912 (*left to right:* Edna Chase, Martha Moller, Marie Lyons, and Grace Hegger)

itors from behind a Chinese Chippendale desk and asked them to wait in the conservatory."

But it hadn't always been so. At first, during Turnure's tenure—lovely alliteration—the atmosphere had been decidedly no frills. But all that changed after Condé Nast, a gentle, fastidious law school graduate and perpetual number cruncher, bought the magazine in 1909. As he rose, the magazine did as well; as he himself became more dressy, the offices associated with his enterprise spiffed up accordingly. Nast had arrived in New York in 1897 to work for *Collier's Weekly.* Within a decade, he'd begun putting together the magazine empire that still bears his name. His acquisitions at the time he bought *Vogue* included *House & Garden;* later, in 1913, he added *Vanity Fair* to the mix. Originally called *Dress,* then *Dress and Vanity Fair,* it was at first conceived as encompassing fashion, too, although Nast soon reconfigured it to focus on politics and the arts instead. "Where do you date intellectually?" asked an ad for the magazine. "Your clothes, your house, your car, even your dog are in the mode of 1927, maybe even 1928. . . . But what is the date of your ideas?" Such contributors as Sherwood Anderson and Alexander Woollcott—the leading writers of the day—were on hand to keep readers up to date.

Nast was a solid midwesterner who'd had the good sense to marry up. His wife, the former Clarisse Coudert, was "slender, suave, and frighteningly chic," as one *Vogue* editor described her. While Clarisse turned out not to be a permanent acquisition, the elegance she'd brought with her proved indelible; after being in her orbit, Nast became known for serious refinement—in his dress, his way of entertaining, his very aura. His wife was the daughter of Charles Coudert, a cofounder, with his two brothers, of the international law firm known as Coudert Brothers, which was established in 1853. An amateur interior decorator, it was she who first gave *Vogue* the rarefied environment it deserved. Inevitably, "sophistication crept in upon us," as the magazine's editor, Edna Chase, put it. (At some point, Clarisse's efforts would be revamped by the legendary decorator Elsie de Wolfe, a style-setting American residing in France who was frequently written up in *Vogue*.)

Chase presided over her fiefdom from an ornately furnished office; her desk was pale yellow, its vertically grooved legs were highlighted in blue. Elsewhere in the room there was an elegantly diminutive chest of drawers and a marble-topped occasional table. Maidenly secretaries typed discreetly in niches. A starched-uniformed maid went over the editors' offices daily with a feather duster; for a time, her duties also included wheeling a trolley through the halls each afternoon at half-past four, proffering tea and cookies, until Chase banned the practice as being too disruptive. "It seems that only the British can serve tea during business hours without demoralization," she sniffed.

The refined, ladylike decor was deceptive. *Vogue* was a business, after all, and Chase ran it ferociously—and with great success—exhibiting the toughness and decisiveness that's a prerequisite for the job of editor of a fashion magazine. She was a certifiable, fire-breathing dragon. She didn't waste time on niceties and thought nothing of cutting her editors to the quick as required. But she lived *Vogue* and got the job done. The magazine was healthy under her tenure, and it remained that way. For decades, Chase brought results, and Condé Nast was eternally grateful to her for it. They worked closely and harmoniously together. She filled the pages with a mix that scarcely varied—acres of fashion and society news. He, endlessly, kept the numbers in check.

When Carmel began working for Chase as an assistant editor she was thirty-four, yet her boundless energy and enthusiasm—not to mention a naïveté that even she, in later life, found remarkable ("I was as pure as the driven snow")—made her seem younger. Chase was only a decade older, but seemed more than that. Descended from New Jersey Quakers, she was dour and, as she was the first to admit, entirely without humor. She dressed primly and pinned her wavy gray hair back in a way that made her seem ancient. She dated from antiquity, in magazine terms, having first joined *Vogue,* in its circulation department, in 1895, when she was eighteen. In 1914, Nast appointed her as editor, and there she stayed.

Chase recalled Carmel's hiring somewhat differently than her employee did—it was just one of numerous differences in the way they viewed the world. The editor described herself as a friend and fan of the White family—she even shopped at T.M. & J.M. Fox, among other Manhattan emporiums—and stated that it was she who had determined that the younger White daughter should be hired. "Carmel, I felt, had a flair for fashion," she pronounces in her 1954 memoir, *Always in Vogue,* in that wonderfully consistent imperious voice that seems to come so naturally to fashion editors of her vintage.

Nast was an entirely different figure. He was an immensely gracious man, and he ensured his staff's loyalty with his warm manner. "Even at his busiest in the office, he always stopped in the hall to ask some personal, unbusinesslike question that made you feel a part of his life, not just part of his organization," one staffer recalled. He was unwavering in his enthusiasm for his new employee. He considered Carmel's hands-on experience in fashion to be an asset, and he admired her ability to get along with anyone—an important talent for a job that involved contact with such disparate groups as department store executives, Seventh Avenue manufacturers, fashion artists, professional models, advertising salespeople, socialites, and photographers. Carmel was popular with all of them, as well as others on the magazine's staff. And she was a favorite of some of her office neighbors as well, notably Frank Crowninshield, the relentlessly charming editor of *Vanity Fair,* which, later in the 1920s, after both magazines moved to 420 Lexington Avenue—perennially known to Nast staffers as 420 Lex—became *Vogue*'s neighbor on the nineteenth floor.

Nast must have seemed like a fairy godfather to Carmel. He was always accessible: "The open door was Condé's policy," Chase wrote.

> *Anyone could push his head in. They could ask him a question, he'd take care of their problems, speak on the telephone, maybe vanish for a moment into the little washroom adjoining his office, where he had a private wire for beautiful women and stockbrokers, emerge, and continue the conversation. That kind of multiple activity stimulated him and he enjoyed it.*

Carmel fell right into the social swim of the magazine. She meddled benevolently in the lives of her coworkers, something she adored doing, always. She called them "Dodie" and endless other Irishisms, and threw herself into their stories, encouraging them in love affairs, consoling them over breakups, rejoicing over proposals. She had an "extra instinctive feeling about people," someone on her staff later said. "She was deeply interested in people, all kinds of people," adds another. "She'd have lunch with a Seventh Avenue cloakmaker and she'd come back with just as much enthusiasm as if it had been the Prince of Wales."

At *Vogue,* with its deep-set snobberies, she was a blast of fresh air. In many ways, her boss was, too. Nast was an unusual man. He loved glitter, glamour, to be surrounded by famous names, yet he had a down-to-earth quality that seems distinctly midwestern; "he had great simplicity and gentle manners," a *Vogue* editor recalled. If he developed a taste for almost ludicrously young women, you sense that it was their relative simplicity that attracted him as much as anything else.

And while he may have eaten in the world's finest restaurants, he favored ice cream and plain, all-American food. He and Chase frequently lunched together at Horn & Hardart's Automat, perhaps the most unglamorous, if gimmicky, restaurant in fashionable New York. Its clientele—which didn't include many other media moguls, needless to say—would buy their pot roast special and apple pie à la mode by dropping small bits of change into glass-covered cases—a kind of jukebox of food. The meal itself may have been "quick and dirty," as Nast affectionately called it, but the way you obtained it was refreshingly new.

By all accounts, Nast and Chase worked beautifully in tandem, putting out a magazine that little resembles the one that bears its name today. "They were a perfect team," Alexander Liberman, the future editorial director of Condé Nast's magazine division recalled. In 1921, when Carmel signed on to *Vogue,* the magazine, to modern eyes, looked quaint. But by the end of the decade both its look and the fashions it contains—dresses that reveal the body, hemlines that stop just below the knee—seem much closer to our sensibilities today. To peruse the 1920s in *Vogue,* from one year to the next, is to see a world that looks anachronistic slip away, replaced by something that seems suddenly, shockingly, almost of our time.

In these early issues, photos were rare. Instead, under art director Heyworth Campbell, the magazine was full of sketches of fashionable people, places, and, of course, clothes. Some drawings look suitable for a Victorian nursery, as innocent and old-fashioned as anything Kate Greenaway might have drawn. But that changed abruptly in the mid-1920s, after the witty Spanish artist Eduardo Garcia Benito, who signed his work with his last name only, was brought in to freshen up the book. Benito lived in Paris, a city that had been awakened to modernism by the seminal Exposition Internationale des Arts Décoratifs et Industriels Modernes in 1925, from which the term *art deco* was coined. With its heavy black lines, copious white space, and Bauhaus-influenced typefaces, Benito created a dummy of the magazine that swept Campbell's florid, sentimental designs away.

The magazine's art deco–influenced covers, of the mid-1920s in particular, project an idiosyncratic glamour that has retained its sophistication over the years. Drawn by such period artists as Helen Dryden and Georges Lepape, they were often realized in the bright, harlequin palette of Diaghilev's Ballets Russes, the dance company that had first electrified Paris in 1909, not just with movement, but with its costumes, sets, music, choreography—its very style. *Vogue*'s covers were a doorway into a world of unspeakable glamour. There's an insouciance about the idealized, chic women they depict, posing with children with hoops, peacocks in full plumage, and other unexpected sights. They seem to dwell in an impossibly elegant universe, one just beyond our own. Like the best, the most addictive, fashion publications, *Vogue* had an unattainable quality, drawing its readers in while gently excluding them at the same time. (In this way, nothing in the magazine world has changed.)

A famous cover by A. E. Marty of a veiled woman in a cowboy hat, sitting sidesaddle on a bucking zebra while clasping bright red reins, caused a sensation when it ran in the January 15, 1926, issue. The *New York Herald Tribune* even ran an editorial on the subject, stating that "Mr. Condé Nast almost persuades us that style is an American invention" and adding that "once in a while convention and novelty make a highly useful team." *Vogue* promptly reprinted this wry, flattering essay in its own pages, saying that the editorial had pleased the magazine because of "*Vogue*'s desire to promote all that is new in art (so long as it is inherently good and has the intangible quality of chic that characterizes all the material in the magazine) . . ."

During the time that Carmel was at *Vogue,* in the 1920s, fashion underwent a revolution, one largely caused by Coco Chanel, whose stripped-down aesthetic lent itself beautifully to mass production. Carmel, of course, had foretold this, but she couldn't have known—or did she?—how profoundly, and completely, everything would change. As the magazine asked rhetorically in its 1922 thirtieth-anniversary issue, "Would anyone believe that the female hour-glass figure of thirty years ago could be straightened out and flattened into the long ghost-like silhouette of today?"

Even high-quality clothing could now be manufactured, rather than made by hand. As Douglass correctly predicted, this latest development would soon drive her own and other dressmaking establishments into financial ruin. (The Depression, of course, would help the process along.) "The day the readymades started coming in," she told her daughter in the Dublin cadence Carmel loved to imitate, "with a dar-rt here and a dar-rt there, I knew I was finished." Early in the 1920s these smaller emporiums still managed to stay afloat: in May 1922, several styles by Molyneux and Chanel, all credited to Fox, were photographed in *Vogue*. But the shop would not be carrying them, or indeed anything else, for long.

That a store was mentioned at all was an indication of how much fashion magazines, too, had changed. A woman perusing *Vogue* just the year before might have fallen in love with the fashion it contained—a beribboned robe de style by Jeanne Lanvin, for example—but she wouldn't have been given a clue about where she might acquire it. As often as not, she'd tear out the page and bring it straight to her dressmaker to copy. But in 1922, just as clothes began being made in quantity, *Vogue* started crediting stores. (It took decades, though, for any fashion magazine to mention ones outside of New York.)

In those days, *Vogue* took its readers' upper-class status, or at least their aspirations, for granted. Its pages scarcely hinted at the existence of any other socioeconomic group. Articles on the "Basis of Good Breeding" and the chicest way to uniform one's chauffeur crowd its pages. The editorial section of each issue began with a portrait, usually of a titled subject—the Countess of Oxford and Asquith, say, or the Comtesse du Bourg de Bozas. Often, the lensman who shot it was an aristocrat himself; "How many of our photographers had titles in those days!" as Carmel once exclaimed. The most famous of these was the Baron Adolph de Meyer, known as "Gayne," whose melodramatic portraits and fashion shots were part of the magazine from the time he was hired by Condé Nast as a contract photographer in 1914. "He developed a technique of glamorizing the subjects by means of a veiled lens and ethereal lighting," as one *Vogue* editor put it. For eight years, de Meyer's baroque, theatrically lit portraits and fashion shots were a staple of *Vogue*. If their subjects seem stilted to us now, it's worth remembering that, then, everyone's did. As the photographer George Hoyningen-Huené has pointed out, "Women had to pose for large 8 by 10 cameras, and since the manipulating of these cameras is very slow, they all looked as though they were posing. . . ."

Working for the magazine at the same time, Hoyningen-Huené aimed for a different look. "I tried to make [models] look the way we saw them, not as if they were posing for static portraits. I think that was the first innovation." A master of studio lighting, he created fashion shots that were more like scenarios, sometimes staging entire parties peopled with languid, impossibly beautiful men and women in evening clothes. Like de Meyer, Hoyningen-Huené was a baron, and operatic in temperament. Although his title was authentic—his mother was an American, an ambassador's daughter, from Grosse Point, Michigan, his father a Baltic baron—others were more dubious. Baron de Meyer's baronetcy, for example, was an honorary one that was supposed to have died out with his father.

The magazine's focus was seriously Eurocentric, especially given how far away the Continent was in those days—a week or so by sea. Yet *Vogue* casually chatted about doings on the French Riviera, then a newly minted resort, as if the average reader might dash right over in her new motorcar, a Nash, perhaps, or a two-toned, two-door Oakland Sensible Six. Paris is mentioned almost as often as New York. And certain European aristocrats, such as the Princesse Faucigny-Lucinge and the Honorable Mrs. Reginald Fellowes—goddesses of the 1920s—were ubiquitous. There were so many venerable Gallic titles in *Vogue*'s pages in this period that it seems inconceivable that the French Revolution ever took place. A surprising number turn out to be held by American girls. It's all very reminiscent of Henry James, with tarnished Old World titles finding new luster after the generous application of New World cash. And, of course, homegrown American upper-class beauties (more horsey, less chic, than their European counterparts) were also featured—Whitneys, Biddles, and more.

The amount of leisure, not to mention money, implied in these pages is staggering. "New York Spends Halcyon Days at Newport," one *Vogue* headline read, as if the canyons of Manhattan had emptied out. "Paris Builds Barricades of Fur" (the mind boggles) reads another. The women who weren't professional

Portrait of Carmel Snow, photographed by
Cecil Beaton at Condé Nast's apartment, 1929

models tended to be socialites, and their lives don't sound, how to put it, terribly deep. A pudgy, dog-walking, teenaged heiress named Diana Dalziel—later to be known as Diana Vreeland—"just returned from Palm Beach," one photo caption solemnly informs us. Oh. Even so, *Vogue* had an intellectual side that sometimes filtered through. Aldous Huxley and Virginia Woolf contributed to its pages in the years Carmel worked there, and the magazine did try to keep its readers abreast of cultural doings, critiquing C. K. Scott Moncrieff's new English translation of Marcel Proust's *Remembrance of Things Past* as "leaving much to be desired," for example, even as it described the author himself, with delicious understatement, as being "introspective."

When she first went to *Vogue,* Carmel still aspired to write; in the course of her years there, though, this goal dissipated and she became, inexorably, an editor. She and Chase would tussle over Carmel's writing, which had "an airy insouciance about it that appalled me," Chase wrote. "I used to edit her letters and gradually trained her into the more conventional paths of business usage, although I think she found it prosy stuff." It's impossible to discern now what Carmel's literary contribution to the magazine might have been. Was it she who penned such wonderfully ludicrous conceits as "*Vogue,* the Ancient Mariner charts the sea of fashion"? Sadly, we can never know.

Years later, Carmel would recall being told by William Nichols, editor of *This Week,* a syndicated Sunday magazine, that "being a writer manqué . . . is almost a qualification for being an editor, since editors must be catalysts who communicate through their contributors." In any case, she proved herself to be a born fashion editor, sure of her choices, iron willed as needed. Her delicate Celtic beauty and elegant wardrobe—courtesy of trips to Paris and the workrooms at Fox—didn't hurt, either, and she soon became a favorite guest at the fabled, uninhibited parties that Nast and another legendary magazine man, *Vanity Fair*'s Crowninshield, gave together at Nast's Park Avenue apartment, where her dance partners might include George Gershwin or any number of New York's Four Hundred.

By this time, Nast was on the way to amassing a fabled fortune. His first marriage, to Clarisse, had ended in 1919; two years later, Crowninshield moved in with Nast. Their relationship was by all accounts a platonic one, a kind of Boston marriage between men. For the next decade, until Nast married again, the two bachelors were seen everywhere together, everywhere, that is, that was fashionable—theater openings, nightclubs, charity balls. Starting in 1925, when Nast bought his legendary thirty-room—yes, *thirty*—duplex penthouse apartment at 1040 Park Avenue, with its ballroom and its glass-enclosed terrace, he became famous for his dinner dances: "the most glamorous parties I've ever been to," in the words of one *Vogue* editor. And they weren't just for stuffy society types. "Everybody who was invited to a Condé Nast party stood for something," wrote Diana Vreeland, who attended them in her youth.

People in the arts mattered more to Nast than such august, if relatively useless, people as Mrs. Hermann Oelrichs or Mrs. Stuyvesant Fish, although he always enjoyed sprinkling such Social Register types among the crowd. His guest lists also included Fred Astaire, Katharine Cornell, Rube Goldberg, Edna St. Vincent Millay, and more. And there was no snobbery to it. Everyone from his magazines was invited, "from the stockroom, the messengers, the typists, the editors and right on up," as were "a dozen or so of the most wanted call girls in New York," according to Ewart "Red" Newsom, a former writer at *Vanity Fair.*

The evenings swelled with swing music, bootleg liquor, undiluted talent. The backdrop was money. There were buckets of champagne, acres of flowers—$30,000 worth of roses for one party alone. The rooms themselves, featured in the August 1, 1928, issue of *Vogue,* were almost too rich to digest. Elsie de Wolfe had filled them with things of fabled provenance—an eighteenth-century Chinese-accented black-and-gold lacquer table that had once been in the collection of the Duke of Beaufort or, from the same century, Chien-Lung wallpaper that had graced the walls of "Beau Desert," the Marquess of Anglesey's stately home. It lined Nast's famous ballroom, an extraordinary space in which to entertain. The room's palette of salmon pink and bluish green flattered everyone, and its sheer size—a hundred could sit down to dinner in the adjoining terrace alone—imparted a grandeur, a social heft to almost any group.

It's no wonder Carmel wrote that "in the Twenties, life was at its most glamorous." Even before she became "Miss White of *Vogue,*" she was a social light in a young, fast-moving New York crowd—the so-called Flaming Youth of the Twenties. Her connection with *Vogue* added still more events to an already-packed calendar. She still gravitated toward the theater crowd: one lifelong friendship began after she saw *A Bill of Divorcement,* the 1921 Broadway hit. Her own witchy intuition told her instantly that the dark beauty who played the daughter would be famous. The girl was Katharine Cornell, and, of course, Carmel had it right. Her life, and career, would be marked by such moments; "I've always been attracted by what I can, by some kind of Irish clairvoyance, *foresee* in an artist," as she put it. She became, in time, "terribly close" friends with both Cornell, whom she called "Kit," and her husband, the theater producer Guthrie McClintic, attending parties at their house on Beekman Place (then, amazingly, a relatively low-rent district) and socializing with their friends, many of them either famous or about to be so, among them Noël Coward, Beatrice Lillie, and Gertrude Lawrence. Adding to the intrigue, perhaps, was the persistent rumor that McClintic and Cornell were each homosexual, and that their marriage was, as the French put it so delicately, a "white" one.

At the magazine Chase was feared, even respected, but hardly universally liked. So when Carmel came along—popular, gregarious, fun—the older woman saw her as a threat. While she was glad to have such a hardworking, talented young protégée, and happy to take credit for her discovery, it's clear from Chase's memoir that Carmel's success, and particularly the deep, abiding esteem afforded her by Nast himself, was unnerving to the older editor. She may have been formidable, but she was deeply insecure, an impression confirmed by Alexander Liberman, who remarked on Chase's "deep inferiority complex. . . . There was a great sadistic trait in her."

There are moments when, as Chase writes about Carmel, a deep, unexpected sadness percolates up through her words. "Carmel Snow's personal life I sometimes envied," she wrote. "She and her sisters [sic], her brothers, and sisters-in-law were a close-knit, warmhearted conclave. Having myself been the only child of an only child and possessing but one chick of my own, I used to think wistfully of their big, gay, overflowing gatherings, lighted by their Irish wit and charm." It's telling that, when talking about her young staffer, Chase mentions jealousy up front. Like Douglass, she envied the younger woman's beauty and talent. It must have felt to both women that, while they had peaked in their professional and personal lives, Carmel had ample time in which to come into her own.

Chase's comments are measured ones, more than measured, actually: when talking about her former protégée she seems to seethe. "She was so good, when not distracted . . ." is one barbed remark she directs toward a woman she once valued over anyone else on her staff. "She was keen about the work, full of enthusiasm and verve, but her actual business experience was nil . . ." is another. As is

> *She had native good taste, which had been cultivated and developed by her work. She had ability, poise, and an engaging wit, but there were lapses. She was capable of originating fine ideas, though, like a spotty golf player, her follow-through was weak.*

Even Carmel herself said she looked "rather sulky" in a 1922 photograph of the *Vogue* staff, seated, as she was, next to the editor who treated her, at least intermittently, with such opprobrium. But Chase's aspect is also revealing: regal in a fur collar, she looks down with icy disapproval, even contempt, at the young woman at her side. As Liberman put it: "She was a very down to earth lady, and her assistants were much more brilliant, and that's why she quarreled with Carmel Snow, because Carmel Snow was much more brilliant."

In her first years at the magazine, Carmel and Chase would socialize together from time to time. In April 1921, the pair gave a lecture on makeup, a par-

Vogue's editorial staff in 1922. *Front row left to right:* Carmel White, Edna Chase; *back row:* Lois Long, Nina Ryan, Heyworth Campbell, Agnes Bright

ticularly hot topic in a year that saw the invention of the first waterproof mascara (by Elizabeth Arden, who'd just opened her first salon in Paris). At a dinner afterward given by Ruby Goodnow, the two editors joined Carmel's sister, Christine Holbrook (by now also the mother of a daughter named Carmel), and a group of irreverent male friends who, Goodnow noted, became "hysterical at the talk of 1251 rouge, and Swedish hair powder, and bella donna and transformations, and lipsticks." Later in the same month, Carmel and Chase together attended the huge opening dinner of the Ambassador Hotel, a grandiose, marble-columned structure on Park Avenue that had been decorated by Goodnow, with leather paneling on its walls and a Roman gold-and-green motif in its opulent restaurant.

Carmel dressed for such occasions in clothes by Vionnet and Chanel, who had only recently changed all the rules, first to scandal, then to acclaim, by dropping the waistline to the hips. Virtually every other designer followed suit. "Women entered the second decade of the Twentieth Century shaped like hourglasses, and came out of it shaped like rolls of carpet," as Alison Lurie so unforgettably described it. Another writer, Cecil Beaton, compared the female figure of the 1920s to "cooked asparagus." Carmel also favored the Anglo-Irish designer Captain Edward Molyneux (who pronounced his name, with British perversity, "Mollinucks"). Decorated for bravery in World War I, Molyneux had gone on to become one of Paris's leading couturiers, creating pure-lined, elegant clothes of luxurious fabrics. His

> *clothes had an "understated" look that I appreciated more and more as I began wearing them. My personal philosophy about fashion was at last beginning to form: Clothes must be subordinate to the personality of the woman wearing them. She must express her personality, in terms of color especially, but the costume mustn't outshine her.*

The clothes of the 1920s—like the era itself, with its speakeasies and flappers—have long been reduced to a cliché. Waists headed downward, as we all know, and the silhouette became radically more slender. Women, well, some women, seemed sylphlike overnight, their swan necks emerging from bateau necklines. Cloches and other smaller hats replaced the heavy, even ridiculous numbers of just a few years earlier—just the style to complement the decade's new bobbed and marcelled hairstyles. "Chic started at the eyebrows" is how Chase summed it up. "To show the forehead would have evoked a scandal."

Although the period's look seemed almost static, lingering forever, there actually was some variety. Hemlines rose and fell. Early in the decade, skirts were ankle length; later, they crept higher. Dresses were unstructured, none more so than Chanel's, and if there was a certain sameness to it all—the dropped waist was, quite simply, inviolable—it seems understandable. After decades, even centuries, of being trussed up, the public reveled in something more forgiving. If the 1920s were "gay" in that old-fashioned sense, it was in part because women, at last, could move.

As Carmel's social life expanded, her home life seemed to become evermore constricting. Most unmarried daughters in those days stayed at home until they wed, so Carmel remained with her mother and various unmarried brothers—all of whom delighted in poking fun at her increasingly high-fashion outfits.

While these comments were mainly lighthearted, Douglass's, typically, were not. Over the dinner table and elsewhere, she never let up, telling her daughter that her career couldn't last. Her withering remarks might alight on anything, including Carmel's fashionably marcelled hair, ironed in stiff rows, like a series of frozen waves: "The thir-rd time this week she's been at the hairdresser's, and look at *her hair*." Self-esteem hadn't been invented yet, of course; the entire concept, especially as applied to one's children, would have seemed preposterous. Even so, Douglass's attitude was extreme. Carmel recalled that "from the moment I arrived at *Vogue* the day seldom passed without a phone call from my mother to check up on my performance."

Sometimes work and home mixed. At Carmel's request, Nast stopped by the Navarro Apartments one night to coach her in the seemingly endless details of magazine layout—she claimed not to know the difference between a title and a caption. Long after their famous rift and for the rest of her life, she would credit Nast with teaching her everything she knew. Crowninshield, a relentlessly sociable creature, who relished his evenings with the Whites, was another visitor to their home in the Navarro. He was a favorite of Bridget Keogh, the opinionated, funny maid that Suie, one of Douglass's sisters, had found for the family in Dublin. Bridget called the large, boisterous family "a circus" and would delight them all by mimicking visitors after they left. She adored Crownie and did a wicked imitation of his turning up "jauntily at our door in his frock coat, hands behind his back, eyes peering over his spectacles, twinkling with the joie de vivre he always brought with him."

A gentleman caller who fared less well was Conger Goodyear, an industrialist and art collector in his thirties who, in 1929, would become the first president of New York's Museum of Modern Art. Goodyear once rang the bell only to be greeted by a suspicious-looking Bridget, who was becoming increasingly alarmed by Carmel's apparent resistance to settling down. "Are you married?" the servant demanded. When Goodyear admitted that he was, she said, without missing a beat, "Then you're no good to Miss Carmel," and closed the door in his face.

Carmel also spent time with Crowninshield. Their relationship was platonic, as all of his relationships with women seemed to be, but fun for both. They'd go to opening nights on Broadway, holding hands, retreating afterward to Hicks, a popular soda fountain, for ice cream. Or they might dine at the Hotel Brevoort, a restaurant in a Greenwich Village hotel that was a favorite among French expatriates and one that was, for Carmel, "a nostalgic reminder of Paris to me." Another favorite was the Coffee House Club, founded by Crowninshield as an alternative to the stuffy Knickerbocker Club. There, Crownie introduced her to one suitor after another, among them Abram Poole, a socialite and portrait artist who's probably best known for his dramatic, stylized, 1923 portrait of his wife, Mercedes de Acosta, a wonderfully colorful character who wrote, dabbled in mysticism, and was said to have been the lesbian lover of a truly astonishing number of the era's great actresses, among them Katharine Cornell, Eva Le Gallienne, Greta Garbo, Marlene Dietrich, and more. Surely, Poole found Carmel, however spirited, to be weak tea by comparison. Another escort she met through Crownie was Charles Hanson Towne, known as "Charlie," who was then the editor of William Randolph Hearst's *Harper's Bazar* (the second *a* in the magazine's title was added in 1929). It must have been an interesting pairing: the competition between *Vogue* and its rival fashion magazine, known by *Vogue* staffers as "Harpie's Bazaar," which had been founded in 1867 and lagged far behind *Vogue* in both circulation and advertising sales, was fever pitched even then.

Carmel also met Stanton Griffis, a future American ambassador to Egypt, Spain, and other nations, through Crowninshield. This encounter would change the course of New York theater, since she then introduced Griffis, who was an "angel," i.e., a financial backer of plays, to Goodyear, and the two went on to produce some of Katharine Cornell's most successful productions, including the stage version of Michael Arlen's hugely popular novel *The Green Hat,* a book that more or less defined the 1920s, becoming a cautionary tale for its Flaming Youth. Its plotline, in which the protagonist, Iris Storm, commits dramatic suicide by driving her Hispano-Suiza into a tree, had an alarming effect on the nation's young, as described by one of them, the actress Ilka Chase (who just happened to be Edna Chase's daughter): "Romantic young women were much influenced by it and went round being gallant, doomed, and as promiscuous as their luck allowed."

At about this time, as Douglass had predicted, Fox closed its doors; a victim of market forces, it had slid from success to obsolescence more or less overnight. Its proprietress was left without an enterprise to run for the first time in thirty years. Still, she was hardly a candidate for idleness. With all of her children engaged in one work or another, she had many lives to preoccupy her; with Carmel, the only one to choose a fashion career, the urge to meddle proved to be particularly strong. But Carmel was increasingly launched on an exciting, independent life of her own.

Despite her mother's meddling, she had every reason to feel secure in her job. Nast himself was behind her, and it didn't get better than that. The publisher described her as "keen as mustard" in a memo to Chase. For Nast, she was a find—lively, pretty, eager to learn. Happily, for their professional relationship, she was only that. "What he liked in girls was something much hotter than I was, so there was no hint of romance in our relationship," Carmel explained. Instead, he set out to "mold his new fashion editor into a figure of fashion."

Then and now, fashion encompassed far more than clothes. It was a way of living, thinking, being. Dressing well was the minimum; living well was the goal. Surrounding oneself with fashionable people—something Nast did almost compulsively—was work. It took time to mingle with and attract the right sort. The reward was a kind of immortality, a sense of being, however briefly, at the center of the world.

As part of Carmel's indoctrination into the fashionable life, Nast began inviting her to weekends at Newport, where he was at home in some of the grander houses, including the Breakers, the seventy-room Italianate palazzo commissioned by Cornelius Vanderbilt Jr. in 1893, the same year he began to back a new magazine called *Vogue*. She also accompanied Nast to some legendary Adirondack hunting lodges—enormous, chaletlike, log structures in the mountains that were owned and frequented by many of the same ultrarich New York families who made Newport the place to be each summer. These camps offered a unique rusticity—the Sagamore, for example, had its own private bowling alley—with plenty of room for servants, of course. Before such visits, Carmel strategized over her wardrobe with the intensity of a general deploying his troops. She had tons of clothes, let's face it, thanks to Fox, but the need to look fresh every weekend was a pressure, even so. "On Monday I would send everything to be cleaned and freshened for the following Friday," Carmel writes. Her weeknights were fully charged, too. She was often at Nast and Crowninshield's dinner parties, where she might find herself seated next to just about anyone—a country club squire, a famous entertainer such as Fred Astaire, even what she laughingly referred to as a "presentable gigolo."

By 1923, she was hiring her own assistants and supervising fashion shoots, choosing and styling the clothes to be featured, and, in one way or another, enabling photographers to do their best work. One of these was Edward Steichen, who had been recruited that year over lunch with Nast and Crowninshield to become chief photographer for Condé Nast Publications, shooting celebrities for both *Vanity Fair* and *Vogue* and also doing fashion for the latter. Steichen, a former painter, had surprised the pair—shocked would be more accurate—during their meal at Old Delmonico's by asking for an outrageous sum of money, $35,000 annually at a time when, as Steichen's biographer, Penelope Niven, has pointed out "the average yearly salary in the United States was less than $1,500." Nast, the inveterate bookkeeper, was stunned by the figure, although perhaps also quietly impressed by Steichen's nerve. In any case, he agreed.

Nast also offered the great photographer, in passing, the chance to do his fashion work without credit on the assumption that Steichen would be loath to have his name associated with such a frivolous enterprise. But here the photographer surprised him again. Rather than seeking to deny the connection, he seemed to embrace it, even asserting that he'd been the first to make serious fashion photographs in the first place. (His series of ethereal group shots of models wearing floor-length Paul Poiret gowns—influenced by Oriental art and surprisingly unstructured for their time—had been published in the French magazine *Art et Décoration* in April 1911). In truth, there was some competition for the title of first fashion photographer, with de Meyer generally acknowledged as coming in ahead. The latter had jumped ship to *Harper's Bazar* in the early 1920s, an action that infuriated Nast (the competition between the two publishers was perennial) and no doubt helped to pry open his wallet as far as Steichen was concerned.

Steichen's decision to work for Nast made him, handily, the highest-paid fashion photographer in the world. It also shocked his contemporaries, notably Alfred Stieglitz, the pioneering photographer who had championed Steichen since he'd turned up, aged twenty-one and clutching prints of his work, at the New York Camera Club in 1900. Stieglitz was an enormously influential figure in the movement to have photography accepted as an art form. By the early 1920s, he'd founded the Photo-Secession group, edited the quarterly *Camera Work,* and opened 291, his seminal gallery in New York. In his own work, he'd moved away from painterly influences and special effects to something more naturalistic, which he described as "pure photography."

Stieglitz had been unstinting in his support for Steichen, even describing the younger man, in 1913, as "the greatest photographer living; in fact the greatest that ever lived." But he, like many others, couldn't fathom how an artist of this caliber could make such an abrupt, calculated-seeming detour into the heart of the commercial world. When Steichen made the move, it altered forever his relationship with his mentor, according to Stieglitz's biographer, Richard Whelan. "From then on, Stieglitz would sneer at Steichen as an artist whose ambition and greed had led him to prostitute himself."

But Steichen, then in his mid-forties, had endured a bitter, seemingly endless divorce, along with the financial worries that are the usual lot of a young artist. He had debts to pay off, years of them, and he was philosophical about his choice. As it happened, he would shoot some of his greatest portraits for Condé Nast—among them a pensive Katharine Hepburn, eyes closed, all cheekbones and upswept hair, and a wary Paul Robeson, dressed in an officer's uniform, looking sidelong at the camera (both done in the 1930s for *Vanity Fair*)—as well as some striking fashion work for *Vogue.* Transcendently lit (at Condé Nast, Steichen worked with artificial light for the first time), his portraits, particularly his theatrical ones, were "amazingly knowing," in the words of a contemporaneous critic in the *New York World-Telegram;* they seem to both reveal and conceal, challenging the viewer to discern the real person beneath the pose.

And so one of the greatest living photographers turned up at *Vogue.* "It was a tremendous coup to get a great artist like Steichen to photograph fashion," Carmel wrote. "And it was my first coup that Steichen and I immediately clicked." And they did. Carmel was frequently at the studio Nast had provided for Steichen at the Beaux Arts Studios on West Fortieth Street. "I waded into this work with a will to bring out everything I could in the model and the costume," she later wrote. "I used to kick off my shoes when I went into the studio, borrow a pair of slippers from the prop closet and set to it." She chose the clothes to be photographed as well as the model who would wear them. His favorite was the wide-eyed, black-haired Marion Morehouse, who would later marry the poet e. e. cummings and, later still, become a photographer herself. Carmel guided the course of their photographic sessions so that the best of both came through. And, crucially, she kept things light, infusing the high-pressured atmosphere of a fashion shoot with humor and fun. Steichen relied on her from the first.

His first fashion sitting for *Vogue* was done in Condé Nast's apartment at 470 Park Avenue. The photographer had planned to shoot the model in natural light—he had never used any other kind before—but was diverted by an electrician on the job who kept asking him where he should set up the klieg lights that most other photographers used. To humor him, Steichen had him set up a row of them, then requested a couple of sheets. "No one at a photographic fashion sitting had ever asked for bedsheets," he later recalled, "but Carmel Snow [then White], fashion editor [sic] at *Vogue* at the time, had a policy that a photographer should have whatever he required, and no questions asked." When the sheets appeared,

Steichen folded them, then draped them on some chairs in front of the bulbs. The diffuse light that resulted transformed the scene, allowing, as Carmel put it, "Steichen's marvelously luminous quality to come through."

During his years at Condé Nast Publications, Steichen would become ever more adept in his use of artificial light, as so many of his images, among them a deeply atmospheric 1927 picture of strapped shoes, full of reflections and shadows, attest. He never failed to credit Carmel for her help with his work. "When I started making photographs for *Vogue,* I had a great deal to learn about fashion, so I have always felt grateful to Carmel [White] Snow for the real interest she showed in fashion photography and for her invaluable assistance at fashion sittings." Almost a decade later, just before the Museum of Modern Art in New York mounted its 1961 retrospective of Steichen's work, he and Carmel were interviewed about their working years together. "You never interfered," Steichen told the editor, who was by then retired. "You always encouraged. When things were going badly you didn't say anything, when they were moving in the right direction I got a pat on the back."

From the first, Steichen and Carmel had an exceptional rapport: soon, he was requesting her presence at each shoot. At Steichen's request, Chase wasn't invited. Since she was constantly critical of Carmel, her absence only contributed to the young editor's delight in working with the photographer. "I always went to Steichen's sittings with such joy, as if I were taking the picture myself! His severity never frightened me—it was all *fun.*" Even so, a Steichen portrait of Carmel in this period had a kind of shy formality to it. Standing amid some shrubs and vines, the graying but still-youthful-looking Carmel, wearing pearls and a classically low-waisted ensemble of the 1920s, stares almost ruefully off into space.

Some, including the photographer Lillian Bassman, have said that Steichen was in love with Carmel, even broaching the subject of marriage, but at this distance, and in the absence of surviving letters between them, this seems impossible to verify. But Carmel does mention in her memoir falling in love with a divorced man at about this time. Not everyone thought Steichen was the one. As a former colleague recalls, "She said that she learned everything about art from a lover of hers, and I don't think it was Steichen." An editor who lived on Long Island as a child and knew the Whites recalled rumors of Carmel's involvement with a local millionaire who had an estate in Wheatley Hills—which would seem to narrow the field to Conger Goodyear, an art lover who owned a vast tract of land in that township. Whoever it was, such a relationship could go nowhere, given Carmel's deep Catholicism ("I take the dictates of my Church with great seriousness," she wrote). If it were Steichen, so much the worse. The photographer wasn't just divorced, he was notoriously so, complete with a messy, and very public, trial and allegations of adultery, apparently false, brought against him by his unstable first wife. If there was a hint of a romance between him and *Vogue*'s appealing assistant fashion editor, it must have peaked quickly and ended without rancor. By 1923, he had married Dana Glover, a long and happy union that would last until her death. His working relationship with Carmel would endure for another decade.

Indisputably, Carmel and Steichen shared a passion—a passion for work. Steichen couldn't have cared less about fashion, but he did care about making beautiful photographs, and Carmel, endlessly respectful of his talent, did what she could to help the process along. "His position as an artist was this: 'Anything I have to do interests me,'" she recalled.

> *If I said of a dress, "This is important," he made it important. . . . He always did what I* hoped *he would do. Ours was a wonderful combination because we never said to each other or to the model, "I want you to do this or that."* We insinuated *what we wanted and because of Steichen's genius, we got it.*

And so they turned out spread after spread.

In one 1927 photograph, Marion Morehouse stands before an ornate fireplace, resplendent in a sleeveless, asymmetric-hemmed Jean Patou dress of crepe Roma with rhinestone trimming. The brilliance of this shot, and so much of

Steichen's fashion work, lies in its composition, its stark contrasts. Seen against the dark interior, the dress seems almost iridescent, highlighting the pale palette, the simple flowing lines that were typical of Patou. Steichen would have been the first to acknowledge that this quiet masterpiece, and others, owed much to the Irishwoman who had buzzed behind the scene. As he told her decades later, "If you enjoyed our work together, I enjoyed it twice as much. If you learned, I learned twice as much." From a man at the peak of his reputation—he said these words toward the end of his life, when honors were pouring in from around the world—it was extraordinary praise.

Back at the office, Carmel would review the photographs with Nast, seeing them, she said, from Steichen's point of view, perpetually trying to ensure that the shots he favored would make their way into print. She and Condé continued to have a strong rapport—office wags used to say, teasingly, that "Edna Chase is Condé Nast's wife and Carmel White his mistress." No doubt fueled by Nast's admiration for his young protégée, Chase was ceaselessly critical of Carmel; her caustic comments sounded a dour leitmotif in the young editor's working day. "It was almost like being back under my mother's thumb," Carmel wrote.

Even so, she flourished at *Vogue,* which, for all the competition among its staff, "basically was an integrated, affectionate, family," according to Chase. Carmel worked her staff of junior editors so hard that they called her "the cossack," more or less good-naturedly. Her staff included another fashion assistant—and beauty—named Pauline Pfeiffer, one of a long line of women with whom Nast was said to be in love, as well as Lois Long, a flapper who came to work for the magazine as a copywriter in 1922, when she was twenty-one and fresh out of Vassar. (By 1925, she'd moved on to *The New Yorker,* a charmingly eccentric new magazine that had been founded that year, where she would write about nightlife and fashion under the pseudonym "Lipstick" for more than forty years.) One staffer, Clare Brokaw, would later become famous—notorious, actually—as the talented writer (and social climber) Clare Booth Luce. She and Carmel were on friendly terms when both were at *Vogue.* Still, Luce, in her two-faced way, didn't hesitate to describe Carmel, years later, to a rising German photographer named Erwin Blumenfeld, as "one of the ugliest of the ugly career-women who are so plentiful in America."

Carmel was a very hands-on editor of fashion copy, as one young writer, Dorothy Googins, recalled. Hired by Carmel in 1924 to write editorials and captions for the magazine, Googins routinely saw her copy "Vogued," and now and then rejected outright, sometimes from as far away as Paris, from where Carmel would send cables saying, "I don't think it publishable." At one point, when Googins wrote that "black lingerie is so chic this year and so practical because you never have to launder it," Carmel reacted with quiet horror. "We won't use the last line" was her cool response.

In the mid-1920s Carmel acquired what Chase described as "an exceptionally able assistant," Frances McFadden, a niece of her old friend Abram Poole. McFadden had first approached Carmel when she was just out of Wellesley College about writing a freelance article; when she learned that the topic she favored was of no interest to the young editor, she slinked away, thinking that that was that. But it wasn't. As Carmel wrote: "My intuition had spoken . . . and nagged me all summer." By fall, she'd summoned McFadden to meet Nast, who subsequently offered her the tough, all-encompassing job of managing editor—basically making the magazine run. She and Carmel would work side by side for the rest of McFadden's career, a fact all the

Carmel's "exceptionally able assistant": managing editor Frances McFadden. Photograph by Louise Dahl-Wolfe

more remarkable when you consider that she resisted fashion consciousness almost completely," as a colleague put it. "She went around with a ribbon in her hair." Too, too un-*Vogue.*

Carmel often hired on impulse. Sure of her instincts, she didn't hesitate to pursue someone, like McFadden, who seemed right for the job. One young hire, Eleanor Barry, radiated glamour and had an infectious sense of fun. "She was a delight to me from the moment I first saw her," Carmel wrote. Unfortunately, Barry was out the door quite quickly when, writing a lonely hearts column for the magazine, she answered the question "Is it all right for a nice girl to let a nice boy kiss her?" with a one-word telegram to its author. Unfortunately, from the magazine's point of view, the word Barry had chosen was the wrong one. Such a response would never have gotten by Miss Caroline Duer, a kind of resident censor whom Carmel called "the duenna of *Vogue,* whose arbitrary decision about what was 'ladylike' seemed to me *passé.*" Not to mention Mrs. Chase.

There were three editorial conferences an issue, one in which the magazine was planned, a second while it was in progress, and a third after it had been "put to bed," in magazine parlance, i.e., sent off to the printer, in which staffers debated its relative merits. Things we now take for granted were then the cause of heated debate. Colored nail polish was introduced in 1925; the decision to show hands tipped with a bloodred shade on the cover of *Vogue* sparked furious discussion at the magazine. Other attempts, such as a recurring one to feature strapped shoes—so vulgar!—as street wear in its pages were squelched, in horror, by Chase herself. "Inappropriate, unsightly, and dirty," she sniffed.

Carmel sparred with Duer, as well as Chase, and for all her warmth and humor, she, in turn, could strike fear in the hearts of her underlings. One staffer described her as having piercing "gimlet eyes." Although Lois Long thought her "severe," the two soon became friends. Carmel admired Long's light touch as a writer, and she would lend her all-important Chanels—an impossible acquisition on a copywriter's salary—as needed for social events. Then, as now, a serious wardrobe was a necessity at the magazine, and when Carmel wrote that "*Vogue* was a mass of intrigues in those days," she was mainly referring to the relentless competition about clothes. Staffers negotiated feverishly about what they would wear to Nast and Crowninshield's soirees. If one editor was going to turn up in her dressy red Chanel crepe de chine suit, she'd want to make damn sure that the girl down the hall would be limiting herself to white. And so it went, endlessly.

Fashion editing is a behind-the-scenes art; it's hard to know by looking at a given page from whose imagination it might have sprung. Chase oversaw everything in Carmel's early years. But by 1926, when the latter was promoted to fashion editor, the choice of which clothes to feature became very much her own. The job was multifaceted. As Grace Mirabella—who held the same job decades later, in the 1950s—has described it,

> *what fashion magazine editors do is report and write stories, just like any other journalist. In our case, however, the reporting consists of going out and seeing manufacturers and designers, checking out what's going on in lingerie or shoes or accessories or separates, then "editing" that "text" of reported material not just by choosing words, but sorting through racks of clothes, and then picking the clothes that fit together to make a coherent story in pictures. In a successful fashion feature, the pictures, rather than the verbal captions, tell the story: through their setting, or their style, or their lighting, or their mood, they make the clothing speak—not just about a way of looking, but about a way of feeling, or of being.*

Carmel reported not just to Chase but to the art department, a place Bettina Hill Wilson (who would later, under the name of Bettina Ballard, hold Carmel's job at *Vogue*) aptly described as the "nerve center" of the magazine. Here she met frequently with both the art director and Chase, going through the process known as a "run-through," in which an editor stakes out her pages for the next issue, discussing which fashions she wants to feature, who should photograph them, and who should model the clothes. Each issue started out as a series of miniaturized pages pinned to a bulletin board in the art department. The order and contents of these pages was always in flux, increasingly so as the deadline to close the issue approached. Bettina Ballard described a ritual that even now, with technology available that was unimaginable then, remains essentially the same.

> *The night before each issue would go to press the top editors would stand before the board, enjoying their last chance to pull the magazine apart and put it together again more effectively, sometimes in violent opposition, sometimes in complete accord, each editor instinctively favoring the placing of her own pages but struggling to be fair about the best ultimate effect for the magazine.*

Through banter and untold drama, somehow, every two weeks, a magazine was born.

Once she became fashion editor, Carmel began attending the Paris openings, traveling to the French capital for three weeks at a time, and sometimes longer, as other detours and duties piled up. She was no longer a glorified spy, as she'd been during the years that she'd gone with her mother, but an editor, there to review hundreds of garments, discern which ones might appeal to her readers, and, in one way or another, transmit them to the world. The choices she made might change a couture house's luck, perhaps for a season, perhaps forever, or it could destroy it just as easily. It was a delicate, near impossible task.

The combined workrooms and showrooms—known as couture houses—of the French couturiers erred on the sumptuous side, as a description of Chanel's premises, published in *Vogue* in the mid-1920s, makes clear. Everything, "chairs, carpet, woodwork, ceiling, everything a warm and lovely beige. There was perfume in the air, as there always is at Chanel's—subtle, exotic, sophisticated beyond words. There were great shaggy, gorgeous fabric flowers, new at the time...." There were no runways in fashion houses in this period. Instead, editors, buyers, and other visitors sat on dainty chairs in a given designer's "house" while models, typically fleshier, less airbrushed-looking than their counterparts today, circled the room at the same level as their audience, each carrying a small cardboard sign on which was written the number of the style she was wearing. They moved quickly, to discourage the "copyists" who fed off the Paris couture, drawing styles for exact reproduction all over the world. "You stole what you could and bought what you had to," said Elizabeth Hawes, a designer and former "sketcher" herself, who, like many in that low trade, earned her living by pretending to be a buyer, but copied the styles that passed by instead. "It wasn't considered stealing. It was just business," she wrote in *Fashion Is Spinach,* her famous 1938 disquisition on the fashion trade.

An editor had to make snap judgments, then, after the show, arrange for the fashions she'd chosen to be brought to the magazine's photography studio on the top floor of a building on the Champs-Elysées. In a pinch she might carry them by the armful, along with shoes and accessories, herself, with or without an assistant (the Paris office, then located on the rue Edouard VII, was always understaffed). The clothes were often accessorized with jewels borrowed from Cartier or Van Cleef & Arpels. The choice of photographer to use would depend on the year, the mood, even the fashions to be shot. It might be George Hoyningen-Huené, who worked out of Paris for *Vogue* in the 1920s, or a lesser-known, yet up-and-coming talent such as Cecil Beaton, who had made an apparently effortless leap from writing and illustrating to photography, and had begun coming over to Paris on the boat train from London to work on assignments for the magazine. In 1925, another new talent turned up, a Philadelphia-born surrealist painter named Man Ray, who was eager to try his hand at fashion photography, too. His portrait of the Honorable Mrs. Reginald Fellowes, a ubiquitous Parisian style setter, known to all as "Daisy," in the February 1, 1926, issue looks formal, even tortured, scarcely hinting at the boldness and daring that Ray would soon bring to the form.

Photo sessions during the collections tended to start late, after the buyers had left the couture houses. The models were usually imported from the States, traveling on their own dimes and earning next to nothing, all for the brief immortality of having their photographs in *Vogue.* After some late-night sessions, Carmel, models, photographer, and Paris staff would troop across the Champs-Elysées to Colisée or the venerable restaurant Fouquet's, which stayed open forever, to share a meal while waiting for the proofs to be developed. As dawn broke, Carmel would select the best shots for the magazine, arranging for them to be sent first by train to the northern French ports of Cherbourg or Le Havre, and then by boat across the Atlantic to the editorial offices in New York. Later that morning she'd be back at the collections, racing from one design house to the next. Sleep was a distant memory.

It wasn't just the pace but the secrecy, as a model who worked for Carmel in Paris pointed out.

> *It was a frantic experience because the collections were shown during the end of July and had to appear in the fashion magazines' October issues. Not only were the couturiers competing with each other, but the fashion magazines competed as well, so everything was very secret. The models used to go from one place to another swathed in sheets to prevent anyone from seeing and copying what they were wearing. Spies were everywhere.*

On the first trip for *Vogue,* Carmel stayed at the Westminster, worked around the clock, then shopped for herself and socialized in her tiny slivers of free time. "My first allegiance was to Chanel, because the freedom of her clothes was so congenial to me." She bought suits and her first "little black dress" from the designer, including one made of "chenille with a tie belt and sleeves just over the shoulder." She also stopped in at Callot Soeurs on the avenue Matignon, founded by three sisters in 1895, where Nast had offered to buy her a dress as a present. Such an offer was thrilling since the Callots specialized in evening gowns of great intricacy; they were often embroidered and realized in richly colored organdy or chiffon. What set Callot apart "was a daring in combining colors generally believed to clash to prove they were perfect complements of one another," as an early customer wrote.

When she shopped for herself, Carmel was no doubt offered the minuscule prices, known as the "prix de jeune fille," offered to the young and socially prominent or, even better, the more-or-less nonexistent ones, reserved for "mannequins du monde." (Women in either category gave a fashion house enormous cachet.) Like all clients she would have had at least three fittings per outfit, until each one fell exactly right. It would be hard to overstate the level of perfectionism involved.

Carmel attended the Vionnet show with a young Chicagoan named Main Bocher, then a fashion illustrator living in Paris, who would later become the couturier Mainbocher. There, she succumbed to an almond green dress and a gray-and-white tweed coat with the same green fabric as a lining—an outfit that turned out to be a "sensation," she reported, when she wore it in New York. Bocher also brought her to the new house of Augustabernard, which made sinuously draped gowns for evening and chicly unadorned suits for day, and to the inventive Louiseboulanger (combined names were obviously "in") who, at around the time Carmel first saw her designs, had daringly—and anachronistically—added trains to her newly lengthened skirts; later, she'd bring back the bustle, too. She shopped for hats at Reboux, *the* hatmaker of the day, where customers lined up to have felt cloches molded to their heads. She had her hair bobbed by Antoine, a Polish-born genius and former sculptor, who caused a sensation in 1924 by dying the gray tresses of Lady Mendl (aka Elsie de Wolfe) an unforgettable shade of blue, something Carmel, now almost completely white-haired herself, soon emulated. And she always shopped for her family; one niece, Nancy White, recalls her aunt delivering on extravagant promises, bringing home Paris dresses of rose pink or sky blue.

Carmel drank up the city. "Paris has *always* been glamorous for me, from the time I first went there as a schoolgirl," she later wrote.

> *"I think it's because it's a place that worships quality, as I do. The* best *of everything. That, of course, is why Paris leads the world in fashion. Because the workmanship and the fabrics, as well as the designers, are the best that can be found. Because there's* time *for quality. Because people* care *about quality. . . .*
>
> *To me Paris is a city where millions of clever hands are at work, always inventing something that has never been seen before—a new twist, a new cut, a new stitch. American designers haven't found that fund of auxiliary talent to draw on.*

She felt more alive in Paris than anywhere else. She had been born in Europe, after all, and remained "more European than American," in the words of one relative, Kate White. She spoke French—idiosyncratically, it's true. "She had an accent" is how the couturier Hubert de Givenchy describes it, with his habitual tact. "It was sometimes not easy to understand her. Maybe in her head it was clear. . . ."

Part of Carmel's mission on her 1926 trip was to recruit Bocher, who had become Paris fashion editor of American *Vogue* in 1922, to head up the new French edition of the magazine, which had been founded the following year—a mission that failed because no financial agreement could be reached. "Main has always had a healthy respect for the value of his work and won't settle for less!" she wrote. While the Paris edition was a separate magazine, it, like British *Vogue,* which was started in 1916, shared some editorial content with its American counterpart. All the *Vogue*s, which were overseen by Chase, pooled their intelligence. Having a presence in Paris was critical not just for fashion but for getting a bead on European cultural life and on the all-important doings of socialites. French society is close to impenetrable for outsiders; having well-connected natives on staff opened it up, somewhat, for a clamoring readership.

And there was no one better connected in the 1920s in Paris than Solange d'Ayen—a duchess, she was the daughter-in-law of the Duc de Noailles, one of the oldest titles in France. A Parisienne of staggering chic, the striking, copper-haired d'Ayen was first a consultant, then on staff at *Vogue.* She was "the person I most wanted at that time to fashion myself on," Carmel said. Through d'Ayen, as well as through her own efforts, Carmel got to know the cliquey social set known as *le tout Paris,* even dining with Chanel, whose clothes she favored, early in her editorial career. Carmel's French trips were social triumphs as much as professional ones; as such, they were yet another irritant for Edna Chase, who, while no doubt glad for the magazine's sake that Carmel was well received in the French fashion world, must also have envied the ease with which she navigated it. (Chase herself hadn't crossed the Atlantic for the first time until 1919, and her French was nonexistent.)

As Carmel rose through the ranks at *Vogue,* she chafed under its limitations. She yearned, for example, to move fashion photography out of a studio setting. She once bought a photo of women on a balcony by the photojournalist Margaret Bourke-White to a meeting at *Vogue,* only to have it dismissed by the rest of the staff as "just a snapshot." Later, after she suggested that a fashionable couple be photographed in their private plane, "I was told that *Vogue* didn't use outdoor shots!" But the idea stayed in her mind. Another frustration was a social one. She may have been having the time of her life, but she was still unmarried, which was social death. She was in her mid-thirties—ancient for the era—without a prospect in sight. The divorced man she'd cared for, whoever he might have been, was out of the picture, although she hints that the pain she had experienced over him was not. She found a cautionary tale in the sufferings of one of her colleagues. Like Carmel, Pauline Pfeiffer was a devout Catholic in love with a divorced man. She agonized over whether to marry him, a move that would qualify her as an adulterer in the eyes of the Catholic Church. "Her decision was torture to her," as Carmel wrote. In the end, love won out, although perhaps not for as long as she'd hoped: the man in question was Ernest Hemingway, and Pfeiffer would become the second of his four wives.

Carmel's home life had changed—her mother had moved to 510 Park Avenue, and two more brothers, Victor and Jim, had married and left home. So she was left with Desmond, and the haunting sense that all the siblings close to her age

Carmel Snow with her brother Desmond and three of Tom White's children (Nancy, Carmel, and Thomas Justin White Jr.) 1921

had moved on to their own lives. She socialized madly, gaily, with an increasing sense of desperation. "I tried to resolve my emotional turmoil by spinning around faster and faster." A woman in the era couldn't easily go off to live alone. It would be marriage, or life with mother. No wonder she was out, night after night.

She moved from one social circle to another. Through her friend Jane Grant, wife of the first *New Yorker* editor Harold Ross, Carmel began frequenting the house in New York's dicey Hell's Kitchen area that the couple shared with two *New Yorker* writers, Alexander Woollcott and R. Hawley Truax. This semicommunal living arrangement was notorious at the time, as was Woollcott himself, a man loathed and idolized by turns whose love/hate relationship (mainly the latter) with Grant would last for as long as they did. Their house was known for its men-only poker games and its "after-theatre parties that brought the 'Vicious Circle' of the Algonquin Round Table together with many celebrities who admired, envied or feared them." One of these, of course, was Dorothy Parker, the writer, critic, and all-round wit who had been a caption writer at *Vogue* before becoming a drama critic at *Vanity Fair.* Carmel had known her for years.

Another friend was Anita Loos, the author of *Gentlemen Prefer Blondes,* the wildly successful novel about the misadventures of a flapper heroine named Lorelei Lee. Newsstand sales of *Harper's Bazar* had tripled after the book was serialized in that publication in 1925. Men formed a large percentage of the novel's audience (James Joyce was said to be a fan), and therefore the magazine's;

as a result, men's advertising was included in a women's magazine for the first time. Loos was the toast of New York but not quite sure how to navigate it all, so Carmel took her and her husband, John Emerson, under her wing, escorting them to chic parties all over town. "Our click was immediate and it extended to our clothes. We were both dressed by Chanel, later by Mainbocher . . . ," Carmel recalled. *Gentlemen Prefer Blondes* resonated with Carmel, too. Like so many, she waited avidly for each installment of the book in the magazine that everyone called *The Bazar.* The novel's popularity taught her a lesson:

> *I think I determined from the moment I read the first installment that if I were ever the editor of a magazine I would publish fiction, which* Vogue *refused to publish. Though our business as a fashion magazine was to show fashion, our business as journalist, it seemed to me, was to make an exciting book.*

When Carmel's "Miss White" days finally did come to an end, it was by way of her old friend Ruby Ross Goodnow, who was then living in a brownstone in Manhattan's West Thirties. Goodnow had a reputation for being fast—Carmel's mother refused to allow her daughter to go to her friend's parties, which were full of artistic people, among them the sculptor Gaston Lachaise and the illustrator Rockwell Kent—but the facts of her life hardly confirm this. She was certainly showy, having shocked New Yorkers back in the 1910s by painting the ground floor of her house on Eleventh Street bright pink (she favored attention-getting hues). By "fast," Douglass probably meant divorced, which was considered morally dicey at the time and which Goodnow had become in 1923, after sixteen years of marriage. The following year she became engaged to Chalmers Wood, a vice president of the New York Stock Exchange, and after her marriage became known, professionally and otherwise, as Ruby Ross Wood.

Wood was increasingly influential, both as a decorator and as the proprietress of Au Quatrième. Like other of Carmel's friends, she began appearing in

Vogue in the mid-1920s, contributing a story to an interior decorating number in 1926. The same issue, in an article on a New York town house decorated by Elsie de Wolfe, featured a painted mirror overmantel, done in chinoiserie style, by Carmel's brother Victor, who, besides painting portraits and landscapes, worked with interior designers on decorative projects, too.

Chalmers Wood was an avid fox hunter who lived with a friend and fellow sportsman, George Palen Snow, whom everyone called "Pa" at Rolling Hill Farm, a rambling white house in the Long Island town of East Norwich, a pretty, still-rural-seeming village on the North Shore of Long Island, not far from the patrician enclaves of Locust Valley and Oyster Bay. Carmel's first meeting with Palen, in the early spring of 1926, was not auspicious. She and Ruby arrived for a visit, only to be told that the two men were out golfing. By the time the pair did turn up, ages later, straggling home in high spirits following their game, the women were fuming: "Who did these men think they were, keeping two busy New York women waiting?" Carmel wrote. Sensibly, and with revenge in mind, she concentrated on another man present—Jim Curtis from Boston, who became a frequent escort—ignoring Snow altogether.

She began dating Curtis, now and then consenting to let the man she refused to call Pa—it would be Palen or even Snowy, thank you very much—to take her to dinner

George Palen Snow on horseback, c. 1920

dances at New York's Pierre Hotel. Palen was tall, reasonably attractive, well mannered. But he was rough around the edges, most agreed, and he had a debilitating stutter. Still, he wasn't divorced, as most of the men Carmel dated were ("to be expected in unattached men my age"), and he had an enthusiasm for the outdoorsy pursuits he loved, such as gardening, hunting, and golf, that she found appealing. "There was a boyishness about this big man in his forties that you couldn't resist." When spring turned to summer, Carmel began spending most Sundays at Rolling Hill Farm, which Palen owned, where her suitor helped her up onto horses, walked her through games of golf, and in general attempted to make his world hers. His efforts failed dismally, a fact that neither he nor Carmel seemed to notice.

All important messages were sent by telegram in those days; they had a certain poetry that e-mail could never hope for. The trick was to keep your sentences short and punchy and to expect "STOP" once a message was transformed into cable-ese, to punctuate each line. The cable that decided their fate was too short even for "STOP." Carmel was scheduled to go to Paris for the collections in the fall, the first time the couple would have been separated since they'd met, and Palen would have none of it. "MAY I SAIL ON THE MAURETANIA WITH YOU? REPLY PAID." he wrote. Her answer was two words, "REPLY ACCEPTED." Somehow, both understood that this was code for a honeymoon. People married quickly in those days, of course, shockingly fast by our standards, but this strained convention, even so. Palen gave her a family ring, an "enormous, big, gorgeous emerald, square cut—a rock," in the words of an editor who worked with Carmel. The couple scheduled their wedding for Armistice Day, November 11—a frantic pace. There would be no French trousseau such as Christine had enjoyed, no crammed-full Paris trunk. Instead Carmel ordered hers from Manhattan retailer, Peggy Hoyt.

Some women didn't see Palen's appeal—he was a bit of a bumbler, and his stutter was severe—but he was kind and patrician, a fact that dazzled Carmel. "Socially, he was desirable," as Eleanor Perényi, an editor and writer, put it. His parents, Mary Palen and Frederick A. Snow, were from old New York families; at the time their son married, they were living in both Southampton, Long Island, and in Aiken, South Carolina—a foxhunting mecca—where they'd migrate each autumn and spring. That town was almost as terminally elegant as Southampton in those days: "The smart world loves Aiken in springtime," according to *Harper's Bazaar* (which by now had acquired its second *a*).

Palen, who had grown up in Manhattan and had graduated in Harvard's class of 1904, "was an eighteenth-century gentleman," in the words of Brigid Snow Flanigan, his youngest daughter. Although he had a seat on the New York Stock Exchange, he wasn't often in town; he preferred the country, where he rode to hounds and experimented with various mulches for his garden. He wasn't incredibly rich—"not well-to-do but comfortable," in Flanigan's words—but he was a step up, a steep, near-impossible one, for an Irish girl. By all accounts, Carmel adored the trappings that accompanied her new station in life. One of her sisters-in-law was shocked to hear Carmel crowing, "I'm going to marry Palen and I'm going to have a personal maid!" according to a niece, Julie Groupp. "She was very cold about it. My mother was quite shocked."

That Palen was a catch was confirmed by the reaction of Chase, whose own fairly modest origins, especially when compared to people who filled their pages (who tended to be megarich or megatalented, rarely both), was an abiding source of chagrin. "Well," she said dourly after Carmel broke the news. "You certainly know how to do things." Which was, infuriatingly enough for Chase, the truth. Another person who had a strong reaction was Steichen. He'd been scheduled to shoot for *Vogue* on the day Carmel's hastily planned engagement was announced. When Chase appeared in her stead, announcing the news, Steichen stormed off the job, saying, "You surely don't expect me to work after *that* news!" He came around to the idea, eventually, and even presented Carmel with a wedding portrait.

There couldn't be a church wedding—Carmel was Catholic, Pa Episcopalian—and Carmel envisioned a huge gathering, inviting families from both sides, friends by the dozen, including many with whom she'd danced and dined over the past few years. Since the family apartment was too small for such a horde, friends offered their place in the same building instead. The afternoon ceremony, officiated by the Reverend Henry F. Hammer of St. Patrick's Cathedral, was undilutedly Catholic. Carmel was escorted by her brother Desmond; Palen's brother-in-law, Harry I. Nicholas, the husband of his sister, Dorothy, was best man. The bride wore a "gown of cream white satin trimmed with seed pearls and old Burano lace that has been in her family for many years," the *New York Times* reported. Steichen's portrait reveals it to be short-sleeved and tight at the bodice; its lacy skirt flaring out, then dropping to the ground in an asymmetric hemline. Most striking of all is the lacy veil tied snugly behind her head like a kerchief; floor length, it cascades to the ground behind her. Carmel smiles demurely in the photo, looking youthful, in spite of her white hair, even girlish, although she's just a notch under forty.

The only glitch in the proceedings had to do with Palen, who'd spent hours at the Racquet Club dressing in morning clothes, adjusting his top hat to a properly rakish tilt. On the way to the proceedings, he realized that he hadn't brushed his teeth and dashed into a pharmacy to buy a toothbrush and paste, begging the pharmacist for a place to brush. The sight of the groom, bending over a sink and clutching a toothbrush, his top hat still perfectly angled, left Nicholas, who had accompanied him, overcome with laughter.

And then there was the problem of their names: a White can't easily marry a Snow with dignity. The predictable jokes are exhausting to contemplate. (Carmel claimed never to have considered using her maiden name professionally for that reason.) Even the priest became befuddled. When he asked Palen to repeat the phrase, "I, George Palen White," the groom burst out with "I, George Palen *Snow*" in a loud, authoritative voice—and without a trace of stammer—instead.

The guest list was worthy of one of Condé's gatherings, a mixture of society figures—Mr. and Mrs. Winthrop W. Aldrich, Mrs. Gordon Auchincloss—with people from magazine publishing and the arts. Both Nast and Crowninshield attended—it's easy to imagine these most elegant of men at their most expansive in such a crowd. Mr. and Mrs. Russel Sard, the assistant secretary of the navy and his wife, were also there, along with such well-known artists as the violinist Efrem Zimbalist; Ruth Draper, the legendary actress and monologuist; George Bellows; and Rockwell Kent. Carmel's teacher Henri turned up, of course, as did Ruby Wood, who had introduced the couple, and Harrydele Hallmark, who had helped to launch Carmel's career. And, as the bride noted, many of her "beaux" were also there, including Jim Curtis, by then married himself.

Carmel claimed to scarcely remember the reception—she was too much in the thick of it for that. Years later, her sister-in-law, Dotsie Nicholas, recalled that Crowninshield, at his smooth, glib-talking best, had toasted the "thousand and one heartbroken men" Carmel was leaving behind. Nicholas also noticed—as who could not?—the enormousness of the White clan; all five of Carmel's siblings were in attendance, as were numerous others, including her niece and goddaughter Nancy—her brother Tom's eldest child—with whom Carmel was especially close. Nancy, age eight, sounded the only sad note at the proceedings when she complained to her aunt despondently that "I won't be *yours* anymore." The *Times* soberly reported that "Mr. Snow and his bride will pass their wedding trip abroad." The destination was obvious, as was the nature of the trip. As Carmel wrote in her memoir, "Our honeymoon in Paris had to be combined with business for me, a foretaste of our life together." While she worked, attending the collections, checking in with couturiers and buyers, supervising photo sessions, Palen would continue his leisurely, gentleman's life, this time on the other side of the Atlantic.

Carmel would later describe Palen as being "an attorney who in conjunction with his father represented a building loan society"; a member of the New York bar, he would join his father as a partner in the real estate and insurance firm of Snow & Snow at 230 Park Avenue. Still, he, like many men from established eastern families, scarcely worked, at least not by our standards today. In the case of the Snows, as with so many other members of the WASP establishment—they ruled then, remember?—the fortunes had long been made, the clubs founded and joined, the great houses built. It was a matter of keeping busy with various pursuits and with keeping one's end up socially. Most men married wives for whom this could be a raison d'être. Palen did not, a fact he seemed to accept with equanimity. He also didn't request, as many men of his station would have done, that his wife give up her job. As late as the 1950s, even later, American women seeking to work for fulfillment, rather than out of necessity, often had to ask their husbands' permission to do so. And many men refused it. To Palen's enormous credit, there's no evidence that he ever even broached the subject with Carmel. He was right not to, of course. "She never would have given it," as her niece Nancy White pointed out.

The couple stayed at the Westminster, where, Carmel recalled, every morning a call would come through from the American ambassador, Myron T. Herrick, a friend of Palen's parents, arranging various expeditions for Palen to take with the ambassador's son, Parmelee; in the evenings, Carmel and Palen would often dine at the embassy, then located on the place d'Iéna. On this trip she lived a Paris she scarcely knew, before or since; normally, during the collections, she'd spend her evenings dining late with fashion's usual odd assortment: aristocrats, mad artists, couturiers, models, some of them rumored to be opium addicts (then all the rage in Paris). It was effortlessly decadent—something she enjoyed from a safe distance. While her honeymoon might have been "a good introduction to my new life," as Carmel put it, it was a distinct anomaly: her Paris would always consist of hard chic, bohemian gatherings, backbreaking work.

Not much remains of their honeymoon, not a diary fragment, not a reference in a letter, not a living mem-

Carmel and Palen Snow, 1930s

ory. We can only assume that Carmel took the man she had just married through the city she loved, and that he joined her on her adored postmass Sunday morning strolls through a place "where I know my way around as no other city in the world." Perhaps he even suffered through some of the fashion shows and parties that were the stuff of her days and nights during the openings, that year and for many more to come—even though his new bride liked to tell people that "dear Palen doesn't know a skirt from a dress." You could find anything in the French capital at that time, up to and including Josephine Baker, the shockingly sensual, jazz-infused American singer and dance sensation. A brothel near the Left Bank church of Saint-Sulpice featured prostitutes dressed as nuns. And a wildly fashionable restaurant served up high-heeled, naked waitresses along with fairly traditional bistro food. But mainly Palen followed his own pursuits, perhaps taking in the races at Longchamp or Auteuil or even striking out on horseback through the bois de Boulogne, as any serious rider might have done, while Carmel went after her own terribly different ones. It was a pattern that would endure for all their married days.

4 an elegant life

In a way we felt we had all married Palen. . . .

—Edna Woolman Chase

THE COUPLE RETURNED HOME from Europe in mid-January 1927 without a hitch, unless you count a quite predictable conflict involving the new Mrs. Snow's need to smuggle. Palen had bought her a pearl ring on her wedding trip. "I knew, though he didn't, that the pearl could be unscrewed from the setting, and he was horrified when he caught me unscrewing the pearl as we made out our Customs declaration. He made me screw it right back. . . ." She did, although it may have been one of the last times that duty was actually paid on her purchases abroad.

Back in New York, Carmel stepped up to a privileged life, spending her first married winter in a suite at New York's Barclay Hotel, where she and her husband stayed until the spring, when they opened Rolling Hill Farm for the summer season. The rumpled-looking Palen remained a cipher to some in Carmel's fast-moving circle, in part because, given his speech defect, he tended to be fairly quiet. He was the yin to Carmel's yang. "I didn't get it," one longtime colleague of Carmel's said of the apparent attraction between the clothes- and fun-loving editor, who tore through life at breakneck speed, and her staid, slow-moving, new husband. "She had so much personality and Palen had not nearly as much" was her niece Nancy White's cool assessment. His life revolved around outdoor pursuits—riding, hunting, gardening (he was inordinately proud of his compost heap)—and, as such, took place at a far remove from *Vogue.* Still, in their first years together, with his spending more time in New York, he was game enough and could be prevailed upon to tear himself away from his mulch to make an appearance at a cocktail party.

They began a strenuous social life. "Naturally our friends wanted to entertain us" is how Carmel puts it. Her boss, Edna Chase, had a whole other take on it, writing with weary melodrama that after Carmel's marriage

> *our vicissitudes began. In a way we felt that we had all married Palen, as the life he wanted to lead, the holidays he wanted to take and the parties he wanted to go to became Carmel's primary interest and she sought to rearrange her* Vogue *schedule accordingly.*

Chase pointed out that Carmel was now socializing with a crowd in which the women spent their days playing bridge, their evenings dancing, and their mornings sleeping off the night before. Carmel skipped the resting and card-playing parts—but then, hadn't she always? And even Chase had to concede that when her fashion editor "got to her desk in the morning she was as alert and able as ever."

Chase credited Carmel's staying power to the curious fact that

> *she could literally sleep on the dance floor. Several of us, who might find ourselves briefly in a nightclub or at the same party, had seen her do it time and again. She was a good dancer and her body went on waltzing or fox-trotting or tangoing while her consciousness was in temporary or deep eclipse.*

Carmel's ability to seemingly doze through critical moments, while somehow remaining aware of her surroundings, would always be a part of her legend. Some have said there was a medical reason—narcolepsy, perhaps. Still others just credit it to a kind of supernatural aura she had, or at least liked to project. She loved to tell how little sleep she needed, or food, for that matter.

Chase's other gripe was about Carmel's sudden need to take time off the job. She was clearly rankled by the fact that the younger editor "had married a man who could indulge in resort life when so minded." The talented, vivacious, popular Carmel was a threat enough; that she should acquire a husband of independent means must have seemed particularly cruel. Chase, by contrast, had the garden-variety kind of husband, the type who had to work. Some of the couple's trips were to see Palen's parents, whom Carmel called "Ma Dear" and "Pa Dear," just as her husband did. Mary, her mother-in-law, was formal in the way that was then appropriate to her age and class—she almost always wore a veil (the gossamer kind that ladies wore with hats to church back then, not a chador)—but she leavened it with a wicked sense of humor. While Carmel professed to adore her, some relatives have said their relationship was more complicated than that; Ma Dear had been known to drive a wedge, intentionally, between Carmel and Palen at times, causing conflict. Even so, the young couple spent ample time with the elder Snows, going down to see them at Deodara, their house in South Carolina, reveling in the warmer climate. The rest of the year, when they were at home on Long Island, the newlyweds would head out to see them there. Carmel confessed to being "amused by the formal magnificence of her in-laws' Southampton life." Their immense, many-gabled, three-story house, called Gardenside, on the maple-lined Ox Pasture Road, was run by a staff of ten.

If their backgrounds differed widely, it didn't seem terribly important. They shared a sense of humor—the "most important bond," in Carmel's assessment. Her account of their first months together, which she wrote more than thirty years after her wedding, is suffused with joy. "I was in love; and when I became pregnant that first spring of my marriage, my cup of happiness was full." She was almost forty, ancient for the time, in childbearing terms, and "the knowledge that I was going to have a child gave me a sense of fulfillment that only a woman of my age could understand." She worked through most of her pregnancy, keeping up her New York social life with Palen during the week, and spending weekends at Rolling Hill Farm, which they considered to be their permanent home.

When on Long Island, they spent time with Chalmers and Ruby Wood, who were living in nearby Syosset in a "one-story Malmaison sort of house," as *Harper's Bazaar* later described it, that Wood had designed herself. Palen's sister, Dorothy, and her husband, Harry Nicholas, had a house on thirty acres just behind the Snows. Both Nicholases rode with the venerable Hartford Hunt at Monkton, in Maryland, a fact that, a few years later, would land them in the pages of *Vogue* in an article on the Hartford in which Nicholas is described as "MFH of Meadowbrook for thirteen seasons and . . . one of the most knowledgeable horse and hound men in the country." (No wonder he and Palen were close.)

And the Whites were amply represented: Tom and Virginia, whom Carmel and Palen saw often, had settled their family at a house called Willowbroke in Lawrence, and Victor and his wife, Margaret, were soon installed in nearby Woodmere. It was a time of growth for the close-knit Whites, who had become one of the better-known clans in eastern Long Island. "They were just firecrackers," recalls Laura Pyzel Clark, who would later work with Carmel. "It was great fun to be around them." Another editor who grew up in the area and knew the family by reputation recalled the group as being very "large and very country clubby."

It was also a time of growth for *Vogue*. In 1927, Carmel's first year as a married woman, Edna Chase was listed as editor on the magazine's table of contents page for the first time. (It could hardly be called a masthead, since hers was the only name on it.) In its understated way, this move signaled a new direction for fashion magazines. Over the next decades, the names of editors would become increasingly public, until they acquired a mystique of their own, becoming celebrities in their own right, as they are today. It's hard to imagine the sight of Chase at a society function, or even just walking down the street, causing the same kind of excited speculation that, say, Anna Wintour, the endlessly chic, long-time *Vogue* editor, has done in our time. Mild curiosity, perhaps, but not the what-was-she-wearing, who-did-she-talk-to kind of interest.

In mid-April 1927, *Vogue* moved to expanded offices on the nineteenth floor of "the new, towering Graybar Building," as the magazine described it, at 420

Lexington Avenue, just next to Grand Central Station. *Vanity Fair* moved as well, which meant that some of Carmel's more stimulating friends and acquaintances, Crownie, Dorothy Parker, and the like, were still to be found making wisecracks down the hall. In the same year, Main Bocher at last agreed to take over French *Vogue*. He was an unruly employee—the Paris office seemed to be full of them—a gifted, if intermittently effective editor. His own talent, which was prodigious, was an endless distraction. Besides his abilities as a couturier, he was also an aspiring singer; *Vogue*'s Bettina Ballard recalled that he was forever interrupting the working day to dash off to voice lessons. In spite of its colorful staff, the French version of the magazine looked far stuffier than the American one into the 1920s, with page after page of brides posing in their wedding regalia, and excruciatingly fawning stories about the latest—and dullest?—society events, among them a Regency Ball, covered in the August 1928 issue.

In an era when expectant women rarely worked, Carmel was the energetic exception. "I always felt so well during my pregnancies, I worked until the last possible moment." She probably even attended the Paris collections in August, when she would have been about six months along. There was, as always, much to see. Women were newly bare, their hems heading up toward the knee; their sleeves, in the case of evening dresses, disappearing altogether, replaced by slender straps. In general, less fabric was used, and that which was tended to be diaphanous. With dresses so flimsy, coats took on new, cozy proportions.

One new name on the Paris fashion scene was soon to be a much-pronounced one: Elsa Schiaparelli. The aristocratic Italian designer—Schiap to her friends—whose career had been nurtured by Patou, had begun selling her witty sweaters at her apartment on the rue de l'Université earlier in 1926. Her career had catapulted forward after Anita Loos began wearing her tweedy black-and-white pullover of Shetland wool with an illusory bow knit into its design. Knitwear jump-started Schiaparelli's career (then in her thirties, she'd scarcely designed anything before). She conjured up one inspired sweater after another, including a trompe l'oeil design that gave the illusion that the wearer was wearing a blouse and red string tie, and which *Vogue* called "an artistic masterpiece." These early designs were immensely, almost insanely, popular with both the public and the ever-present copyists. Schiaparelli's bow sweater was picked up by one American wholesaler then, in a flash, appropriated by numerous others. It was so brazenly purloined that within eighteen months, *Ladies' Home Journal* was offering a pattern of it, without attribution, to its numerous readers.

After the frenzy of the collections, Carmel retreated to Long Island, where the rest of the summer seemed to pass in a dream. She and Palen took their holiday in a shack at Montauk Point, at the far, unglamorous tip of Long Island (an isthmus, actually)—only miles from Southampton but light-years away in every sense—and there, in an atmosphere of Bohemian splendor, they waited for their first child to be born. "I knew how I wanted to spend my summer vacation: as a beachcomber," Carmel wrote. When Pa Dear and Ma Dear came to visit, "they thought we were *lunatics*!" she reported. There were numerous reasons to be shocked. They were living—heavens!—with only one servant, the quirky, amiable Bridget Keogh, and the well that supplied the house, if one could dignify this residence with such a name, had gone dry. And, Bridget notwithstanding, the place was a mess. "Palen had been brought up with James, *the* perfect butler valet to look after him. He simply steps out of his clothes like a fireman and leaves them where they fall. Bridget had been too busy fetching water to pick them up, and our house looked like a slum."

In short, it was perfect. Carmel described that season as "the happiest summer of my life." A snapshot of the two of them, bundled up against foggy weather and reading peaceably in deck chairs, exudes cozy domesticity. If there was any negative aspect at all, and, mainly, there was not, it was that here—perhaps inspired by Montauk's incessantly crashing surf?—Carmel began to have the recurrent dream of drowning that would revisit her, even in more landlocked places, for many years to come.

Their first child, a daughter named Carmel, was born in November 1927, about a year after her parents' marriage. She first saw the light of day where the chicest New York babies then did, at Miss Lippincott's Sanitarium at 667 Madison

Avenue, which for years had been conveniently located just above the Colony Restaurant: "where all the smart world went for lunch or dinner," according to *Vogue.* The restaurant had moved around the corner in 1926, to 30 East Sixty-first Street, but it still supplied Lippincott's with food as chic as its clientele. "Champagne and gourmet meals flowed upward along with a stream of visitors." Among these was Bocher, then passing through New York, who came bearing baby clothes from Lanvin. "Babies were *dressed* in those days," as Carmel put it.

To the modern reader, who just might have been tossed out of a hospital within hours of delivery, Carmel's three-week postbaby convalescence sounds dreamy. And her leave-taking from Miss Lippincott's was downright ceremonial. She wore a fashionable "coming out" hat, designed to celebrate her "emergence from pregnancy" by her old friend Jessica Daube, the milliner, who had moved from Bendel's to Bergdorf Goodman—a gift that Daube would repeat after each of Carmel's pregnancies. Carmel hired a "stylish English nanny," and she and Palen moved in with her mother, spending the winter at the family apartment at 510 Park Avenue. Even after such a long postpartum rest, Carmel had a trained nurse named Dunny to take care of her. It's no wonder that the elevator "was constantly popping up and down because I felt so well after the three-week period you spent in hospital in those days, I was on the go the minute I was let out."

In this same year, Tom was promoted to manager of Hearst's magazines, among them, of course, *Harper's Bazaar,* invariably referred to as *The Bazaar.* It was the enemy, however it was called, and the fact that Carmel's favorite sibling was now directly involved in it was worrying for Nast. "He knew of Carmel's affection for her brother, and blood, he reasoned, was thicker than printer's ink," Chase wrote.

> *He said to me one day, "Edna, I have a feeling that Tom will eventually want Carmel to go over to Hearst and I don't think she should be with us unless she's under contract. As a matter of fact, I've suggested it to her."*
>
> *"'What did she say?'"*

"Condé shrugged. 'She was indignant. She said nothing would induce her to work for Hearst, she wouldn't dream of it, and she gave me her word to that effect.'"

Then Nast was on to other things. Carmel had hired a new employee that year on his recommendation, the latest in a never-ending stream of pretty young women, qualified or not, whom he steered toward jobs at the magazine. The latest one was a Miss Leslie Foster, late of Lake Forest, Illinois. Still in her twenties, Foster was the exact same age as Nast's daughter, Natica, and had very much caught his eye. They were married late in 1928, very happily for both, apparently, and the newest Mrs. Nast began her married life by befriending her new stepdaughter—they would become inseparable—and adjusting to her newfound wealth. (She wouldn't need to get used to it for long.)

That same year, the Snows took a place at 115 East Forty-eighth Street, according to the Social Register, which that year included Carmel in its pages for the first time. (Her brother Tom had already entered its rolls upon his marriage to Virginia Gillette.) Other Whites would follow, including Tom and Carmel's artist brother, Victor, who was included after his marriage to the former Margaret Wood. The Whites were a newsworthy addition to the list for the simple reason of their religion: Catholics were then scarce, if not entirely unknown, in this annual directory that had been founded by Louis Keller in New York in the nineteenth century primarily as a list of families who could trace their ancestries back to that city's early Dutch and English settlers. Palen would have had to have applied to have his wife included, providing letters of recommendation from other listees; had she been rejected, he might well have seen his own name dropped.

The register provides a snapshot of Carmel's new life, if one with a limited view. She joined the Colony Club, not to be confused with the restaurant of the same name, where Ma Dear also belonged, a women's organization on Park Avenue that caters to society ladies who lunch. It's hard to imagine that she ever had the time to go; even so, belonging was a kind of minimum requirement for a woman of her class. It was the only club that would ever be listed by her name. Palen, of course, adored the club life—in the mid-1920s, he belonged to seven, from the Piping Rock on Long Island to the St. Andrews Golf Club—a mecca for golfers—in Scotland.

Once the Snow daughter, inevitably known as "little Carmel," had passed out of infancy, she was cared for by her nanny on Long Island while her parents stayed mainly in town, returning to East Norwich on weekends. Now that there was a Mrs. Snow in residence, this white clapboard house lost its rough edges, becoming cozier. "It was a big, rambling house, most attractive," one early visitor recalled.

> *It looked comfortable and warm. Mrs. Snow had a terrific hand inside, there were lovely couches and comfortable country furniture. There was nothing put on, it just looked like a very warm, wealthy place. There were nice big armchairs and pillows, pretty pictures on the wall.*

The dining room was painted a periwinkle blue, a shade Palen loved, the chairs covered with bright chintz.

It came to life with frequent dinner parties, orchestrated by Carmel, who couldn't cook, particularly, and, more to the point, didn't have to, with a formulaic simplicity that served her well. At East Norwich she settled into a lifelong pattern of having her cook prepare one excellent, yet simple meal—a clear soup, game or squab, salad, cheese—which she would bring out at countless dinner parties until, gradually, some courses were supplanted by others. Palen, a crack shot, would supply the main course in hunting season, and he always made the salad dressing. The atmosphere was shabby chic, long before the term was coined. "There may not have been quite enough knives and the knife blades were steel and they may have been a bit rusty but whatever she put her hand to turned out to be perfection, charming, and right," one relative recalled.

Carmel was a meticulous housekeeper, instructing her cleaning person to a degree of perfection that had been instilled in her by her mother. One friend and former employee remembers Carmel reciting the edict: "Silver must be shining, furniture polished, with lots of polish on the floor." The staff at Rolling Hill included the always-entertaining Bridget, generously relinquished by Douglass, and a Scottish chambermaid who had worked for Palen's family for years. If it sounds grand, it's good to remember that, in the 1920s and for decades afterward, a servant or two was the norm at many, even middle-class, American homes.

Becoming parents didn't put a damper on the couple's social life—a nanny makes a difference. Carmel described weekends on Long Island that sound almost frantic, what with dances on summer nights in vast, Gatsby-esque houses and weekend lunches, often hosted by the Snows, on the terrace the couple had installed for that purpose. Carmel emulated Condé Nast's example of inviting people from all walks of life (presumably without the call girls), then seeing what came of the mix. Her New York friends—artists, actors, magazine people—would be tossed in with Palen's country club chums. And the Snows kept in touch with some of their more notable neighbors, including Corinne Roosevelt Robinson, a published poet and sister of President Theodore Roosevelt, whom Carmel and Palen visited at her Oyster Bay home.

Although Carmel didn't gravitate toward the sporting life, she still, as a fashion editor, thrilled to the look of it all, long before Ralph Lauren came along. She wrote rapturously of watching the international polo matches at the Meadow Brook Club and of Saturday fox hunts where

> *the turnout of the field was in its most stylish period, the men in "pinks" or black shadbelly coats, the women (except for the redoubtable Mrs. Hitchcock, who rode astride) in dark-blue sidesaddle habits with silk hats and veils—all of them mounted on the most beautiful animals.*

The only time Carmel rode in a hunt herself ended in tears of pain—hers, not the fox's: the riding habit and boots that she'd ordered in London at the end of her honeymoon turned out to be agonizingly small.

OPPOSITE: **An Edward Steichen portrait of Carmel Snow and her daughter Carmel, summer 1929**

The couple wasn't grounded, the way so many parents are, in their first child's first years. Palen would head off to various locales with hunting, fishing, or yachting in mind, while Carmel kept up her biannual forays into the center of the fashion world. Her trips to the French couture were a highlight that never dimmed. Both her duties, and the magazine itself, were expanding. By now there were four *Vogues,* American, British, French, and a German edition that had been founded in April 1928. As editor in chief of all four, Chase was spending increasing time in Europe, where there seemed always to be a crisis of one sort or another.

One took place in the mid-1920s at British *Vogue,* which was then edited by Dorothy Todd, who was a friend to the Bloomsbury Group—and, not incidentally, a lesbian. Todd, who had little interest in clothes, had brought a distinctly literary slant to the magazine, while slighting fashion, an agenda that Nast decided was inappropriate. He determined that Todd should go. She "refused to make any concessions for the reading public," according to the English writer and legendary gardener Victoria Sackville-West, who reported on the events in a letter to her diplomat husband, Harold Nicolson. After Nast fired her,

> *she then took legal advice and was told she could get £5,000 damages on the strength of her contract. Nast, when threatened with an action, retorted that he would defend himself by attacking Todd's morals. So poor Todd is silenced, since her morals are of the classic rather than the conventional order. . . .*

Nast's ruthlessness in this instance comes as a shock. Mainly he was known for his extreme courtliness, at least with favored employees, whom he would sometimes reward with extraordinary generosity, even paying off Chase's mortgage at some point, in a (very welcome) surprise gesture. It was easy to forget that he was a businessman, above all, and in that guise he could move quickly, and without mercy.

Happily, Carmel was very much in favor. Nast promoted her to editor of the American edition in the spring of 1929. "We needed a resident editor in New York who could be continuously on the job," as Chase said. Nast had been urging Chase to "establish my succession," as she put it—another reason, no doubt, for Carmel's promotion. With this step it seemed obvious that she was in line to ultimately assume Chase's job. By May 11, she had ascended to the masthead, along with Bocher, for the French edition; Alison Settle, who had replaced Todd at British *Vogue;* and Dr. L. O. Mohrenwitz in Germany.

It was a difficult position. Chase could never truly relinquish the day-to-day running of American *Vogue,* where, after all, she had been the boss for years. When she was out of town, Carmel had some autonomy, but when the boss returned, it became clear that, truly, she did not. Chase's assessment of the younger editor's performance was characteristically double bladed:

> *A great deal of the time she acquitted herself admirably although I could not always condone her methods. I was often annoyed when I returned from one of my prolonged working bouts abroad to find that the New York staff efficiency had degenerated, the costs had mounted, and that our trade and advertising interests were neglected.*

She doesn't name names, but she doesn't need to. At such moments, Chase would call the staff together for a kind of pep rally, in which she acknowledged the difficulty of putting out a twice-monthly publication. "Slipshod methods cannot and must not prevail if we are to maintain our position of leadership." Chase, quite simply, ran the place, and whatever noises she made about her succession had a hollow ring: it was increasingly obvious to Carmel that her boss had no plans to step down. "Under her I'd be a subordinate and I was beginning to find that position as intolerable as I found it under my mother."

Meanwhile, the managements of *Vogue* and *Harper's Bazaar* had entered a period of détente. For years, Nast, Chase, and the rest of the *Vogue* staff had fumed as employees of Hearst's magazine division casually poached editors and contributors—artists, writers, photographers—to Nast's magazines, pouncing on new talent as soon as it had proven itself, typically offering to double salaries and pile on other amenities if the prospective employees jumped ship. (While this was often successful, it sometimes resulted in Hearst also coming away "with some very fine lemons," as Edna Chase's spirited daughter Ilka Chase once wrote.) Nast, too, had certainly hired, and perhaps even lured away, his share of his rival's disgruntled employees. In the late 1920s, however, the two publishers entered into an agreement "not to molest each other's staffs." For a while, the poaching stopped.

Still, Nast personnel were on the move. Before too long, Carmel's counterpart at Paris *Vogue,* Bocher, resigned "in a dispute over the size of his salary," according to Bettina Ballard, who had been working at the Paris bureau. Bocher had been "brilliant," this editor wrote; not quite, according to Chase. Within eighteen months of leaving the magazine he'd transformed himself into the designer Mainbocher, known for his understatedly elegant clothes, with a fashion house on the avenue George V, the first such establishment on this illustrious Right Bank street, which runs between the Champs-Elysées and the Seine. His successor at *Vogue* was Michel de Brunhoff, who signed on in 1929 and proved to be a much more stable employee; he and Solange d'Ayen were "an unbeatable combination," one fashion insider reported.

ABOVE: Edna Chase, *Vogue*'s editor in chief, with art director Dr. Mehemed Fehmy Agha, 1937

OPPOSITE: Carmel Snow with the designer Mainbocher in Paris, late 1920s

As the 1920s progressed, *Vogue*'s American edition reflected an increasingly modernist sensibility. This was due partly to Carmel's influence—she traveled in artistic circles, both in Europe and the United States, and was forever coming up with new ideas. But by 1929

there was another factor at work. The pages changed drastically, and for the better, that year after Nast lured Dr. Mehemed Fehmy Agha, an art director of Turkish descent, born in the Ukraine, away from the moribund German *Vogue* to oversee the look of not just *Vogue,* but *Vanity Fair* and *House & Garden,* too. Nast urged Agha to revamp the look of the magazine, using Benito's layout of several years earlier as a guide. All three publications promptly leaped into modernity with bold, solid typefaces replacing the coy, italic ones that had been the norm. Agha explored the limits of the double-page spread—using two pages to tell one pictorial tale—a powerful tool in fashion pages ever since. "Agha removed the frames and sometimes the margins, and enlarged the photographs or filled whole pages with them, put together to tell one fashion story." Layouts became daring, inventive, calling attention to themselves in a distinctly unladylike way that must, at first, have seemed very un-*Vogue.* Frames around photographs disappeared, and there was white space everywhere. All that emptiness may have seemed wasteful to some, but it looked modern then, as it does to this day, and it cast everything displayed within it in a flattering light. And isn't that, in a fashion magazine, the point?

Carmel was an early, even instant, champion of the new art director. He was "as inscrutable as a cup of black coffee to me, but I instinctively felt he was right." She warmed to his "new European style of layouts," which she described as "a complete departure from the static, stilted look of all American magazines at that time." He was after boldness, in a word—drawings that weren't froufrou as so many then were, and huge, luscious photographs—a move that, Carmel noted, was "vigorously supported by Steichen and me." Nast also approved, writing in a memo to Chase that the monocle-wearing, multilingual Agha gave "impressive evidence of his intelligence" and adding that "for the first time in the twenty-one years that I have been running this shop the work of the art department . . . is being lifted from my shoulders." Beginning in 1928, the covers, which had always been shown with a border, began to be "full bleed," that is, their images leached right to the edge of the page. The illustrations themselves seemed to jolt ahead. Benito contributed numerous covers, including, in 1929, a neon-bright one that seems presciently psychedelic. By the next year, even the table of contents had some wit to it, with sophisticated drawings dancing up and down its margins. Some of these, including one of diminutive servants unfurling a long, narrow carpet, might have escaped from the pages of the witty, idiosyncratic *New Yorker,* whose staff frequently overlapped with *Vogue*'s.

Chase had once described, unforgettably, the staff of German *Vogue* as "actors cast in the part of office workers," which made the efficient Dr. Agha, who had a doctorate in political science and was a former student of Le Corbusier's, even more of a find. "Nast said the only thing he salvaged out of German *Vogue* was Dr. Agha," a *Vanity Fair* writer of the era recalled. From its founding, this Berlin-based enterprise seemed as doomed as the *Lusitania.* Even before Agha jumped ship to New York, the magazine had begun to list, and then to sink. It would disappear beneath the waves, to prolong an agonizing metaphor, in the fall of 1929.

With the advent of Agha, as well as Carmel's rise up the masthead, the magazine assumed a forward-leaning slant. It wasn't just its appearance but what it contained: at times it assumed the look of a catalogue of avant-garde art and design. The February 1928 issue, for example, showed Man Ray photos of the house of the Vicomte and Vicomtesse Charles de Noailles entirely done by the furniture designer Jean-Michel Frank, then the reigning interior designer of his day; a later feature shows the strict Paris dwelling of one Mademoiselle Charlotte Perriand, the young designer (she was then in her early twenties) whose furniture, created in collaboration with Pierre Jeanneret and Le Corbusier and still very much in style, had been a sensation at the the 1929 Salon D'Automne. Her apartment, located "under the eaves of an old house on the rue Bonaparte, that street so suggestive of Paris of a century or so ago," was done entirely in black, white, and gray. It had a "severe and practical simplicity," this otherwise-flattering story notes, adding that the dining room, in particular, had "something of the impersonality of a cafeteria."

The magazine's covers were still illustrated—many by Georges Lepape—and seemed to favor elegant women gazing languorously out over water, at distant cityscapes, or in one case, at a ship in an orb. In one, a woman scrutinizes a compact mirror, the New York skyline reflected in the background. Illustrators were invaluable to magazines in those days: it was their covers, after all, that translated into newsstand sales. One of the greatest fashion artists to emerge in the 1920s was an American-born Parisian named Carl Erickson, who signed his work "Eric," and whom Carmel helped to transform from a callow midwestern youth who didn't know beans about fashion into one of the most sophisticated illustrators around. (*Life* magazine described him as "small, unpolished and ill at ease in salons.") When he first began to work at *Vogue,* Carmel and Pauline Pfeiffer, who had joined *Vogue*'s Paris staff in 1925, would take him to Ciro's, one of Paris's hottest nightclubs, with branches in Deauville and Monte Carlo, "to show him which women were stylish, and I always concentrated on the styles I thought the Duchesse d'Ayen would approve."

Eric acquired sophistication in spades, at least on the page. He stayed in France for years where his wife, Lee, acting as his agent, would endlessly lobby French *Vogue* on his behalf. Like other fashion artists, he often sketched from models, a process that wasn't very different from a photography sitting. An editor would select the clothes and accessories to be drawn and, with guidance from both artist and model, chose the pose the latter might adopt; the slightest detail had to be rendered by the artist with what must have sometimes seemed to be a dreary exactitude. One of Benito's daughters, Isabel LaMotte, recalled that "the fashion editors drove him crazy," accusing him of not drawing the darts in the right place and other crimes. Her father, she adds, "wanted us to be fashion editors to get even."

At other times, an illustrator would have to work from memory, an immensely difficult task, as George Hoyningen-Huené, who worked as an illustrator before taking up the camera, recalled. "I would have to go to dance places and night clubs and to the races and remember clothes. . . . I could remember over a hundred dresses in every detail, after about two hours' work. Then I would go home and start sketching." The best illustrators could convey the essence of a garment in a few nuanced lines, as Eric demonstrated time and again, drawing a white crepe marocain resort ensemble by Jean Patou, for example, with crisp precision.

One of his best-known *Vogue* covers, depicting a woman posing with a black-gloved hand under her chin against a pinkish background, conveys in its chic simplicity the very essence of the magazine. Not surprisingly, Agha wanted more Eric-like illustrators at *Vogue,* ones who could supply "bold brush strokes with life in them," in Carmel's words. In contrast to the new *Vogue, Harper's Bazaar,* its main rival, seemed as dated as a silk sachet. There was something floral about all that italic print; its look was as dusky and old-fashioned as tea rose wallpaper.

Although her authority wasn't final—Chase was very much her overseer—Carmel flourished in her new job. The increased responsibility suited her temperament; she loved being in charge. She worked closely with Agha, and admired him, but she, like others on the *Vogue* staff, lived in dread of his sarcasm, which spared no one. She never forgot a lesson she learned from Nast in this period: "The day the Art Director is stronger than the Editor is a bad day for the magazine." This truism would serve her for the rest of her career.

Editing involves passing numerous quick judgments in the course of a day—what sounds right, what looks right, what will work—and Carmel, who moved at warp speed, could make them on the run. As fashion editor, she'd zeroed in on which garment to feature, what photographer or illustrator to use, how a shot or drawing might be played in the magazine; when she became editor, her scope widened: besides overseeing *Vogue*'s fashion reporting, she also weighed in on what features should appear. But decisions could be hard to make at *Vogue,* where a governing-by-committee culture prevailed. "Nothing could be decided without getting the opinions of fifty different people, from the editor to an office girl," Carmel wrote, adding that

> *I have never had much faith in meetings and opinion polls. . . . I believe that the editor of a magazine must make the decisions, and if the editor operates by intuition, as I do, he or she must be guided by instinct. For myself, I adore decisions. I'm frankly bored by meetings and conferences. . . .*

For all the changes, the underlying *Vogue* formula remained intact. A socialite's portrait always appeared in the first editorial pages. Royals were still very much in evidence—Lady Louise Mountbatten, the Princesse de Faucigny-Lucinge—with an occasional multicultural name, such as HRH Princess Paul Chavchavadze (in June 1928), tossed in. Another species, the good old American do-gooder, turns up, personified by such stalwart, hardworking figures as "Mrs. George W. Patterson, Junior, mother, aspiring writer, active in the Junior League and the Shipping Board." And there's a new portrait of the much-photographed Honorable Mrs. Reginald Fellowes—still "the most elegant and most talked about woman in Paris," according to Bettina Ballard—on the occasion of the publication of her first book, *Cats in the Isle of Man.* (Is it cruel to call this title underwhelming?)

The magazine wasn't aimed at the youth market. Refreshingly, there wasn't such a thing, or at least not one that mattered. "The French didn't believe that true chic could be attained much before the age of 40," an early client of the haute couture, Alice-Leone Moats, recalled in the 1970s. "They were convinced it took a long time to learn the art of dressing and to develop an individual style . . . by then, when a woman's looks were beginning to fade she *had* to have chic or she had nothing." Fashion magazines targeted the older woman, giving tips for giving one's gray or white hair an elegant look, presenting a portfolio of styles with the sage headline "To Age Gracefully Is an Art." There were no tight faces, no desperately starved bodies in evidence.

The magazine paid great attention to culture, and it's easy to see Carmel's hand in it all, particularly in an appreciative piece on Henri, her friend and former art teacher, who died in July 1929. Its contributors included the most-talked-about writers and critics of the time. Clive Bell, the British art historian, and the painter Augustus John contributed essays on art, and short stories by such exalted authors as Colette and Virginia Woolf were included in the magazine.

Vogue was still a place where a girl from Fargo or Kansas City could take part in the life of Europe or New York. Paris and the Riviera seemed to be just around the corner, and there was always social news to catch up with from Newport, London, and anywhere else that rich Europeans and Americans congregated. Less glamorous, but still critical to the *Vogue* reader, were reports on such denizens of Waspdom as the Brookline Country Club and the town of Oyster Bay. Frequently, too, the magazine reflected the sometimes numbing frivolity of its time. "You'll never feel more like 'dressing up' than you do aboard ship" one ad reads. The ceaseless assumption of a privileged life can feel, at times, almost suffocating.

Steichen contributed a prodigious number of photographs to *Vogue* through the 1920s, including a fashion shot of a model in a striking, horizontally striped Chanel cape with matching skirt and a wonderfully unsettling portrait—the sitter looks almost deranged—of one of the great actresses of the day, Eva Le Gallienne. His fellow lensman, George Hoyningen-Huene (who had dropped the acute accent on the last *e* for an American audience), was now shooting in New York as much as in France, contributing both portraits and fashion. And Cecil Beaton had become ubiquitous—his photographs of society figures were now a *Vogue* staple.

Beaton was twenty-four and bursting with both talent and attitude when he whirled through Manhattan on a first trip to the United States in 1928. He was charming on the surface, wicked in his mind. His reaction to the interior decorator Elsie de Wolfe, upon their first meeting, was typically outrageous. "She is the sort of wildly grotesque artificial creature I adore," he confided to his diary. (They would later become great friends.) He social climbed relentlessly and had the temerity to be dismayed when one Mrs. Vanderbilt, to whom he had presented not just one but two letters of introduction from well-connected friends, didn't bother to include him in a large dinner party she hosted during his stay.

Beaton had met Chase in London at some point and begun contributing drawings to the magazine. Upon his arrival in the States, the magazine opened its doors: Chase met him the day after his boat docked; four days later, on November 13, Nast hosted a lunch in his honor. Steichen, who Beaton described as "a good looking, goatishly-fawnish grey-haired man," was among the attendees, as was Crowninshield, who thoroughly impressed the young Briton with his legendary charm ("Wise, kind, witty and extremely knowledgeable"). Beaton was new to photography—he had an eye but also a lot to learn. Nast arranged a meeting with Steichen. Their encounter was fraught. Both he and Nast were deeply condescending toward him, or so Beaton imagined. "I felt like a humiliated schoolboy and said quite honestly that my photography was so amateur that I felt it might cease to exist any moment."

Steichen complimented his drawings, but thought his photographs were too painterly—an assessment with which Beaton agreed—and even, disconcertingly, that some were "rotten." In spite of this, Nast asked the young man to photograph his daughter, Natica. The shoot was "an agony," according to Beaton. He was as ignorant about lighting as Steichen had once been.

> *I had no idea of the negative potence and there was no unshaded bulb that I could put behind the sitter's head to give an effect of sentimental radiance and without this I am lost. The photographs I took I am sure were merely poor imitation Steichen.*

Soon after, he was summoned to the *Vogue* offices by Chase, where he learned to his shocked amazement that his portrait had been well received. She introduced him to Carmel, whom Steichen described as "looking like a fox terrier," a comment made stranger by the fact that, to her great joy, she was pregnant at the time—she had conceived again at about the time young Carmel turned one (a pregnant fox terrier?). Carmel offered Beaton one assignment after another while two of her assistants, including Margaret Case, helpfully made lists of the goodies he was to produce.

"This meeting was very satisfactory," Beaton reported. "Mrs. Snow... seemed pleased with me, and we arranged that I should do various jobs for her." One of these was to report on New York nightlife, with Eric, in town from Paris, in tow. Beaton was notoriously catty—his unexpurgated diaries, full of dish (and worse) were published in 2004—but not when it came to Carmel. "Mrs. Snow has the most satisfactorily ordered life," he gushed. "She is never flustered by the vast amount of work to be done at the office, yet has time to devote to her husband and children [sic], a house in New York [sic] and another in the country, while still she manages to travel to Europe." Even when pregnant her energy was boundless, and she took it for granted that everyone else could keep up. (Often, they couldn't.) The itinerary she concocted for his story on nightclubs made Beaton wilt. "She said, 'Well, that night you'll go to the movies after dining at the Caviar. You can try Casanova later. And this will be a good night to go to Harlem.'"

Although Carmel thrived on this kind of schedule, she also learned first-hand of its perils when her second child, a son they named Palen, was born prematurely on May 22, 1929, something she blamed, in part, on "combining hard work on *Vogue* with an unusually strenuous social life." Palen, caught off guard by his wife's early delivery, was off yachting when the boy was born, and Carmel was left to go through the worst ordeal of her life by herself. Two weeks after the birth, when it became clear that the infant couldn't survive, she cloistered herself away with him. "My mother was hurt because I wouldn't allow her into the room—only a priest—when the baby was dying, but it was *my* battle. I had to see it through by myself." Young Palen died on June 23. The pain of this loss lingered for both Snows; the lack of a son, which, as it turned out, was a permanent situation, was particularly grievous for Palen.

To be in mourning in New York at this time was to be out of step. The city was full of people who were giddy with prosperity, obsessed with investments, drunk with the prospect of infinite wealth. It was a bubble waiting to burst, but that wasn't clear to those floating within it. They were just enjoying the upward ride. Investments had become a national obsession. As British journalist John Brooks, who arrived in New York in 1929, reported: "You could talk about Prohibition, or Hemingway, or air conditioning, or music, or horses, but in the end you had to talk about the stock market. . . ."

But all of that would quickly change. In just two months, September and October 1929, the market lost 40 percent of its value. On Black Tuesday, October 28, it crashed altogether, losing "in that one day of trading $14 billion in value."

The next day, the *New York Times* put a human face on a catastrophe they called "the most disastrous and far-reaching in the history of the Stock Exchange."

> *Groups of men, with here and there a woman, stood . . . watching spools of ticker tape unwind and as the tenuous paper with its cryptic numerals grew longer at their feet as their fortunes shrunk. . . . The crowds about the ticker tapes, like friends about the bedside of a stricken friend, reflected in their faces the story the tape was telling. There were no smiles. There were no tears either.*

Crowds gathered at the Stock Exchange at Broad and Wall Streets hoping to witness history being made, but "actually they saw little enough—bankers whom they did not know by sight hurrying in and out of the office of J.P. Morgan & Co. across the way, other sightseers, a special detail of policemen and a few political speakers who addressed the noonday crowds near the Sub-Treasury Building. By the end of November, investors had lost $100 billion in assets. And Black Tuesday wasn't the last of it. After a brief rally in 1930, the Depression settled in. The market continued falling until July 1932; it wouldn't recover for another twenty-two years.

Condé Nast was one of innumerable wealthy Americans who saw his fortune wiped out. His magazines were thriving, reaping huge profits, but "the biggest percentage of Condé's wealth was on paper in Wall Street," Chase wrote, adding, with almost comic understatement, that " . . . he had always been a little naive about investments and the business of stocks and bonds." Nast hadn't acquired much property, given his wealth; when his investments evaporated, he had little else. He was in terrible shape, although you couldn't tell that from *Vogue,* which ran a cheery piece in the January 18, 1930, issue about how "the terraces of Mr. Condé Nast's penthouse has been transformed by one of Lady Mendl's minions from stark nudity to a thing of mirrored phantasy." An article that ran later, by Ruby Ross Wood, on how to furnish a new apartment on "nothing at all" seems more realistic, given the timing.

Others at Nast's company were affected in various ways. At *Vanity Fair,* Crowninshield—who claimed not to have a financially savvy bone in his body—sold off his Condé Nast shares just before Black Tuesday dawned at a phenomenal $93 a share, its highest price. It was entirely blind luck. After the crash it dropped to $48, and then, disastrously, to $2. The Snows, by contrast, were hard hit. Edna Chase recalled Carmel saying, "Palen has lost so much money," but there's no record of how much, and it never seemed too apparent to those on the outside. Still, Palen's wife's salary became more useful, perhaps even indispensable for the first time. Chase, too, had lost money, although she'd been shrewder than her boss, having put most of her money into real estate. Even so, she was poorer than she'd been and, for this reason, claimed that retirement was now a more distant possibility than before.

Such news must have been yet another blow for Carmel, who had been led to expect, she claimed, that the magazine would soon be hers to run. But, mainly, she was in a haze of grief. The death of her baby "so far overshadowed the effect of the 1929 crash on my life, I was scarcely conscious of a depression outside my own." It may also have affected her life in a way she never guessed: Edna Chase told some in *Vogue* circles that she'd decided to fire Carmel during this period. "Mrs. Snow had done something that Mrs. Chase didn't like and she was going to get rid of her," Benito's daughter, Isabel LaMotte, recalled. When the pregnancy ended so disastrously, though, Chase was so upset that she dropped the idea.

It took Cecil Beaton to bring the essence of postcrash New York to *Vogue*'s readers. Five months after his first, wondrously successful visit, he returned to a very different environment. "Last year," he wrote, "everybody talked about the stock market and excitedly exchanged reports of their new gains and successes while ordering a dozen orchids," he wrote in a story entitled "This Year and Last," which ran in January 1930. "The band played 'Making Whoopee.' Now, the same people still have the same topic on their wagging tongues, but it is a gloomy tale of woe that is being told by a million courageous tragedians, and the band plays 'Without a Song.'" Another observer who noted the difference was the astrologer Evangeline Adams, whom Carmel had met after, literally, landing in her lap during a stormy Atlantic crossing from Europe. "This little woman in a too-youthful hat covered with cherries had some kind of supersensory power that I immediately recognized. . . ."

Arrested early in her career for "fortune-telling," Adams had since become eminently respectable, writing books that are still in print and building a client base said to number a hundred thousand. The financier J. P. Morgan was her most famous client (and what better advertisement for her abilities could there be than that?); others included Enrico Caruso, the tenor; and a certain Mrs. Snow. Adams's obituary in the *New York Times* charted the difference in her client's preoccupations, both before and after the crash. "With the generality of her clientele the chief interests, in a class by themselves for popularity, were love and money. Before the depression, love ranked first. Since January, 1930, money has taken first place."

There was a certain protocol to it all, Beaton observed. "One is still grand, but one is poor—the new poor. It is vulgar to be rich and extravagant, and it is bad taste to give a large party, even if you can afford it. Even if you haven't lost money, you must pretend you have." The young photographer worked for *Vogue* during the length of his stay; when, at some point, and in spite of the tenor of the times, Carmel offered him a raise, her comments revealed a lot about the culture of the magazine. "Now you know, Beaton, you're very valuable to *Vogue* because you are a personality," she told him. "We have so many clever and intelligent people working for us but few are personalities and it's very important to us that you're happy." Carmel usually rewarded genius well. And the snobby, colorful, omnitalented Beaton was just the sort she adored.

At about this time hemlines fell, almost as abruptly as the market. The trend had been launched by Jean Patou, who had had enough of the low waist of the 1920s and hemlines inching up above the knee. He cinched in the waist—no one had seen one for a decade—and dropped his hems to the ground. Women had become used to the ease of movement the shorter lengths afforded, and there was a certain amount of resistance: "Can you see them in the subway?" asked Hattie Carnegie, the outspoken Austrian-born dressmaker and retailer (who'd adopted the name of the richest man in America—Andrew Carnegie—upon her arrival in the United States). Yes, actually, and in the *métro,* too. Women on both sides of the Atlantic quickly accepted the newly demure look, even though it rendered much of their wardrobes obsolete.

Chanel, who had been among the first to yank skirts up, quickly dropped them back down again. Others followed. "Patou and Louiseboulanger (with Mainbocher at *Vogue* egging them on) led the way for longer skirts," the fashion historian Caroline Rennolds Millbank reports. "Augustabernard, Molyneux, and Valentina emphasized the silhouette's slimness by stripping it of extra decoration. Madame Grès paid homage to the classically narrow figure by draping her jerseys around it." Soon, in the inexplicable way of fashion, women with trailing skirts looked more modern, more entirely with it, than their knee-baring counterparts. Just over a year later, though, the trend was reversed: *Vogue* decreed that the "average length for daytime dresses is now 12–13 inches off the floor." In deference to the newly rediscovered waist, "new corsets, carefully fitted," became the basis of the 1930 wardrobe. Hats were worn low, pulled down to eyebrow level. Other fashion developments reported in *Vogue* seem a bit less earth-shattering, if not downright forced, including the classic headline "Galoshes Attain Smart Standing" (what a relief). Schiaparelli was still a rising star, achieving a kind of canonization when she was photographed by Steichen in a black-and-white ermine scarf–collared suit of her own design.

Thomas Justin White

Late in 1929, Carmel discovered that she was pregnant again. Her joy this time was tempered, given her disastrous last experience. In any case, she soldiered on, resolving, as always, to work to term. On the home front, the Snows remained peripatetic, moving from one city residence to another. Their lives seemed particularly gypsylike in 1930, when records indicate that Carmel spent weeknights at either her mother's residence at 510 Park Avenue or at two other Upper East Side addresses, 502 Park Avenue or 155 East Seventy-second Street, the latter two temporary rentals of one sort or another. To confuse things further, her brother Tom White had taken a place at 501 Park Avenue, just across this broad, canyonlike avenue from his mother. In doing so, he was following a pattern once described by William Randolph Hearst's top financial adviser, John Francis Neylan:

> *Most of Hearst's top executives . . . drew enormous salaries, bought homes on Park Avenue, then spread out to country places on Long Island, and before you knew it they became yes-men because they felt they had too much to lose to argue with Hearst. In times of stress, with a few notable exceptions like Tom White, their loyalty was very thin.*

The Snows finally settled down that year when they moved into an apartment in the newly built forty-one story Ritz Tower on the northeast corner of Park Avenue and Fifty-seventh Street.

Not surprisingly, given all their peregrinations, Carmel, Palen, and young Carmel, now a toddler, were counted twice in the 1930 census: once at Rolling Hill Farm, then again at the Ritz Tower. While their daughter, Carmel, was usually on Long Island in the care of Rebecca Lucas, an English nanny, when the census takers came to call both were in New York with the Snows, as were a married couple of servants named George and Edith Hall.

Early that year there was awkward news: a former mistress of Palen's presumably floundering, like so many, in the postcrash economy, was bringing a $250,000 suit against him for breach of promise, claiming that he'd said he'd marry her, then jilted her to marry Carmel. "She threatened to expose their love nest and make a scandal," a family member says. "She threatened to tell the newspapers and give them love letters." The woman in question was Marion Hurley, a former Ziegfeld Follies girl and artist's model and altogether, from the Snows' point of view, very much NOOC—not of our class. Still, there she was, ineffably linked with her former lover in the pages of the *New York Times,* which ran a story on May 20, the day after the case went to trial, with the unfortunately damning headline "Former Show Girl Says G.P. Snow Broke Promise to Wed Her."

One can only imagine the elder Snows' reaction, and that of their friends, and family, and Carmel's friends, and on and on. For a conservative WASP family of the era such an association was, how to put it, deeply unfortunate. Worse still, Ms. Hurley had made an appearance in the same newspaper in 1924, when she was one of a team of professional models hired by the New York specialty store Best & Co. to demonstrate new corsets, including the Madame X Relaxing Girdle, to its customers. There it was, boldfaced and in large, if erratic type: "MISS MARION HURLEY who has been declared by noted artists to be the MOST PERFECTLY FORMED WOMAN IN AMERICA will be one of the models."

At the trial, a sobbing Hurley testified that she had "wept almost constantly," with serious damage to her health, ever since Palen wrote to her in 1926 saying that he intended to marry "another woman." There's no indication why she waited so long to bring her suit or, indeed, much else. In any case, the case was quickly put to rest. A court document indicates that it was settled on the day the story appeared in the *Times.* It seems safe to assume that a transaction took place, Ms. Hurley was mollified, and the matter was dropped.

A month later, early in the morning of Monday, June 23, Palen's father, Frederick Snow, died in Southampton and was buried two days later at St. Andrew's Dune Church in the same town. The following week, on June 30, Carmel was back from the funeral and sitting at an office meeting—her least favorite part of the job—when Dr. Agha, noticing that she seemed distracted, asked if he could take her home. "No, I think you'd better take me to the hospital," she replied. Her second daughter, Mary Palen, was born within the hour. (The baby was named for both Palen and Ma Dear.)

Carmel cut short her stay at Miss Lippincott's: "Perhaps because my last stay there had ended so unhappily," she wrote. Gone were the carefree, gossipy lunches with friends over chicken hash and other WASP fare from the Colony's kitchen. She left New York City altogether, traveling by ambulance to visit the recently widowed Ma Dear in Southampton. As the vehicle rounded a corner on a winding rural road, it crashed headlong into an oncoming car. Carmel's left hand was deeply cut; amazingly, there were no other injuries. A priest, happening by the accident scene, asked if the baby had been baptized. When told that she hadn't been, he took care of it on the spot. Upon arriving in Southampton, Carmel downplayed her injury and had the finger stitched up by a local doctor. From that point on, "because he did a clumsy job the first finger of my left hand always pained me a good deal. . . ."

Mary Palen's early life followed the pattern set for her older sister: she was cared for by nannies on Long Island during the week while her mother worked in town, sometimes with Palen, when he wasn't hunting or fishing elsewhere. Carmel, for her part, would go fishing on behalf of her magazine, chasing down fashions, supervising fashion editors, courting contributors, lining up articles. Or, rather, for the magazine that was hers but not hers. Her relationship with Chase continued its up-and-down course, as erratic as Carmel and Nast's was consistent. The publisher would later describe it as "not merely a close and confidential business relationship, but an intimate personal, almost family relationship as well." Their mutual devotion was such that, when Condé and Leslie Nast's daughter, also named Leslie, was born in 1930, Carmel was named her godmother.

The Depression had settled in and, as Chase pointed out, *Vogue* in the early 1930s was anemic "compared to the corpulent volumes of the [1920s]. Editorially we tried hard to give the magazine a practical aspect and to give the reader a greater variety of models, and despite the general poverty our circulation began to mount." The magazine kept up its bright facade, exuding opulence in the face of the economic rubble all around it. It gave its readers the illusion that everything, even the most exotic corners of the globe, was somehow within reach.

Solange d'Ayen contributed an article on traveling to Egypt, putting her considerable imprimatur on the Rome Express train that ran from Paris to Genoa. What to wear in the desert? A coat and traveling rug by Schiaparelli, of course, perhaps casually tossed into a Louis Vuitton butterfly trunk. (La Duchesse d'Ayen recommended both.) An August 1931 feature on a house party in Sidi Bou Said, Tunisia, showed Diana Vreeland, now looking mature and every inch the future fashion icon, with Reed, her equally sleek husband.

In the early 1930s, the first color photographs appear in the magazine, gradually and very artificially. "At first it became more of a liability than an asset," as Steichen has written, "for it brought forth an orgy of color. Instead of colorful pictures we had coloriferous images." He considered color to be a whole new medium and it was; his first *Vogue* color shots, which ran in 1931, seem woefully overbright and unrealistic, as color would in the hands of many photographers for years to come.

However difficult they found this transition, photographers were still highly prized. When word filtered to Nast that Cecil Beaton was being courted by *Harper's Bazaar,* Nast fired off a telegram to William Randolph Hearst at his *Los Angeles Examiner.* Its language was both steely and courtly and, as such, quintessentially Nast.

> SORRY TO BOTHER YOU WITH THIS DETAIL BUT TOM WHITE I AM TOLD IS ENROUTE BETWEEN CALIFORNIA AND NEW YORK SO I HAVE NO RECOURSE BUT TO YOU STOP BAZAAR EDITORS ARE MAKING CECIL BEATON AN OFFER VIOLATING OUR TWO OR THREE YEAR OLD AGREEMENT NOT TO MOLEST EACH OTHERS STAFFS STOP HAVE HAD NO WORD BAZAAR'S WITHDRAWAL FROM OUR ARRANGEMENT SO HAVE SURMISED THIS IS BEING DONE WITHOUT THE KNOWLEDGE OF HEADQUARTERS STOP WITH BEST REGARDS AND APOLOGIES FOR BOTHERING YOU STOP CONDE NAST

The cable worked, apparently, for Beaton remained, a fact that, within the decade, Nast would come to regret.

Whenever Carmel suggested a child- or baby-related story, her staff would teasingly suggest that another young Snow must be on the way. A clue came in the early 1930s, when young Carmel Snow, enchanting, shy, and aged about five, was photographed by Rosamond Pinchot in a story called "A Preview of New York Society," with the solemn caption: "Carmel is the daughter of Mr. and Mrs. George Palen Snow. Her hobbies are hoops and her dog." Sure enough, in the spring of 1932, Carmel was pregnant again with what she was sure would be her last child—she was now forty-five. If the news rankled Chase, she doesn't mention it. Instead, she writes, "We treated her as a favored daughter and began to look upon her offspring as *Vogue* descendants."

Such warmth wasn't entirely reciprocated. Carmel chafed constantly: "My judgment on *Vogue* continued . . . to be disputed by Mrs. Chase, just as my brilliant managing editor's [Frances McFadden's] judgment was often disputed." When a clipping service sent in photographs of England's Queen Mary taken over decades, wearing the same style of hat, "the toque that she made famous," McFadden captioned it " 'A Lady who is too Great to change her Fashion,' and I immediately passed it. Mrs. Chase overruled me." This kind of second-guessing never stopped. And every time Chase promised, yet again, that Carmel would soon succeed her, there'd be some grim indication that it wasn't to be. Carmel might learn that Chase had made the same offer to someone else or, even worse, that, as she once heard, she was planning to demote her to society editor—an unspeakable humiliation. It became clear to Carmel that "my wings as an editor were beginning to sprout, but at *Vogue* I would never be able to use them."

Looking back, all the signs seem to point, inexorably, in one direction. But in late 1932, of course, they didn't. The magazine went on; her pregnancy progressed. Roosevelt was elected, although there's no indication how she felt about this, or indeed any other, political event. (Palen was a Republican.) *Vogue*'s American edition had hit its stride with covers by Eric, including a pastel of a fashionable couple on horseback riding past a signpost reading VOGUE, and articles by Beaton, back in New York and wittily skewering its notables, and now frequently contributing photographic portraits, including one of Mrs. Winston Churchill, as well. The magazine was, once again, thick with fashion.

For the fourth time, Carmel worked until the end of her pregnancy, then, just before her baby was due, wound things up at *Vogue,* knowing she wouldn't be back at her desk for weeks. She began her maternity leave, if it can be called that—no such accommodation was made for working women in those days. Ma Dear's companion, Cookie, an indispensable part of the older woman's life since her husband's death, pitched in to help, packing Carmel's overnight bag and delivering it to Miss Lippincott's, which had been renamed Harbor Sanitarium.

The next day, Carmel went to a matinee of *Another Language,* a Broadway hit, written by Rose Franken, that had just opened to acclaim. The impending birth preoccupied her, and she was anxious about the gender of her child. "For Palen's sake I was desperately eager to have a son." As she watched the play, in which a new husband struggles between loyalty to his domineering family and his free-spirited young wife, she became aware of a growing discomfort in her stomach which she, at first, attributed to indigestion caused by eating a green apple. The next minutes were a struggle with two halves of herself. On one side there was the ever-inquisitive editor who couldn't leave until she knew if Stella and Victor's marriage would survive. The other was more businesslike. "Now, Carmel," she told herself, "you've been through this before. You know it's not that apple; you've got to leave the theatre."

She did, finally, halfway through the last act, hailing a taxi and proceeding at full speed to her mother-in-law's apartment at 150 East Seventy-third Street. When she got there, Ma Dear's companion was on the phone in the entrance foyer. "Whatever you're doing, Cookie," she called, "put that right down because I'm on my way to the hospital and this baby is coming as fast as it can." The image of ladylike Carmel standing with her legs crossed, urging her off the phone, was a story that Cookie would tell and retell for the rest of her days, as was the experience of hurtling toward the hospital in a taxi, wondering which of her clothes she should remove to wrap around the baby after its imminent birth. She loved to recount how, twenty minutes after their cab pulled up at the hospital, she heard a newborn's cry and exclaimed, "Don't tell me that's the Snow baby!" It was.

Carmel had been anesthetized from the moment of her arrival, and young Brigid—"a beautiful baby," according to her mother—had been delivered without a doctor in attendance. ("They always try to save the doctor," she quipped.) Within half an hour she was back in her room, happily chatting with the still-distressed maid. "Well, Cookie, we had quite a party, didn't we?" she asked, before speculating about how *Another Language* might have turned out.

Cookie had desperately tried to reach Palen, who, as it happened, was immersed in a golf game on the course at the Piping Rock Club, one of his favorite haunts. "When we knew we had another daughter I begged her to spare him the news as long as possible," Carmel recalled. She later learned that Palen had been "pretty gloomy" when he heard, while she, of course, "was exhilarated, as every new mother is. . . ." The baby had been born at term and was healthy, which, of course, was a triumph. The usual festive postpartum period unfolded, complete with room service, via the Colony, and an ever-changing cast of visiting friends and family.

One of Carmel's visitors was Nast, who stopped "in the next day to kiss me goodbye before once more sailing for Europe." Any qualms she may have been harboring about her working life had evaporated with "this new joy," and her encounter with the publisher was, as always, a warm one. For the rest of his life, he would quote Carmel saying from her hospital bed that "if you were to fire me today I'd be back tomorrow, I love my work so much." Carmel, who felt increasingly oppressed by working with Chase, never remembered saying these words herself, although she was ready to concede that, given her state of postpartum bliss, anything was possible.

A few days later, another visitor appeared, this one a stranger: Richard Berlin, the head of the Hearst magazine division and a colleague of Tom White's (who was then out of town). *Harper's Bazaar* was not doing well, Berlin told her, and the management at Hearst thought that if Carmel took over as fashion editor it could be brought to life. Perhaps to her own amazement, Carmel was instantly drawn to the bait. "What Mr. Berlin offered me was opportunity and *challenge,* as irresistible to me as it was to my mother." The job was at least nominally a step down—its current editor, Arthur Samuels, would remain in the top post—but there would be no Edna Chase and her salary would be the same. And the offer, it transpired, had filtered down from William Randolph Hearst himself—not a bad ally to start out with.

Carmel accepted.

She must have been shaken herself, both by the magnitude of the decision and the ease with which she had made it. After she left a message for Chase, asking her to come to the hospital, the latter hurried over, "sick with fear that something had happened to the baby or [Carmel] herself." When she got there, she found Carmel sitting in a rocking chair, apparently calm. When she told Chase of her decision, the older woman was "stunned. I sat beside her for a long time unable to speak."

Nothing prepared Carmel for the maelstrom that ensued. When Chase did find her tongue, she let loose. "*Vogue* trained you, *Vogue* made you, now you propose to make out of *Vogue*'s rival a copy of the magazine that trusted you!" she thundered. Even in her memoir, written more than twenty years after the fact, Chase's white-hot fury comes through.

> *She was fully aware of the keen rivalry between* Vogue *and* Harper's Bazaar *and she was now throwing over all that we had built together over the years to go to work for the man who, Nast felt, had tried assiduously and continuously to undermine his property and bribe away his best people. This was a procedure that Carmel herself had always condemned and had worked to protect us against whenever she got wind of it.*

Extreme decisiveness was Carmel's forte. Her decisions were quick, well reasoned, and final. And such, Chase discovered, was the case here. The older woman begged, threatened, cajoled. She urged Carmel to wait until Nast had returned from Europe so that they could discuss it face-to-face. But Carmel was unmoved. "She turned her face away and said, 'No, I have made my decision.'"

Chase's reaction wasn't unique. "Before I knew what was happening the entire staff of *Vogue* was grouped around my hospital bed arguing, pleading, threatening." This kind of session was duplicated more than once. At one point, Chase even turned up with Leslie Nast, now separated from her husband, who had felt so close to Carmel that she'd asked her to be her daughter's godmother. "Mrs. Chase thought the mother's presence might arouse some sense of conscience in the treacherous editor," Condé Nast's biographer has written. It did not.

5 changing sides

Your treacherous act will cling to you . . .
—Condé Nast

EVEN IF SHE PUT A BRAVE FACE ON IT, Carmel must have been unnerved. She immediately turned to unseen forces for help, no doubt praying furiously—and cabling others to do so. She also checked in with her astrologer, Evangeline Adams. "When I asked her for the stars' advice, she said, as I already suspected, that Mrs. Chase was *not* planning to retire, that I must accept this offer, but that I must not sign a long contract because within two years I would be worth twice as much to *Harper's Bazaar*." The stars were on her side.

Even so, the pressure mounted. There were more operatic scenes, with staffers turning up at the hospital. "This is Treason!" some shouted, in Carmel's recollection. From others she learned that Chase, marshaling sides, had begun "extracting loyalty pledges." Fortuitously, she neglected to ask Frances Mc Fadden for one, probably because she was a freelancer, rather than a member of the staff—an omission that would serve Carmel well. ("It was my Irish luck, I think, operating again.")

Soon enough, she heard the reaction of Nast himself, who had by then arrived in Paris, where he'd received cables from both Carmel and Chase bearing the news. In later years, Carmel claimed not to have anticipated the effect her decision produced. She even professed to believe that Nast, postcrash, would be relieved to no longer have to pay her salary, which was substantial (Carmel—like Chase, Agha, and other key members of the staff—was well paid, while the magazine's underlings typically were not; as bandleader Eddie Condon, whose wife once toiled at a fashion magazine, once put it, they typically paid "prestige and thirty-five dollars a week.") If Carmel really believed this, she quickly learned otherwise. Nast was devastated—so much so that he cabled his friend Harry Yoxall, the business manager at British *Vogue,* asking him to hurry over from London to be at his side. By the time Yoxall had crossed the Channel and arrived in Paris, Nast, despondent, was drunk. It was only the second time in his life that the abstemious publisher had been in this state (the first time being on his honeymoon with Leslie when, at her insistence, and against his better judgment, he ordered a second martini). Yoxall put him to bed.

After he'd slept it off, "Condé began dissipating the profits of a year on long, long cables to me. . . ." Carmel reported. Whatever was said had little effect. Three letters survive from this period, and they are fraught. Published here for the first time, they articulate each party's point of view with dismaying clarity. One can only watch as the gulf between these two former allies widens, until neither can be glimpsed from the opposite shore.

By the time Nast sat down to write, on December 20, 1932, he was back in New York where Carmel, presumably, was preparing for the holidays with her family. If she'd hoped for Nast's forgiveness, she was very, very wrong. He addressed the letter to her mother's residence at 510 Park. The opening paragraph set the tone:

> *Dear Carmel:*
>
> *I have cleared my desk, after my return from Europe, and can now answer the cablegram which you sent me to Paris, in which your intention to go to the* Bazaar *was announced, along with your statement of reasons, excuses, expressions of regret, sentiment, good will, etc. There was not a sincere or genuine line in that message. Those who break their word always build excuses—a "case" with which to square their consciences.*
>
> *Here is the simple truth in this affair:*

There does not often arise, in the management of a business, a tie of honor so binding as that which existed between you and me. Its binding character arose not only because your word was pledged, but because the circumstances under which that pledge was given were so unusual as to make the promise, for a person of character, an invisible one.

The first of these circumstances was the constant and long-repeated raids conducted over a period of fifteen years, upon the personnel of my organization, by Harper's Bazaar. *No one was more familiar with this disorganizing type of competition than yourself, of our watchfulness against it, and of the various measures taken by us to defeat it, and no one was more outspoken as to its unfairness than you.*

The second special circumstance was the appointment of your brother as manager of the very property in whose behalf those raids had been conducted. You were quick to realize that, because of this appointment, a situation had arisen which was so unusual that you would have to deal with it clearly and beyond any question of misunderstanding. Accordingly, and without delay, you came to me and said that I could dismiss from my mind the danger involved in your brother's appointment as Manager of the Bazaar. *You said that while blood was thicker than water, no combination of circumstances could persuade you to join the* Bazaar *staff; that no contract covering this situation was necessary because you were willing to give me your word of honor that you would never desert the* VOGUE *staff for the* Bazaar. *That pledge was made originally to me. Subsequently it was repeated before Mrs. Chase, and from time to time throughout the five-year period you took occasion . . . to reassure me by the repetition of that pledge . . .*

Nast went on to say that "no one has ever confided a more thorough, a more implicit, a more unquestioning faith in another than I confided in you." He attributed her departure from his magazine to greed, saying that Carmel had broken a promise for financial gain and reprimanding her in the severest terms. "Had you broken your word in financial circles as you did with me, you would never again have been engaged by a reputable institution in Wall Street." He talks at length about her "prestige and honor," and her presumed loss of both. He even resorts to the cheap trick of telling the unpopular schoolchild that everyone else in the class hates him or her, too. "I may also tell you that many men and women in social and business circles—some of them more your friends than mine—have gone out of their way to tell me what a contemptible thing they thought you had done."

And so it goes, for three typewritten, single-spaced pages.

Along the way it implies, even states, that Carmel made the move for money, to compensate for Palen's losses in the crash. It implies that, since she announced her resignation, she'd been poaching on *Vogue* talent. It implies a lot of things. But nowhere does it acknowledge what Samuel Goldwyn so famously said, that "a verbal contract isn't worth the paper it's written on." And nowhere does it acknowledge the force that really drove Carmel away: the formidable, vaguely unpleasant personage of Edna Chase. Had Chase been willing to step down, as both she and Nast had promised, perhaps disingenuously, time and again, nothing would have held Carmel back at *Vogue.* At times, even Nast seemed to be nudging Chase toward the door; surely he wanted Carmel in her place? But in his infinitely courtly, infinitely loyal way he would never have pushed.

As Carmel predicted, the older editor stayed in her post, without budging, for another twenty years. The clear implication of Berlin's offer was that, given the right performance—and how could it not be, with Carmel's energy and drive?—*Bazaar* would soon be hers. By reputation, and in fact, Arthur Samuels had little real interest in being editor in chief beyond commissioning literary pieces from the writers he coveted for the magazine. He was a domino ready to fall.

There are great gaps in their stories. Both Nast and Chase maintained that Carmel had plotted for some time to join *Bazaar,* waiting for Nast's boat to leave New York Harbor before she did so. But Carmel explicitly says Berlin docked at Harbor Sanitarium after Nast had embarked for his more distant port of call. And she makes a point—perhaps too much of one?—of saying that her brother knew nothing of Hearst's offer.

> *He was appalled when he heard what had happened in his absence. It was only when Dick Berlin assured him that "Chief" [as Hearst was known to his employees] himself wanted me (as far back as 1922 Mr. Hearst had expressed his opinion that a woman editor was needed for* Harper's Bazaar*) that Tom withdrew his opposition. From then on he was my chief adviser on matters of policy.*

Carmel Eitt, Tom White's daughter, recalled her father insisting that he'd had nothing to do with his sister coming to Hearst. And a niece remembers hearing that he'd been against it. "Tom didn't want the whole family working for Hearst," says Julie Groupp. And yet the idea that White knew nothing of the plan to recruit his sister sounds a false note, especially in the light of correspondence between Hearst himself and an earlier editor of *Harper's Bazaar* named William Martin Johnson, who wrote to the publisher, seeking employment, in early 1929. Hearst told Johnson to contact Tom White at the company's magazine division, saying, "He is more familiar than I am with the details of the magazine situation." It seems unlikely that the bid to hire Carmel would have been beneath his radar.

All we can really know, all these years later, is that an offer was made and Carmel accepted it. For all of Nast's much-invoked decency, his self-righteous horror at the step his former protégée had taken, she was right to act as she did. As someone who worked with her, Geri Trotta, says, "When destiny calls you don't hang around in the wings." Carmel's judgment didn't fail her in this instance. She had always had an exceptional eye for talent; in this case, the gift she believed in, and would go out on a limb for, was her own. That it was disloyal, there's no doubt. And yet, wasn't Nast somehow complicit in allowing Chase to continue talking of her retirement while becoming ever more vague about when it might actually occur? The trouble is, he was loyal to both. Yes, Carmel did betray both Nast and his organization, but she did so in the course of expressing her faith in something higher, the creed of excellence—the "top quality" she loved so well—that she subscribed to all her life. Nast worshipped at that altar, too. Part of her must have thought that, when Nast saw the virtually limitless nature of her new job, he would forgive her for acting as she did. Society editor at *Vogue*? Thanks anyway.

And so she moved on to the magazine she would later call "the impersonal love of my life." And she did so denying Nast's allegations to the end. She always maintained that, since she technically took a step down, from editor to fashion editor, the salary she was offered was the same—even though, as Chase reported, Hearst's "famous 'find out what they pay So-and-So and offer him double' was a well-known cliché in the publishing world." And she maintained, too, that she never moved to steal any of Nast's employees. But Nast, in a postscript to his letter, refers to Steichen telling her, after she approached him to cross over to *Bazaar,* "Well, Carmel, I couldn't do it." Nast added that "Steichen was bound to me by a bond of loyalty only, which he was not willing to break. But *you* were bound to me by a bond of honor which immediately your private interests were concerned, you were willing to break without hesitation or remorse."

The last clause can't have been true. Surely she hesitated, surely she regretted, if only the loss of Nast as a friend and mentor. As for whether she tried to woo Steichen away . . . for all her denials, she would have been foolish not to approach him—still the greatest photographer of the day!—hoping to capitalize on their long-held, mutual affection. Carmel is careful in her memoir to seem blameless. But surely she wasn't above reproach?

She denies, too, that she approached Frances McFadden, whom Chase herself described as "exceptionally able." Carmel's version of how this key lieutenant ended up at *Bazaar* is a classic: "I simply sent Frances off to Evangeline [Adams] who told her that she was about to receive a very advantageous business offer which she should accept." As she tells it, even McFadden took a dubious view of this sequence of events. (She "insists that I tipped off Evangeline Adams and induced her in some Machiavellian way to urge Frances to follow me to the *Bazaar*.") But Carmel truly believed, and insisted to McFadden, that only the stars had been in charge. "The next day, when Dick Berlin phoned Frances out of the blue with his offer, what could she do but accept her fate?"

Carmel answered Nast's letter on December 23.

510 Park Avenue
Friday Night

Dear Condé:

I'm so sorry to see by your letter that you feel as bitterly as you do—so bitterly that evidently there is nothing to discuss; only to say I never tried to take Steichen, or said a word to influence Frances or approached another person in your organization, and have no intention of doing so.

I hope you will have a Happy Xmas and that the New Year will bring you hapiness [sic].

(signed) Carmel

Nast responded the following week.

January 7, 1933

Dear Carmel:

I would not write you again if it were not to point out to you that, as usual, when you are in a difficult position, you attempt to befog the issue.

Your statement that my letter is "so bitter that there is nothing to discuss" completely ignores the question at issue. The issue between us is not my bitterness, but your act. Were I less bitter or even wholly indifferent as to what you have done, it would not, in any way whatever, alter the fact that you had welshed on your word and betrayed a friend.

You haven't the courage to face squarely your own conscience and the opinion of your social and business friends with the truth as to what you have done. In order to calm your conscience and to protect your reputation, you will undoubtedly continue your efforts to befog the issue, but the record in this case is too clean and clear-cut to be thus befogged. Your treacherous act will cling to you and your conscience and your reputation today, tomorrow, and during the years to come.

Very sincerely yours,

No further word would pass between Carmel and the man she always said had taught her everything about fashion. There would be no turning back. "It was the only incident in his business life on which I knew Condé to be implacable," Chase wrote in her memoir. "To the day of his death, he never spoke to her and never forgave her." And that was that.

6 *reinventing* harper's bazaar

I wanted to reflect in my magazine not only fashion . . . but everything that interests the kind of woman who reads expensive fashion magazines . . .

—Carmel Snow

AFTER CARMEL GOT OUT OF THE HOSPITAL she never went back to *Vogue.* Instead, after playing out the now-familiar routine of a new baby—long convalescence, nanny at home—she went to work in premises that had nothing to do with ornately carved antique desks or leather-bound fake books. The Hearst magazine offices were housed on two floors in a former hotel at 572 Madison Avenue, then mainly a low-rise area of brownstones and town houses, with a famous old drugstore, Henry Halper's, known to all as Halper's and the destination of choice for cucumber-and-watercress sandwiches, downstairs. It looked "like a small-town newspaper office," Carmel wrote. One can just visualize the yellowing linoleum, the rickety, utilitarian furniture. A decade earlier, she had been dazzled by *Vogue.* At *Bazaar,* she was, by her own description, "appalled."

And it wasn't just the office. Executed mainly in black and white, with relatively few photographs, the magazine itself was frankly dowdy, much more so than *Vogue.* Like its rival, *Harper's Bazaar* was founded in the nineteenth century, on November 2, 1867, to be exact. If its name sounds familiar, it's because the trio of brothers behind it also created the publishing house bearing their name, as well as two other magazines, *Harper's Weekly* and *Harper's Monthly* (which survives to this day). Their third magazine, *Harper's Bazar,* was the brainchild of one of the brothers, Fletcher, who gave it the subtitle of a "Repository of Fashion, Pleasure and Instruction." Originally a sixteen-page weekly, it became heftier, and a monthly, in 1901.

When it was acquired by William Randolph Hearst in 1912, the magazine joined the ever-expanding list of publications owned by a man who was becoming "the nation's most powerful publisher."

> *By 1930, he owned twenty-six daily newspapers in eighteen American cities. His Sunday papers accounted for more than 20 percent of the total national circulation. There is no way of even estimating how many Americans saw his newsreels or listened to the radio programs or radio stations sponsored by his newspapers.*

Hearst's magazine holdings included *Cosmopolitan, Good Housekeeping, World Today,* and *Hearst's Magazine.* (He would later acquire others, including *House Beautiful,* in 1933.) His reach was extraordinary, and he made full use of it, employing the

> *power of the media to set the national political agenda, first as a muckraking, progressive trustbuster, then, in his seventies, as an opponent of the New Deal and a stalwart anti-communist. He set the topics, dictated the tone, and edited all the editorials in his papers. . . .*

Hearst was a dynamo. Besides opining, ceaselessly, over the airwaves and in print, he served in the U.S. Congress and narrowly missed becoming the Democratic nominee for president in 1904. And he was, of course, stupefyingly rich. His art collection was legendary, and, at the time Carmel went to work for him, he had extensive real estate holdings, among them San Simeon, his Julia Morgan–designed folie de grandeur in California, as well as numerous properties in Manhattan. His employees called him "Chief" and quaked when his famously dogmatic memos and cables, invariably beginning with the words "Chief says . . . ," appeared in their in-boxes. The Hearst organization was an anthill, populated by hardworking drones, all doing the boss's bidding. (One of these, of course, was Carmel's brother, Tom White, who had just been promoted to the position of general manager of Hearst's newspaper division.) The magazine division hierarchy was housed at 959 Eighth Avenue and referred to, with dread, by the *Bazaar* staff as "Eighth Avenue" or, more often, "Fifty-seventh Street." It was these underlings, Richard Berlin and his crew, who were the interface between the magazine and the fearsome Mr. Hearst.

A few weeks after Carmel started at *Bazaar,* McFadden came to join her, as did her secretary. "It was a clean sweep of her department," Chase wrote resignedly. Another new employee was Cookie who, soon after Carmel left *Vogue,* quit Ma Dear's employ—not a very riveting job, except, of course, for visitors in active labor—to join Carmel's staff. She, too, arrived by way of Adams, who, when reading her astrological chart, asked who the CS was whose initials were turning up everywhere. "Carmel Snow had cropped up in Cookie's life before this, of course, but our association after that reading was inseparable for many years, as the stars foretold, for she came to me at *Harper's Bazaar* as my social secretary." Another early hire was Eleanor Barry, the young editor who had been summarily fired from *Vogue*—and who had never been forgotten by Carmel.

No doubt it was to Nast's advantage that Carmel's relationship with her spiritual adviser was short lived. Adams left this world suddenly on November 11, 1932—a death the seer had herself foretold—moving on to a place far removed, presumably, from rivalrous fashion magazines. No one else from *Vogue* jumped ship at this point. By now, the Condé Nast organization had banned all its personnel from talking to Carmel. Some, such as the artist Benito, who had worked closely with her at *Vogue,* were taken aback by the vehemence with which this edict was enforced. "As soon as Carmel Snow went over to *Harper's Bazaar* she may as well not have ever existed," recalled one of Benito's daughters, Carmel Semmes (named for Carmel, her unofficial godmother). "My father was stunned. You couldn't even pronounce her name in front of Mrs. Chase."

It wasn't a good time for Hearst, as it wasn't for most of America. Unlike Nast, Hearst had scarcely been affected by the crash; most of his holdings were in real estate. Even so, "the effects of three years of economic downturn were beginning to hit home," according to his latest biographer, David Nasaw, and in December 1932—the very month in which Carmel exchanged her last letters with Nast—Hearst cut salaries by a staggering 39 percent. While most of the Fifty-seventh Street drones were well paid and could withstand such a reduction, the rank and file of the Hearst organization could not, a fact that caused Tom White to resign briefly in sympathy, although he quickly returned to the fold.

Bazaar's cast of characters was reminiscent of *Vogue*'s. There were the usual underpaid society girls, stunning receptionists, imperious white-gloved editors. Presiding over all of it was Arthur Samuels, who had taken over the editorship in the fall of 1931 from Carmel's old friend Charles Hanson Towne, who was still contributing short stories and poetry to the magazine. Samuels was a dim satellite of the Algonquin Round Table who, while entirely unmotivated in terms of fashion, was committed to bringing great fiction to the magazine, which he often did: his September 1932 issue alone included works by Dorothy Parker, Robert Benchley, and Victoria Sackville-West. Not all of it was sublime: there were other writers in its pages to whom history has not been kind, Hugh Walpole, for one. Still others, such as the fashion-conscious Elizabeth Finley Thomas, seem to have disappeared without a trace. One of her short stories began with the unprepossessing words: "Standing there, in her wisp of pale chiffon, the light catching, here and there, the facet of a diamond among the tulles and lace . . ." Oh dear.

Visually, *Bazaar* seemed trapped in a time warp. Samuels "never bothered with the look of the magazine," Carmel wrote, and the magazine's unnamed art director, to her Agha-trained eye, was "perfectly terrible." The covers had become the franchise of the Russian-born, Deco-ish artist Erté, whose real name was Romain de Tirtoff, and who had derived his *nom de dessin* from the way his initials, RT, were pronounced in French. He'd begun his career as a fashion artist and designer and was so in demand that he was said to have "flipped a coin to decide whether to go to *Vogue* or *Harper's Bazar.*" His cover women were inescapably of the 1920s—an unfortunate situation, given that it was 1932—coolly elegant, almost vexingly unreal.

The magazine's photographer of choice was the Paris-based Baron de Meyer, who had left *Vogue* for *Bazaar* in 1923 after Hearst offered him a twelve-year contract at three times his *Vogue* salary. He contributed essays as well as the heavily retouched, silvery images that were his trademark, and, by the time Carmel joined the magazine, his distinctive theatrical signature seemed to run below every photograph. These strongly back-lit, formally posed images had once been revolutionary but, to Carmel's eyes, were no longer. And de Meyer himself, who was both flagrantly homosexual and recently widowed from the colorful Olga—another "white marriage"—seemed as fatigued as his pictures. He was already in his sixties, and the long years with Olga, socializing on many continents and dabbling, like so many Paris artists in the 1920s, in opium, cocaine, and other drugs, had taken their toll.

The work of another titled *Bazaar* photographer, Baroness Antonie "Toni" Von Horn, a young German who was de Meyer's equivalent in New York, wasn't much more exciting. Her portraits and fashion shots seemed static, at least in the eyes of Carmel, whose mandate, upon being hired by Hearst, was in part to freshen up the look of the magazine. *Bazaar,* like *Vogue,* loved having contributors who were aristocrats; even so, their titles could carry them only so far. Both de Meyer and Von Horn "sounded more distinguished than their fashion photographs were," was Carmel's dry assessment.

Bazaar's reigning fashion editor, Kathleen Howard, a former opera singer, worked in close tandem with her sister, Marjorie, who held the equivalent job in Europe. Since Samuels was impervious to fashion, they had that aspect of the magazine sewn up. In a 1931 talk to the Fashion Group, the organization for fashion professionals, including buyers, editors, and advertisers, that had been founded in New York that year, Kathleen Howard described the sisters' working relationship, using an analogy that one can only assume grated as much then as it does today:

The editorial pencil of Harper's Bazaar *has two ends, like every other pencil. One is the blunt, business end which is personified by your humble servant; the other the sharp, incisive, I think excellent end and which is wielded by Marjorie Howard in Paris, my sister.*

Certainly something about this team had begun to grate with Carmel, who noted with ill-concealed satisfaction and no further detail that the sisters were gone from the magazine by summer.

The anonymous art director, too, was soon history, presumably also nudged toward oblivion by Carmel. From this point on, although technically still only a fashion editor, she took over. She brought in a photographer, Ruzzie Green, to act as art director, and her office became command central of the editorial department. "An exciting aroma of intrigue always pervaded her office," McFadden once wrote. It was true even then.

"Things began to hum," Carmel wrote.

Because all was confusion at the beginning, and pretty amateurish, what was agreed on one day might be abandoned the next. If I decided that an issue had to be done over, new sittings were hastily set up and night after night Ruzzie Green, Mary Hanshon, the production manager, and I sat up till all hours remaking the book.

And it was, from that point on, very much her "book," as insiders refer to magazines. She was soon the de facto editor in chief, to Samuels's quite understandable annoyance.

He had been in the habit of locking his office door so he could read in peace the stories and novels he bought for the Bazaar. *Now there was no need to lock the door because nobody went near him. My office, Samuels said, was like Grand Central Station—his like Grant's Tomb.*

Her door remained open, as it would do for the length of her career. If Samuels offered resistance, it didn't add up to much. Carmel took charge, and that was that.

She went straight to the new. She urged her staff to "Do it! Try anything!" A conference table, placed in her office, became the locus of a meeting that never quite adjourned. Everyone alit there at one point or another—art director, junior editors, assistants. "The enthusiasm of my new associates was high because I always gave them the green light; I knew only too well what constant discouragement can do to an enterprise." Some ideas were inspired, some mad, some a bit of both, such as the new front-of-the-book feature called "Dog Bazaar," geared toward fashionable canines and their owners, that would be a beloved part of the magazine for decades to come. (Its editor, Chase Harindean, yet another beauty, used to arrive at the offices accompanied by two great danes.) Whatever. As Carmel later wrote: "A magazine can, and should, take chances," and it did. Everything happened at a frantic pace. When any contributor asked her what the deadline for an assignment—whether a sketch, photograph, or text—might be, she inevitably answered, "The day before yesterday."

Every meeting had the same goal: to create an exciting monthly magazine that looked new, that knew everything, that could, most importantly, out-*Vogue Vogue.* Carmel had a hand in everything. During this period,

I adopted the custom I used throughout my life at the Bazaar *of "putting the book on the floor"—laying out photostats of every page in the coming issue so I could see it as a whole and mull over it while I sat at my desk. My photographers have told me that it was a chilling experience to watch their masterpieces walked over by everyone who came in to see me, but since there were photostats it didn't do the masterpieces any harm. . . .*

She revamped the way each issue's pages were laid out, in a way her staff found hair-raising, by rearranging them, often at the eleventh hour. The orderly, yet ever-changing rows of paper, splayed out across the carpet, would be shuffled frequently, like an outsize deck of cards.

"We photographed fashions I believed in . . . and even with inferior photographers we began getting results." Edging into the top spot, Carmel learned on the job, a circumstance that's impossible to imagine taking place in our time. By today's standards, she was under no pressure at all. She doesn't mention any talk of newsstand sales and circulation figures, at least in her early years. And while it's true that she now and then was obliged to feature the dreary styles that generations of *Bazaar* fashion editors have called "pearls of little price"—designs by important advertisers that, now and then, just had to be shown in the magazine—this didn't arise too often. Her main obligation was to her readers and to her own taste.

And in this she was off and running. The magazine, while often late to press, became more lively overnight. It burst with ideas, some wonderful, some disastrous, as almost any issue demonstrates, perhaps none more so than the one of October 1933, which soared with a sublime Salvador Dalí–painted cover—a long way from Erté—only to crash and burn over a tacky story on hairstyles that featured photographs of miniature clay heads. Other ideas seem inspired, including a fashion spread on lingerie, in the September 1933 issue, in which bras and girdles were shown beneath impeccably tailored, transparent plastic clothes. The typeface became bolder, with cleaner lines, and it could do surprising things: one headline, in August 1933, started vertically at the bottom left of one page and continued to the top, where it took a sharp right angle and marched horizontally across the facing page. Layouts were jazzed up, with lots of white space. Even the work of longtime contributors, such as the artist Reynaldo Luza, seemed livelier, sitting, as they did, more inventively on the page.

And there was wit to it all—that dash of daring. Captions became livelier: "Fifty million ermine can't be wrong," read one, showing a society figure, Mrs. William T. Emmett, in an ermine wrap. There seemed to be no limit to what the magazine would discuss. It took a strong stand for buying clothes made by unionized workers, for example, exhorting readers to

> *lend the weight of your prestige to the cause quietly and effectively over your own luncheon table or after dinner with the creme de menthe, by refusing to listen to any more boasting about those wonderful little dresses that cost practically nothing at all.*

Another early story, in an entirely different vein, featured a fortune-teller named Dolly, who, in the absence of Adams, would become "a permanent fixture" in Carmel's life. Fashion, too, hit some high notes. "It Is Conventional to Be Extreme" ran a headline in April 1933, one of the first issues in which Carmel had a hand.

> *Women who wouldn't have been seen dead in padded shoulders a year ago are wearing them now and loving the lift they give them. . . . Inhibitions in regard to lace gloves are melting. No one thinks twice about wearing big swirling footman's frogs or circus clown hats of queer décolletés or full backs or any of the other trade-marks of this spring.*

It was all part of the deco-influenced look of the 1930s, with its monochromatic sensibility. (Headlines from this period refer to "The Chic of Thin Black"—how contemporary is that?—and "The Modern Polar Effect of Dead Black over White.") Clothes were tailored, narrow, with hems grazing the midcalf. All women wore hats, the wildest, as usual, came from Schiaparelli, who, continuing on her inventive course in clothes, too, conjured up an evening cape that season that ballooned out like a spinnaker at the back. Vionnet was in top form, contributing diaphanous dresses, including one arresting, drapey number in iridescent lamé. Her flattering bias cuts influenced everyone, giving "elasticity to the fabric long before Lycra was invented." A new designer, Alix, who offered beautifully draped, classically simple clothes, would, years later, become known under her surname, as the deft, mysterious Madame Grès (pronounced like "dress"). Mainbocher, in his third season, contributed long afternoon dresses and short coats with surprising touches—fur sleeves on one, a leopard back on another—while Chanel's tailored suits, as always, provided an understated counterpoint.

Carmel herself was wearing Molyneux, a designer who seemed to come into his own in the 1930s, showing streamlined, practical clothes with fewer pyrotechnics than some of his colleagues: "A Molyneux *ensemble* differed from one by Chanel or Vionnet by its rejection of the details of dressmaking; he preferred the simplest lapel, the least complicated color scheme." His fashions were eminently practical—perfect for a working woman with both a social life and a family. His afternoon dresses in patterned silk, combined with matching three-quarter-length coats, could go easily into evening. Many of his clothes could be dressed up or down by the addition, or removal, of another element—a jacket, say—often in sumptuous colors.

Now in her forties, Carmel had lost the fresh prettiness of youth, perhaps, while moving into a look that was distinctly her own. She was small featured and as thin as a pencil. She was pale on top, like Kilimanjaro; her prematurely white hair—once reddish brown, fiery like her character—was part of her signature, just as much as her impeccable suits and the sound her high-heeled shoes (she had hers custom fitted by a Madison Avenue shoemaker, who used only the finest Italian lasts) made as she clicked decisively down the halls. "Every morning she looked just crisp and marvelous," a former employee reports. "We'd love to see what she was wearing."

Although she dressed up, always, carrying alligator pocketbooks and wearing pearls and the like, there was still an offhandedness to the way she put things together, a breeziness that was distinctly, almost quintessentially American. "She was impeccably well dressed," says Hubert de Givenchy. "When she arrived at a collection she overshadowed everyone else with her elegance." Long before frighteningly thin society women—indelibly dubbed "social X-rays" by journalist

Tom Wolfe—were invented, Carmel (who was skinny out of vagueness, or a fondness for alcohol, or both, in any case not because of vanity) was a living example of how well sinewy women can look in clothes. Everyone who worked with her, it seems, comments on her immaculate brand of chic. "She was as neat as a pin," one editor, Dorothy Wheelock Edson, says.

Like many women who are focused on fashion, Carmel arrived at a style that would serve her, with only minor variations, for the rest of her life. The formula never varied: simple pumps of excellent last, a small circular hat—"She wore a hat all day long with a little veil," one editor recalls—and "exquisite suits in beautiful sweet tea colors," according to Babs Simpson. "She looked very seductive. I don't think people usually mention that. She was piquant looking with her lovely figure and great legs. . . . She wasn't classically beautiful, but she was piquant and charming." Like a Frenchwoman, she rarely wore earrings; she wore her emerald engagement ring, of course, and, often, a broach—a favorite was the enormous one she was said to have had made up by the jewelry designer Jean Schlumberger, "the size and shape of a macaroon," as the journalist Janet Flanner once described it, and "composed of her mother's fine big diamonds." (Its attribution is tentative. Some, including Nancy White, said it was made by the Sicilian Fulco Santostefano della Cerda, Duke of Verdura, aka Fulco Verdura, who arrived in New York from Paris at about this time: "I think she probably took whatever family jewels there were and said to Fulco, 'Make me a pin,'" White says. Others, including one of her daughters, attribute it to Cartier. Wafting behind her, always, was Jean Patou's Joy—a talcumy, floral mélange that smells dated now, but then seemed as sharply new as its creator (a marketing genius who—brilliantly, and with great success—advertised his scent as "the costliest perfume in the world"). Like almost all ladies of her time, Carmel wore only lipstick and face powder—in later years contained in a heavy gold Verdura compact with a starburst motif.

Although nominally not the boss, Carmel had become one, adored and feared. She was no longer "the Cossack," as she'd been known at *Vogue,* but "Bossy," a nickname that would endure. Her most immediate impact was on the look of the magazine: she was its de facto art director just as much as its editor. Working side by side with Dr. Agha, and Benito before him, she had absorbed much that was revolutionary about their work. Now, with Green, some of both men's design tricks turned up, although never with quite the self-assuredness that had been theirs. Stamp-size photos lined up at the side of the table of contents; other photos seemed tossed, higgledy-piggledy, across the page. And color photography, inevitably, appeared; it was still a hit-or-miss business, with some lensmen, Ruzzie Green among them, managing it well, while others turned in pictures that looked alarmingly fake.

At about this time, Carmel began

> *my lifelong habit of waking early to read newspapers and magazines before I went to the office, tearing out any item I thought might be useful. I also read advance copies of books I knew people would be reading, and I always arrived at the office with a bagful of scraps—clippings, notes on things I'd read, memos about people or fashions I'd observed at the theatre or at parties or in restaurants. By always keeping my eyes open I "spotted" unknown girls who later became well-known models.*

Whenever Dorothy Wheelock Edson ran into her in the elevator, "she'd never waste a minute," the editor recalled. "She'd say, Dorothy, don't you think that we should photograph so and so? She had so many things on her mind, a lot of it about features that had nothing to do with fashion." It was all about keeping your eyes open. When she saw something, or someone, who interested her, she always followed up. After reading and admiring Janet Flanner's famous "Letters from Paris" in *The New Yorker* for years, Carmel approached the Indiana-born author, asking her to contribute to *Bazaar*—which she did, becoming a close friend in the process.

In the May 1933 issue, Carmel's name appears on the masthead for the first time, below Arthur Samuels. So does the story on Queen Mary's hats that so offended Chase, a cheeky, irreverent series of photographs showing how little the monarch's puffy, meringue-shaped headgear had evolved. (It must have been delicious finally to see it in print.) A Von Horn fashion shot of a flower-encrusted, white organdy evening dress by Henri Bendel, in the same issue, seemed infinitely more sultry than anything the young German had shot before.

There was a noticeable jolt to the copy, too. Where once it was treacly ("satin of several varieties is very important in the midseason mode"), it became punchier, more precise, as in "Lanvin takes bias bands of white satin and silver lamé, twists them together and binds the twist about the head like a Ballets Russes turban—the most becoming line in the world." There's an irony to it now, a sense that fashion is ephemeral, amusing, sometimes deranged. Writing about a new blouse style, the anonymous writer urges readers to "remember that one silly, solitary flower like a daisy, stuck on the front of your white sailor, is the new nonsense that makes sense in fashion." If Snow's changes appalled some of the senior staff, they didn't worry Hearst, who had long been concerned with the look of the magazine, even writing to Charles Hanson Towne in 1929 to complain about overly decorative borders and backgrounds. With this once seemingly moribund title becoming livelier with each passing month, the publisher could scarcely object.

Carmel headed off to the Paris collections in the spring of 1933, as usual, only now she was flying the flag of her former rival. If there was awkwardness at first, it didn't last, and she and *Vogue*'s Paris staffers soon were carrying on, at least when Chase wasn't around, just about as warmly as ever. "It was not considered very loyal in *Vogue* circles to be friendly with Carmel Snow, but the Paris office was uninfluenced by this feeling," Ballard wrote. "In Paris they could get away with it." The only real tension came from *Bazaar* itself; Marjorie Howard, still the Paris editor, was said to be "perfectly furious" at being upstaged by Carmel's presence.

In Paris, "I was very much on the qui vive to develop artists for the *Bazaar*," Carmel wrote. Many of these were brought to her attention by Daisy Fellowes, a half-French, half-American heiress to the Singer sewing machine fortune who had become "the personification of the hard Thirties-chic that came in when

Schiaparelli became the rage." But many were artists Carmel had known in Paris for years: her sleepless, apparently inexhaustible, visits to the collections were crammed with dinners with artists; she once even went off to visit Paul Cézanne, regaling her relatives with tales of her studio visit, in which the great artist had wiped his paintbrush off on his dog. Sleep, presumably, was reserved for East Norwich.

Carmel corralled the endlessly gifted, endlessly self-inventing Jean Cocteau—whom Janet Flanner called "the most indestructible talent in Paris," remarking on the "sense of astonishment that Cocteau aroused with everything he laid his pen, pencil, or imagination to between the two World Wars." There was nothing he couldn't, and didn't, do: besides drawing, playwriting, painting, writing ballets, and designing theater sets and costumes, he published an acclaimed novel, *Les Enfants Terribles,* in the early 1930s, and would go on to make iconic avant-garde films. "The passage of time seems neither to wither nor even to interrupt the hothouse ripeness of his talent," Flanner wrote. It's no wonder that the plaque on the building where he lived for years in his red apartment on Paris's rue Montpensier, overlooking the Palais Royal, says that he "lived and shone" at that address. He was dazzling, and soon he was in *Bazaar,* contributing a line drawing of a Chanel robe de menton in the simple, evocative style that was so characteristically his. A later sketch of Chanel demonstrated his exceptional ability to evoke a personality, an outfit, in just a few clear lines. It's all there: the designer standing with arms akimbo and angled hips, the wondrous simplicity of her floor-length dinner dress, the cheerful, unrepentant gaudiness of her faux jewels.

Carmel reeled in the Hungarian artist Marcel Vertès in Paris, too, whom she knew, as everyone there did, from the work he was doing for Schiaparelli, designing bottles and packaging for her line of perfumes (all of which, in that period, began with the letter *S:* Shocking, Sleeping, and on and on), as well as his famous print ads in what Carmel called his "deliciously frivolous style," each page crowded with satyrs, naiads with flowers in their hair, violin-playing dogs, and other ephemeral creatures. This diminutive artist's numerous contributions to *Bazaar* included a charming piece he wrote and illustrated after visiting New

York for the first time, where he found himself surrounded by "skyscrapers"—by which he meant not buildings but the ubiquitous long-legged American women. "They stride like giantesses, looking only forward."

And then there was the portly Christian "Bébé" Bérard, a huge—quite literally—figure in Paris theater, a gifted artist, and a major Paris gossip, who was a friend of Carmel's and more or less everyone else in fashionable circles at the time. Bébé had attended Paris's Académie Julian, where he'd studied painting and, incidentally, also earned his nickname: pinkish and rotund, he indeed resembled a baby. He was the greatest set designer in France in his day, designing for the ballet as well as for the Comédie Française. He was particularly known for his "superb, fresh and vital" sense of color, in the words of an admirer, George Hoyningen-Huene.

Bérard's influence in the beau monde was enormous. "In Paris it was considered that a word from Bérard could make a hat shop or break a dressmaking establishment," as Cecil Beaton has written. "Whether it was a matter of a new shop, the latest interior, actress, or play, his opinion counted more than anyone else's." He was close to numerous couturiers and, as his friend Boris Kochno, the writer and ballet librettist, has pointed out, had a true instinct for fashion—when it came to others, that is: his chicer friends consulted with him endlessly on how to dress. His detailed suggestions about styles frequently turned up in one form or another in the collections of his designer friends. He himself often resembled a madman, albeit a stylish one, wearing a huge oversize scarf at the neck, a flower or two pinned to his paint-splattered worker's clothes, and pulling his equally stained-looking Maltese dog, Jacinthe, behind him on a leash. "His normal appearance was nerve-shaking," as Edna Chase described it.

By the early 1930s, Bérard was just over thirty and well known as an illustrator and set designer. He was a talented painter, an art form he neglected for practical reasons: a profligate user of drugs, he was in constant need of cash. "Bébé was so heavily on drugs that you'd be sitting with him at lunch and his beard would just get dripping wet, he needed a fix so badly . . . ," Thornton Wilson, who spent part of his childhood in Paris (and would later become Carmel's son-in-law), recalled.

Carmel knew Bérard the way she seemed to know everyone in Paris, from a thousand late-night dinners at such places as the Mont Blanc and the art-encrusted Provençal restaurant called La Méditerranée on the place de l'Odéon, decorated with fanciful murals by Bérard and Cocteau, among others, that survive to this day. Marlene Dietrich used to lunch there daily when she was in town; in later years, the American writer Carson McCullers, impossibly young and new to Europe, once almost silenced the teeming restaurant by turning up in blue jeans—long before anyone in Europe had ever seen such a garment.

"And what fun we had at those dinners!" Carmel recalled. "In Paris *everyone* is interested in fashion—that's one of the joys of working there." Those assembled might include Cocteau, the composers Auric and Poulenc, ambassador's wife Evangeline Bruce, Nancy Mitford, and Marie-Louise Bousquet, whose famed salons at her cramped apartment attracted "the century's tycoons of art and industry," as Truman Capote has described it, among them Aldous Huxley and Pablo Picasso, as well as a smattering of French aristos. Out at night in Paris, eating wasn't the point. "Marie-Louise says that I was always urging people to 'eat well,' though I barely touched the food on my plate," Carmel recalled.

ABOVE AND OPPOSITE: **Carmel Snow and fashion colleagues at a Paris restaurant, August 1937**

She decided early on that the perpetually broke Bérard could be a gifted fashion illustrator, and she promptly put him to work. Or tried to. It wasn't always easy. "Almost all the work was done the minute after the very last minute, George Davis, who'd first met Bérard in the 1920s, once wrote," partly because he enjoyed the drama of editors and agents howling deadlines, partly because he lived constantly in the most acute physical and moral distress." It's no wonder that *Life* magazine, in a 1937 article, described

Bérard as "perhaps the strangest of all the strange people recording Paris fashions for U.S. publications."

Ballard, who later worked with him at *Vogue,* once described his routine:

> *Bébé usually appeared about six in the evening set to work through the night. His black beard was full of spaghetti and little active pets who lodged there and he never dreamed of wiping his brushes any place but in it. He had a slashing wit and the wickedest tongue in Paris, but he could still draw more graphically than he could talk. He was ambidextrous, drew equally well with both hands, and he'd pick up pencils or brushes and before he'd finished describing a party it was before your eyes on paper, the drawing room where it was held, the women in their elegant dresses—the evening had come alive.*

They came alive without faces, a fact that drove Hearst to the brink—he called the artist "Faceless Freddy"—but set Bérard's work apart. In one sketch, a faceless clotheshorse with a swanlike neck imparts an impossible elegance to a black taffeta Molyneux cape and ostrich-plume fringed hat. Many of his accomplishments were either ephemeral, such as theater sets, or designs for private use, including wall panels he created for the houseboat, designed by Jean-Michel Frank, of the Vicomte and Vicomtesse de Noailles. As a result, hauntingly, years after his death there remained "little to prove that a deeper talent existed," as his friend Ballard once wrote.

For Bérard and others within "the realm of the gifted and tormented," as Ballard once so aptly described it, it was a time of extraordinary fruitfulness—and decadence the rest of us can scarcely imagine. Flanner called the period "that strange 1930 Paris literary epoch of drug addiction." Opium was the rage—at times, Cocteau and Bérard were, quite literally, yellow with it—a drug that became less appealing as the wages it exacted became clear. As Cocteau wrote in his hallucinatory "Opium," a tract he penned in a detox clinic in the course of a twelve-day period spent without sleep, the drug was "the only vegetal substance which communicates the vegetal state; through opium we obtain an idea of that other speed known to plants." In other words, you had only to smoke it to approximate the mental condition of a ficus tree.

Were artists more artists in the Paris of this era? They were uninhibited, to say the least, and could be wildly undisciplined: the machinations involved in getting Bérard, who was apt to disappear for days, even weeks, at a time, to actually produce something could be heroic. That any editor was willing to take on the challenge speaks volumes for his talent. In general, Paris artists seemed vastly less businesslike than their New York counterparts, with the clear exception of the soberly efficient Eric, whose wife so ably lobbied the *Vogue* offices on his behalf.

At about the time of Carmel's first visit to Paris for *Bazaar,* there were intimations that Eric was unhappy at the Condé Nast publication. His wife let it be known that he was doing more fashion work than he liked, when what he most wanted was to draw "portfolios" for the magazine—multipage spreads on a travel destination or other subject of his choice. The *Vogue* team became concerned, particularly when Carmel was around, that these grumblings would be picked up by their rival, with the result that Eric would be snatched up by *Bazaar.* Paranoia about Eric was so intense that one editor even confided to Mrs. Chase that she was worried about leaving Paris at the end of the collections before Carmel, who always stayed for a week after the showings were over to have her wardrobe fitted for the next season, lest she try to lasso *Vogue*'s favorite artist.

But Carmel was busy netting a bigger fish. After she returned to New York, the magazine announced, in the text of a caption beneath an arresting pen-and-ink portrait by Cocteau, that Daisy Fellowes—"the most elegant and most talked-about woman in Paris," in Ballard's words—had signed up to be *Bazaar*'s new editor in France. She was an amazing catch, as the magazine couldn't resist pointing out. "Her entry into the world of journalism created a sensation in Paris, for the clever lady is herself the very source of fashion. She is the woman in Paris society for whom the dressmakers love to create. . . . Everything she touches has style." Her job was, essentially, to be herself, with the most attendant publicity as possible. Fellowes would be the first in a line of influential Parisiennes who would serve "as a sort of honorary underpaid assistant who would pave the way for [Carmel's] visits," according to Ballard.

The magazine had scarcely had a presence in the City of Light before (in Carmel's eyes, Marjorie Howard didn't count). Suddenly, its credentials were impeccable. Fellowes's every move was studied, photogenic. No one could touch her for elegance. "I remember her appearing at the collections with Mrs. Snow, always with spotless white gloves and one long stemmed red rose in her hand," Ballard recalled.

"She simply blurred everyone out," Carmel added.

> *For many years she headed* haute couture*'s unpublished list of best-dressed women, and because of her wealth and her reputation for chic, she could coerce dressmakers and even manufacturers into carrying out her whims and could thus greatly influence the styles.*

One year, Fellowes ordered matching sequin jackets for all her evening gowns—an instant trend. At another point, she caused a scandal by turning up at the August collections wearing bare, tanned legs and a cotton piqué dress. The ensuing uproar—no stockings? Cotton in town?—was loud, but short lived. Soon, everyone who was anyone was bare legged and swathed in piqué. When Fellowes gave up leather gloves in favor of cotton ones, it was rapidly as though the former had never existed. They simply could no longer be found in the stores.

"A coverlet made of black ostrich feathers—a dress bearing fresh orchids on its train—nothing was too extreme for Daisy Fellowes," Carmel wrote. "She always wore her jewels in duplicate, exactly the same jewels on both hands and arms. . . ." And on and on. She was Schiap's mannequin mondaine—also known as "a mannequin du monde"—which meant that the designer supplied her clothes for free, or just about, knowing that having them worn by Fellowes was the best advertisement money could buy. It's no wonder that Fellowes's entry into journalism was a "sensation," according to Carmel. The September 1933 issue immortalized her, looking resplendent in a silvery Louiseboulanger dress with winglike tulle sleeves, in a flamingly bright de Meyer color portrait.

From a distance, all the hoopla seems almost comic, especially for an American magazine. Did they really care about Daisy Fellowes in Des Moines? In any case, they most certainly did at *Bazaar.* It wasn't just her American fortune that the magazine adored, but her European blue blood. She was a veritable Almanach de Gotha in her own right: born Marguerite Séverine Philippine Decazes de Glücksbierg, the daughter of a duke, niece of the American-born Princesse de Polignac, and the former wife of the Prince de Broglie. Her husband, the Honorable Reginald Fellowes, was the son of Lady Rosamund Churchill and the grandson of the seventh Duke of Marlborough.

Fellowes was a novice as a fashion writer; sometimes her candor—such as when she described struggling to get into an awkwardly structured Mainbocher dress—provoked pained reactions from the couturiers. Although she contributed articles from time to time, work definitely wasn't her thing. Wildly temperamental, she'd receive awed American buyers and others while "lying on a chaise longue under an awning on her upstairs terrace, generally wearing Chinese silk pyjamas of bright peacock blue" at her stunning showcase of a house in Neuilly-sur-Seine. She wasn't nice—few of those ultrachic Parisiennes, who lived to upstage one another, were—and she was beyond dramatic, at one point cabling her resignation to Hearst in California because someone in the office in New York had the temerity to change some of her fashion copy. (In this case, she was nudged gently back into the fold by Carmel, who made the sly point, "I enjoy doing battle but I'm perfectly willing to employ diplomacy first.")

Most of Carmel's battles at this point had to do with Samuels, who, along with Hearst's Richard Berlin, had tried to block her idea of including a feature on the Hay diet—a wildly complicated business of assessing starches and proteins—in the September issue. Diets had never been featured in a fashion magazine before, and neither man could see why they needed to be now. Carmel prevailed, but not before she and Samuels "almost came to blows." The story was an instant hit, so much so that *Bazaar* ran another piece about it the following month. Soon afterward Carmel was back at the ramparts, fighting Samuels over some Bérard fashion sketches, the first to run in *Bazaar,* which she felt he was trying to downplay in the September issue, a mistake, in her estimation, given the importance of both the artist and his subject—Fellowes again. This style setter was hardly underrepresented in the issue, which included a portrait of you know who in a Schiaparelli blue satin outfit, as well as a photo of her and another Frenchwoman of staggering style, Coco Chanel, dressed in the identical dark blue wool Chanel woolen suit.

When one of Hearst's megalomaniacal, oracular-sounding memos was delivered to Carmel's office, it became clear that, Samuels notwithstanding, the September issue had impressed the person who mattered most. "Chief says everything a woman would want to know [is] in this issue." It's no wonder that, before too long, poor Arthur Samuels put down the manuscripts he was forever reading, opened his eternally closed office door, and quietly went on his way. Carmel must have known that the magazine would soon be hers.

Every aspect of it, to her mind, still needed work. Fashion had long been an indoorsy business. Even fashion features on skiwear, bathing suits, and the like tended to be put together in a photographer's studio. Sure, some women had been photographed, here and there, walking chicly down the streets of New York or various European capitals wearing the season's fashions, but that was the extent of their movement. Gradually, in the pages of *Bazaar,* all of that changed. More action shots seemed to appear with every passing issue. Carmel had already begun using a French photographer named Jean Moral, who liked to shoot outdoors (although even his walking women seemed to have a static quality). In a story called "Weekend in Quebec," written by the statuesque Eleanor Barry, she and some of her glamorous friends modeled "two of Patou's divine new ski suits" and other skiwear while frolicking in the Canadian chill; in these unattributed photographs, one snow-covered girl laughs uproariously after being rescued after a fall.

In late 1933, a young Hungarian news photographer named Martin Munkacsi—a complete unknown in the States—began turning up in *Bazaar*'s pages; in one of his shots, a model leaps across a puddle in a Parisian street, her umbrella open. Carmel found Munkacsi through another Hungarian, artist Frederic Varady, known as Fritz, who'd drawn a department store ad she'd liked in one of New York's then-numerous daily newspapers. ("How lucky I was in my Hungarians!" Carmel would later write, referring to Vertès, too.) She'd already heard of Munkacsi; both Agha and Steichen had spoken of him admiringly. The photographer had known one displacement after another, moving from his native village in Hungary while still a teenager to work as a newspaper reporter in Budapest. Later, in his twenties, he was off to Berlin, where he became a photojournalist, traveling the world for the Ullstein Press.

When it turned out that Munkacsi, who lived in Germany, happened to be in New York on a two-day visit, fate seemed to be at work. "I remember my joy at thinking, this man is here!" From the time she first saw it, Carmel "immediately grasped the potential of the Hungarian's work," according to the photo historian William Ewing. In truth, she wasn't alone, Stieglitz and Agha had seen it, too, even showing his work to an unreceptive Condé Nast. The difference—all the difference—came from Carmel's persistence. If she wanted something, she never let up, and she wanted Munkacsi from the first.

It was October 1933 when Carmel first met Munkacsi, and the December issue, which had a Palm Beach theme, was already "closed," as they say at magazines, meaning that it was just about to be sent off to the printer. Every page of its content had been fixed; photos had been taken, drawings done, articles written. Even so, Carmel wasn't satisfied, particularly with one fashion spread that showed models posing in bathing suits before a painted backdrop. With Munkacsi in mind, she determined to reopen the issue—a misdemeanor, at least, in the magazine world—and have him reshoot the swimsuit pages. He had never taken a fashion photograph in his life, but Carmel was undeterred.

It was fall and brisk out, to put it mildly, and when it came to finding a beach, the Long Island Sound, near the East Norwich farmhouse, seemed logical enough. The Piping Rock Club, one of Palen's haunts, was a natural choice: it was nothing if not private. "The day was cold, unpleasant and dull—not at all auspicious for a 'glamorous resort' picture," Carmel wrote. "Munkacsi hadn't a word of English, and his friend seemed to take forever to interpret for us." The model, a socialite named Lucille Brokaw, another Carmel discovery, was "blue with cold," she recalled. The photographer began making wild gestures. "What does Munkacsi want us to *do*?" Carmel asked his friend. It soon became clear that Brokaw was to run toward the camera. Given the temperature, she was off like a shot. "Such a 'pose' had never been attempted before for fashion," as Carmel put it. The result was history.

And history of a particularly American kind. Brokaw was a home-grown beauty, "an American girl in *action,*" as Carmel described her, and the image of her tearing ahead seemed to sum up the spirit of a nation. Seen today, this famous shot is not a particularly beautiful one, nor is the model, really, and the clothes aren't even particularly clear. But it conveys movement and life and fashion. It all seems to fly by: Brokaw's hip-length beach cape, her stretchy swimsuit with a racing stripe down the side. She herself is the very picture of summer and youth. "It was as nearly alive as a still photograph could be," a *Vogue* editor later wrote.

When the December 1933 issue came out—"late, as usual, of course," in Carmel's words—no one had seen anything like it in a fashion magazine before. Lucille tore through the pages of *Bazaar,* racing through one after another, in one outfit after another, including a striking silver-white satin beach costume that could have been worn on the Stork Club's crowded dance floor. Munkacsi's shots looked blurry and unglamorous, as if they owed more to photojournalism than fashion, which they did, and they showed the feel of an outfit at the expense of its all-important details—heresy in the fashion world. They broke every rule in the book. Chase was among the loudest to take offense, dismissing it as "farm girls jumping over fences," a comment Carmel adored, pointing out that it "illustrates why *Vogue* remained static and 'ladylike' when *Harper's Bazaar* became lively and exciting." But many others were more positive. Even so, before too long, Carmel began to hear censorious rumblings emanating from the direction of her boss.

Hearst had all sorts of ideas of what was appropriate content for his publications. He had numerous pet peeves and a particular dislike for swearing. As he wrote, amusingly, to one of his editors in 1916:

> *If any writer writes any such swearword [sic] into any article or story, please eliminate the word. And if the word alone cannot be eliminated, eliminate the paragraph. And if the paragraph cannot be eliminated, eliminate the story. If the author objects, eliminate the author.*

There was nothing funny or lighthearted about another one of his strictures, his de facto ban on publishing photographs of African Americans. When one *Bazaar* editor wanted to publish a portrait of a black actor, "it was made known to her that, while nothing existed on paper that disallowed this, it would be difficult to do," according to Ann Thomas. "Anything that did not mirror middle White America was hard to get published." One editor, challenging this, wrote to Fifty-seventh Street at Carmel's suggestion and received a long letter back saying that the "Hearst Organization has no restrictions on anybody at all." Reassured, she ran in to tell her boss the news. "Mrs. Snow, they say it's fine," she said. "Are you stupid?" Carmel snorted. "Can't you read between the lines?"

Hearst had absolute control. "Nothing got into the Hearst papers without his approval," David Nasaw says. Publications that weren't making money were a constant target; ones that did well, or at least attracted the right attention, remained unscathed. His criticism could be withering, as a *Bazaar* editor in the 1920s experienced. Once, after looking over an issue of his *Harper's Bazaar*, he telegraphed its editor, Henry Sell, "I find the ads fascinating." But with Carmel, as with a select few editors he admired, he tended to be hands off. "He placed tremendous faith in individuals and gave them a good deal of latitude in many directions. . . . His normal procedure was not one of nagging or interfering in detail."

But when Hearst saw Munkacsi's grainy, unorthodox photos, it was clear to him that his new editor had gone too far. Before too long, Carmel was summoned to San Simeon "to discuss Munkacsi's work." As it happened, the photographer himself was planning to be in California on the next leg of his American journey, so she arranged for him to meet her there. Hearst, who had perhaps hoped never to see this photographer again in the pages of his magazine, discovered that he would soon be hosting him at San Simeon instead.

Few things scared Carmel, not even the Chief. But it was early in her tenure, so she may have had some trepidation as she made the three-day-long trip across the country by train to California to meet her volatile boss. Arriving at Los Angeles's Union Station in the evening, she probably took the eight-fifteen P.M. train, as most of Hearst's guests did, streaming northward up the coast to the central California town of San Luis Obispo, where they'd arrive in the middle of the night, before being shepherded into a car for the ninety-minute drive over dirt roads to San Simeon. They'd arrive, finally, by the coastal highway, glimpsing the towers of Hearst's castle—floodlit for special effect—from miles away. As they approached, they could hear the sometimes deafening sound effects—roaring lions, howling baboons—that emanated from his five-hundred-animal private zoo.

Completed a decade earlier, San Simeon was the very heart of Hearst's empire. Set on 275,000 acres of land, two thousand feet above the Pacific, it consisted of a vast, Mediterranean-style, four-story, 115-room castlelike structure called "Casa Grande," "containing treasures from all over the world and set amid a paradise of horticulture." It was surrounded by a villagelike configuration of guest cottages—each smaller than the main one but, even so, grandiose—joined together by colonnaded Italian gardens.

Architecturally, it was over the top, a pastiche "of decorative schemes and arrangements [Hearst] had seen in European castles and cathedrals, and which he wished to incorporate in his own palace." Its interior decor was equally eclectic: Hearst had filled it with treasures from all over the world, some of outlandish provenance, as one young visitor, Ilka Chase, who visited San Simeon when she was a young actress living in Hollywood, discovered, after being told that the cute bed she'd been sleeping in, the one with the cardinal's hat engraved in the headboard, had belonged to none other than the scheming, austere Cardinal Richelieu, France's prime minister under Louis XIII.

A disparate blend of houseguests rotated through San Simeon's thirty-eight bedrooms, from Winston Churchill to any number of movie stars to the gossip columnist Hedda Hopper. Studio heads, Irving Thalberg and the like, would find themselves sharing weekend time with less auspicious characters, radio executives from Hearst's vast network, perhaps, or starlets by the carload. Among the latter was Marion Davies, who, "sometime in the spring of 1926 . . . replaced Millicent as Hearst's de facto West Coast wife and hostess at San Simeon."

On this first visit, Carmel recalled being "met by . . . herds of wild animals running across the road." She was also, happily enough, greeted by a human specimen: a butler who had stayed up late for her arrival and who showed her to her room. "When I finally reached my bed, which had belonged to Madame de Pompadour, I fell into a grateful sleep that was broken early the same morning by the roaring and howling of Mr. Hearst's private zoo." One can scarcely imagine what Munkacsi, who had been born into a "large and impoverished family," according to William Ewing (and who was, incidentally, sleeping in a bed that had belonged to that saintly eighteenth-century beauty, Madame Récamier), must have made of it all.

The next morning, desperate for coffee, Carmel asked for a breakfast tray, but was told that meals were served only in the castle's Great Hall. (Hearst didn't approve of breakfast in bed.) She wandered down to the vast dining hall, and I do mean down. The stairs seemed endless: "It was like following a mountain stream toward civilization," says John Michael White, repeating an oft-told family legend. (Carmel's brother Tom, a frequent visitor to San Simeon, used to say that it was the only place where he'd fallen downstairs while getting out of bed.) The enormous, flag-lined dining room was impressive, with its enormous Gothic fireplace, one of several on the property, and a massive refectory table at which eighty people could comfortably sit—and did so, night after night, as the restless Hearst entertained. "I was about to try again for a cup of coffee when a little figure popped up from behind the huge sofa in front of the baronial fireplace," Carmel recalled. "It was Charlie Chaplin, who had come down for the same purpose but hadn't had the nerve to brave the kitchen. I got us our coffee."

With its ubiquitous movie stars and astonishing luxury, San Simeon often cast an unnerving spell on Hearst executives summoned there to meet the boss. Which was all part of the plan. He would call meetings there for precisely that reason, one of his early biographers pointed out. And then, more potent still, he'd have them wait.

> *These were high-salaried men of prestige and authority in their own spheres, but when they reached the castle their importance was pricked like a balloon. Although Hearst might see immediately someone on urgent business, it was his habit to make others wait from a few days to a week, or more. Already intimidated by the grandeur of their surroundings when they arrived, they would feel the remnants of their self-assurance ooze away as hours and days passed and they conjured up reasons why he might be displeased. They could swim or ride or meet glamorous film people, but they could not get drunk [one of San Simeon's numerous house rules], and their enjoyment of all this was marred by the audience with the unpredictable tycoon that lay before them.*

When they finally found themselves cloistered with the man they'd come to see, they might be finished off by another weapon in Hearst's arsenal, his notoriously icy and unrelenting stare. "His secretary, [Joseph] Willicombe, privately advised editors that the best thing to do was to stare right back at him," according to a Hearst biographer, W. A. Swanberg. When Carmel went to see him in San Simeon for the first time, Hearst was seventy and as formidable as ever. But there's no evidence that she was intimidated. In fact, you could argue that it was Hearst himself who had the disadvantage in their dealings. What wouldn't one give to be a fly on the wall in his Gothic study, dense with rare books and manu-

Guests at Heart's San Simeon during Snow and Munkacsi's visit. In the front row: Carmel Snow (*left*), Marion Davies (*second from right*), Charlie Chaplin (*right*)

scripts, when the short, balding Hungarian, still so close to poverty, and the tiny, steel-willed Irishwoman were ushered into an audience with the fearsome publisher? The great man was uneasy—he'd decided that Munkacsi was "just a snapshot photographer"—and he was quite sure he didn't want him in the pages of one of his publications. Carmel had been called across the country to defend herself, essentially, yet she cannily treated the visit as a social call, introducing a man who barely spoke English to one of the richest men in creation as if his acceptance into the latter's empire was a foregone conclusion.

Carmel had been warned by her brother Tom not to push for a contract for Munkacsi, given the dim view Hearst took of the photographer. But she wasn't to be deterred. She smoothed the way at San Simeon, within earshot of braying zebras, shrieking exotic birds, and the like, then shrewdly waited until she was back in New York before pressing Hearst to sign him on. What happened next was inevitable, so much so that it seems like a waste of ink to write it down. How else could things have turned out? Hearst's better judgment was neatly overruled and "a contract was drawn up with Munkacsi's name on it," Carmel wrote.

To everyone's surprise, though, Munkacsi declined to sign it, saying that "he had no desire to leave Germany," according to his daughter, Joan Munkacsi. Instead, he returned to Berlin, resuming his contract with Ullstein. But the winter of 1933–34 wasn't the best time to make such a decision as Munkacsi, who was Jewish, soon discovered. Gradually, Jews were beginning to be fired at Ullstein and, indeed, everywhere else. "My father saw it happen but, as with everyone, he couldn't believe it would become what it became," his daughter says. For a while he seemed immune—his name didn't sound particularly Jewish, and the Nazis needed photographers. He began working for the *Berlin Illustrated News.* His moment of awakening came in the spring of 1934 when he was castigated for photographing a banana in a still life on the grounds that "bananas are not an Aryan fruit." He was soon on the boat with his family. "He came to the U.S., walked into *Bazaar,* and said 'I'll take that contract,'" Joan Munkacsi says. He was one of the few photographers to have one, according to Gwen Randolph Franklin, who came to work at the magazine at about this time.

Hearst, presumably, never knew what hit him. Carmel routinely stood up to him, sometimes unwittingly, as she'd done at about the time of her California trip when, unaware that Hearst had banned any mention of Norma Shearer in his pages, she featured the popular actress in a photo spread in *Bazaar.* Shearer, the wife of MGM's Irving Thalberg, Marion Davies's longtime mentor, had been given the famous "Hearst silent treatment" because she'd beaten out Davies, who just about no one accused of knowing how to act, for a part in the *Barretts of Wimpole Street,* then compounded her crime "by making it a smashing success." Thalberg should have known better; soon after, Davies left MGM for Warner Brothers. As for Carmel, she was informed too late of her error by perturbed associates, but the Chief himself never complained.

"One thing Mr. Hearst liked about me," Carmel later wrote, "was the fact that I seemed to be the only living being except Marion (of whom I got to be very fond) who wasn't afraid of him." It was an enviable position to be in, and it would serve her well in her struggles with "Fifty-seventh Street" for years to come. "We fought editorial battles over hair dye, over bikinis," Carmel recalled. "I forget all our battles." It must have come as a surprise to no one when, later in 1934, she was promoted to the job of editor in chief.

Within months of Munkacsi's signing on, models in *Bazaar* were racing up sand dunes and executing perfect, impossible dives, seeming to fly horizontally across the page. One Munkacsi female, dashing naked around a swimming pool, was the first nude to be shown in a fashion magazine. By the time the August 1934 "college issue" was published, it was hard to imagine that any young American female ever stood still. "The most outstanding and best-dressed type of college girl" was shown in all her glory, dashing, running, walking, and, of course, modeling new fashions, including a "heavenly shade of green velveteen cut à la Chanel." This was the first issue with a collegiate theme to run in a women's magazine; Carmel began the trend, which continues to this day, after a survey by *Bazaar*'s advertising department showed an enthusiastic response. (Some of the campus trends the magazine reported were downright bizarre. At Vassar, the reader is told, the chicest coeds "wear bright shawls over their heads like Czechoslovakian immigrants while going from class to class when the Poughkeepsie winds blow free. . . .")

Fashion photography was a new art at this point; there weren't many who practiced it, and even fewer after Carmel canceled de Meyer's contract in 1934. (Six years later, in an unexpected tribute to de Meyer in *Bazaar,*

The photographer Martin Munkacsi and Carmel Snow on the boardwalk at Atlantic City

he was described, in the time-honored, weaselly manner, as having "retired" at that time.) Since fashion photographers were in great demand, with little competition in sight, everything conspired to indulge them. Many had outsize temperaments, none more so than George Hoyningen-Huene, who stormed out of sittings with alarming frequency. He'd been based for years in Paris—where he was known for going to bed early and avoiding meat, both things that seem incomprehensible, if not downright mad, to the French—and was now, increasingly, working in New York. Like his photographs, the lanky, balding aristocratic Hoyningen-Huene was almost impossibly elegant; his behavior, however, was not, and his volatile personality was a constant worry for the Condé Nast staff. So much so that, when the time came to renegotiate his contract, in the summer of 1934, Dr. Agha traveled to Paris himself to suggest, among other things, over lunch that the photographer might try to tame his behavior on the job. By numerous accounts, Hoyningen-Huene reacted instantly, knocking over the table between them and announcing, as he stormed from the dining room, that he was on his way to call Mrs. Snow, in town for the collections, to see about going to work for *Bazaar.* "I'm on the street, and you can have me!" he allegedly said to Carmel. In her telling, Agha was still wiping sauce béarnaise off of his lap when Huene returned triumphant, saying that he'd been hired on the spot.

Given the state of French phones even well into the 1970s, such a tale sounds too efficient to be true; there's plenty of other evidence, too, that it took the photographer a while to make the leap. But he did stop photographing the collections midstream, a huge potential catastrophe for *Vogue* that was averted after a young unknown named Horst P. Horst, a former architecture student who'd turned up in Paris in the late 1920s to work for Le Corbusier, then begun taking photographs at the suggestion of Dr. Agha, stepped in to finish the job. "I was just a little German boy, no titles, no nothing," Horst recounted years later. Not for long.

Perhaps Hoyningen-Huene did overturn the table, perhaps he did race to call Carmel. But his

OPPOSITE: **Carmel Snow *(left)* supervising a Hoyningen-Huene fashion shoot for *Bazaar* in Paris, August 1937 (Huene is at right)**

decision to leave *Vogue* took a few agonizing days to unfold. Nast sent various emissaries to appease him, including Edna Chase, and Huene vented to each and every one. "Agha was the wrong person to deal with me. If I leave it's Agha's fault," he told one New York–based *Vogue* editor, in town for the collections. "Agha said Condé wanted to chastise me, that I was a naughty boy! No one has ever chastised me, and I don't intend to let them start now." He did finally make the move to *Bazaar,* soon working, at his preference, from New York instead of France. And, by all accounts, he never got easier. He was a tyrant at sittings. "I always insisted on complete silence, no noise, no music, no muttering behind my back." One model who, years later, would fall apart under this regimen was a future star named Lauren Bacall. "He posed me like a statue.... Whenever he said, 'Hold still,' I started to shake. I was a disaster. He was not pleased. *I* was not pleased. Not pleased? I was suffering. I hated him."

Vogue retaliated, of course. Chase snatched up Bérard, luring him away from *Bazaar* in 1935 with the help of his great friend Solange d'Ayen. With her whispering in his ear, and with, presumably, the cash he was perpetually short of on the table, how could he have refused? But it was a sad move for everyone, the artist most of all. Unlike Carmel, who adored Bérard's work, Chase never really did; in fact, she loathed it, and only ever published it halfheartedly. She would never have fought for better placement of his work in the magazine, as Carmel had done. And her reasons for going after him were suspect: "She kept him on only because she knew I wanted him," Carmel seethed. And she was right.

7 *assembling the team*

Surprise, change, shock!
—Alexey Brodovitch

We were like family there, and we became Snow's children.
—Louise Dahl-Wolfe

ABOUT SIX MONTHS AFTER she returned from San Simeon, Carmel was off to another outsize Hearst residence—a real castle, this time—on a similar quest. It all started in April 1934, at the Thirteenth National Exhibition of Advertising Art, held at the Art Directors Club in the RCA Building, in New York's Rockefeller Center, where Carmel had been sent by a photographer named Ralph Steiner, who sometimes shot shoes and accessories for *Bazaar.* Knowing that Carmel was perpetually on the lookout for fresh talent, Steiner suggested that she see the work of a friend of his, a graphic designer named Alexey Brodovitch, who had put together the show.

> *The day before the exhibition was to open, I went over to a big hall still in utter confusion, step ladders and paint cans standing about, and I saw a fresh, new conception of layout technique that struck me like a revelation: pages that "bled," beautifully cropped photographs, typography and design that were bold and arresting.*

Carmel had been on the lookout for an art director from soon after she'd first crossed the threshold of *Harper's Bazaar;* Ruzzie Green had always been, to her mind, a temporary solution. She wanted a bold modernist, one who, like Dr. Agha, could bring the most far-reaching design to the typically more conservative American audience. Finding Brodovitch among the chaos, where he was overseeing the exhibit's installation, she acted with characteristic decisiveness and speed. "Within ten minutes I had asked Brodovitch to have cocktails with me, and that evening I signed him to a provisional contract as art director."

Carmel may have met him in the most American possible setting, on the thirty-fourth floor of a building in Rockefeller Center, the art deco–ish cluster of buildings in downtown Manhattan built by John D. Rockefeller in the 1930s, but this dapper, exceptionally polite man was as Russian as they come. "He was very self-contained," says Mary Fullerton Faulconer, who was once one of his students. In part, this had to do with language. Like many upper-class Russians, he'd been raised speaking French; his English was another story. "It was very poor," according to Faulconer. "He had no small talk. He couldn't go to parties because he couldn't talk."

Like Agha, also born in Russia, Brodovitch had arrived in the United States after years in Europe. He'd fought for the czar in World War I, then later against the Bolsheviks; after his family fled to France, in about 1920, he became part of the legion of well-educated White Russians who took whatever job they had to in order to survive. Like Hoyningen-Huene, another escapee from the Bolsheviks, he "joined the thousands and thousands of Russian refugees who really were not brought up to do any manual labor or had any particular profession." Many, famously, drove cabs. Newly married to Nina, a nurse Brodovitch had met in 1918 after being wounded in the White Army, he began his Paris life as a house painter. Within only five years, he'd made his name as a graphic designer, imposing his clean-lined, provocative vision on books, catalogues, posters.

Recruited to establish a department of advertising at the Philadelphia Museum of Art's School of Industrial Art (PMSIA), Brodovitch arrived in the United States in 1930 to discover that most of his students were oblivious to the disparate avant-garde movements—constructivism, futurism, fauvism, and more—that, reverberating about Paris, had made it such an exciting place for an artist to be. The Bauhaus, in this group, was a nonstarter. Instead, his Pennsylvania students were busy creating "beautiful, technically flawless pictures . . . from a nineteenth-century tradition of romantic realism," according to Virginia Smith.

In his classes at PMSIA, and particularly his famous Design Laboratory seminar, which he instituted for his advanced students in 1933, he set about shaking things up. He appropriated Diaghilev's famous imperative, *"Etonnez-moi!,"* urging his students, repeatedly, to surprise him. "He'd seduce you and your brain into doing anything he wanted you to do," as Mary Faulconer put it. "He was an incredible teacher. It was like Russian hypnotism."

Carmel knew instantly that Brodovitch was the man for the job, she also knew that the Chief would need some persuading. She asked Brodovitch to create a dummy of a visually reconceived *Harper's Bazaar,* giving him two weeks to get it done. Back in Philadelphia, he rounded up some of his ablest students, Mary Faulconer among them, and set to work with them on a sample issue. They pored over recent *Bazaar*s, with Brodovitch complaining bitterly about Erté, a familiar figure from his Paris days, who seemed to be on every cover and whose allegiance to art deco seemed almost aggressively old guard. As they looked through the pages, he kept saying, "Dis Erté must go!" Faulconer recalls.

They made two dummies, each consisting of double spreads of fashion shots, accessories, and more. (Neither one survives.) "For Brodovitch . . ." Kerry William Purcell writes,

> *the repetitive presentation of skirt lengths and different colored gloves had to be reinvigorated. Each design had to be fresh. Searching for "shock value" on every page, Brodovitch constantly referred to those artists who influenced his formative years in Paris. He would encourage his students to "appropriate" a particular style, with statements such as "Do it in the manner of Cocteau, but do not imitate Cocteau."*

They aimed for a mix, Faulconer says. "We'd illustrate fiction, then he'd say 'We're going to do a perfume double spread.' Then he'd say we were going to do shoes and I'd do that and I did all this kind of feminine stuff. He wanted to give them lots of choices." The result, she says, was "very attractive, very modern. It looked great."

Carmel thought so, too, and rushed to show the results to her boss. "When I heard that Dick Berlin was going over to see Mr. Hearst at the castle in Wales he had recently bought . . . I announced that I was going along." All of Fifty-seventh Street, it seemed, tried to discourage her: "Sometimes you have to wait for weeks before the Chief will even talk to you," Berlin and others warned. Undeterred, she set out for England and from there to St. Donat's in Wales, once described by the *New York Times* as "the most perfect Norman building in Great Britain."

Set on thirteen hundred acres in Glamorganshire, just west of Cardiff, this 135-room castle was just the sort of folly Hearst seemed to adore—huge, unruly, grandiose. The old man, who had been hankering for a castle, had succumbed to its charms after seeing photographs of it in the horsey British periodical *Country Life*. He bought it for the equivalent of $120,000, then tossed in a million dollars more in the form of furnishings and improvements. Thanks to an earlier renovation, it already "had electric lights, bathrooms and all modern conveniences," the *Times* reported. It also featured a portcullis, banqueting hall, even a tilting yard—useful, presumably, for guests who might feel the urge to joust.

Hearst was a shopaholic on a gargantuan scale; inevitably, he dispatched scouts all over Britain in a mission to fill the place with perfect antiques. He may have hoped to make of St. Donat's a kind of Celtic San Simeon, or perhaps a companion piece to Wyntoon, his Bavarian extravaganza in northern California, but it didn't really work. It was too far from California, where he spent most of his time, and his visits to it were rare. And besides, not everyone approved of his tenancy. A scandal had erupted in Britain after Hearst bought and dismantled a medieval tithe barn in 1929, intending to resurrect it at St. Donat's. And, more ethereally, a *New York Times* article the year before reported that local villagers had seen "a wraith in flowing robes" wandering the grounds. Apparently, a sixteenth-century inhabitant, one Lady Stradling, having vowed that "she would return to earth and haunt the castle if it should ever change hands," had come back to do exactly that.

Alas, the only specimens Carmel encountered during her visit were all-too-human ones. Hearst executives seemed to be there by the dozen, which, as it happened, only helped her cause. "I think I was lucky on that visit because he was bored with the second-helpings of wives that some of his associates had brought with them." She snagged Hearst after dinner on the first night of her stay.

> *"I came here to show you a dummy for the kind of magazine I'd like* Harper's Bazaar *to be," I said.*
>
> *"But I think* Harper's Bazaar *looks very well," he said in that high, squeaky voice of his.*
>
> *"Unfortunately,* Vogue *looks better," said I.*
>
> *"Well, why don't you get the dummy and show it to me."*
>
> *When he looked at it he said, "Well, if you want this man, go ahead and get him."*

Mission accomplished. By eight the next morning, Carmel was on her way to the collections in Paris.

When Carmel was in the French capital she became someone else, slipping into a private orbit that was charmingly, idiosyncratically her own. And it wasn't all work. She'd attend mass at least once a day in one of a constellation of favorite churches, from the musty, intimate Sainte-Clothilde to the neo-Grecian grandeur of the Madeleine. She'd make time for card readings with her favorite fortune-tellers (she considered those practicing in France to be more skilled than their extra-lucid colleagues in New York). In Paris in this period, she gravitated toward a certain Rive Droite hauteur, the reassuring feeling of solidity that unerring quality, going back over time, can impart. She loved the city, she said, because "it's a place that worships quality, as I do: *The best* of everything." She was drawn to timeworn places where the historical figures she admired might have sat centuries before. She adored, for example, the venerable old Le Grand Véfour restaurant, a place of deep crimson velvet banquets, elaborate chandeliers, and unbelievably polished brass, where, through heavily curtained windows, one can peer into the gardens of the Palais Royal, where Louis XIV used to play as a child. With its pâtés and fruits de mer, the Véfour's menu is the very heart and soul of the French haute bourgeoisie—but none of that mattered to Carmel, who was indifferent to food. Drinks counted, though. She favored bourbon in this period, which she pronounced, with sly irony, like the French dynasty. Even at the finest restaurants in Paris, and therefore the world, she ate sparingly, while drinking to happy excess.

Although Carmel was in Paris well into August, she was heard back in the United States in the middle of that month, giving a radio address about upcoming fall and winter styles. Although the broadcast had been advertised in *Bazaar*'s pages as being direct from France, it really wasn't—such a thing wasn't possible yet; instead, it featured prerecorded interviews with Paris designers, outlining coming trends. On the recordings, their accents made their English seem incomprehensible. When someone at the radio station had the bright idea of hiring actors to read what they'd said, a full-blown fiasco was born. Everyone sounded fake. For weeks after returning from Europe, Carmel was teased by buyers and wholesalers wherever she went: "Yep, that's good old Schiap. Know her voice anywhere."

Brodovitch, who'd agreed to join *Bazaar,* was in the French capital that summer, too, on a long talent-hunting detour—a trajectory he would undertake annually through the 1930s—before beginning work at the office that fall. His Paris connections served him well. The first artist he bagged was the American surrealist painter Man Ray, né Emanuel Radnitsky. Ray wasn't an unknown in America, or, for that matter, to Carmel: he'd begun his photographic career with the designer Paul Poiret back in the early 1920s, and had appeared in *Vogue* as early as 1925, contributing fashion shots—in one case a magnificent art deco–influenced Chéruit dress—and other photos, including ones of a Paris logia, designed by Jean-Michel Frank and belonging to the Vicomte de Noailles. But to rope him into working exclusively for *Bazaar* was a coup.

Ray photographed the Paris shows for the magazine for several seasons, almost always with a difference—sometimes showing the same dress from several different angles, for example. He was a tireless innovator. He came up with his famous "Rayograph" technique after he discovered that objects—a small funnel, a thermometer—placed directly on photographic paper in the darkroom, left distorted impressions of themselves on the page. At the time he began working for the magazine, he was living with the American model/photographer/writer Lee Miller, another early *Vogue* contributor who now sometimes photographed for *Bazaar*. Ray was deeply in love with Miller, a free spirit who slept with whomever she pleased, whenever she felt like doing so, and it wasn't a happy thing. "I looked like an angel, but I was a fiend inside," she once confessed.

Miller's best work would come later, as a photojournalist; still, she shot some interesting things during her time with Ray, including a portrait of a far-eyed beauty rendered unforgettably mysterious by the fact that it had been solarized, a process she happened on in 1929, after she accidentally opened the darkroom door while developing Ray's portrait of Suzy Solidor. In a flash, literally, the lines of the print that should have been dark became light, so that the print resembled a negative; best of all, there was a kind of nimbus around Solidor's nude figure, a line of light that had a mystical quality—particularly pleasing for a surrealist. Ray dubbed the process "solarization" and ran with it, refining it through tireless experimentation. For a time Miller kept up with it, too: her solarized portrait of an "Elizabeth Arden beauty" ran in the March 1934 issue.

Ray figured prominently in Brodovitch's first issue, in September 1934, contributing "fashions by radio," as the magazine called them, Rayographs of Paris styles. It was a mad idea, really: Ray cut out the shape of a dress or other item of clothing on a piece of cardboard, covered it with the garment's actual fabric, then beamed the whole thing by radio wave to the magazine. The advantage was speed, of course—an actual Paris fashion, even if it wasn't quite recognizable as one, could reach America on the very day it was shown. Art was a by-product: these "clothes," had a hallucinatory look on the page that must have been a revelation to many readers.

Ray's work was that of an unrepentant sensualist, as one striking photo, of models posing naked beneath translucent nightgowns, seen in profile and lit for maximum exposure, attests. Another famous shot, of a reclining woman in a patterned silk beach coat by Heim—white, with little brown foxes printed on it and far too elegant to be mixed with sand and surf—takes one of his more famous paintings, *Observatory Time—The Lovers,* which features a giant pair of lips floating across a landscape, as its backdrop. As the model reaches toward them, the lips seem to float away. It was no longer as with de Meyer, or even Steichen, enough just to show a woman directly posing for the camera. Now, models seemed to be doing something else, even if what they were up to couldn't be captured in words. Ray broke "the stranglehold of reality on fashion photography," as the photographer Richard Avedon later remarked.

Another artist Brodovitch went to see that summer was the painter Salvador Dalí, whom he encountered at Dalí's Paris home in an atmosphere that was suitably surreal. "A butler ushered him up a stairway lined with surrealist paintings and objets trouvés into an enormous room containing only a table on which sat Dalí wearing a fantastic robe," Carmel later recounted. Brodovitch's request that the artist contribute to *Bazaar* was firmly rejected. Dalí "was very supercilious about doing any work for a fashion magazine"; so much so that the art director left empty handed. On his next visit, though, Brodovitch took Carmel along, at which point "my reputed 'charm' (and cash, doubtless, which I must again have wrung from Dick Berlin) accomplished our purpose." Soon, Dalí was in *Bazaar,* introduced as someone "who paints the way Gertrude Stein writes."

His first fashion feature, entitled "Imaginative Suggestions for This Summer in Florida," included drawings of evening gowns that were literally unreal—one was made of coral, the other of roses. The store credits were original, to say the least: "Not any of these are at Bergdorf Goodman, Marshall Field, or Bullock's Wilshire, California." Later, Dalí would also contribute an article he'd written on surrealism in Hollywood, along with a surprisingly figurative drawing of Harpo Marx. But it wasn't all surrealism. One of the Paris artists whom Brodovitch persuaded to contribute to the magazine at this time was the fauvist Raoul Dufy, who weighed in with a winsome painting of American buyers at a fashion show—not, to put it mildly, this artist's usual turf—that captured "the heat, the smoke, the tension, and the hour: 5 to 8 P.M."

From the outset, Carmel and Brodovitch had an exceptional rapport. They shared a strong visual aesthetic, particularly appreciating great photography, and total commitment to their jobs. Both worked intuitively. One of the art director's assistants recalled watching him shuffle "dozens of photostats of various sizes until he 'saw' the right one for the page." Carmel, too, knew it when it came along. She never failed to heed Nast's advice about the importance of the editor retaining the last word; trusting her judgment, Brodovitch never seemed to resent it. "Mrs. Snow respected Brodovitch enormously. Everyone did," says Geri Trotta, who was then just out of Barnard and working at the magazine for $18 a week. One Brodovitch watcher, Mary Faulconer, whom he'd tapped to work at *Bazaar* as an assistant art director, was astonished to see that her taciturn former teacher was entirely in Carmel's thrall. "He worshipped her. I'd never see him admire someone like that. He admired her more than anything. He'd really do his best work for her. Mrs. Snow, he adored." As assistant art director, she had to seek Carmel's approval for every layout. "She was very stimulating just to be around. You'd know that her eye was going to have the right judgment."

Melancholy-eyed, yet with a naïve, almost slapstick sense of humor—Russian wit, Faulconer says—Brodovitch put everything into his meticulous, quietly precise work. "His life was right in that magazine." He was a constant presence at *Bazaar,* inscrutable, short-tempered, spare with words, and yet, somehow, adored. Clearly, he was in New

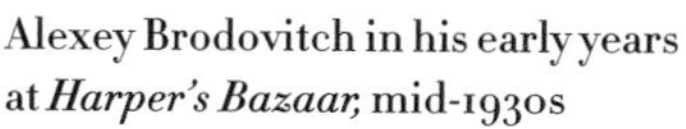
Alexey Brodovitch in his early years at *Harper's Bazaar,* mid-1930s

York to stay. He signed a lease on an apartment at 239 East Seventy-second Street, a broad, expansive street on New York's Upper East Side, that October, moving in with his family. His personal life was sad, even tragic, and it never became less so. His wife was fierce, by all accounts, and their relationship seemed loveless. She was even rumored to be mentally ill. And yet there seemed to be no question that they'd separate. In that era, and from their culture, this would have been too drastic a remedy; and besides, they were held together by their son, Nikita, known as Nicky, who had severe physical and emotional problems. He was most likely hydrocephalic, the photography critic Andy Grundberg has theorized; in any case, he was "slow" and incapable of living on his own. His recurring misadventures—nothing, it seemed, could ever go well for him—were a constant trial for his parents.

The marriage that did work for Brodovitch was his working relationship with Carmel. "They were a couple of such subtlety," says the photographer Henri Cartier-Bresson. Their mutual respect was infectious: "They were going to take over the world," in the words of Mary Faulconer. Grundberg puts a Freudian spin on all this, saying that Brodovitch turned to his coworkers "to compensate for the conflicts in his family life," but you could look at it otherwise, that his work at *Bazaar* was his real life and that those he shared it with were another kind of family, one with which he could share his life's passion, with levity and blessedly little pain. He was close to some of the magazine's contributors, too, notably Reynaldo Luza, a talented South American illustrator who "was the son Brodovitch never had."

Brodovitch also turned to alcohol as, increasingly, did Carmel herself. It was something else they shared, and, as the years went on, it became clear that if you wanted to get any business done at *Bazaar*—as at many other offices in this post-Prohibition era—you should make a point of doing so before lunch. Complicating matters was the rumor that Carmel had Ménière's syndrome, a disorder of the inner ear that can cause vertigo and problems with balance, which, even when she hadn't been drinking, meant that she was wobbly on her feet. "Sometimes she appeared drunk," as Avedon put it. "But sometimes she *was* drunk." Of course, the liquid lunch was endemic in New York publishing at the time, as it was in other professions. "It was the same way at *Mademoiselle,*" said Faulconer, who worked at both magazines. "All the editors would discuss big ideas in the morning, yak yak yak, then they'd go out to lunch and have three or four dry martinis and after lunch they'd have completely changed. . . ."

Like any artist, Brodovitch created his world on a daily basis. It was a place of serenity that was all his own. Diana Vreeland would later say of Brodovitch:

> *He loved white paper, the more the better, and it was very hard indeed for him to allow even the most beautiful blow-up of a Cartier-Bresson photo to spoil the immaculate clarity and whiteness. . . . [O]ne felt that when he was alone with his white paper, he was resting in the snows of his native Russia, and finding a purity and cleanliness he could not find elsewhere.*

The hyperbole is classic Vreeland; still, there's truth at its core. (Even so, it's hard to imagine Brodovitch, who so admired great photography, resisting adding it to a blank page.) The minute Brodovitch arrived, the look of the book changed. There seemed to be a clear theme running through each issue, as well as immense variety: there might be old-fashioned watercolors on one page, black-and-white photographs, perhaps with bright stars or ribbons dropped into the margin, on the next. Even the Old Guard looked freshened up, as in one Hoyningen-Huene photo depicting two women floating along in a canoe, one with her hand trailing in the water, wearing diaphanous organdy dresses—in one case by Hattie Carnegie, in the other by Vionnet. It was a far cry from the sophisticated drawing rooms that were this photographer's usual turf.

Artists and designers mingled on the page—and in life: Salvador Dalí is shown painting his *L'Instant Sublime* at Coco Chanel's house on the Riviera in one issue. Another features a Louise Dahl-Wolfe photograph of a pensive-looking model in a Schiaparelli tunic dress standing next to Brancusi's *Miracle* at New York's brand-new Museum of Modern Art. There were illustrations by Ludwig

Bemelmans, who would later invent a little girl named Madeline, and, for the first time, an appearance by Babar the elephant, in a spread by his creator, Jean de Brunhoff, brother of the editor Michel de Brunhoff, who had replaced Bocher at Paris *Vogue*. Punctuating it all, with clocklike regularity, were formal portraits of Miss Marion Davies, the silent-screen actress whom Hearst adored but would never marry for political reasons and in deference to his wife, who lived apart from him on the East Coast, never quite reconciled to her husband's more-or-less permanent absence. It was the audacity of the mix—elephants, actresses, clothes—that set *Bazaar* apart. "She absolutely turned it inside out with this new energy," says Geri Trotta. As the art and cultural historian Calvin Tomkins has written, "It was the magazine editor as auteur."

Much has been discussed about whether Agha influenced Brodovitch or vice versa. As Purcell has pointed out, "The truth is probably more a case of shared influences—with neither Agha nor Brodovitch being the first to utilize the techniques in question." Both adhered to Bauhaus constructivist principles and, in their European years, would have been well aware of the striking graphic developments taking place in Continental magazines. But Brodovitch was the more dynamic designer. His layouts made news as when, in the November 1935 issue, he illustrated a story on New York nightlife first with a shot of dancer Eleanor Powell, her legs kicking, looking as if she's about to twirl right out of the magazine. In a series of sequential photographs, the Spanish dancers Ramon and Renita dance up one page, then fly down the next, culminating in one large photo, daringly set at a forty-five-degree angle. It's not just the images—Munkacsi at his most dynamic—but the layout itself that makes this spread come alive

Other personnel included Paul MacNamara (who would later make his name as director of publicity for the producer David O. Selznick), a whiz of an advertising man for whom "no promotion scheme for increasing advertising or circulation was too fantastic. . . ." Carmel poached him from *Vogue,* where he'd been advertising manager and "learned the highly successful Nast method of advertising and promotion straight from the horse's mouth," according to Caroline Seebohm. His publicity stunts on behalf of *Bazaar* could be harebrained, including one unrealized scheme involving a cover that could be played as a record, one that would include both a commentary by Carmel on the Paris collections *and* a Lucky Strike commercial. Another MacNamara publicity extravaganza involved distributing cages of carrier pigeons to advertisers, retailers, and manufacturers all over New York, including one that Schiaparelli, who was setting sail for Europe, released in New York Harbor. One bird, sent by a local jeweler, was carrying a diamond, possibly a fake, that was never found.

Then there was a beauty editor named Carola Kip, a glorious beauty herself, who after watching how Carmel ran the magazine—on pure instinct, adrenaline, and the edge of chaos—once had the temerity to suggest that there was room for improvement. "My haphazard methods of editing must have outraged her, because she began drawing up elaborate blueprints on how the magazine should be run." Oh, dear. As Kip stood at her desk, outlining these innovative procedures to her boss, Carmel, devastatingly, didn't bother lifting her head from the task at hand—choosing layouts for the next issue—not even pretending to take the young staffer seriously. "I frankly hadn't the least intention of changing my methods. How could I? I learned not to exhaust myself on things that wouldn't work and turned my attention to something else." Presumably, Kip got the message. On the plus side, Kip, too, turned out to have a gift for promotion; Carmel watched in wonder as some of her unheard-of schemes bore fruit. When she suggested that *Bazaar* offer its readers perfume samples if they sent a dollar in to the magazine, publisher Fred Drake reacted with skepticism. "But when ten *thousand* dollar bills had to be bailed for transport to the bank, he was transported with joy."

The staff also included a seemingly endless series of fashion editors, not career women, exactly, but "lively young women who had too much vitality to expend it all on social life." These young editors were expected to work, if not to earn (that famous "prestige and . . ."), and their jobs seemed to become ever more challenging. Once "Munky," as they called Munkacsi, joined the team, they began going out with him on location, a place where all manner of crises were just waiting to occur. Technological changes were also behind this stampede to the outdoors, as Seebohm has pointed out.

> *Largely owing to the development of new, light, flexible cameras such as the Leica, the Rolleiflex, and the Hasselblad, and the introduction of increasingly high-speed film, photography had discovered a new identity, light-years away from . . . formal studio portraits. . . .*

Location shots became the norm, with all their attendant pressures. "We rocketed from success to disaster, skirted lawsuits by the skin of our teeth, and always came out laughing." One *Bazaar* editor, Wilhela Cushman, who soon moved on to *Ladies' Home Journal,* scored points by conjuring up an elephant for a Munkacsi shoot (from Barnum & Bailey circus), long before this kind of thing had ever been done before, then securing permission to photograph it in the New York Botanical Gardens. Carmel "encouraged competition among my fashion editors," she wrote. Her "girls" craved her approval, and she was deft at withholding it, as necessary, to make them work harder. "You'd do anything to please her," one editor recalled. Carmel was unapologetic about the way she drove her staff. "She would use people and throw them out," Babs Simpson adds. "She was known to have said to somebody or other about a beauty editor, 'Oh, we'll squeeze her like a lemon and throw her away.'"

Carmel loved having girls of a certain pedigree—"tall, cool Vassar graduates," as the humorist S. J. Perelman once described them—on her staff. Eleanor Barry was one of this genre; another was Louise Gill Macy, formerly of Hattie Carnegie, who joined the staff in 1934 after Carmel sent a cable to her while she was on vacation that read: WON'T TAKE NO FOR AN ANSWER. REPORT HARPER'S BAZAAR WHEN YOU RETURN. Snob appeal always worked. Editor Laura Pyzel Clark recalls being floored, during her job interview at *Bazaar,* when Carmel looked her dead in the eye and asked, "Darling, who do you know?" When the girl answered that she was working for Alfred Vanderbilt, Carmel said, without hesitating, 'That's fine, you'll be the men's editor." When Clark sputtered that she wouldn't know how to do such a job, Carmel responded breezily, "You'll know." Good looks also helped. An attractive staff translated into business for the magazine, as editor Melanie Witt Miller discovered on a trip to Paris, when Carmel asked her to remove her wedding and engagement rings: an available-seeming young editor had more allure than one who wasn't. Another staffer recalled being sent by Carmel to attend fancy parties, if only briefly, to keep the magazine's name in the air. "She told me to find out who'd be the most important person in the room, go up to them, make yourself known and mention *Harper's Bazaar,*" Laura Pyzel Clark reports. "Then you can find the kitchen, grab something to eat, and leave. Just make sure they know you've been there."

Carmel adored it when her staffers had glamorous admirers. "It may be my passion for romance that influenced me in choosing them," she admitted in her memoir. There was a certain vicariousness to it all: her editors' affairs with important men might as well have been her own. Macy and Barry, she wrote, "were the girls with the most glamorous—and prominent—beaux in New York. Macy's included Jock Whitney and Robert Benchley. Barry was friendly with the very married Vincent Astor, who was said to have bankrolled her chic apartment on East Fifty-sixth Street and with whom she traveled on his famous yacht, the *Nourmahal* (which, before coming to *Bazaar,* she'd reported on in a 1932 issue of *Vogue*). It was even rumored that Astor had offered to leave his wife in order to marry her, but was turned down by Barry, who thought he was too stodgy. Her other admirers included the Earl of Warwick and Allan A. Ryan Jr. "Mrs. Snow was a terrible snob," says Lillian Bassman, "so the fact that Barry was running on yachts and carrying on with the Vanderbilts and people was a big seller with her."

Carmel adored matchmaking, and did so with a passion. "She loved men, she loved romance, all that sort of thing," says Gloria Moncur, "and it came out in her work." But at times she went too far, as when she urged Ryan, the grandson of the financier Thomas Fortune Ryan, to marry the very fetching Barry. "The Ryan thing was a disaster because he didn't want to marry her and Mrs. Snow bullied him into it," says Babs Simpson. Barry duly left her job, as women did then, to take up domestic life. But her marriage to Ryan, which took place in January 1937, lasted for a millisecond, apparently: according to one New York newspaper, Mrs. Eleanor Barry Ryan, who, as her name indicates, had already separated, signed a lease on an apartment down the street from her husband in the following month. (She divorced Ryan on the grounds of cruelty in May 1941, becoming Mrs. Lawrence Lowman the following month.) No doubt Carmel's distress over Barry's misguided alliance was real, but there was a certain officiousness to it, too. As Thornton Wilson put it:

> *She always liked the girls that worked for her to have problems. She always said, "Poor Suzy Q. Isn't it terrible that her husband has gone out and done something vile and I have to take care of her?" She thought of herself as a family and she made a big fuss about that sort of thing. She thought* Bazaar *was a family affair. She was really the big mother.*

At one point in poor Barry's romantic travails, Carmel took action. As Mary Louise Aswell wrote:

> *[Jean] Moral, who took outdoor shots of collection dresses in Paris, had sent Carmel a cable: "Crise sentimentale. Impossible deux pages séptembre." The same day a letter came announcing that Barry's heart was broken. Carmel promptly summoned them both to Ireland. Wherever they visited she would leave them in the hall while she slipped in to prepare a welcome for them. "Very unhappy in love," they could hear her whisper. "Not with each other." Since Irish hearts are all susceptible to romance, their welcome was warm.*

Bazaar continued to outpace *Vogue,* scoring one first after another, including a major coup in 1936 when Carmel learned from Marion Davies the scandalous fact, known to an inner circle of Londoners, that King Edward VIII, who had been on the throne for less than a year, had fallen in love with an American divorcée, Wallis Warfield Simpson. Carmel promptly commissioned a Hoyningen-Huene portrait of this controversial, if beautifully dressed, woman, only to discover after the boat carrying the film from Europe docked, that it had been delivered to Hearst himself, then in New York, by mistake. Naturally, the minute Chief saw the portrait, he wanted to publish it in his newspapers—a major exclusive—and he informed Carmel of his plans to do so.

Incensed, Snow dispatched an assistant, Jean Chiesa, who later became executive editor of the magazine, to face down Hearst at his apartment. But Hearst's practiced secretary successfully kept Carmel's lieutenant at bay. At which point the editor stormed over there herself. As Chiesa later described it: "The door swung open. In came Mrs. Snow like a little Irish firecracker. She marched straight into Chief's private office, and when she came out, she had her photographs in hand." Poor Hearst was toast. The portrait ran that May, in *Bazaar,* of course, and although many by then knew the significance of the woman in question, no one could quite let on. (*Time* magazine would be the first to break the story in the United States.) The caption that ran beneath it was a model of knowing restraint. "Mrs. Ernest Simpson, the most famous American in London, wears a Chinese dinner dress."

Carmel continued to experiment with *Bazaar*'s look and content, and she continued to bring in new talent. She bagged one of her greatest catches in 1936, after Fellowes handed in her resignation after a year or so on the job—for real, this time.

> *I had been looking for a replacement for Daisy Fellowes—not as our Paris editor, necessarily, but as someone who would make news for* Harper's Bazaar. *In Mrs. T. Reed Vreeland, a fashionable young woman who had just returned from Europe with her banker husband, I found her. She reflected for us the new world of the International Set, and in addition she earned the undying respect of the Seventh Avenue market because of her daring originality and taste.*

Vreeland had been living in London with her dashing and perhaps not-terribly-brilliant husband, T. Reed Vreeland, a banker. She was an extraordinary creature, whose gift for self-invention and whose wonderful pronouncements—"Pink is the navy blue of India," that sort of thing—which so lend themselves to parody, would, years later, bring her not just to the attention of the fashion world, but far beyond.

Carmel had known of Vreeland, the former Diana Dalziel, for years: her photograph ran several times in the 1920s in *Vogue* at the time Carmel worked there—one of them was captioned, "Miss Diana Dalziel, one of the most attractive debutantes of the winter, is shown entering her Cadillac"—and their paths must surely have crossed at chic gatherings in New York. Always elegant, Vreeland had become radically more so during her years abroad. "For her fashion is of the essence, she thinks, lives and breathes it," as *Bazaar* later wrote. By the time Carmel sighted her again, dancing at New York's St. Regis Hotel in late 1935, it was clear to her even across a crowded room that Vreeland was a born fashion editor. It wasn't just her white lace Chanel dress with a bolero top that drew Carmel's attention, but that elusive thing called style. Vreeland emitted it; it was as tangible as the white roses she'd pinned that night into what Carmel described as her "blue-black hair."

Vreeland had been back from Europe for only six months and was living on East Ninety-third Street, then the far reaches of the Upper East Side. "I was going through money like one goes through . . . a bottle of scotch, I suppose, if you're an alcoholic," she recalled. So much so that she'd been actually looking for a job—an act that was almost aberrant for a young mother of her class (the couple had two sons). At the time of her encounter with Carmel, Vreeland had been closing in on a job at the venerable *Town & Country* magazine, a far more conservative Hearst title than *Bazaar*. But then Carmel, with her nose for talent, pounced. Asked by a journalist years later why she'd taken the job, Vreeland answered in her usual disarming manner. "Money. Why does anyone work for anything else?"

Vreeland's memory, as is well known, was a bit loose with the facts, starting with the actual year in which she was hired. (It was probably 1936, not 1937, as she claimed.) As for the story of her debut in the fashion world, which has been told and retold, frankly, who knows what's true? The sighting by Mrs. Snow probably was, but as for the rest . . . In *D.V.* the long stream-of-consciousness memoir that even she has described as "faction"—i.e., a mixture of fact and fiction—Vreeland recalled receiving a phone call from Carmel the day after the party.

> *"But Mrs. Snow," I said, "except for my little lingerie shop in London, I've never worked. I've never been in an office in my life. I'm never dressed until lunch."*
>
> *"But you seem to know a lot about clothes," Carmel said.*
>
> *"That I do. I've dedicated hours and* hours *of very detailed time to my clothes."*
>
> *"All right, then why don't you just try it and see how it works out."*

There are other versions. Eleanor Barry, the young *Bazaar* editor, claimed to have been the first to have met with Vreeland the day she came in to the magazine, after she'd been summoned by Carmel. Barry's reaction was as decisive as Carmel's had been. "She knew instantly that Vreeland was something special," Barry's niece, the author Roxana Robinson, recalls. According to Mildred Morton Gilbert, an assistant to *Bazaar*'s merchandising editor who went on to a long career at *Vogue,* ultimately becoming executive editor, Carmel cultivated Vreeland even before she'd returned from Europe. The instant she was back in New York, Gilbert wrote, Vreeland became a presence at *Bazaar.*

> *She used to come in once a week to talk and the whole thing was that she just gave Mrs. Snow a stream of consciousness. Mrs. Snow would take that and edit all the material and relate it for use in the magazine. Diana was so full of ideas and a very colorful woman herself, but she needed an editor, and Mrs. Snow was that.*

One way or another, this fantastical creature, who would become with age only more so, turned up at *Bazaar*. You could argue that she was created there, for "Diana wouldn't have existed if it weren't for Carmel Snow," as Babs Simpson, whom Carmel recruited as Babs Domerico from Lord & Taylor to work "at the lowest possible thing in the fashion department" (literally, this time, for $35 a week) under Vreeland, puts it. Frederick Dalziel Vreeland, known as "Frecky," agrees: "Carmel Snow started my mother on the way to her career. My mother would have been nothing without her."

In later life, Vreeland was funny, outrageous, so given to exaggeration that you couldn't believe a word she said, and yet, somehow, all of it was true. At least in spirit. Her vivid, nutty pronouncements are so much of what people know about her now. But in real life she was also something far less glamorous: like Carmel, she was an energetic, utterly disciplined, hard-driving female professional in an era when such an entity was rare. Years later, Richard Avedon would describe Vreeland as "without exception the hardest working person I've ever known." Her taste was her gift, and she never stopped refining it. For all her apparent frivolity, her life, along with her matchless persona, were mainly constructed out of very hard work.

Vreeland was in her thirties in the 1930s and much less of a caricature than she would become. A Munkacsi photograph that ran in the January 1936 issue of *Bazaar* captures her striding, daringly confident, down a New York street, a felt hat by Suzy, the Paris milliner, clamped jauntily to her head, a nutria cape fanning out behind her as she walks. Not a detail of her outfit has been left to chance, from the gloves of supple leather to the crisp, pointed collar of her blouse. Her midcalf suit here is unattributed; in this period, though, she favored nonstop Chanel. (She would later turn to Mainbocher, almost exclusively.) The new fashion editor dressed "like a blond," *Bazaar* noted, and was "never long out of her favorite color combination—oyster beige with white." She, too, had a signature scent—hers was actually a bath oil, by Prince Matchabelli, worn as perfume.

Like Carmel, Vreeland was deeply invested in Europe. Paris was the center of everything for her, too, yet at *Bazaar* it would never be her turf: Carmel wouldn't have given up her biannual visits there for anything in the world. (She would take other editors, though. McFadden sometimes accompanied her, as did Eleanor Barry and, occasionally, both.) Since Carmel only went to the American openings that caught her eye, Seventh Avenue, the epicenter of American fashion, became Vreeland's beat, one that she professed to adore.

> *I tramped the streets. I covered the waterfront....*
>
> *I'd walk home those sixty blocks alone all those years. I loved the fur district, and that's where I'd walk when I finished working....*
>
> *I was so happy when I was down on Seventh Avenue. I was always going up rusty staircases with old newspapers lying all over the place and the most ghastly-looking characters hanging around... but* nothing *was frightening to me. It was* all *part of the great adventure, my métier, the scene.*

Like other editors in this era, Vreeland worked closely with dressmakers, giving feedback on collections, suggesting new avenues to explore. "Her concept of being a fashion editor is to create fashion... to motivate it, not simply to report what Seventh Avenue has to offer," Ballard, her counterpart at *Vogue,* once wrote.

Who knew that Vreeland was a recovering gum chewer? Apparently so. "The first thing she did was to get rid of her gum," reports Geri Trotta, who was "an ant, a very observant ant," in her own words, on the *Bazaar* staff at the time Vreeland was hired. The fashion editor's first days on the job weren't auspicious. Taste or not, you needed experience to do the work, and Diana had none. "I knew so little when I started. I must have terrified them." One of her first ideas was to eliminate handbags. Why not? The idea came to her on a day she was wearing a Chanel pantsuit "with pockets inside, not on the outside like pockets are today." (The fact that she'd turned up at the office in trousers was in itself astonishing since, as Charlotte Seeling has pointed out, "It was only in 1939 that *Vogue* showed women in pants and sweaters for the first time.") Bursting with excitement, Vreeland shared her inspiration with one horrified editor after another until Carmel quickly brought her entire train of thought to a careening stop. "Listen, Diana, I think you've lost your mind. Do you realize that our income from handbag advertising is God knows how many millions a year?!"

From the outset, she, Carmel, and Brodovitch formed a tight trio, tearing down the halls, meeting for endless conferences in the art department or at the much-used conference table in Carmel's sunny corner office, which overlooked Fifty-sixth Street and Madison Avenue, with its honking traffic and rush-hour crowds. Just floors above, her corner workspace might have been in another world. "It was like going into fresh fields full of apple blossoms when you went into Carmel's office those early days," as Vreeland famously described it. "There was always a divine smell in the room. The windows were always open, as if to everything new. Everything was so light, so sure, so concentrated."

With its gray-painted French provincial desk and chintz-covered couch and chairs, it looked more like a well-appointed living room than an office. This was long before ergonomic office chairs, or even just swivel ones: the redoubtable editor perched on one of those French, wood-framed, armchairs that's known as a fauteuil. The room was full of framed photographs of her family, including ones of her children that had run in the magazine—the girls were occasionally pressed into service to model children's clothes. On her desk there was a bust of Nefertiti, the Egyptian queen, a gift from a friend who thought it resembled Carmel (who didn't agree, but displayed it anyway). Still, the editor had a regalness to her bearing that would become more pronounced with time.

Here, Carmel interviewed job applicants and conferred with her staff. She was always rushing—they all were—so she rarely removed her hat. "Lady editors in those days were famous, and much caricatured, for wearing hats all day long—at their desks, to lunch, to bed." To bed? "A hat seemed to proclaim you in the fashion business, much as a plastic helmet identifies the construction worker today." But surely Carmel rushed more than most? As Trotta recalled, "Her factotum, Jean Chiesa, used to even follow her into the bathroom. She'd continue taking dictation while Mrs. Snow urinated. You see, she never wasted a minute. She worked like crazy." Carmel wore white gloves, as all ladies did then (Vreeland, too), and one staff member recalled that, when you conferred with her in her office, she might put them on and take them off compulsively, hardly seeming aware that she did so.

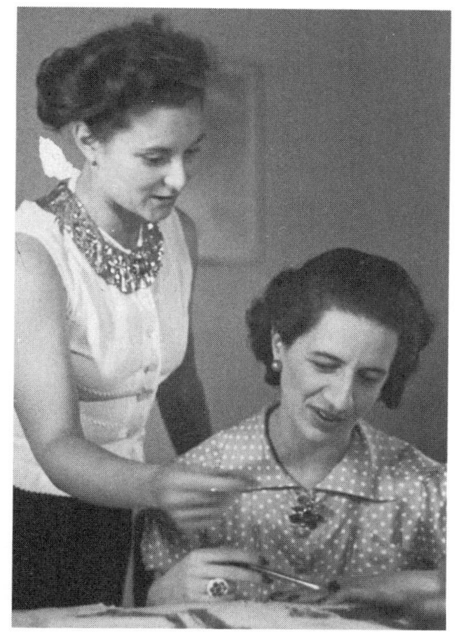

Diana Vreeland during one of her first years at *Bazaar* (with Shopping Bazaar editor Peggy LeBoutillier), 1937

Carmel, Brodovitch, and Vreeland "were three extraordinary people who respected each other for their own domains, it was an amazing sort of triumvirate," says Adrian Gilbert Allen, known as A.G., who worked in both the art department and on the editorial staff under her maiden name, Adrian Johns. They could count on each other to have quick opinions, decisive moves, impeccable taste. But this wasn't true for everyone. Wilhela Cushman recalled Carmel yelping "It isn't good enough!" when one of her junior fashion editors brought in an outfit to photograph that didn't meet her standards. Such words were never directed toward Vreeland, whose fashion sense was unerring. "She was a great innovator and had good ideas. She was great at sittings, which were the mainstream of the *Bazaar,*" editor Laura Pyzel Clark recalls. "She was tops on a sitting," a photographer added.

> *You'd be given a dress to do and you had to make a picture. The shape of the dress did not please; there would be nothing about the garment that had even a touch of inspiration; you'd be disgusted—and then you'd appeal to Diana to help brighten up the dress, and her eye would*

come to the rescue. She'd always produce something, like the addition of a scarf, to help liven up your photograph.

Another recalls shooting a kimono-style dress while Vreeland went on a riff about geishas. "She'd say a geisha girl would stand this way and bend her knees that way. She knew her paintings. She really was fantastic with that. She knew the makeup the old masters used." (The great, unanswered question is, How?) An editor who worked with her remembers her as "a great comic figure. She was an original. She once said to me, 'You and I know that the British navy has always worn silk underwear.' She really said those things and we all religiously copied them down." One might find such comments ridiculous, but they had an exceptional longevity; they stayed in the mind. "These little fetishes about how things should be crept into your life in some ways," another editor adds. As Cecil Beaton has written about Vreeland, she had "a poetical quality quite unexpected in the world of tough elegance in which she works. . . ."

Wildly imaginative, Vreeland sometimes had to be reeled in, according to Richard Deems, who began working as an ad salesman at *Bazaar* in 1939, eventually ascending to the Hearst Corporation's board of directors.

Carmel understood [Vreeland's] limitations. Vreeland got so enthusiastic about so many things that Carmel had to edit her. Diana was always posing, very theatrical, she'd clutch her throat and say "The whole issue must be about fuchsia." Carmel would quietly say "Diana, we'll do four pages on fuchsia." She was always the boss.

It wasn't always serene. "Vreeland and Carmel had their rows . . . and their differences of opinion," Carmel's niece Nancy White recalled. "I remember lunching with Carmel one day and Vreeland was in the same restaurant and I knew they'd just had one hell of a row. . . . But Carmel thought Vreeland was great." Frederick Vreeland adds: "There was enormous mutual respect with no side to it." It didn't hurt that their fiefdoms were separate ones. "They were not in competition," as one photographer put it. "They were in two different worlds." The triumvirate they formed with Brodovitch fed on nervous energy—no wonder they were all reed thin. They dashed up and down the halls, cigarettes in hand (all except Carmel, who never smoked). Alcohol also played a part: their lunches became more liquid as the years went on.

It was a rarefied atmosphere, but managing editor Frances McFadden could be counted on to bring things down to earth. McFadden's looks and manner had a severity that was belied by her character: she was warm and humorous and, like her boss, an enthusiastic gossip. (Carmel adored "a juicy piece of scandal," Dorothy Wheelock Edson says, something McFadden could often supply.) Staffers always knew when Carmel and McFadden's first-thing-in-the-morning meetings were in session by the peals of laughter sounding down the hall.

McFadden called Hearst "the God Almighty of the magazine," but her admiration for Carmel had no such edge. In later years, she parsed her former boss's gifts:

> *One of her talents was her ability to absorb impressions quickly (she was always in a hurry) yet accurately (with devilish accuracy in some cases). She knew where every seam in a dress was placed without feeling it . . . she could walk into a room once and tell you everything important in it. Her intuition was particularly keen with people. She saw beauty before the fledgling herself realized she was going to be beautiful . . . and cleverness just by looking into a pair of eyes. . . . She could move from one milieu to another without confusion. . . .*

Cecil Beaton echoed the thought: "So attuned is Carmel Snow to her atmosphere that she often anticipates what other people are about to suggest, and can telepathically finish thoughts and sentences for them." No wonder the critic Kenneth Tynan later described her as being a mystical combination: "Half Irish . . . and half Inca."

Carmel was now on top. "She was the height of everything—taste, posture, toughness," Faulconer says. The latter was key. Still in her forties, she needed to project absolute authority. It was a necessary transformation, as another editor in chief, *Vogue*'s Grace Mirabella, discovered later on:

> *Diana Vreeland had been right when she'd told me, the first time I went in her place to the Paris couture, that I was "too approachable" and needed to put some distance into my manner. . . . Now, I pulled rank. I decided that there would be no more nonsense.*

At some point, Carmel did, too, transforming herself into a boss, the person whose vision could sustain a magazine. She could be ruthless, as Erwin Blumenfeld, the German photographer, recalled:

> *The sharpest fashion journalist ever, her nastiness was stimulating. Totally tight-fisted whenever anyone wanted something; fantastically generous when she wanted something from you. Her secretary once assured me proudly that she would have murdered her old mother without a second thought to get a good spread in* Harper's Bazaar.

Blumenfeld was scarcely heard to say anything nice about anyone; even so, it's a scathing portrait. Exaggerated, but not entirely inaccurate. Carmel could be beyond cruel to those who threatened her or in whom she didn't believe, which may be why one young southerner, Mary Lee Settle, a stunning former house model for Traina-Norell who later worked for *Bazaar,* could perceive her as "the coldest woman I've ever known," while others speak of her exceptional warmth. "She mostly didn't seem like a scary fashion person," says Margot Wilkie, a family friend of Carmel's. "She seemed like a warm Irishwoman." If she liked you, if she thought you had talent or style, if you put the magazine before anything, her affection could be boundless. For others, it could be limited indeed.

She was the "the heartbeat of the magazine," as model Mary Jane Russell put it. "The day didn't begin at the office until Carmel came up in the elevator," an editor wrote. Once she stepped off it, another one adds, "you knew the world had changed." By now Carmel's hair was tinted like Elsie de Wolfe's, but in a more extreme color, a look she adopted after a Paris hairdresser—probably Antoine, her perpetual favorite, although she could also be seen chez Guillaume—bluing her hair to make its white whiter, left the chemicals in for too long. It might be powder blue one month, lilac the next; whatever the *couleur du mois,* it retained the same intensity.

Carmel's mood filled the corridors, which was mainly a good thing. As fierce as she became, she never lost her infectious, and very Irish, sense of fun. And even if her accent had long since been downgraded to an inflection, she was inescapably from the Emerald Isle, capable of trotting out Irishisms like nobody else. She'd call call people "a sketch," or, as she used to do when heading out into Seventh Avenue with one of her favorite young fashion editors, say, "Take me arm, dear, and pass as me wife." She might describe someone as being "as old as Kate Carney's cat" or call a certain shade of brown "the color of dun-ducketty-mud."

At times, though, she had "the temper of the world," according to one of her nieces, "and she'd lose it like she pressed a button." So much so that Jean Chiesa once analyzed her boss's notorious fury, making the distinction between "Wrath, or real RAGE," which might leave Carmel's interlocutor "bereft of speech and minus a logical

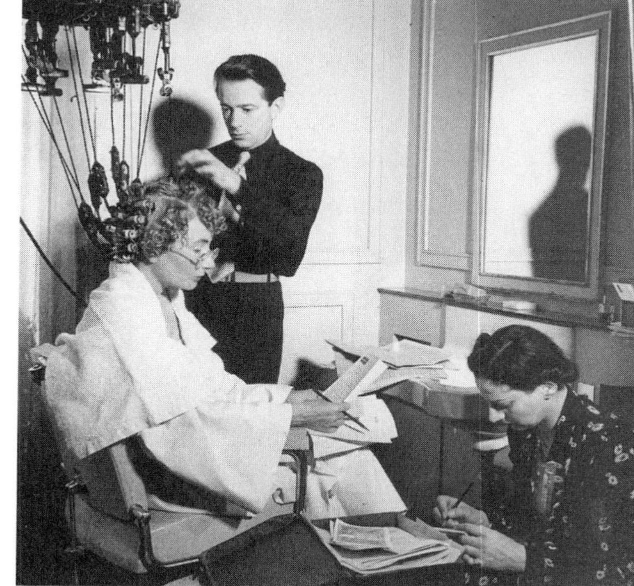

Carmel Snow dictating a radio address to a secretary at Paris hairdresser Guillaume, 1937

thought in her head . . ." and "False Wrath," which "was reserved for the intelligent person who just was not getting on with the job at hand and needed to be jolted into reality. . . . This calculated temperamental outburst also left the recipient speechless but seemed to produce results." It was all the work of "a consummate actress," in Chiesa's view. It could also flare up unexpectedly. A photographer, Lillian Bassman, says Carmel once slapped her across the face after she ventured the opinion that marriage was overrated (unbeknownst to Carmel, the young assistant was living with her future husband, photographer Paul Himmel, at the time). It was a reaction the young woman couldn't make sense of at the time, or ever since.

Magazines are ultimately about commerce, not art, and Carmel had to keep a constant eye on the bottom line. The kind of naïveté Vreeland exhibited about handbags couldn't—and didn't—survive for long. Market research may have been in its infancy then, but there was plenty of evidence about what covers sold, what stories were popular, what readers wanted to see in their magazine. *Bazaar* hit a high note after Vreeland began putting together her "Why Don't You?" columns in 1936. Some were harmless enough, such as "Why don't you turn your old ermine coat into a bathrobe?" or "Why don't you stick Japanese hair-pins in your hair?"—why not indeed?—while others were laughably fey, such as the famous "Why don't you rinse your blond child's hair in Champagne, as the French do?" Still others, such as "Why don't you go serenely out in the snow in a court jester's hood of cherry red cotton velvet?" sounded downright deranged. A few are notorious: "Why don't you wear bare knees and long white knitted socks, as Unity Mitford does when she takes tea with Hitler at the Carlton in Munich?"

The best of these lodged in the brain, demonstrating Vreeland's keen marketing sense. As Cecil Beaton has pointed out:

> *It can be seen that Mrs. Vreeland's column was directed towards an imaginary upper-income bracket in a magazine whose circulation was largely due to the average American woman. The psychology of this, however, was shrewd and appropriate. At the height of a depression, to*

> *list such things as fanciful as porcelain stoves brought back from Europe or beds from China gave the reader a feeling that a sentiment* de luxe *(and hence the perverse, the capricious) was still operating.*

In 1938, S. J. Perelman wrote a famous satire that ran in *The New Yorker,* inspired, he wrote, by "months of restlessly reading Diana Vreeland's new 'Why Don't You?' column in *Harper's Bazaar.*"

> *If a perfectly strange lady came up to you on the street and demanded "Why don't you travel with a little raspberry-colored cashmere blanket to throw over yourself in hotels and trains?" the chances are that you would turn on your heel with dignity and hit her with a bottle. Yet that is exactly what has been happening for the past twenty months in the pages of a little raspberry-colored magazine called* Harper's Bazaar.

Other satires followed in that magazine, by Perelman and others. Vreeland recalled Carmel writing to editor Harold Ross in protest, saying that "it was very upsetting for such a young girl to be criticized." But Vreeland herself saw it otherwise. "Good heavens! I was in my thirties at the time and very flattered." At another point an unnamed *New Yorker* writer overstepped the reportorial line, in Carmel's view, by recounting a private conversation in print, a transgression she solved by having "a flaming row" with her old friend Ross. One way or another, the parodies stopped for a while. But then, eventually, they came back: like *Vogue, Bazaar,* with its sometimes hallucinatory fashion copy, would provide comic material for *The New Yorker* for decades to come.

Everyone seemed to have a reaction, including Hearst himself, who sent Vreeland a touching, handwritten note saying how much he enjoyed her column. One "Why Don't You?," impudently revised, became bathroom graffiti at a famous men's club in New York, as well as at some decidedly less blue-chip venues all across the country. Carmel doesn't specify which one was so honored but, to my mind, "Why don't you lift your blue wool Mainbocher skirt to show a candy-striped petticoat (Bloomingdale)?" seems as good a choice as any. Vreeland's column lasted only a few years; she later claimed that she lost interest in part because people—Carmel, presumably—began to interfere, insisting that she include such earth-shattering nuggets as, for example, the fact that Daisy Fellowes's daughter and her groom had left the church where they were married in a two-in-hand. For as long as they lasted, Carmel took a pragmatic view of the hoopla they caused, writing that "publicity is publicity and since 'Why Don't You's' are quoted today, a quarter of a century later, they achieved exactly the purpose I hoped for." Now, of course, a great deal more time has passed, and the WDYs—and, indeed, Vreeland herself—show no signs of fading.

All through her early *Bazaar* years, Carmel continued to cross paths with her former boss Edna Chase. The two served on a fashion jury together, judging a fabric design contest, in 1934. They retained an icy distance, perhaps nodding to each other to acknowledge the other's presence; in any case, nothing more. ("Carmel goes her way and I go mine," as Chase put it.) But then, daringly, in 1936, Carmel decided that enough must at last be enough and wrote to Chase suggesting that they meet. The *Vogue* editor's somewhat melodramatic response must have been a disappointment:

> *Thank you for your kind invitation to dine on Friday. I wish I could accept, but the old relationship that existed between us was so made up of our long years of work and play together that when you threw that all aside in order to build up the property of the man who had been our meanest rival, you killed in my heart an affection and a faith that nothing but your own words could have destroyed.*
>
> *Our friendship was not built on trivialities, Carmel, it was welded from the joys and struggles of mutual accomplishment and a common interest. I still feel too keenly the sorrow of this whole situation to be able to see you in the old familiar way.*

I often think of you and the children and hope that they are all well. In my heart I do you the justice to believe that you too have suffered.

It must have been galling for Chase that one of the key finds of Carmel's early years was an inadvertent gift from *Vogue.* The photographer Louise Dahl-Wolfe was a colorful figure. She resembled a nun, albeit one who walked around with a seven-pound Graflex around her neck (until damage to her vertebrae caused her to change cameras), and her earliest portraits had been good enough to bring her work to the attention of Frank Crowninshield, who had wanted her for *Vanity Fair* (which had folded in 1936, becoming incorporated, in name at least, into *Vogue*). But Dahl-Wolfe, who was fiercely independent, refused to work in a company studio, as Crowninshield required. "I'm of an independent mind and need my own surroundings," she said. Ultimately, the photographer slipped through Condé Nast's hands altogether after she met with *Vogue*'s Dr. Agha on a day when the cantankerous, wondrously plain photographer, having been ill, looked particularly peaked.

"This is the work of a Louise Dahl-Wolfe who is making a great effort to learn photography," he wrote in a notorious memo to Nast. "She has taste but on account of her advanced age—about forty-eight—perhaps a little too late." Dahl-Wolfe, who was actually in her thirties at the time, later told an interviewer that Agha's "criticism was merciless . . . I just wanted to go through the floor." It was a bad mistake, one that Agha compounded by accidentally returning the photographer's portfolio to her with the incriminating memo still inside. Dahl-Wolfe's next stop was to see Brodovitch, who was impressed by her black-and-white portraits. That she had some experience photographing fashion, and in color, only added to her appeal. "From the moment I saw her first color photographs I knew that the *Bazaar* was at last going to look the way I had instinctively wanted my magazine to look," Carmel wrote.

Trained in both art and interior design, Dahl-Wolfe had been a student of color since her art school days back in San Francisco, where she was born. "You have to study color like the scales of the piano," she wrote in her memoir. "It's really scientific." In her early years, "when not faced with a deadline, she worked with her little camera on experiments with Kodachrome, experiments that were to set a new standard for color photography," according to Frances McFadden. It was a shrewd investment. Soon, Dahl-Wolfe would "revolutionize the *Bazaar* as Munkacsi and Brodovitch revolutionized it, because she developed color photography to its ultimate," in Carmel's words. Its importance was absolute. You could see the color of a dress—an enormous development.

Carmel wanted more color in *Bazaar,* but was shrewd enough not to force it on a photographer who couldn't—or didn't want to—handle it. The Hungarian-born photographer André Kertész, who contributed fashion and other photographs to *Bazaar,* recalled that Carmel had never pushed him in that direction. "She understood that my genius was for black and white." In the mid-1930s, color was the great leveler. Magazines wanted more and more of it; photographers who wanted to survive had to master it overnight. It tripped up even some of the most accomplished black-and-white photographers, rather in the way that the introduction of "talkies" immediately eliminated squeaky-voiced silent-movie actresses, Marion Davies among them, from the field. Some lensmen, like Hoyningen-Huene, gamely took up the challenge, contributing a color page or so per issue. But the adjustment wasn't easy: at their most awkward, his shots had a colorized look. And this was true for others, too. The learning curve was so steep that, in the early days of Kodachrome, "The Eastman Kodak company sent technicians with each of the three huge one-shot cameras that had to be used with brilliant klieg lights" to help photographers get it right, according to Steichen.

The hands-off policy that both Brodovitch and Carmel took with their contributors was largely what drew Dahl-Wolfe to *Bazaar.* It was fine with them if she worked out of her own studio, in the Sherwood Building at 58 West Fifty-seventh Street in New York, rather than from one of the two *Bazaar* ones on the fourth floor at 572 Madison, one of which was then used by Hoyningen-Huene, the other by James Abbe Jr. And Carmel agreed to allow Dahl-Wolfe to correct her own engravings, a critical move. Although "it was reported that she drove the pressmen mad with her perfectionism, at times, pulling proof after proof in pursuit of the perfect balance of shades," the results were luminous, as photo after photo makes clear. A shot that ran in the September 1939 issue of a frostily elegant blonde, seated at a restaurant banquette in a velvet Hattie Carnegie suit, looking pensively ahead, her face reflected in the shiny black table before her, demonstrates how this photographer's elaborate compositions, combined with her nuanced sense of color (in this case, gold and green), set her work apart.

Dahl-Wolfe was one of the first to use color extensively on location, something technical developments were making easier than ever before. The development of the light meter meant that photographers no longer had to guess at f-stops and shutter speeds, and the new, lighter, smaller-format cameras gave them greater flexibility. Where once Dahl-Wolfe relied on her Graflex, even occasionally hauling along a forty-pound English camera called a Studio Mines (dubbed "Dahly's Folly" by her husband, artist Meyer "Mike" Wolfe), she now worked with a Rolleiflex or a Contax when she and Vreeland headed off on location.

By all accounts the pair enjoyed an excellent working rapport. "There was an extraordinary immediate communication of her seriousness," Vreeland once said, approvingly, of Dahl-Wolfe. Once, on location with the photographer in the Southeast, one assistant whispered to another, "Now we're going to see Diana discover the South." True to form, the fashion editor stepped out of the car and, as if on cue, spying some wisteria, exclaimed, "What a divine vine!" to much hidden merriment all around. Dahl-Wolfe sittings were always accompanied by a "chorus" from the photographer, in Carmel's recollection. Dahl-Wolfe would perch on a stepladder or whatever was at hand (including, precariously, a table on a Paris balcony, when she photographed Bébé Bérard), and call out to those around her, "Higher, get me higher!" She was very temperamental, sometimes capriciously refusing to accept any work from *Bazaar* for weeks on end, at which point Carmel might turn to a mutual friend to lure her back into the fold. "Louise would be on the outs with everybody and Mrs. Snow knew how to handle her—by flattery," says John Esten, who worked for *Bazaar* later, but knew many of the principals involved. "It was Mrs. Snow who was able to keep everyone in line."

Like other photographers, Dahl-Wolfe could be stymied by the magazine's perennial "Must List," garments of no particular merit that occasionally had to be shown because their manufacturers were regular advertisers. These didn't come up often, but when they did, they could be a challenge. "That's perfectly ghastly," Vreeland had been known to exclaim, before calling a manufacturer and encouraging it to make some change in the garment that might make it more palatable to *Bazaar*'s readers. "Sometimes, when commissioned to do a fashion or beauty shot that I thought thoroughly uninteresting," Dahl-Wolfe recalled, "I'd call Carmel Snow and she'd say, 'Oh dear, just make a beautiful picture, put just part of it in and that will be fine.'" Besides creating fashion photographs, Dahl-Wolfe kept up with portraiture, her first love, too. And her work was by no means confined to color. In 1938, she went off to Hollywood for the magazine, coming back with black-and-white shots of Bette Davis, Ginger Rogers, David Niven, and others, all done in natural light with a small camera (a Rolleiflex) and relatively fast film—a far cry from the stilted studio portraits of the day.

From the first, Carmel had enviable freedom at *Bazaar*. But it wasn't absolute. After Fellowes, to no one's great surprise, went back to a more leisurely life, Carmel at one point tried to replace her with the Marquise de Vögué, the bearer of an ancient French name that was, unfortunately, spelled the same way as the name of *Bazaar*'s biggest rival. She wired the Chief, asking his permission to move ahead with the hire, but "Hearst, who received the cable without all the little attendant dots and accents, and having probably never heard of the distinguished house of Vögué, thought somebody was making fun of him and nearly burst one of his remaining blood vessels," according to Caroline Seebohm. Another fashionable bearer of an ancient Gaulic name, Anne de la Rochefoucauld, was quickly summoned in her place.

Although Carmel's "own apprehension was largely visual," as she once put it, she loved good writing; still, she didn't entirely trust her instincts with it, as she did with photography. She needed a fiction editor she could count on. Although Frances McFadden served in this capacity, she had proven herself to be even more valuable as a managing editor. The first fiction editor Carmel tapped was Beatrice Kaufman, wife of the playwright George Kaufman, whom she'd known from her days on the edge of the Algonquin crowd. Kaufman joined the magazine in 1936, and while she only lasted a couple of years—her husband's career would soon take them to Hollywood—she became a great friend of Carmel's, even accompanying her to visit Hoyningen-Huene at the house he'd built for himself in Hammamet, Tunisia—"one of the most romantic spots I ever visited." Carmel was besotted with this exotic, dramatically changeable, landscape, with its mystic-seeming distant mountain, the Djebel Zaghouan. "Perhaps because my life has been so civilized ... that visit made an indelible impression on me."

Kaufman, and her successor, George Davis, who first joined the staff as features editor in 1935, strengthened the writing to be found in the magazine to such an extent that a 1938 ad boasted, "Some of the most important fiction being published today . . . appears regularly in the pages of *Harper's*

George Hoyningen-Huene portrait of Carmel Snow, 1930s

Bazaar," citing Christopher Isherwood and Elizabeth Bowen, among other authors. Davis was particularly sympathetic to writers of fiction, since he was one himself: his novel *The Opening of a Door,* which satirized life among the midwestern middle class, had been a surprise bestseller in 1931. "As a chunk of life it is magnificent," Davis's friend W. H. Auden wrote. Marion Davies was another pal of his; it was she who persuaded Hearst to recommend Davis, then even more broke than usual, to Carmel, who, upon reading his novel, promptly hired him. Their relationship was fraught from the beginning, but then Davis's usually were: he was hypersensitive, only a step or two away from being a full-blown paranoid, and seemingly incapable of actually turning up for work. But when he did, he was brilliant. At Davis's own suggestion, Carmel sent him twice to Europe, where he scouted out talent, commissioning such writers as Osbert Sitwell, Christopher Isherwood, Stephen Spender, and W. H. Auden for *Bazaar.*

It was easy to draw talent in. Davis was a wonderfully sensitive editor of fiction, and the magazine paid top dollar. The writer Kay Boyle, whose short stories were, for a time, a *Bazaar* staple, was given $350 for her "Maiden, Maiden," which ran in the December 1934 issue—a very generous sum. (*The New Yorker,* whose attachment to good writing was legendary, paid the same author almost a third less—$250—for another story in the same period.) Later, in 1940, *Bazaar* offered Davis's friend Katherine Anne Porter a staggering $600 for her story "The Leaning Tower." Carmel's interest in good writing was genuine. Fashion editor Polly Mellen, who worked at *Bazaar* early in her career, when she was still Polly Allen, recalls that Carmel was forever encouraging her staff to read—Colette and Oscar Wilde were among her favorites. "She would always say to me, 'You have to reread it, Polly, you'll find something different.' And we all did exactly what she said. Like little sheep." But some doubted the depth of her appreciation. "Personally, I don't think she was cultivated," says the writer and lecturer Rosamond Bernier. "She had a flair and a nose for what might be important. She showed an instinctive flair for what was good."

Carmel adored her geniuses, catering to them, when necessary, because she knew they'd bring results. But she could be scathing to those she judged less worthy. One hapless writer, whose name has been lost to history, once stopped in to see her after sending in a story for her consideration. The girl sat down, eager to hear what the great editor thought, but Carmel, clearly unimpressed, refused to even discuss it. "Who are *you*?" she asked disdainfully. "It was a brutal question and she felt Aunt Carmel was ruthless," says her niece Kate White. "Part of her ruthlessness was her sense of her own genius and decisiveness. . . . She had the perfect eye, and she knew it." Those who clearly didn't weren't worth the time.

On the other end of the spectrum, Carmel continued to stand up to Hearst. In 1937, she knocked down his barricade against allowing blacks into the magazine with consummate ease when she commissioned Munkacsi to photograph the contralto Marian Anderson. It took some doing. Hearst fought back—crassly, and in vain. "I won't have that nigger in my living room," he was reported to have said. Carmel must not have been listening: the photographer's efforts—a two-page spread in which the singer looked celestial—ran in the September issue.

That fall, for the first time, *Bazaar* added an extra midmonth issue, full of coverage of the fall Paris collections, with plans to do the same just after the spring showings in March. Readers of *Vogue,* which came out twice a month, had always been able to get the latest word from Paris in mid-September, while *Bazaar*'s readers had to wait until the following month. In 1937, for the first time, *Bazaar* was able to rush "eight pages of Openings" news into its September 1 issue, according to a *Life* magazine story published that month, but working at such a pace was hardly ideal. The magazine even showed the *Bazaar* office boy, Ulysses Armand, dashing to the gare du Nord with a package of photographs, destined for Le Havre, from where they'd be brought by the *Queen Mary* to New York, to be met by anxious editorial assistants waiting at the dock. (*Vogue*'s office boy was in the same photograph, a crucial few paces behind.) After Carmel neatly trumped *Vogue* by turning *Bazaar* into a fourteen-times-a-year publication, "*Vogue*'s editors gasped," the magazine reported. "Editor Chase rallied her team." All three *Vogue* editions had a combined circulation of 313,000 at this time, while *Harper's Bazaar* had a respectable 203,000 for both its American and British editions. (The latter, founded in 1929, existed independently of its U.S. counterpart, although it ran the same Paris pages, edited by Carmel.) The horse race between *Vogue* and *Bazaar* was closer than ever.

An ad in the September 1 issue, showing Carmel in a simple black dress with pearls, looking demure, delicately pretty, and far younger than her fifty years, trumpeted the issue's importance.

> *Carmel Snow, our editor-in-chief, has been in Paris since June, setting the stage for one of the most dramatic editorial feats in magazine history. Soon, in a special mid-month issue, she gives you the complete story of the recent openings, photographed, sketched, written, edited, on the spot, within sight and sound of the great dressmaking houses. It will be your fashion bible. You and everybody else you know will want it to study, quote and follow its advice on what's new in Paris and good in New York.*

The issue boasted a cover by Cassandre and a changed table of contents page, with a new typeface and logo. The Erté spell had begun to be broken the year before, when Brodovitch himself contributed a cover of a dressmaker's dummy—a recurring image in his work—for the February issue. Adolphe Mouron Cassandre, a Ukrainian whom Brodovitch had known for years, was another artist the art director had hunted down in Europe. His first cover, in March 1937, was captioned "The Key to the Paris Openings"; its imagery—an old-fashioned key, a swirling ribbon, clouds—was pure surrealism. The artist also favored obelisks, statues, floating eyes, and, shades of Paul Delvaux, women who looked as if they were in a trance.

Getting rid of Erté took some convincing. For Hearst, who had signed him to a long contract, he was synonymous with the magazine. "How would you know it was *Harper's Bazaar* without Erté?" he asked, after Carmel wrote to him in November 1936 with some suggested Cassandre cover art, seeking permission to offer a contract to this artist. Hearst replied the next month in a letter that said worlds about himself, his era—and the grudging respect he afforded *Bazaar*'s editor in chief. (Emphasis is Hearst's.)

I think the Cassandre covers are showy—let us say striking, as a more amiable word. I do not know exactly what they mean. I do not suppose it is necessary that I should know. I imagine modernistic art is not good if anybody does know what it means. The idea seems to be to draw something that everyone can put his own interpretation on.

This, then, is good modernistic art and will making [sic] a striking cover; and the twelve covers for the year will be furnished by the same artist in the same definitely incomprehensible style. Thus we will have continuity.

Harper's Bazaar announces its first mid-September Paris fashion issue, 1937

And most important of all, you like them. Therefore, I do not see why we should not go ahead on this basis.

Finally, I do not know of anybody who could do worse, unless it be Picasso; what I really mean is that I do not know anybody who could do better from a modernistic standpoint.

However, please do not ask me to express an opinion as to whether I like Cassandre better than Erté; because I like Erté better, and I would hate to have you know how wrong I am.

I think the little girl picking up the posies is very striking and very charming, and at the same time more or less understandable. That last defect makes it unavailable, no doubt; but otherwise I think it is good.

However I am definitely a back number. I do not like Picasso or any of that kind or crew.

I guess a lot of people do; and if they do, they may be overwhelmingly right. I did not like Roosevelt.

So it was a yes? Carmel terminated Erté's contract soon after. In his autobiography, Erté saves face by saying that he'd already asked to be released from his contract after realizing that something that had been a "challenging and rewarding arrangement had ended by becoming a frustrating chore." Like de Meyer, he would soon discover that his future was over, as far as American fashion magazines were concerned. Both approached *Vogue* at some point, but Chase would have no mercy, even on de Meyer, whose written entreaties from Hollywood bordered on the pathetic. "She found the idea of hiring either man absurd. Anyone who had ever worked for *Bazaar* was "tainted, in her view, forever."

Cassandre was not destined to spend too long at *Bazaar,* no artist was; magazines were increasingly choosing photographic covers over illustrated ones. In 1936, Nast noted that when a photograph ran on *Vogue*'s cover, newsstand sales increased exponentially, and he resolved to run ten such covers on the biweekly publication the following year. At about this time, Hearst began hinting to

Carmel that he'd also like to see a photographic cover on *Bazaar.* But for a while she and Brodovitch resisted.

Whatever one may think of Hearst and his "back number" taste, he undoubtedly spoke for some portion of *Bazaar*'s readership—an important voice for any editor to hear. (It's easy to forget that, in many quarters, even Picasso was controversial at this time.) In a letter written in late 1936, Hearst responded unenthusiastically to some of Brodovitch's innovations ("I do not believe in wasting blank space . . .") and to some of the magazine's contents.

> *The picture, "Schiaparelli's black wool ball-shaped cape," is to my mind awful. . . . The illustration looked to me like a picture of the "Iron Virgin" at Nurnberg [sic], which closed on its victim with iron spikes, and which is exhibited merely to produce a shudder.*

And then he asked, "Do you think it is necessary to make ugly pictures in order to be modern?"

It's easy to imagine Carmel glancing over this missive and, in her own devastatingly dismissive way, putting it down again, then turning her attention back to the task at hand. But she would have been wise to keep reading, for just a few sentences on, Hearst wrote, "I was interested in it" about one story he'd perused, before giving his grudging imprimatur to the magazine as a whole. "I think on the whole it is a good paper," he wrote. In Chief-speak, it was high praise.

8 *parallel lives*

I ran a three-ring circus, with my family, my work and my social life.

—Carmel Snow

AS CARMEL BUILT UP HER MAGAZINE FAMILY, life went on, of course, with her other family—the one she was actually related to—as well. The girls, nicknamed "the Snowdrops" by some of their relations, were growing up in East Norwich, attending the Green Vale School in the nearby town of Glen Head. Their mother spent most of her time working in New York, which she preferred: Long Island would always be more Palen's place than hers.

Rolling Hill Farm was idyllic in lots of ways. It sat on a hill, as its name implies, surrounded by farms and fields, and the house itself, which may have dated as far back as the eighteenth century, was cozy. There was a barn out back and, of course, Palen's beloved compost heap, "the thing he was most proud of," in one relative's words. "He thought it was sensational. He used to go down and look at it a lot." The house seemed made for small children, right down to the large dollhouse in the playroom, but their mother's absence most of the time was a continual source of tension, particularly for the Snows' eldest daughter, Carmel, who was often obliged to oversee her younger siblings while their mother was away. The elder Carmel was a Sunday presence, sometimes a formidable one, to her daughters, who remembered the luxury of spending mornings with her in and around her four-poster bed as she read the newspaper and decompressed after the working week. "They were beautifully brought up, but I don't think that came first in her life," in the words of Babs Simpson.

Snow family Christmas card, early 1930s

There were heartbreaking moments, too many from her daughters' point of view, times when she'd cancel evenings at the theater and other family treats at the last moment to accommodate work obligations of one sort or another. When she was at home she could seem tough, unnurturing. "It was a sink-or-swim atmosphere," a family member recalled. In this sense, her own household wasn't much different from the one in which she'd been raised. "It's in the genes of the Mayne women that they be business-oriented women, not family-oriented ones," as one of her Irish cousins, Veronica Freeman, says. "Carmel was more of a business lady than an affectionate mumsy type."

The pain of her absence was amplified by one simple, glaring fact: she was out of step with society. "It wasn't easy, working back then," said her niece Nancy White, a career woman who came along a generation later. "It wasn't *right* to work." To do so was to be "out of kilter with life as a woman," the fashion critic Bernadine Morris has said. A working, middle-class mother was a rare species in America in the 1930s and '40s. The few there were, like Carmel and Vreeland, must have learned to recognize the occasional iciness of those who, faced with a woman who went off to the office each day, tried them in absentia for going missing on the home front. Still, there's no evidence that either editor took such judgments to heart. Neither was the least bit introspective; guilt didn't seem to enter in.

Even for mothers who didn't work, at least those of a certain class, parenthood then was a much more distant business than it is today. There would be others at home—in the Snows' case a "wonderful maid called Nelly," in the words of their daughter Brigid, and a long sequence of governesses, the last one being a Miss Sperling—to whom the children would become attached. Parents tended to be less demonstrative then. Many of the Snows' time and social station had, to modern eyes, an almost shockingly formal relationship with their children. In some cases, they'd cross paths only in the evening, when, beautifully dressed and on their best behavior, they'd be ushered in for a brief visit with their parents before the latter headed out for an adult evening. And evenings out did seem more adult then. In New York, couples flocked to the Persian Room, the Stork Club, the St. Regis Roof, places to dine and dance, to see and be seen, to be gay in the now-archaic sense.

Such parties were a constant of Carmel's weekday life in New York. As the years went on, she often, but not always, attended them alone, including the glitzy opening of the Rainbow Room in Rockefeller Center in 1934. Magazine editors were far lower profile then—they were worker bees, not queens—still, it was important to make an appearance. And besides, Carmel adored it, turning up, costumed, at another benefit that year, one to benefit the Ecole des Beaux-Arts, the famous Paris school where her brother Victor had been trained. Palen also loved stepping out—"he loved to do the social thing, and so did Mummy," in Brigid's words. Sometimes he'd accompany Carmel, sometimes not. Many social columns list her simply as Mrs. George Palen Snow; Palen was presumably off hunting, boating, fishing, or at home with their daughters and garden in East Norwich. "They lived separate lives, although they did not live apart," as their daughter described it.

When Carmel joined the Hearst family, that company, too, became a family affair. Hearst was an enormous presence in the life of her brother Tom, who was continuing up the ladder of the organization, having been named its first general manager in the spring of 1934. It wasn't an easy task.

> *It was White's job to restore health to the Hearst empire of now twenty-seven newspapers, ten magazines, assorted radio stations and real estate holdings, and a vast art collection. . . . With the Hearst empire close to bankruptcy, White had to cut budgets, consolidate papers, and eliminate losers.*

Everyone seemed to get pulled in. Tom even wrote frantically to his young daughter Nancy at one point, entreating her to help him suggest a birthday present for Hearst—a man who had everything, if anyone did.

> *Would you be thinking for me, dear, and if you want to consult your Aunt Carmel or anybody so that I might strike something for a birthday present for Mr. Hearst. His birthday is on the 29th and, in thinking of a suitable present for him, please bear in mind that he is even older than you are.*

(A joke, of course: Nancy was barely out of her teenage years.)

By the mid-1930s, the Snows were firmly established as hotel hoppers during the week, decamping from the Ritz Tower to the Waldorf-Astoria Towers in the mid-1930s, then back again to the Ritz, where they settled into a suite, more an apartment with amenities, room service, and more. It was their first permanent-seeming city residence since their marriage and, in a sense, it was all in the family, since Hearst had bought the building (disastrously, as it would turn out) back in the 1920s. He and Davies spent the winter of 1936–37 there and frequently, when they were at loose ends for an evening, they'd call down to the Snows' suite to ask them up for dinner. One evening, Carmel and Palen had a prior commitment—"a particularly stuffy dinner party for some very old New York friends of Palen's," as Carmel described it. Hearst, with his empire of yellow newspapers, illicit relationship, and outspoken, even ranting, editorials was anathema in such circles (Vreeland's father, for example, simply refused to acknowledge that his daughter worked for the notorious publisher). Even so, Carmel, impulsively and probably relishing the fireworks to come, suggested that Hearst and Davies come along.

The foursome was greeted by "stiff head bows." Could have been worse. But when Marion began regaling the rest of the company with stories of the notorious Mrs. Simpson and her besotted king—none of which had yet been made public—she had the group, stuffy or not, firmly in the palm of her hand. They may have been scandalized by her tales, and the notorious woman who told them—a rich man's mistress, and a B-movie actress at that—but they left the evening informed, perhaps even charmed.

There were other familiar faces in the building, too, all, like Carmel, in need of a pied-à-terre in Manhattan, among them her brother Tom White, who had given up his Park Avenue apartment, and Jack Neylan, also of Hearst. At some point, not quite by coincidence, the notoriously difficult Eleanor "Cissy" Patterson, who was then both editor and publisher of the *Washington Times,* the first female to hold such a position on a major American newspaper, also moved in.

Hearst was in desperate financial shape at this point, so much so that, by the next winter, "the old boy never came down from the top of the Ritz Tower—apparently there were always creditors downstairs," according to Vreeland. The building itself was part of the problem: by 1937, Hearst was losing $500,000 a year on it alone. Unable to sell it at $6 million, he discontinued mortgage payments on the place, effectively returning it to the bank. With a total debt of $126 million—a truly terrifying sum—Hearst, then seventy-five, gave up financial control of his company. By 1938, he was divesting with a vengeance, selling off holdings that ranged from newspapers to works of art (no Picassos among them, needless to say). He even, with great reluctance, put St. Donat's on the market, where it sat unsold for ages, "a white elephant, eating up good Organization dollars for maintenance, until the British government requisitioned it for use as an officers' training center."

In spite of all this, Hearst continued at the helm of the publications he still controlled, and he continued to live his outsize life, notably at San Simeon, where the cast-of-thousands, weeks-long parties went on. Edna Chase of all people, one of his archrival's top editors, even turned up at one in 1938, escorting her daughter Ilka, who'd befriended Marion Davies. It was a strange circumstance, but, by all accounts, Hearst and the elder Chase maintained a formal cordiality throughout her stay. There was, presumably, little magazine chat between them.

In the winter of 1937, Carmel's niece Nancy came to stay with the Snows at the Ritz during what her aunt called her "coming-out season"—a concept that may seem quaint to us now, but was then a thing of high seriousness. The point was to go from dance to dance, ball to ball, meeting as many young, marriageable bachelors as possible. Other debutantes, no doubt, lived in grander New York abodes than her aunt and uncle's part-time one, but surely none was as exciting! Nancy later told her aunt that the sight of one of her houseguests, the elegant surrealist Salvador Dalí—now happily, and lucratively, contributing to *Bazaar*—with his trademark twirled mustache, had scared off more than one of her suitors.

Nancy White had warm memories of that stay, and of an aunt who, in spite of her relative scarcity on the home front, remained at the center of the extended family's life. "It was she and Palen and their children and Uncle Victor and Aunt Margot and they'd all come to our house for Thanksgiving and we'd go to Carmel's maybe on our way home from the country on Sunday night. We were a close family. . . ."

White never forgot her aunt's generosity to her as a child.

> *I still have a little comb in there when Carmel said "Take something." She had so many gifts. . . . I mean, she was wonderful with children. I can remember going to visit her as I did frequently and I had my elder daughter with me. And I can't remember what it was all about, but Carmel said, "I will do something." And I said, "Don't worry about it." And she said, "Nancy, never disappoint a child." And that was very like her. She was very caring. . . ."*

Even when he was eleven years old, it was clear to Frederick Vreeland, Diana's oldest son, that Carmel was a special kind of adult.

I was aware that this was rather a magical lady, quite fey. All of that was clear to me, that this was a slightly mad lady who was really fascinating . . . She stood very erect, she had stature. She had sort of an aura about her—and I think she never took her gloves off.

As the younger generation was coming up, so an older one was passing. Annie Douglass's health had begun to deteriorate in late 1934. Later on, in a letter, Tom White exhorted his daughters, Nancy and Carmel, to visit, adding that "Carmel, who is almost as busy as any of us, does manage to visit once or twice a week with her." Carmel must have by then recognized that, whatever her differences with her demanding parent, the two were cut from very similar cloth. "Aunt Carmel's genius was in her eye and her taste," as her niece Kate White puts it. "In a sense, that's what her mother had this line on, just this perfect taste. I think she inherited her mother's eye and taste and her sense of her mother's domination and assuredness." Douglass's approval was never quite forthcoming, at least as far as her daughters were concerned. Christine was by then the editor of *Better Homes & Gardens*—a rival to Hearst's *House Beautiful*—working from her home state of Iowa. "When we both made a success of our careers my mother said complacently, 'Naturally, after the education I gave you!'"

Douglass rallied, but fell ill again the following year. She was hospitalized at Harbor Sanitarium, the same hospital where Carmel's children had been born, on May 7, 1936. On her deathbed, she displayed the determination that had characterized her entire life, clinging to life until all of her children, scattered across the American continent, could be at her bedside. She died, two days later, on May 9. A funeral was held for her at the Lady Chapel of St. Patrick's Cathedral on May 11 and she was buried later that day at St. Patrick's Cemetery in Smithtown, Long Island, not far from Tom and Virginia's home. Where once she'd been featured in the *New York Times* and was so prominent a businesswoman that she was frequently quoted there, she was obscure enough after years of retirement not even to merit an obituary in the same paper. Her will divided the bulk of her $328,149 estate, a tidy sum in that era, among her six offspring. Late that year, Carmel wrote to Tom to commend his wife, Virginia, on how she'd tended the site. "The grave couldn't be lovelier. We should be so grateful to her," adding that all the White siblings "who could afford it" should share in the cost of the grave's upkeep. "I certainly feel I should."

It was typical of Tom's wife to have taken on such a task: Virginia was always doing things for her family. Her husband traveled ceaselessly and, somewhere along the way, had become involved with Cissy Patterson, whose family owned and operated the *Chicago Tribune*—the very same woman who had suddenly taken an apartment in the Ritz Tower. Both she and Tom White worked for Hearst; in this capacity, "he and Cissy had crossed swords often and earned each other's respect." He'd known her for some time and had even, at some point, engineered a job at *Bazaar*'s Paris office for her daughter, Felicia. Patterson was a larger-than-life, emotionally exhausting millionairess with enormous personal style. She was charming, a big drinker, and she adored men. In fact, she devoured them, according to her friend Arthur Brisbane, the newspaper editor and columnist, who once described her as a "boa constrictor." As soon as she set her sights on White, who was nothing if not susceptible to charming women, the course their friendship would take became clear. Their affair began in the mid-1930s in Cissy's private Pullman car on a trip to San Simeon. White rode with her to California from Chicago, then came back east in the same way; it's safe to say that by the time he alighted from her railway car, he was a goner. "Again and again, thanks, thanks, thanks, and a long restful sleep to you," he wrote to her.

For Patterson it was full speed ahead. "For a large man, he is very quick on his feet and I don't know whether I can catch him," she confided to Brisbane. After turning up at the Ritz Tower to be near him, she moved on to a rented house overlooking Manhattan's leafy, exquisite Gramercy Park, so that her paramour might feel even more at home. It wasn't long before, as Ralph G. Martin writes in a perhaps-too-imaginative passage, "White's monogrammed pajamas were neatly folded in the bedroom bureaus. . . ." The reader will get the picture.

As a Catholic, Tom would never have considered divorce, in any case, and for whatever reason, he opted to remain married—another Hearst tradition. Their affair was steamy, and thrilling at first, but it could remain only that.

> *Brisbane reminded Cissy of the realities of her situation. He and Hearst, and everyone else, would wink at a casual affair with Tom White, but a serious romance would be regarded with grave disapproval. White had a wife and five children, and he was a distinguished Catholic layman, firmly opposed to divorce.*
>
> *Cissy knew all this and did not care. She even smiled wryly when Brisbane invited her to "supply the intellectual brilliancy, youth, verve, savoir faire and PEP" by joining him and Tom White and Mrs. White for lunch at the Colony.*

Patterson didn't go to the lunch; had she done so, she would no doubt have been impressed. From the outset, Virginia handled the situation with almost unbelievable dignity. She seemed to become stronger and stronger, as a lifetime of letters to and from her husband and children demonstrates. She sent frequent updates on the progress of their children, not to mention an intricate constellation of other relatives, to her husband as he traveled, apparently ceaselessly, for work, pleasure, sometimes both, sometimes on Hearst's private train, sometimes on Cissy's. "He was always in New York or in California, in Wyntoon or San Simeon," his daughter Carmel White Eitt recalls.

Even so, he still managed to spend time with Patterson.

> *Although White had a family to look after and the Hearst empire to manage, he played an increasingly important role in Cissy's life. He advised her on the rental of her Sands Point home, her income tax, her newspaper business problems, he sent her books to read. . . .*

In the early fall of 1936, the couple sailed to Europe together, combining a romantic holiday with business. Cissy, who had spent part of her childhood in Paris, claimed that she wanted to attend the collections in order to write about them for her paper. Tom introduced her to his sister Carmel, who said, "You will surely fall in love with my brother. Everybody falls in love with my brother Tom." Her much-vaunted intuition must have been operating on overdrive. In any case, Cissy didn't miss a beat, answering sassily, "Well, you should meet my brother Joe." Tom and Patterson spent time with William Bullitt, a friend of Cissy's for decades, who had been named ambassador to France that year and had since become "more French than the French themselves," according to another friend, Harold Ickes, then Roosevelt's secretary of the interior. The couple visited him in his sumptuous chateau in Chantilly; when Tom went off on business-related trips, "Bullitt took Cissy to elaborate balls and entertainments. He revived Cissy's memories of their Riviera romance, and then he wooed her again."

> *Patterson toyed with both, weighing one against the other.*
>
> *Bullitt was in his element, and White was not. Bullitt was the more brilliant and White the warmer of the two. Compared with the sophisticated Bullitt, White seemed like an old shoe. Whenever she compared them, Cissy realized that she far preferred White. But in one important area Bullitt had an edge: while White was married, he was not.*

The two men became increasingly infuriated with the situation until Tom stormed away altogether, presumably returning home—where, as always, he'd been gravely missed. "He was always away working," his daughter Carmel recalled, remembering the desolation she and her siblings felt when, one Christmas, "Mr. Hearst snapped his fingers," and her father never quite made it home. "It was such a body blow to the family."

Ultimately, Bullitt proposed, but Cissy turned him down, loath to abandon her position in newspaper publishing for the formal and, she feared, stultifying role of a diplomat's wife. Back in the United States, her relationship with Tom resumed its turbulent course. Their paths became even more intertwined after 1938, when he was named chairman of Hearst. The publisher's financial situation had become desperate. When Patterson, crucially, offered Chief a loan at one point, it was White who took her million-dollar check in hand on Hearst's behalf, whispering "God bless you" to her as he did so. More installments would follow. In 1939, Patterson gave the down-on-his-luck publisher another timely influx of cash by buying both Washington papers he owned, the *Times* and the *Herald,* merging both into the *Washington Times-Herald.*

In that same year, Tom was named president and general manager of Hearst's *Chicago Herald-American;* he was also vice president of Hearst Publishing, general manager of the *New York Journal-American,* and supervising director of the *Pittsburgh Sun-Telegraph.* It was a promotion, to be sure, but a further death knell to his family life. Although he traveled ceaselessly, his main office from this point on was in Chicago. Given his continuing involvement with Patterson, the separation may have worked to his advantage. In any case, from this point on he maintained a residence in the Midwest, as well as the family residence on Long Island.

Although Patterson knew that White was married, she still, in the late 1930s, found herself wishing that he was not. She was a tough businesswoman and she took a businesslike approach to the problem. In the late 1930s, she asked Mrs. White to meet her at the Carleton House in New York. Patterson told a friend afterward that she'd gotten dressed up for the occasion and prepared speeches in advance. She planned to talk about how White needed his freedom and how "it's bigger than all of us," but such words vanished the minute she was ushered into the presence of the calm, matronly Virginia White. "I forgot all of the speeches, and I just said, 'But you see, I *love* him.'" Mrs. White answered, without hesitation, "So do I." Patterson is even said to have offered Virginia a million dollars—for her husband!—but was refused.

At some point, White did try to leave Patterson, according to one relative, but "she simply wouldn't let go of him," Julie Groupp recalls. Still, things between them became distant enough that White moved on to a flirtation with the cosmetics magnate Elizabeth Arden (probably not a full-blown affair, in the opinion of her biographer), with whom he kept company in the late 1930s and early '40s. This particular friendship was irksome to Carmel, and not just because it may have offended her morally: it also cost her magazine some advertising. When Arden's rival, Helena Rubinstein, got wind of the relationship, "she mistrusted the lines of communication [at *Bazaar*] and turned her attention to *Vogue* and the Condé Nast Magazines" instead.

It may have crossed Carmel's mind at some point that her brother's marriage wasn't entirely dissimilar to her own: increasingly, she and Palen ran on parallel tracks, intersecting only infrequently. In the mid-1930s they traveled to Ireland, in part so that she could introduce her daughters to her beloved grandmother Susannah Mayne. Forty years had passed since Carmel and her siblings had scampered about the house and property at Cremorne; the house had long been sold, but its former mistress lived well into her nineties. To Carmel's dismay, their visit came too late: she had news of her grandmother's death, in the Dublin suburb of Blackrock, in a letter from a relative, just before the family set sail. The matriarch's obituary in a Dublin newspaper claimed her as a nationalist, pointing out that her husband, Thomas Mayne, had supported Parnell "and stood by his side, to the end."

Still, Carmel brought the Snows en masse to see other relatives and friends, including her aunt Agnes, Susannah's sister, then almost a hundred. Whenever she came to Ireland, there "was a big fuss in the family, with people putting on dinners," one cousin, Joan Regan, recalls. "They were delighted to be related to such a famous person. They were very proud of her and very envious of her wealth." Her Irish relatives were plentiful, and some were regular recipients of her largesse. They eagerly awaited her packages, which would be full of Paris clothes. "Every so often a gift box would arrive with clothes from Carmel," recalls another cousin, Veronica Freeman. "Sometimes the most gorgeous party dresses for me." Her mother, Elizabeth Cullen Hanlon, the daughter-in-law of Claire Mayne Hanlon, one of Annie

Douglass's sisters, was a great Celtic beauty, with such stunning dark looks that she was said to have once been offered a film contract in Hollywood. Betty Hanlon was "a huge favorite of Carmel's," her daughter recalls, and "she wore the clothes with great élan." Her couture wardrobe was the envy of the family, Freeman adds; they'd be "raging, not that they had the figures and looks to wear them."

For years, Carmel used to stay in the suburb of Ranelagh with her aunt Agnes, the same aunt who, long ago, had accompanied her mother to the world's fair; she'd since married and become Agnes McQuaid (one of her stepchildren would become the archbishop of Ireland). After her aunt died and her own fortunes rose, Carmel moved on to the Shelbourne, the majestic old hotel on Dublin's leafy St. Stephen's Green. There, Carmel entertained her relatives at high tea in the famous high-ceilinged, damask-wallpapered tearoom on the hotel's ground floor, where genteel Dubliners feast on pastries beneath an enormous crystal chandelier, accompanied by live piano music. Veronica Freeman has an abiding memory of being taken in her teenage years by her mother to tea with Carmel, who was dressed "in a Chanel-type suit with mauve-colored hair and long, long cyclamen pink nails. She was very, very elegant." Carmel may well have stayed at the Shelbourne on this trip with Palen, and there were, no doubt, family teas. One cousin recalls that "she was sophisticated, full of life in a very American way. She was the life of the couple." Like other Irish relatives, this one was less taken with Palen. "When he came here he was written off as totally uninteresting," she adds; another cousin describes him, unflatteringly, in a uniquely Irish way: "No top story," she says.

On their 1937 trip, the Snow's social rounds included a meeting with an extraordinary character named Oliver Gogarty, the inspiration behind James Joyce's Buck Mulligan. There were other various glamorous bits of flotsam and jetsam from the magazine world around then, too, including Lady Cavendish—who had often turned up in *Bazaar*'s pages under her maiden name, Adele Astaire, and was then residing at Lismore Castle in the south. For Palen, it was a horsey time—he took the girls to the Dublin Horse Show and delighted in the fishing in County Donegal, an area Carmel also adored: "For me any place on the coast of Ireland is heaven." They returned home to news of another death: Ma Dear, with whom Carmel had had a complicated relationship, died at eighty-three on September 16, 1937, in Asheville, North Carolina, near her Aiken home. She was buried at St. John's Church in Cold Spring Harbor two days later.

The next year, in 1938, Palen, who had occasionally dabbled in real estate development, bought a row of eight tenement structures, called, more genteelly, "low buildings" in Carmel's memoir, on East Seventy-second Street, overlooking the East River, and set to work upgrading them. They were remarkably undistinguished, clones of thousands of other such apartments, built all over New York City to accommodate the poor, many of them, in those days, immigrants from Germany and Ireland. But Palen swept the more depressing accoutrements of such housing—bathtubs in the kitchen, and the like—away. "The architects Sacchetti & Siegel designed an alteration that gutted and combined the eight tenements into four buildings with two-, three-, and four-bedroom apartments of simple finish, many with wood-burning fireplaces," as Christopher Gray has written in the *New York Times.* Other amenities were far from the tenement norm, included built-in bookcases, floor-to-ceiling mirrors, and maids' rooms.

Moving out of the Ritz Tower, the Snows took what Carmel called "the prize apartment" at 541 East Seventy-second Street—a high-ceilinged duplex with rows of windows overlooking the river—for themselves. Carmel always loved a large main room, and this one seemed enormous. (But then her living rooms always tended to be, according to Brigid Flanigan. "Mummy always knocked all the walls down, to the horror of my father.") "It was meant to be a pied-à-terre," Carmel wrote. "There was one very long room on the entrance floor where we dined at one end, with a kitchen and a maid's room and bath. A stairway led down . . . to a large master bedroom and bath." It's not true, as has been reported, that the Snows filled the other apartments with privileged friends, many of whom had also lost money in the crash, as an act of charity; for Palen, it was still a business proposition. But it is true that those who gravitated to these apartments, and

The Snows and Whites gather in Ireland, mid-1930s. *Back row, left to right:* Tom White, Christine White, Victor White, Carmel Snow, Nancy White, Palen Snow, Desmond White, James White. *Front row:* Carmel Snow, Brigid Snow, Mary Palen Snow.

some were indeed their friends, tended to be social—"This was a new building type, the Social Register tenement," in Christopher Gray's droll assessment—and, like the Snows, less moneyed than they'd once been. They may not have been poor, exactly, but they'd had to curtail themselves, financially, as the Depression rolled on.

The buildings were painted black and white, perhaps inspired by another set of converted buildings with similarly painted facades just to the south, in the newly developed Sutton Place, designed by the interior designer Dorothy Draper (and later featured in *Bazaar* as her "smart idea" for "repackaging shabby brownstones"). There was a cobblestoned plaza out front surrounded by benches and trees. Although Carmel is credited with having influenced the building's look, there's no evidence that she was very involved. Perhaps it was she who, with her great awareness of design, brought the Draper structures to the attention of her husband, who then adopted their distinctive color scheme for his own venture. In any case, the row of houses that Palen developed is known to this day as "the Black and Whites" by some of its residents and, even more obscurely, as "Snow Village."

One of the first tenants was a friend of Carmel's named Katharine Loines, whose daughter, Margot Wilkie, recalls attending a lunch at Manhattan's Cosmopolitan Club where Carmel talked animatedly and with contagious enthusiasm about the venture. "She was encouraging people to think well of it. I know that she felt like an adventurer and that she was making something beautiful." Certainly she did so in the apartment's interior, which she filled with beautiful objects, some of lofty provenance, but plenty that were not. As Carmel wrote:

> *After the years spent in hotel suites it was far pleasanter to have my own things around me, including some of my mother's beautiful furniture and glass, and since I've never given up the flowered chintzes I love, and since flowers and open fires are a permanent part of my decor, the long room had a "country feeling" that my city friends enjoyed. It was the setting for many successful parties over the years.*

The result, as in all her homes, was a fresh, country look—"light, bright, with lots of yellow," in the words of one visitor. The effect was "quite simple," but arresting, another says. "She turned everything into something attractive," adds a third. "She had this God-given talent. . . . She had an extraordinary taste about things in life."

The apartment overlooked the river, with its endlessly fascinating movement and light. Carmel had window seats installed so that you could sit and watch, and eschewed the use of curtains altogether. Instead she added lambrequins, shaped boards that cover the top and sides of a window frame, "like theatrical cutouts," in Richard Avedon's words. Ever fond of chintzes, she had them upholstered in the same fabric as her Billy Baldwin–designed couches, which had a beige background with pink flowers and green leaves. The effect was "understated, with a great sense of color," Avedon said, calling it a "lesson in coziness." In later years, she added an unforgettable accessory, the model Mary Jane Russell recalled. "She had little finches that would flutter around and have total freedom. She had little boxes of Kleenex around the room and if the birds had a dropping while she was there she'd have a Kleenex ready and quickly dispose of it."

The East River is hardly the Seine; even then the view across the polluted waterway, with the often-homely structures of Queens across the way, could be distinctly unlovely. There was a roar to it, too: cars tore up the highway, now known as the FDR, that ran along the riverbank. Still, the light and the waterway activity—tugboats, ferries—had a kind of magic to them, providing a respite from the asphalt of Manhattan. The dining area was part of the great room, and Carmel recalled the family watching boats going by during dinner. It was just enough off the beaten track to convey a sense of being "alone at the end of the world," as a superintendent who worked at the complex later put it.

In the early years of the Snows' marriage, when they still had young children, the summers were punctuated by long trips, even though, "to be truthful, I never cared for vacations," Carmel said. (No surprise there.) They might head out west to a ranch or up to Maine's Waspy Dark Harbor, a place where Palen also traditionally went on his own, often spending two weeks at a local inn called the Pendleton while Carmel worked the collections. As the children got older, they were sometimes given the choice between accompanying their father there or going to the Paris openings with their mother. They mainly chose Maine. At first, his wife's long absences weren't easy for Palen to navigate: even as late as the early 1930s, he'd seemed at loose ends during one of his wife's long sojourns in France, his brother-in-law Tom White recounted in a letter to his mother. But time apart, lots of it, began to pattern their lives. Carmel and Palen were far distant in their interests, always. Her trips, her endless preoccupation with life beyond the family, only widened a rift that was there all along.

Carmel was more apt to travel with one or more of her daughters than her husband. She once took her eldest, Carmel, and a young friend to Paris, where they accompanied her as she roamed the fashion houses. The return trip was almost uneventful, except for the usual tension over contraband as she entered the United

States. Smuggling was a misdemeanor under Section 593 of the Tariff Act of 1922, with very real consequences, including fines of up to $5,000, a two-year jail sentence, or both. But none of that worried Carmel, who instructed the girls to cut out the labels on their purchases—including fur-trimmed pantalettes from Piguet that Carmel abhorred—so that no duty would have to be paid. The labels, of course, were formidable, from the best Paris fashion houses, and the girls plotted to keep them as souvenirs. When a Customs officer asked young Carmel to open an eyeglass case, she forgot that it contained the forbidden labels, then watched in horror as "they fluttered down agonizingly slowly," as she described it. The day was saved when her friend, "with split-second timing . . . bent down, scooped up all the labels, and shoved them in her coat pockets." This close call didn't deter her mother at all. She would ask almost anyone to smuggle for her, even roping photographers into the cause, as Gleb Derujinsky discovered one year in Paris, when she handed him label-less dresses by Balenciaga and Givenchy to pack with his things.

It's no wonder that Dorothy Monger used to tease her boss for stopping off at St. Patrick's Cathedral "to say a little prayer of thanks for a safe journey," as she always did at the end of each trip; Dorothy insisted that such gratitude was really inspired by the fact that she'd gotten away with it, once again, as a smuggler. But it could have been any number of reasons: in Manhattan, as in Paris, Carmel seemed to pop into churches at the slightest provocation. As she once said to an editor, "Do you think I could bear all I have to if I didn't stop for a prayer daily?" Many on her staff had the experience of hurtling along with her in a New York taxi, on the way to one appointment or another, when she'd have the cab screech to a halt so that she could dash into a house of worship to pray. The Saint Jean Baptiste Roman Catholic Church, strategically located at Seventy-sixth Street and Lexington Avenue, almost equidistant between home and work, was a favorite.

There were ski trips up to Mont Tremblant in Quebec, an activity that Carmel was hopeless at, as she was at most sports; her sister-in-law Dotsie Nicholas, whom the girls called Aunt Dulcie and who was athletic, like the other

Snows, exclaimed over the "startling effect of my blue curls tumbled in the snow." And, when skiing, that's the position she found herself in most often. (Other Snows, by contrast, tended to remain upright.) Palen often traveled with his male friends in pursuit of something sporting—hunting, fishing, sailing, golf—and, according to some relatives, female companionship, too. "He had nice lady friends that he took out and they went shooting to Scotland," one of these recalled. (As for Carmel, there was never any hint that she had affairs. She was far too Catholic, not to mention in a hurry, for that.) "Mummy had her life and he had his," as their daughter Brigid Flanigan puts it. And it all seemed to work.

Like a migrating bird, Carmel would nest in East Norwich most summers, driven by Davis, the family chauffeur, to work in the city, as required. There were family outings to Jones Beach, also on Long Island, which was then a much less overrun destination than it is today. A family friend, William "Tish" Rand III, recalls watching "Poppy Snow" cook one of his specialties, scalloped potatoes with a creamed sauce, over an outdoor fire, while the Snows' springer spaniel dug messily in the nearby sand, adding an unexpected, and not particularly edible, element to the dish.

Carmel's daughters "all had this great charm," according to a *Bazaar* editor, Laura Pyzel Clark. Their childhoods were very different from Carmel's, almost as if they were being groomed to be as unlike her as possible. It was important to her that they be athletic and/or good horsewomen, for example, and she raised them in a way that was far more sheltered than her own childhood had been. They went with their nannies to exclusive Long Island clubs—the Lawrence Beach Club, the Piping Rock—where they played tennis and swam. Brigid was particularly athletic. "Mummy and Daddy's son died, so I was the boy." Her father taught her to hunt and fish, both of which she adored, and she recalls Pa Dear, her paternal grandfather, saying, approvingly, "She shoots well in the field and she casts a wonderful fly." But such sports-mindedness didn't necessarily pass down to the next generation, as yet another Carmel, Carmel Fromson, one of Carmel Snow's granddaughters, recalled.

Our mother never pushed us athletically with any lessons like that because she didn't want to do to us what her mother did to her and her two sisters, which was to schedule them beyond belief with activities of all kinds, like riding and tennis, especially in the summer.

Work and home mixed at lunches and dinners on Long Island, where Palen's country club friends and Carmel's colleagues would gather on the weekends. The difference between the two camps could be glaring: the Snows were "all sort of shabbily dressed, not nattily dressed," Kate White says. "Palen was old, old, family society, while Carmel's crowd tended to be chicer, more café society." Family members would turn up, particularly Tom and Victor White and their families, who lived nearby, and there'd be various Hearst people as well, editors and even the occasional representatives of the dreaded "Fifty-seventh street." One was Dick Berlin, who became president of the Hearst Corporation in 1943, whom Carmel describes as "a close family friend" although he was often also her bitter adversary. Berlin's wife, Honey, was a socialite who counted the Duchess of Windsor among her closest friends. Like most of Hearst's top crew, the Berlins lived extremely well, with a massive apartment on Fifth Avenue and a summer compound on Canada's Murray Bay.

The Snows' Long Island friends were "not so interesting as Mummy's," Brigid Flanigan says. "You could say they were a bit stuffy." Sometimes the two camps looked at each other across great gulfs. "I was one of the few people who could get along with Palen because of the boredom factor," says Eleanor Perényi, editor, writer, and avid gardener. "We had compost heaps and things in common. I was usually put next to him at dinner because we could talk about compost heaps and things. He was one of the dullest men who ever lived." (Perényi, who'd married a Hungarian baron as a teenager, then written about the experience in a 1946 memoir, was anything but boring herself.) The couple's differing styles were striking to Perényi and others at the magazine. "They had four children and no one could imagine how."

Nancy, Carmel's niece, recalls one family lunch when Diana Vreeland arrived, festooned, as always, with armloads of jangly ivory bracelets. Gazing upon this apparition, one of the Snow daughters, young at the time, exclaimed, "Mommy, she should really have a ring in her nose!" Generally, though, the girls were quite used to strange and talented people wandering loose. "We just learned to accept the wonderful photographers" who stopped by, Flanigan says, recalling that Horst became a frequent visitor after he began contributing to *Bazaar.* (He later bought a house in nearby Oyster Bay.) "He always slept on the porch. He had a sleeping bag but he never came inside. I don't know why." Carmel often invited *Bazaar* contributors home. "Some day—more than anything in the world—I hope that you will come out and meet Carmel, Mary Palen and Brigid," she gushed in a letter to the writer Katherine Anne Porter in 1941. "They are really divine and the husband is very nice too."

The daughters were exposed to all of it. "It was a fascinating life," Flanigan says. They took for granted the idea that famous couturiers would design their party dresses and that their annual photo Christmas cards—three immaculate, beautifully dressed daughters, growing taller and taller—would be taken by a famous photographer (Toni Frissell, say, or Louise Dahl-Wolfe). These were disseminated far and wide. One *Bazaar* editor had a cynical reaction to the card the Snows sent one year, taken by the photographer Paul Radkai and showing the family gathered at East Norwich. "Old Snowy was stretched out and Mrs. Snow was embroidering or something. It looked like the most peaceful party in the world, but the truth is that she was never there."

Of her numerous nieces and nephews, Carmel was probably closest to her brother Tom's daughters, Nancy and Carmel White. Nancy, the eldest, was Carmel's goddaughter, a fact that drove her sister wild with jealously. "I'd argue that Aunt Carmel should be *my* godmother," says her niece Carmel. Aunt Carmel was like a fairy godmother, her sister Nancy recalled.

> *She was just incredibly special. There was an aura to Aunt Carmel that was really remarkable. She'd capture people instantly and she never lost her Irish accent, none of those six children did. My father spoke with a wonderful burr. . . .*

She was tiny and delicate. Nancy and I were five foot seven or so and we towered over her when we were in high heels. She was probably no more than five foot four and she couldn't have weighed more than a hundred pounds. . . .

She had this unique way of walking down the street with you. She'd hug you close, wrapping her forearm around you. She'd always put you on the outside of the sidewalk towards the curb. She'd lean against us and we'd end up with our feet in the gutter. We'd be talking constantly and leaning over and pulling ourselves out of the gutter.

Both girls traveled to Paris at separate times with their aunt. Nancy went when she was just seventeen, accompanying Carmel to the 1934 collections where her aunt put her to work as a completely unglorified errand girl. Nancy's fashion sense had been commented on in the family since her infancy when, according to her sister, "She sat up with the bonnet beautifully placed and from there on she was slated to follow Aunt Carmel." Their trip to Paris inspired her choice of a magazine career—a fact that must have felt bittersweet to Carmel later on. "I remember the joy of watching my aunt ordering hats from Reboux, or Agnes," Nancy once wrote. "I can still feel the excitement of the moment when I fell in love with a coat at Marcel Rochas and Aunt Carmel approved my choice!"

Young Carmel also traveled to Europe with her aunt, in her case to a convent when she was twelve, after "it was decided because I have an ear for languages that I should go off to Europe." Since Carmel was going to Paris for the month, she accompanied the girl to the Pensionnat de Notre Dame in Verneuil-sur-Seine, forty miles outside of Paris, where the young Carmel White, as she was then known, would be spending the year. Years later, when the charismatic young girl became an actress, her aunt was one of her biggest supporters; in May 1939, she accompanied her siblings Tom and Christine to *Kiss the Boys Good-Bye,* a Broadway play in which young Carmel had a part. (To commemorate her role, her proud aunt duly had her portrait taken by Dahl-Wolfe for *Bazaar.*) The fact that

Carmel, Palen, Brigid, and young Carmel at Rolling Hill Farm, Long Island, 1950s

she shared her aunt's name caused certain complications, the actress discovered during this play's run, when the entire cast was invited to a party at Condé Nast's penthouse. "It was so awkward to have the same name and to be accepted into his apartment on Park Avenue," she recalled. "I kept thinking I'd be ushered out." (She wasn't.)

Both girls adored their aunt Car, but she could be brutal, as they both knew. Once, at a family gathering at the Old Mill, Tom and Virginia White's home in Smithtown, Long Island, during a time in her life when she "was hardly the fashion queen," according to young Carmel, her aunt "took one look at me and said 'Car dear, when you want to go shopping next, why don't you call me up and ask me to go with you?' My jaw dropped, it was so deadly." At another party, Carmel let loose on the young girl for the way she wore her hair. She complimented her sister Nancy's style, while denigrating young Carmel's, adding, lethally: "Look at your sister, she's as ugly as an old mud fence, but she does the best with what she has." Nancy, stoically, didn't react then or later, but her surviving siblings were still discussing it—shocked—half a century on. "I think it was the martinis speaking," Carmel White Eitt mused, recalling the scene. It may well have been true. They would talk more frequently, and louder, as time went on.

9 *descending into war*

It is really a commonplace war, since it is simply a fight for liberty.

—Janet Flanner

THE LATE 1930S WERE A TIME OF TRIUMPH AT *BAZAAR.* As Frances McFadden once wrote:

> *On a spring Monday morning Carmel would blow in from the country where she spent weekends with her children, arms full of lilacs, an adorable potato chip Suzy on her blue curls, ready to take on anything. She could trust her blarney to get her out of trouble and she knew she had a big success on her hands.*

That success translated into numbers. From the time Carmel began to work there, the number of its readers had increased from 104,910, in 1932, to 191,333 in the second half of 1938. It was an ecumenical audience: as the magazine itself announced "more men read *Harper's Bazaar* than any other women's magazine," in part, they theorized, "because anyone, man or woman, cannot fail to be excited by the quality of the photography." If the magazine looked the way it did, it was because of Carmel and Brodovitch, far more than Vreeland, who wasn't particularly informed about photography. "If she was going to run a catalogue she'd be happy," one former contributor sniped. "She just wanted to get those damned dresses on a page." Lillian Bassman, a former fashion illustrator who joined Brodovitch's staff as an assistant art director in 1941, recalled hearing Carmel express something similar. "She said to me, 'You know, Diana is a great fashion editor but never let her choose a photo." Vreeland's focus—her genius—was for clothes, and for this she was indispensable. Both she and Carmel stalked the fashion; the look of the book was Carmel and Brodovitch's domain.

Like a Munkacsi photo, this troika—Carmel, Brodovitch, Vreeland—came alive through motion. The three ricocheted among the art department, the fashion department, and Carmel's office, their talk eternally centered on the next story, the next fashion spread. Brodovitch wanted shots that had "journalistic impact, meaning that you stopped at that picture," recalled Gleb Derujinsky. "He believed in the concept of making a picture stand up on its feet and tell a story." Another photographer, Viennese-born Lisette Model, who began shooting for *Bazaar* in the 1930s, recalled that Carmel had "an expert's understanding of photography.... It all added up to ... an extremely intelligent working situation." The three had arrived at a way of putting the magazine together that was, in its thoroughness, unique. After landing an assignment, a photographer would meet with Carmel, Brodovitch, and Vreeland in Carmel's office, along with the models who were either trying out for the job—on a "go-see," as they call it—or had already been hired. As they modeled the fashions, the editors would determine who should wear what, and where in a given issue it would work best.

The editorial pages were laid out, as usual, on the floor, sixty of them, usually, in three rows of twenty each, a process Carmel and Brodovitch had begun to call "laying down the magazine." At first, all the pages would be blank white; gradually, in the course of the month, those blanks would disappear, replaced by dummy pages. (Another version of these, smaller but otherwise identical, was kept in Brodovitch's office.) The editors would—quite literally—walk the photographer through the magazine, explaining where his or her fashion spread would fall, what garments it would encompass, and more. "Brodovitch would say something like, 'Since the last page of Dahl-Wolfe's layout will be color, showing an outfit that's brown and green, you should think about what you're going to follow it with,'" Derujinsky recalled. And Vreeland, in the way that was so artfully hers, might convey with a gesture, a pose, a baroque sentence, the mood each garment evoked and thus, obliquely, how it should be photographed. The issue was conceived as a whole, both in its look and content. Brodovitch would impart a specific rhythm to each issue—"like a flipbook," Derujinsky says. One page might hold one shot, the next two, the third might be a double spread; and this sequence might recur, quite exactly, like DNA. Or, as in a piece of music, a theme might be sounded out, then recur in myriad ways. Such tight structuring lent the magazine momentum and coherence, with each page seeming to follow inevitably from the one before. "Everything went together hand in glove," as Derujinsky puts it.

There was a pedagogic quality to these encounters, recalls Polly Mellen. There were numerous times when a photographer, often Dahl-Wolfe, might resist Carmel's choice of photograph, arguing that another take was stronger than the one that she and Brodovitch had selected and placed in the sequence underfoot. Carmel would then take the shot the photographer preferred and put it on top of the other. "Look at the flow," she'd say, before picking it up again to reveal her original choice. "Now look at this one. Now tell me which picture works better in the magazine." When, as they inevitably did, the photographer acknowledged that Carmel's choice worked better for the magazine as a whole, the editor would say "Good," with great dignity. "I will take this picture for my book."

The art director often worked up two layouts for each page, the A and B versions, offering both to Carmel, who always had the last word. Brodovitch cannily kept tension between them down by deferring some key tasks to his assistants. "If she said 'B,' it was my job to fight for the 'A,'" Bassman says. Carmel often had other factors to consider: "If she did choose the 'B,' it was often a business decision." When she overrode Brodovitch, he seemed to take it philosophically, another former assistant says. "I just never felt he was miffed if she changed something," says A. G. Allen. "And she didn't do it much. He respected her enormously."

Although Vreeland was deferential to Carmel—"It was a question of knowing who was the boss," as photographer Richard Avedon puts it—there was the occasional frisson of competition between them. "In a curious way, I think she resented my taste," Vreeland dropped, with transparently faux innocence, in *D.V.,* the matchless book of her recollections. The fact that Vreeland was enjoined

from working at the collections in Paris—of all places!—grated continually. Carmel had enormous clout in the French capital by then, and the fashions she showcased from there "were often translated into American fashion successes," as even a rival, *Vogue*'s managing editor Jessica Daves had to admit. She was never shy about telling even the most exalted couturier about how to improve his or her line. "Mrs. Snow . . . really helped to create trends because she had a way of looking at collections and picking out ideas that had a future," the publicist Eleanor Lambert recalled. "She would go to the designer and say, 'This is really wonderful, we're going to use it in the magazine and you should do more of it.' Her whole attitude was one of inspired editing."

While both she and Vreeland made suggestions to local designers and manufacturers, nudging American fashion along, in Paris, Carmel alone held sway. "She believed in the French," Bassman says. "The American was something she had to show. She didn't care very much about it. She'd leave that to Vreeland." She was also more exacting when it came to showing French fashion in the magazine: "In America you could do whatever." But such was not the case in Europe, as Bassman discovered later when, with Brodovitch's encouragement, she became a photographer for the magazine. "One time I shot a dress that was made, probably by Jacques Fath, with thirty yards of chiffon. I was so thrilled with the dress that I took the girl out to the bois [de Boulogne] and had her photographed with the chiffon flying." She adored the results, but was

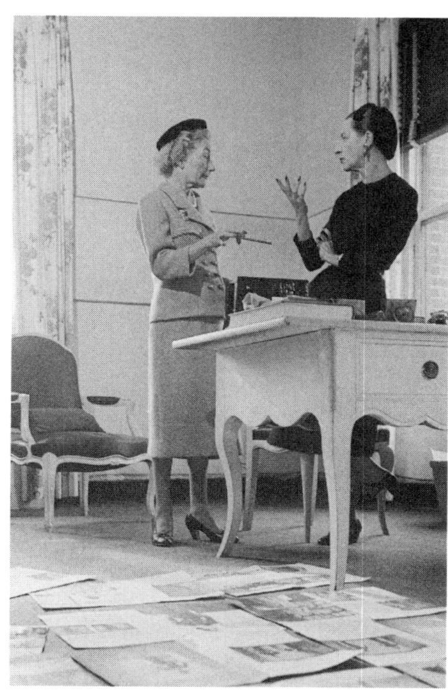

OPPOSITE: **Putting the magazine together in Carmel's office: Carmel at her desk, Alexey Brodovitch (*on floor*), managing editor Bob Gerdy (*standing*), and Jean Condit (*in reflection*), 1952**

RIGHT: **Conferring with Diana Vreeland**

quickly called on to the carpet by Carmel. "Lillian, my dear, you didn't go to the Fath show. That was a column of chiffon and you've taken liberties with it." Bassman had to reshoot the dress. Artistic license was one thing—no one appreciated it more than Carmel—but the magazine had a business role to play, not just an artistic one. As she gently reminded her staff, "We've got to sell the dress."

French clothes still predominated in the magazine. "It was just Paris, Paris, Paris," according to Lambert. Certainly, France was the source of the most inventive designs as a Vertès-illustrated feature on wacked-out accessories, most from Schiaparelli, including gloves with metal claws, a windmill hat with protruding feathers, attests. (Even today, the European imagination, at least in matters of design, seems to take flight more easily.)

A huge fashion influence swept in after Mrs. Simpson married the former Edward VIII, on June 3, 1937, six months after his abdication. Mainbocher made the bride's trousseau and, one way or another, almost every other designer fell into line.

> *In the early summer of 1938 the British royal couple visited France and inspired a neoromantic fashion revival. Even Chanel, the inventor of modern simplicity, suddenly designed evening dresses with very full, stiffened skirts and ornate trimmings, strongly reminiscent of the crinoline which one thought had been given up for good.*

The press may have painted the Windsors as the century's most romantic couple, but few insiders believed it, including *Vogue*'s astute Bettina Ballard, who, upon visiting the couple in their impeccable Paris residence on the Boulevard Suchet, near the Bois, reported to a friend that an almost fanatic neatness on both their parts seemed to unite the pair. There was not a trace of romance in her description of two people entirely obsessed with their appearances—and little else; during her visit, the former king dithered for much of the afternoon on the all-important question of what to wear to dinner.

The late 1930s were a time of shoulder pads; short, full skirts in dusky colors; wedge-heeled shoes, then platform ones. Cotton—once too humble for a certain class of woman—had become the fabric of choice for summer. Hair was worn upswept, a trend so important that the Paris collections were centered around it, according to Edna Chase. In 1938, Schiaparelli launched her famous "circus" line, something Carmel announced on a radio broadcast that February live from Paris over shortwave radio on NBC's Blue Network. Vionnet unveiled a line of Directoire evening gowns, and polka dots were "everywhere." Hats shrank, and veils—which most self-respecting women still wore, if only to church—became more voluminous. And then, as so often happen, fashion seemed to zigzag overnight: in 1939, colors brightened and shoulders resumed their natural contour. "Shoulder pads are in the dustbin," the magazine trilled. Women wore short pleated skirts and pullovers. Hats and veils switched places, with the former becoming more substantial, the latter less.

Bazaar documented all these peregrinations and more. Vreeland's hand was everywhere, not just in the fashion, which she rounded up with a squadron of more junior fashion editors, some of them, like twenty-one-year-old Wendy Iglehart, impossibly young. Many became quickly Vreeland-esque—issuing pronouncements and styling their hair, like their mentor's, so that it was pulled back severely from their foreheads—to the quiet hilarity of others on the staff. Vreeland also meted out the occasional column, such as one entitled "It's New," which ran in the

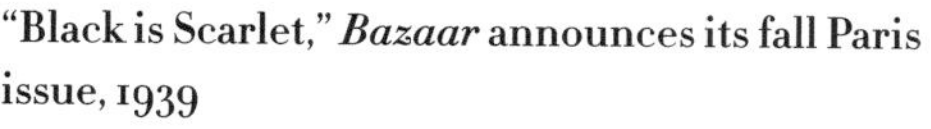
"Black is Scarlet," *Bazaar* announces its fall Paris issue, 1939

March 15, 1939, issue. Such inspired non sequiturs as "It's new to carry an umbrella like an Englishman, even on sunny days" were pure Vreeland. All that was missing was the "Why Don't You?"

Fiction was crackling, with George Davis, who had been the first to translate some of Colette's stories into English, teasing out talent from all directions. He brought in works of such relative newcomers as Dawn Powell, John Dos Passos, William Saroyan "the young whirlwind from San Francisco," and a twenty-eight-year-old John Cheever. The young poet W. H. Auden, who had recently been called by *Time* "the most spectacular poet alive," supplied a Christmas poem in December 1939; Katherine Anne Porter, a new, and much-noticed literary talent, turned up in the same issue. "Two years ago Miss Porter promised *Harper's Bazaar* the very next story she completed," the magazine reported, "though she wasn't at all sure which one it would be." It was, fortuitously enough, her classic "The Downward Path to Wisdom."

Carmel scored another literary coup in 1940 when, after reading a review of Carson McCullers's first novel, *The Member of the Wedding,* an affecting portrait of a young girl, written when its author was not more than twenty-one, sent Davis off to bag the young novelist for the magazine. McFadden bragged later that she'd brought in the young writer "almost straight from Georgia." As a result, two of McCullers's famous novellas, *Reflections in a Golden Eye* and *Ballad of the Sad Cafe* were serialized in *Bazaar.* Carmel admired the latter one so much "that she cut the magazine to pieces one month to be first to print it in its artistic entirety," according to Janet Flanner, who described this as "a revolutionary intellectual act on a fashion periodical." *Ballad* was one of the longest pieces ever published at the magazine, and it was accompanied by a famous, much-reproduced Dahl-Wolfe portrait of the petulant-looking young author who, although twenty-three at the time, looked twelve. She and Carmel promptly became friends.

Keeping up with good writing, fiction or non, was a priority. As Mary Louise Aswell, a later *Bazaar* fiction editor, once wrote:

During my years as fiction editor of Harper's Bazaar *I knew it was worth my job not to let her know when an interesting writer was in town. I'd pop my head in her office to say, "Eudora Welty's coming in from Jackson," and she'd call for her calendar. Dorothy Monger might say, "I'm sorry, Mrs. Snow, you're booked solid."*

Carmel would look over the closely scribbled pages. "Oh—that advertising lunch. Tell them I've been called out of town." On the day of Eudora's arrival I'd help Dorothy extricate Bossy from a meeting, we would often skip out the back via the freight elevator to avoid someone waiting in the front hall to pounce, and then, in those days, we generally walked around the corner to the Savoy-Plaza, where she entertained the people who didn't care about being seen in the fashion world.

The credence given in the magazine to both fiction and just plain great journalism is hard to overstate. In January 1940, Janet Flanner was introduced to *Bazaar*'s readers with a solemnity worthy of de Gaulle. That she was contributing an article about fortune-tellers—Carmel's passion—only made the dissonance more fun. Another piece, entitled "Your Obedient Servant," suggested by Carmel, took the world of servants as its subject, daring to show its well-heeled readers exactly how the people who ran their lives actually lived. The subject, poignantly enough, was none other than Bridget Keogh, who'd worked for both the Whites and Snows. "She told the horrors that servants in very wealthy families had to go through," says Dorothy Wheelock Edson, the editor who brought Carmel's idea to the page, complete with a photograph of Bridget in her diminutive maid's room. "It was a terrible, terrible life."

The magazine was alert to culture in all its forms, at one point presenting in quick succession: a Dahl-Wolfe photo of "the 24-year-old wunderkind of the theatre, Orson Welles"; a portrait of Salvador Dalí and his wife, Gala, in front of his painting *L'Instant Sublime;* a shot of Chanel sewing costumes for the *Bacchanale,* a Dalí ballet; and interior decorator Frances Elkins's Yerba Buena Clubhouse from the San Francisco World's Fair, with its striking red, black, and white motif. One never knew what to expect. In March 1939, Schiaparelli contributed an article—of all things!—to the magazine extolling the virtues of vegetarianism. "Cannibals are supposed to be fierce. Vegetarians are fiercer," it read. "Adolf Hitler and Benito Mussolini eat no meat, drink no wine. On a diet of noodles and spaghetti they've just changed the map of Central Europe." Who knew?

The results dwarfed *Vogue* on every level with the crucial exception of newsstand and advertising sales. They rose during Carmel's tenure, went up and stayed there, but they could never really outdistance *Vogue.* (It's sobering to note that Carmel would probably not have lasted long in her job in our era, when numbers trump everything.) Even so, *Bazaar* was the acknowledged class book, the gold standard, the undisputed leader. "*Vogue* published two issues a month and could use many, many photographs," Vreeland once said, in a rare moment of understatement, "but in my opinion the thickness and lack of refinement in which it was projected made it less attractive than *Bazaar.*" Sometimes even Nast agreed. In 1940, he sent a memo to his staff criticizing a Horst cover photo of an orange silk jersey Hattie Carnegie evening gown. The young photographer had unwisely posed the model behind a table, hiding much of the intricately draped dress from view. Nast was furious.

> *It so happens that* Harper's Bazaar *has reported the same dress, also in full color, in its September 15th issue. In the* Bazaar*'s photograph reporting this dress will be found proof of the soundness of my criticism. So far as the dress itself is concerned, without entering into a discussion of the background, the* Bazaar*'s photograph avoids the many faults of* Vogue*'s. In a word, the* Bazaar *reports the dress—*Vogue *doesn't.*

A couple of years earlier, *Bazaar* staffers must have been relieved not to be working for the competition. In January 1938, a scandal erupted after it was discovered that Cecil Beaton had illustrated an article he'd done for *Vogue* on New York life with an intricate decorative border in which he'd twice embedded the word *kikes* in tiny letters. You may have needed a magnifying glass to read them, but they were undeniably there. Someone tipped off Walter Winchell, the syndicated writer, whom Philip Roth has described as "the most famous gossip columnist in the country, gross and cheap without apology." Winchell was then possibly America's best read—and most feared—journalist. He ruled both on the page (in the *New York Mirror,* his hometown newspaper, and more than two thousand others) and on radio, where he spewed out words at a typhoon pace (he was once clocked at speaking over 225 words a minute) to an audience of about 55 million Americans—and that was in the mid-1930s, when the country's population was only about 127 million. It only took a quick mention for Beaton's world to fall apart. In the ensuing furor, 130,000 copies of the magazine were withdrawn from circulation and, needless to say, this young and talented photographer/writer/illustrator, at Nast's request, resigned from *Vogue.* He wouldn't be seen again in its pages for years.

Beaton's actions seem incomprehensible now, as they did to many then. Explanations have come and gone. What seems likely is that he was perpetuating a ghastly in-joke, aimed at a group of friends who—amazingly enough—might be amused by seeing their sentiments covertly expressed in the glossy pages of a magazine. The fact is that the vocabulary Beaton employed was, in some circles, routine. "In New York, there was an unspecific but recognizable atmosphere of anti-Semitism, particularly in the higher echelons of society," as Caroline Seebohm has written. And while many expressed outrage after Beaton's folly came to light—including, most vocally, Condé Nast himself—there were others who quietly confided to its perpetrator that they found the fuss about it more distasteful than the incident itself. Wink wink, nudge nudge.

An undercurrent of anti-Jewish sentiment was a fact of life in many organizations, and *Bazaar* was no different. "I felt anti-semitism very strongly in that office," the photographer Richard Avedon would later say. Its poison mist permeated the air. Like the many-too-many-martini lunches that Carmel and her colleagues would indulge in at Halper's (also called "The Scalpers" by the *HB* staff for its hefty prices), L'Aiglon, or the Colony's bar, it was part of the vocabulary of a certain class and time. Still, it's a relief to learn that, while Vreeland, a close friend of Beaton's, was known to make exclusionary comments, Carmel was not, according to Richard Avedon. "She was not a snob in the way Diana was. She was not anti-semitic." Vreeland, by contrast "was a Nazi, for God's sake," says former *Bazaar* editor Mary Lee Settle, recalling the notorious Unity Mitford "Why Don't You?"

The Beaton controversy was a setback for *Vogue* in every way and, as such, must have been welcome news to the Hearst camp. And there is a school of thought that says it was somehow fitting that it took place at *Vogue,* which was more socially rarefied than *Bazaar:* "You really had to be a WASP to make it at Condé Nast" then, Geri Trotta recalls. In this period, the competition between the two rivals, always simmering, often threatened to boil over. By now, the informal agreement between Hearst and Nast seemed to have been forgotten. Defections were a regular occurrence, including that of the Paris-based photographer Erwin Blumenfeld, who left *Vogue* in June 1939, in part because he was fed up with that magazine's Paris editor, Michel de Brunhoff. ("He filched every idea that came his way. Nothing was sacred to him . . .") When rumors reached Chase that Bettina Ballard was being courted for a job by Hearst, Nast responded, in a famous memo, by assuring Chase that this wasn't the Chief's style. "It has been my experience over many years that when they want anyone, you don't hear delicate purrings from the cat or the Organization but that they soon go after whomever they want definitely, vigorously, openly and with large bait."

The latter was either not forthcoming or persuasive enough: Ballard stayed at *Vogue* for the rest of her magazine career, eventually taking over the job of fashion editor in New York. But others jumped ship, and the tension over keeping key personnel continues to this day. In 2004, Cathleen Black, president of Hearst's magazine division, told the *New York Times* that Condé Nast Publications had been known to "roll out the wheelbarrow . . . to attract key employees," adding that, "We've been competing with Condé Nast for 100 years." For most, the wheelbarrow at both magazines wasn't particularly full. It was close to empty well into the 1970s, when female editors were still being paid what Grace Mirabella, *Vogue*'s former editor in chief, referred to as "debutante wages." (As she, grossly underpaid herself, was in a position to know.) Women were offered almost nothing on the grounds that their husbands would be supporting them anyway—a breezy assumption that wasn't true for many, including both Carmel, after the crash, and Vreeland who, with her husband Reed, lived consistently beyond her means.

On April 12, 1939, Carmel wrote to Vreeland saying that Berlin, who had taken over the magazine division the year before, would be increasing her salary to $125 a week, as of April 15, for a total of $6,500 a year. In later years, when Vreeland referred to her pay, she seemed to forget a few raises along the way. "I think the Hearsts paid me eighteen thousand dollars a year for twenty-eight years for working at *Harper's Bazaar*. San Simeon must have been where the Hearst money went. I certainly never saw any of it." The editor in chief's salary wasn't much more: a former *Bazaar* editor, Geri Trotta recalls seeing a pay stub in the 1950s that indicated that Carmel was then earning $20,000 a year. Brodovitch, no doubt, did better: almost all men at Hearst, as at so many other organizations, did. If this circumstance seems incredible to us now—why didn't these women insist on raises?—there is this: it wouldn't have been ladylike to do so. Both Carmel and Vreeland were ladies, above all, with all the discipline and rectitude that that noun implies. They played the hands that were dealt to them, for better or for worse, and carried on without complaint. Hearst management "just got away with it, you see," fashion editor Gwen Randolph Franklin explains. It was easy to keep more junior members of the staff in line. "They were always threatening us that there were nine million people who wanted the job," says fashion editor D. D. Ryan, who began her career at *Bazaar* as Dorinda Dixon Prest.

It's no surprise that Ballard, who'd lived in Paris for years and had a bead on everything and everyone there, was stalked by the Hearst crowd: finding the right editor for France, where the fashion crowd can be tough beyond reckoning, was a perpetual challenge. The few who could thrive, such as Daisy Fellowes, tended to be long on glamour, short on work ethic. The job would seem fun, for about a minute, and then it would not. For this and other reasons, Anne de la Rochefoucauld morphed into Mrs. Erickson—of Eric fame, a strange choice, given that her husband was still a key contributor to *Vogue*—and then still another young woman before Carmel, caught short once again, settled on the reluctant figure of Louise Macy (sometimes called Louie), her adored protégée. It was another of her hunches at work.

> *Louie explained to me frankly that her French was strictly the boarding-school variety, but I had a mind that [her] personality . . . would make a devastating impression on the French temperament. How right I was! Within two weeks Louie was the new American sensation in Paris, with beaux lined up to take her out and the couture eating out of her hand.*

Macy was open, fresh, charismatic. Arriving in Paris in the fall of 1938, she scored one of her first coups after she asked Vertès to sketch some lingerie and he, preoccupied with a stage set he was working on, suggested a young unknown illustrator named Christian Dior instead. The future designer's first signed sketches duly appeared in the magazine. That was luck, perhaps, but some of Macy's other accomplishments were not. In an audacious move, and at the suggestion of the Duchesse d'Ayen, she arranged to take over the then-deserted Hôtel Sâlé, a beautiful seventeenth-century mansion in Paris's Marais district (and now the site of that city's Musée National Picasso), for a party in the name of *Harper's Bazaar.* The house was then a virtual ruin, without electricity or other amenities, but the indefatigable Macy pushed forward with her plan, obtaining permission to take it over for the night, then talking to seemingly everyone in Paris, including André Terrail, proprietor of the famous restaurant La Tour D'Argent, as much a Parisian institution then as it remains today, to donate goods and services for nothing or at cost. Carmel missed the results, but word filtered back to New York that the party, lit by nine hundred (donated) candles, was one of the chicest gatherings of prewar Paris. As such, it was an enormous public relations coup for the magazine.

Danger was in the air, although not everyone knew it yet, at least not in America, far from Europe, where events seemed to be marching in lockstep one after the other, all of them ominous, all—so easy to see in hindsight—adding up, inexorably, to war. But politics filter slowly down the halls of fashion magazines. *Bazaar* more than most strived to keep one foot in the real world, including a 1939 feature, shot by Walker Evans, on families living in the Williamsburg and Harlem River housing projects. This is a magazine for *interested* readers, light-years away from today's cool. *Bazaar* might dip into the real world (another piece featured New York's settlement houses), but it could also float quickly away, an elegant cloud, rising above so much.

In the summer of 1939, as world events rushed ominously on, director William Wyler's wrenchingly romantic version of Emily Brontë's *Wuthering Heights,* starring Laurence Olivier and Merle Oberon, was released. *Bazaar* duly put together a story on Olivier, who played the brooding Heathcliff, and on whom numerous women at the magazine—not to mention the world—had a crush. Mary Faulconer had seen the film eight times, so when one of her assistants called her to say that the great thespian was in the waiting room, hoping to see her, she was particularly susceptible to the news. She tore down the hall to Carmel's corner office, where a meeting about the September issue was taking place, attended by a gaggle of editors, among them the very beautiful Lenore Cotten, wife of the actor Joseph Cotten—as famous as Olivier in his day—as well as representatives of Fifty-seventh Street.

> *I opened the door and made a clean move right up to her desk and I said, "Mrs. Snow, I hate to interrupt you but Laurence Olivier is here to see me." Without hesitating she banged her hand on the desk and said,*

"Faulconer, don't you see him alone! I want to be there with you!" whereupon all the editors started putting on lipstick. The whole room was in chaos.

Faulconer raced back to the art department to get the layout she'd done of the star, then tore back to the reception area in a complete state of nerves only to find that it was . . . empty. After one of her assistants confessed to having pulled a prank, she ordered him down the hall to make his confession directly to Mrs. Snow, while she herself waited outside in dread. "Not only could I not face the office again, I couldn't face working there again." She prepared for the worst. But, instead, Carmel appeared, looking downright cheerful and seeming "elated by the whole experience," Faulconer recalled. "That was a very amusing young man who's working for you," the editor said. She sounded similarly euphoric when, at about the same time, she turned up at the office one spring morning with the announcement that her favorite couture evening gown—worth $500, a fortune then—had been sucked out of the car window by the wind during her morning commute. "It sailed out of the car and into the Hudson River," she breathlessly reported. "Can you imagine? I felt like calling to it 'Come back! come back!'"

Carmel made waves in July that year by fearlessly boarding the first eastbound commercial plane, Pan Am's Clipper, to Europe on its first flight. "Isn't Carmel a sketch?" Palen asked McFadden as the two watched her take off from a marshy area off Port Washington, Long Island. She described the experience with joy. Flying was brand new in those days and, as such, terrifying to some. But not to Carmel. "I'd fly to the moon if I could," she wrote.

You parked your car in the bushes and walked through a field to the water's edge, where the great bird floated in the harbor among all the little pleasure boats. I was the only woman passenger. A strong off-shore breeze almost blew away my Suzy hat as I walked down the shaky wooden pier.

The flight would take almost thirty hours; the destination was Lisbon and ultimately, of course, Paris. Within a few years, Carmel would be "making the trip regularly in those slow old planes that always stopped at Gander, Newfoundland, to refuel."

She was also in the news that year after she and her old friend the designer Hattie Carnegie "broadcast to the world the behind-the-scenes story of the Paris openings," as the magazine described it—live this time—over the CBS network. An ad in *Bazaar* mined the first broadcast's inherent drama. "What new fashions will make history, when Mrs. Snow's eyes light on them and send them sizzling over the short waves?" The ones that did came from the Spanish designer Cristobal Balenciaga, who had left his native country after the outbreak of the Spanish Civil War, opening his maison de couture in Paris a short while later, in 1937. He made his debut in *Bazaar* in October 1938 with a black cloqué crepe-lined coat. "Balenciaga projects a new quality into the couture, a definite personality into the fray," the text read. "There's a flavor of Spain about his whole collection."

What set him apart, always, was simplicity of his line. "Nothing is more mysterious than simplicity, it can't be described nor copied. Simplicity is fullness, nothing more, nothing less." The designer had started out with a couture house in his native town of San Sebastián, then opened ones in Barcelona and Madrid. At first he sold copies he'd made of French imports, mainly from Chanel; he also picked up other lines, which he'd scout out twice yearly at the French collections. Then he began designing himself. Even in his earliest work, his fashions, with their

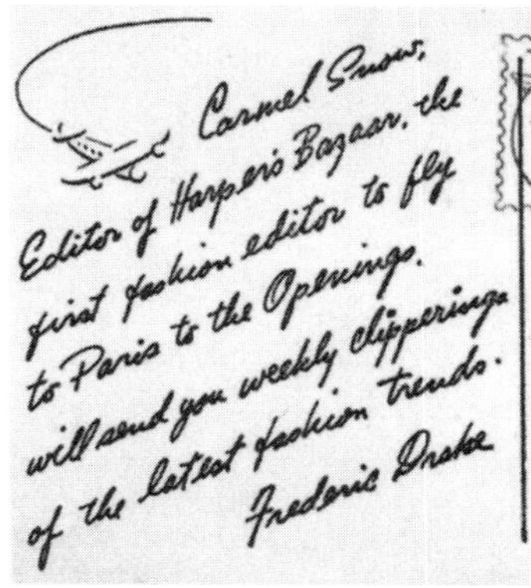
Carmel Snow,
Editor of Harper's Bazaar, the
first fashion editor to fly
to Paris to the Openings.
will send you weekly clipperings
of the latest fashion trends.
Frederic Drake

Two sides of a publicity postcard announcing Carmel as "the first fashion editor to fly to Paris to the openings," 1939

bold lines and impeccable tailoring, made news. "His is a Spanish as well as a French elegance," Carmel said, adding that "he is one of the fashion Greats of all time." She burned to bring his work to her readers. When photos from his collection were held up by British censors in Bermuda, she cabled her sister Christine, as well as her daughters' nanny—both devout Catholics—exhorting them to pray. "They did, and the pictures arrived," she writes matter-of-factly.

Such cables took wing frequently during her years at *Bazaar,* often directed to Christine, as well as to her son, Father John Holbrook, after he became a Catholic priest. "Every time something happened in New York I'd get a cable saying 'Jack, pray hard,'" Holbrook says. "That would be all. At that point, I'd destroy the telegrams and pray. I'd pray as if the world was going to come down. I'd never know what happened. That was the only contact I ever had with her...." While she often thanked him later, assuring him that his efforts had been a success, "I never ever learned what it was that I was praying for."

In August 1939, Carmel headed again to Paris, where the threat of war colored everything. The Nazis had invaded Czechoslovakia six months before, on March 15, and Poland, which both France and Britain had agreed to defend against German aggression, was under threat. In a letter to *Bazaar*'s readers that ran in the September 15 issue, she wrote:

> *Today I see another Paris. In the last week it has become, almost overnight, a city deserted. The taxis have disappeared from the streets. All the telephones are cut off. You can walk for miles without seeing a child. Even the dogs—and you know how the Parisians love their dogs—have been sent away. No one who has been in Paris during these distressing days of suspense will ever forget the silence of the city or the courage of the women of France. As man after man is mobilized, these Frenchwomen go about the work of their daily lives without a trace of hysteria. It is not a moment of mass courage but of individual heroism. From the première [the most expert dressmaker in any fashion house]*

to the little black pinafored girl in the workrooms, each accepts the inevitable with a calm that leaves one awed.

The ominous pressure of impending war combined with a more familiar one: the rush to get material into the September issues. In some ways, all was as usual. Carmel, like her fashion colleagues, resumed the frantic pace that was as much a part of the collections as great clothes, with panic and inspiration mixed in a euphoric rush. Their nights ran late. As Hoyningen-Huene described it:

Immediately after the photography was over and the negatives had been processed, proofs would be numbered and, wet as they were, presented on large blotters to the editor for selection. Then the retoucher would go to work, after which the final print was made, fixed, washed, dried, captioned, and rushed to the boat.

Early in her career, she'd developed a system by which she'd sleep upright in bed in her suite at the Hotel Westminster, invariably wearing pearls with her lacy Paris nightgown. Photographers, anyone, could just walk in. The light was always on—"She was terribly afraid of the dark," according to Mary Jane Russell, a model who later traveled with her to the collections. If she was asleep, she'd shoot bolt upright, instantly awake, and reach for the almost comically large magnifying glass that she kept on

Selecting photographs with photographer Louise Dahl-Wolfe in Carmel's Paris hotel room

her bedside table. She and the photographer would then go through the proofs of the photos he or she had just taken, choosing the best for the magazine. A mad scramble would then ensue to get their choices to the courier who would race to the Gare Saint Lazare, from where the trains would leave for Cherbourg or Le Havre and a waiting ship. Connections could break down at any time. Once, in a desperate moment, Carmel enlisted "a portly young man I'd met in New York"—the soon-to-be-famous liberal columnist Joseph Alsop, who was then working as a staff reporter in the Washington, D.C., bureau of the *New York Herald Tribune*—to take an envelope of photographs to the magazine's offices in Manhattan. Meetings in her Paris hotel suite might take any form. As Lillian Bassman recalls,

> *One time I walked into her suite at 6 A.M. and she was sitting in the tub completely made up with the pearls—she was never without her pearls—and a hat on her head. The waiter was whizzing around bringing croissants and things. She was perfectly at ease sitting in the tub. I wish I'd had a camera. It's like a painting by an old master, that little Irish face.*

On August 29, when photographer Erwin Blumenfeld met Carmel for the first time, she was in a decidedly different mode. Blumenfeld, who had recently jumped ship from *Vogue,* was known for his daring photography; he often experimented with color and darkroom techniques. His first fashion spread had just run in *Bazaar,* a dizzying sequence of women posing on the Eiffel Tower, one in a stunning Molyneux dress of pale gray chiffon. At the time he and Carmel met, she was heading out the door, on her way to board the *Queen Elizabeth,* the Cunard liner, as it stopped in Normandy on the way to New York. Like so many of Blumenfeld's descriptions, this one has a distinctly negative tinge. Still, it's a classic.

> *Like every female fashion editor in every Hollywood film she was sitting in regal splendour surrounded by carefully orchestrated "I'm-*

just-about-to-leave-town" chaos, with huge bouquets of orchids, champagne on ice and telephones. Porters were forever carting the same suitcases in and out. Carmel was dictating letters and telegrams to three different secretaries at the same time, with precision, wit, and outrageous virtuosity and a total lack of soul. She acted as if she hadn't seen me arrive. Then all of a sudden she stretched out all three hands for me to kiss and assured me with an enormous smile that according to her latest top secret information, all dangers of war had disappeared. Peace in our time. Again.

As Blumenfeld arrived, Carmel was desperately trying to set up a photo shoot with none other than her brother Tom's rival, Ambassador William C. Bullitt, and his nubile daughter Anne. According to Blumenfeld, she was dictating cables to hold the cover for a double portrait, in color—something that, by the way, hardly sounds likely: portraits of middle-aged men, even ones accompanied by lovely young daughters, aren't likely to sell fashion magazines. But his description of Carmel's wily maneuvering, including composing flattering letters to the ambassador and his assistant and anyone else who might help, rings true. Blumenfeld was less than enamored of Carmel—he described her, quite unnecessarily, as "looking as beautiful as only ugly American women know how" and "fifty something, with pale blue-rinse hair and a drinker's snub nose"—and he seemed appalled by her machinations. But he really shouldn't have been. She was an editor in chief, and she would stop at very little to get her story.

In this case, it didn't work. The ambassador canceled at the last moment, saying his daughter was already on a boat bound for Philadelphia. In the retelling, it was instantly clear to the photographer, if perhaps not those around him, that war was on its way. And other signs, even tiny ones, were revealing. Carmel told him, in passing, that "in the hotel they had already started taking away pillows from the guest rooms to use in military hospitals, and replacing them with little notes of apology."

Although his allegiance was now to *Bazaar,* Blumenfeld wasted little time recounting the story of Carmel's aborted photo session to de Brunhoff, his former boss at *Vogue.*

> *When I told him it had been cancelled he beamed with plain delight that* Harper's *had lost this journalistic coup. Pretending he had stomach-ache, he got up and went to cable New York about this (or possibly "his") victory. He came back to the table, still exulting, a long quarter of an hour later. Only then did he realize that this meant there would be a war. He stared at me without saying a word, and shed a tear or two.*

A day or so later, on the morning of September 1, the Germans invaded Poland. Two days later, in response, France and Britain declared war on Germany.

By then Carmel was on her way home. In a letter to his wife, written on September 14, Tom White reported that his sister was back in New York and looking well but "deeply concerned about the conditions in France. Apparently the last week there was a very tragic one with all the French houses closing down—people being put out of work and men going away in mobilization." Many fashion houses were shutting their doors, or at least considering doing so, starting with Louiseboulanger. And *Bazaar*'s contributors seemed to be scattering to the winds, including Cassandre who, shaven and unrecognizable, had joined the army, where he was ordered to organize "a theatre entertainment for his regiment." Some still brought in work, such as Vertès who, on two-day leave from the army, sketched some wonderful vignettes of wartime Paris for the magazine.

The November 1939 issue of *Bazaar* confidently reported that "the French couture is carrying on.... The French have decreed that fashion shall go on, even in the dark, anxious nights. Though no one wears full dress, everyone makes an effort to be as elegant as possible, not only for the morale of their friends, but to keep up France's greatest industry, on which so many workers depend." The designer Lucien Lelong had been demobilized and was heading up the Chambre

Syndicale de la Couture, the French trade group that had been founded by the couturiers decades earlier initially to fight piracy. He and the other couturiers were furiously doing their bit for the war effort, including Lanvin, who was designing uniforms for women. Foreign buyers, barred from entering France, were making their purchases through intermediaries. But some of the fashions that came with war—including flashlight umbrellas and "white accessories that shine out in blackouts"—seemed unlikely to make their way to the States.

In a long "Letter from Paris" the next month, Louise Macy, who had been vacationing in New York when war was declared and had hastened back to the French capital, reported that, in surprising ways, life there was going on as before. Maxim's, the eternally popular restaurant, famous for its "Billy-by" mussel soup and still the place to be seen, especially on Fridays, when formal dress was required, was packed, and "the Crillon Bar has taken on a huge popularity." But of course there was no end of differences, starting with the *Bazaar* Paris offices themselves, where, Macy wrote, blackout curtains were on order. Blue lampshades, designed to augment these drapes, could be bought on almost every street corner.

Fashion, that eternal scavenger, quickly absorbed the fact of war. Blue, the very shade of those ubiquitous blackout lampshades, was suddenly "the color of Paris," picked up by seemingly every designer. Not surprisingly, there was a new pragmatism in the air. A striking cerise jersey suit—with a body-hugging, gold-buttoned jacket and a "flair skirt over bloomers" that fell just below the knee—featured in *Bazaar,* didn't just provide "warmth for coatless Paris," but was eminently practical for use on bicycles which, in the absence of gas, had become the transportation of choice. Since so many women rode them, and, in any case, leather was rationed, designers came up with jackets and coats with oversize pockets to use instead of handbags. Some styles had a militaristic edge, among them a Molyneux wool coat with epaulettes, while others reflected "no war influence at all," as Macy put it: Alix, for example, showed jersey day dresses with matching coats and some exquisitely draped (a given with this designer) silk dinner dresses.

The wartime Parisienne's "uniform is a suit, it may be tweed, or jersey, or soft wool," the magazine said, while extolling the virtues of "comfortable shoes that transport you without benefit of limousines." Designers still at work included the gifted newcomer Balenciaga, Patou, and Robert Piguet, who had trained with Poiret and who relied on an army of freelance designers (including, early in their careers, Dior, Givenchy, and the American James Galanos) to produce beautifully cut suits and dresses. He and Molyneux began turning out outfits to wear in air raids. Every designer was under strain, with many on their staffs involved in war work of one kind or another. Chanel, at this point, had only one fitter left.

Even the chicest, richest members of *le tout Paris* found their lives quickly changed. The formidable American-born decorator Elsie de Wolfe, reduced to living without servants, at one dinner party served her guests corned beef hash, albeit on an elegant table decorated with autumn leaves on silk yellow cloth, according to Macy, who dropped in at de Wolfe's famous residence, the Villa Trianon at Versailles. (It was a far cry from her prewar extravagances, which had included a circus ball at which she officiated, dressed as a ringmaster and holding a giant whip.) The party was all about Chinese checkers, the game of the moment in both France and the United States. Elsie was "mad about the game and liked only to win," according to Bettina Ballard; her guests, who, besides the fashion crowd, might include Noel Coward and a smattering of Anglo-American diplomats, knew they were invited only to lose. On the night of Macy's visit, the usual glamorous clientele showed up looking surprisingly unadorned, including Daisy Fellowes in "the plainest of dark blue suits"—"plain" not being a word usually associated with this goddess—and Schiaparelli in a "country skirt" and heavy tweed jacket. Characteristically, this exuberant Italian brightened things up by wearing blue woolen stockings with red clocks on them. She was right to make them fun: there would be lots of thick legwear in the cold winters ahead.

On January 15, 1940, a veritable flotilla of fashion editors, press representatives, and designers, among them Claire McCardell, then in her early thirties and a rising star for her ingeniously cut, very casual—and therefore very American—

clothes headed to Europe to see all this firsthand. They boarded the S.S. *Washington* in New York, "bent on helping a great industry which, despite the war, must keep alive to give employment to the thousands of fashionworkers in France," as the magazine described it. Illustrator Reynaldo Luza turned photographer to document the occasion. There was a "wonderful feeling of camaraderie on shipboard, like the spirit of the old transatlantic boats," the magazine claimed. "All rivalries forgotten. Bendel loved Bergdorf. Bergdorf loved Saks. Even *Vogue* loved the *Bazaar*." It sounds unlikely. One can only imagine the sentiments both Carmel and Chase felt, far off in the wintry Atlantic, finding themselves captive together on a Europe-bound ship. A Luza photograph captured a windswept Carmel on board, suited, the inevitable Suzy on her head, looking exhilarated—travel, adventure, had a rejuvenating effect.

The group disembarked at Genoa, then took a special train, "arranged for by the couture, which was desperate for our assistance," according to Carmel, from Italy to Paris's Gare de Lyon. The twenty-four-hour trip was a trial—the train was crammed with soldiers, there were no lights or heat, and access to the toilet was blocked by mountains of luggage. For these Americans, who were so far from experiencing war themselves, it was a miserable experience, but not for Carmel, who took pride in scarcely needing sustenance or sleep and even claimed to rarely urinate. "If I weren't a 'goddess' about natural functions I would have suffered as most of my fellow passengers suffered on

BONWIT TELLER

HIGHLIGHTS FROM YESTERDAY'S

PARIS BROADCAST

by CARMEL SNOW, *Editor of Harper's Bazaar*

☆

"There's a new kind of coquetry" said Mrs. Snow, "the utmost feminine guile to hold the eyes of one man, rather than catch the eyes of many."

New "gentlewoman" look in the quiet, ultra-sophisticated gray to brown palette we launched this week. Soft, disarming dressmakery clothes in the new neutrals. Throughout the Shop

☆

"Brown accessories. With the grays and beiges, shoes, bags and gloves in brown leathers."

Hot Amber—our warm, golden syrup brown in shining-surfaced crocodile bags and shoes.

Custom-Tan Calf—our polished antique-looking saddler's tan, launched by us in Urbanite☆ shoes. Two Bonwit expressions of the turn towards brown. Shoe Sàlon, Second Floor

☆

"The bloused top. Accentuating the smooth restrained hipline, the slim-skirted look."

The bloused coat—by Clare Potter. Town and Country coats with the new bloused top, the smooth flowing hips. In creamy corduroy, 59.95 Red cashmere, 69.95 Town and Country, Fifth Floor

Bonwit Teller

FIFTH AVE. AT FIFTY-SIXTH ST.

☆Reg. U.S. Pat. Off.

A 1940 specialty store advertisement featuring Carmel Snow

that trip that took twenty-four hours to reach Paris without food, drink or sleeping accommodations." They arrived in Paris to find the city blanketed in snow. It was the last time for years that the American fashion crowd would descend on the capital. They found it remarkably unchanged. "The city was settling into what was to be its normal wartime routine," as Edna Chase described it, noting that, while Maxim's was still packed, "the number of uniforms, and the gas masks and tin hats stacked in the checkroom testified that times had changed."

It was the time of the "phony war," as the Americans called it—the *drôle de guerre* for the French—referring to the nine-month-long lull in the action after the invasion of Poland, which had collapsed in September 1939, surrendering to the Germans early the next month. War was on, but, until Hitler went on his western offensive in May 1940, few symptoms of it manifested themselves. Food was still available and fashion continued to evolve. Carmel went to see the usual suspects, among them Lanvin, Molyneux (whose clothes she still wore almost exclusively), and "the almost-immortal Worth." While she found that they'd done good work under near-impossible conditions, their new styles seemed far less inventive than those of Balenciaga.

The March 1940 *Harper's Bazaar* announced with great fanfare that its six pages of Paris fashions had been "posted by Clipper in a Paris snowstorm, delayed at Lisbon and again at the Azores, held up by high seas in Bermuda, brought to earth at Charleston. . . ." And it brought the reader's attention to the heroics of the magazine's contributors, including Man Ray, now painting full-time, who had returned to Paris from the south of France (he would soon move on to Hollywood) for a photo shoot of the photographers and staff artists who were serving in the French army, among them Jean Moral, Cassandre, and Vertès. Louise Macy, whom the magazine described as "devoting her free time to French war charities," was also there. All "joined Man Ray in a rush of day and night sittings in studios with windows taped to avoid shattering should the dreaded bombs fall."

Soon enough, there was nothing phony about the war at all. In April, both Denmark and Norway fell to the Nazis, followed in a matter of weeks by the Low

Countries—Luxembourg, Holland, and Belgium. By early June 1940, Hitler's army had broken through the French fronts on the Somme and Aisne rivers and was on its way to Paris. On June 10, Italy declared war on France. Within days, the last government members had fled the capital and Paris was declared "an open city" by the French commander. An estimated million people streamed away from the capital by foot and on every imaginable conveyance. The writer Francine du Plessix Gray, then a child fleeing the French capital, has described

> *a cacophonous din of bleating horns, fire trucks, ambulances, ice-cream vendors' vehicles, funeral carriages, municipal street-sweeping trucks, tourist buses racily labeled "Paris La Nuit," even wheelbarrows and prams mingled with the chic limousines, sports cars, family sedans. . . .*

Among the refugee-packed trains heading out of town were fourteen that were crammed full of government archives and records—"not very reassuring evidence of the government's confidence in its ability to hold the capital," as Willis Thornton, the author of a book on the liberation of Paris, has pointed out.

By June 14, Paris was occupied; German units goosestepped down the Champs-Elysées to the sound of a military band sounding out from the Etoile. With breathtaking audacity, they mounted an enormous black, white, and red Nazi swastika on top of the Eiffel Tower—the very symbol of France; other buildings so festooned included the palace of Louis XVI at Versailles. Wehrmacht sentry boxes in the same colors appeared around every government building, from the Chambre des Députés to the Palais du Luxembourg. To those in America, France seemed to go out like a light, as if an enormous blackout curtain had dropped. Fashion news trickled out for a time: in the summer of 1940, what was to be the last of the couture for years was reported on in both *Vogue* and *Bazaar*. But two issues later, Paris was over, its fashions—indeed, all of it—sealed off from the free world.

bazaar *ascendant*

Every issue . . . is full of a special sort of zing*!*

—*Harper's Bazaar*

AS SOON AS PARIS WAS TAKEN OVER, Carmel began frantically cabling Louie Macy, whose parents were dead and for whom she felt responsible, begging her to return to the States. But Macy stayed on, sending her staff home to their families and running the office herself. She spent her nights distributing food and first-aid supplies to refugees with the help of another American girl, before finally succumbing to Carmel's entreaties and returning to New York. She boarded the S.S. *Manhattan,* appropriately enough, which sailed from Genoa in early June, with thirty-three hundred on board, three times its capacity; among its passengers were Macy and Schiaparelli's young daughter, Gogo, whom the designer had entrusted to Macy's care.

Carmel's devotion to Macy was such that she made a place for her in New York by asking another editor, Gwen Randolph Franklin, who was "sort of in charge of sportswear," in her own words, to leave. "She took me out to lunch and she said, 'Gwen, you've done such a wonderful job but, dear, I've got to let you go. I've got to bring Louie back from Paris and I don't want to discuss this.'" It was all said casually, as if she were debating what to order from the menu rather than relieving an editor she admired of her job. Franklin was furious and promised to tell the story to everyone she knew in New York, but Carmel seemed entirely unfazed. "I don't think she even reacted. She was terribly clear about that sort of thing with the staff. She was full of Irish blarney."

From then on there were only rare flickers of news from the Paris staff: in late 1940, photographer Jean Moral managed to send an envelope of photos of occupied Paris to the magazine in New York, which were duly published; later, an unnamed contributor, described in the magazine as being "imprisoned in a concentration camp," had a friend smuggle out some shots he'd taken of the signs to be found in Paris shops—a dispiriting collection, including "Closed No Meat" and "No Wool Whatever." (That photographer was probably Erwin Blumenfeld, who had been in a series of French camps, including one in the Moroccan desert, and who, before long, would make his way with his family to the safety of Greenwich Village.) But the fate of other *Bazaar* contributors was unknown for much of the war. Many faced enormous suffering, which their American counterparts could too well imagine, without being able to help.

Blumenfeld implied otherwise in his memoir, stating that he'd at one point cabled Carmel via an officer at an internment camp for assistance, without receiving a reply. But wartime communication was spotty, at best; anything might explain her silence. The day after the photographer arrived on American shores he turned up at *Bazaar* to find her surrounded by the usual frenzy. When she made a cavalier-seeming suggestion that they have lunch sometime "so you can tell me your war stories," it solidified his belief that she was callous to both his sufferings and those of all Europeans. The tenor of the magazine, which was full of sympathetic stories about their plight, contradicted this view entirely. Even so, he was off and running.

> *Carmel Snow dominated the tiny, boiling hot private office. Without getting up, without looking up, she delightedly gave me her orders as if we had never been separated by two years of world war. "Blumenfeld! Talk of the devil! Two of Huene's pages are impossible and he's gone off on holiday again. We have to have the September issue finalized by tomorrow. Run up to the studio and do some fabulous retakes."*

He duly ascended to a *Bazaar* photo studio "high under the roof" where, in those pre-air-conditioned days, he clocked the temperature as "a hundred degrees and a thousand percent humidity." He slaved all night to shoot eight pages, then fell asleep in a chair. Upon awakening, he was handed a note by Carmel deducting $100 per photo from his fee, since he'd done the shoot using the magazine's equipment and studio. Even so, he walked away with $800 for the night's work, a sum that must have seemed incredible to a recent escapee from Europe's cauldron.

The issue he worked on, that of September 1, 1940, was "the first issue of *Harper's Bazaar* that has ever appeared without fashions from Paris," the magazine announced on one of the sparest layouts Brodovitch ever produced, black words looking funereal on a desolately white page. The magazine transformed as the world around it did, extolling practicality and declaring war on such indulgences as "eccentricity, exaggeration . . . strapless decolletages." While it extolled the virtues of American fashion, the absence of France, and everything it stood for, seemed as stark as war itself.

The fashion news in the States at this time was trim: skirt lengths were "an atom shorter than last year's"; suits ruled still, albeit ones with longer jackets or peplums of contrasting fabric; coats had an easy fit. For *Bazaar* readers used to Carmel's Francophilia, this issue's very Americanness—its red, white, and blue layouts, its "Editor's Guest Book" introducing a rash of Seventh Avenue designers, among them Bonnie Cashin and Vera Maxwell—must have seemed downright foreign. The French were gone, as if they'd vanished from Earth. They were so missed in the pages of the magazine that, at one point, Louise Dahl-Wolfe resorted to photographing a fashion spread of models posing against architectural models of France's great monuments. It was a cardboard Paris, but it would have to do.

Everything changed. Illustrated covers had been on the wane at other publications, but not at *Bazaar*. Hearst had long wanted to join the photographic pack, but Carmel and Brodovitch kept the illustrated covers coming. Chief became so exasperated that he penned a famous memo to Richard Berlin, then head of his magazine division, asking, "Have you any influence with Mrs. Snow? I KNOW I haven't." Berlin nagged, too, but also got nowhere. And then the impasse broke. The cover of the September 15, 1940, issue featured a photograph of a blonde model in a dark blue Forstman suit, her hand raised in a pledge to the colorfully waving Stars and Stripes beside her, a skyscraper—that quintessentially American form—in the background. "The call for color" was the cover's somber, yet fashion-conscious, cut line. Hearst and Berlin were thrilled. "The best gal-darned cover I have ever seen," Chief wrote in a memo. Illustration wasn't over—there would be some glorious covers by Vertès, among others, in the months, even years, ahead—but it was on the wane.

The magazine in this period rang with a nationalistic theme. Layouts were heavy on the red, white, and blue, sometimes accompanied by patriotic stars. The message to readers was to conserve, conserve, conserve. A wartime ruling, the L-85, first mandated in 1943, then amended the following year, limited the amount of material that could be used, and *Bazaar* urged its readers to do the same. "Keep right on wearing the slim, abbreviated silhouette that uses minimum yardage." Hems narrowed; all dresses seemed to taper at the bottom. And almost all the clothes shown—and advertisers—were solidly American; their names—Arthur Falkenstein, Ron Barach—perhaps unfamiliar to readers schooled on Chanel and Patou. (And to us.) Carmel had always "liked to encourage the American designers to be independent of Paris but respect Paris as a source of fashion," according to Eleanor Lambert. "She did a great deal to establish the importance of American designers." Never more so than during the war, when there was little alternative.

The misfortunes of the French fashion industry translated into a rare opportunity for America. Fashion magazines needed to fill their pages, and there were all sorts of talented designers just waiting to be discovered. In the October 1940 issue of the *Fashion Group Bulletin,* Carmel gave a call to arms, asking the American fashion world—at that time, so far behind the French—to do all it could to catch up. "We are starting late, but the truth is we are just being born. We've got to experiment and all the way down the line—in design, fabrics, buttons, buckles and the whole bag of tricks." She didn't just blame the industry, but American women themselves. The very casualness that gave them such a fresh, distinctive look could also be their undoing.

> *On the whole the American women have too little personal point of view about their clothes. They grab a new dress and go out to dinner. They never have a dress rehearsal. They want to look like everyone else. They won't take chances. Yet they want to look well dressed. Often they don't deserve to look well dressed. They haven't done enough about it. They care passionately but ignorantly.*

Fashion was education, she insisted, speaking more frankly to this trade group than she ever would have to her readers. "Taste can be taught. . . . I've watched the models who pose for us. Little girls from small towns, coming to New York wearing dowdy dresses. After a year of modeling, they learn good taste."

The war gave a jolt to American fashion. Working mostly with Louise Dahl-Wolfe, Diana Vreeland photographed American clothes all over the place, including, in early 1941, Miami and Cuba, then a chic vacation spot catering to rich visitors from the United States. On one location shoot, Vreeland headed off to Arizona with Dahl-Wolfe and a crew that included her assistant Hazel Kingsbury, Dahl-Wolfe's assistant, and two models, a half-Polish, half-Scottish beauty named Wanda Delafield, and the comely Bijou Barrington, a new mother who took time out from the shoot to absorb the joyous news, delivered by letter, that her baby had sprouted two teeth. When one of the mannequins fell ill, the model-slender Vreeland stepped in, posing for a famous shot in the January 1942 issue, leaning against a fake stagecoach stop on a deserted movie set, inevitable cigarette in hand, wearing a cinch-waisted rayon-and-cotton suit from Henri Bendel, a seafoam green silk scarf tied smartly at her neck.

Back at *Bazaar,* the population was, as usual, in flux. In October 1940, a key player appeared in the form of Dorothy Wheelock—a young writer who contributed an amusing story on insomnia among the famous. A blurb in the magazine quoted her as saying that she was "thirty-two, anti-social, and a country girl at heart." (Wheelock would later become Dorothy Edson when she married.) Referred by Kathryn "Fuffy" Abbe, a young woman fashion photographer, this funny, energetic, "stirring stick of a woman," as Carmel would later call Edson, was soon on staff as an assistant to the fiction editor. In this capacity, "a stirring stick" was very much required: one of the new assistant's tasks was to rouse George Davis, who often wouldn't rise from his alcoholic stupor until afternoon.

"You call George and tell him to get in here!" Carmel would cry out. Invariably, Davis promised to turn up but, when four o'clock rolled around and he still hadn't, someone from the staff, often Dorothy Monger or Cookie (the former had become Carmel's "business" secretary, while the latter was still her social one) would head off to fetch him at his brownstone on Middagh Street in Brooklyn, a kind of Bohemian madhouse he shared with an endless stream of artistic friends, including Auden (who called the place "our menagerie"), Benjamin Britten, Paul and Jane Bowles, and Richard Wright, and where all sorts of antics took place, including, on the more printable side, séances with the dead. Here Davis was known to play the piano in the nude, "bed hopping was standard, meals were communal and parties were an outrageous concoction of circus acts and transvestites," as one journalist recalled. When Davis did finally appear at work, there was usually more drama in store. Phobic about buying clothes, "he dressed so badly and looked so unkempt that when he went into 572 Madison the door people asked him to use the back entrance," Geri Trotta says.

Davis was one of the more colorful members of the *Bazaar* "zoo," as Brodovitch called the staff. "George had the nastiest tongue I've ever encountered," said Pearl Kazin, a writer who later joined the editorial staff. "He had that look of a rotten peach. You had the feeling that if you pressed your finger into his skin, the dent would stay." Although flagrantly homosexual, Davis had become engaged to Gypsy Rose Lee, the famous stripper, a liaison Edson first learned of after Davis, who had a morbid fear of banks, asked her to deposit a check Lee had written to him with the naughty comment, "I earned a quick buck under the bridge." Their affair, or whatever it was, was both salty and ill fated, with Davis continuing his encounters with a crowd that fell distinctly in the category of rough trade. When he turned up at *Bazaar* one day with a black eye from someone he'd picked up the night before, the office was abuzz. Frankly, he had to go. And he did. "He just sort of drifted away," Dorothy Wheelock Edson recalls.

Actually, he stormed out, as he'd done at regular intervals over the years. The cause of his fury was Carmel's treatment of two writers he admired, Katherine Anne Porter and Glenway Wescott. In the summer of 1940, Carmel offered $300 to Wescott via Davis for his short story "The Pilgrim Hawk" on the condition that he cut it down by a quarter to fit in the magazine. Wescott was suitably outraged. As he wrote to Porter, who was a close friend: "I'm not awfully conceited about my past perfection as a writer; but I think I may boast that I have never written a story which could be cut as much as a quarter and still live."

In January 1941, Porter had a similar experience with her story "The Leaning Tower." As she recounted to Wescott:

> *Our bizarre friend, Caramel Ice, accepted the story with love and kisses, sent me my check, assured me it would appear whole in one issue of her magazine, and there followed the comfortable silence which should mean all is going beautifully. . . . On the 18 of January I received a letter from her and a bulky package I hoped would turn out to be proofs. It was in fact a typewritten copy of my story* after *it had been most expertly disemboweled by a Mrs. Aswell, who helps to edit. It is true the story was longer than any of us expected, but on the other hand it was meant to be published in two parts. The letter from Mrs. S . . . explained with all the effrontery in the world that they had decided the story would not go well in two parts and were so anxious to publish it they had cut it to fit their space requirements for February.*

Davis battled Carmel on both writers' behalf, protesting such drastic cuts, only to crash headfirst into the brick wall of Carmel's legendary determination. The impasse was total; she wouldn't budge. He resigned in a fury, as he'd done before, then later came back asking to be rehired—another familiar gesture. Only this time, Carmel refused. The story, probably untrue, swept through the halls of *Bazaar* that Davis had fallen to his knees and begged to be rehired, only to be rebuffed again.

In any case, Porter withdrew the story from *Bazaar* by telegram the minute she saw the edited version. Carmel cabled back, begging her to reconsider. Porter replied in another cable that "the story, in its edited form, had shifted the emphasis and changed the point; I could not allow it to appear in that form." She then fired a cable off to Wescott, asking for the contact number of his literary agent. "Mrs. S... said, if I could not consent to her publishing it in edited form, she feared she would have to give up her rights in it. I fear she will, too. In fact I am dead certain she will." The author then waited in agony for Carmel to return her manuscript, apparently her only copy(!), half suspecting that the editor might somehow lose it in revenge. She kept offering to return the hefty fee she'd been paid—$600, an amazing sum for the period—but Carmel never responded and, for a time, Porter thought it might be hers to keep.

She and Wescott entered into furious correspondence about the ogress they called, variously, "our bitch goddess on the slick paper job," Mrs. Cold Carmel, Caramel Fudge, and Caramel Ice. In a letter to Wescott penned from Yaddo, the writer's colony in Saratoga Springs, New York, Porter wrote:

> *Caramel Fudge is really making quite a spectacle of herself. Who* was *it who told me—I think it must have been John Cheever, who was here lately—about* Harper's Bazaar *looking down its nose at the* New Yorker *for taking on the war so seriously. Very vulgar attitude, thinks* H's B. *They, on the contrary, have taken a new lease of life and gayety [sic], have had the excuse to fire out several of their paid staff and replace them with rich career girls who will live on their incomes and work for nothing....*

This is an "aspect of the class-war that I think nobody expected," Porter adds, but, in truth, the rich-deb-fashion-assistant phenomenon was as old as fashion magazines themselves. As for the comment about the magazine's coverage of World War II, it seems only fair to point out that, deep in the war years, *Bazaar* seemed to be all war, all the time, only filtered through a prism of fashion. It may not have been the same conflict that *The Atlantic Monthly* witnessed, but it was a deeply serious business all the same; the magazine was forever exhorting its readers to do more for the war effort.

But then Porter's accusations got darker.

> *Darling, the real point is this: Mrs. S . . . is rather more than Nazi-ish in her leanings, she was a little disappointed at what my story was leading to; she hoped, she said at lunch, I would manage a good word for the poor dear Germans. I was not interested in managing either a good or evil word for anybody or any nation: I was really telling a story. I explained this to her. She seemed satisfied. . . . The cutting as done makes it a harmless sweet little affair showing how really good and caring the Germans are. . . . Now I never denied they have good qualities, I would not willingly slander even an enemy, but I will not have my story mangled, and least of all by* that *staff of editors. . . .*

One can't return to this lunch and replay this conversation. But in all fairness, the comments Porter attributes to Carmel don't sound like her—the most Francophilic of all editors—at all. They sound more naïve, if not obtuse, about the nature of fiction than anything else. But Porter was in a rage—a quite understandable one, from a writer's point of view—and she was eager to take Carmel down many notches in the process. She was strapped financially and burning to buy a house she'd fallen in love with in Saratoga Springs, New York, but, she sniffed, "not at the price of letting Carmel Snow edit my stories. I can manage the affair without that. . . ."

In another letter to Wescott, Porter expressed contempt, not just for Carmel, but for the whole phenomenon of fiction-publishing women's magazines.

> *I made an exception of* Harper's Bazaar *on account of George Davis, but I have always been uncomfortable, more than a little apologetic in my mind, about stories of mine appearing there. Yet, if they would publish them as I wrote them, and I wrote them without regard to their tastes, and would pay me well for them beside, why, then what was lost except perhaps a little shade of vanity in my fantastic and enviable reputation. . . .*

Of Carmel, she wrote:

> *C.S., so far as concerns me, does not exist at all, what she thinks or feels about the matter is nothing, and my guess is that she can* do *nothing, short of destroying my manuscript, which I do fear rather. . . . I don't trust her, I never did, naturally, but I did attempt negotiations with her because of her real desire to have another story. . . .*

Wescott wrote back with suggestions on reselling the story, opining that Carmel "may be even unusually ruthless at the moment because she is sincerely sorry for herself—as once victimized by those who have 'artistic temperament'—on account of the tragic farce of Gypsy the Gyp and poor George." He warned Porter that "she probably wants the story just as she has edited it, to fit in somewhere; and she may try to delay and weary you into letting her have it."

Davis was, by then, back at *Bazaar,* apparently as an assistant to Mary Louise Aswell, who had been freelance editing for the magazine and was being groomed to replace him. "He's gone back to Snow on his hands and knees, as a kind of office boy," Wescott reported. Carmel must have taken him back out of sympathy—the impoverished Davis was more strapped than ever after his protracted encounter with "Gypsy the Gyp," which, Wescott wrote,

> *turned out to be a pecuniary operation in the end; pecuniary ruination for Geo—it cost him almost as much to have his moral standing raised as it has cost other richer men to have theirs lowered. So I heard. . . . Perhaps Snow herself inspired the romance as a means of getting George on the rebound, at less than a living wage. I think she [Snow] does do things like that quite unconsciously; and no doubt when she finds out what she has done she weeps a-plenty to her confessor, Money Magdalene, with blued hair, and he imposes fearful penance. . . .*
>
> *At any rate George telephoned me last night; and I wonder whether it is to tell me his sad story, or somehow to do Snow's bidding about yours. . . . I won't trust him for a bit. I don't trust men while they are in women's clutches like this. . . .*

So Carmel was the devil incarnate, although one who was religiously inclined. (The reference to "Money Magdalene" seems to be a blatantly anti-Catholic slur.) In any case, Davis didn't last at *Bazaar,* in any capacity, for much longer. He contributed freelance articles for the magazine on cultural subjects into 1941, even receiving a generous Christmas bonus from Carmel at the end of that year. But after that he was, for the most part, gone from its pages.

The editor never learned how much she was held in contempt by Porter, a writer she very much admired (who ended up publishing "The Leaning Tower" in the literary magazine the *Southern Review,* a place where "I need not be ashamed of the company I keep"); she continued to stalk her literary prey. Correspondence between Porter and Carmel seems to have taken place in a parallel universe. All is polite, a bit removed, and there is no reference to Mrs. Cold Caramel at all. Flattery was a frequent strategy. "It has been a long time since we've had the distinction of publishing anything with your particular quality, and I covet it," Carmel wrote to Porter a few years after "The Leaning Tower" fiasco. Porter answered evasively, while privately reiterating her vow never to publish fiction in *Bazaar* again ("Although she's asked me for stories since, I haven't sent anything and shan't . . . ," she told a friend, a novelist and short-story writer named James F. Powers).

Still, she did accept journalistic assignments from *Bazaar,* including one on Yaddo—where Porter was again hard at work. Carmel commissioned an article on the place, which Porter duly wrote. But when it turned out that the other writers in residence at Yaddo at that point weren't particularly exalted or, crucially, even attractive, she balked at paying the writer for her efforts. Without glamorous ink-stained wretches the story couldn't fly photographically. Porter immediately sent the piece to *Vogue,* as well she should have after this dicey episode. But her epistolary relationship with Carmel continued, with her dangling the editor along while Carmel tried to persuade her, over the years, to contribute. Even sought-after contributors could be called to task, as letters from Carmel to Porter attest. "I have to confess that I have been very much disappointed to see your name several times in *Vogue,*" she wrote to her in April 1942.

As for George Davis, he and Carmel remained friends. Her affection for him was genuine; she even wrote to Gypsy Rose Lee at some point (before that relationship dissipated) to thank her for her support of him. Even after Lee moved on, Davis's liaisons with high-profile women continued, culminating in his 1951 marriage to the German singer Lotte Lenya, then widowed from Kurt Weill, the German-born composer of *The Threepenny Opera* and other works. After news of the marriage made its way to *Bazaar,* Carmel sent off a congratulatory telegram. Others on the staff were shocked, not because Davis was a homosexual, necessarily, but because Lenya "was the homeliest woman in the world," in Dorothy Wheelock Edson's words. "I was amazed he'd ever marry her." No doubt, fame, both Lenya's and Weill's, was a draw. In any case, Davis moved on to Fleur Cowles's *Flair* and from there to *Mademoiselle,* where he would reign as fiction editor for eight years.

Davis's tenure at *Bazaar* has since been justly celebrated, not only for its picturesque eccentricity, but for the writers he introduced to the magazine, sometimes publishing them for the first time. Truman Capote's biographer, Gerald Clarke, has described it as a "remarkable, but little-remembered, moment in American literary history, when fine fiction found a nest in a forest of lingerie ads." Actually, fiction had a place at *Vogue* and *Harper's Bazaar* both before and after Davis; it was the quantity—and quality—of it that set his tenure apart. And he was succeeded, at *Bazaar* at least, by some talented counterparts, starting in July 1941, when Mary Louise Aswell, a former *Atlantic Monthly* editor and "a gentle soul," in Edson's estimation, joined the staff.

Recently divorced, Aswell was under enormous pressure in her personal life; no sooner was she on the job, it seemed, than she left to enter "the nut hatchery," as Edson calls it—a sanitarium in White Plains. Edson was given time off to visit Aswell, with the approval of Carmel, who also saw to it that the new fiction editor's job was waiting for her when she was released. "Carmel Snow was so wonderful to my mother," Aswell's daughter, Mary Doll, recalls. "She saved her life. My mother was coming off a divorce and a breakdown, and she hired her. She was so distraught not having custody of her children. Carmel just picked my mother up." She was forever making extra efforts on behalf of Aswell's children, her daughter recalls, once even having a complete set of designer doll clothes made for her, including a beautifully cut miniature Balenciaga coat in pale green and pink. "My mother was so thrilled because it was one thing she could do for her children, give them a taste of fashion and New York."

If Carmel liked you, there could be no one more human. In 1941, when Roy Faulconer, the husband of Mary Faulconer, Brodovitch's first *Bazaar* assistant, died in a tragic shooting accident, she penned a simple, heartfelt letter to his widow. "I know how truly you loved each other, and I can realize what all this means to you." Similarly, after Harry Hopkins's idealistic young son, fresh out of high school and eager to defend his country, was killed in the Asian theater toward the end of World War II, she was quick to type a note to her "Dear, dear

Harry," empathizing with what "must be for you a most complete and utter heartbreak." And her warmth to young people on her staff could be disarming. "I felt her kindness all the time," Jane Strong says, who worked at *Bazaar* under a married name, Jane Bouché.

In spite of her inauspicious debut, Aswell's tenure was triumphant for *Bazaar*. In 1943, the magazine beat out all others with six stories each in both *The O. Henry Prize Stories* and *Best American Short Stories* for that year, even though, as Aswell would later say, "The literary department was the absolute stepchild of the Hearst organization." The next year saw the publication of *It's a Woman's World: A Collection of Stories from Harper's Bazaar,* edited by Aswell. Trusting her editors completely, Carmel tended to rubber stamp their selections if she was too busy to read them. And so a poem called "The Postures of Love" slipped through. Despite its suggestive title, it wasn't sexual in nature; even so, it roused the interest of the ever-observant Fifty-seventh Street, confirming their worst fears about the avant-garde nature of Carmel's magazine. "The Hearst management was always alert to accuse me of becoming too daring for their established rules," Carmel wrote. A scandal threatened to erupt, with no one quite taking the time to parse the poem's meaning; at one point the post office even threatened not to deliver the issue. When Carmel read the poem, coming across a disturbing passage in which a man kissed a woman's "nape," she was sent into a panic. "I can't hold my head up walking down Fifth Avenue," she moaned to a friend. But she was soon reassured by Edson, who explained that the word in question referred only to the back of the neck. Carmel could be naïve beyond imagining, by modern standards, and sometimes vetted ambiguous passages with Aswell, saying, "Now, Mary Louise, I know you are a lady to your fingertips and have beautiful judgment, but are you sure this story is all right?"

The nape incident was an example of her "invincible ignorance in certain fields," as Carmel herself described it. There were others. One day, when Edson arrived at the office she heard more than the usual hilarity emanating from the corner office, where Carmel's ritual morning meeting with McFadden was taking place. The managing editor, who had never been married, was, like Carmel, astonishingly naïve about certain things. As Dorothy passed by the office, she heard Carmel say to McFadden, "There's Dorothy, she knows everything," and called her in.

And then Carmel—her boss, let's not forget—looked her dead in the eye.

"Dorothy," she asked calmly, "what do homosexuals do?"

It was clear, to the young editor's horror, that the two older women wanted the complete, intimate, physical lowdown. Scrutinized by both editors, she scrambled for time. Edson knew exactly what homosexual sex was all about—and she had no intention of describing it to her boss and her cohort. "I did some quick thinking and I thought, 'If I simply tell them they'll think I invented it.' They'll think, 'That dirty girl, let's get rid of her.'" Happily, Edson had seen a review of a book on male homosexuality in a New York newspaper just days before. She seized on the memory, clutching it like a lifeline. Feigning ignorance on the subject, she mentioned the book to the editors. "Order two of them," Carmel said, without missing a beat. "I want them right away!" And the young editor, breathing numerous sighs of relief, was soon back on her way down the hall.

Carmel's innocence even extended to contraception, as an American model, engaged to a Frenchman, discovered when she asked her advice on the subject.

> *To tell the truth, as a good Catholic I hadn't the remotest idea what a contraceptive was, so I just concentrated on persuading the model that it would be wonderful to have a child, something to remember your husband by in case anything happens to him in the war.*

When Aswell was first offered Davis's job, she told Carmel "It's impossible, I don't have the clothes." But she was quickly initiated into one of the time-honored ways that young editors became well dressed at the magazine: by buying its editor in chief's castoff wardrobe. Carmel went through clothes quickly, preferring to keep only a few things—perhaps a half-dozen suits—in her closet (a habit her daughter Brigid has inherited). And, of course, they weren't just any garments. They never had labels, for one thing, since they had invariably been smuggled in, one way or another, from France. Their designers were almost always Parisian, although the occasional Hattie Carnegie or other American label—and in that case they really did have labels—slipped in. (Carnegie, like many other New York specialty stores of the period, featured imported clothes in its East Forty-ninth Street emporium, as well as its own ready-to-wear and custom designs. No less a continental fashion plate than the Duchess of Windsor had been known to have clothes made up for her at Carnegie.) And few designers were represented. At some point in the 1940s, Carmel made the transition from Molyneux to wearing Balenciaga, almost exclusively. She also occasionally still opted for Chanel. But no matter who designed them, they were almost always lined in the white silk the couturiers knew to use when making something up for Mrs. Snow. They also sewed green ribbon into the lining of her coats, just above the hemline, so she could know from a distance, even in a crowded coatroom, which one was hers.

News of an impending sale traveled quickly. Cookie would discreetly pass the word; soon, the corridors would be abuzz with the news. "We'd have a little sale in the office," Bassman recalled. The *Bazaar* women fought over the garments, exercising all sorts of gyrations to make them fit. "The fat, the skinny, the tall, the short—we could all wear Mrs. Snow's clothes," reports Edson. (Most, but not all: Edson, being even more minuscule than her boss, had to turn to a seamstress to make hers work.) The secret to their wearability wasn't just desperation, but the wizardry of Balenciaga. As Ballard has written, "His suits fit any number of sizes by some miracle of cut." One editor, Eleanor Perényi, reports that many of Carmel's clothes came with her signature scent—Joy, of course; in the case of one suit Perényi purchased, it remained embedded in the cloth despite numerous dry cleanings.

There was a set protocol. Carmel always offered her clothes for sale to acquaintances first—among them Anita Loos and Charlie Chaplin's down-on-her-luck first wife, Mildred Harris Chaplin, who'd married the actor in 1918 when she was only sixteen, only to find herself divorced three years later. (She would die tragically, after many hard-drinking years, in her early forties.) Carmel would send a limousine full of clothes around to Chaplin's house; from there it was on to Loos. Any leftovers would be offered to her staff. And they didn't come cheap: one outfit might cost $25, another $50, at a time when some of the women buying them earned less than that in a week. Of course, being haute couture, their true value was much, much higher. No one seemed to know if Carmel had bought them in the first place or accepted them as gifts. The latter, Lillian Bassman thought. "If she paid anything, it would be nominal."

Dorothy Wheelock Edson's seamstress, for one, found the whole business unseemly, saying, "I don't like you paying so much for Mrs. Snow's clothes." But Carmel gave things away, too, including an ingeniously simple Mainbocher wool cape—when spread out on the ground, it formed a perfect circle—that Bassman wore for years. Hats were another giveaway, with Edson a frequent recipient. ("In those days we all wore hats, can you imagine?") When Carmel was pleased with someone, she might send other things their way, as model Mary Jane Russell discovered when, after a particularly arduous trip modeling the Paris collections, Carmel let her loose at Christian Dior's *maison de couture* to buy anything she wanted. Any remaining garments might be shipped to relatives, such as the young Kate White, who laughs now as she realizes that she was "naïve enough not to realize that she was sending me her discarded Diors."

Life changed, of course, after the Japanese attack on Pearl Harbor on December 7, 1941, and America's subsequent declaration of war against Japan. *Bazaar* went to war in its own way, using superb photographers and journalists to document the conflict, including a photo spread by W. Eugene Smith of a junior officer aboard a U.S. battleship—and all in the context of a fashion magazine. The shortages that were so much a part of European life came home. Rayon stockings replaced nylon ones after that fabric was appropriated by the government for the manufacture of parachutes. The results were awful, but there wasn't any choice and twenty-five million dozen pairs were duly made. "Be the first to launch them," the magazine begged its readers. Gas was rationed and leather was scarce—a 1944 ad for Bergdorf Goodman's Delman line of "wooden-soled fun shoes" contained the magic phrase "Non rationed!"

Endless *Bazaar* features set out to help women cope, including "Tips for the Servantless Life," which basically taught upper- and middle-class American women, for whom cheap help had been a way of life, how to clean house. In 1942, after Davis, the Snow's chauffeur, went off to fight, Carmel had to resort to the notorious Long Island Railroad for the summer months, when she commuted to work from the country each day. Traveling within her vicinity could be perilous, as Eileen Ford discovered one day when she and a friend, Carol Philips, then on the *Vogue* staff, were standing in Penn Station—the beautiful, Stanford White–designed ironwork one, not the mall-like structure that replaced it—preparing to board a train to Great Neck. The two women weren't wearing hats and gloves, a huge no-no at the time. "We had put them in our pockets and Mrs. Snow really chewed us out," Ford recalled. "I remember she said, 'Where's your hat, young lady?' Carol almost died." (Ford went on to cofound the famous modeling agency, Ford Models, with her husband, Jerry, in 1946.)

Carmel bypassed Penn Station altogether after she discovered that Dorothy Wheelock Edson and her husband, Wesley, who worked in advertising, drove in to Manhattan from their home in Oyster Bay each day. Wesley Edson instantly became Carmel's de facto chauffeur. The trouble with this arrangement was that, given the martinis-at-lunch situation, Carmel's day was apt to end prematurely, in midafternoon. "I'd call my husband on Wall Street and say 'Can you leave?'" Edson recalls. "Mrs. Snow wants to go home." The truncated days were just part of Carmel's summer routine, which also involved lengthy time off, usually on Long Island. (She was such a rare aestival presence at *Bazaar* that when a young student of Brodovitch's named Irving Penn came to work in the art department for a couple of summers in the early 1940s, he scarcely ran into her at all.) So the Edsons, too, quite unwittingly, saw their summer hours reduced.

Their commutes with Carmel were entertaining: the editor in chief had that peculiarly Irish talent for talking nonstop, something she seemed able to turn on and off like a faucet. Wesley Edson was amused to hear his funny, outspoken wife become demure, even silent in her boss's presence, saying, "Yes Mrs. Snow, no Mrs. Snow," as the older woman spoke. (She'd once asked Dorothy to call her Carmel, but the young editor couldn't bring herself to do it. "I could no more call her Carmel than call her Jesus Christ. I called her Mrs. Snow, very respectfully." Others shared the feeling; even Brodovitch, Carmel's contemporary, always called her Mrs. Snow. She in turn called him simply Brodovitch.) At the other end of Carmel's commute, on Long Island, life went on, war or not, undisturbed. The summer was a time of picnics, beach visits, sports. She attempted a Victory Garden, with no particular success, catching poison ivy in the process. "Palen has such fixed ideas, especially on the sacred subject of compost heaps, he allowed me only the outlying districts of our garden to grub in."

It must have been a painful moment for her when, at the end of one summer, on September 20, 1942, the New York papers announced that Condé Nast had died after suffering a heart attack at his apartment at 1040 Park Avenue the day before. In its obituary, the *New York Times* noted that the sixty-eight-year-old "Mr. Nast's magazines are distinctly 'class' publications" and went on to describe a stellar career, a man who'd made a fortune, worked for charitable causes, won

Bazaar's theater editor Dorothy Wheelock Edson on location with photographer Paul Radkai

numerous awards, including being voted "one of the ten of America's best-dressed men." What it didn't describe was the increasingly desperate loneliness of Nast's old age, a period when, divorced from a woman he'd adored, and far poorer than he'd been before the crash, he consoled himself with a succession of young women, including numerous of his magazine employees, who, fearing for their jobs, dated him, some scarcely able to contain their boredom and most wriggling away when, inevitably, he lunged at them in the taxi taking them home.

The funeral was held three days later at the Roman Catholic church of St. Ignatius Loyola on Park Avenue, just blocks from Nast's apartment. About eight hundred people attended, some from New York society (Mrs. Vincent Astor), others from the world of magazines (Raoul Fleischmann, the publisher of *The New Yorker*). It was a class production, of course. Nast's pallbearers included Henry R. Luce, the founder of *Time* magazine; the financier Bernard Baruch; and his friend and former roommate Frank Crowninshield. Even so, for a man who had been known for his festive, extravagant parties, the ceremony was austere. "The low mass with no flowers and no music seemed sadly unlike him," as Bettina Ballard, who attended, wrote. About half the mourners were Condé Nast employees, in Edna Chase's estimation. She was among them, as was Margaret Case. And at least one former employee turned up, much to Chase's astonishment. "As I walked sorrowfully up the aisle of the church, I was staggered to see Carmel Snow on her knees saying her rosary," she recalled decades later, her outrage still palpable. "She knew how Condé had felt toward her. I wondered what was in her heart at that moment." But for Carmel, there was nowhere else to be. "I could not *not* have been there, he had been such a part of my life."

After coal was rationed, she and Palen closed the East Norfolk house and moved into the city for the duration of the war. By now, their two older daughters had left for the horsey precincts of Foxcroft, the famous Virginia boarding school, which, conveniently enough, provided stables so that some of its girls could bring their horses to school. The choice of such a blue-chip institution was not accidental: Carmel wanted only the best for her girls. "It was all about elevating one's position," D. D. Ryan says. For the duration of the war, Rolling Hill Farm became a summer home, opened up each year during the girl's spring vacations from school, then closed again in the fall. When young Carmel and Mary Palen returned from Foxcroft that first winter, they crowded with their mother into the master bedroom of the Black and Whites, now packed with two single beds and a double one, while Palen slept in the maid's room on the ground floor until, as his wife wrote, he began complaining about the proximity of "too many naked women" and decamped to one of his clubs. Once her sisters were back at school, Brigid, who was in fourth grade at the nearby Brearley School, took over the maid's room and Palen was coaxed home again to share the master bedroom with his wife. In later years, she rented extra space in an apartment next door for the girls to sleep in, Edson recalls.

The middle daughter, Mary Palen, resembled her mother most, with a "wide-eyed face that looked so like my own, it startled me sometimes." She had always been different. Her mother described her as "a mystic child" and one with the most original way of expressing herself." She was adored by her father, who, Carmel reported, used to say, "When Mary Palen comes home, joy enters the house." But there was something else, too. She was "an off-horse," in Edson's words, someone who didn't quite fit in. She seemed slow, a bit in her own world, something that one cousin, Kate White for one, could identify with, saying, "I was more the Mary Palen type, going into ecstasies over sunlight and wearing who knows what." But the adults around her were becoming concerned. In August 1941, the eleven-year-old girl was sent off to stay with her aunt Virginia in Smithtown while her mother was in Paris. In a letter written later that month from Chicago to his wife, Tom wrote that "Carmel hadn't told me she was going to leave Mary Palen with you. I can imagine what a time the kid has had. She is everything you say." It's the first intimation, at least on paper, that Mary Palen was troubled. His words are cryptic, but the girl's problems would become more clear.

A vulnerable child is a challenge for any parent, but perhaps particularly so for one whose working life takes place in the very unreal universe of fashion magazines. The lives of Carmel's staff, whom she only saw part-time, must have seemed uncomplicated by comparison. And besides, even the antics of its more brilliant, high-strung members, such as George Davis, tended to be amusingly picturesque. They had their share of "nervous breakdowns," a phrase that seems to have all but vanished now but was once used as a convenient catchall to describe a wide range of human suffering, from depression to psychotic breaks to simply an inability to cope. Another staffer, scandalously enough, was rumored to be having an affair with her brother.

There were Cinderella stories, too, ones that made it seem as if one really could be kissed by a prince, then ascend permanently into a more celestial realm. One played out in the summer of 1942, when Louie Macy, like so many *Bazaar* ingenues before her, left her job to marry. She'd made a good alliance—something Carmel adored—and the magazine reported more than once that its former Paris editor was now betrothed to Harry L. Hopkins, a former secretary of commerce and head of the Works Projects Administration. Hopkins had been President Franklin Delano Roosevelt's personal envoy to Britain early in the war, and was then based in Washington, D.C., where he worked as FDR's special assistant. He was also the president's "closest friend, and his unofficial confidant," as *Bazaar* reported. (Macy, for her part, was making her own wartime contribution by racking up hours as what the magazine described as "probably the country's most famous nurses' aide.) By now, Carmel was a member of the Clothing Bureau of the War Production Board, which Hopkins headed. At one point, in Washington for a meeting, she visited her former protégée in the Lincoln Room of the White House, where she and her husband were living, something Carmel reported on with girlish excitement. "Many decisions affecting our destiny were made there, with Louie at the center of the world."

Later that year, an almost unbelievable tale unfolded after a gorgeous teenage drama student named Betty Bacall was introduced by a friend to Nicholas de Gunzburg, a fashion editor on Vreeland's staff. Niki de Gunzburg was another extravagantly mannered aristocrat, a baron who had washed up from wartorn

Europe earlier in 1942—yet another larger-than-life figure in an office that teemed with them. He was said to have inherited a fortune, then resolved to spend it all after being diagnosed with terminal cancer. He did so by giving "a party that lasted a year," according to one *Bazaar* contributor. Only, later, he discovered that he wasn't going to die after all—hence the need to go to work.

Bacall was then eighteen and living with her mother on New York's Upper West Side. She'd been born Betty Persky, then had her name changed to Bacal, half of her mother's hyphenated maiden name, in childhood after her parents divorced; earlier in her teenage years, after she resolved to be an actress, she'd changed it to Bacall. Whatever she was called, she was ambitious and funny and had a beauty that's hard to define. She seemed slinky and knowing, yet still, somehow, a kid, and an unspoiled one at that. It was a seductive combination, and de Gunzburg knew immediately that this was someone whom Vreeland very much needed to meet.

Ushered into the legendary editor's office, Bacall found herself in the presence of "an extraordinary-looking woman . . . at a desk covered with papers, photographs, boxes with bits and pieces of jewelry, scarves." Vreeland was

> *very direct in manner and speech. She stood up, shook my hand, looked at my face—with her hand under my chin, turned it to the right and to the left. She saw I was awkward, not made up, far from the perfect model. She asked what I'd done before, I told her—it was practically nothing and some time back. She said, "I'd like Louise Dahl-Wolfe to see you. We're having a sitting tomorrow—could you come to the studio? It won't take long. . . ." I was scared to death. . . .*
>
> *The next day I went to the appointed studio at the appointed time. There was a sort of dressing room, rather like the theatre—make-up lights around mirrors, canvas chairs, clothes on hangers, and boxes of accessories, all of which, I was to learn, were permanent fixtures at fashion sittings. The studio was a large room with lights, backings—*

and Dahl-Wolfe and her cameras. She was a rather short, stocky woman whose sandy hair was pulled up tight in a bun or braid on the top of her head. A friendly, open woman who was number one in her profession.

And so Bacall's brief, pivotal career as a *Bazaar* model began. "From that day on," she wrote, "my life would take a different course." Vreeland saw what was exceptional in the skinny, ambitious young actress before her, saying, "Betty, I don't want to change your look." The sitting, and those that followed, were memorable for being fun. "I'd say anything that came into my head—about acting, the theatre, my being an usher. A lot of it made them laugh—though all through it, Dahl-Wolfe never looked up from the camera, never really took her mind off what she was doing. A total professional."

Bacall had Carmel's instant approval and quickly became one of the magazine's favorites. She was endlessly in its pages, a striking face in a crowd in her first spread, in February 1943, in which she and other models posed in bright white "lookout blouses," inspired by Paris's unlikely blackout chic. She was one of several models on the page, but she was so sultry, her gaze—what would come to be known, so famously, as "the Look"—so seductively direct, that the other girls might have been forgiven for just packing up and going home. Another shot in the same issue, showed her reclining in "celestially inspired rayon and wool pajamas" by Claire McCardell.

That spring, Bacall headed to St. Augustine, Florida, on a location shoot with Dahl-Wolfe, Vreeland, and another model. At the end of the shoot, they found themselves stranded: northbound trains from Florida were packed with American troops. Bacall recalled watching, fascinated, as Vreeland lied to the railway's management, insisting dramatically that Bacall was her pregnant daughter, in order to secure the young girl, for whom Vreeland felt responsible, a seat on a troop-packed train back to New York. Telling such tales didn't perturb Vreeland at all. "Mother had no sense of right or wrong," her son, Frederick Vreeland, has said.

By this time, it had already hit. On the basis of the blouse feature alone, letters flooded into *Bazaar* asking if the young beauty had an agent and how she could be reached. At least two were from well-known names in Hollywood—David O. Selznick, the producer, who wanted Bacall to act the part of a *Bazaar* model in a film called *Cover Girl,* and the director Howard Hawks, whose attention had been drawn to the eye-catching photograph by his wife, Slim Hawks, aka Kitty Hawks, one of those überchic women—Babe Paley, Millicent Rogers—that *Bazaar* so adored. (Carmel had already pounced on Hawks, cannily photographing her in her own stylish wardrobe and, in so doing, inventing her, as Hawks herself acknowledged. She had the kind of chic that transcended designers. As Bill Blass said, "Slim had no affiliations. She did it herself.)" Carmel and Vreeland encouraged Bacall to take on the Selznick project, the one that took models as its subject, mindful of the publicity it would bring to the magazine. But Bacall, after long consultations with her family, ended up deciding that Hawks's offer was the more promising one. It was the right choice. The film she debuted in, *To Have and Have Not,* became a classic while Selznick's quickly sank from view.

Fame would strike like lightning, fast and blindingly bright. Just before it did, Bacall posed for the cover of the March 1943 issue, one of Dahl-Wolfe's stranger efforts, in which the young actress, wearing a midnight blue suit by the American designer Philip Mangone and a peculiar lacy skullcap by Hattie Carnegie, stands with a winsome expression before the dramatically lit glass door of the American Red Cross Blood Donor Service—sounding yet another note in the magazine's ongoing patriotic theme. (Brodovitch was underwhelmed by this image, apparently. He thought Bacall looked "too 'decadent' for a cover featuring the Red Cross," according to Carmel.)

In the same issue, Bacall gazed into a hand mirror while standing in the window of the outsize, majestically high-ceilinged living room—all soft colors and floral combinations—of the Snows' apartment in the Black and Whites. By the time these images were on the newsstand, Bacall had been claimed by Hollywood, where she would become known as Lauren Bacall. Her modeling career was obsolete. Even so, her picture still turned up in *Bazaar,* sometimes in shots taken months earlier, at other times in portraits from Hollywood. Their captions told her story as she moved from being "Lauren Bacall of Warner Brothers" to a "brand-new leading lady" filming *To Have and Have Not* with costar and soon-to-be-husband, Humphrey Bogart. When it was released, Bacall was everywhere, overnight, featured on the cover of *Life* with the cut line "New Movie Find" and in countless other publications. In its magnitude, it was a success experienced by very few, which makes the young actress's loyalty to *Bazaar* all the more remarkable. She sat for another Dahl-Wolfe portrait in 1944, with a text by Slim Hawks. And she even turned up as late as 1945, after filming *The Big Sleep,* to model a pair of knickerbocker pants ("the niftiest thing in Paris") for the magazine.

A new feature debuted in Bacall's cover issue of March 1943: "Junior Bazaar," a kind of magazine within the magazine, geared to the younger generation ("fair and younger fashions in sizes 9 to 17"). It was a daringly original idea—the youth market wasn't even a concept then—and it, too, was a hit. Started on a trial basis, it quickly became permanent. "The *clamor for more* was so great we couldn't resist." Carmel said. The section also functioned as a proving ground for young talent. Six pages or so per issue fell in this rubric, usually shot in their entirety by a relatively inexperienced photographer who hoped to work his or her way up into the main magazine. One of these was Lillian Bassman, who'd taken up photography with Brodovitch's encouragement, but was still employed as an assistant on his staff.

Junior Bazaar had been Carmel's idea, and it remained a special interest. As Bassman became increasingly involved in the section, she found herself going out with Carmel at the end of each day while the editor had too many drinks, after which "I'd pour her into a taxi," Bassman recalled. The latter was, in her own description, "sort of the bohemian child at the *Bazaar*" with "none of the social credentials" that Carmel adored. Even so, they had a strong bond, forged through work. Carmel admired Bassman's taste—a rare compliment—even soliciting her to shop for her own children's clothes, something she herself scarcely had time to do.

At some point, it dawned on Bassman and other *Bazaar* staffers that their fearsome boss, who spent so much of her time as a single woman, was lonely. "She couldn't stand to have an evening alone. She'd ask if I knew anyone she could have dinner with," Dorothy Wheelock Edson recalled. Or she'd say, "You have such an interesting life, Dorothy, could I go out with you and your husband?" And so she'd tag along, here and there, at one point joining Edson when she was entertaining Peter Kavanagh, the scholarly brother of the noted Irish poet Patrick Kavanagh and an eccentric figure who lived in New York where he ran a hand printing press, cranking out literary works. The antipathy between Kavanagh and his countrywoman was swift and sure; Edson never knew what, if anything, provoked it. But at some point over dinner each began to confine his comments to her alone. Kavanagh resolutely avoided looking in Carmel's direction; she, retaliating, did the same. It wasn't a good evening.

A teenage Lauren Bacall on the cover of *Harper's Bazaar*, photographed by Louise Dahl-Wolfe, March 1943

"The next day I went marching into Mrs. Snow's office," Edson said. " 'I know you hated him,' I said.

" 'I know those Irishmen,' Carmel replied, seething as she did so. 'They were brought up on potatoes and that's all they've ever known.' " When Edson asked Kavanagh about the experience, his response was eerily the same. "I know that kind of woman," he said. "She should be whipped every day of her life." So much for the sentimental Irish. Carmel tended to view some Irishmen with suspicion, even advising a startled young New York buyer named Jeanne Eddy, who would later become a fashion designer, to steer clear of her rich and well-connected, upper-class Irish beau and spend more time with a less impressive (on paper, at least) American admirer instead.

In the absence of any news—fashion or otherwise—from Paris, there was space to fill, and Carmel decided to expand the magazine's theater coverage, promoting Edson to the job of theater editor. Such a job would be unlikely on a fashion publication today, but it was all part of Carmel's philosophy. As she once said: "It is not by chance that the *Bazaar* published fiction and articles on travel and the theatre and movies and music in its pages. All these go to make up the climate of fashion, and to be in fashion one must be very aware of the weather. . . ."

Frances McFadden left the magazine for the rest of the war, heading to London where she worked as an editor at the Office of War Information. Eleanor Barry Ryan fetched up at a couple of unlikely spots, at the Brooklyn Navy Yard, where she worked as inspector, and at a New Jersey munitions factory. Carmel, too, when she could manage it, did her bit, giving speeches, visiting with women war workers, even, at one point, launching a ship during Barry's tenure at the navy yard. Barry recalled her arrival there with amusement: "Suddenly, when Carmel walked in with her blue hair and immaculate white gloves, there was a chorus of wolf whistles over the racket." No doubt she adored the fuss, but her mind was increasingly elsewhere. McFadden's absence was a real loss. Without her, Carmel noted, the magazine "continued on momentum, it sometimes seemed to me." Just as, during World War I, Carmel had longed to follow her sister to Europe, she yearned, once again, to be in the midst of it all, like McFadden. "And almost as if this time a *younger* sister had preceded me, again I wanted above everything to get abroad, too."

11 "seeing and feeling everything"

Paris was her whole life.

—Lillian Bassman

Every visit was crammed with seeing and feeling everything. . . .

—Bettina Ballard

HARDLY ANYONE MADE THE JOURNEY from America to Europe at the height—or rather, in the depths—of World War II. And especially not in the deep winter of 1944–45, when German U-boats still patrolled the Atlantic. Certainly, almost no one from the notoriously fickle, notoriously frivolous world of New York fashion did so, even if the ultimate destination was Paris, where, somehow, the haute couture had managed to continue all through the war. Since the fall of France, travel there had been far too dangerous to contemplate.

The Germans were routed out of Paris by the Allies on August 25, 1944. The city is "all lovely and saved," a famous Parisian, Gertrude Stein, wrote in *Bazaar.* But even after General de Gaulle made his triumphant entrance into the city, the following day, Americans, forbidden to travel, stayed away in droves. That is, all but one of them did. Then in her eleventh year as *Bazaar*'s editor in chief, Carmel had no intention of sitting out the war in the dreary safety of Manhattan. "The minute Paris was liberated I began bombarding Harry Hopkins with requests for a visa so that I might see for myself what the couture was doing and report on it to America," she wrote.

In August 1944, Carmel wrote to Louise Macy Hopkins at Maine Chance, the pioneering beauty resort that Elizabeth Arden opened in 1934, telling her that she had applied to the Immigration and Naturalization Services (INS) for permission to enter France as a war correspondent. "They are anxious to have me go and on their part will do everything they can to expedite matters," she assured Macy. Still, there were numerous hurdles to clear—among them approval from the FBI, the army, and the navy. She appealed to Hopkins to ask her husband to hurry things along.

> *What I am terribly worried about is that if I have to wait until everything is passed upon in the routine way, it will be too late—too late to do any good to the magazine and too late to help the French Couture reestablish itself as an important branch of French industry.*

And then there was the nagging fact that *Vogue* was poised to cover the collections: "De Brunhoff and Vogel are there at the moment with an open office getting sketches and photographs over."

Carmel begged Macy to be discreet about her request: "If *Vogue* got wind of it they would try to get ahead of me." She hoped to leave the country by October 1. "What do you think, Honey" Louie Hopkins scrawled on top of the letter before, presumably, passing it along to her husband. But Hopkins, sensed that granting such a frivolous-seeming request during wartime could be a political disaster for Roosevelt, who was running for reelection against New York governor Thomas E. Dewey, was inclined to wait until the election was over before moving ahead.

Still, Carmel pushed on, begging Macy to lunch with her in New York ("This thing is so terrifically important that I would like to have a second to talk it over with you") on her way back from Maine. Hopkins joined the two women at a Manhattan restaurant that September; in a letter just afterward, Carmel again begged him to intercede. "Wasn't the President wonderful Saturday night!" she gushed, pandering to her interlocutor by referring to the first speech of FDR's presidential campaign—they were blessedly short in those days—one that his rival, Dewey, derided shortly afterward as "a speech of mud-slinging, ridicule and wisecracks." It's one of the few instances in which Carmel referred to politics in print.

Carmel next heard from Hopkins in early October when, anticlimactically, he got in touch with her to request bound volumes of *Harper's Bazaar* for the period of his wife's tenure there. Carmel seized on the request, never forgetting to remind Hopkins of what she, in turn, was after. She did the same to Louie Hopkins, too, at one point forwarding her a copy of an ad that *Vogue* was running in various print media "stating that their Paris office is opening." It must have felt like a knife in the side not just to Carmel, but to Louie, too, who had, after all, worked at *Bazaar* for almost fifteen years.

Harry Hopkins wrote again to Carmel on October 14—two weeks after she'd hoped to depart for Paris—again on the subject of the bound volumes of *Bazaar,* which he hoped to present as a Christmas surprise for his wife. Poor Carmel must have been ready to promise anything. In a telegram to the White House two days later, she assured his assistant that she would come through. She also pushed—why not?—for permission for Dahl-Wolfe to take a portrait of his boss, assuring Hopkins that the photographer "adores the President—to the point of ecstasy—and longs to photograph him."

Favor piled upon favor, flattery upon flattery. (Collecting the *Bazaar* issues of Louie's tenure "was a joy," Carmel wrote at one point. And on and on.) At some point, she apparently asked Louie Hopkins for her husband's help after Brodovitch's troubled son, then in the armed forces, could have faced a court-martial after going AWOL. Hopkins intervened; the matter was resolved. And time passed. Carmel must have been frantic. But she played it cool, at least on the page. Finally, after the election was over and FDR was safely assured of another four years, word came that she could leave. She did so on December 7 but not before sending an effusive thank-you note to Hopkins ("If it wasn't for you I never could have done it"), along with a request for access for Dahl-Wolfe to photograph, not just the president, but some "of the men who are making history today—both in military and civilian life."

And then she was off. By then, it was the beginning of a European winter that promised to be paralyzingly cold. But that was the least of the obstacles to making the trip. The Allies had turned a corner—the invasion of Normandy had taken place in June, and American troops had captured their first German city, Aachen, in the fall. Still, no one could predict when the long war might end. And the Germans were not going to go down without a fight. By the time Carmel left New York, they were gearing up for their counteroffensive in the Ardennes; it would flare up in mid-December, becoming known as the Battle of the Bulge. But even such an enormous clash couldn't keep her away.

The Nazis might have been only freshly routed from the capital, but there was no question that she would go. The City of Light drew her to it like no place else, and her four years away from it had been an agony. "Paris, to anyone in the fashion world, was delirium . . . ," as the model Dorian Leigh has said. Besides, Carmel loved a challenge, and she had her well-deserved reputation as a woman of daring to protect. "The Whites are not quitters," as Snow's spirited young niece and namesake, Carmel White, then also in France, where she was working for the Red Cross, wrote in a letter home at this time. No matter how ladylike the older Carmel was, and whether she admitted it or not, she liked the dramatic gesture. The act of going would add to her legend. "A sketch," as Palen put it, indeed.

To avoid the treacherous North Atlantic, she chose an almost unbelievably circuitous route, hopping from one prop plane to another in an era when air travel was neither commonplace nor particularly safe. It's hard to reconcile the toughness of this journey with the figure cut by Carmel, who was then in her mid-fifties. She always looked proper, beyond proper, really. No matter what time the flight or how primitive the airport, she dressed for the occasion in the beautifully tailored suits that had long been her uniform. Thus attired, she headed south from New York to Miami, where she caught a flight to the Caribbean island of Trinidad, just off the coast of Venezuela. From there it was on to Caracas, where she hopped across the southern Atlantic to the Senegalese capital of Dakar, in West Africa. For all the exotic scenery she passed through, she lingered nowhere. Europe was her goal—the rest, merely a backdrop. From Africa it was on to Lisbon—during the war, the crossroads of the world—and then Madrid.

She arrived in neutral Spain on December 16, the day the Battle of the Bulge began. She checked into the Ritz, a haven after such an arduous journey, and savored every luxurious detail—"better food and better service than I have ever seen in my life." As she wrote to her family:

December sixteenth, Saturday

Hotel Ritz, Madrid
My Darling Palen and Children,

Here I am at the most expensive hotel in the world and also the one with the most class and swank, at least as far as I have ever seen. We arrived in Lisbon the night before last at five in the morning, and as no one had slept the night before, we were all a little on the ragged side. However, the Hotel Avis, which is the hotel I stayed at the first time I crossed on the Clipper, is luxury and comfort combined, so you can imagine my joy when I found myself in a huge double bed with linen sheets that smelled of lavender and a bath tub fit for the Rajah Bong. After the filth of South America, I just reveled. But since I wanted to leave at once for Madrid, I got off last night on the train, the tops of luxury as it is here today, which means you got a meal on the train and slept with a nice strange lady.

Anyway we arrived in Madrid, I took a bath, got my clothes pressed, and went down to lunch. The food on the trip had been pretty awful, you know you don't complain because it doesn't help you but I had cold roast beef and salad that only Brigid could appreciate. Heaven.

The following day, she wrote again:

Sunday

Mr. Balenciaga called yesterday afternoon and took me out to dinner last night. As the restaurant was very pretty he took me up to see the second floor where the private rooms are. He opened the door of one room and there having a most delicious dinner and sounding very merry were ten or twelve Japanese! Imagine.

This morning I went to Mass at the Cathedral. Magnificent, such altars, and a beautiful service. Then Mr. Balenciaga took me to the Flea Market.

For about one half hour we walked about looking at the people and then we came to a section where they sold lovely things. I bought for myself an old decoration to wear with suits, made in 1867, the date marked on it. Divine. I got another one for Carmel. You will adore it, Carmel, and wear it with suits, afternoon dresses, etc.

The wearing of such military medals, which Carmel adopted after her return to New York, would become a fad.

Her next missive was brief.

Monday

Darling children and Palen—

I am off tonight with a wonderful letter from the French Embassy here—which I will need—as after I leave the Spanish frontier I will be lucky to get a seat on a train.

She did get one, as it happened, and in the time-honored way: by slipping a hundred-franc note to the French conductor who boarded the train after it passed through the Pyrenees from Spain. After changing trains in Bordeaux, another hundred francs secured her a place in a second-class compartment. It was December 22 by then, three days before Christmas, and it was so packed "I thought a fly couldn't get on the train," she said. As they had been on her last trip to Europe, the aisles of the train were too crowded to permit access to the dining car, or even the toilet, which, while awkward for most riders, scarcely mattered to Carmel since, among her many superhuman attributes, besides rarely needing to urinate and never feeling the cold, was that "food and sleep are unimportant to me." (One wonders how her fellow travelers managed . . .) To alleviate the suffering of those passengers who did have human needs, she dug deep into her carry-on bag and shared what she found.

> *When I passed around the box of chocolates Balenciaga had given me in Madrid, my companions kept saying, "For four years we have tasted nothing like this." The chocolates were all we had to eat for more than twenty-four hours.*

Telegrams to Europe had become a hit-or-miss business, so no one knew that Carmel was coming; who would have imagined that she would make such a trip? No one was there to meet her when her train pulled into the steamy, hectic Gare de Lyon. Happily, she'd shared her train compartment with a worker from Citroën, the automobile manufacturer, who took pity on this delicate-seeming, yet indefatigable foreigner who was "as thin as a sparrow," according to her niece Nancy White. This man became Carmel's *ami de voyage,* helping her to carry her luggage down the steep steps to the Métro. Carmel, who had never set foot in a subway before, was both astonished and appalled. "As I was soon to discover . . . the doors of the Métro were never completely closed because they couldn't be—each doorway contained half of three people, the other half hanging outside." She was stunned at what people hauled onto the underground trains. "They'd take in a piano. You even have live geese as they are coming up for Christmas. Their legs are tied together and they quack, quack, quack all the way." In spite of such conditions, "you never hear a complaint or a cross word. They just say, 'You don't know how much better this is than when the Germans were here.'"

Arriving at night, her first impression was of "silence and blackness and rain. But the smell of Paris!" Gasoline was almost impossible to come by; there were no taxis and few cars. The place de la Concorde was a silent void. And the air seemed almost alarmingly clean: even in once-busy streets, you could detect a whiff of the Ile-de-France countryside. Carmel arrived at the Westminster on foot. Although she'd long earned a reputation as a demanding guest, the staff greeted her with astonishment and great warmth. "Permit me to embrace you," she recalled them saying, almost as one, before leaning over for a hug. She found the same tearful welcome repeated wherever she went; no one could believe that she was there. The appropriately named Westminster had been commandeered by the British who had designated half of it for military use. As a result "at the hotel she once all but owned, she now is pushed off into a back room in the annex," her niece Carmel White reported.

City life was endlessly disconcerting. Like the Parisians, Carmel woke to the call of roosters, since the hungry populace had begun keeping all manner of farm animals in their apartments. Each weekday morning and, again, at five o'clock each evening, when businesses were legally obliged to close, the streets were loud with the clack-clacking of wood hitting pavement: in the absence of leather, everyone was wearing wooden clogs. During the day, carts and rickshaws, fashioned from dismantled cars, were ubiquitous. Some, called velotaxis, were pulled by bicycles. There were even horse-drawn carriages in evidence. It must have seemed like another world.

Parisians seemed shell-shocked. "The population of Paris is still a mass of uncoordinated individuals, each walking through the ceaseless winter rains with his memories . . . ," Janet Flanner reported in *The New Yorker* on the very month Carmel arrived. The effect on their notorious surliness was miraculous: they were "politer and more patient in their troubles than they were in their prosperity," Flanner reported. Everyone faced innumerable hardships in the course of each day. Although it rarely gets light before nine in the morning in a Paris winter, the electricity was turned off a half hour before. It only resumed sporadically before going off for good at the stroke of five. Because of its British contingent, the hotel had electricity into the evening, although hardly very late. Invariably, the letters Carmel sent to her office in New York ended in the same way: "Goodnight—it's late and I can't run the typewriter any longer. . . ." Because there was no coal, there was no heat. At most Parisian hotels, hot water was available for bathing only on Friday and Saturday mornings. Guests were given two towels, a bath-sized one and a smaller one, to last the week. Given the lack of bathing opportunities, they easily sufficed.

Food was scarce. "No Parisian, worker or capitalist, patriot or turncoat, important or obscure, has enough of everything," Flanner reported. "Nourished by liberation, warmed by the country's return to active battle, Paris is still, physically, living largely on vegetables. . . ." (Weekly rations for a family of three were half a pound of meat, three-fifths of a pound of butter, and nine twenty-fifths of a pound of sausage.) Even at the once well-appointed Westminster, the menu was grim—watery soup, a vegetable, something sweet and undefinable for dessert. The only bread to be found had an ominous grayish cast to it and the texture of burned sawdust. The deprivations of war, Carmel discovered, had brought a whole new set of manners with them. "Since I never eat bread I found that when Janet Flanner or a girl from the office came into my room before my breakfast tray was removed, they went right over without a word of excuse and finished every bit of bread and jam."

Carmel started her first day in this disconcerting environment with a long telephone chat with her very homesick niece and namesake, Carmel White. "We fell all over each other verbally," the girl recalled. Young Carmel was continuing in her aunt's footsteps by working in wartime France as a staff assistant for the Red Cross, in her case stationed at a "rest camp" where troops from the Thirty-sixth Division stayed on their way to and from combat. (Her touching, observant letters home were intermittently published in *Harper's Bazaar*.) But there wasn't much time to visit. Almost as soon as she was awake, the editor headed off to the American Red Cross HQ at the Gare St. Lazare—her old stomping grounds—to embark on a five-day trip to see the work being done by that organization in eastern France. She was determined to do "a better than good job," she told her office in New York, for an upcoming story on the Red Cross for the magazine. To achieve this goal, she enlisted Henri Cartier-Bresson ("not only the best photographer in France, but a darling," as she put it) in her cause.

Cartier-Bresson was in his mid-thirties at the time and on the cusp of the worldwide fame that has been his ever since. He had been married since 1937 to Ratna Mohini, a Javanese dancer whom he'd met in Paris. Unobtrusive, almost bland-looking, he seemed far younger than his years; Carmel described him as "looking about nineteen though he must have been thirty." (Actually, he was thirty-six.) Yet he had already packed in far more living than most people his age. Inspired by Munkacsi's work, he'd begun photographing as a teenager, wandering among villages in Africa and Europe with his Leica, taking particularly moving photographs of Spain during its civil war. Active in the French Underground movement in the war's early years, he had been captured by the Germans in June 1940, spending thirty-five months in a prisoner-of-war camp, during which he attempted to escape—twice—before finally succeeding on his third try. An admirer of James Joyce, "I had a copy of *Ulysses* under my arm when I was captured," Cartier-Bresson recalled. "And I had *Ulysses* under my arm when I escaped."

Cartier-Bresson's wartime photographs, his silent commentaries, shock still, conveying a wealth of emotion in the simplest terms. One 1944 image, which shows a Resistance soldier lying dead by a fog-bound bridge traversing the Rhine, has the powerful simplicity of a haiku poem. In a few strong lines, it says everything about the waste and senselessness of war. Another famous image, taken in the Dessau concentration camp and depicting an infuriated refugee confronting a Gestapo informer, epitomizes what he so famously called the "decisive moment" (a dubious translation of the title of his 1952 book *Images à la Sauvette,* perhaps more accurately rendered as Pictures on the Run), that fraction of a second in which a person or a situation is ineffably revealed. Cartier-Bresson's genius lay in his ability to capture this almost mystical circumstance, in a myriad of diverse situations, over and over again. It added up to "a great general contemporary record of our time, sensitively seized by one man's eye and his camera lens," in Flanner's words.

By the time Carmel worked with him, the young Frenchman had worked mainly on the Continent, although he'd already made one working trip to the United States; soon he'd fan out, bringing back unforgettable images from the farthest reaches of the world. His photo-taking techniques were already the stuff of legend. He'd tape the shiny metal parts of his camera with black tape, to attract as little attention to the apparatus, and the man who carried it, as possible. He took advantage of his own unremarkable-seeming appearance, moving gently through the world, making the ordinary seem extraordinary, capturing moments as they unfolded that might have gone unnoticed by someone else.

He and Carmel set out for the city of Nancy, in Lorraine, and its environs, "as close as you could possibly get to the front," Carmel later wrote. They had an immediate rapport. "She was a remarkable woman," Cartier-Bresson recalled years later. They traveled together for five days, she taking notes, he photographing, together documenting the effects of war, including "villages we passed through where there wasn't a breath of life: Houses, stables, churches blown to atoms." The very landscape seemed putrid: Carmel was repulsed by the sight of bloated, rotting dead cows in fields, bovine victims of land mines. It's hard to imagine another photographer who could do greater justice to such desolation. The images Cartier-Bresson brought back juxtapose relentless physical destruction and a shell-shocked populace—among them, strikingly young Red Cross workers, driven by idealism—with the timeless landscape of eastern France.

The photographer, too, was impressed by his traveling companion. "She was very intuitive," he recalled. "She guessed at people." He later said that he learned from Carmel's witchiness, her much-vaunted sixth sense, to trust more in his own intuition. "I owe her a lot." He was also struck, as so many were, by her eating habits. "She didn't nourish herself. She never ate." And when she did it could be idiosyncratic. One niece, Kate White, recalls one phase in which she ate only *blanc de poulet.*

On her return to Paris, Snow shared her notes and impressions with Flanner, who wrote the text that accompanied Cartier-Bresson's photographs in the

March 1945 issue of *Bazaar.* These were a striking addition to the magazine, sandwiched as they were between pages of fashion commentary—superb photography in its own right, but more than a little frivolous by comparison. But so ingeniously edited was *Bazaar* in this period that it hardly seemed to be so. The magazine seemed to make the point that, for all the well-documented evils of the world, there was joy, beauty, and pleasure to be had, too. It's just that they weren't often tossed together in the slick pages of a fashion magazine.

In its next issue, it went further, publishing Cartier-Bresson's searing photographs of wounded soldiers being evacuated from outside the Dutch town of Nijmegen, after Operation Market-Garden, the Allied plan to capture bridges in the German-occupied Netherlands, failed, with catastrophic losses for the British. Cartier-Bresson would contribute, intermittently, to *Bazaar* for years. And Carmel's support for him went beyond just giving him assignments; in 1947, she lent him $400 to help defray his share of the cost of founding the Magnum photographic cooperative, which he created in Paris that year with fellow photographers Robert Capa and David Seymour, who was born in Poland as David Szymin and known as "Chim."

Back from her trip, Carmel went straight to work, setting up shop in her hotel room, where she fielded visits from couturiers, fashion assistants, photographers, journalists, and more. Dining with her niece on January 3, she told her that "people at home really have no idea of what war is," a statement the young woman, who had been working with soldiers on their way to and from the front, found deeply ironic. ("She is here as a civilian and sees it all with different eyes. I saw it with army eyes.") Even so, the younger Carmel had to concede that, on her trip, her aunt had "managed to get herself far closer to where the fireworks are than I have." She expressed concern for her welfare, noting that her aunt had none of the military privileges that she herself had as a Red Cross worker. For any civilians, finding adequate food was a challenge. "She is invited out plenty but even so—it is ghastly," the younger Carmel wrote home.

When Carmel went to lunch with Benito, the Spanish illustrator with whom she had first worked at *Vogue* in the 1920s, she was thrilled to be served beautifully prepared French cuisine, with no end of fresh-seeming ingredients. "Oh, but you don't lack anything over here, you just have wonderful food," she said to one of the couple's daughters, Isabel LaMotte, a story that soon became a part of the Benito family legend, since finding any sustenance at all had been near impossible. "Carmel had no idea what we went through to present her with a decent lunch," recalls another Benito daughter, Carmel Semmes. The editor's elegance, in the midst of wartime Paris, was striking. "Mrs. Snow still had a beautiful figure and was dressed very nicely in a red jacket with gold buttons and a black skirt. We thought she was very chic. . . . She had great authority."

In one of her first evenings in Paris she joined up with a triumvirate of Paris friends—Janet Flanner, Bébé Bérard, and Marie-Louise Bousquet—at the latter's tiny walk-up apartment on the top floor of 3, place du Palais-Bourbon, just across from the eighteenth-century edifice where *Vogue*'s Paris offices were housed. Bousquet was at the very heart of *le tout Paris.* Her malicious tongue was legendary, as was her generosity to artists of all kinds, many of whom, by way of key introductions and general moral support, she helped along in their careers. They, among others, gathered each week at her famous salon, which she had begun with her late husband, Jacques Bousquet, a playwright, librettist, and actor, back in 1918. On the night Carmel dined at the Bousquet apartment, "the electric lights were uncertain, the evening chill, but a hard-come-by lamb roast warmed us," Flanner wrote. In a burlesque moment, Bérard wrapped his old mackinaw around him and, pulling along his ubiquitous dog, Jacinthe (described by Flanner as "multicolored" because of splattered paint), paraded in front of the others to hilarity all around, demonstrating the styles he'd already seen at his friends' couture houses, which Carmel had yet to visit. *"Ah, c'ést épatant, chère Carmel, c'est l'élégance de Paris,"* he said. It was, as Flanner recalled years later, "an astonishing scene."

No doubt Carmel also stopped in, as she so often did, to one of Bousquet's salons. Held between five and seven each Thursday, they were "the mirror of Paris, famous into the heart of Texas," as Christian Dior once wrote. Anyone might turn up—past attendees included Aldous Huxley, Pablo Picasso, the *couturier du jour,* and on and on—but with many of these leading lights dimmed, in one way or another, by war, attendance was drastically reduced. Now, Bousquet's visitors were mainly "war correspondents who had discovered her wit," Ballard recalled.

Like everyone, Carmel went everywhere on foot, occasionally resorting to the Métro. When she didn't walk, she climbed. The diminutive caged elevators that are so much a part of Paris life functioned even more erratically than usual as an intrepid American fabric buyer, who also made it to France against all odds that winter, remarked. "Ninety percent of them are not operating because of the shortage of power, and when they do run, it is necessary to walk down." Given how much ground Carmel needed to cover, it's no surprise that she ended each day in a state of physical collapse. "The poor lamb literally staggered upstairs to her room one day after walking a good ten miles . . . ," Carmel White wrote to her mother. Not surprisingly, and for the first time in a long time, the editor found that she didn't need sleeping pills to sleep.

On her daily forays out to the fashion houses, she was repeatedly impressed by the simple, everyday heroism of the French, starting with "my little fitter at Balenciaga," whom she visited in the course of buying her "one splurge" (with the prevailing prices, who could afford more than one?)—a suit with a snug bodice, rolling peplum, and fashionably rounded shoulders. When her longtime fitter kept dropping pins, she excused herself by saying, with a humility the editor found heartbreaking: "I regret, Madame, my hands used to be so quick, but now, you understand, they don't seem to work as they used to." Given the temperature, nothing could. At Cartier, just down the rue de la Paix from the Westminster: "The shop was freezing, and the incongruity of looking at the most extravagant jewels in the world in an icy room can't be imagined. . . . It was so cold that everyone wore gloves."

With every encounter, Carmel pieced together more information on how the French fashion world had survived the occupation. After the fall of France, the couturiers had found strength in the leadership of Lelong, the head of the Chambre Syndicale, who urged them to join forces against such diverse enemies as endless shortages—silk and wool, for example, two mainstays of any couture line,

LEFT: **Carmel and a Paris assistant dashing through the Paris streets, late 1930s**

RIGHT: **Thwarted by a Paris elevator**

had all but disappeared—rampant unemployment, and the Nazis themselves, whose threats to the industry seemed never ending. When the Germans first took over, they decreed that only certain designers would be authorized to continue working, presenting "a reduced collection to a reduced clientele," and closed down two of the most prestigious houses—Balenciaga and Alix (who, having sold her company, along with her name, was now known by her surname, Madame Grès). The Spaniard duly left for Madrid, but was able to return to France and reopen his maison de couture almost immediately, in September 1940, in part due to pressure from the Spanish government. As for the inventive Grès, a master draper, she was allowed to join the ranks of functioning wartime couturiers only after promising to reveal her "style secrets" to Nazi specialists who would then, presumably, pass them on to German designers. She agreed to this wholeheartedly, thereby ensuring the reopening of her business, then delayed endlessly, trotting out one excuse after another to explain why the occupiers would just have to wait one more week. In the end, just as she'd planned, she never actually did come through with the goods.

Some foreign designers fled altogether—to the disapproval of their French counterparts, who interpreted their flight as cowardice. Molyneux retreated to his native England, which hardly turned out to be a haven, for the duration of the war. He escaped France by slipping onto a coal barge just before the Nazis arrived. British *Vogue* painted the scene: "In the midst of the coiled confusion, the terror, and the soft soot came Molyneux's former batman, his butler for twenty years, the dry, thin, efficient Pawson, in a white jacket, carrying a tray with glasses and a shaker of Martinis." (Just the kind of story that, true or not, a magazine writer of any era might find irresistible.) Mainbocher also left, returning to the United States, more prosaically, by airplane and presumably without his own butler. He would rebuild his fashion empire in New York, not returning to live in Paris until his retirement in 1971.

Schiaparelli and Chanel, longtime rivals, acted, exceptionally, with one mind, planning to head south to unoccupied France. Chanel closed the fashion part of her business saying that she didn't want to cater to war profiteers. In truth, the fact that she had been cohabiting with a German officer, Hans Gunther von Dincklage, a former diplomat and spy known as "Spatz" (sparrow) made fleeing the easiest course. She was still in Paris, though, at the time of Carmel's visit. "She is not in business and she was going in one morning as I passed and she was dressed in a little blue jersey jacket," the editor noted, adding that "all jackets are a little longer than are permitted by our regulations." One aspect of Chanel's business—a little number called Chanel No. 5, which the designer had created, to enormous, lifelong profit, in the 1920s—was thriving, with lines forming outside her former fashion house on the rue Cambon. "They can't buy perfume until twelve but at nine o'clock the queue starts outside of Chanel's place and that queue is doubled down to the rue de Rivoli and if Chanel opens five minutes after twelve, there is practically a riot." The people in line, mainly American military men, were scrambling to buy their girlfriends the one thing that actually seemed affordable in postoccupation Paris—in spite of rampant inflation, scent, inexplicably, had risen only 100 percent over prewar prices, a rate much lower than other goods. "Perfume is the cheapest thing in Paris," Carmel told the Fashion Group. All were selling well, but none more so than Chanel No. 5, in part, Carmel theorized, because of its simple name, which worked so much better than "the poor boys saying 'L'amour Toujours' which they couldn't remember."

It was this fragrance, more than anything, that allowed Chanel to live with such fabled insouciance. Rich lovers, she had learned, didn't last forever, but a popular perfume certainly could. Thanks to it, her exile from Paris was a luxurious one, spent partly on the Riviera, where she converted her house into a billet for French and Allied soldiers, and partly in Switzerland. Although she told the world that her retirement was permanent, later events would prove otherwise. As for Schiaparelli, she transformed her Paris house into an emergency hospital, then moved her operations to Biarritz. Not long afterward, upon arriving in America on a lecture tour, she was asked by a reporter about a brooch she was wearing. "It is a phoenix," she answered, in a much-quoted remark. "A bird which, after being burned, rises again from the ashes and grows in full beauty. It is the symbol of France." For a long time, though, such optimism must have seemed unrealistic. At the time of Carmel's trip, the phoenix was still very much in cinders. It wouldn't rise again for years.

Only about twenty couture houses continued to function during the occupation, and only on a very reduced basis, presenting a total of about a hundred garments per season. They were continually harassed by the Germans, who would close them down for "flouting restrictions" and other infractions. Of all the threats the couturiers faced, none was more pernicious than the Nazis' often-stated goal of relocating the industry to Berlin and Vienna, incorporating it into the German apparel trade. For the designers, such a move was unthinkable. "French fashion exists in Paris, or it does not exist!" thundered Lelong, who is widely credited with having saved French fashion in this period. Through ceaseless, ingenious procrastination—shades of Madame Grès—he and some of his designing colleagues ensured that the industry, however tenuously, would stay where it belonged. Lelong served as an intermediary with the occupiers on other fronts, too, endlessly working, for example, to procure enough fabric for himself and his colleagues. The departure of the Germans in late summer had cleared the way for what was widely known as "the first free demonstration of the couture since 1940," held in the fall of 1944. These weren't "openings," even in name, and there was scarcely a foreign buyer in sight; still, they were seasonal styles served up, for the first time in years, without outside interference.

The occupation may have been over, but the war itself was not. Its suffering was still unfolding. The Holocaust was under way, although no one outside of the inner circle of the Nazi Party could know the full extent of its evil machinery. Still, it had become clear that few Jews who endured the forced deportations to Nazi "work camps" ever found their way back. The Gare d'Austerlitz seemed to ring with the echoes of thousands of deported children, wrenched from their parents' arms, never to return. The atmosphere in Paris was every man for himself, as Bettina Ballard recalled—a far cry from the prevailing self-sacrificing mood in Britain, where even the king, famously, waited his turn. Parisians instead pulled whatever strings possible to get ahead, to escape, to wring out sustenance from depleted ration books. The black market flourished, in currency, food, everything.

Even in the rarefied world of haute couture, no one was immune. Each had suffered his own war, and suffering was very much the operative word. When Carmel came across members of her old crowd, she found them dramatically changed. Ballard, who returned to Paris at about this time, gives a horrifying example when she describes her reunion with her former boss, de Brunhoff.

> *He had aged twenty years in the four and a half years since I had seen him. His only son, he told me, at seventeen had been hunted down on a farm by the Gestapo and shot, along with several other boys, on the suspicion that they were part of the resistance. "Why did it have to be him? He was so young—I wanted to teach him all I knew about editing." He seemed completely dazed by it still, by the uselessness of it. . . .*

No one, "rich or poor, has been spared," Carmel noted. "Each one has her own private grief, each one shares the larger grief of her country." The überchic Solange d'Ayen, former fashion editor of French *Vogue,* was among the hardest hit. Is suffering more grotesque when juxtaposed with elegance? Imprisoned in the notorious Fresnes prison, she had lived and slept for months in the same beige Balenciaga dress, washing it daily as part of a much-clinged-to routine in solitary confinement—where she was kept in limbo, without even a book to read, uncertain of the fate of her husband, Jean, who had been imprisoned before she was. She saw him only once after her release, as he was being marched, stone-faced and forever changed, down a suburban street on his way to being transported to Bergen-Belsen, the infamous transit center in Lower Saxony, a concentration camp in all but name, where thousands died of starvation and typhoid each month. Like so many, he never emerged. His wife would be tormented forever afterward by the fear that he might somehow have learned before his death about the accidental wartime demise of the couple's only son. It's no wonder that, as Ballard wrote, after visiting d'Ayen, "Looking at her, I felt that I was seeing her ghost." Carmel, too, was moved, expressing unbounded admiration for her bravery. "She is the most wonderful woman I have known in the world," she told the Fashion Group.

For a week, Carmel went about her Paris rounds accompanied by her young niece, who recalled sitting in "beautiful, lavish, plush" lobbies feeling "*de trop* and like a country cousin" while her chic aunt met with couturiers and the like. "When she was making appointments to go places she'd say, 'I have a little niece.' I'd say, 'Aunt Carmel, I'm twenty-six years old!' " When Carmel's old friend actress Katharine Cornell turned up, on the tail end of a tour of *The Barretts of Wimpole Street,* playing to American troops and others in front-line villages in Italy and France, the editor kept young Carmel close at hand. "She knew that the contact with Cornell would be advantageous to me," the girl recalled. Both current and former Carmel Whites accompanied the venerable actress, then in her early fifties, on a shopping trip "to some couturier place where there was the most magnificent coat lined with mink," according to Carmel White. She described it in a letter home as

> *a coat that C.S. said was "perfect, my dear, simply perfect for Miss Cornell." It was perfect at that. I can no more tell you the price of it than I can get home, for you wouldn't believe it. Neither can Cornell, but I have a hunch that she will get it all the same. Your sister is to blame, if the woman goes bankrupt.*

In the end, the great actress's finances were saved by wartime regulations that made it impossible to take such a large amount of cash out of the United States.

Hardly any buyers were in Paris in this season; if they had come, they would have been unable to buy—prices had shot up insanely with many goods costing five times, even more, of what they had earlier in the war. "Over and over they'd say, 'We realize, Mrs. Snow, that even Mr. Bergdorf Goodman doesn't buy clothes at this price,'" Carmel told the Fashion Group upon her return. Unable to import a photographer—it had been hard enough getting over there herself—she relied mainly on illustrations to show the new styles, with occasional shots by whichever local photographer could take time away from wartime tasks, among them Jean Moral and Maurice Tabard, a character of a man who, in prewar days, used to be seen riding around Paris on a large aluminum tricycle.

Carmel published fashions from Paquin, where a new Spanish designer named Antonio Castillo was debuting, as well as from Piguet, Lanvin, and Madame Grès. In general, clothes had a sloped shoulder line ("everything is round"), with padding used to make it so. Skirts and dresses had a fullness in front, with draping around the hips. One of Balenciaga's dresses, a glorious silk evening number of midnight blue satin, embroidered in black paillettes, particularly caught Carmel's eye. Other fashions were almost eerily pragmatic, such as Schiaparelli's Shelter suit, a zip-fronted, low-waisted pantsuit designed to be worn in bomb shelters. Every designer, it seemed, had stories to tell, most dramatically Patou, who took

Carmel around his office, its walls pierced with bullet holes. "When the Gestapo came here, they just shot up the wall to show how quickly the papers had better be produced." She had brought six months of issues of *Bazaar* with her, which she circulated among the designers, and was cheered to receive compliments, not just on the magazine but on the American styles that, in the absence of any competition from abroad, dominated its pages for the first time.

Snow almost always melts on the sidewalks in Paris, and rarely builds to slush, so it seemed miraculous when, one day in that desperate winter, the city streets were suddenly powdered with white. Working in her hotel room that morning, it took a while for Carmel to realize what was wrong: the clack-clacking of Parisians going to work, a sound Flanner likened to horse's hoofs, had been muffled into silence. ("You miss it," the latter reported.) Late that first snow-filled day, on the way back to the Westminster, Carmel witnessed a charming tableau, when "about fifty of Schiaparelli's young midinettes poured out into the Palace Vendôme and had a snowball fight with our G.I.'s, all of them laughing, flirting, singing. It was a delightful scene."

In the city's churches, Carmel discovered, all was dark and cold. She prayed, as she always did, daily, stopping in at some of her favorite places. Attending mass at the Madeleine, one gray, wintry day, she found it lit only by two altar candles, leaving most of this cavernous, eighteenth-century space as black as a cave. "When the priest went to the pulpit to make the sermon his voice seemed to come out of the walls, and the Sanctus bell rang from where you knew not," she reported, sounding thrilled in a girlish way.

For all the austerity of the war years, and in spite of everything, as Ballard noted, fashion didn't die.

> *My friends in Paris still talked about hats, about clothes, and the usual fashion-world gossip. They would bicycle or take the Métro any distance for any semblance of a party—often carrying their fancy hats in boxes on their handlebars and putting them on at the door. This deliberate effort to continue their lives as usual dated from their years*

under the German occupation when they had not wanted to be cowed by the enemy whom they despised.

Parisiennes, in their inimitable way, managed to dress with style no matter how many shortages they had to endure. One of the first things Carmel noted was how people's clothes were "darned exquisitely." Many were tricked up in an artful way, drawing attention away from areas that had been worn or repaired. Enormous collars, ceramic buttons, and fanciful patches, it was discovered, could hide a multitude of sins.

But the wartime fashion landscape hadn't always been so chic. In the first days of the conflict, "People wore clothes made out of blankets and curtains," recalls Isabel LaMotte. "It was like *Gone with the Wind*." In a November 1944 radio address, *Vogue*'s de Brunhoff traced the ebb and flow of Paris fashion during the war:

> *The first winter was bulky. Everybody wore everything they had at once; coats, overcoats, layers of garments. The next winter, even colder, produced newer shapes, planned during summer for warmth and everlasting qualities—dull by themselves, but embellished by gay hats, colorful accessories. By the third winter the Nazis could be taunted. The big wooden shoes became fancy creations instead of farmyard utility. Hats soared to balance the silhouette. Last winter was the season of contrast and exaggeration. Lumberjack coats and such practical outfits alternated in wardrobes with the most extravagantly wasteful dresses that could be imagined, to tease the enemy and flaunt the regulations.*

Many designers had reacted ingeniously to wartime deprivations. Since ribbon wasn't rationed, it appeared everywhere for a time, curling brightly from hats and even stitched together to form bright, multicolored fabric, which was then used for dresses and blouses. Schiaparelli fastened buttonholes together with dog leashes and chains. And Lanvin came up with gas mask holders in bright felt or dusky tweed.

By the time of Carmel's trip, voluminousness reigned, with huge skirts and billowing sleeves all the rage. Americans, hearing about this mode from a distance, had reacted with outrage—fabric was scarce in Europe at the time, and the French had received numerous donations of material from the United States. The French certainly weren't using material sparingly. But, up close, Carmel discovered that many of these apparently fabric-rich creations had been conjured as much from sleight of hand as from actual cloth. Through careful straight and bias cutting, the ever-resourceful couturiers had made these garments seem more ample than they actually were.

There was a limit, though, to what could be done. Since metal and leather had been confiscated for war purposes, accessories were particularly hard hit—hence the wooden clogs. Some women had gone so far as to take their old pocketbooks to shoemakers to have them transformed into shoes. Most upsetting of all, to Carmel's mind, was the fact that "there is no quality in France. The quality is appalling. All of the raw materials are gone." Lots of fabrics were made of "dreadful ersatz stuff"; everything was diluted, with wood fibers added to wool, and so on. ("It is a mixture of everything in the world.") In spite of this, she added, "the plaids they have made are the prettiest colors I have ever seen in my life."

The French millinery industry faced an extra challenge when the tides of fashion, as well as of war, briefly turned against them. Suddenly, and for no apparent reason, Parisian women began to appear in the streets bareheaded or wearing snoods. Before too long the pendulum swung back—from the sublime to the ridiculous, you might say—and big, extravagant hats became the rage. Women swanned through the streets wearing enormous berets, some loaded down with feathers, artificial flowers, and the like. Others soared a foot into the air, including home-made, fantastically high, upholstered Charles X turbans. Fur was added, here and there—rabbit or even cat, the only pelts available. "You should see the hats!" young Carmel wrote to her sister Nancy at this time.

> *Darnedest thing you ever laid your eyes on. They are awful big most of them and there is ribbon or tulle over everything. . . . There are*

> *mammoth plaid jobs built up on the order of a beret or inverted cuspidor types that are hideous. You would go mad.*

Not all millinery news was grim. Couturiers had begun making their own hats; some, such as Balenciaga, doing so for the first time. "His hats are charming," Carmel told the Fashion Group.

Other looks were not. Many theories have been trotted out to account for the rise of what Carmel described as "grotesquely fantastic Zazou fashions," which flourished, for both sexes, beginning in 1942. The look was jive, and some historians, Valerie Steele among them, have traced it, linguistically and stylistically, to the "zoot suits" then flourishing in certain corners of the United States. Zazous, as the men and women who wore it were called, favored a look that was unapologetically bizarre: long jackets, flared trousers, thick-soled shoes. It was all part of what Flanner called "the strange chic of the female Zazous, along with no hat, an artful, absolutely terrific pompadour, a strict, tailored suit with a full skirt for bicycling, and hanging from the neck, the inevitable cross." They wore outsized versions of these Christian symbols around their necks and carried another, unexpected accessory: "long, crook-handled umbrellas" taken everywhere, rain or shine. It all added up to a kind of sartorial nihilism, a comment—complete with exclamation point—on fashion, war, occupation. "Perhaps on some semiconscious level, flamboyant fashions were a way of denying the humiliation of defeat," Valerie Steele wrote. Which sounds about right. Zazou was a gift of ugliness, specially wrapped and delivered to the Germans.

While Zazou began at street level, for a time it had an equivalent in haute couture, which also displayed an ugly side. In 1943, *Life* magazine, reporting on "the first sizable collection of French creations to enter the U.S. since the German Occupation," described them as "vulgar exaggerations of famous silhouettes. The dresses brief but at the same time overly draped; rather than use simple fabrics sparingly, couturiers used loud ones to compensate for restrictions."

The magazine blamed the "sorry state of the couture to the French having to cater to German tastes." The rich customers who had kept it afloat before the war were long gone. Couture prices were more astronomical than ever, and they drew in a new, less savory, clientele.

> *The people who were buying at the moment were the new black-market rich, with a vulgarity that was too dreadful to be believed. They were the people who had traded with the Germans and were still making fortunes trading among themselves, and they were the explanation of much that went on in Paris: the awful hats, the women in expensive clothes whom you wouldn't be seen dead with. . . .*

Of these, the lowest specimen was what Carmel called the "black market woman."

> *She is the most dreadful-looking woman in the world. She could be very easily, if you were in France, your butcher's wife and during the Occupation she may have made millions dealing with the Germans. She isn't France. She has nothing to do with France. She is a woman who has come up overnight. She will be gone tomorrow. She has what we call her "hot money" and she wants to get rid of it as soon as she can because she is going to be asked to account how and where she got it. She has no idea of value therefore she is spending it like a lunatic and she is one of the reasons the prices are as high as they are.*

Some French couturiers later insisted that they intentionally came up with substandard designs—wacky head coverings, broad-shouldered, ungainly looking suits—in this period to give such women the fashion they deserved. It wasn't hard to do. "The Germans . . . had such an inferiority complex about French fashions that almost anything could be put over on them," Lelong told Ballard. To Edna Chase's mind, such fashions evolved as a way "to discourage the hausfraus." If so, it was a well-kept wartime secret. For what must be the only time in the history of couture, clients were allowed to leave the great fashion houses convinced that they epitomized the height of elegance, when in fact they looked grotesque. Incredibly, its victims didn't seem discouraged at all. It's delicious to imagine the giggles that might have emanated from behind closed doors as the fraus of generals and other Nazi brass walked to their chauffeured cars, looking ridiculous—and proud of it. No one, from the première to the lowliest of its sewing girls, would have given the game away.

Toward the end of her European stay, Carmel moved on to London, again with Cartier-Bresson in tow, where the Blitz was eternally under way, buzz bombs and all. Again, they traveled through small, sometimes desolate villages—these ones in Kent—photographing aid workers along the way. She was moved by what she saw, admiring the English for "what they have suffered, what they have gone through, their self-discipline, their self-sacrifice." While there, she caught up with two *Bazaar* alumnae: McFadden, her "right hand" of so many years, and that survivor Daisy Fellowes, then sojourning in the land of her well-born husband.

Carmel made her way to Albany, the famous Georgian building off Piccadilly, that was built in 1802 as a residence for the Duke of York, to visit the young playwright Terence Rattigan in his "sets," as Albany's rarefied residents traditionally call their apartments. Rattigan was then in his early thirties and making the difficult transition from being a writer of light drama to something more substantial *(The Browning Version, Separate Tables).* "There in his freezing flat," Carmel wrote, "I found Lady Cunard, looking like a parakeet with the feathers in her hat; and Daisy, a little older, a little stouter, and wearing (as did everyone in England) a dress that had seen gayer days." Even for those of us who have only known the Honorable Mrs. Reginald Fellowes from afar, such a description comes as a shock. (Stout? In a faded dress?)

Back in Paris, "I felt that new talent was emerging," Carmel added. Nothing could have made her happier. She turned again to Cartier-Bresson to photograph a feature on promising young fashion designers, among them the Viennese-born Mad Carpentier, "who practically grew up at Vionnet," according to the magazine, and Colette (then the chief designer for the venerable former saddlemaker Hermès), for the April 1945 issue. The latter had created the *Canadienne,* a short jacket with a round collar, rounded shoulders, and a strictly defined waist that was one of the season's hottest looks; designed to be worn while bicycling, as everyone still did in Paris, it was chic, practical, and *everywhere.*

When the shoot was over, Carmel's work was done. She'd been away from her home and family for four months on a voyage that had been far more difficult than she would admit. "It was a totally bewildering exercise for her," as her niece Carmel White wrote in a letter home. "It was arduous and unknown." It wasn't just the foraging for food, the trekking through city streets, but the loneliness, too. Usually, on her Paris sojourns, as her niece wrote, "she'd be completely sheltered and taken care of and suddenly there she was, unheralded, unknown, unshepherded. It was much, much harder than she ever let on." Still, you can sense from Carmel's own description of her departure how reluctant she was to tear herself away from Paris, where daily life remained stubbornly in crisis mode. The city needed her, and it was so full of talent and people she loved.

Finally, in mid-March, she took her leave. She caught a train to Cherbourg, where she boarded an uncomfortable passenger boat, accompanied by the huge duffel bags she now favored over steamer trunks. (She would later move on to Louis Vuitton.) She reported a calm voyage. It was certainly a more direct one than she had taken on the outbound journey. But her idea of calm doesn't sound relaxing by anyone else's standards—as she told her friends and family, almost casually, upon her return, the trip was marred by the occasional depth bomb, aimed by Allied destroyers at German submarines. And there were also discomforts on a smaller scale: Carmel, who shared a crowded stateroom with five other women, opted not to use the drawer that had been allocated for her clothes. "When I opened mine, cockroaches which reminded me too vividly of South America walked out, so I quickly shut it again. . . ." It was a long way from even wartime Paris.

12 new faces, new names

Carmel Snow taught me everything I know.

—Richard Avedon

Carmel was a rascal.

—Sarah Tomerlin Lee

CHRISTMAS HAD COME AND GONE, and she hadn't seen her family for months. She must have been astonished, on her return, to find how much her daughters had changed. The girls were busy with their studies, and young Carmel, who was graduating from Foxcroft that year, had been accepted to enter Vassar College in the fall. Palen was mainly absent. By now, "they only got together for major holidays," in the words of a relative. It's no wonder that few who worked with Carmel ever met Palen, or heard much about him. There were just little snippets of things—one editor recalls Carmel describing him, at about this time, as "older than God!"; she told another that she'd sent him off to stuttering school ("It didn't work at all, but she tried"). From about the 1940s on, he's scarcely even mentioned in her memoirs. "I don't think he mattered much," a former colleague says.

In April 1945, Carmel recounted her European trip to an audience that included Chase and other fashion journalists, buyers, and executives from such

Carmel, Palen, and society hostess Elsa Maxwell at the theater in New York City, 1945

specialty stores as Bonwit Teller and Saks Fifth Avenue, as well as others in the industry. Her tales of the deprivations of Paris life must have seemed very far away to these members of the Fashion Group, comfortably ensconced, as they were, in the Biltmore Hotel, just steps from Grand Central Station, with heat and food and transportation to spare.

The war in Europe ended the following month. "V-E Day here was like an occupation of Paris by Parisians," Janet Flanner reported in *The New Yorker*.

> *They streamed out onto their city's avenues and boulevards and took possession of them, filling them from curb to curb.... The people in the crowds seemed to draw nourishment from each other, and the strength to go on down one more street, up one more avenue.... The marching masses lived on air and emotion.*

Church bells pealed deafeningly all across the city and cannons were fired from both the Invalides and the Louvre.

From a fashion perspective, Europe's agony should have been America's gain: homegrown designers had had an exceptional opportunity in this period, one that some believed had been squandered. The model Dorian Leigh wrote:

> *During all those war years, fashion had ceased to exist, even in the United States, and, for quite some time after the war, it lacked a sense of direction. Not that American designers were incapable of innovation, they simply weren't accustomed to being on their own, cut off from any communication with their captive capital. No one knew which way styles ought to go....*

Years later, Carmel told the designer Norman Norell that "American designers really came into their own after the War, not during the War as some of us used to think." Ultimately, the deprivations of the war years enhanced designers' creativity: as the fashion historian Caroline Rennolds Milbank has written, "Being given specific limitations spurred them to be more inventive, and with everyone limited in the same way, competition to solve problems resulted in excellent design." It may be true that "the minute Paris opened up all they wanted was French fashion again," as Babs Simpson puts it; even so, American styles had more of a place in the magazine than ever before.

Ready-to-wear was on the rise. "It was modern, it was democratic, and New York had proved that it was stylish." In the 1940s, the nation's top-of-the-line designers in this category, such as Norell, designing for Traina-Norell, Adele Simpson, and the Paris-born Pauline Trigère, "were perhaps more important than couture." There was couture of a sort, too, but only the work of a few New York designers, such as Mainbocher and Charles James, who'd started his own business in Manhattan in 1945, and featured "often asymmetric, usually draped clothes" in luxurious fabrics, approached the standards of the Paris couturiers. In any case, as Ballard pointed out, it wasn't right to compare them with the French. Americans weren't really interested in haute anything. They preferred sportswear. In fact, such designers as Vera Maxwell, Clare Potter, and Claire McCardell, were inventing it, particularly the latter, "the first designer to take the category of sportswear and make it answer to every possible need," according to Milbank. "Golf skirts and bathing suits were just as important to her as evening clothes." It was a distinctly American approach, one tailored for a country that was rapidly becoming more suburban than anything else.

When a key nonfashion figure, Frances McFadden, returned to *Bazaar* after the war, the magazine functioned much more smoothly again. New talent kept emerging, some of it impossibly young. In the mid-1940s, Carmel was surprised to see a young blond boy lurking around the office. Although he was born in 1924, the writer Truman Capote managed "to look all of thirteen," according to a note in *Bazaar*'s "Editor's Guest Book" section. (He was actually twenty-two.) He'd just published his first short story, "Miriam"—an eerie tale of a young girl who moves in with a widow and tries to take over her life (or perhaps not)—written in

Capote's spare, almost surgically precise style. It ran in June 1945 in *Mademoiselle,* which, under fiction editor George Davis—now, presumably, showing up for work?—had become as formidable a publisher of fiction as *Bazaar.*

"I saw 'Miriam' in *Mademoiselle,* and I said, 'This is somebody we've got to get for *Harper's Bazaar,"* recalled features editor Mary Louise Aswell, whose tenure, Carmel recalled, was an "island of placidity" after the wild excitement of Davis's. "When this little thing, this little sprite turned up, I told him, 'I want to see anything you've got.'" What he had was "A Tree of Night," which became his second published story after *Bazaar* ran it in October 1945. It offered ample evidence of what the magazine described as the author's "agile, unconventional eye." Other Capote stories would soon also grace the magazine. When Aswell first brought Capote to a cocktail party at the Snows' apartment, Carmel assumed he was the younger brother of someone on her editorial staff and, not realizing that this slight, boyish creature was actually full grown, offered him a glass of milk. When she learned who he was—one of the magazine's great recent discoveries—she quickly changed tack and, to the accompaniment of laughter all around, fetched him a martini instead, "the first of many that Truman and I have downed together over the years. . . ." He became a frequent presence, both in Carmel's life and at the magazine. "Carmel and Diana Vreeland were both fascinated by him and adored him," Aswell recalled.

Another young man who turned up at this point was Richard Avedon, an aspiring photographer who had grown up with fashion. Until the Depression, when it closed its doors, his family had owned a specialty store called Avedon, located in Manhattan at Fortieth Street and Fifth Avenue. After high school, he'd made his way into the merchant marine, where, among other things, he was put to work taking identification photos of recent recruits. He'd long been interested in photography. His first subject had been the Russian composer Sergei Rachmaninoff, who lived on Manhattan's Riverside Drive, in the same building as Avedon's grandparents. At the age of ten, and armed with a box Brownie camera, he'd stalked the composer on the back stairs, finally enlisting the doorman's help.

"I posed him against the fire hydrant outside, snapped the picture, and he said, 'Thank you very much.' It was very heady," Avedon told Charles Michener for a *Newsweek* magazine cover story in 1978.

A decade or so later, when he was in his early twenties, Avedon went after Brodovitch with the same fervor. He'd experimented with photography when he was in the service, taking pictures of other sailors in action; by the time he was discharged, he knew that he wanted it to be his career. Inevitably, he was drawn to *Bazaar,* by then "one of the most fervently admired magazines in America," as Dodie Kazanjian and Calvin Tomkins have written. The quality of its graphic design set it apart, making it a magnet for any aspiring photographer. "Nobody could believe such a magazine existed," according to Avedon. By the mid-1940s, it was also, for the first time, on a par with its rival in both advertising revenue and circulation—at that time, both *Vogue* and *Bazaar* were printing about two hundred thousand copies a month. For Avedon, too, it was an ancient touchstone. "My family subscribed to *Harper's Bazaar,* it became my window and Munkacsi's photographs my view."

Avedon resolved to get Brodovitch, who "was legendary at the time," to look at his admittedly scant portfolio. It was an insanely ambitious idea for a novice, but Avedon wasn't going to let it go. "I'd have a weekly appointment to meet with him and he would cancel every one. I'd dress up in my best suit." For weeks, as he stepped off the elevator, *Bazaar*'s receptionist would greet him by shaking her head. "She'd say, 'He's cancelled again,'" Avedon recalled. And so it went. At one point, he even dropped some prints off at Brodovitch's residence, by then on Fifty-seventh street, only to regret it when he next turned up at the magazine. "Don't ever do that again!" the same receptionist snarled. The photographer later estimated that he'd made fourteen thwarted visits to *Bazaar,* for appointments that would vanish, miragelike, at the opening of the elevator door.

It was Avedon's persistence, far more than his work, that impressed Brodovitch, he later learned. ("He always said I had 'elbow.'") And his appearance was timely. Avedon later learned that Brodovitch was "just fed up" with two of the great photographers he'd worked closely with for years—Hoyningen-Huene and Dahl-Wolfe—with their outsize egos and tendency to make scenes. "They demanded all kinds of things," including reshoots, Avedon says. "They were older, they had tantrums."

Dahl-Wolfe was still pulling her disappearing acts, sulking after one perceived slight or another; it would take all of Carmel's coaxing to bring her back into the fold. She made a huge scene in the mid-1940s when Toni Frissell, who had left *Vogue,* approached *Bazaar* hoping to sell some war photographs that she'd taken in Europe. Carmel had known Frissell for years: the photographer had actually started her career as a caption writer at *Vogue* during Carmel's time at that magazine. Good war coverage was hard to come by; Frissell's photographs seemed heaven-sent. Carmel was all set to publish them when "Louise Dahl-Wolfe made a fuss—even when assured that Toni Frissell wouldn't be allowed to shoot fashion," Frissell's daughter, Sidney Stafford says. Carmel insisted that Frissell was essential, "as I had no war correspondent"—in vain, according to the editor, who recounted the scene in a letter to Frissell. "Her reply was she would leave if *anything* of yours appeared in the magazine."

Carmel added that she was

> *so upset by the whole matter I hardly trusted myself to write—knowing I would say too much.*
>
> *When July appeared, Louise refused to take any September pictures—colour or otherwise—unless I assured her I would not use you.*

So Frissell, and some much-needed war coverage, was out. Not many could get away with such antics. "Dahl-Wolfe was a horrible person," one editor says, "although if she loved you she couldn't do enough for you." But she was essential to the magazine, in Carmel's view, and she indulged her as necessary.

By contrast, Avedon was so eager to ingratiate himself at *Bazaar* that "I would do anything Brodovitch asked," he says. He took a series of fashion shots of model Dorcas Nowell (nicknamed "Doe"), who would become his wife. After Nowell took them on a go-see to *Vogue,* Avedon received a call from Alexander Liberman, who had become art director of that magazine in 1943, saying that he was interested in the young photographer's work. "I said, 'Mr. Liberman, I'm going to work for *Harper's Bazaar.*'" Decades later, he tells this tale with incredulity—"For anyone of that age to turn down *Vogue*!"—but also to make a point. "It tells you something about the aura of the magazine."

Brodovitch hadn't even consented to flip through the scrapbook Avedon had made of his pictures. He finally did so, without seeming impressed, until he came across an ID snapshot Avedon had taken of twin recruits, one in focus, the other blurred. Brodovitch had found his fashion work to be derivative; this image hinted that it might not always be so—it had a dynamism that might translate well into fashion. "If you can make something like this . . . ," he ventured. Avedon went back to work, even signing up for Brodovitch's classes in layout and other aspects of design and ultimately even his Design Laboratory class, which had been resurrected at the New School for Social Research in New York in 1941.

> *It was about a six-month period that I kept experimenting with what he was interested in. I began to take courses at the New School, but he was so formidable. . . . He had me experiment for a long time and when he liked [my latest photographs], he said "I want you to meet Carmel Snow."*

Avedon's impressions of his first visit to the editorial offices of *Bazaar* were so vivid as to be almost hallucinatory: Carmel's hair (bright blue at the time), editor Alice Morris wandering barefoot down the halls. . . . And then there was Vreeland with her shellacked coiffure, pencil-length cigarette holder, oracular voice.

She had the kind of depth that superficial people sometimes have. She pretended to be everything. . . . There was this line in an Enid Bagnold play at the time. "She's like old porcelain, she's cracked, but for the better." That was the feeling you got a little bit about all of them. . . . They all talked in that Noel Coward way. I was like a spy in this other country. Really *another country. I had certain values that were not shared, social values. I had worked for civil rights.*

Equally amazing was the ease with which a neophyte photographer might enter the magazine's inner sanctum. On the day he met her, Carmel's office door was, as always, ajar. "You just poked your head around the door and she invited you in." When she saw his newest fashion work, including an image of a kooky-looking, overweight friend, wearing a striped top and perched on a pair of stilts, "I knew that in Richard Avedon we had a new, contemporary Munkacsi. I sensed that with his keen, seeking intelligence he would develop into far more than a striking photographer of junior fashions. . . ."

Avedon's first pictures appeared in *Harper's Bazaar* in the October 1944 issue; a month later, in a brief profile in the magazine, he was quoted as saying, "I want to be a fireman when I grow up." (You had only to glance at this picture to see that he was still a kid.) Although he actually debuted in the main section of the magazine, it was in the Junior Bazaar section, toward the back, where he was, at first, featured most. On about his third assignment, he wandered into Vreeland's office, located on the long hall that ran between the art department and Carmel's corner office, to find the editor sitting behind her desk while Niki de Gunzburg fussed around a staggeringly beautiful model in a bridal gown in the center of the room.

Mrs. Vreeland never looked at me. She cried, "Baron!" Beside her stood Baron de Gunzburg, the only male fashion editor in the world, a pincushion hanging like a Croix de Guerre from a ribbon at his throat, and she cried, "Baron! Baron, the pins!" She took one pin and walked swinging her hips down the narrow office to the end. She stuck the pin not only into the dress, but into the girl, who let out a little scream. Diana returned to her desk, looked up at me for the first time and said, "Aberdeen, Aberdeen, doesn't it make you want to cry?" Well, it did. I went back to Carmel Snow and said, "I can't work with that woman. She calls me Aberdeen" And Carmel Snow said, "You're going *to work with her."*

Working for *Bazaar* was like taking on a new family, he recalled, complete with "father, mother, crazy aunt." (I think we know which one that was.) He soon saw that more than eccentricity united the trio. "There was a dedication to excellence of such a degree." For Avedon, *Bazaar* was an education. "It was a teaching place. They were constantly training. It was in their nature." By his own admission, he had a lot to learn: "I'd never read Colette, I'd never read Proust, I'd certainly never been to Paris. . . . All I knew about elegance was from Lubitsch movies, from Astaire and Rogers." Brodovitch was entirely visual—he'd always ask Avedon, "What have you seen?" Carmel, on the other hand, would talk "as much about a piece of fiction," he says, as something in the visual sphere.

Avedon was an immediate presence at the magazine. "He was a little spot of a fellow, always hopping about," one editor recalls. He had enthusiasm and style—for a while he wore his tie as a belt, emulating Fred Astaire, whom he'd photographed for *Bazaar*. He used to work in his own studio, just blocks from the magazine, and tear down Madison Avenue, fresh from the darkroom, with wet photographic prints in hand. "I ran to Carmel, Brodovitch, and Diana with joy, with pleasure." Early in his *Bazaar* days, he did a shoot of Katharine Hepburn, a huge star at that time, who'd been featured in the magazine since the early 1930s. When he went over the contact sheets with Carmel, he was surprised to see that the photo that was clearly superior, to his mind, wasn't the one she favored. "She said, 'Dick, I know this is a better photograph but there's something in the eyes in this one. . . . ' And she was right."

Vreeland was a huge part of his training. "She never told you what to do. She came in on a slant." She could be inscrutable on a photo shoot. Once, faced with a nondescript model in a nondescript dress, and drawing a complete blank on how to present either one, Avedon begged Vreeland to "just give me some notes on how you see this thing!" Instantly, the fashion editor was off, channeling that greatest of all channelers, the Oracle of Delphi. "Just imagine Cleopatra," she said, in a drifty voice.... "Just imagine Cleopatra, that young girl.... Everyone around her is so old.... She's walking on a roof...." Whether this clarified the matter or not, Avedon doesn't say.

Of them all, "the one I related to was Carmel," he says. "She was approachable." Vreeland, on the other hand, was

> *very different—cold, removed, flamboyant—where Carmel was humane and warm and funny. Vreeland had contempt for photography, interestingly enough. She was a snob, and very condescending. She'd say hello to the woman scrubbing the floor, and know her first name, but for years she called me "Aberdeen." I never felt that sort of condescension from Carmel or from Brodovitch. They always lifted me up.*

Carmel was "conspiratorial" with him from the first, Avedon recalled, and always accessible. "She said, 'You never have to call to make an appointment.' She said, 'Just poke your head in the door.'" When he did so, "She seemed to have all the time in the world." It was an amazing position for a young photographer to be in, but a friend in the fashion business quickly brought—or tried to bring—him down to earth. "She said, 'The day she can't use you, you'll never get her on the phone.'" Avedon recalled. "She said, 'Just learn this, and learn it fast.'"

Carmel gravitated toward this young photographer as she did to all people of exceptional talent, particularly in the visual sphere. She seemed to know their capabilities before they could guess at them themselves. She took Avedon under her wing, as she had done with so many others, from Munkacsi to the young fashion editors—Eleanor Barry, Louise Macy—who had so brightened her days. She hovered and coaxed. From the start, Avedon saw her as "a warm person who was going to support you. You were never a threat." She wasn't political in the office politics sense, as others at the magazine were; with her, there were no games. Instead, she "exuded a sense of trustworthiness." In the words of a *Bazaar* staffer: "She wasn't dictatorial, she was just in charge."

Like so many who worked with her, Avedon felt that she incited him to ever greater creative heights. As with others, once she trusted him, she left him to do his work. The flip side to this was that she never wanted to know about problems, the interview you couldn't get, the negatives that got lost. The results were all that counted. Carmel assumed one could do anything and thought nothing of asking someone to run out and find a yacht for a location shoot in the middle of winter and on very short notice, then dress it up as grandly as possible, as she once did of a young staffer named Denise Fitch, then Denise Lawson-Johnson, who later became accessories editor. Barely out of her teens, Fitch duly scrambled in response, as many had done before her, even using her family's silver to set the scene. "You never said no to Carmel Snow," she explains.

Avedon was soon all over the Junior Bazaar section while also intermittently appearing in the regular magazine; by January 1947, he'd done a *Bazaar* cover, a casual shot of a model on the beach wearing tiny shorts and a long pullover by American designer Carolyn Schnurer. As with Munkacsi, Avedon's women *moved*—laughing, waterskiing, jumping. But while, even in his fashion work, Munkacsi never seemed to have left photojournalism, the younger photographer was somewhere else. His images were crisp, sensual, optimistic, sometimes gauzily romantic.

Some surprising faces turn up in the magazine at this time, including a fresh-faced Jacqueline Bouvier, photographed by Avedon in the mid-1940s. (Her sister, Lee, now known as Princess Lee Radziwill, would become an assistant to Diana Vreeland at *Bazaar* a few years later.) Real-life models were briefly in the ascendant after Carmel read a Cholly Knickerbocker column that said: "Away with those skinny models, with the hawk faces, who look like picked birds. Let's fatten them up. . . ." Carmel agreed wholeheartedly, and fired off a memo to all *Bazaar* photographers to that effect.

> *I have been passing photographs taken for the August issue in color.*
>
> *One thing stands out clearly; that is, the photographs taken of girls who are barely professional models . . . have infinitely more appeal than the professional, skinny model.*
>
> *I am told that . . . the photographers prefer to use the old-line models, who are too skinny for the modern idea of beauty. The fashion for curves was set by Dior.*
>
> *Do believe me when I say the average reader, looking over both* Vogue *and* Harper's Bazaar *are [sic] sick to death of the type of model both magazines are using. There are many beautiful American girls, and I think that photographers should be flexible enough to get their eye in for the new type. . . .*

There's no evidence that this made a bit of difference. Such movements toward using "real," i.e., realistically unthin, women as models, which recur periodically in the fashion world, never seem to work. In any case, this one fell flat: In the 1950s, *Bazaar* was as full of impossibly lithe, impossibly beautiful women as ever.

Avedon's debut wasn't a threat to Munkacsi: he'd given up taking pictures after a serious heart attack in 1943. But it certainly was to Dahl-Wolfe. "Dick came in when he was twenty-four years old and he turned out to be the boy wonder," Dorothy Edson recalls. "It was terrible for Louise, who'd done so much for the magazine for so long." Brodovitch liked Avedon "very much better than her and she was very jealous." While Avedon professed to admire Dahl-Wolfe's work, he was also, in a sense, stealing it. So it's not surprising that there was great enmity between the two photographers. And for all Dahl-Wolfe's accomplishments, in some ways her work suffered by comparison, seeming dated, even fussy, when compared with Avedon's more clean-lined look. While Brodovitch was said to increasingly find Dahl-Wolfe's work dull, both photographers still had their place, according to Edson. "What Brodovitch knew was that having Louise and Dick in a single issue was marvelous. They complemented each other in the most wonderful way."

Dahl-Wolfe was known for her elaborate compositions and backdrops; Avedon's compositions, by contrast, seemed effortless; his backgrounds—seamless white paper, as often as not—daringly simple. Everything about his work looked new. Which isn't to say that Dahl-Wolfe's *Bazaar* career ended at this point—she would continue with the magazine until 1958, contributing hundreds of photographs, almost ninety of them covers. But she would never again be unchallenged, a situation that worked nicely for the magazine: like Condé Nast before her, and countless magazine editors since, Carmel wasn't above fostering a little competition among her contributors to goad them into doing better work.

As for Hoyningen-Huene, he was already winding down, for reasons of his own, when Avedon came along. (He'd end his career, like Man Ray, in southern California.) Still, there was a certain passing of the baton between him and Avedon and it wasn't without ambiguity. Hoyningen-Huene, who rode a bicycle to work, first encountered Avedon when he was carrying his bike into the elevator of the Hearst building. "Are you the new photographer?" he asked the twenty-two-year-old. Avedon replied that he was. "Too late," said Hoyningen-Huene. "Too late," implying, perhaps, that commercial considerations had taken over and that the great, glamorous days of fashion were gone.

But, in fact, they'd only changed. Even Avedon's approach to models—those key, yet unsung figures—was different, as Leigh, who modeled for both him and Dahl-Wolfe, has written:

> *Dick wanted his models to look like real people wearing real clothes, he wanted real expressions on their faces and genuine reactions to their surroundings. . . . Instead of using the "still life" approach, which meant*

asking a model to strike a pose and freeze, he kept her moving, sometimes moving around her himself with his camera in his hands, keeping up a conversation, explaining what he wanted her to feel and portray, always telling her how well she was doing, making her feel she was the most beautiful creature on earth.

It was a time of particularly strong photography at *Bazaar.* Bill Brandt, that most mysterious of practitioners—and one of the shyest men on earth, according to *Bazaar*—turned up frequently in its pages after being corralled by Brodovitch in Europe. Brandt, who had briefly apprenticed with Man Ray in Paris, was known to stage some of his most powerful documentary works. However he achieved it, his work had a disturbing effect. Among other images, he contributed a brooding (is there any other kind?) portrait of T. S. Eliot to *Bazaar,* as well as some moodily dramatic images of Haworth in Yorkshire, the house where the writer Emily Brontë once lived. To achieve this effect, "Brandt spliced together two different negatives to get a convincingly lowering sky." The result was so powerful that when associate editor Mary Lee Settle, an American who was homesick for Britain, where she'd spent the war years, came upon them in the *Bazaar* art department, she was inspired to flee an atmosphere she loathed—New York, the magazine world, Carmel herself—and decamp back to London just as soon as she could get out.

Many *Bazaar* features at this point were non–fashion related: a Lisette Model spread on a place in Long Island "where old Broadway players go to retire"; a "playlet" by Betty Comden and Adolph Green; a report on the United Nations Commission on the Status of Women; photographs of Paris by Brassai (another Hungarian, whose real name was Jules Halasz) and André Kertész; an article on Jean-Paul Sartre ("the most talked-about writer in France today") by his companion, Simone de Beauvoir, illustrated by that famous Cartier-Bresson portrait of him standing broodingly on the pont des Arts, the pedestrian bridge that crosses the Seine.

The French photographer arrived in New York for the first time in 1946 on the occasion of a retrospective of his work at the Museum of Modern Art. He came early to do assignments for *Bazaar* and identified himself so closely with the magazine that he listed his address in *Current Biography 1947* as 572 Madison Avenue. In an inspired moment, Carmel paired him with Truman Capote, who had been born in New Orleans, and sent them both off that summer to do a feature on that city. The two had an immediate rapport. The photographer nicknamed Capote "T," a habit that would last a lifetime; for his part, Capote wrote to Mary Louise Aswell that "I like Cartier-Bresson extremely."

Beyond that, the assignment was a dog, from Capote's point of view. The two fanned out in the scorching heat, hoping to capture New Orleans on the page. "I've never worked so hard in my life," he wrote to Aswell the following week, "and I hope never to again." Still, "Notes on N.O.," which ran in October 1946, was an eye-opener. "New Orleans streets have long lonesome perspectives . . . ," Capote wrote, "in empty hours their atmosphere is like de Chirico and things innocent . . . acquire qualities of violence." Such affecting Cartier-Bresson photographs as "Chartres Street, After the Rain" and a shot of absorbed-looking Cajun gamblers sitting, cards in hand, on a filigreed New Orleans porch, didn't seem to fit in either category, just hovered ambiguously somewhere between. It was on this trip that Cartier-Bresson took his famous portrait of Capote, posed on a wrought-iron garden chair, surrounded by enormous tropical leaves, looking scrawny, narcissistic, sultry, young. This by-now-endlessly-reproduced picture wasn't necessarily to its sitter's liking. In mid-August Capote wrote to a friend, "Yes, Cartier has done some portraits (they are very strange, I must say, but the photography is, of course, beautiful). . . ."

Returning to New York, Capote was infuriated, naturally enough, by the usual Hearst tactics about expenses. He wrote to Aswell "They sent me a bill for my fare down there . . . can you beat that?" Only they unwisely chose to do so before they had his article in hand; sensibly, Capote chose to withhold it until the offending bill was withdrawn. "The Hearst Corporation . . . was notoriously stingy with its writers" when it came to expenses, according to Gerald Clarke. Things went smoothly from there. Capote wrote to Aswell that "I went with Cartier to

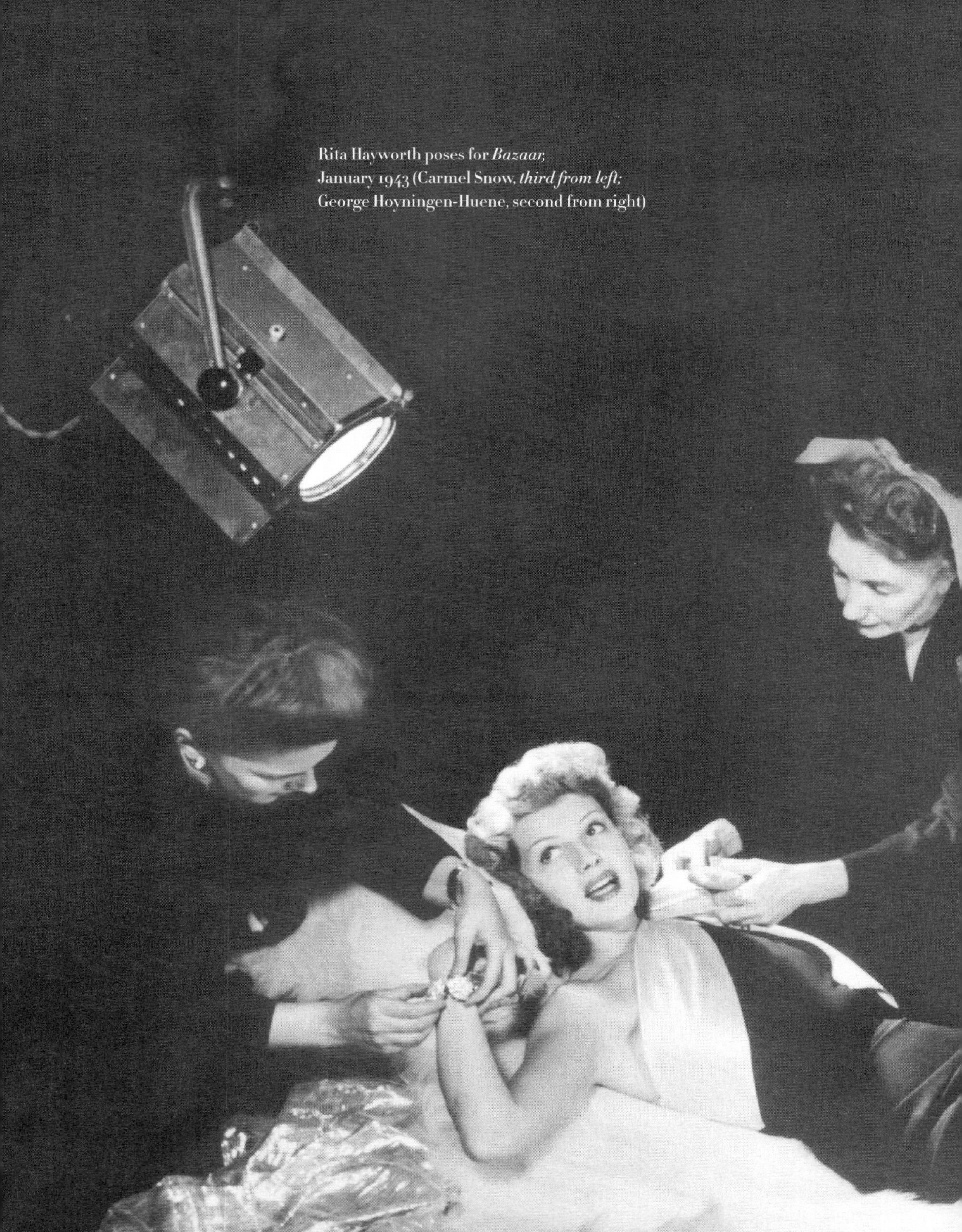

Rita Hayworth poses for *Bazaar,*
January 1943 (Carmel Snow, *third from left;*
George Hoyningen-Huene, second from right)

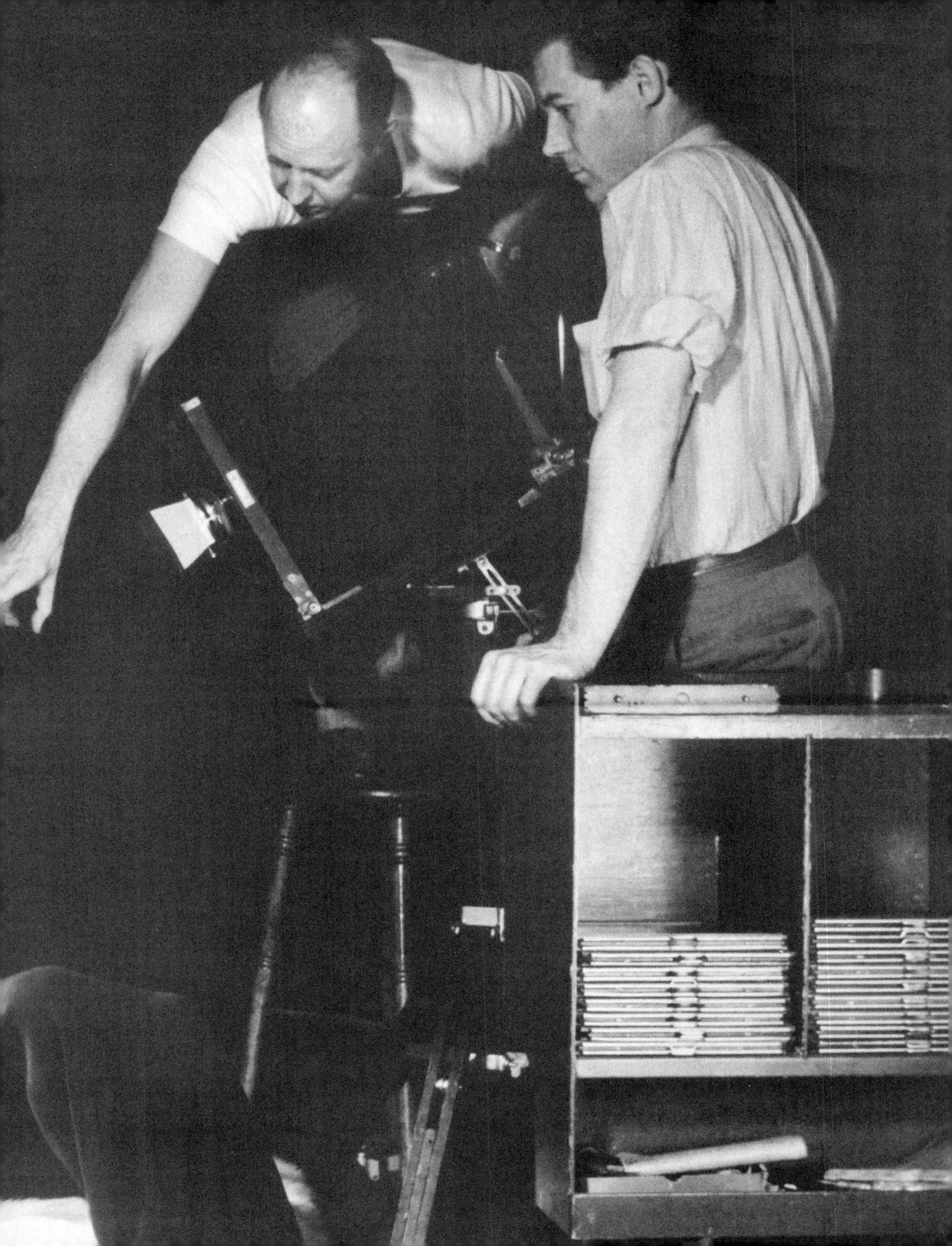

McFadden with the N.O. pictures, and they were all crazy about them; they are really very wonderful. . . ." His text was similarly received; Aswell, who had become a close friend, cabled her congratulations to Capote soon after reading it.

The young writer would go on to contribute frequently to *Bazaar*—his story "The Headless Hawk" ran in November 1946; many others would follow. In July 1951, the magazine ran the first chapter of *The Grass Harp,* with its cryptic first lines: "When was it that I first heard of the grass harp? Long before the autumn we lived in the China tree . . . ," describing it as "the year's most eagerly awaited new novel." As his letters reveal, Capote was gushingly affectionate toward his friends, and counted several of *Bazaar*'s editors in that category, not just Aswell, but Pearl Kazin, the sister of the writer Alfred Kazin. Like Katherine Anne Porter, Capote also fell victim to overzealous editing at *Bazaar*—and protested loudly. In this case, Carmel quickly took his side. As he wrote to Aswell,

> *I think the folks at the* Bazaar *have lost their minds. You should have* seen *what Helen Eustis did to an article of mine! I wrote them a letter that would have tickled your heart. Anyway, they are now publishing the original. Oh God!*

The organization's attitude toward expenses was as scandalous for photographers as for everyone else. Avedon recalls being given $2.50 to provide lunch for his entire studio during a shoot. Models who traveled to Europe were given hotel accommodations and a $600 fee for more than two weeks of backbreaking work, seven days a week, including late-night photo sessions, then expected to pay all other expenses themselves, including airfare and meals. Even so they clamored to go to the Paris shows, "the most exciting event of the fashion year. . . . To 'do' the French collections was to put on the loveliest, most luxurious clothes designed by the world's greatest couturiers . . . ," says Dorian Leigh. "Any model gladly would have paid the magazine for the privilege of going," something that Hearst management knew all too well.

Bazaar staff members didn't fare much better. "Even editors on location always had to fight for enough money to pay their travel costs," Babs Simpson recalls. "No one was ever given enough money for trips. You'd have to fuss to get more." The approach to salaries was similar: even the most seasoned editors rarely made more than $100 a week. Carmel sometimes found ingenious ways to circumvent such restrictions. Once, when Dorothy Wheelock Edson's salary had reached that figure—topped out from Hearst's point of view—Carmel found a way to supplement it that fell below the organization's radar, by paying her an extra fee of $50 a week to "read manuscripts," Edson recalls. "She did that for years and years." And Carmel was generous with expenses: "I could take my mother to lunch and say it was Edith Sitwell," Edson says.

Photographers weren't particularly well compensated at *Bazaar;* "they paid less than anybody," according to Lillian Bassman. Still, they clamored to be in the magazine for the context, the chance to have their work showcased along with the best photographers in the world. Avedon recalls making $75 to $100 a page—more than adequate at the beginning of his first ten-year contract with the magazine, less so toward its end. Such written agreements were rare. In 1949, Carmel deftly turned Toni Frissell down for one on the grounds that "we have no contracts," although this wasn't entirely true, shrewdly assuring her that Fifty-seventh Street, in all its habitual unreasonableness, was to blame.

In the summer of 1945, Carmel headed back to Paris to see the couturiers' offerings. There were far more than during her last visit; this time, too, there were other Americans in attendance. She went by plane, at a time when air travel was improvisational at best. There weren't many flights at all, and those that did exist could be unpredictable. "We would come down for hours at Gander, sometimes we were thrown off the plane for days at Shannon," recalled Bettina Ballard, by then on *Vogue*'s New York staff. The two editors were on the same flight. Ballard described Carmel as "always amused and amusing under the most trying circumstances." She was also up to her usual racket, this time smuggling in the reverse direction. She looked "like a bloated bear with the inside of her coat hung with cartons of American cigarettes for Marie-Louise Bousquet," Ballard wrote. *Vogue*'s Rosamund Bernier, then known as Rosamund Riley and working as that magazine's European features editor, came across Carmel and Bousquet lunching on *omelettes aux fines herbes* and, of course, martinis, just after Carmel deplaned. Their mood was euphoric. "Think of it," one of them trilled, "we can have a martini in Paris and a martini in New York on the same day!"

The dispatches Carmel sent home revealed her enthusiasm for Paris's revived fashion scene. Designers favored a "hippy look," she reported; curvy jackets that fell to midcalf were worn over straight skirts that seemed daringly short, falling just below the knee. Schiaparelli, now back from the United States (she'd passed most of the war years in, of all places, New Jersey) showed a Directoire-inspired collection. Carmel delineated "two strong silhouettes, including a straight sheath, shown at Balenciaga, Lelong, Piguet, as well as a rounded, more baroque one, with longer, fuller skirts that "exaggerate natural curves, enormously feminine," also on view chez Balenciaga.

Back in America, shortages were ending—a ban on colored leather was lifted; and, in late 1945, nylons returned—and the nation began entering a postwar boom. As advertising revenue rose, Hearst and his executives became increasingly interested in expanding the Junior Bazaar pages into a magazine in their own right. This younger version of *Harper's Bazaar*—"a magazine covering the world of fashion, people, events, ideas for girls thirteen to twenty-one"—was a pet project of Carmel's. "My heart's soul is now in this," she told a potential collaborator. Thanks to her own three daughters, she knew her target audience well. *Junior Bazaar* wasn't the first in this market—*Seventeen* had been founded by Walter Annenberg in 1944—but even so, it was a bold move: after all, *Vogue* didn't launch a similar project until *Teen Vogue,* which began regular publication in January 2003.

The seventh floor of 572 Madison was given over to the new publication; it hummed with activity all through the summer of 1945. "The new magazine, I think is going to be good," Carmel told a young photographer, promising that it would have "all the distinction of the *Bazaar*." Trips to the *Junior Bazaar* offices were derided as "slumming" by some editors of the magazine that, inevitably, became known as Big *Bazaar,* but they never felt that way to Carmel: "A confused world of novices in ballet slippers and wide hair ribbons, an atmosphere of slightly amateurish fervor, was just to my taste." Among the ingenues was Melanie Witt, the magazine's fashion editor; Lillian Bassman, its art director; copywriter Maeve Brennan; and Anne Bullitt, the cover shoot no-show and daughter of Ambassador Bullitt, who had given up teaching French at Foxcroft to join the new magazine's fashion staff. Barbara Lawrence, late of *The New Yorker,* signed on as features editor. Best of all, from Carmel's point of view, her beloved protégée Eleanor Barry Lowman returned as *Junior*'s editor. Once she did so, Carmel's "trips to the seventh floor became frequent and joyous," she wrote.

The editors were like sorority sisters let loose in the grown-up world. A photograph of the editorial staff, taken on the job, shows them to be impossibly fresh, small-waisted, and young. Brodovitch's name was on the masthead as art director—he insisted on it, Bassman says—but this "highly gifted young woman," as Carmel called her, really ran the show. Still, she remained under Brodovitch's stewardship, just as Barry remained under Carmel's.

The editorial staff of *Junior Bazaar,* 1945 (*left to right, starting second from left*): Melanie Witt, Lillian Bassman, Eleanor Barry Lowman, Ann Campion, Maeve Brennan

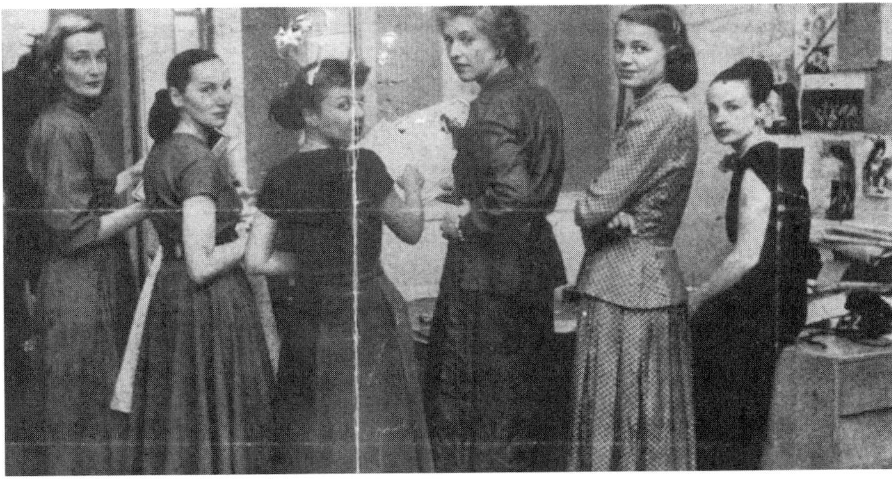

Bassman came up with lively, kinetic layouts. "It was really very innovative and lots of fun," she says. "It was completely different from the *Bazaar* and yet it had a family feeling to it. We did all the layout tricks we could think of. We'd walk on the beach and talk about the issue for weeks." She brought in a new group of young photographers, including Gleb Derujinsky. Another, Toni Frissell, was suggested by Carmel, who found that *Junior Bazaar* provided a neat solution to the impasse caused by Dahl-Wolfe's refusal to allow Frissell to work for *Bazaar*. "I think a splendid thing has happened for you and for me," she wrote to the photographer, telling her about *Junior Bazaar* and adding that she wouldn't use Dahl-Wolfe for this publication because she was "too closely identified with the *Bazaar*." She promised Frissell both fashion and feature work on *Junior*, which was gratefully accepted. Before too long, Frissell also infiltrated *Bazaar* itself. Dahl-Wolfe, for once, had been cowed.

Looking as fresh and colorful as the young women who put it together, the magazine debuted with the November 1945 issue. One cover, in particular, caught the spirit, with an Ernst Beadle black-and-white photograph of a young woman, taken from the back, shooting an arrow toward a distant target. Carmel called the magazine "a proving ground of young talent," and it was: many of its contributors went on to distinguished careers. Bassman, who began taking photographs for *Junior Bazaar*, moved on to be a regular contributor at *Bazaar* (and beyond). Leo Lerman, the magazine's entertainment columnist, would make his name on the editorial staff at Condé Nast. Melanie Witt (who was later Melanie Miller) became fashion editor of *Glamour* and then, for twenty years, editor in chief of British *Vogue*. And the elegant, Irish-born Maeve Brennan went on to become an associate editor at *Bazaar* in 1949; later that year, she joined the staff of *The New Yorker* as a writer, contributing short stories and nonfiction pieces both under her own name and as the pseudonymous "Long-Winded Lady," who turned up in the Talk of the Town pages for years. (She also returned to *Bazaar*, in a sense, contributing short stories to the magazine in the early 1950s.)

The ponytailed Brennan dressed with great originality, wearing all black in an era when such a concept applied only to widows, William Maxwell once said,

"To be around her was to see style being invented." She revered Carmel, her fellow Irishwoman, for her wardrobe and chic, but she was scared to death of her, too. Bassman recalls having to almost force Brennan over the threshold of Carmel's corner office for meetings—and in this she was not alone. "A lot of people trembled before Carmel," says Luc Bouchage, a Frenchman then working in the art department.

Barry may have been editor, but Carmel's presence was often required. At one point, when the magazine was about to publish a bathing suit spread by photographer Genevieve Naylor, in which a black man could be glimpsed swimming in the same body of water as a group of frolicking models, all of Fifty-seventh Street seemed to rise up in protest. "They made holy hell about that," Bassman says. "They didn't want that published." Carmel had already broken Hearst's stricture about showing African Americans in his publications—Munkacsi's photographs of Marian Anderson had done that in the late 1930s—but the fashion pages were sacrosanct, and she took on this battle, too. "She put her foot down and she won," Bassman says, adding that she had Fred Drake, the magazine's publisher, "around her little finger." The yes-men beneath him could only fall into line. Carmel would prevail again later when she published a stylized nude shot by Avedon that handily broke the stricture against showing two breasts in a Hearst publication. (Interestingly, one alone didn't count.) And in 1947, she published the first photograph of a bikini (in a shot by Toni Frissell) to appear in an American fashion publication.

Carmel mothered the *Junior* staff, sending them encouraging memos, reveling in their problems, proffering advice. "One's relationship with Carmel was always personal," as Aswell has written. Melanie Miller, who went from being a junior fashion editor to taking over that department, found the situation ideal: "She was tough but she was kind. I had complete autonomy. I did what I wanted to do." As so often happens, Carmel found things to be more difficult with her own children who, one relative says, were growing up with little emotional support in an environment that could be "very brutal, especially when Carmel was drinking." Mary Palen, who some said was the prettiest of her daughters, had long been the one Carmel had thought could be groomed to follow her at *Bazaar.* "She expected her to be the successor, but she wasn't up to it," according to a family friend. "Given her personality, she was not happy at all with that kind of pressure that was put on her," another adds. The girl was "fragile," in Avedon's gentle assessment. "She was original."

The photographer remembers attending a late-night dinner party at Carmel's New York apartment at which the gaminelike Irish actress Siobhan McKenna was in attendance, along with the writer Flannery O'Connor and others, when Mary Palen, then in her midteens, casually walked through the combined living and dining room on her way out the door, a pair of roller skates tied together by their laces slung over her shoulder.

"Where are you going, young lady?" Carmel thundered from her place at the head of the table.

"Forty-second Street" was the girl's reply.

"Not in that dress with that belt," Carmel answered.

Avedon doesn't recall if Mary Palen did end up on Forty-second Street that night. But he remembers being amazed at the deft way Carmel diffused the situation. "The thing was defeated, but I mean it was very tense." At another point, Mary Palen—evidently an enthusiastic skater—wanted to get a job as "an errand girl on roller skates," according to Dorothy Edson, a request that was sharply vetoed at home. Eventually, her mother helped her into employment at the Museum of Modern Art. Mary Palen "wasn't tough enough," her cousin Kate White recalls. "She was an Irish lass living in the midst of this tightly constructed world." She tested her mother continually, crying out for attention from a parent who could never give it in the measure the girl deserved. She seemed continually out of step. "She didn't fit into the groove Mrs. Snow wanted for the rest of the family—the best schools, and all that," Edson remarks. Carmel adored her children, but she wasn't introspective or given to self-doubt. She didn't believe in psychiatry, according to Edson. There was no question of getting the girl help.

In February 1946, Carmel returned to Paris for the first spring collections since peace was declared to find that the city—which "looked as if it had fainted" during the war, in the words of the photographer Jacques-Henri Lartigue—had begun to revive. Cars could be seen again, and even some buses, but gas was still scarce: Lucien, Carmel's chauffeur, kept cylinders of the precious substance affixed to the roof of his car. Heat was still spotty enough that when photographer Maurice Tabard shot an assignment in the *Bazaar* studio, the shutter of his camera froze. And finding good food, even in the culinary capital of the Western world, wasn't something you could count on. One night, Carmel was surprised to find herself in a sumptuous restaurant where there seemed to be no food shortages at all. It was only after the police raided the place, bringing her meal to an abrupt end, that she realized that its ingredients had come from the black market, still very much in operation at this time. A *Bazaar* feature entitled "Paris Working Girl 1946" brought the dire straits of post-war Parisians home to American readers by following a malnourished young couture worker (employed by Molyneux, who had returned from Britain) as she went through her day, returning home at the end of it to "a cold-water flat and an empty larder."

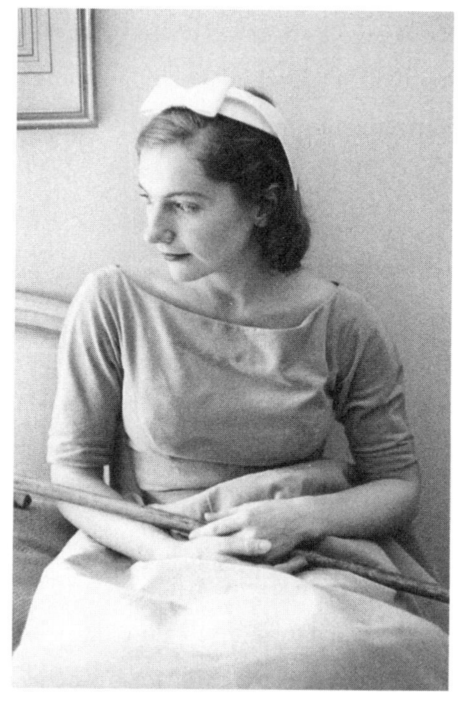

Mary Palen Snow

Ever alert to those whose connections could help *Bazaar,* Carmel had hired Marie-Louise Bousquet as Paris editor. Bousquet had been affiliated with the magazine since 1937, but the official title and her appearance on the masthead were new. It was another shrewd move: Bousquet seemed "to be everywhere, posing hands on feverish brows, promoting kindness, friendships, helping to launch talent, and, in general, serving as the brilliant Florence Nightingale of fashion . . . ," as Cecil Beaton put it. The salary was pitiful, but less so than it might have been, since Helena Rubenstein, a friend to both Carmel and Bousquet, took it upon herself to supplement it, not just with cash, but with a car, which the very arthritic Bousquet needed to get around. "They earn *nothing* on those magazines," Rubenstein said at the time. It was a clever tactic, of course—in this way, the beauty mogul probably thought that she'd receive favorable coverage in *Bazaar.* And Bousquet would zip around Paris in her tiny Simca for years to come.

In appearance Bousquet was light-years away from such elegant predecessors as Daisy Fellowes. She was "wacky looking, with her red-dyed wig," in Avedon's description. Crippled with arthritis, she walked with a cane. Her brown eyes were so close set that they gave her a simian appearance—she looked like "a sprightly little monkey," in a *Vogue* editor's words—a resemblance Avedon exploited brilliantly in a 1950 portrait, where she cuddles a stuffed ape. One *Bazaar* editor describes her as "an ugly woman with a wonderful sense of fashion. She wore silk or organdy blouses. You'd see this crisp organdy on this little gnomey, gnarled figure—it helped, but not much." Bousquet was rumored to resort to artificial means to keep her spirits up. "She was always on some drug or another," says Bassman. "In the middle of the evening, she'd disappear into the bathroom for two minutes, then she'd come out all cheerful." The drug of choice was probably cocaine, then far easier to obtain in France than in the United States. "It was very common in those circles," Bassman points out.

Bousquet's effervescent, if not quite benign, personality was a draw. "She had very lively brown eyes and obviously a lively intellect. People came [to her salons] because of her," according to Rosamond Bernier. Vreeland was mad about her. "She is the most adorable and wonderful woman in the whole wide world," she wrote to a *Bazaar* staffer at one point. "She is old and she is young, and she is the embodiment of the spirit of France." Bousquet's gatherings weren't just social ones: they provided much-needed income, too. Like others with friends among the couturiers, Bérard among them, Bousquet would be compensated each time a new customer turned up, on her recommendation, at one of their *maisons de couture*. She returned the favor by contributing to the support of young artists.

In any case, her soirées hardly broke the bank. "She had no money and it was very modest," Bernier recalls. The formula behind them never varied. As Truman Capote wrote:

> *The drinks are bad, the rooms too crowded; but the hostess, ruffing herself like a parrot, banging a gold-headed cane as though it were a gavel, mincing and moueing and making oh horrid mischief, can be forgiven—yes, all.*

According to Ernestine Carter, an American who had moved to London during the war, "The drink, served in eyecups, was undiluted lime juice . . . supplied from embassy and army commissaries by Madame Bousquet's admirers." Whatever they were served, everyone who mattered seemed to turn up, and plenty who didn't, too. In the way of these things, "those you wanted to see the least came the most often," Carter adds. Significant meetings took place there—the American composer Ned Rorem, then a Paris resident, met his longtime idol, Marie-Laure de Noailles, yet another chic emblem of the 1920s, at the salon, as well as the American playwright Thornton Wilder and a certain Mrs. Snow. The latter might shanghai almost anyone to Bousquet's: at one point she brought young Frederick Vreeland, Diana's college-aged son, along. Extraordinary sights were on display, including, in one instance, the diminutive, preternaturally childlike Capote sitting blissfully on the lap of the severe-looking Janet Flanner, a sight Rosamond Bernier, for one, never forgot.

Bousquet became an integral part of Carmel's Paris life. Their friendship was forged on their mutual Catholicism, as much as gossip, martinis, and fashion, and Bousquet often accompanied the editor when she stopped in at the church of the moment—Saint-Clothilde, the Madeleine—to pray. Although an editor once described Bousquet as "the most completely alive person I've ever known," she was no match for her Irish American colleague, who tore among fashion houses, photo sessions, and runway shows without ever seeming to flag. "When Carmel arrives in Paris she makes me feel twenty years younger," Bousquet once complained. "When she leaves I feel a hundred and sixty." During the collections, Bassman adds, Carmel "worked like a son of a bitch."

The meals they shared seemed lethal. "They'd have a marvelous lunch and they'd come out holding each other up," says Leigh. "They'd stagger into the showrooms." Carmel's drinking was an increasing problem, perhaps more so in Paris with its nonstop social life and exhausting physical demands. Vreeland joined the chorus, writing unkindly that Carmel

> *was a great personality in Paris then. Everyone knew this crazy, brilliant Irishwoman. Drunk or sober, they adored her. . . . And she was often very drunk—I don't mean tipsy. She would talk absolutely brilliantly—but she couldn't get up and walk.*

However true this was, however often, it scarcely seemed to cloud her judgment. And it never made her less intimidating. Ernestine Carter, an editor at *Bazaar*'s British edition, was told by her magazine to stay during the collections at the San Régis, an elegant small hotel on the rue Jean-Goujon that had supplanted the Westminster for Carmel, becoming "already my second home." (Its appeal was partly based on convenience—*Bazaar*'s Paris offices had relocated to 18, rue Jean-Goujon.) But Carter determined that "Mrs. Snow's proximity made this too dangerous," and opted for the Matignon instead. Carter wrote:

> *In 1946, she was a distant, awe-inspiring figure with her immense chic, her blue hair, blue spectacles and her entourage of secretaries,*

assistants, photographers, the odd debutante and, above all, that darling of Paris, naughty, witty, minute Marie-Louise Bousquet.

The terror Carmel inspired may have worked in her favor—everyone wanted to keep her happy—but it wasn't deserved, Carter later determined.

She had been pictured to me . . . as a kind of ogress—ruthless and unscrupulous. I was terrified of her. When I was told that Carmel wanted to meet me again, I was tempted to take evasive action. I'm glad I didn't, for when I knew her she was none of these things.

Carmel and Bousquet were inseparable at the shows, sitting side by side at one after another. One couture watcher, Celia Bertin, described Carmel as "impassive, absent-eyed, with her curious faraway air" and Bousquet as "gesticulating, humorously ecstatic." Carmel always glided in at the last moment, taking her seat imperiously, and speaking only to a chosen few, a technique that made her seem to rise above the rest. "She was impeccably dressed," recalls the couturier Givenchy, who knew her at the very start of his career. "When she arrived at a collection she outshone everyone with her elegance." By then, "Everyone treated her like a *grand personage des collections,"* adds Bettina Graziani, at that time the top runway model in Paris. (She modeled for Jacques Fath before becoming Givenchy's star assistant.)

For Carmel, a show wasn't just about the dresses and suits going by, but part of a long continuum.

It is fascinating to me to see the birth of a new idea in the spring collection, and then to spot the same notion in the autumn line, matured and polished, maybe a little modified, like a fruit that has ripened during the summer. Sometimes the reporters miss the prophetic dress—the biggest fashion is not always the most obvious. Often a buyer will see it, and then deliberately skip it, knowing that her customers would find it too extreme. A magazine can and should take chances that a merchant can't. If I think a dress is important I don't care if it has been bought or not. I mark down the number in my little red book and give it to Avedon or Louise Dahl-Wolfe. The photograph usually evokes both praise and criticism. But I just sit back and wait. For I know that six months, maybe a year, later the public will be ready for it and the fruit will be plucked.

She had a way of watching a fashion show that her competitors, had they only known how, would have loved to imitate. "She used to sit at the collections looking as if she was asleep," recalls Susan Train, *Vogue*'s longtime Paris editor. "But every single time a dress of any interest walked by she seemed to wake up. She never missed a trick." Givenchy concurs: "She saw absolutely everything, every detail. She had a vision of each collection that was astonishing. She registered more than anyone else. Her talent was enormous. Madame Snow understood."

Ballard recalled that "Carmel Snow and Bousquet laughed and clowned in their seats before the shows began." But when the clothes came out, their reactions were vastly different. Bousquet would whisper "sublime!" over and over while Carmel sat stone-faced, as inscrutable as a cat, sometimes even sleeping. Or perhaps not. "She wasn't asleep, just being very cagey," insists Jeanne Eddy, then a buyer for Lord & Taylor. Whenever a junior editor accompanied her to Paris, Carmel would poke her in the ribs as a style that interested her went by. "I would take down the number so *Vogue,* which sat across the way, wouldn't see what she was up to," Laura Pyzel Clark recalls.

After the shows, Carmel wasn't beyond some sly maneuvering, according to Ballard:

Carmel Snow at the collections

She would say, in her low Irish voice that always sounded as if she were chewing her words, "Now, Bettina, of course in New York we have to pretend to be rivals, but you know that here we are all friends, and I don't mind at all if you know every model I'm taking. Just between us, what did you think of that collection we saw this afternoon? If you have any idea what we could possibly photograph from it, I wish that you would tell me—I can't think of a thing," reminding me of the old boarding-school technique of giving a confidence hoping to fish out many more from the girl you gave it to.

Carmel found a more willing spy in Bérard, who had none of Ballard's "schoolgirl loyalty," as the latter pointed out. He'd cheerfully "sketch on the tablecloth what we'd asked him to draw for *Vogue* from the collections and also what he preferred himself, giving just as much fashion help to the *Bazaar* as he ever gave to *Vogue.*"

In appearance, Bérard and Bousquet were dissimilar—he Buddha-like, she tiny and wizened—but they were twins in their encyclopedic knowledge of everyone and everything of interest in Paris, as well as in their love of malice; their "clever and wicked sallies were invariably at someone's expense," Ballard wrote. Bousquet wasn't any more loyal than Bérard, as later events would prove. She loved to imitate Carmel's "mannerisms and her low voice, the way she talked through her teeth," Babs Simpson recalled.

Subterfuge was still a routine part of fashion. A 1955 article in the *New York Times* reported that "style-snitching espionage agents have already burrowed deep into the industry," with "pattern pilferers" responsible for tens of millions of francs in lost revenues each year. The tricks were endless. Some designers' in-house photographers sold prints to manufacturers; seamstresses spirited away patterns from work; one American woman even swooped in one year, buying up couture clothes, then flew home, where she charged a hefty fee to manufacturers who wanted to see her wares—and copy them.

Spying was also part of a fashion editor's job. Jeanne Eddy recalls feeling surprised and flattered when Carmel invited her to visit her in her hotel room the morning after a show.

> *She said, "I like to go over things in the morning when I'm having breakfast." She knew what she wanted in the magazine. I think she wanted to include the thoughts of someone from the retail business, to mix it in with what she thought. She'd always say, "What are you getting for Lord & Taylor?" She just wanted some additional input. It worked into a regular routine each year.*

But Dorian Leigh paints a darker picture:

> *Finding out which designs were being bought by American buyers was not a matter of asking the buyers outright; one buyer didn't want another buyer to find out what her store would be offering that fall. An editor also couldn't ask a designer point-blank which of his designs were best sellers because, naturally, the designer wanted to give the impression to the other designers that* all *his designs were selling well. So an editor had to meet with buyers and designers . . . and cleverly get them all to give her the information she needed without their being aware of it. Then the editor had to arrange with each designer to borrow the precious fashions during the night, when they wouldn't be in use. And all this without revealing her knowledge to any other magazine editor!*

A familiar figure went missing at the shows that year: Chase had finally retired, at least nominally, and been replaced by her longtime associate Jessica Daves (to the disappointment of Ballard, who'd hoped for the job). For ages, Carmel had been the de facto queen of the collections, with Chase a close second; now there was no competition at all. Daves, who'd started at *Vogue* as fashion merchandising editor in 1933, was highly respected, but she had an enormous handicap in her looks. She resembled "a bunch of old laundry," in the words of one editor; another adds that "she looked like a cook." (Pace, Nigella Lawson.) Grace Mirabella, one of her successors, delivers the coup de grâce: "Everything about her was unappealing."

Try as Daves might—and consider the ammunition she had, working for *Vogue*!—she remained deeply, intractably unchic, a bizarre circumstance for someone in her milieu. Geri Trotta, who went on to write freelance articles for *Vogue* after leaving *Bazaar,* recalled attending a meeting at Daves's office. "I remember seeing all these elegant new hats on Jessica Daves's desk and thinking 'Oh boy, they're about to go.' Nothing could survive that dowdiness." Her chic-proof appearance colored everything. As Mirabella has written: "There were frequent humiliations—the couturiers in Paris consistently failed to recognize her and treated her with some disdain."

Adding to Daves's problems was the predictable one that Chase didn't fade away as promised; rather, she lingered endlessly, attending meetings and second-guessing her successor's every move. "It was agony," says *Vogue* editor Catherine di Montezemolo. Age hadn't improved Chase, to put it mildly. "She was a grump. She never smiled. She was one of those awful old ladies." Carmel must have congratulated herself, once again, for having gotten out when she had.

Tough as she was, awful as she was, Chase remained emotionally vulnerable on one subject at least, as Rosamond Bernier discovered over lunch with Chase, after she joined the *Vogue* staff.

> *Mrs. Chase began to speak of Carmel Snow, and as she talked Rosamond Riley [Bernier] was astonished to see tears suddenly begin to course down the cheeks of the tough old editor and businesswoman. By then Carmel Snow had been gone thirteen years.*

The 1946 spring showings were all about length and slenderness. Clothes were so tight that season that, at one couture house, while Carmel was being measured, the fitter said, "Forgive me, Madam, if it martyrizes you," while pulling the measuring tape around her waist tighter and tighter.... There was a 1913 influence at work, of all things, that year, a clear nostalgia for a prewar place and time. The line was so retro that Carmel corralled an old veteran, the illustrator Lepape, whose slender, long-waisted vamps had so defined the 1920s, to interpret that season's fashions for the magazine. Carmel was thrilled to find that Lelong's house had been moving in a new, exciting direction since a relatively unknown former illustrator (and *Bazaar* contributor) named Christian Dior—"Tian" to his friends—had signed on as its chief designer. So promising was this middle-aged neophyte that in 1946 Carmel commissioned Cartier-Bresson to take his portrait for the magazine. In her report to the Fashion Group that season, she encouraged her audience, still skittish about going to postwar Paris, to make sure that they did so the following year. "Lelong has a new designer whose collection was sensational—full of ideas. His name is Christian Dior."

At the end of the collections, in the routine chaos of air travel at the time, flights were canceled and some buyers found themselves stranded in Europe, unable to get home. Some didn't see New York again for weeks. Inevitably, a few vowed never to return, only to forget such promises the next season when fashion, once again, lured them en masse across the Atlantic. There they found that couture's predominantly narrow line was continuing. *Bazaar* used some suspiciously familiar drawings to show dresses with newly defined waistlines by Molyneux and Balenciaga, along with classical columns by Madame Grès. (These distinctive, faceless drawings, signed SAM, fooled no one: Bérard, still under exclusive contract to *Vogue,* was earning a little extra money on the side.) Schiaparelli came up with a pleasingly padded-looking jacket, a standout among all the slender dresses and suits. And, as in latter-day Manhattan, everyone seemed to be wearing black, including Lanvin's "ultramodern sheath of black crepe." It was a nuanced shade, the magazine assured its readers. "In Paris, black is never dead black."

In a climate of austerity and tightness, only Lelong, for whom Christian Dior designed, was showing cascades of fabric: one of his evening dresses was "a waterfall of pink tulle," the product of a designer who once wrote, "The most important principle in dressmaking is to follow the direction of the material . . . one must always obey the natural movement of the cloth." It soon became clear that Carmel's predictions about Dior, with his exceptional draping skills, had been borne out. He was clearly the one to watch. With the help of a wealthy backer, Dior set up his own *maison de couture* at 30, avenue Montaigne that autumn. In just three months, he did the interior design, trained models and staff, and, not least, of course, designed the first fashion line to bear his name. His impending debut collection was the talk of Paris for months.

At fourteen, Dior had been told by a fortune-teller that "you will make your living from women, and it is by them that you will succeed," a prediction that seemed unlikely: having grown up in a wealthy family, he didn't anticipate having to make a living at all. But by the time he was thirty-five, his family's money had dissipated after one crisis or another and he had to go to work, initially as an illustrator, signing the fashion drawings he contributed to newspapers and magazines with his nickname, "Tian Dior." His appearance was unprepossessing: Cecil Beaton described him as looking "like a bland country curate made out of pink marzipan." He was "disarmingly sweet," in his friend Bettina Ballard's assessment, with "an almost desperate shyness.

Dior's career, he wrote, began before the war when

> *Marie-Louise [Bousquet] introduced me to Mrs. Snow, the editor of* **Harper's Bazaar.** *It was then that I began to have a place in the world of fashion which, even a short time before, had been entirely unknown to me.*

Besides publishing his early sketches, Carmel commented, guided, critiqued. "She brought him to the fire, as she brought a lot of people to the fire," in her niece Nancy White's words. With this kind of encouragement, from Carmel and others, he emerged as a designer, working first for Piguet in the late 1930s, then Lelong, who was never a particularly inspired couturier. The fashions Dior designed in his name were the best of Lelong's career.

In response to the air travel fiasco of the year before, and with suitable fanfare, TWA added an extra flight on February 1, 1947, to accommodate people traveling from New York for the spring collections. Forty American buyers and journalists made the trip, less than the prewar volume but much more than the year before. Lucie Noel, reporting for the Paris edition of the *New York Herald*

Tribune, described a "certain Louis XIV flavor" about some of the showings and "a distinct Amazon feeling" about others. Molyneux's dresses had a nipped-in waistline; Lelong showed a "slender, harmonious feminine silhouette." And the ever-resourceful Schiaparelli had gone "into forest and farmyards for some new motifs."

Christian Dior was the last to show. Even before his first collection, which was unveiled on the freezing cold morning of February 12, 1947, word was out that it would resuscitate haute couture. A huge crowd gathered outside his gray-awninged entrance. Seated on a fauteuil in the deeply, understatedly chic, gray-and gold-decorated salon, *Vogue*'s Bettina Ballard recalled being "conscious of an electric tension that I had never before felt in the couture." As always, Carmel took the place of honor, an elegant settee upholstered in gray velvet. "*Harper's Bazaar* was the sofa," Dior wrote, as if describing a law as inviolate as gravity.

There was a strict protocol. The canape—Carmel's throne—was Mount Olympus. Lesser gods and goddesses perched on lesser peaks. The fauteuils were for other people who mattered, the gilt chairs for hoi polloi. "There was a world of hierarchical difference between an armchair . . . and a gilt chair," reported Ernestine Carter of *Bazaar*'s British edition, who learned this lesson the hard way when, at an early Dior show, the first she'd attended, she was solemnly shown to a fauteuil. As she took her seat, she heard great merriment all around her, something she understood only later on. "I was an innocent and didn't realize that a joke was being played on Mrs. Snow." (The hilarity came from Carmel's imagined reaction, finding a novice among the grandees.) "No show ever began until Mrs. Snow arrived," according to Dior. She was always not late, exactly, but on the cusp; all eyes would be on her as she glided to her seat. She'd perch in her place of honor, Bousquet at her side.

At Dior's debut, Bérard—a key supporter of the designer's, who'd helped in almost every aspect of his house's opening—sat on the floor with Jacinthe, his "absurd puff of a dog," as George Davis described it. The legendarily homely Daves, of *Vogue,* sat across the way. At ten-thirty, "we were given a polished theatrical performance such as we had never seen in a couture house before," Ballard recalled. Models began circulating, swiftly and with military precision, as the style numbers of their outfits were called out, as always, in both French and English. And then there were the clothes. Of the several lines Dior presented, the sensation was the Corolle. It featured an extravagantly full skirt—some measured as much as forty yards in circumference—rounded bust and hips, and an impossibly tiny waist. Its shoulder line was the rounded one the French refer to as *pauvre.* Its hemline stopped exactly one foot above the ground. Dior topped these ensembles off with hats of his own design, typically pillboxes, some held on with gauzy fabric tied beneath the chin.

Dior had a genius for color, and it was very much on display. He mixed neutral colors—navy, gray, black—with shades he called scream red, Longchamp green, earth of Paris, porcelain pink. The fabrics were light; these were spring fashions, after all—cotton, dotted twills, mousseline. The prototypical New Look suit was a two-piece one called "Bar," which had a full skirt of black wool crepe and a tight-waisted jacket of pale pink shantung. And then there were such extravagances as the "*panthère,*" a belted dress in an animal print pattern, as its name implies. (Dior, like most designers, gave names to each style.)

The line was "a brilliant nostalgia," in Cecil Beaton's words. The huge pleated skirts, inspired by the black, floor-length ones worn by Marseilles fishwives at market, called to mind the hourglass silhouette that had prevailed in la Belle Epoque, two world wars earlier. It was feminine with a vengeance: "The essence of femininity," *Bazaar* later called it. The artistry behind it was exceptional: pleats were stitched down twelve inches from the waist, hand-pressed and flared to the hem. Most styles, for greater smoothness through the middle, buttoned in back. They gave woman, at least those who had waists in the first place, first-rate figures, one that was 100 percent illusion: Dior's flat-chested models were wearing "pink felt false bosoms," according to *Harper's Bazaar,* and "all his dresses have little Basque girdles sewn inside."

The applause began early in the show and never stopped. The clapping got louder and louder as buyers, friends, journalists, editors, and hangers-on realized the import of what they'd seen. "My God what have I done?" the designer is said to have cried as it gathered force at the end. The portly, mild-mannered designer burst into tears. "God help the buyers who bought before they saw Dior!" Carmel exclaimed, referring to the fact that many American buyers had already headed home. "This changes everything." And then, or perhaps later, she said the words: "It's quite a revolution, dear Christian. Your dresses have such a new look."

No one knows exactly when these famous lines were uttered. No less an authority than Susan Train, *Vogue*'s Paris editor, who started her long and storied career for that magazine in about this period, has been able to pinpoint exactly how these words passed from Carmel to her interlocutor. Theories have come and gone. The most likely explanation is that they were called out in the tumult at the end of his show. But there are other theories. One journalist claimed that Carmel wrote them in a note the following day. Another that a Reuters reporter, overhearing her comment, called it down to a colleague in the crowd waiting outside on the avenue Montaigne, who then telegraphed it around the world. Yet another theorized that Carmel cabled the term back to the *Bazaar* offices in New York.

However they were said, the words *New Look* locked in the phenomenon. They had the exact degree of authority that such assured fashion deserved. In their succinctness, they implied, even insisted, that, to remain chic, every image-conscious female in the Western world would have to sign on. And they did. "From one day to the next he made our poor wardrobes seem ridiculous," wrote Françoise Giroud, who witnessed Dior's collection as a young reporter for *Elle,* then a very unglossy weekly. "Nothing could save our skirts, which were too short, too straight." It's no wonder that *Elle* (which had only recently been founded by Hélène Lazareff, who'd trained under Carmel at *Bazaar* in New York during the war), called it, "The collection that knocked out the entire world," and proclaimed in its March 4, 1947, issue that "everything that shines is Dior." The show was the "sensation of the season," the Paris edition of the *New York Herald Tribune* wrote. Some of the buyers who had headed back to the United States were said to have turned around, returning to France to stock up on Dior.

As for the deeply modest designer himself—branded by *Time* magazine as "the undisputed king of couture"—he was in a state of shock.

> *On the night before the first collection, the one which introduced the "New Look," if I had been asked what I had done and what I hoped from it, I should certainly not have spoken of "revolution." I could not have foreseen the reception that it was to have.*

At a celebratory dinner after the show, Bérard presented Dior with a drawing of 30, avenue Montaigne that the designer would adopt as his signature, reproducing it on scarves and, seemingly, everything else for the rest of his career. He also proffered some invaluable advice to the deeply shaken designer, telling him that this undisputed triumph would be something he'd have to live up to for the rest of his days: "You will have to compete against yourself." It was a point that Dior wasn't yet ready to concede: "Success was too new, too unknown a poison" for him at that moment, he later wrote. But in short order he would understand Bérard all too well.

Even so, he moved from strength to strength: the next year, when he presented his spring collections, gendarmes had to be called in to control the mob on the avenue Montaigne. Also in 1948, Dior took a critical step when he signed a deal with Prestige, a New York hosiery company, to produce nylon stockings under his name. Shrewdly, he held out for a royalty agreement, rather than accepting the flat fee he was initially offered. It was the first licensing agreement undertaken by any designer, one of many that would enrich his coffers in the years ahead.

Carmel was the first in the United States, and probably the loudest, to trumpet this very feminine silhouette, a radical change from the austerely tailored look—a kind of uniform for civilians—that had prevailed during the war. "It was because women longed to look like women again, that they adopted the New Look," she wrote. "The change was due to a universal change of feeling, of atmosphere. Fashions, I believe, aren't *put over* on women." Between copyists and buyers, the style was quickly in the stores. Even American designers benefited. "Seventh Avenue

In the front row at Dior, 1950s: Michel de Brunhoff; Bettina Ballard and Alexander Liberman, of *Vogue,* to the left; Avedon and Carmel on the right

joyfully discovered that every dress in every closet in the U.S. had been outmoded at one stroke." *Bazaar* covered Dior to such an extent that at one point Carmel wrote to Dahl-Wolfe, who was about to photograph the designer yet again for the magazine, to refrain from promising him that the image would ever run. "Every day and in every place I go, I get criticized about the amount of publicity I am giving him and, as we have already published his picture in the magazine, I would much rather give publicity to his models."

Women made all sorts of sacrifices to wear the new clothes. The German photographer Willy Maywald, who worked for Dior for years, once described a scene that took place as a young Swedish model, married to a rich South American, left a fitting at the House of Dior. "Carmel Snow was there and congratulated her on her dress. "Yes," replied the client, "it is the most amazing dress I have ever seen. I can't walk, eat, or even sit down." Carmel asked the hapless girl what she'd purchased. The list that followed was extensive—"five cocktail dresses, six coats, and twelve suits, all from Dior"—and she'd also bought from other designers. Then the editor moved in for the kill: "That's all?" was her crushing response. The poor girl, digging herself in deeper, explained that she lived in Rio, and that these items were only for her to wear in Europe. Given such enthusiasm, it's no wonder that, before too long, the House of Dior was earning one and a half times what all the other fashion houses put together were bringing in.

For all the ecstatic press it engendered, there were some—and still are—who saw something insidious taking place. In *The New Yorker,* Francine du Plessix Gray called the New Look "the dumbest misnomer in the history of finery," adding:

> *It turned the clock back to the restrictive folderol of la Belle Epoque, and evoked alarmingly regressive models of femaleness: women as . . . displayers of their men's wealth and status—women who need to be helped into cabs, who required huge trunks in order to travel with their finery, and maids to help them dress.*

It wasn't just women's clothes that Dior seemed to be yanking back to an earlier time, but their role in society, too. During the war, they'd learned that they could do anything: run subways, take over munitions factories, and on and on. Afterward, they had to be nudged, gently and persistently, through advertising and other means, to return to their places in the home, relinquishing their jobs to the men who, back from the war, needed to work. It was a subtle but persistent message. And the New Look fit into it hand in (white) glove.

Dior's triumph was only a more extreme example of what takes place, to some degree or another, in every fashion season. It's that "universal change," Carmel mentioned, that something in the air, a feeling that, somehow, gets translated into fabric and line. Year after year, fashion capitalizes on our deep-seated need for change, for transformation, for the illusion, at least, of progress. It marks off a moment, providing a kind of milestone between one and the next; on rare occasions, as in the New Look, it becomes history in its own right. It "was a success only because it reflected the mood of the times," Dior wrote, "a mood that sought refuge from the mechanical and impersonal in a return to tradition." Its ecstatic reception, he theorized, was a correction to the work of such designers as Schiaparelli, who "had moved the border of elegance backwards to the limits of the bizarre."

Carmel's staff always waited eagerly to see what she was wearing each morning, but never more so than on her first day back in the office after a trip to France. "There was a letdown, always, when she was away," Aswell has written. "When she came back from Paris, bringing the world with her, to her staff it was like their mother's return home from a party." Of course, we all knew what she put on that year. Practically no one in America had seen a New Look outfit up close. The silhouette was so radical that no less a discerning critic than Vreeland—cruelly kept away, as always, from fashion's front lines—almost lost her cool. "Carmel, it's divine!" she cried, studying her sloped-shouldered New Look suit. "It makes you look *drowned*." (Vreeland would later call it the "guinea hen look," presumably for its trussed-up qualities.)

The April 1947 issue of *Bazaar* reprinted the Cartier-Bresson portrait of Dior, only in a much larger version, and with a solemnly worshipful caption: "He is revolutionizing daytime fashions as Poiret did in his day and Chanel in hers." By the time Carmel debriefed the Fashion Group a few weeks later, the New Look was unstoppable, and her speech (written by Frances McFadden in this period) was ramped up to match. "Dior saved Paris as Paris was saved in the Battle of the Marne," she said at one point. Fashion had come back to life. In the United States, the old look didn't go down without a fight. It came down to legs: American men wanted to see as much of them as possible; Dior's dropped hemline didn't suit their purposes at all. Others complained that all that material, used so soon after the war, added up to a scandalous waste. Something called the Town Meeting of the Air debated the New Look as if it were a kind of conspiracy, a hoax being put over by the French on Americans, but such voices were quickly drowned out.

Even the *Wall Street Journal* weighed in, publishing a survey on its front page that said that most people approved. Resistance was futile.

When Dahl-Wolfe, who always splurged on one couture outfit when in Paris for *Bazaar,* wore her New Look suit while photographing a willowy mannequin, herself dressed in a Dior tailleur, this comic image—the dwarflike, almost exuberantly homely photographer, Rolleiflex at the ready, trailing a goddess in human form, both women dressed alike—was wired by a news service around the world. "She wore it with aplomb around New York, enjoying the sensation it created," McFadden wrote. And sensation was the word. When Bettina Ballard appeared in Manhattan in "1947," a style in which pleats were released "twelve inches below the waist to form a tremendous flounce," in *Bazaar*'s description, the editor literally stopped traffic. Her outfit "gave me a brief moment of fame," she wrote. "Even taxi drivers asked me, 'Is this the "new look"?' so quickly did the expression become part of our everyday vocabulary."

Few in the United States had heard of Dior before; overnight, everyone had. On Dior's first post–New Look visit to America, columnist Walter Winchell, who "saw them acting lovey-dovey together," according to John Michael White, one of Carmel's nephews, concluded that they were having an affair, and published an item to that effect. "*Flash!* The romance of the year is between Carmel Snow at *Harper's Bazaar* and Christian Dior." The two were close—Dior had even treated Carmel to a session with Madame Delahaye, his favorite fortune-teller (like Carmel he consulted one before every important decision)—but he was gay, so such an insinuation was absurd. The designer reacted lightheartedly, sending Carmel a dozen roses addressed "To my fiancée" and signed "Tian." Carmel, less sanguine, stormed off to a lawyer. "You can sue him because he says you're unchaste," he advised. But Carmel, who was vain enough, misunderstood and was appalled at the implication that she might not be attractive to men. "Do you think I want to tell the world that I'm unchased?" she asked, in horror—and dropped her plans to sue. Palen, outraged, and stuttering more than ever, was heard to ask, "Who is this fellow Winchell? I'll horsewhip him." He didn't. Carmel did, however, score a rare retraction from Winchell, who wrote, "Same magazine, different girl." (That wasn't true either.)

Lawyers came in handy one Friday in August 1947, though, when Carmel asked a *Bazaar* assistant working for her in Paris to help out on a photo shoot the following day. When the young woman said she couldn't because she would be getting married that day at noon, alarm bells sounded in Carmel's mind. The employee in question was the tobacco heiress Doris Duke, then considered to be the richest woman in the world—with a net worth estimated to be as high as $200 million. Carmel had been uneasy ever since she learned of Duke's involvement with the darkly attractive Dominican playboy Porfirio Rubirosa. He was famously attracted to superrich women—another of his wives was Barbara Hutton, the Woolworth heiress—and, perhaps not coincidentally, so well endowed that, half a century later, those outsized, theft-proof pepper grinders wielded by waiters in better restaurants are still informally known, in Europe at least, as "Rubirosas." Worse still, the couple, both in their thirties, planned to wed at the Dominican Legation, where Rubirosa was a chargé d'affaires, a move that could have cost Duke her American citizenship.

A 1947 news clipping of Louise Dahl-Wolfe in a New Look suit, photographing a model wearing the same

Carmel had originally hired Duke at the request of Hearst management. She had turned up at 572 Madison on her first day of work in an oversized beaver coat and was assigned to share an office with beauty editor Sarah Tomerlin Lee. While Duke was rumored to be interested in fashion, few could tell that, or indeed, anything else about her: she was so timid that she rarely spoke. "Doris was rather dumpy. Without vitality. She was almost mute, and seemed extremely sad to me," Lee said. "She was so shy it was miserable for her. In meetings, she never made a remark or asked a question." Carmel took the young heiress under her wing. "She must have been intrigued by Doris's wealth," said her niece Nancy White. Not particularly attractive in the first place, Duke became instantly more chic, which led White to suspect that her aunt had begun choosing her clothes. When the girl expressed an interest in working in Europe, Carmel arranged for her to be a correspondent for *Bazaar* in Paris. She went to work for Bousquet in March 1947, without terribly impressive results. "I don't think Doris contributed anything but a certain glamour," in the words of Nancy White.

When Carmel heard that Duke had taken up with the notorious playboy, she resolved to keep her as busy as possible—never more so than during the collections. But clearly not busy enough. It was just before five o'clock on a Friday afternoon in August, back in a time when Paris, even more than today, really does empty out for the month. "I went into action," Carmel wrote. By some miracle, she reached Hearst's French lawyer, who said that the wedding should not go ahead unless Duke was represented by counsel. Carmel insisted, Duke acquiesced, and when she married the next day, on September 1, 1947, "a battery of legal talent was there to represent the interest in one of the largest fortunes in the world," according to Carmel. News accounts confirm the speed with which Carmel moved. According to the *New York Times,* the wedding had been originally scheduled for early the following week, then moved up to Saturday, presumably at the groom's request, in a bid to avoid the presence of lawyers altogether.

Carmel Snow with Christian Dior, model, and student designer at Parsons School of Design, New York, 1953

The paper described the bride as being tall, blond, and "glittering with diamonds." She wore an ankle-length green taffeta Dior New Look dress, chosen by Carmel. As for the groom, he was dressed in a dark striped suit—and infinitely poorer than he might have been had Carmel not been moved to action on his bride's behalf. (She was one of two official witnesses to the marriage.) "Reversing the usual wedding procedure, the bride, bridegroom and their guests drank champagne and whiskey toasts and ate cakes before the ceremony," the *Times* noted, making the whole thing sound deceptively festive. But the real reason for this topsy-turvy schedule was that it gave the lawyers enough time to finish their work.

"At the outset the two had looked like adolescent lovers," according to Joseph Kingsbury-Smith, a friend of Duke's and one of the guests.

> *But Rubi's mood changed when two men carrying briefcases arrived. They were lawyers from the law firm Coudert bearing a prenuptial agreement for the groom to sign. The document stated that Rubi, in marrying Doris, renounced any claim to the Duke fortune. "His face was quite a picture when the two lawyers walked in. He looked like one of those fierce black Miura bulls about to charge a red cape," recalled one guest. "I've never seen anyone madder. But he signed. There wasn't much else he could do."*

According to the *New York Times:*

> *During the ritual, Senor Rubirosa . . . smoked a cigarette. He ground it out in time to exchange rings with the bride, placing on her finger a small band of rubies, while she put a gold band on his finger. Each smiled frequently at the other.*

But behind the mask, Rubirosa was seething. The paper noted that the couple had signed "a notarized matrimonial contract"—a rarity in this era—just before the vows were exchanged. Its terms were not disclosed.

"I suppose the bride was no more grateful than the groom at the time, but subsequent events have happily changed her feeling about my interference,"

Carmel wrote cheerily. These "events" included constant, chronic infidelity—the groom was going at it with a maid within hours of the service—and, inevitably, divorce. The marriage lasted thirteen months. Duke's relationship with *Harper's Bazaar,* on the other hand, would endure for years: the magazine continued to cover her goings-on and, how to put it, her money, for years, publishing a piece on her "Shangri-La in Hawaii," for example, in May 1957.

Carmel may have shepherded Duke to safety, but she found things harder with her own children, notably Mary Palen, the most free spirited of the three girls and, by many accounts, the most unhappy. Carmel returned to New York to continued trouble with her middle daughter. "I had long ago determined that I would try not to dominate my children," she wrote. "I let them make their own mistakes, which they frequently did." But some who knew her say otherwise—that, while she adored her daughters, they were expected to bend to her will. This approach might have been effective with Brigid and Carmel, more docile by nature, but it wasn't with Mary Palen. "She wasn't dominated by her mother as much as the others," according to Dorothy Wheelock Edson. "She was the only one who seemed to be trying to kick off the braces."

Carmel's difficulties at home were compounded by a severe disappointment in work. In spite of her belief in it, *Junior Bazaar* folded. After May 1948, the date of its last issue, its pages were again incorporated into *Bazaar* itself. With the postwar economic boom subsiding and advertising becoming more scarce, the Hearst organization decided to pull the plug on the magazine, a decision Carmel very much regretted: "I think we could have made *Junior Bazaar* into a formidable rival of *Mademoiselle* and *Seventeen.*" Dick Berlin told her that Hearst higher-ups thought that too much of her attention had been siphoned off into the new project. "I suppose that was true," she conceded. "The new always fascinates me."

The news surprised many, including Tom White, who, like many in the organization, learned of it from an April 2 memo from the Hearst administration headed "Harper's Bazaar and Jr. Bazaar." In a letter written that day to his daughter Nancy, he described the news as "startling," adding that "the *Bazaar* thing sets one back in the example of how quickly it came and how quickly it departed." Hearst himself was behind the decision to discontinue it, according to Melanie Witt Miller. The magazine announced *Junior*'s demise along with the news that *Bazaar* had reached a circulation of 350,000. Starting in June 1948, the words "incorporating Junior Bazaar" were added to *Bazaar*'s cover; a corner of the main masthead listed the section's (very reduced) staff, headed by Martha Stout, who had replaced Barry as editor. Melanie Miller would become its fashion editor. The section was longer than it had been when it was last a part of *Bazaar* itself; as always, it was heavy on fashion, but also had regular feature stories, including a photo essay on a young rider.

As time went on, Carmel, like a character in a nineteenth-century English novel, became increasingly preoccupied with marrying her daughters off advantageously. "She was unquestionably a social climber of the first order," Perényi says. At one point Carmel was approached by Rose Kennedy, who was interested in finding eligible young Catholic women for her three sons, a plan that—disappointingly, from Carmel's point of view—never came to pass. In later years, after Rose's son John F. Kennedy was elected president, Carmel's eldest daughter, Carmel, loved telling people that her date was supposed to have been Jack.

With or without the Kennedys, "she married her daughters off very well," as Perényi has noted. The first to go was Carmel, who was betrothed to R. Thornton Wilson Jr., a Princeton graduate then working as an investment banker, on June 10, 1948. On a page of soft-focused wedding portraits in the society pages of the *New York Times,* Carmel Wilson's portrait stands out for both realism and quality: the wide-eyed beauty looking directly at the camera had been photographed by Dahl-Wolfe.

Wilson was wealthy and a descendant of John Jacob Astor, facts that certainly appealed to the bride's mother, and the wedding was an extravagance, with nine ushers and nine bridesmaids, mainly friends from Foxcroft and Vassar, as well as both the bride's sisters; Mary Palen was the maid of honor. "Mrs. Snow was thrilled with Carmel's match," reports Ann Murphy Vose. "It was a coup. Not only was he very social—he was an Astor—but his stepfather was someone big in government" (Wilson's mother was married to R. Sumner Welles, then undersecretary of state). Since Wilson was an Episcopalian, the service couldn't take place in a Catholic church. It was held in the ballroom of the very traditional Colony Club instead, which was transformed into a chapel for the ceremony, with a Catholic priest presiding, then metamorphosed back into a ballroom for the reception. Toni Frissell took the wedding pictures.

Carmel prepared for the festivities by brushing up her dancing skills at a New York dancing school. "Naturally I didn't care to be less nimble at my daughter's reception than at my own!" Young Carmel's satin-and-tulle wedding gown was a gift from Mainbocher. (Carmel passed it on to her favorite New York fortune-teller for *her* daughter's wedding the following year, a detail Mainbocher adored. "It's just like you to do something like that," he told her.) And, of course, the wedding was featured in the pages of *Bazaar,* in a two-page spread, shot by Dahl-Wolfe, complete with fetching, flower-laden bridesmaids, some with distinguished surnames—Dillon, Goelet—and all dressed in hoop-skirted organdy.

The Snows at Foxcroft, 1948 (young Carmel shows her engagement ring to *Bazaar* editor Laura Pyzel Clark in the background).

Wilson was a fun-loving, colorful figure who would go on to work in advertising and public relations, become a keen supporter of the arts, and co-own the popular Ermitage Restaurant in Manhattan. He was also a wickedly funny raconteur—"a riot of a man" according to D. D. Ryan—who "would regale many people at the golf club out in Oyster Bay with funny stories about Palen." The Wilsons settled in on Sutton Place, and young Carmel took up a life her mother never would have considered for herself: that of a charity- and society-minded socialite, whose life revolved around her husband.

Carmel was thrilled that her eldest daughter was settled, but her complacency didn't last for long. Word came on July 9 that her beloved brother Tom, then only sixty-three, had died the day before in Chicago. The timing was strange: another brother, Peter Desmond White, an industrialist, had died on a business trip at the age of fifty-nine only two months earlier. That had been bad enough, but the demise of Tom, one of her favorite siblings, was a real blow: they'd been allies, always, since long before the days when, new to America, Tom had shot pats of butter to the ceiling, hoping they'd fall on his sister's head. The funeral, held at St. Patrick's Cathedral on Fifth Avenue, was crowded with representatives of Fifty-seventh Street and beyond; among the mourners was Tom's mistress Cissy Patterson, whom his widow, Virginia, classy beyond all imagining, had made a point of inviting.

And Carmel's worries about Mary Palen, who was set to enter Bryn Mawr that fall, seemed to grow only more intense. At some point, "she cracked," in Avedon's words. According to Edson, Mary Palen had "a nervous breakdown"—that phrase again—and was institutionalized more than once, at least on one occasion at Payne Whitney, a private psychiatric hospital in New York. "Mrs. Snow was very secretive about her daughter being mentally ill," Edson says. "She said, 'Dorothy, my daughter is going to be as well as your daughter.' She said it disapprovingly, as though I were responsible. She hated talk about anyone being sick. She really couldn't handle it."

Mary Palen did get to Bryn Mawr, where Mary Stair Dempwolf, a fellow member of the class of 1962, found her to be "shy and quiet and very much in herself, but delightful when you chatted away." Another classmate, Francine du Plessix, was, by coincidence, the stepdaughter of Condé Nast's Alex Liberman. The two girls became friends, although not because of their shared fashion roots. "I kept very aloof from my parent's fashion world," reports du Plessix, who would become known as a writer under her married name, Francine du Plessix Gray. At some point during this time, Mary Palen was diagnosed as schizophrenic and "was never really independent after that," according to one relative. One can take the diagnosis with a grain of salt—the condition was notoriously overdiagnosed in that era—but it must have been devastating. Her parents, quite naturally, were distraught, perhaps even more so since, as Perényi reports, the editor "once broke down and told me that [Mary Palen] was her favorite child." Carmel's home life had been on autopilot for most of her married days—with her schedule it had had to be. Now it very much wasn't.

Work went on, of course, with its unforgiving deadlines. It wasn't a question of throwing herself into it; Carmel had never done otherwise. But now her attention was compromised as it had never been before. During this period, when she went to Paris, she'd ask her sister Christine to come to New York to keep an eye on the girl. At one point Mary Palen ran away, to her aunt's terror, and was eventually returned by the police. It was a turbulent time, both for the girl and those around her. Eventually, she would improve, even go on to marry. But her well-being was a concern for years. It's no wonder that, when Carmel became the first radio commentator to report directly from Paris on fashion in August 1948, she ended each broadcast with a message to her family—a wish, even a prayer, that in her absence they'd keep well and safe.

A Snow family Christmas card from the 1950s at the time of Mary Palen's hospitalization

13 *triumphing over all*

Mrs. Snow, as usual, triumphs over all.
—Dorothy Wheelock Edson (in a letter to Kenneth Tynan)

Richard Avedon was restless. It had been several years since the young photographer had found his way into the pages of the greatest magazine of his time. With awesome speed, he'd infiltrated its pages until he'd become as much a part of the magazine as the estimable Dahl-Wolfe. He was all of twenty-five. One peak, though, remained to be climbed. Early in 1948, he confronted Carmel as the time for the spring collections approached. Take me to Paris with you, he said, or I'll move over to *Vogue*—a terrifying threat.

Covering the French collections was the pinnacle for a fashion photographer; nothing else could substitute. By trying to force Carmel's hand, Avedon took a risk, but it was a calculated one. Given the mutual affection that he, Brodovitch, and Carmel shared, he must have known that he would prevail. But there was a natural obstacle—a huge one—to his going in the form of Dahl-Wolfe, who was expecting to accompany Carmel to the collections, as always, that year. Nothing would be worth her wrath if she found herself supplanted. And besides, "Dahl-Wolfe was invented by Carmel," as Avedon has said; the editor's affection for the photographer, and longtime support of her career, was genuine.

Such human complications were Carmel's meat and drink. A solution would be found, and it was. "Carmel recognized Dick's threat as genuine and arranged for him to go to Paris *secretly*.... It was a strictly undercover operation," according to Mary Louise Aswell. Avedon, the self-described "little guy in a black suit with shiny black hair parted over here..." did end up in the French capital, but so did Dahl-Wolfe, while an operation was mounted to keep the latter in the dark. Taking Avedon was a shrewd decision. Although he was now shooting regularly for the magazine, he was new to the collections and their round-the-clock demands. To try him out as a backup photographer made eminent sense.

Dahl-Wolfe went to Paris a week early to scout for locations. Avedon flew later with Carmel. Their adventures began on the plane ride over. "She put her coat over my lap and said, 'I don't put on my seatbelt,'" adding, conspiratorially, that General Eisenhower didn't either. And then she began to talk, indulging in that Irish national pastime. "She talked through the night, telling me the story of her early life in America." They stayed at the San Régis, only meters from Dior, a hotel "known only to those who heard about it from someone else," according to Dorian Leigh. Carmel commandeered the penthouse suite, a space with an unsavory history: during the war, she told Avedon, the hotel had been requisitioned by the Nazis, and her own suite had been reserved for the führer himself.

From the moment they arrived, Avedon and Dahl-Wolfe led parallel lives. It seems incredible that the editor got away with it, and on numerous occasions she almost didn't. At one point, when Dahl-Wolfe appeared unexpectedly at Dior, Avedon and Carmel leaped into a dressing room to avoid being detected. And there were other near misses. Collection weeks had long been a time of subterfuge—think sheet-wrapped models sneaking through streets—now there was a hidden photographer as well.

On this trip Avedon was initiated into the whole Paris shebang, beginning with early-morning strategy sessions in Carmel's suite, overwhelmingly fragrant from the bouquets sent by the couturiers, "in the exchange of compliments we intersperse with inevitable rows," as she put it. She conducted meetings

> *while she was barefoot and dressed in a slip, although always of course wearing pearls She'd dress as we talked, talking to me the whole time. She walked out as this vision. It was like someone going on stage with the speed of a theatrical change. No time was wasted.*

She had even been known to receive selected guests while in the bath. In later years, Sally Kirkland, the fashion editor of *Life* magazine, recounted a similar scene.

A late-night meeting with Richard Avedon, Hotel San Régis, Paris, 1950s

> *You know the first act of* Rosenkavalier*? While the Marschallin in the opera is drinking her morning chocolate and getting dressed for the day, she receives her lawyer and her major-domo and a milliner and a perruquier and some orphans and an animal vendor and an Italian tenor. Well, the Marschallin had a quiet morning compared to the morning I once spent with Carmel.*
>
> *Carmel said . . . "come tomorrow—is a quarter to eight too early for you?" So I said, "Oh no, not a bit too early." I practically had to stay up all night to make it, but I got there at a quarter to eight, and of course I was about two hours behind Carmel. She'd been up at six to get some outfits from Balenciaga for Avedon to photograph. She'd been stone-cold naked under the suit she'd put on so it was easy for her to get back into her nightgown, which was the way I found her—she'd kept her pearls on, though. And that hotel suite was in full swing.*
>
> *Two telephones were going full blast, with a secretary in the sitting room to pick up one phone when Carmel picked up the other beside her bed. There seemed to be a thread running through some of the calls: "Number* seventy-seven *and Number* seventy-three *. . . No, no, those are the two," so I gathered that those were the O.K. Balenciaga suits, and that the calls were the postmortems Carmel always holds after showings. If she made a call herself she'd start right in, very low, sort of like a*

conspirator: "Hattie, this is Carmel. What did you think of Balmain's collection?" . . . "Larry, this is Carmel. . . ." and so on and so forth.

In between phone calls Carmel dictated cables—very good ones—bawling out the home office for some monstrous commitment they'd made, giving direct answers to questions and good advice on the periphery of the collections, such as telling Dupont not to give up hope, Givenchy had used nylon in his collection—all very clear and concise and quick.

Some jewelry person came in with samples he spread out on the bed next to Carmel's, then a lingerie lady with same, then a man from the studio with some layouts for approval; Marie-Louise Bousquet hobbled in for the day's gossip; Avedon rushed in with his contact prints. Carmel picked up her magnifying glass, peered through it at the sheets of tiny pictures for three minutes, then began puncturing the ones she wanted with a pencil, all the time talking or dictating.

Suddenly in came a woman who walked straight past all of us into the bathroom. Nobody paid the slightest attention to her. I saw her open a bag she carried and begin laying out some kind of instruments on a table. When she came into the bedroom Carmel said Bonjour, stripped down the sheet to expose her flank (gents were still standing around of course), the woman gave her a poke with a needle, and away she went.

Well, by nine-thirty, when Carmel got up to dress for the day's first fashion show, I was ready to go back to bed.

The injection, by the way, was probably vitamin B_{12}—Dahl-Wolfe got them in Paris, too—although given the pace Carmel sustained, one can be forgiven for wondering if it wasn't combined with something less legal. Whatever the source, nonstop energy was required. Her mission after the war was nothing less than "to help revive the French luxury business by whetting the vast, lucrative American appetite for its wares," as Judith Thurman has written.

Avedon hadn't hired any models for the trip—that certainly would have given the game away—but he brought his wife, Doe, with him instead. There were numerous restrictions on models in those days. For one thing, they, like any other contributor, had to pledge allegiance to their respective magazines: "Both *Vogue* and *Harper's Bazaar* felt they should have exclusive use of their models," according to Dorian Leigh. "A model couldn't go back and forth between the two without losing friends at one of them." And there were other rules, such as the unwritten one that said that no mannequin could do more than two collections with the same photographer—term limits, in a sense.

Mary Jane Russell fell afoul of this one in the early 1950s, after she'd done two collections in a row with Louise Dahl-Wolfe. When the time came for the next showings, the photographer went looking for a model—"calling Eileen Ford three times a day," in Russell's words—but couldn't find anyone who seemed right. Weeks went by, the departure date was approaching, when Russell received a call from Carmel saying, with a laugh, that Dahl-Wolfe "is interviewing people looking for the next Mary Jane Russell," and asking if the real one would save them a lot of trouble by agreeing to travel for the magazine once more. Others were often hired in France, including two of the better-known House of Dior models, Lucky and Rénée.

Dorian Leigh had her turn when she went to Paris with Avedon for two years in a row, beginning in 1949. As always, it was a frenzy. One night, during an all-night session at the *Bazaar* studio, in a nineteenth-century building just across the perfect, compact place François Premier from the San Régis, Carmel helped her into an extraordinary Dior creation,

> *an absolutely marvelous dress, a mass of pearls and sequins and everything. [Carmel] zipped me up in it and I said "Imagine having this cleaned." She answered "Don't be ridiculous. He'll tear it off of you. You'll never have to have it cleaned."*

This romantic, even Gothic flight of fancy was pure Carmel. The scenario she outlined was hardly far-fetched—like so many American models loose in Paris, Leigh seemed to be pursued frantically by every man she met. Her life at home, though, was very different than the editor supposed; Carmel was surprised to learn in the middle of a photo shoot that the slender, impossibly young vision before her was already a mother. "Madam, the model has three children," Avedon told Carmel, photographing Leigh as she posed in the place de la Concorde.

The clandestine photographs Avedon took during this first, surreptitious trip to France were published in a double spread in the June 1948 Paris issue. The shots, of two striking evening gowns—dotted swiss Schiaparelli, white tulle Dior—were done, as the captions inform us, "in the extravagant poses fashionable in the days of Nadar." Avedon worked with a large-format camera, an eight by ten, which did perfect justice to the *Bazaar* studio's cubic proportions. His model was framed, lovingly, dead center. His shot took in the whole scene, right down to the artificial ways in which he'd created his vision: the cloth draped under the skylight, dappled light filtering through; the painted backdrop paper. All artifice was apparent, a very sophisticated conceit for so young a photographer. After years of working with a Rolleiflex, "which gives you too much information and feels too easy—as if the camera is taking the picture," working with the larger-format equipment was a relief, Avedon later said. Still, it would, by his own admission, take him years to master.

By now, all photos, sketches, and copy generated in Paris were sent back by air—saving more than a week each time. The Paris staff knew the schedules of Pan Am flights to New York, and even which pilots flew them, and would bring the material directly out to the planes on the runway at Le Bourget. Someone from the New York office would then be dispatched out to Idlewild, as Kennedy International Airport was then called, to meet the flights at the other end. This direct approach wasn't only faster—it beautifully bypassed Customs, too.

One can imagine the fireworks when, after the issue went to press, poor Dahl-Wolfe—the veteran—took in the extent of her betrayal. If she reacted as she

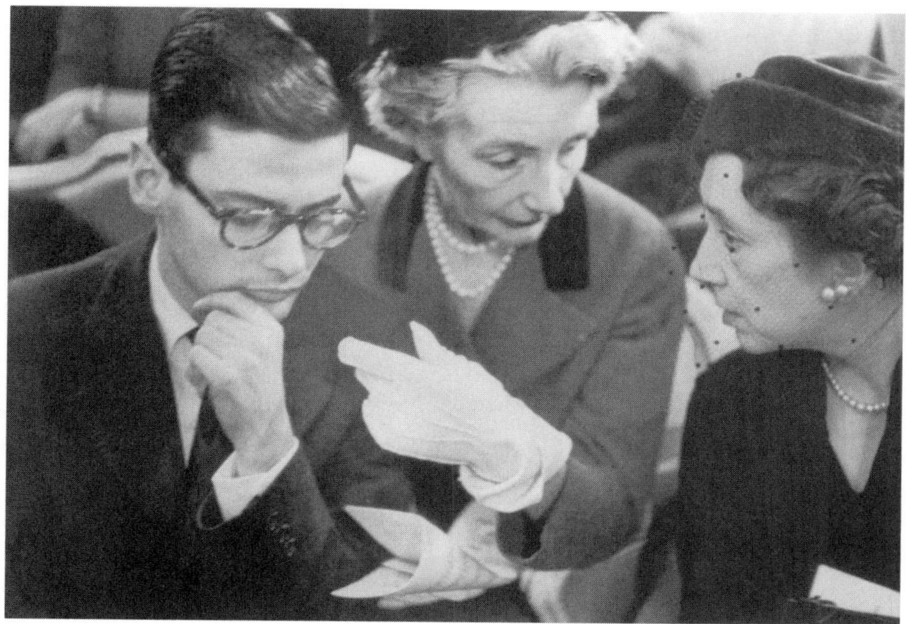

Richard Avedon, Carmel Snow, and Marie-Louise Bousquet at a Dior fashion show, 1948

often did, she would have stayed away, in a fury, from the magazine for days. Still, she didn't leave for good. "It took all of Carmel's genius for diplomacy to keep both her valued photographers on her staff, but she did," Mary Louise Aswell wrote. From then on, for years, Avedon was a frequent presence at the French openings.

Dahl-Wolfe also went and other photographers occasionally had a turn—among them Lillian Bassman, whose softly focused, deeply feminine images were a distinctive presence in the magazine at this time. When Bassman was elected to go instead of Avedon, not long after the latter's triumphant Paris debut, Avedon, who was a close friend of hers, defused a potentially awkward situation by throwing a party to celebrate. Gleb Derujinsky also occasionally went, contributing, among other things, a famous series of photographs of the model Carmen posing in front of a man on a ladder, a lamplighter, who was busy illuminating one of the streetlights—they were still gas in those days—in the place de la Concorde. One photographer hired to do the collections for *Bazaar,* the German-born Karen Radkai, loved telling how, as she was saying good night to Carmel at two or three in the morning after a shoot, the editor said: "Now, Karen, we've had a busy time and I'm sure you're tired. So have a good rest and sleep late and don't call me before seven o'clock."

The next year, Leigh prevailed upon Avedon to take her sister along to France, too. Since the girl in question was a young, redheaded beauty named Suzy Parker, not a lot of arm twisting was involved. Parker had started modeling with the encouragement of Leigh; as with Bacall, a *Bazaar* cover (in Parker's case, when she was only fifteen) helped to launch a career: she would go on to become one of the most famous models of all time. Both Texas-born women were knockouts, but Leigh was surely the more astounding character. Then in her mid-twenties, she was a mechanical engineer by profession—one who also claimed to have published sonnets in *The New Yorker.* Endorsed by Vreeland and Dahl-Wolfe, she landed on the cover of *Bazaar* on her very first assignment. Later, Truman Capote, once her neighbor in an apartment building on Lexington Avenue in New York, would base the flighty, promiscuous, borderline criminal Holly Golightly, the protagonist of his novel *Breakfast at Tiffany's,* on Leigh, or so she claimed. (In this, she wasn't alone. As Gerald Clarke has written of Capote, "Half the women he knew, and a few he did not, claimed to be the model for his wacky heroine." There were so many claimants that the author began to call it the "Holly Golightly Sweepstakes.") In any case, modeling wasn't Leigh's last stop: she later founded her own agency for models in Paris, wrote cookbooks, and more.

Bazaar had rented an old prewar taxi that year; in it, the magazine's crew careened from one appointment to another. For Avedon, Paris time with Carmel

Richard Avedon and Carmel on location at the Paris Opéra

"was all teaching—through gossip, through conspiracy." She introduced him to Bérard, even, at one point, he says, to Colette, by then one of the national legends of France. "She wanted me to be exposed to everything. She wanted me to read the writers she was publishing. It was all through stories and great daring."

At the shows, Carmel, beside him, kept up a running dialogue, telling wickedly witty tales in her deep Irish voice about everyone in the room, which

Carmel and Dahl-Wolfe in a lighthearted moment in the Paris studio, 1950

mannequin was having a secret liaison with which married aristocrat, who was a lesbian, and on and on. Avedon was startled to hear her whisper at one point that very sedate-seeming Madame Grès was involved in a ménage-à-trois. Great funniness was part of it: "There was nothing but laughter, nothing but stories." Babs Simpson, attending the shows with Carmel at one point, recalls that "she'd call over the girl with the most hideous possible dress on and say to me in front of her, 'You've got to have this! It's just your dish.'" At which point both women would dissolve into giggles.

On later visits Carmel would insist that Avedon leave his shoes out for polishing in front of her hotel suite door, rather than his—purely to give John Fairchild, who became Paris bureau chief of the influential *Women's Wear Daily* in the 1950s, something to gossip about. In time, Fairchild would transform the sedate trade journal, founded by his father, into the self-described "fashion bible" it's become today, one that, besides presenting in-depth coverage of the industry, "raked over the personalities of high fashion: the couturiers and their socialite clients," as Teri Agins puts it. Even before he did so, he was fair game. Anyone was. "Everything was like that, it was work out of joy," as Avedon puts it.

When Carmel was in town, the magazine's photo studio was a hive of frenzied, buzzing activity. "We all worked around the clock. There was just an enthusiasm . . . ," Avedon says. Messengers, editors, assistants ran in and out; photo sessions lasted until dawn. Some people never seemed to leave, leading Dahl-Wolfe to liken the place to a boardinghouse. "Even taxi drivers took their meals there with us," she wrote. The place was run by André Gremela, a darkroom technician and, in Avedon's words, "perfect artisan," who'd worked with a dynasty of *Bazaar* photographers, going back to Hoyningen-Huene. "He performed magic in the darkroom," Mary Jane Russell recalled. A wardrobe assistant named Olga completed the team. The studio was tiny.

> *There was hardly enough room to unpack the dresses. In a tiny kitchen on the mezzanine, a maid cooked French lunches, and the darkroom smelled of the garlic sausage on Gremela's breath. He never slept and was always wearing a soiled lab coat. Every night, he'd string clotheslines from wall to wall and hang up the negatives to dry, making his prints the next morning, one at a time, in his simple trays.*

For Gremela and others, Avedon's work was a revelation.

> *The pictures Dick had taken were so different from anything he or any other fashion photographer had done before that everyone who saw them got excited. . . . They were particularly admired by the French fashion photographers who had been cut off from anything new for many years.*

Harper's Bazaar's Paris staff, 1956 *(front row, left to right)*: Marie-Louise Bousquet, Louise Dahl-Wolfe, Carmel Snow. Technician André Gremela is on the ladder.

The tools Avedon took for granted—seamless white backdrop paper, electronic flash attachments—were looked upon by his French counterparts with envy, being almost impossible to obtain in Europe at this time. They were part of what made his work look new. Another substance he relished—natural light—was easier to come by. "I was interested in the challenge of shooting with no props, no artificial light, no background, little help," Avedon has said, "just a dress, a model, and her pensive beauty in isolation."

On free evenings, the young photographer might join Carmel and members of a shifting cast for group dinners in Paris—a ritual, then as now, of the collection season. They'd meet for drinks at the Ritz or the Plaza Athénée, then head off to somewhere farther afield, perhaps to Le Cheval Noir, on the outskirts of town, or Le Coq Hardi in the bois de Boulogne. Anyone might turn up. Later, Carmel sometimes included favorite niece Kate White, a midwesterner then residing in Paris, taking as much pleasure in the company of this glamour-free young relative as in the couturiers, artists, and titled Parisians with whom she also dined. "I was living in a maid's room then, but she always had time for me," White recalls. Frederick Vreeland, Diana's son, who spent many family summers in Paris, recalls attending dinners with Carmel where his tablemates included the likes of Bérard and Cocteau. "Carmel moved easily in these magical circles in Paris. She was accepted in these magical circles long before my mother was. For a college kid this would be very impressive stuff."

Vreeland herself went to the collections for *Bazaar* on one occasion, in the 1950s, and it was not a success. "Carmel took her only once to Paris and she'd never take her again," recalls fashion editor Gwen Randolph Franklin, who rejoined the *Bazaar* staff in the early 1950s, insisting on equal billing with Vreeland when she did so. (Only one editor, Patricia Cornwell, had managed this before.) "Diana was like a designer—a creative—and also wanted to throw her weight around," Franklin says. "That was too much competition, as I see it." Vreeland was appalled by what she found in the very epicenter of the fashion world. She "fled in horror at the frenzy of it," according to Ballard. "Bettina . . . how can you work in this confusion night and day? How can you understand fashion smothered like this?" she asked. "The sheer terror of it, the indignity!" It was just the atmosphere that Carmel adored.

Carmel's Paris entourage expanded with the years. When both her secretaries, Dorothy Monger and Cookie, retired due to ill health, she replaced them with Catharine Stewart Dives, who began accompanying her boss to Paris, taking the room next door at the San Régis and working on captions and correspondence that were dispatched by courier to New York each night after Carmel went to bed. Everything was accelerated. Kate White recalls her aunt calling her in the hotel lobby as she waited there one evening to say she was on her way down. "I can remember her saying, '*Je descends,*' which meant, more or less, 'Clap your hands and get the chauffeur at the door.'" Everything, including drinking, was conducted with great efficiency. Since "she loved dry martinis, and lots of them," as Givenchy puts it, she adopted a system to ensure that they'd be close at hand. Laura Pyzel Clark recalls that, after attending the shows with Carmel, "we'd go up to her room and she'd order '*trois martinis secs s'il vous plaît tout de suite.*'" One of the three drinks was for Clark, who would only sip politely at it. The others were for Carmel, who liked to know that, when she was done with the first, she could move right on to the next.

Diana Vreeland at Brigid Snow's wedding, 1952

Church figured in, of course. As Kate White recalls,

> *I was with Aunt Carmel and she picked me up, driving with a chauffeur when she suddenly said, "Kate dear, we're going to stop by this chapel." The chauffeur said to me, "Madame Snow comes in every afternoon." I knelt on the prie-dieu and Aunt Carmel sat before me. She looked like a*

> *ten-year-old girl. She was not Carmel Snow giving orders, she was in front of someone much bigger than she was to whom she owed attention.*

A new, more earthly companion was Balenciaga. Carmel had known—and championed—this designer for years, since he'd opened his first fashion house in Paris in 1937, showing black, long-sleeved tight-bodiced dresses. *Vogue*'s Ballard, who also attended his debut show, recalled finding these offerings modest indeed. But she later realized that she was

> *too inexperienced a fashion editor to foresee the genius of this gentle Spaniard or to dream that he would dress the most elegant women in the world. It took Carmel Snow, of* Harper's Bazaar, *with her wise, experienced fashion eyes, to understand and to push the talent of this unknown man from his very first collection.*

The designer was notoriously reclusive. "Balenciaga, as usual, was not in evidence," Carmel wrote teasingly a few years later. "I don't think that anyone has ever seen him in person."

Balenciaga's architectonic clothes, designed in his fashion house on the avenue George V, had a strictness, a purity of line that made them immediately recognizable. He was "an absolute master of the cut," in the fashion writer François Baudot's words. His own premiere, Madame Feliza, described him as having "the precision of a surgeon." It wasn't just about style, but about technique. "He was the architect of the Haute Couture. You could have fantasy, ideas, but what counted was the construction of a dress. . . . He was the man of the straight line." Although he was little known in the United States, even into the 1940s, this wasn't true in France, a point that was driven home to one American editor who, ensconced in a Paris taxi just after Dior burst onto the scene, was startled to hear the driver ask, "So now Monsieur Balenciaga has some

OPPOSITE: **Carmel Snow at the Gare Saint Lazare, Paris, undated. Photograph by Richard Avedon**

competition, no?" (As Carmel liked to point out, *everyone* in Paris is interested in fashion.)

For years, Paris's couturiers had been swimming against the tide—the flood, even—of the tiny-waisted New Look. But Dior's canvas- and tulle-lined fabrics, his padding and artifice, were anathema to the Spaniard (as they were to Chanel, who famously said, "Dior, he doesn't dress women, he upholsters them"). By contrast, Balenciaga felt that fabric should speak for itself, that a woman's body, and the way it moves, should dictate the design of her clothes, not the other way around. The Spaniard went his own way, always, following his own strict inspiration, only changing his silhouette, as Ballard has pointed out, every six years. Even Dior, whose vision was so different, revered Balenciaga, calling him "the master of us all." "He was deep, without detours," Hubert de Givenchy says of him. "I worked with Fath, Piguet, Lelong, Schiaparelli, but when I met him, I saw that I knew nothing."

Carmel dated the start of her friendship with Balenciaga to August 1946, after Bousquet brought her to dine in his opulent avenue Monceau apartment, with its satin-lined walls, rare bronzes, and Louis XVI furniture. "This was the first time I had really talked to Balenciaga—and how we talked! It was enchantment all around." So much so that Lucien, her driver, whom she'd ordered for ten, had to wait in the car for four more hours until both women emerged.

If Balenciaga was relatively obscure in America, that changed almost overnight during the fall collections of 1950, when he unveiled the barrel look, which in the witchy way of fashion, managed to make the New Look seem dainty, overblown. As Carmel wrote in the September issue:

> *After his opening there was a five minute ovation, but the "monk of the couture" still refused to appear. Almost no buyer has ever met the mysterious couturier, yet the Balenciaga look—elegant, individual, never casual, never theatrical—is the epitome of fashion today.*

"This year's suit has ROUNDED lines, ROUNDED armholes . . . ," Carmel told the Fashion Group. "A new Paris suit makes the suits of last year look angular and skimpy." Many of these pieces, including a wool ensemble with an outsized, smocklike jacket and a narrow skirt that stopped just below the knee, would look avant-garde if worn today. The palette of this superb colorist tended to Goya shades—"the color of Spanish earth and rocks and olive trees." His hats were simple; Carmel favored his pillbox, and she wasn't alone: it became a classic in the 1940s and remained one for as long as women wore hats. "Why has this great dressmaker come into his own?" Carmel asked in a fashion-industry newsletter.

> *It's because he builds clothes for the WOMAN not for HEADLINES. He knows a woman's body better than any living dressmaker. The dash of a Balenciaga dress lies in* a bold, vigorous affirmation, *in the* forceful *use of the* colors *you see in Spanish paintings. [Emphasis hers.]*

His fashion shows were usually "tense performances," Carmel wrote. "Where Dior collections had a Mozartian lightness and grace, Balenciaga's were paraded with sombre solemnity," in Ernestine Carter's words. His couture house, unlike Dior's, was unadorned, its atmosphere austere. His models, dubbed "monster mannequins" by the fashion world, were ferocious, including one, named Colette, who moved

> *with her Dracula walk, her big head low like a bull ready to charge, her shoulders hunched down, her arms swinging low, and a look of almost violent hatred on her face as she passed, concealing the number of the dress from the spectators.*

(This trick was one played by many models. "They took a very wicked pleasure in putting their number in a pocket or holding it upside down," Susan Train recalls.)

"One never knew what one was going to see at a Balenciaga opening," Vreeland once said. "One fainted." Or more. In the winter of 1951, Balenciaga unveiled the "*semi-ajusté*" or semifitted suit—sharp-collared, pulled tight in the front yet loose in the back, ballooning behind like a spinnaker. The suits were classic Balenciaga—plain lines, little trim—but they billowed out behind to a shocking degree. It was "a total break with the New Look," according to Marie-Andrée Jouve, and, indeed, everything else. In showing these styles, the designer turned his back, once again, on everything he'd done before.

As the loose, asymmetric styles came out, the audience "sat there hating them," Carmel recalled.

> *"Why should a woman look like a house?"—you could feel their hate in the room. Instead of the screams and* Bravos! *that greeted Dior, there was an uneasy silence when the showing was over.*
>
> *I was seated as usual in the front row, and I stood up. I began to clap. No one joined me. I simply continued to clap, slowly, deliberately,* loud.

The aftermath was turbulent. "Everyone screamed that women would never accept this too-big-for-you look," Ballard wrote. Some journalists sniped that the suits were "badly adjusted," not "semi-adjusted." But Carmel continued her applause in glossy pages a few months later, calling the designer's new cut "a revolution" in *Bazaar.* The traditional spring Paris issue burst with Balenciaga, eclipsing every other designer, with the near-exception of Dior. And, sure enough, its readers came around.

Needless to say, the editor's demonstration had a career-enhancing effect; a definitive book on Balenciaga even uses the chapter heading *"Madame Snow Applaudit"* (Mrs. Snow applauded) to describe a turning point of his career, at least as far as the United States was concerned. Before this editor—ouch—took a stand, Balenciaga was considered too far out for an American audience. But afterward, "the fashion world began to pay attention," Carmel wrote. "The rest is fashion history." It was also more evidence that, as she said in a lecture a few years later: "You can't keep an exciting fashion down, and it's no use trying. Fashion is an element mysterious as uranium and just as explosive, but light—lighter than air."

Light or not, acclaim wasn't necessarily the outcome the great designer—a recluse, who loathed the press—was after. "His Spanish sense of dignity is outraged by publicity," Ballard once wrote. "The more journalists plead for stories, for clothes to photograph, the more the entire house of Balenciaga closes itself into its shell." He wasn't fond of customers, either: he'd slip into his *maison de couture* through the back door so as not to encounter them.

Most revolutionary, from an American point of view, was his concept of *cursi,* that Spanish word for which there's no English equivalent. Perhaps "vulgar" is the closest word. Editor Anne Hopkins Miller recalls Carmel explaining that "if you wore blue shoes and and you feel you have to have a blue bag that's what Mr. Balenciaga would call *cursi,* which basically meant bad together. Carmel felt that anything that was too contrived was *cursi,* bad taste." To tell conforming American women of the 1950s that their bag and shoes shouldn't necessarily match was subversive indeed. But they listened, apparently, and gradually yet another useless fashion convention loosened its hold.

After the clapping incident, Carmel and Balenciaga's relationship, already warm, heated up. "Balenciaga was Carmel's tenderest spot," as Aswell has written. Like Dior, he had impeccable taste, and a string of beautifully appointed country houses. Carmel visited him at Igueldo, his house in San Sebastián, "the Spanish watering place near the little fishing village where he was born." Furnished with "beautiful, rather uncomfortable, Spanish antiques," she found this residence to be "as remote and simple as his personality." Even so, she returned numerous times, often with Bousquet, and at one point with her teenaged daughter, Brigid, and one of her Foxcroft classmates. Carmel also visited his seventeenth-century residence near Orléans. Although she claims to have once sent a very young and very talented man named Hubert de Givenchy to see Balenciaga there, bearing a letter of introduction that she had written, Givenchy recalls first meeting Balenciaga through Marie-Louise Bousquet. In any case, Givenchy went on to apprentice with the Spanish designer, before opening his own fashion house in the French capital in 1951. His debut collection was impressive enough that it landed him in *Bazaar* as "the new name to know." By the fall of 1954, the magazine was reporting that "his whole collection has real authority and technique, as well as ideas. Givenchy is now among the top designers."

Carmel's enthusiasm for Balenciaga seemed to intensify with every passing fashion season. "Ours is an intuitive relationship that simply ignores the language barrier," she wrote with girlish enthusiasm. "I speak no Spanish, he speaks no English, our French isn't especially competent—but I never once doubted that I could understand all that he was saying." One night they sat up till dawn together while he told her the story of his life—one that had, they discovered, strange parallels with hers: both had fathers who had died young (Balenciaga's was the captain of a fishing boat) and widowed mothers who had opened dressmaking establishments (although Señora Balenciaga, unlike Annie White, actually took up sewing herself) in order to support their families.

Balenciaga took frequent cures to Switzerland for sinus trouble and chronic nervous exhaustion and advised Carmel to do the same. She went to one once, in Zurich, for a day—and bolted. Leisure wasn't her thing and, besides, "I'm afraid I have yet to *finish* a course of treatments for anything." It was he, too, who suggested the revitalizing shots that had become as much a part of Carmel's Paris routine as fortune-tellers and La Méditerranée. As Nancy White once told a cousin: "In Paris, Aunt Carmel lives on martinis, French pastries and vitamin B injections."

The story of their friendship, as told by Carmel, sounds downright romantic. Certainly for her it was. Her marriage had long lacked passion; Palen's attentions were elsewhere as, for that matter, were her own. In this romantic vacuum, her feelings for this intense Spaniard could only bloom. Just as she venerated his precise tailoring, exquisite materials, futuristic cuts, she came to worship Balenciaga as a man. Inevitably, Paris wags began gossiping, maliciously, about the editor's unrequited crush. "A lot of people said she was in love with him, which I completely understand," says Givenchy. "He was so very talented." Susan Train adds: "She was totally in love with Balenciaga. She was mad, insane, about him. She never let him alone. Given that he was a shy, reclusive man, this kind of exhausted him after a while. It drove him crazy." Carmel had already given up other designers to wear only his clothes. But now her fittings took place at his apartment among the antiques, where the designer fussed over her outfits "endlessly until they entirely pleased him, often suggesting changes in color—I think he took pride in the way I wore his creations."

He must have, since he designed one of his classic suits for her, "because I have no neck," as she told Ernestine Carter. He first showed this loosely fitted jacket with a collar set away from the neck in the early 1950s, then did a variation of it each year. "The stand-away collars allowed women, and their pearls, to breathe," in the mystical words of Jacqueline Demornex. Calling it "the great suit of our time," Carmel adopted it as a uniform, ordering it in seemingly every fabric, every shade. (Avedon has an abiding memory of her wearing a watermelon-colored one during a period when her hair was bright lavender.) She loved the way the suit's collar, set away from her face, made her neck seem longer. Since the look was stark, she softened it with a silk scarf, which she was taught to tie on the bias, with cool perfection, by Balenciaga himself. This tradition passed from one pair of fashion hands to another: years later, Carmel showed her niece Nancy White how it was done; she, in turn, passed that knowledge on to Geoffrey Beene. The American designer included scarves, knotted in just this same way, in his collections for the length of his career.

Taciturn and difficult, Balenciaga extended his friendship to very few. So when he began sending bouquets to the San Régis, as many other designers did routinely, to greet Carmel on her biannual arrivals in France, the gesture seemed entirely uncharacteristic. Inevitably, the editor put a romantic spin on it. "She was in love with Balenciaga from afar and she misinterpreted every sort of business thing she did as something part of a romance that she imagined," Avedon recalled.

One day, over lunch with Balenciaga, at Le Grand Véfour, Carmel spied the great French writer Colette (who, like Cocteau, lived in one of the apartments in the adjacent Palais Royal) at a table across the room. By then an invalid, Colette had been carried down from her apartment to lunch with Carmel's old chum Anita Loos and the actress Paulette Goddard. The editor beckoned both women to her table, knowing that they both admired Balenciaga, before going off to introduce herself to the writer, whose work she'd published for decades, including the winsome story "Gigi," which appeared for the first time in America in *Bazaar* in 1946. "When I performed the introduction, without a moment's hesitation, without even glancing at each other, both women curtsied to Balenciaga as Englishwomen curtsy to royalty." It was a reaction she understood.

She herself copied this worshipful gesture, at least figuratively, by promoting his career at every imaginable opportunity. And the designer made it easy, again and again, by the daring way he leaped from some new, previously unimagined silhouette to another. He never stopped breaking rules—indeed, he refused to acknowledge that any existed. His chemise or "sack" dress, a simple sheath that eliminated bust or seam darts, which he designed in the mid-1950s, was in its way as radical as the New Look, but it had nothing like the Dior fashion's popularity. "The dresses were so unusual that we put them on backwards at every fashion show," said Dorothy Fuller, then a fashion director at the Chicago department store of Marshall Field & Co. "We only discovered that later on." Once

Carmel Snow and Cristobal Balenciaga in New York, 1952

again, Carmel set out to turn the tide of public acceptance for her beloved friend. As the *New York Times* reported in its issue of September 21, 1957: "Carmel Snow, editor of *Harper's Bazaar,* defended the controversial new chemise dresses from Paris yesterday by saying they were neither 'sad sacks' nor 'sexless.'" Her advocacy never flagged. When Fuller's successor, Kathleen Catlin, put in an order for the dresses, she received a cable from Carmel commending her on taking such a risk. "My dear, how courageous!" Such tactics worked, apparently. As Teri Agins points out, "By the late 1950s, every smartly dressed woman in America donned a chemise, and the style lasted through the 1960s."

Convinced that it perpetuated copying, Balenciaga had a pathological hatred of the press. In 1958, both he and Givenchy infuriated buyers by changing the date of their collections to a full month after everyone else's, "to prevent leakages and copies of his pet ideas before they can appear in American stores," according to the *New York Times,* thus obliging American buyers who wanted to see their work to return to Paris a second time each season. Both designers offered to make an exception for Carmel, but as Ernestine Carter later reported, "she scornfully declined to accept different treatment from that meted out to her colleagues."

Carmel herself didn't offer such treatment to any designer. She may have loved Balenciaga, but she featured his clothes in her pages because she thought they merited the space and attention, and for no other reason. Had his talent vanished overnight, her friendship toward him might have continued, but his clothes would no longer have been seen in the pages of *Bazaar.*

As long as she believed in you, she nurtured you along, as Marc Bohan, whom she'd known for years as a designer for Patou, discovered.

> *She looked at collections from a business point of view, how individual clients would react, how stores would react. After a collection she'd take me out to lunch and explain exactly what worked and what didn't. [*Life*'s] Eugenia Sheppard did the same sort of thing. There were no flowers or compliments. . . . She was very, very professional.*

Editor Geri Trotta—the "observant ant"—perched on Carmel's desk, *Bazaar,* 1950s

To Bohan's surprise, "there was no 'copinage,' with Carmel Snow as there was with everyone else, except for Eugenia Sheppard," meaning that neither would promote a designer, or a style, without merit. It was never a question, as it was known to be with other editors and journalists, of covering a collection because it seemed fashionable to do so or because its creator was a friend.

No matter how much Carmel did for Balenciaga, even she could fall out of favor with the mercurial designer. One day his head vendeuse barred her from entering one of his shows "because he was afraid she'd break the fashions before anyone," according to Geri Trotta. Infuriated, Carmel threw her handbag at the woman, before storming out. It was a burst of temperament—surely not the only one to take place in the fast-paced, high-stakes collection season—but its sole witness, Marie-Louise Bousquet, "instead of shutting up about it, spread the word all over Paris," Trotta reports. Carmel's sidekick, who had a distinctly poisonous side, seemed strangely happy at this turn of events. "She would work any angle," Trotta says. "She was jealous of Carmel. She was so pleased that Carmel had been barred from Balenciaga's collection."

At one point, Carmel and the designer became so estranged that a young fashion assistant from the magazine, Barbara Slifka, accompanying her mother to Paris, where the older woman was shopping, was asked to sit out the show in the dressing room "because I was with *Harper's Bazaar*." Later in this trip, Slifka innocently asked Carmel if there was anything she could do to help her while she was in France. "My dear, I've been covering these collections for years. I don't need any help" was the frosty response. (Actually, as it turned out, there was one thing she could do.... Before Slifka knew what she'd agreed to, she, like so many before her, found herself returning to America with a few extra, label-less clothes in her bags. . . .) On the plane back to New York that year, Carmel sat next to an unidentified American designer who asked herself, rhetorically, in the course of their long transatlantic conversation, if it was worth traveling to the collections, given the pressure and expense. And then she answered the question herself. "I've never worked harder than I did in Paris—but I'm not tired, I'm stimulated—comforted by all the beauty—and I've got enough inspiration for four years in my pocket." No doubt her seatmate agreed.

All that inspiration, the sheer love and energy that Carmel expended on behalf of France and its fashion industry was rewarded on April 13, 1949, when the *ordre de chevalier de la légion d'honneur* was bestowed upon her by the French government. "Please do come," she wrote to Nancy White, who had become director of fashion at *Good Housekeeping,* another Hearst title (and one her famous aunt had been known to deride as "Good Housecooking"). "I do wish I could ask Del [Nancy's husband, magazine publisher Ralph Delahaye Paine Jr.], but as I am only allowed ten people in all and have to include about five business people, children, husband, etc., I am afraid I can only have you," she wrote. It was a small, immensely proud group: Palen and the girls, young Carmel's mother-in-law, Mrs. Sumner Welles, Frances McFadden, Richard Avedon, and

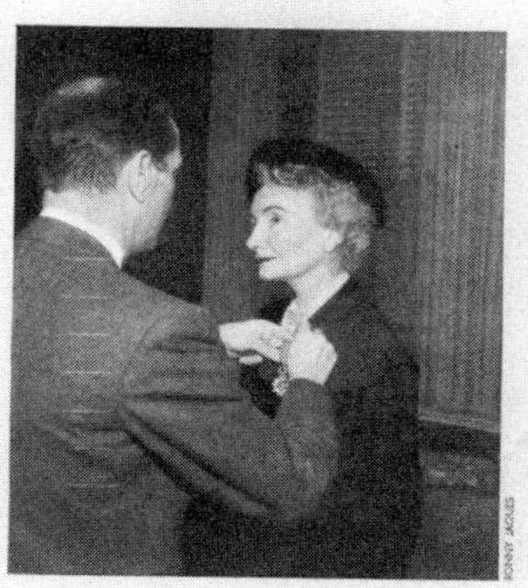

Harpers Bazaars Editor
Receives the LEGION OF HONOR

• It is with great pride that we report that our editor, Carmel Snow, has been made Chevalier of the Legion of Honor. On April 13, in a simple ceremony, M. Ludovic Chancel, Consul General of France, presented the decoration in the name of the President of the Republic, citing Mrs. Snow's long friendship for France, her influence since the end of the war in re-establishing the prestige of French art. French crafts and French design in the United States. Carmel Snow estimates that she has covered the Paris collections at least sixty times. She visited France twice during the war, once in the winter of 1940, and again in the dark winter of 1944–45, when she flew to Paris to carry to her old friends and through them to thousands of workers in the fashion trades a message of confidence and friendship. The little red ribbon which Mrs. Snow wears in her buttonhole is a recognition that international understanding is promoted not only over the conference tables, but in daily business, and particularly by a respect for and generous understanding of talent and skill.

"Harper's Bazaar's Editor Receives the Legion of Honor," *Harper's Bazaar*, June 1949

Nancy White all gathered at noon at the French consulate, then located in Rockefeller Center. The award was presented by Ludovic Chancel, the consul general, in the name of President de Gaulle, in gratitude for "Mrs. Snow's long friendship for France, her influence since the end of the war in reestablishing the prestige of French art, French crafts and French design in the United States." She was rewarded for her absolute loyalty. In her daughter Brigid's words, "I never saw her in an American-made suit, that's why she got the Légion d'honneur." A tribute in the magazine just after noted that "Carmel Snow estimates that she has covered the Paris collections at least sixty times."

Bérard had made a "charming memento" of the occasion—an elaborate sketch of the award, festooned with decorative ribbons and motifs, and signed by some of the people she loved the most in Paris, among them Dior, Balenciaga, Schiaparelli, and Molyneux. It was a particularly treasured gift, since the troubled, addicted, hugely talented Bérard had died unexpectedly two months before the ceremony, on February 12, 1949, at a theater where he'd been designing the costumes and sets for a play by Molière with his usual extraordinary artistry, conceiving the costumes in shades of gray "with rare little flames of color," as his friend George Davis described them. He'd had two strokes and been warned by his physician not to return to work, but the doctor's words were futile. Bérard died "as he had lived for many years," Flanner noted in *The New Yorker,* "while working, after midnight, in the Marigny Theatre." (Fittingly, Molière himself had expired the same way.) "Bébé was our blood donor," Cocteau cried when he heard the news. "How can I work? I have lost my arms." Is it too cynical to imagine that, over at the *Vogue* camp, there was a certain satisfaction in knowing that Bérard might have been gone, but at least he wasn't working for *Bazaar*? In any case, Chase, true to form, didn't pass up the opportunity to chastise him posthumously.

> *We used to think it was an overdose of drugs that killed Bérard, but there is a school that holds to the theory that it was bread. Everything on earth was wrong with him including high blood pressure and diabetes. His*

doctor told him that he wasn't to eat bread, but he craved it. Along with the opium and liquor binges he'd go on bread binges, gorging himself with it, thrusting it down his throat like a ravenous animal.

So Bérard was there, in spirit and in sketch, at least, when Carmel had her moment of triumph. From then on she had the red ribbon symbolizing the French award sewn just below the collarbone, on the left, on all her clothes, up to and including her San Régis bathrobe. On clothes that had no ribbon, a tiny rosette "began appearing in all her buttonholes," according to Hopkins. It's strictly forbidden for anyone who hasn't won the award to wear such symbols of course: Carmel duly instructed her staff buying her clothes to remove the ribbons before they wore them, which they sometimes did. One day her daughter Brigid, then a student at Barnard College, wore one of her mother's jackets to school only to be confronted by a French professor who asked, quite reasonably, "Aren't you a bit young, miss, to be wearing the Legion of Honor?"

By now Carmel was in her sixties, and a legend. One staffer, Jo Jeanne Millon Barton, who worked as a secretary to Melanie Witt Miller, editor of the Junior Bazaar section, recalls Carmel "thrilling the secretaries" simply by walking by. Although she looked her age, even older, Carmel, like her mother before her, seemed to become more decisive and powerful with every year. "She was Mrs. Snow and she was blue haired and when she stepped into a taxi everyone stopped to look at her," Avedon recalls. She'd lunch at chic restaurants, such as the Colony or L'Aiglon where "everybody knew her," A. G. Allen says. Or at the Pavillon, a restaurant that "she'd done a lot to create," according to Truman Capote.

New York was hers, just as Paris was. A portrait, taken by Derujinsky in this period, shows Carmel seated at her desk, her head cocked to the side like a bird's, looking almost preternaturally alert. In the background, chintz curtains on one side and a whimsical painting on the other seem to hint at two sides to her character—the one traditional, rooted in upper-class Ireland and New York; the other irresistibly drawn to the newest, and most imaginative, in art. Characteristically, Carmel is wear-

Carmel Snow at her desk at *Harper's Bazaar,* 1950s

ing pearls, two sets of them, one three stranded, of smaller beads, the other, a single one, of larger ones. Her Balenciaga has an off-the-shoulder look; her white pillbox, designed by him as well, is set smartly toward the front of her head. In her right hand, she holds a writing implement—a blue pencil? Her beautifully manicured left hand, the three-fingered one, rests matter-of-factly on an outsize layout page.

After years of pain, Carmel had had her index finger on that hand amputated in about 1951. The discomfort remained for years, and she would later conclude that her decision to have the operation was a mistake. Sometimes, as she pointed out, teasingly, she was perhaps *too* decisive. After it was removed, she had no apparent self-consciousness about the missing digit, as Flanner remarked. "She merely used that hand with a strange widened grace." When she counted on her fingers, the way we all do, she inevitably included the missing one, too, Avedon recalled, although it was long gone.

The magazine in this period reflected the usual daring juxtapositions—one 1949 issue showed photographs of *le tout Paris*—among them Dior—dressed in extravagant, artful costumes for a costume ball given by the Comte Etienne de Beaumont, while, a few pages later, photographer David Seymour documented Polish youth playing nonchalantly in the rubble of the Warsaw Ghetto. There were wonderful portraits, not just of movies stars, politicians, and the like, but of key socialites, such as the formerly camera-shy C. Z. Guest, who, like so many, was snared by a wickedly persuasive Diana Vreeland.

When first asked to model, the beautiful blonde replied that she couldn't because her husband and his family absolutely hated publicity of any sort. Diana looked her straight in the eye and said, "But they'll never know, my dear." Diana absolutely and completely seduced me right then and there. And I believed her, that's the amazing part.

For all its disparate ingredients, the shock value of the early years of Carmel's tenure at *Bazaar*—the eye-opening layouts, avant-garde clothes and art—had been tempered. Both fashion and graphics had become tamer, like the times. Still, there were moments of great inventiveness. There are the famous shots—Avedon, Dahl-Wolfe—many of them often reproduced, such as the one of Dorian Leigh, clad in a gray flannel, flounced-sleeved Dior dress, euphorically embracing a cyclist from the Tour de France. But also striking are the everyday fashion shots, the unsung images that don't turn up in retrospectives or illustrated books, such as Avedon's picture of a trio of models wearing outsize silk coats (by Norman Norell for Traina-Norell), topped with "curve hats" by John Frederics—huge swoops of brim that might have been worn by monks, albeit polka-dot-wearing ones, in medieval Europe. And whoever actually penned the words, the copy for a piece on "India pink," is pure, delicious Vreeland: "This year's pink, the pink of the East, pure fresh and singing against sunburned skin."

A new magazine, one geared to the latest in the arts, flared up in this period, when Fleur Cowles, an old acquaintance of Carmel's from the New York magazine world, created *Flair,* her legendary rag. The magazine had "spectacular backing," according to Capote, and a no-less-spectacular editor—the well-connected, if unruly, George Davis, who had left *Mademoiselle* in 1949. Visually, it was the opposite of Brodovitch, so chaotically imaginative that it bordered on kitsch. As the *New York Times* noted: its "windowed covers, die-cut pages and foldout features sent it to stardom and doomed it to failure as an expensive folly. . . ."

Fleur Cowles knew Carmel

> *when I was running* Look. *But when I started* Flair *I was enemy number one.*
>
> *"How dare anyone go into the class market?"*
>
> *For me* Harper's Bazaar *was not a competitor. I didn't want to be like a magazine at all. I never did two issues that were like each other.*

Of Carmel, she says: "I never crossed her path if I could help it. She wasn't a warm, motherly person. She was not what you'd call a friendly figure. Everyone looked up to her but they didn't necessarily like her." She once told a *Bazaar* editor that Carmel was so hard that she made "concrete seem like ice cream." But concrete endures and *Flair* didn't—it ran for only twelve issues, from February 1950 to January 1951, and Davis was gone even before it folded.

In late 1950, McFadden finally retired, her departure hastened, Carmel thought, by a particularly noxious piece of marketing: a "Sunset Pink" promotion to introduce a new train called the Sunset Limited to *Bazaar*'s readers. The magazines editorial and marketing departments came together on this one—never a particularly comfortable fit. In any case, the January 1951 issue was awash in a rosy hue, from its cover, which featured a sleeveless pink Larry Aldrich linen dress, through numerous advertisements—manufacturers had trotted out myriad rose-shaded products, from belts to underwear, for the occasion—down to the editorial pages, which featured not just pink fashion, but pages highlighted by blocks of the same shade. The whole thing must have appalled Brodovitch; in any case, it "was too much for Frances McFadden," Carmel noted, "who forthwith retired from the *Bazaar* to write. With her, much of the joy went out of my office work." The managing editorship was a crucial position—"she really depended on her aide-de-camp very much," as Edson puts it. But few could touch McFadden's unique combination of crack organizational skills and literary acumen.

The search took on comic proportions. When Rosamond Bernier of *Vogue* received a message asking her to lunch with Carmel and Vreeland, she knew that a job offer must be in the wind—the détente between Nast and Hearst on the subject of hiring each other's staff had long since dissolved. But she was shocked to discover what they had in mind.

> *I'd never had a job before. I can't imagine why they called me, except that I spoke French and I was relatively presentable. It was a fluke. There was Carmel Snow in her neat little Balenciaga drinking her martini before lunch. I remember Diana arriving very late. She came loping in and said—I've never forgotten it—"I've just been to the most divine funeral." They grandly offered me to be managing editor. I'd never done anything! It was ridiculous.*

Loyally, Bernier reported on the offer to the retired-in-name-only Edna Chase, to which the latter responded with that offhand, ego-demolishing instinct that was so effortlessly hers. "She said, 'Ridiculous child, ridiculous child, you couldn't possibly do the job,'" Bernier recalls.

Other candidates approached the magazine, among them George Davis. For Carmel, his overture—and for a job involving not just editing but management!—must have been too rich. Her reply was tactful, affectionate—and about the firmest no imaginable.

> *Knowing Frances as I do, I cannot regard her departure as temporary, and for that reason I must look for someone who can be considered a Rock of Gibraltar for some time to come. I have the greatest respect for your editorial talent, George, both for your creative ideas and your ability to work with authors, but knowing this magazine as you do, you know how many things are involved in the job of a managing editor—and these other facets of the job—working with promotions, handling decisions when I am away, etc., etc.—are, I think, not your forte.*

Putting it mildly. She went on to say that "you have a very rare talent, and I do appreciate it," and to suggest that he freelance for *Bazaar* and others. Ever the editor in chief, she made sure to push for first dibs. "I'd like to feel that we would be the first to consider your ideas, as they come to you." Davis's editing career ended here. He went on to become a full-time writer, although, sadly, one known more for the intractability of his writer's block than for anything he actually produced. Although he was forever planning to write another novel, "like his friend Bébé Bérard he had too many other interests and distractions to concentrate on his work," Carmel noted. "He was an inveterate collector, of objects, of gossip, of people. He hadn't Bébé's tragic vice [i.e., drugs], but he was every bit as experienced a procrastinator."

The search for a managing editor got increasingly desperate: "Mrs. Snow would go to a cocktail party and say to whoever was at her elbow, 'Who would be a good managing editor?' from among the guests," Edson recalls. She finally hired a man who had been vetted by her astrologer, according to Bassman. But the stars, alas, must have been off course. "He collapsed on the job," she adds. "The poor guy left after six months, he had such an ulcer. He just couldn't deal with the Vreelands." Others came and went with alarming rapidity—as if spinning through a well-oiled revolving door.

Beyond her Paris trips, which bookended the year, Carmel took numerous smaller ones at about this time, including one in about 1950, when she and her daughters headed down to Haiti for Christmas and New Year's. Mary Palen's friend Francine du Plessix Gray, who accompanied them, recalled deplaning at Port-au-Prince.

> *My lasting memory of Carmel Snow is of going down the steps single file behind her, exiting the plane. She emanated this marvelous smell of "Joy." She had this great head of white hair and this Balenciaga tweed suit and I thought, "When I grow up this is what I want to be like." I thought, "This is true elegance." It was the elegance of a mother*

superior. She was a brilliant, alcoholic mother superior. I was in awe of her. I loved the kind of haughtiness of her style.

Once on the island, "we were given a lot of leeway," du Plessix Gray recalls. "She went her own way, reading, pondering, drinking." Other travel companions included the American designer Jane Derby, née Jeannette Barr, who had opened her own ready-to-wear business in New York in 1938 (and whose company would be taken over by Oscar de la Renta decades later), as well as Russel Carpenter, another friend. There is no mention of travels with Palen. "One never saw the father," says du Plessix Gray.

At about that time, a very young Polly Allen, later Polly Mellen, came to work for *Bazaar,* fascinated by all she saw and utterly enamored of Vreeland. "It was love at first sight. . . . She was the most ugliest [sic] woman you ever saw and the most fascinating woman you ever saw." From her first interview at the magazine, she was intrigued by the two editors' complementary styles. "Carmel was a strict lady. No bullshit. She's strict. She's demanding. She's disciplined. She's Catholic. Discipline, but humor—and a businesswoman." The fashion editor was something else. "Designers who thought Mrs. Vreeland was a bit outré, they'd talk to Carmel, who was so down to earth."

Polly Allen Mellen's debut was tenuous. She was undone by the fashion she had to photograph at one of her first sittings—"they were like the maid's clothes!"—and baffled as to how to style them. They had to be reshot, by her estimation, seven times. At this point, Carmel decided to call a halt, saying to Vreeland, "We cannot keep this young woman," but the latter demurred, saying, "Yes, we can, please Carmel, I see something in her." And she prevailed. (In time, of course, Polly Mellen would become almost as well known as her mentor, revered for her offbeat eye.) There was another close call after Mellen intentionally had a dress she considered ugly photographed *both* inside out and backward. The designer was "a nasty man," in Mellen's words. He was also a friend of Carmel's. Say no more.

She wasn't fired. But other editors were in flux, including the indispensable Mary Louise Aswell, who left to retire in 1956, succeeded first by Pearl Kazin, her former assistant, and then by Alice Morris, "who took over the fiction with brilliant assurance." There was office gossip, of course. An editor named Constance Woodworth—"glamorous!" in Mellen's description—on Vreeland's staff, was said to be having "a mad affair with Serge Obolensky," the suave man about town. "We were always tittering about that," says Anne Hopkins Miller, who started at *Bazaar* in the late 1940s as a secretary to fashion editor Patricia Cornwell before moving on to work with accessories editor June Dickerson Cuniff, who had "the best taste in the world."

For young women, fresh out of college and embarked on their first real jobs, *Bazaar* was an unusual experience. Miller remarks that it was only after she'd moved on to other employment that she discovered that not every office was as packed with brilliant people as the magazine had been. In fact, most places turned out to have no resident geniuses at all. When she started at *Bazaar*, the designer Billy Baldwin, who had spruced up Carmel's office at some point, outpasteling and outchintzing her earlier efforts, seemed to be "always rushing in to chat with Carmel about something." (He'd also done Vreeland's office, as well as the famous red "garden in hell" living room in her Park Avenue apartment.) Vreeland herself "used to sweep through like the empress of Ethiopia, talking to the help. Everyone, even Joe the electrician, adored her." Then there was Brodovitch, "always running down the hall with big blowups" in his hands. "I loved him with a passion, sad, tortured guy that he was." (His son was by then employed as a delivery boy at the magazine.) Meetings in Carmel's office were more crowded than ever, with a number of editors circumnavigating the pages on the floor in their stocking feet.

Miller was embraced as if by family. On her first Christmas at the magazine—the first she'd ever spent away from home—she returned to her apartment one afternoon to discover that Avedon had left a fully decorated Christmas tree at her door. And one day Carmel "called me into the office and said, 'Annie, I wondered if you'd like to have a little Schiaparelli'" and handed the astonished young staffer a red velveteen sack dress. More would come, including "The very best thing she gave me"—a shawl-collared Balenciaga coat of brown melton wool.

Carmel Snow and her first grandchild Thornton "Toto" Wilson, 1950

A milestone passed in 1950: Carmel and Palen became grandparents that year, when their daughter Carmel's first child, R. Thornton Wilson III ("Toto"), was born on May 16 at LeRoy Sanitarium, formerly known as Harbor Sanitarium and the same place where Carmel had given birth to her daughters. With Toto's arrival they assumed new identities—she became "GanGan" and he "Pardy"; their grandchildren would multiply, as they tend to do, in the years to come.

Toto was meant to have been a Catholic. As his father, Thornton Wilson, recalled,

> *When Richard was born . . . I signed the papers with reluctance. I went into this priest's office on Seventy-ninth Street and I said, "I don't believe in signing." He was an Irishman and he said, "Oh, Mr. Wilson, it's just a formality. It's just a formality. Forget it. It doesn't mean a damn thing." I signed the paper to make the wedding possible. You agree to bring your children up in the Catholic tradition. I'm an Episcopalian.*
>
> *So the minute Richard was born the priest was waiting outside in the foyer, and I went down to my father's apartment on Sutton Place and he said, "Are you having some trouble up there?" And I said, "Well, yuh, a little bit." So I said, "The old lady's there with the priest and they're all ready to come and baptize Richard." He said, "Give me that telephone*

and give me the number." He got her and said, "Wilson here." He said, "What's the name of that child? Will you spell the child's name for me? Does it begin with a 'W'? Let's go through it, W-I-L-S-O-N. Who's picking up the tab for all this stuff? Wilson, right? All right," he said, "God damn it. You lay off my grandson and my family and we'll have none of that goddamn nonsense. And you tell that priest to get the hell out of there." And you know, she didn't say "boo" to him. They became great, great friends. That's the only time I think anybody ever defied her.

Ultimately, Carmel Wilson converted to Episcopalianism. Just after the birth, the new young family headed out to Rolling Hill Farm for a stay of several weeks with their new baby. On their return to New York, Thornton was surprised to find a bill in the mail from his notoriously tightfisted father-in-law: Palen was asking for rent for the trio's three-week-long stay.

By the early 1950s, Carmel was in her mid-sixties and it was becoming clear—perhaps even to her—that she couldn't go on forever. Certainly, Brodovitch was winding down. He'd long done work on the side, including the blurry, evocative photographs he took of the Ballets Russes de Monte Carlo while the company toured the United States in the 1930s, published in a limited edition by a small New York publisher in 1945. Later, he and editor Frank Zachary together created *Portfolio* magazine as an American version of *Graphis*. "It was probably the inherent constraints of the fashion magazine that partly accounted for his burgeoning interest in projects beyond the confines of *Bazaar*," as Kerry William Purcell has written. In other words, *Bazaar*—which Brodovitch, in more disparaging moments, had been known to refer to as "the catalogue"—was becoming increasingly stale.

Portfolio was a tour de force of graphic design. Anything might be found there—a kite designed by Charles Eames; an Apollinaire poem, "Il Pleut," its words sprinkling graphically down the page like the rain that is its subject. It must have been a euphoric experience for the art director to be freed from such mundane considerations as hemlines and "pearls of little price." It also began to encroach upon his time, something Carmel, who missed nothing, soon realized. Worse yet, some *Portfolio* meetings were held down the hall in the art department—in short, right under her nose. Just before one was to begin, Zachary looked up to see the formidable editor in chief standing in the doorway. Her eyes met his. "Mr. Brodovitch works for *Harper's Bazaar,* not for *Portfolio,*" she said, speaking calmly and concisely. "So I took the hint," Zachary recalls. "I picked up my marbles and left."

Whatever lift Brodovitch received from this dream project was tempered in its first year, when he was struck by a Hearst delivery truck on Fifty-seventh Street, injuring his hip. "He walked around the office on two crutches. I think he was racked with pain," Miller recalls. "He'd come off the elevator looking ravaged," adds Bassman, who took over the art department for a year while he recovered, taking the pages out to East Hampton—where the Brodovitches had a weekend home—for his comments and/or approval. His absence was a particular loss to the spirited group of photographers, including Bassman and her husband, Paul Himmel, Arnold Newman, and, briefly, Diane Arbus, who took his famous Design Lab class, which had been convening in Avedon's studio since 1947. It was a grim period for the Russian, whose life rarely seemed much brighter. "He became very disenchanted with the world," Avedon says. "He became a really hard drinker."

Carmel lost a key ally, sometimes even an unwitting one, in 1951, when William Randolph Hearst died on August 14 that year, after a four-year illness. He was still involved, if erratically, in the day-to-day workings of his publishing empire, still keeping close tabs on his editors and their publications. According to his son, Bill Jr., they would hear from him

> *at ungodly hours . . . long after we had gone home and to bed. . . . Pop didn't repeat instructions. So editors and publishers had to snap out of their slumber quickly; several kept notebooks beside their phones. We*

feared missing any instructions because the old man would surely recall them.

For Carmel, Hearst was an old adversary, but also a kindred spirit. Like her, he was unabashedly himself, unafraid to express an opinion that might differ from anyone else's. For Hearst, she was a rare find—someone as independent-minded as he. It's hard not to admire this publisher in some ways, in spite of his eccentricities, repugnant prejudices, and sometimes unsavory political beliefs. If he believed in someone, and he believed in Carmel Snow, he could be disarmingly open-minded, too. He abhorred the new, particularly in the visual domain—it wasn't just Picasso he detested, but seemingly every other modern artist. Yet for twenty years he allowed Carmel and Brodovitch, confirmed modernists, to show as much that was new in their pages as any fashion magazine before or since.

Changes were coming to the magazine world, ones that transcended Hearst or any other publisher. Years later, Louise Dahl-Wolfe wrote:

On thinking back my memory is haunted still by a remark that Carmel Snow made to me sometime after the end of the war: "My dear, life will be very difficult in the future." I realize now that she was talking about the coming world of technology—the machine age, a commercial age.

She could as easily have been talking about the creeping commercialization of fashion magazines. Advertisers increasingly held sway. There were more and more "musts," things that had to be shown, whether they merited it or not. Still, there were pockets of resistance. In the early 1950s, Shopping Bazaar editor Jane Strong accepted an ad from a company that offered "pearlized baby shoes," a service in which infants' first footwear was made into permanent keepsakes. Strong soon found herself summoned to the sales department, where she learned that "the ad girls wanted me to run a photo" of these horrors in her pages. (By placing an ad, they were entitled to coverage, in the advertiser's view.) In a panic, she raced down to Carmel's office, located on the floor below. "I said, 'Mrs. Snow, what should I do?'" The editor didn't hesitate: "You certainly don't want anything to do with that." With her blessing, Strong declined.

Even so, "little by little we were being forced to do the shabby business," as Perényi puts it. The notorious "Must List" began to be distributed to editors in the 1950s, which listed which advertisers' fashions had to be shown in the magazine. Some found ways around this, including Vreeland, who, when she was unable to find a garment worth photographing among the manufacturers on the list—and it happened—might approach one to ask that they change a color combination or tool with a design until they came up with one that merited space in the book. In general, the more ad pages a manufacturer took out, the more coverage was expected in return. Lilli Ann, the San Francisco clothing manufacturer, advertised on page 3 of the magazine for decades; at some point it became the norm that once a year an outfit of theirs would be featured on a *Bazaar* cover even though, as Perényi points out, "Carmel wouldn't have been caught dead in a Lilli Ann suit." Such arrangements would become more commonplace—at *Bazaar* and elsewhere—in the years ahead.

Harper's Bazaar covers from the Snow years

THIS PAGE, TOP: **Erté illustration, 1933**

OPPOSITE PAGE, TOP LEFT: **Cassandre illustration, 1937**

OPPOSITE PAGE, TOP RIGHT: **Brodovitch illustration, 1936**

THIS PAGE, BOTTOM: **Avedon photograph, 1951**

OPPOSITE PAGE, BOTTOM LEFT: **Dahl-Wolfe photograph, 1951**

OPPOSITE PAGE, BOTTOM RIGHT: **Avedon photograph of Audrey Hepburn, 1956**

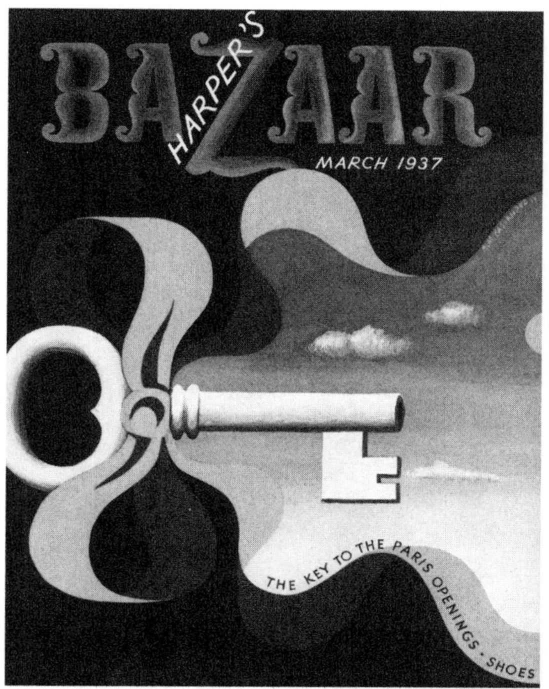
HARPER'S
BAZAAR
MARCH 1937
THE KEY TO THE PARIS OPENINGS · SHOES

HARPER'S
BAZAAR
TRAVEL
CALIFORNIA
FLORIDA
CRUISES
WHITE
DRESSES
BATHING
SUITS
PRINTS
HATS
FRANKLY FORTY
JANUARY 1936
50¢ 15 FR. IN PARIS. 2/6 IN LONDON.

BAZAAR
The Gala Season
Christmas Gifts
November 1951
60 cents
65 cents in Canada

Harpers
BAZAAR
April 1956
Incorporating Junior Bazaar
FLOWERS:
IN FASHION
IN ART
IN BEAUTY
60 cents

14 ideal daughters

Success in fashion . . . means having a finger on the pulse of the times.
—CARMEL SNOW

Fashion people . . . always seem young in spirit.
—CARMEL SNOW

WHEN BRODOVITCH HIRED A YOUNG ASSISTANT named Adrian Gilbert Johns, known as A. G. after the initials of her first and middle names, in the early 1950s, she became a kind of ideal daughter to Carmel, the latest in a long line. A. G. (whose name became Allen through marriage) was the daughter of Sandra Johns, who had contributed fashion illustrations to the magazine since the mid-1940s. Carmel was rarely even introduced to staffers in such a lowly position as Allen's, but after a while the strikingly attractive, well-dressed young woman in the art department caught her eye and she began inviting her to her home in the evenings to talk. Along the way, "we became friends," A. G. says. "We went to the movies or she'd take me to the theatre. She just became a part of my life." In Carmel's words, she was "almost like a daughter to me."

When Allen's mother headed off to Europe for a couple of years in the mid-1950s, Carmel invited A. G. to move into the Black and Whites, where the young woman felt immediately at home: "Nelly would bring me breakfast in bed." Sensing that she had editing potential, Carmel transferred her from the art department to the editorial staff, where she became an associate editor. Allen's presence was an uncomplicated pleasure in the way that sometimes only non-family members can be. With her daughters married or in college, there was room to fill. And while Allen describes the Snows as "wonderful with each other, you always felt a real affection," their paths crossed increasingly rarely, according to one relative. "They only got together for the major holidays." The cordial distance that characterized their relationship left Carmel frequently alone—never her favorite state.

"I loved her dearly," Allen says of Carmel. "She was a mother to me—and I needed one." Once in Carmel's orbit, her life changed. She recalls "incredible nights, like Carmel, Cartier-Bresson, and I having dinner in her apartment. I was just riveted. It opened up a whole life." The French photographer recalled one meal where Palen joined them, too. "She didn't let her husband talk! She said, 'Stick to your horses and your whiskey.' He didn't dare." Cleveland Amory, the writer and wit, was another frequent guest; there were numerous others. The pair went to endless movies, the theater, the opening of the Guggenheim Museum in 1959. Even after Allen moved into her own apartment, Carmel "would do just lovely things for me," the young woman recalls, including passing the occasional plum assignment her way. At one point, Carmel sent her down to Washington, D.C., in the company of Dahl-Wolfe, to interview a new and very dashing young politician, Senator John F. Kennedy, for the magazine.

There's something poignant about this picture; it offers a peek behind the mask of the imperious, famous editor. "I never really understood why she liked me," Allen says. "I was very shy." But from a distance, her appeal seems clear. She was straightforward, gentle, not remotely tough or temperamental like so many of the larger-than-life figures who crowded the editor's days. Another young editor friend of Carmel's was Laura Pyzel Clark, whom she tended to see on weekends.

> *She'd call me up and say, "Darling, come over and we'll go out to Long Island and we'll spend the day." She had a Cadillac with a top down. She'd have a couple of belts and off we'd go. She drove like an Englishman in the tropics, with one hand on the horn. She'd drive through everything. We had a ball.*

In a way, it was a continuation of the Barry/Louise Macy phenomenon; Carmel seemed to thrive on taking young women under her wing. "She really thought of me as a daughter. She seemed to be looking out for me," Allen says. In her case, too, Carmel acted as matchmaker, once again encouraging a relationship that perhaps should not have been. "She arranged for young Carmel and Thornton to have a dinner party and put me next to him," Allen recalls. "She engineered it. He became my first husband." She even gave the couple a wedding at her apartment. The marriage, however, didn't last.

One of Allen's friends was a young illustrator named Andy Warhola. The artist had moved in 1949 from Pittsburgh to New York, where he shared a roach-infested apartment with an old art school friend, the hyperrealist painter Philip Pearlstein. He turned twenty-one at about the time his first assignment—a sketch of shoes for a fashion feature in *Glamour* magazine—went to print. The magazine inadvertently dropped the *a* at the end of his last name, the rest being history. Shoes became his specialty, oddly enough, although, of course, not for long.

For a young freelancer, *Bazaar* was the summit, one Warhol effortlessly scaled. A famous story about how he was hired at the magazine—long a part of his legend—has since been debunked. As Bob Colacello has written:

> *Years later, Andy loved to tell me tales of what he called "my cockroach period," and his favorite has been repeated in every book written about him. He'd never forget the day, it goes, that he finally got an appointment to show his work to Carmel Snow, the white-gloved editor-in-chief of* Harper's Bazaar. *When she opened his portfolio, he said, a cockroach crawled out and ran across her desk, and she felt so sorry for him that she gave him an assignment. It never happened—not to Andy, anyway. Philip Pearlstein says that it was* his *appointment,* his *portfolio,* his *cockroach—and that Mrs. Snow was so horrified that he didn't get the job.*

However he got there, "*Harper's Bazaar* was essential in establishing Warhol as the most sought-after illustrator of women's accessories in New York," according to Calvin Tompkins.

Photos from this period show Warhol to be balding, with darkish hair, a very different look from the straw mop he'd later adopt, wearing obvious wigs as a statement of . . . whatever. "He looked a little funny," Allen recalls. Another friend describes him as "very unattractive, he had pinkish skin and colorless hair. He spoke with this lingo." A *Glamour* editor who worked with him recalled him emitting a constant series of "faint expletives: 'Gee—'Wow'—'Really'—'Oh'—'Ah'—'Er.'" He was, in short, unimpressive. "It was just Andy, the shoe artist who we used. He was very sweet," Allen says. "He was so not known then. He was just little Andy. He did such good work for us. It was nothing like the Andy he became." Few, if any, guessed that he would be the future sensation of Pop Art, avant-garde film, and beyond.

The *Bazaar* staff watched in fascination as, bit by bit, this shy, unprepossessing youth transformed himself. "He had his bulbous nose fixed and got that wig," Allen says. He hung out at the magazine, a strategy that struck some people, including Vreeland, as strange. "He was always at *Harper's Bazaar*. Everyone adored him, but he perplexed me a bit. He never seemed to have much to say or do." Warhol was a clever freelancer. "From the beginning he would charm more work from art directors with little handmade gifts, special personalized drawings, limited edition illustrated books. . . ." In 1954, he distributed copies of one of the latter, featuring sketches of cats, to many on the *Bazaar* staff. "He always knew which side his bread was buttered on," according to Vreeland.

Warhol created his drawings by a three-step process, sketching his subject, then tracing it onto another surface, usually blotting paper, in ink. He'd then press this wet image onto yet another piece of paper, often in multiple versions. His work (unlike his appearance in this era, which, for obvious reasons, earned him the nickname "Raggedy Andy") was meticulous. He delivered it to *Bazaar* and other clients in a brown paper grocery bag, which merited him another nickname, "Andy Paperbag." In an exhibit entitled "The Golden Slipper Show or

Shoes Show in America," held at the Bodley Gallery in 1956, Warhol fantasized on paper, often with gilt touches, about the footwear of such idols as Mae West (by coincidence, the very woman whose figure inspired the famous hourglass-shaped bottle of Schiaparelli's Shocking perfume). He brought this same conceit into the pages of *Bazaar:* in a feature on celebrity footwear he naughtily assigned Truman Capote a pair of plant-filled high-heeled mules. James Dean, rather more flatteringly, merited a cuffed cowboy boot with spurs. (The uneven, faux-naïve handwriting, written across these pages, so characteristic of his graphic work in this period, was done by Julia Warhola, the artist's Czech immigrant mother.) Warhol's early work has a gentle wit to it—he entitled one shoe print "*à la récherche du shoe perdu*"; his future was there, nascent, in the way he put every-day objects into a new, unexpected context; in his fascination with working in multiples; in his obsession with fame. Some of his more striking work from this pre-Pop period was done in gold leaf and ink.

Warhol must have experienced the shortest starving-artist phase in history: within minutes, it seems, of his arrival in Manhattan, he'd become a successful commercial artist. By the mid-1950s, the personality-packed sketches of elongated shoes he did for I. Miller, the New York shoe emporium, which ran each week in the *New York Times,* "had every agency in town hot on his trail," according to Tina Fredericks, a former editor at *Glamour,* who had been among the first to hire him. (He earned an Art Directors Club Award for this campaign in 1957.) By the time he turned thirty, Warhol had bought a town house on the Upper East Side—presumably without the roaches, or at least only with ones of the upwardly mobile kind. As Colacello has written, "by 1970, Andy Warhol was already the best-known artist in the world. . . ."

Warhol had an entourage from his earliest Manhattan days, long before his famous Factory was founded; it would eventually include superstars and all manner of hangers on. One of the former was Brigid Berlin, just out of her teens and the daughter of Carmel's nemesis/friend at Hearst, Dick Berlin. For a time Brigid worked at *Bazaar,* doing various menial tasks. She soon fell in with Warhol, who

gave her the name Brigid Polk—a homonym of "poke"—to commemorate her habit of injecting herself with speed right through the cloth of her blue jeans.

Needless to say, her Hearstling father, Dick Berlin, "thought it was a disgrace," according to Catherine di Montezemolo, a *Vogue* editor at the time. Polk acted in *The Chelsea Girls* and in a film called *Andy Warhol's Pork,* which featured unflattering phone calls from her mother, Honey Berlin—secretly taped by her daughter—in which she nagged the girl to lose weight, get away from Warhol, and on and on. One can only imagine how her father's boss, the puritanical Mr. Hearst, would have reacted. Years later, Warhol insisted that he started his new magazine, originally known as *Inter/VIEW,* "to give Brigid something to do." It must have seemed like a cruel joke to Berlin, by then retired, who'd always hoped that his daughter would inherit his editorial interests. Instead, she became the receptionist at the magazine, which would later change its name to *Interview.*

By the 1950s, *Bazaar* was giving new prominence to American fashion. Vreeland still stalked Seventh Avenue, of course, and Carmel even turned up at the occasional New York fashion show when rumors of an exciting new designer, such as Geoffrey Beene, reached her ears. "She was one of the very few people of her caliber who would come to see what a young unknown was doing," says James Galanos, who opened his fashion house in California in 1950 and whose career Carmel championed from the start. Polly Mellen never forgot being chastised by her in Paris one year after she skipped a fashion show by an unknown designer. "Carmel said, 'You must go to every show. How do you know that this isn't going to be the hottest collection of the season?'" Characteristically, she ended the conversation on a positive note. ("She never gave you an insult," Mellen says.) "She said, 'I believe in you and your eye. I want to hear what you thought of it. Go now and see the collection.'"

At about this time, another young talent, Bill Blass, then working for a New York manufacturer, came to the attention of Niki de Gunzburg who, although he'd left Vreeland's staff to go to work at *Vogue,* was still friendly with the gang at *Bazaar.* More than friendly, actually. For years he sent copies of the

OPPOSITE: **Carmel Snow (*left*) with managing editor Robert Gerdy at the Italian collections, 1952**

fashion reports he filed from Paris for *Vogue* simultaneously to Vreeland at *Bazaar.* In any case, "He told Carmel Snow and D.V. [about me]," Blass said. "They were at *Bazaar* then and they visited me at Anna Miller. It was as if the Queen of England herself had decided to visit." Blass and others joined the ranks of designers in the United States—including Norell, Adrian, Trigère—who were conjuring up a style of their own. They had a practicality in common, favoring, as McCardell once said, "buttons that button and bows that tie." Nothing was extraneous; everything had to be there for a reason. (One designer, Herbert Sondheim, entertained his Seventh Avenue cohorts for years with tales of his megatalented musical prodigy son, Stephen, a name that would soon far outshine his own.)

The fashion map expanded in other directions, too: in July 1951, Carmel headed off to a showing of Italian fashions to be held before the Paris openings. It was the second one held—the first had taken place in February of that year. Both spotlit Roman designers, among them the Contessa Simonetta Visconti, known as Simonetta, whom Ernestine Carter described as "dark, fiery" and "the reigning queen of the 'Alta Moda of Rome'" and Alberto Fabiani—known as the "prince of tailors"—who also signed his creations by his first name alone. (The pair, bitter rivals, shocked the fashion world when they married the next year.) Four buyers from what the Italians called the "boutique sector," including Emilio Pucci, also showed. Their fashions ranged from elaborate bouffant evening gowns—"I have seldom seen more luscious fabrics," Carmel reported—to "gay, correct" sportswear, with not much in between.

The Italian showings were new; no one from abroad seemed to know whether to take them seriously. When word came that Carmel, who'd been entreated to attend by a Seventh Avenue designer, Hannah Troy, would be attending, Italy leaped instantly onto the fashion map. "As the most powerful single figure in the world of fashion, her presence was an occasion," Carter wrote. Certainly it was for Simonetta, who planned to unveil her collection in an alfresco fashion show on the grounds of her mother's elaborate villa outside of Rome. Every detail was locked into place when the worst-case scenario unfolded: it rained. Simonetta, temperamental to begin with, fell apart. Entreated to bring the show indoors, she refused altogether, shooing the audience away. But not before, hysterics notwithstanding, she made certain that the person who mattered most would see her work. "We later discovered that when Simonetta withdrew, she had taken with her Mrs. Snow, who had been given a private view of the collection," Carter wrote.

By the following year, 1952, the shows had expanded exponentially: three hundred buyers turned up, rather than the eight of the year before." The big open square between the Grand Hotel and the Excelsior looked like an extension of Seventh Avenue," Carmel wrote. Nine fashion houses took part, as well as sixteen sportswear and boutique designers. The star of the show was a nineteen-year-old Roman, Roberto Capucci, whose work provided an exuberant contrast to that of the older Italian designers. The best of these fashions had a casual, yet aristocratic air, an offhand opulence that was all the more striking for being understated. Carmel was particularly taken with Italian fabrics and knitwear, especially the delicate work of Marchesa di Gresy as well as, in a different vein, "Emilio Pucci's smart, original sportswear."

"The world of fashion was expanding," she wrote. It wasn't always smooth. The competition between north and south in that country is perennial; no sooner were the Florentine shows established than eight Roman designers set out to outdo them by showing their wares two days earlier in Rome. Eventually a compromise was reached, in which accessories and boutique fashions would be shown in Florence and the "alta moda"—haute couture—in the Italian capital. By the end of the decade, of course, Milan would trump both cities, becoming the center of the Italian fashion world. Given her influence, it's no surprise that Carmel was soon awarded the Stella della Solidarietà, the star of friendship, for "fostering the renaissance of Italian artisanship."

Carmel chose Irene Brin, a columnist for *Corriere della Sera* and other Italian papers, as Italian editor; she was photographed for *Bazaar* in her baroque, cherub-encrusted, carved wooden bed, where she claimed to do most of her writing for the magazine. Brin, who was married to Gaspero del Corso, director of the

Galleria dell' Obelisco, Rome's best-known modern art gallery, knew everyone in the Eternal City and "made my visits to Rome a round of lavish entertainment," Carmel wrote. But Brin's visits to the United States weren't quite the same. "Mrs. Snow was awfully jealous of her for some reason," says Edson. "She never liked her." Given the geographical distance between them, their paths crossed only rarely. Still, Brin turned out to be short-lived, and not just at the magazine. "She had a marvelous figure but she was starving herself," Edson says. "She didn't eat anything. She'd eat one oyster for dinner. She evidently killed herself that way." And all this before anorexia nervosa was a household name.

Another who jumped on the Italian bandwagon was Elizabeth Arden. The shrewd beauty mogul (and intimate friend of Tom White's) had had a clothing line for years; she'd once hired a talented novice named Charles James to be the first in-house designer at her famous empire of red-doored beauty salons. (He left to open his own business in 1945.) Others had followed. On the lookout for someone new, Arden asked Carmel to keep an eye out in Italy for a suitable designer. She bagged one easily, at Fabiani's show, where the best dresses in the line had been designed by one Count Ferdinando Sarmi, and wired Arden with the news. The dapper Italian was soon at work (and, often, at loggerheads) with the willful Miss Arden in Manhattan.

The Italian collections were held in "great, high-ceilinged palazzos," in Carmel's words, an environment where many aristocratic designers, among them Simonetta, di Gresy, and Pucci, felt quite at home. "I am the first member of my family to work in a thousand years," Pucci, an American-educated marchese from a centuries-old family, announced imperiously in *Life* magazine. The designer's family seat in Florence, the Palazzo Pucci, was stuffed with treasures, among them a massive Botticelli given to the family during the Renaissance. It's no wonder, then, that his clothes seemed to combine the quattrocento with the space age, juxtaposing daring colors—pistachio, pink, powder blue—and distinctive swirly designs, many done in such strange and original fabrics as Helanca, a Swiss material that could stretch to five times its actual size. A champion skier, Pucci had begun his career in the Swiss Alps, improvising ski outfits out of elements that were radical at the time: stirrup pants and stretch tops in vivid colors no mountain had ever seen before. (Before he did so, skiwear had consisted of woolen plus fours, available in just two shades, gray and blue.) A chance encounter with photographer Toni Frissell, then on a ski holiday, went the way they so often did with this smooth Italian, with Frissell developing an instant crush on the designer. She shot some action photos of his clothes, and sent them off to *Bazaar.* When they saw their potential, Carmel and Vreeland moved into action bringing them to a key buyer, Marjorie Griswold of Lord & Taylor, who was credited with having developed Claire McCardell's career. Griswold, in turn, showed the designs to the manufacturer White Stag, which began producing them in 1948.

The results, photographed by Frissell in Zermat and modeled by socialites, appeared in the December issue that year with a brief cameo by Emilio himself, seen adjusting the leather strap that ran like a stirrup under one skier's foot—another Pucci innovation. The clothes, which included two-piece ski suits and a parka in yellow tie silk, earned him an immediate following in the United States. He then moved on to sportswear, coming up with a pair of short, side-zipped, casual trousers—the original Capri pants—which sailed out of the boutique he opened, his first, on that island in 1950. To tease his illustrious relatives, scandalized that he would actually go to work, Pucci kept a scrub brush and pail near the store's entrance; he'd drop to his knees and start scrubbing the floor whenever family members or friends stopped in.

When the designer, who became known for a time as Emilio of Capri and Florence, designed a bright, stretchy skirt that Carmel thought would go over well with her readers, "Mrs. Snow somehow or other got Saks [Fifth Avenue] to reproduce [it] and that started off the whole Pucci fashion thing," Babs Simpson recalled. Before long, he'd settled into the bright, infinitely wearable, stretchy line of clothes with which he's identified today. "Because we Americans were so color-starved after the war, viewing his work for the first time was like seeing fireworks," one American retailer, Stanley Marcus of Neiman Marcus, said.

Born in Naples in 1914, Pucci was a strange-looking man, with uneven features and an unpleasant mien, but his success with women was undeniable. He was "a famous swordsman," Laura Pyzel Clark recalls—and she's not referring to the way he wielded an epée. The designer Oleg Cassini, a fellow Florentine who grew up with Pucci, once described his friend as having "a certain nervousness caused by a desire to be the ultimate victor in the arena of sex." As youths, the pair had "planned our conquests of visiting American girls with the precision of a military campaign." (Young Italian women, being closely chaperoned, were off limits.) Pucci's conquests included Edda Ciano, Mussolini's then very-married daughter, whose own father had betrayed her to the Nazis; Pucci succeeded in rescuing her, then smuggling her to the Swiss border; but he was caught, imprisoned in Milan's San Vittore jail, and tortured by the Nazis, ultimately attempting suicide in prison.

He didn't succeed and, after his release, returned to his playboy ways. His technique could be startling, as the model Dorian Leigh discovered one year when she modeled for *Bazaar* in Rome, working with the photographer Genevieve Naylor. The jet-lagged Leigh had just arrived from New York when Naylor introduced her to Pucci over lunch. Afterward, the model was taking a nap in her hotel room when the wily designer let himself in, wheeling a room service cart and dressed in one of the faintly ludicrous outfits he favored—translucent white silk shirts with rolled sleeves and an upturned collar, with pants in the same fabric. Reader, he pounced. So persistent was he, in fact, that one writer has described the encounter as a "near rape." Awakened—and appalled—Leigh managed to escape. The frustrated Pucci, in a classic bit of dialogue, asked the glorious brunette: "Dorian, don't you know that Italians are the best lovers in the world?"

"That may very well be," she answered, "but I'm going to choose the Italian."

Pucci "was a ruthless man," Babs Simpson says. "He was a terrible character but Mrs. Snow was mad about him because he was so successful." By about 1954, his styles, and particularly his "tight, bright pants," had become a "ruling passion with American girls," Carmel once told a lecture audience. What she neglected to mention was that they became a ruling passion in her household as well. "At one point Mary Palen was having an affair with Emilio Pucci," recalls Laura Pyzel Clark. It was more than just a passing attraction, a friend adds. "Mary Palen fell in love with him and wanted to marry him. Carmel would have nothing to do with it." From a mother's point of view, it was a worst-case scenario: the Italian was almost forty, about fifteen years older than her middle daughter, and infinitely more experienced. His reputation as a womanizer was hardly a secret. In short, to a young, impressionable girl, he had limitless surface appeal. No wonder Mary Palen's mother was distraught. "Carmel was terrified for her child," Clark says. It wasn't just that the designer was alarmingly suave, with a mania for seduction; it was the transparency of his motives, the discomfiting sense that at least some, if not all, of the girl's appeal had to do with the influential position held by her mother. "He started to pursue Mary Palen because it was good business," Babs Simpson states.

Frissell "was just horrified" by this turn of events, according to her daughter, Sidney Stafford. "She felt very responsible because she'd introduced them. She was very concerned about the repercussions of that. I remember her worrying terribly about that." That Mary Palen was particularly vulnerable only made the situation that much worse. When her daughter flew off to join Pucci in Italy, Carmel, never one to sit back, moved into high gear. It took a bit of time. "At one point, Carmel asked me to go after her and bring her back." Laura Pyzel Clark recalls. "I said, 'Carmel, I can't do that. I'd do anything in the world for you, but I can't do that.' I told her I didn't think I could handle it, and I didn't think it was right, either." On the other hand, McFadden—"a stiff moralist," in Dorothy Wheelock Edson's words—had no such qualms and was soon winging her way across the Atlantic. It's not clear if she brought Mary Palen back or just persuaded her to come back on her own. However it happened, Carmel "broke off the relationship," according to fashion editor Gwen Randolph Franklin. Things settled down, ultimately, and the crisis passed. (Both parties went on to marry others, Pucci to Cristina Nannini—twenty-four years his junior—in 1959, and Mary Palen to Victor Rossi in 1967.)

In her own life, Carmel seemed ever more restless. "Her one weakness was that she loved new people. She was stimulated by new people," says Dorothy Wheelock Edson. "Sometimes I felt that I was her procurer. She'd say, 'Dorothy, you know everyone in town. Is there anyone around I should have dinner with?'" There was, as it happens, fairly often: Edson, who was responsible for *Bazaar*'s theatrical coverage, knew everyone in the theater world and beyond. In December 1951, she mentioned to Carmel that Kenneth Tynan had arrived from London, and the two women joined him and his wife for dinner at Casanova, on the Upper East Side. Not long out of Oxford and on the rise for about as long as he'd been alive, the young drama critic had come to New York with his American wife on a work-churning trip that included visits to such glossy magazines as *Vogue* and *Mademoiselle.* They'd sailed on the French liner, the *Île de France;* as Tynan wrote, teasingly, to Carmel later on, during the crossing he'd been "fearfully île on the *Île.*"

The choice of restaurant was auspicious: Casanova had been started a few years earlier by an enterprising Viennese immigrant named Max Loew who had come to New York for the first time after a fortune-teller predicted that he would open a restaurant there, describing the building in detail. Alighting in Manhattan, he wandered the streets until he found it, at the busy thoroughfare of Seventy-ninth Street and Second Avenue. (Did everyone manage their careers by soothsayers in those days?)

As for Tynan, then twenty-four, he was brilliant, charming, handsome, flattering; Carmel loved him, quite predictably, from the outset. While dazzled by him, she and Edson were unimpressed by his dismayingly uncharismatic wife, the former Elaine Dundy, née Brimberg, of New York, who, among other attributes, had an "oddball face," according to Kathleen Tynan (who, as Elaine's successor, was perhaps not the least biased of observers). Carmel and Edson giggled together afterward about the sheer weirdness of Tynan's clothes, in particular "a green iridescent suit," as later described by Shana Alexander, the future journalist, who met him on the same trip, and a rivetingly peculiar pair of yellow shoes. Never mind, both wife and wardrobe would soon be behind him—incinerated in the blinding heat of his meteoric rise into the distant galaxies of international theater. In short order, Tynan would become famous for playwriting, criticism, and beyond, up to and including an oddity that could only have burst from the 1960s—*Oh! Calcutta!*—a sex revue that played for ages both in London and New York. (Whatever.)

Tynan and Carmel were mutually enchanted. As Kathleen Tynan would later note in her biography of her husband, over that one meal Tynan "ensnared the legendary Carmel Snow at *Harper's Bazaar*." This prefix was by now part of Carmel's name. She'd become "the legendary Carmel Snow," just as Tynan would become "the Legendary Kenneth Tynan," and at an outrageously early age.

The young critic wrote to Carmel immediately upon his return to London to pitch a story on Noël Coward. She resisted the idea at first, believing that Coward had been done to death, given that the playwright had first conquered the London theater world with *Hay Fever* in 1925 and had had rather a lot of triumphs—among them such famous plays as *Blithe Spirit* and *Private Lives*—ever since. But Tynan nimbly turned Carmel's prejudices around.

> *I'm told you think Coward passé. Now this is really shocking; and quite unhandsome of you, don't you think, when one remembers that Coward has contributed a new kind of human being to the hierarchy of fictional inventions—the Coward hero, the flustered, staccato sophisticate . . .*

Sure enough, Carmel published Tynan on Coward later that year, timed to coincide with the opening of his play *Quadrille.* The extended caption Tynan contributed packed more information into a centimeter than one would have thought possible. As for the flamboyant Coward himself, whose antics had hardly diminished after thirty years in the public eye: "At fifty-two, he describes himself, referring to that touch of the Orient in his appearance and demeanor, as 'that rather splendid old Chinese character actress.'"

In the spring of 1952, Carmel took Tynan to dinner in London with Rebecca West, the English novelist, who was then at the height of her fame. The author of such novels as *The Thinking Reed* (1936), a merciless view of life among the rich, she covered the Nuremberg trials for *The New Yorker* in 1946 and, the following year, was on the cover of *Time* as the "Number One Woman Writer in the World." Tynan described her with characteristic, offhand causticity:

> *She bristled and barked staccato orders at me, and threw gauntlets in all directions. How can a woman contrive to be a non-Smoker and yet look all the time as if she were chewing a cheroot? She seems to me to be Kensington's reply to Colonel Blimp: and yet the best journalist of our time.*

The magazine was full of theater in this period, all of it steered by Edson, who often brought Carmel along to Broadway openings. Tynan, who started writing a monthly profile for *Bazaar* in the early 1950s, was critically important to the magazine—and vice versa. As he later wrote: "To be given virtual *carte blanche* to run riot across the pages of *Harper's Bazaar* was about the most encouraging thing that ever happened to me as a young writer." His pieces were hugely entertaining, tending to compliment and skewer their subjects in equal measure. "It's wonderful when it isn't you" was the actor John Gielgud's comment.

"I used to correspond with [Tynan] a great deal," says Dorothy Edson. "He was our European connection. He could tell me everything that was going on in Europe in the theater. He'd tell us who was hot on the English stage and we'd send one of our photographers over." Cecil Beaton, who had resurfaced, was frequently called into action, contributing what he coyly referred to as "snapshots" in correspondence with Edson, including his famous image of a ravishing, reclining Marilyn Monroe. "Ms. Monroe's entourage is *ghastly,*" he confided, in a letter to the theater editor, adding that he had "Many funny stories I'd like to tell you about her meeting the queen."

Edson was a key lieutenant of Carmel's, but even she wasn't safe. Only a few were—Brodovitch, Vreeland, McFadden; later, Jean Chiesa and Aswell, too. Only the toughest tended to survive, the latter wrote. "What she really respected was a force equal to her own." All of which was true, but Carmel also had another, disarmingly gracious side, exemplified by what Aswell called "the Unnecessary Note," which she describes as "the word of thanks or appreciation or criticism that means twice as much because most busy executives never find time to send it. [Carmel] always found time, even if she had to scrawl it herself. And flowers!" Examples are legion: "You are a wonder! divine—and adding glamour to *Harper's Bazaar,*" was a one-line letter she wrote to Toni Frissell at one point. In a longer massive, she thanked Diana Vreeland for the "wonderful, terribly hard work you did . . ." To Melanie Witt Miller, who'd left *Bazaar* to take a job at *Glamour,* she gushed that "I was heartbroken not to say goodby [sic] to you."

Yet Carmel's management style could be treacherous: "She always had a pet genius, and I was it for three months," recalls Mary Lee Settle. "She'd think you were the most wonderful person and the most talented person, then Boom!" Edson always felt the threat. "She was terribly fair. . . . She loved new people and new ideas but then she'd get tired very easily." When she did, things could get dicey. The victim might be warned by a stray comment or perhaps just a look. The trick with Carmel was to realize that nothing was without meaning, nothing offhand. For experienced Carmel watchers the signs were obvious. Edson once learned, on the basis of one appar-

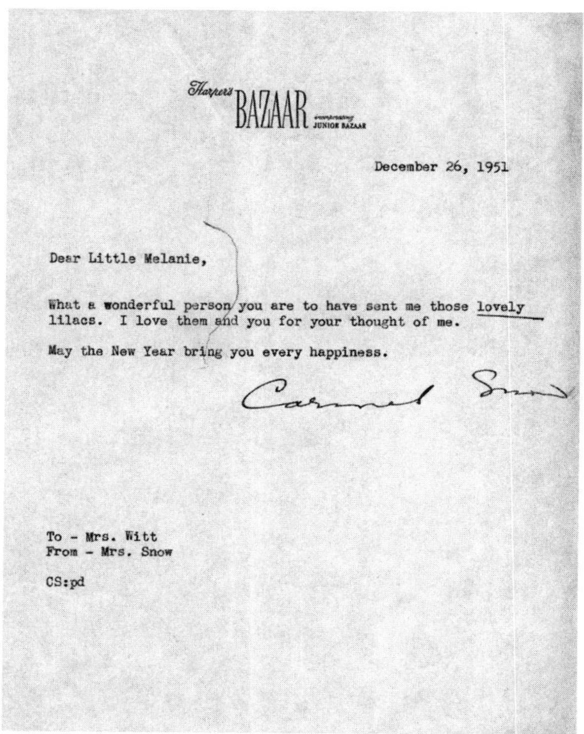

Harper's BAZAAR incorporating JUNIOR BAZAAR

December 26, 1951

Dear Little Melanie,

What a wonderful person you are to have sent me those lovely lilacs. I love them and you for your thought of me.

May the New Year bring you every happiness.

Carmel Snow

To - Mrs. Witt
From - Mrs. Snow

CS:pd

One of Carmel Snow's "unnecessary notes"

ently casual remark, that her future was in doubt. "She said, 'Look at Dorothy. She has all these ideas. Sometimes she has too many ideas.'" The only way Edson could last at *Bazaar* for seventeen years ("a high point of my life") was by cannily learning to navigate her boss's ups and downs. She figured out to lie low when her boss was in a certain—hasn't-she-been-here-too-long?—kind of mood. "She'd get a kind of turtle-eyed look. I thought I'd just stay out of her sight for a while." Once it passed, Edson was wise enough to know that her safety was only temporary.

"She was quite ruthless about getting rid of people if she got down on someone or didn't think she was doing a good job," she recalls. No one was immune. At some point Carmel put together a new rubric at the magazine, one that seems prescient, given the current real estate mania, on interior design. (She'd instituted a similar column back in the 1920s at *Vogue*.) A young woman—"a very clever girl," in Edson's estimation—was hired as decorating editor. Carmel found her amusing, and she became a frequent dinner guest at the Black and Whites. But when the section didn't quite work out as Carmel had hoped, she became a scapegoat. As Dorothy Edson recalled,

> *She decided one time that she didn't want her around anymore. So she invited her to her house for lunch, all alone. She served a lavish meal and then asked her, just like that, "Wouldn't you be happy some place else?" That was the way she did it. You always knew, if she asked you to lunch alone, it was trouble.*
>
> *She invited me one time when I'd been at the magazine for about five years and my heart shrank. I knew . . . that was a sign. When the time came that she leaned over and asked me that question I got my Irish up. (Well, not my Irish, I'm Episcopalian.) I said, "Mrs. Snow, I need this job!" so she backed down. It's the only time she ever did. It was really scary. She could be ruthless.*

And sometimes merciful, for she was known occasionally to help people she'd fired to find other jobs. But one way or the other, it was over. More over, perhaps, than they could imagine. "When they left her magazine they went out of her life," Aswell has written. "The day after unsatisfactory associates left the *Bazaar,* they might not be recognized on the street. It wasn't a cut, a social snub. They simply weren't there for Carmel. It was an odd, chilling phenomenon."

Carmel may have been terrifying, but she inspired devotion. "I truly loved her," Edson says.

> *I never hated her, even when she was so mean to me. It's just that she loved new people. She loved me when she needed me and I did such a good job. When she was mean I was hurt like a schoolgirl. I'd go off and pout for a few weeks. Then she was so glad to see me when I reappeared.*

"Towards the end of her career she became more and more peremptory," Aswell said. Ruthless was another word that, more and more frequently, was applied to Carmel. It was the ruthlessness of an artist with a vision who will do anything to see it realized. "There was only a limited time left for her to make sure her high standards were maintained," as Aswell put it. "A good editor must be ruthless." And she is right. It's all about snap judgments, making decisions that are quick and final. And Carmel was the mistress of just that kind of assessment.

In magazines, the key lies in getting the right mix, both on the page and in the staff. If a story isn't strong enough or an image weak or an editor not quite pulling her weight at the conference table, then they must be dropped without a second thought, replaced with something better. It's all about keeping one's eyes open. As Carmel taught Avedon, indelibly, one photograph may be better in every technical sense, but if another has a certain, unforgettable something about the eyes, or anywhere else, if it reveals more about its subject, then that's the one to use. "She showed me what was good and what was bad in my pictures, and in the fashions. She's the *only* editor whose judgment I could rely on," he has said. And her judgments never wavered. "Without casting more than a glance at an illustration, photograph, or dress she is able to sum up its value," Cecil Beaton said. "She makes split-second verdicts and never goes back on them. She is not afraid of mistakes." Perényi recalls going to a fortune-teller with Carmel, one, she says, whom

> *everyone was going to at the time. Carmel wasn't impressed. She said, "My dear," in that deep, very sexy voice—literally a whiskey voice— "That woman was a fool. She told me I was brilliant and intelligent and I'm neither of those things. The reason I've succeeded is that I can make up my mind instantly one way or the other. I don't hesitate. That's the secret of my success."*

Surely George Hoyningen-Huene, who had left fashion photography behind, bitterly regretted his decision to show Carmel an unflattering, revealing shot he'd taken of his friend Greta Garbo at some point in the early 1950s. Diana Vreeland told the story:

> *At the time when Garbo was at her* most *mysterious and remote, George showed Carmel a picture he'd taken of her just for himself. He'd promised never to publish it, and anyway to him it was like the picture of a lost child would be to a bereaved mother. Carmel calmly announced that she was going to keep it, and she was going to publish it. We* all *protested. Carmel said, "I don't care if George rots in* jail. I want that picture."

The fact that Hoyningen-Huene was by then living in Los Angeles and no longer working for the magazine is a crucial element to this story. He had become expendable—a dangerous thing to be. As Aswell points out, "She was extremely fond of him as a friend. But her magazine came first. It always did—after God and her family."

And, perhaps, Balenciaga, whom Carmel was still hellbent on launching in the United States. She'd already brought him to America in 1952, a catastrophic move, given his lack of English and general hostility toward all but a handful of close friends. Thinking that Balenciaga's perfume line—which then consisted of three scents: Le Dix, La Fuite des Heures, and Quadrille—should be distributed in the United States, she recommended a perfume rep in New York, who also represented Lanvin. It must have taken some persuading, since, as Ballard has written, "Whenever he is offered impressive sums to do a wholesale line in America, or to license his name for something that he has not designed, he shrugs his shoulders and says, 'What would I buy? I have a car and too many houses.'"

Influenced by Carmel, he succumbed to temptation. In September 1953, a new president was named for Balenciaga Perfumes. In announcing the appointment, the *New York Times* said the executive would be "responsible for the sale and promotion of Balenciaga perfumes in the Western hemisphere." But the appointment was a disaster, according to Givenchy. "He didn't serve him well, almost destroying his line. He did his best to destroy Balenciaga." Rather than cultivating a selective image for the perfumes, they were distributed everywhere, including the cheapest retail outlets imaginable—with a predictably disastrous effect on the couturier's reputation. "Balenciaga suffered enormously," Givenchy adds.

> *It was an error of judgment, but he didn't hold it against Madame Snow. She was a demanding woman. Sometimes Balenciaga had to say, "No, Carmel, I'm sorry." They would have huge arguments but they were never really serious. She was unconditionally attached to him, and she was right to be.*

With her children scattered, or settled, Carmel could travel more extensively than before, not just for long weekends visiting friends like Balenciaga, but on extended visits to new places, new climes. She went to Greece for the first time at the request of the American designer Muriel King to inspect workshops that she'd organized as a way to promote Greek handicrafts. Such a mission was right up Carmel's alley—wasn't it her father's passion for local, cottage industries that had brought her to America in the first place? She combined her workshop inspection visits with more tourism, and even had tea with Queen Frederika, "who shared my interest in the fabric industries. . . ." As Frances McFadden pointed out:

> *In twenty-four hours in Athens, Carmel* experienced *Greece, because she was able to put out of her mind other things and concentrate, not on a guide book, but on her own feelings for this new place, these new people, this great building, this Parthenon. . . .*

In April 1953, Carmel was back in Europe on "one of the few holidays I ever thoroughly enjoyed." The destination was Italy, where her friend the director John Huston, with whom she occasionally spent long drinking evenings in Paris, was filming *Beat the Devil,* starring Humphrey Bogart and Gina Lollobrigida. Another friend, Truman Capote, had written the script.

Capote described her arrival:

> *So Carmel came, and greatly increased what was already rather a houseparty atmosphere: Huston danced attendance, Bogart whispered dreadful things in her ear, oh she was having a "perfectly divine time, darling"; not only that, but she had taken charge of the picture—aspects of it. She said Miss Jones' costumes were wretched; Miss Lolloetc's [actress Gina Lollobrigida] worse. Her young new discovery was sent for: a pale boy seven feet tall—Hubert Givenchy, who arrived from Paris with his own small entourage. Even gayer grew the gathering; even grayer the producer's face. And Carmel, who had come for a weekend, stayed a week.*

And then, before anyone knew what was happening, she was gone. She turned up one morning with her white gloves on and "a bonnet pinned to her lavender coif" (surely not?), with a boy following behind, carrying her luggage. According to Capote, the following dialogue ensued:

> *Bogart said, "Why, honey, what's wrong? Ain't we chic enough for you?"*
>
> *She said, "My dear man, compared to you my life is lived in a salt mine. No, it's just that now I must straighten my face and stop having fun."*
>
> *She got in her car; Bogart leaned in and said: "Well, remember, I like you, hon. You're a very ballsy-type type."*
>
> *Mrs. Snow, the Mrs. Snow, regarded him coolly for a moment, then said, "Am I? Well, so are you. Bye-bye, tough boy."*
>
> *He said: "Bye-bye, tough gal."*

Recounted like a true scriptwriter. Although Capote saw her numerous times in the 1950s, he later wrote that he would always remember her best "departing with the shine of that far-gone April day. Somehow those two automatically associate themselves in my mind, Bogart and Carmel. Isn't that odd?"

Quite.

While the movie tanked—"Pleasant enough piffle" in the words of one critic—its costumes were stellar.

Back in Europe for the collections that summer, Carmel took a detour to the land of her birth to celebrate nothing less momentous than "Ireland's first fashion show." There had long been wonderful handicrafts to be found all over Hibernia. While there was a prevailing Irish style, one that was rooted in a national love of natural fabrics and a commitment to the country's rural character, there wasn't fashion, at least by New York or Paris standards. That is, until a dark-haired young designer named Sybil Connolly—a "personable milk-skinned Irish charmer," in Bettina Ballard's words—came along. Working with such traditional local materials as tweed and lace, she alchemized them into solid, contemporary fashion, wearable not just in Ireland, but beyond.

Connolly, who was then designing for the Dublin store Richard Alan, was known for her textiles, among them a crystal pleated linen that was said to take nine yards of material for each yard of finished cloth. "It's a shame to have such beautiful fabrics, such resources for fine handiwork and not use them in fashion," she told the *Dallas Morning Post.* Connolly recycled with brio, taking the red flannel traditionally used for petticoats in Connemara, for example, and turning it into huge billowing peasant skirts. She made one skirt out of men's linen handkerchiefs, another of striped linen tea towels. No wonder *Bazaar* praised her "intuitively facile hand."

It's unclear how Connolly's work first came to Carmel's attention, but once it did, she set out to promote it, arriving in Ireland in July 1953 with a group of fashion journalists and buyers in tow. "I loved her country things, and her charming use of Irish tweeds and muslins." She brought Avedon along, and they stayed at the Shelbourne, where, as always, she invited friends and relatives to join her for afternoon tea. On this trip, or perhaps a later one, she was offered Irish coffee at breakfast, only discovering after it arrived that it was one-third whiskey. Polly Mellen, who was with her, recalled that Carmel was shocked, appalled . . . and drank it anyway. It became an integral part of her Dublin mornings.

Connolly's fashion show was held at the atmospheric Dunsany Castle, twenty minutes from Dublin and the part-time home of Lady Dunsany, one of Connolly's clients. Her husband, Lord Dunsany, was "Ireland's grand man of letters," *Bazaar* wrote, a professor and dramatist whose plays reflected "his undiminished contempt for the evils of this and perhaps other worlds." Let's hope he was away from home when the hordes of disparate fashionistas stormed the castle. The visiting Americans, in any case, were charmed. The designer "bewitched us all into buying her models and filling our editorial pages with them," Ballard wrote. Carmel certainly did so: Avedon's photographs of Connolly and her fashions ran in *Bazaar* in October 1953.

For Carmel it must have seemed as if her life had come full circle. Connolly used local women—shades of Peter White—to produce some of the same materials that had once so impassioned both Carmel's parents, right down to Carrickmacross lace, a favorite of Connolly's and the very material that Annie White had insisted on bringing to Chicago sixty years earlier. Now, on visits to her relatives, "Carmel would tout Irish designs," her cousin Joan Regan says. "I remember lots of talk about Sybil Connolly."

Inevitably, Carmel began working to persuade the young designer to bring her fashions to the New World. "Carmel had a lot of influence on putting Sybil Connolly on the map in America," recalls her cousin Veronica Freeman. "She took her to New York and took her around and it was a great success. She launched her in the U.S." The designer's trip in the fall of 1953 was a triumph: she was featured on the cover of *Life* magazine with the headline "Irish Invade Fashion World," and reported on all over the place, including the very influential *Saturday Evening Post,* where she was quoted as saying, "I'm a freak in Ireland," because she had a career. "Carmel was all over her, giving her lunches and dinners and all that," says editor Laura Pyzel Clark. "It was wonderful for Carmel to promote her Irish friend." The publicist Eleanor Lambert also pitched in: between her and Carmel there was no greater entrée into New York. After a successful fashion show in Manhattan, they arranged for another to be held in Texas.

Carmel accompanied the designer to Dallas that October. On the plane, she showed Connolly the program of the upcoming show. As Veronica Freeman recalls,

> *When Sybil Connolly saw the prices listed she got an awful shock. They were double the prices in New York. Carmel sort of said to her, "My dear, these are the prices for Texans. You have to do this in Texas; if you don't, they think that they're not good quality." She explained to her that unless they were priced like that they'd consider them to be rubbish.*

The show "was a great success and they paid those prices," Freeman adds. In Texas, as everywhere, both customers and the press fell under the Irishwoman's spell. Connolly returned to the United States—and to her expanding following there—twice annually throughout the 1950s, until it became three-quarters of her client base. Her American fans would soon include Jacqueline Kennedy and Elizabeth Taylor.

Other designers were also in the news. In this same period, Dior—a masterful self-promoter—made headlines by raising his hemlines, then repeatedly posed for photographers all over the world, with a mannequin and a tape measure, demonstrating the new length. As Carmel told the Fashion Group, the news wasn't huge in the United States, where skirt lengths had been shorter for years, but in Europe, where "women have been wearing their skirts quite long and looking old in consequence," it was a radical step. "He chopped the skirt, and youth took over," she said.

The next year, Coco Chanel, after fourteen years away from Paris, and the couture, "calmly set about producing 'Chanel' again," at the age of seventy-one. She decided to finance her return collection by having "Marie-Louise Bousquet query her boss at *Harper's Bazaar* in New York about a direct sale of Chanel originals to Seventh Avenue ready-to-wear," according to Axel Madsen. As soon as Carmel got wind of the designer's plan to return to fashion she offered her support, saying that she knew of an American manufacturer that would be interested in reproducing the line. "WHEN WILL YOUR COLLECTION BE READY STOP ARE YOU COMING TO NEW YORK WITH COLLECTION," Carmel asked in a telegram to Paris on September 24, 1953. "WILL BE HAPPY TO HELP YOU," she added.

Chanel answered with a letter on September 30, 1953, in which she explained that "during the summer I got the idea that it would be fun to go back to work, because work is all my life"—a concept the editor certainly understood. Carmel's enthusiasm was unstinting and, as it turned out, unnecessary. As soon as the perfume company that produced Chanel's famous scents learned of her plans, they offered to finance her comeback, and she no longer needed Seventh Avenue's help.

Even so, everything seemed stacked against the designer. It was only natural for Parisians to assume that her fashion instincts had faded during her long exile, spent in Switzerland and the south of France. And no one had forgotten that she had lived at the Ritz with a Nazi during the occupation. Her return collection in February 1954 featured numerous future classics, among them braid-trimmed tweed suits with silk blouses that matched their linings, quilted handbags, signature buttons, and acres of gold chains.

The reception was frigid—at least on the day of the fashion show. The newspaper reviews were scarcely warmer. No one was willing to grant Chanel anything. Except, as it happened, Carmel, who commissioned a laudatory essay entitled "Mademoiselle Chanel" from their mutual friend Jean Cocteau ("There is nothing of her era that she has missed," he wrote) for *Bazaar*'s March Paris issue, accompanied by a famous Dahl-Wolfe portrait of the knotty, complicated designer. And then there was the public. When the clothes hit the stores, they sold beautifully. Millions of women bought them, all around the globe, and Chanel was made. Again. At a time when male designers were "wallowing in extravagance," according to Charlotte Seeling (with Dior, no doubt, at the head of her list), Chanel's work remained true to itself, blissfully unchanged. "Only a woman could think that way," Seeling wrote, describing her newest styles as, "simple, practical, wearable, and elegant."

On this same trip, Carmel found that Paris was thriving.

> *The Marshall Plan had by then done its work. Europe was miraculously reviving; arts and crafts were flourishing; new fashion centers were springing up. And perhaps because my career was drawing to a close, Paris seemed to belong to me—or I to Paris—more than ever before.*

Back again the following fall, Carmel welcomed Dior's new slim "H-line" look, a low-belted style that accounted for its name (the belt forming a horizontal bar like the one in the letter *H*), renamed it the more American-user-friendly "Flat Look," and featured it all over her magazine. By the next season, she was championing the designer's "Tulip Look," which approximated the shape of that flower, seen upside down, with its dropped shoulders, rounded hips, and narrow hemline. The New Look had gone by now, without leaving a trace.

Carmel returned from Paris to news of another sibling's death: her brother Victor, the New York artist, died on April 23 at the age of sixty-three. The *New York Times* noted that his work "was represented by a frieze at the Theatre Guild and by murals at the Waldorf-Astoria Hotel and the International Telephone and Telegraph building in New York," among other projects.

Later that year, in November 1954, Brigid Snow, then twenty-one, was married to Peter Flanigan, whom Carmel described approvingly as "a descendent of a Limerick family," which also happened to be a wealthy one. It was another victory for Carmel, who so wanted to see her daughters married well. The first Catholic wedding among her daughters, it was celebrated by a nuptial mass at the Church of St. Ignatius Loyola, where Carmel's sister, Christine, had been married so many years before. Dahl-Wolfe contributed a wedding portrait, and model Mary Jane Russell helped with the bride's makeup and hair. Both the bride and her mother were dressed by Balenciaga. Brigid wore an elegantly cut wedding gown with two bows at the back. Carmel, dressed in a formal suit of heavy silk brocade—"a good red," in Edson's words—was no less resplendent. And not by accident. "The convention of trailing draperies for the mothers of bridal couples had long seemed senseless to me—why shouldn't mothers appear in the most stylish clothes they can find for the most important event in their lives, next to their own weddings?"

It's hard to overstate the effect of her choice, which she topped off with an ermine hat. "When she walked up the aisle wearing that suit with her little white hat I thought, 'I would give my life for that suit,'" Edson says. Others, apparently, thought otherwise. One can almost hear the whispered comments. It was too short, too bright—red, at a wedding?—too futuristically cut. "My Balenciaga outfit was criticized by some conventional ladies of the Colony Club, but I didn't care tuppence," Carmel wrote. Her daughter Brigid adds: "It was not the thing to wear in weddings for her generation. That suit stopped the reception. It was a *cause célèbre.*"

Carmel Snow and Coco Chanel at Carmel's New York apartment, January 1953

(And yet another lesson in the power of fashion . . .)

If Edson was struck by the sheer beauty of Carmel's outfit, she was even more surprised when, two weeks after the ceremony, Cathy Dives came by to ask her if she might like to buy it. (By now, should anyone be surprised?) "I snapped it up for fifty dollars," Edson reports.

Brigid's husband must have known early on that he'd married into an extraordinary family. But surely that lesson kept being reinforced? The Snows for years had an oversized, red satin, tufted couch in their living room. (To this day,

Carmel's grandchildren recall gleefully somersaulting on it when they were small.) It functioned as a piece of furniture, but also as a kind of stage. When Peter Flanigan, Brigid's future husband, first came to call on the family, he entered their apartment to find an apparition sitting on this bright, almost gaudy piece of furniture. It was a child, apparently, but clearly a terribly sophisticated one, flamboyantly dressed in a bright blue smoking jacket, and with such an effeminate manner you had to think it was an act. (It wasn't.)

There weren't many such visions to be seen at Dillon, Read, the New York investment bank where Brigid's up-and-coming suitor spent his days. But the courtly young man introduced himself as if meeting such a creature was routine.

"I'm Peter Flanigan," he said.

"I'm Truman Capote," the apparition answered in his signature babyish voice. The conservative Mr. Flanigan kept his cool; even so, his wife, Brigid, later confessed that "the whole thing was too much. He almost died." This encounter between two vastly different species became yet another affectionate, living-with-Carmel family story, one that would be repeated for years.

At Brigid's wedding: Carmel Snow (in the controversial red suit) and the groom's mother, Aimée Flanigan, in back; the Snow daughters—Carmel Snow Wilson, Mary Palen Snow, and Brigid Flanigan—in front

15 *being eclipsed*

There is no single trial harder for a woman to face than to step out of the spotlight—especially after a long and honored and glamorous tenure. . . .

—MARCIA DAVENPORT (*HARPER'S BAZAAR,* JULY 1938)

LIFE WENT ON, PERNICIOUSLY. There was Carmel's reputation, which kept growing. To those starting out in the fashion world in the 1950s, such as Geraldine Stutz, then an editor at *Glamour,* she was an intimidating figure—solid, distant, regal. "Mrs. Snow was the grand eminence of . . . the fashion world," Stutz says. "She was wonderfully colorful and marvelous in every way. She was the cynosure of all eyes. She was wired into fashion in the most extraordinary way."

But then, as the decade progressed, there was another Carmel—delicate, under threat. Stutz recalls sighting her at the Paris collections (her first, Carmel's umpteenth) in this period.

> *She was physically very frail. She had bones showing all over the place, little bird bones. She was a little unsteady, sometimes after lunch, and sometimes generally. Dick Avedon was the great cavalier of all time. He was ever attending, he'd put his hand under her elbow. She really needed to have somebody to watch over her. Dick was there and he adored her. They used to have it out, but he adored her.*

By now, Carmel was almost seventy, beyond retirement age, and she wasn't young for her years. "When she was sixty-eight she seemed like an old woman," Avedon recalled. "She was tottering on her feet." Nevertheless, she kept up her usual pace, keeping her hand in everything, traveling for the magazine.

She ruled *Bazaar* more single-handedly than ever. Although she kept looking for a managing editor who "could begin to replace Frances McFadden," she never quite succeeded. She hired a few, in succession, but none seemed to last for long, perhaps because, as Aswell and others pointed out, she herself was becoming more and more demanding. During this period, she relied on her executive editors, Jean Chiesa and Mary McDonough Phillips, to manage the day-to-day workings of the magazine.

Carmel Snow at the Paris collections, spring, 1956. Drawing by Feliks Topolski.

In August 1954, she hired the novelist and critic Anthony West as features editor. West had incredible credentials, both in terms of his lineage and for the all-important gossip factor that Carmel adored: he was the son of the British novelists Rebecca West and the much-older H. G. Wells, who, at the time of his son's birth, in 1914, had been fifty—and married to someone else. Wells had died in 1946, but had made his reputation decades earlier with such works as *The Time Machine* (1895) and *The Invisible Man* (1897). His *War of the Worlds,* turned into a radio drama by Orson Welles after the war, had sown panic across America and beyond, with its realistic depiction of Martians landing on Earth.

The son of these two luminaries had made his own name, notably as a literary critic for *The New Yorker.* Still, he floundered at *Bazaar.* "A stout man and quite superior, he was rather bewildered by the whole thing," Edson says. During his tenure at the magazine he published *Heritage,* a fictional account of a son torn

(*From right*) Carmel, Richard Avedon, and Marie-Louise Bousquet at a Dior collection, mid-1950s

between two high-powered, world-famous parents who weren't married to each other. It was a hot topic (and the first chapter, needless to say, was published in *Bazaar*). But he was gone soon after. "Guess he made so much money with *the* book he didn't need us, and besides I don't think he was too happy here," Dorothy Edson wrote to Tynan.

In late 1955, Ann Murphy Vose, *Bazaar*'s sportswear editor, was invited by one of the magazine's biggest advertisers, Bernhard Altmann, a Viennese knitwear manufacturer that went back four generations, on a press trip to that city to commemorate the reopening of the opera house of the famed Vienna State Opera, which had burned for two days and two nights at the end of World War II. The Austrian capital was only just "coming back from the war," Vose says. "The opening of the opera was a huge thing. Mrs. Snow heard about the trip and she wanted to come." She had only to ask. Carmel enlisted Cartier-Bresson to photograph the event and, from the time the *Bazaar* entourage, which included executive editor Mary Phillips, arrived in the Austrian capital, "we couldn't have been treated more royally, from the car and chauffeur put at our disposal to the apartment filled with flowers and chocolates, complete with personal maid." The opera was Beethoven's *Fidelio,* a fitting choice for its chorus alone—"O Freedom! Art thou once more ours!" As it played, thirty thousand citizens thronged the sidewalks of the adjoining streets in a driving rain, listening to the music as it was piped outside. The opening "was an enormous deal in Vienna," Vose recalls, "such a big deal that when you drove to the opera people along the side of the streets clapped."

For Cartier-Bresson, who hated opera "because he couldn't understand how one could watch and listen at the same time," according to his biographer, Pierre Assouline, the assignment was less than joyous. He survived it "by placing himself in a corner so he could listen without having to look." And he shot, of course, acres of photographs of the crisply formal Viennese, from the Austrian president on down, in attendance, their faces revealing far more than they suspected, as so many of this photographer's subjects seem to do. The opening was followed by a fancy ball, at which "the young girls of Viennese Society" and others waltzed to the "Blue Danube," just the kind of thing the Viennese do best; ditto, the next morning when a mass was sung by the Vienna Boys' Choir.

Coverage in *Harper's Bazaar* was ecstatic—"The new building is as perfect for sound as it is for spectacle"—and went on for page after page. The last one was the payback: a double-page spread, shot by Avedon, of a ripe-looking Suzy Parker in knits by Bernhard Altmann, including a two-piece evening dress of pale blue cashmere, with a square neckline edged in black.

In this same period, Carmel traveled back to Ireland, this time accompanied by her friend, the Polish-born beauty product whiz Helena Rubinstein who—to the editor's delight—always called her "Caramel." The two women went to see Sybil Connolly, whose career Carmel was still very much behind. And she also trav-

Carmel Snow (*second from right*) in a box at the 1955 reopening of the Vienna State Opera

eled closer to home, when, in May 1955, she gave a speech at the College of Home Economics at the Drexel Institute of Technology in Philadelphia. Her talk, probably written by Eleanor Perényi, had an elegiac quality: it was the summing up of a philosophy, a life, a career. Again and again, she chipped away at the subject of fashion, what it is, where it comes from, pointing out, famously, that "elegance is good taste *plus* a dash of daring." Her images tended to the airborne: "Fashion is an element mysterious as uranium and just as explosive, but light—lighter than air," she said at one point; at another, "Inspiration comes out of the air we breathe. And that air is free for all."

Back in New York, on Fifty-seventh Street, much less ethereal discussions were taking place. The men of the Hearst organization had come to believe that *Bazaar*'s editor in chief was obsolete. "Carmel was failing," says Dick Deems.

> *She was failing in many ways. About three years before she retired I said, "Carmel, why don't you select someone to work with you and train such a person?" and she stared at me. She didn't give me an answer. She*

didn't lift a finger, but she looked at me as if to say "This is my fiefdom." It was her baby.

And she went back to her work as if nothing had been said.

On the home front, Carmel enthusiastically welcomed a new rash of grandchildren: her daughter Carmel gave birth to her second, yet another Carmel, in 1952, and in 1955, Brigid Flanigan had her first, also a daughter, and also one who shared a first name with her mother; young Brigid's sister, Sheila, was born the following year. During this period, the neighborhood around the Black and Whites seemed to be declining, with some disturbing side effects, i.e., rats. After a burglary, the Snows decided that it was time to move. The robbery itself was minor—a neighborhood boy had climbed in a window and stolen Champagne from the refrigerator—but it seemed like a symptom of change, and not for the better. (As for the theft, Carmel brought charges, then dropped them after the boy agreed to pay her back. When he did so, she returned the funds, secretly, to his mother.)

The decision to move was a reluctant one. There were certain things that Carmel determined that she could not live without—that river view and a living room so open and enormous it seemed to go on for a city block. Needless to say, given these requirements, the search was protracted. But then, in 1956, it was over, when the Snows took over a rambling apartment at 530 East Eighty-sixth Street. Best of all, there was family nearby: Thornton and Carmel Wilson lived with their small children on the other side of the building on the same floor. The living room issue was neatly solved by knocking out two partitions "to Palen's dismay," including one between the living and dining rooms, to create just the kind of vast central area Carmel adored. She decorated the place with her usual élan, filling the living room with floral prints and color; the red couch, once again, took center stage. The walls were full of photos of friends, and there was a wonderful, color-shot painting by Raoul Dufy above the mantelpiece. ("Dufy is pleasure," as Gertrude Stein once wrote in *Bazaar*.) As always, Carmel kept the apartment full of cut flowers, and there she entertained, usually in solitary splendor, wearing floor-length Balenciaga housecoats, in mauve and other pastels.

Carmel never acknowledged the conversation with Deems, just as she resolutely ignored all of the hints, large and small, that came increasingly her way. She never entertained the idea of a possible successor at her magazine. The inevitable was coming, but she refused to face it. She seemed to think that by staring it down, as she'd down so many adversaries over the years, it would somehow go away. She continued to run *Bazaar,* but on increasingly shaky ground. In mid-July 1956, Charles Rolo replaced West as features editor. Rolo was a glamorous figure—born in Egypt of British parents, educated at Oxford and the Columbia School of Journalism. He came from the *Atlantic Monthly,* where he'd been a Middle Eastern and European correspondent before becoming its literary editor. Worldly and suave, he was just the sort Carmel swooned over, and Dorothy Edson, for one, found her role diminished as a result. "I was there a long time but then she fell in love with Charles Rolo, sort of a man about town. She liked him and she hired him. She didn't replace me but I wasn't as welcome as I'd been." As with Balenciaga, it was for Carmel a friendship with a bit of a crush. And he was a companion for her lonely evenings.

Another newcomer was Barbara Slifka, who joined the *Bazaar* staff just out of college for $37.50 a week ("They don't get many college graduates for that," she says). She started on Vreeland's staff, working for D. D. Prest (who had become D. D. Ryan, having married Barry Ryan, of the same family that her long-ago predecessor Eleanor Barry had married into—and, alas, with the same results: this union, too, ended acrimoniously). Vreeland then was "far more interesting than she became in her later years," Slifka says. Like others, she found that the venerable fashion editor had a certain, unexpected naïveté. She recalls strolling along a Manhattan street with Vreeland one day when the latter was wearing a very-attention-getting black-and-white pony-skin jacket. "She was walking down the street, saying, 'Don't you think there are such odd people on Madison Avenue today?'—but everyone was looking at *us*!" When Slifka pointed to a red Jaguar convertible, exclaiming at how ostentatious it seemed, Vreeland contradicted her. “My dear,” she explained, “that’s like tying a red ribbon in your hair!” Slifka understood entirely. “That’s why Diana was wonderful. She had the big picture.”

Wonderful or not, the fashion editor could be impossible to work for: the day came when Slifka “could stand it no longer,” she says. “You either liked Mrs. Vreeland or you didn’t. I went to Mrs. Snow and said I couldn’t bear it another minute. She knew exactly what I meant.” Slifka ended up taking over Shopping Bazaar, a bit of a thankless task, since this catalogue-type section featured all sorts of unappealing items, from accessories to kitchen items—“Heart-shaped baskets for serving Coeur à la Creme,” anyone?—some tossed in as a payback to advertisers. “You had to find it and photograph it and write the script,” explains Carmel’s daughter Brigid, who, like her sister Carmel Wilson, once did time as the section’s editor. “The script was always about ‘the most beautiful blah-blah.’ ”

Now just below seventy, Carmel reigned serenely as ever over her staff. Even as viper-tongued a critic as Cecil Beaton was in her thrall. He’d begun free-lancing for *Bazaar* again, shooting, among numerous other portraits, a 1956 one

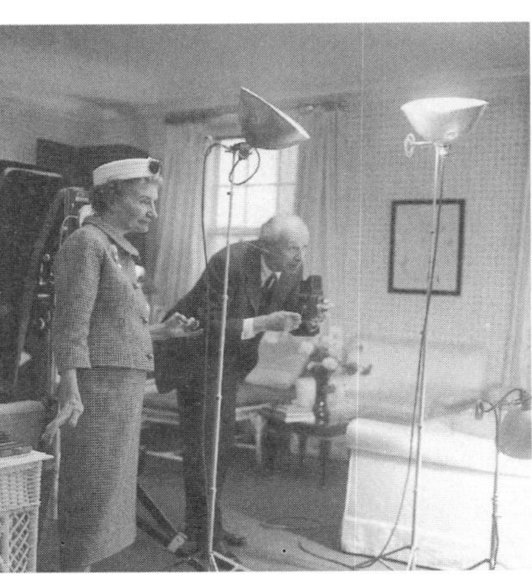

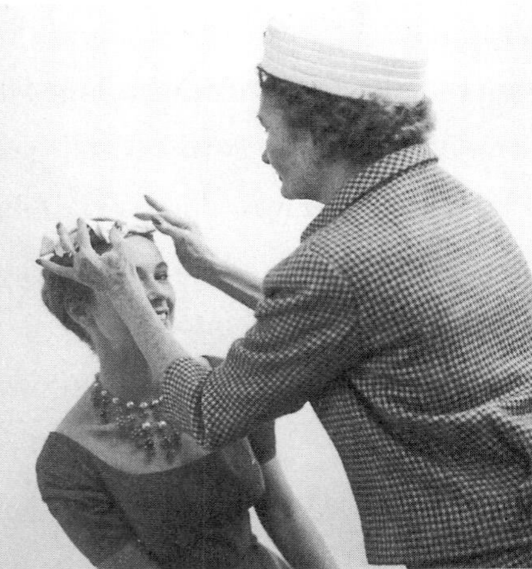

ABOVE AND CENTER: Carmel Snow with photographer Cecil Beaton during a 1956 photo shoot of the actress Vera Miles

RIGHT: Beaton’s Vera Miles portrait, as it ran in the July 1956 issue of *Bazaar*

OPPOSITE: Richard Avedon and Fred Astaire on the set of *Funny Face,* 1955

of the young actress Vera Miles, who was then starring in Alfred Hitchcock's *The Wrong Man.* Thirty years after he'd first met—and been awed by—Carmel, Beaton's experience of working with her was little changed. "Despite all her years on the staff [she] has never lost her innate enthusiasm and lettuce-crisp enjoyment. She is an inspiration," he wrote in his diary, praising "the offhand way in which she whipped up her confectionery with the slightest effort. She worked with the minimum staff, and seemed to enjoy the impromptu."

In 1957, *Bazaar* was immortalized, in a way, with the release of the movie musical *Funny Face,* directed by Stanley Donan, scored by George Gershwin, and inspired by the real-life goings-on at the magazine. The character of Maggie Prescott—played by Kay Thompson, a high-strung, nightclub-singing, Eloise-writing, one-woman extravaganza—was based on Vreeland, "except for the Balenciaga hats," according to A. G. Allen; that touch, of course, came from Carmel. Thompson strutted through the film, making weird pronouncements, concocting unlikely trends ("Think Pink!"). Fred Astaire played Dick Avery, inspired by Avedon, who falls in love—and who wouldn't?—with a dreamy young intellectual with top model potential played by Audrey Hepburn (who'd been a real-life *Bazaar* cover girl just the year before). Other parts were played by such *Bazaar* staples as the models Dovima and Suzy Parker. The whole thing was over the top, yet wickedly true to life.

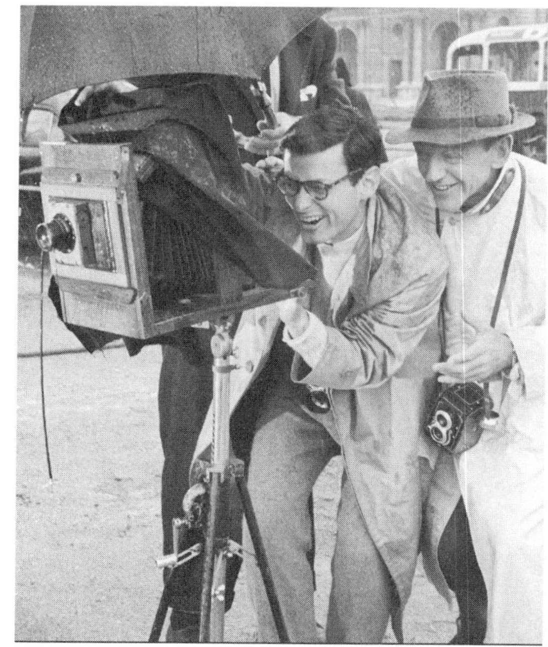

Carmel supported the movie to such an extent that she and the magazine received a "thank-you" in the film's closing credits. Avedon had the title of "special visual consultant" to the movie, and the *Bazaar* staff pitched in to help; Slifka recalls that "in the accessories office we painted all the accessories pink" as props for the film. The whole staff, it seemed, trooped off en masse to its first screening in New York, just before its commercial release. The movie is a broad parody of the fashion world, which, God knows, lends itself to such a thing. It was merciless, in its way, particularly in its depiction of Vreeland, who came off, quite frankly, as ludicrous, waving a long cigarette holder and waxing incoherent. As the movie, which borders on high camp, rolled on there were titters in the audience, but a stony silence emanated from the direction of Vreeland. When the show was over and the lights restored, the editor got up with great dignity; as she left the screening room she uttered one brief sentence to the young editor at her side. "Mrs. Vreeland marched out saying, 'Never to be discussed,'" Slifka recalls. And the movie wasn't, ever, at least in her presence.

In the same year, *Harper's Bazaar* dabbled in the newly minted medium of television, collaborating with Dave Garroway on the *Wide, Wide World* television show on March 31, 1957, beaming the fashions featured in the magazine's April issue to an audience of thirty million. An Avedon photo showed the "almost imperturbable" Dave Garroway, the show's host, being attacked by a frenzied model—all in fun, of course.

Whatever Hearst management thought of her in this period, Carmel was still very much the editor in chief, routinely making difficult decisions. Beth Levine, a shoe designer who worked for her husband's firm, Herbert Levine, which made high-end shoes, recalls that, in about 1957, she came up with a line of pointed-toe, open-back styles that, by accident, ended up being offered as an exclusive to both *Vogue* and *Harper's Bazaar.* Carmel and Vreeland had already decided to feature the style, and had even had it photographed, when word came in that the rival magazine was planning to do the same and was not inclined to back down. "Finally *Harper's* had to pull it and *Vogue* showed it," Levine recalled. The wasted money and effort was considerable, but Carmel, apparently, didn't hold a grudge: to Levine's astonishment, she featured another shoe from the same line on *Bazaar*'s cover just a few months later. "Carmel Snow was not in the business of having petty fights," Levine says. "She was in the business of doing her job. I thought it showed great integrity and understanding."

She still had a hand in everything as a very junior, Japanese-born photographer and former Brodovitch assistant named Hiro discovered when he began contributing to *Bazaar* in 1958, at the age of twenty-eight. Hiro, whose name was actually Yasuhiro Wakabayashi, had done only a few assignments for the magazine, and had dealt mainly with Brodovitch, when he was invited, along with others on the staff, to a party at the Snows. There, he was surprised to discover, the editor in chief he'd met only in passing before was "very acutely aware of what was going on at the magazine. I was startled at how aware of every detail she was. She knew exactly what I was doing at any time."

For this young Japanese photographer, who would become known for his surprising, sometimes surreal images, the sight of the *Bazaar* team at work was indelible. "Sometimes I'd come into the office when they were closing an issue and I'd see Carmel Snow and Brodovitch working together, laying the layout on the floor. I won't forget it." These encounters had taken place so often that, to a new arrival, it must have seemed as if the pair, and the editors around them, were taking part in an ancient ritual; the art director and editor knew each other, and each other's taste, so well by then that they scarcely needed to talk.

Like Carmel, Brodovitch was receiving increasing recognition; he won the Robert Leavitt Award from the American Society of Magazine Photographers in 1954. But at around this period, he began to fall away. There were moments of high inventiveness, among them a December 1954 cover with bright stars silk-screened over an Avedon image of a model wearing a pale satin Madame Grès evening coat, lined in curly white wool. Even so, A. G. Allen, who had gone back to work in the art department as Brodovitch's assistant, remembers that

> *It got to the point where Brodovitch was not interested in the* Bazaar. *He was tired. . . . He'd gotten so jaded with the whole business. There was a year or so when he just stayed in East Hampton and I would do the*

layouts and I would go out in a limousine once a month. I'd really learned his kind of spacing and placement. I was really kind of doing what he would do. I'd have a couple of drinks and go back.

Carmel and he rarely crossed paths outside of the office. "I don't think Brodovitch saw her socially," says Allen. "His wife Nina and he loved animals, but not people. I don't think he saw anyone from *Bazaar.*" His home life remained turbulent—perhaps tragic is the better word. His son, who had a lifelong fascination with fire, may have been behind the destruction of the family's country home in Phoenixville, Pennsylvania, a farmhouse that went up in flames in 1956, destroying not only most of Brodovitch's negatives from *Ballet,* his greatest work, but his collection of signed lithographs by Picasso and Matisse. The family's East Hampton residence would burn a few years later. At about this time, the art director set about "drinking himself to death," one observer says.

Carmel was heading in the same direction, some believed. "In the later years I realized she was drinking a lot," her niece Kate White says. "She was pickled in alcohol and that was sort of preserving her." At some point she seemed to slide over into drinking, not just at meals and in the evening, but throughout the day. "Carmel Snow used to keep a bottle of vodka in her desk toward the end of her career," says Trotta. "She'd take a nip from time to time. There was no trace of it on [her] breath. It was a perfectly safe drink from that point of view." Her propensity was well known. She didn't always go to New York fashion shows—usually only when she was on the scent of a hot new designer—but when she did, those who ran them learned to be prepared. One retail executive recalls that, when word came that the famous editor would be attending a show at her store, "my job was to stand at the elevator and wait for Mrs. Snow and guide her to her seat because it was always a two-thirty show and she'd been out for lunch and she'd obviously had too much to drink. I'd take her arm and guide her to her seat. She was always very polite."

People accommodated Carmel's alcoholism in a way that seems unfathomable to us today. She was surrounded by enablers, in the current parlance. There's no record of anyone confronting her on the subject. (So many others, after all, were in the same state.) Eleanor Perényi, who took over the task of writing Carmel's Fashion Group speeches after McFadden departed, recalls working on them together at the East Eighty-sixth Street apartment, where they would go over the latest styles, which Carmel would have spirited back from Paris. "She'd work fine all day but at five o'clock in would come Brigid with a great big stiff whiskey in a Manhattan glass. In a little while she'd be half seas over. It didn't take much. She didn't weigh twenty pounds soaking wet." The whole procedure, to the younger editor, was dispiriting.

Back in New York, the climate at *Bazaar* was changing—painfully, from Carmel's point of view. Increasingly, business considerations trumped aesthetic ones. The elegant, understated covers that had reigned for so long—great photography and fashion for its own sake—were beginning to resemble those found on newsstands today, with large, attention-getting cut lines. (One from the mid-1950s, "Sex Enters the Ice Age," must be one of the first, if not *the* first, to use that so-recently-forbidden word to sell a magazine, an idea that has become by now, how to put it, deeply old.) Both Carmel and Brodovitch were being overridden by the Hearst establishment much more frequently, ironically enough, than when the Chief himself was alive.

"The last two years that Carmel was there it was a real fight to keep a certain freedom," Allen says. "I watched it changing. That was a very sad time for all of us, when we had to do much more for advertisers." And what they wanted counted more and more. It was no longer enough for *Bazaar* to be brilliant or to elevate its readers, apparently unmoved by the fact that its numbers were eternally second to *Vogue*'s. The push was on to sell more magazines, so that advertising rates, and therefore revenues, would rise. Carmel was still at the top of the masthead, but the control that had been so assuredly hers for a quarter of a century was slipping away. The tension was becoming palpable, as was the chat, whispered and otherwise, about how long she could continue in her job. The pressure kept building; it got to the point that, on her evenings out with A. G. Allen, Carmel—so gifted a talker—seemed scarcely able or willing to speak.

At about this time, Mary Butler, a secretary at *Town & Country* magazine, was at a Fashion Group show with a coworker, Margaret Thilly, when the latter whispered to her that the great Carmel Snow had just entered the room. The editor, "who was super shaky on her pins" at that point, was being guided to her table by Nancy White. "The buzz at her appearance was noticeable and reverent," Butler reports. "To see an icon and someone once so powerful fading and almost a ghost was difficult. She was such a frail little thing to have been such a giant."

And then the inevitable happened. "After three years we thought from a management standpoint that we had to make a decision," Deems recalls. In early 1957, Carmel was told that her tenure would end within the calendar year and that her successor would be coming to work by her side to make the transition easier. Carmel could still cover the Paris shows after her retirement, acting as a paid consultant to the magazine. It was "a bargain with the devil, that she could continue to go to the collections," in Dorothy Wheelock Edson's words. "They paid her to do those pages." It was the only consolation. "As long as I am alive the chances are I shall always cover the Paris collections," she said.

The search had gone fairly smoothly, with the Hearst organization settling on a choice from within its family of magazines. Her identity, though, must have come as a shock: it was Nancy White Paine (who would later become Nancy Thompson, but always use her maiden name professionally), Carmel's goddaughter and niece, who was fashion editor at *Good Housekeeping.* In the Hearst organization's view, White was up to much more than that particular magazine, which aimed to teach its readers exactly what its title implies. "She had gone to Paris," Deems said. "She was a much more rounded fashion editor than just selecting fashion images for *Good Housekeeping.* Carmel and her niece were very close. We thought it was a good move because Carmel steadfastly refused to do anything."

It must have seemed like a cruel joke. For years, whenever the subject of grooming Nancy for her job had been raised, by her brother Tom and others, Carmel had rejected the idea on the grounds that the young woman wasn't tough enough. "Aunt Carmel said of Nancy. 'To do this kind of job you have to be a fighter and Nancy is not a fighter,'" Kate White recalls. Carmel had occasionally, over the years, talked about potential successors, had even entertained hopes for Mary Palen in this regard, but Nancy was not the person she had in mind. "They had two very different approaches," adds White. "Nancy would go and analyze a fabric and say, 'That would stand in the wash.'" In short, "Good Housecooking." For Carmel, that same piece of fabric might speak volumes about where fashion had come from, and where it might end up.

The news of her imminent demise at *Bazaar* came as a blow to others, too. "When Mrs. Snow got the word that she was no longer going to be editor, Diana Vreeland went in and said, 'Was my name mentioned?'" Edson recalls. "Mrs. Snow said, 'Your name never came up, Diana,' incensed at the very idea that Diana could take her job." Some believe that Carmel took a more proactive role than she ever acknowledged in ensuring that *Bazaar*'s editorship would never go to her colleague. "The rumor was that when Carmel Snow had retired as editor in chief at *Harper's Bazaar*, she urged the men running Hearst Magazines to pass Vreeland over for the job, arguing that she lacked the discipline and judgment to head a magazine," Grace Mirabella wrote. Allen concurs with this view, adding that Vreeland "was a brilliant fashion editor who should never, ever, be editor in chief of a magazine."

It wasn't a hard point to get across. Virtually no one at *Bazaar* thought Vreeland could handle an executive role. Her eye was the thing—and her legend, of course—not her management skills. "Carmel was much better," Nancy White said. "Much. Vreeland was always late with her pages, she was always late with this and always late with that. She was this wonderful prima donna with marvelous words coming out. But you can't really run a railroad that way." Even as distant an observer as the couturier Marc Bohan felt that "Diana was a bit above reality. Her business plan wasn't always obvious." In particular, the advertising department—now more important than ever—was anathema to her. "She was impossible with advertisers. She snubbed all the advertising department—quite rightly," Eleanor Perényi says. "She was much too eccentric and really frankly original. [Hearst management] couldn't take it." As for Vreeland's subsequent claims that she ran the magazine in

Nancy White, 1950s

Carmel's later years, they're probably best left untouched. She could say anything. Her humiliation at being passed over must have been absolute.

White began working at the magazine in early 1957 and her name appeared on the masthead as assistant editor, just under her aunt's name, in April of that year. It was the second name listed, and it would soon supplant the first. The time that followed was an agony. Carmel refused to acknowledge her niece's existence, attempting to do her own work as if nothing had changed. And she didn't do so tranquilly. "From the moment we brought Nancy over, Carmel wouldn't tolerate her, wouldn't work with her, and was constant trouble," Deems says. "We had trouble getting the magazine out. Suddenly everything that had gone so well was high confusion."

White had adored her aunt since before she'd cried out at her wedding, "You won't be mine anymore." She had been "thrilled to death," she wrote, when her famous aunt sent her a note in January 1948 complimenting the fashion pages she'd done for that month's *Good Housekeeping*. "I've shown it to everybody within a radius of 50 miles." The two women had their profession in common, as well as the strange fact, noted by many on the *Bazaar* staff, that their new editor in chief *pro tem* was also digitally challenged: The tips of two of her fingers had been missing from birth. The transition to the top of the masthead can't have been easy—in fact, it sounds impossible—but White seems to have managed it with grace. "She behaved toward her aunt the way Dick behaved toward her," according to Stutz, that is, with absolute solicitousness. It wasn't reciprocated. It must have been mortifying for White, relatively young for the job, and following in such famous footsteps, to see how little Carmel thought of her. "I think she was very intimidated by her aunt," says Carmen dell'Orefice, who knew both women at the beginning of her long modeling career.

Somehow the magazine kept being published, and somehow it continued to surprise. It may have lost the visual zing it had had when Brodovitch was in his prime, but the ingredients were still there. During this period it included an article on plastic surgery—a radical concept at the time—as well as some previously unpublished stories by Anton Chekhov that had just turned up in the Soviet Union. An American woman, a patient of a certain Dr. Lamaze in Paris, reported on the miracle of painless childbirth. An eerie blurred early photograph of Elvis Presley ran not long after Cecil Beaton's famous image of Marilyn Monroe did, along with his accompanying text calling her "a make-believe siren, unsophisticated as a Rhine maiden, innocent as a sleepwalker." (Really?) Warhol was still a familiar credit, his fifteen minutes of obscurity clearly behind him. And Bacall was back, on the eve of the opening of her new MGM film *Designing Women,* looking deliciously world weary, although still in her early thirties, sexy as always, posing in a square-cut velvet cocktail dress by Larry Aldrich, a cigarette holder clasped in her left hand.

Another beauty, Tanaquil Le Clercq, the New York City Ballet star, looks beatific, photographed in her New York hospital room after having been struck down by polio the year before. And there are others, always others, among them a blond teenager named Brigitte Bardot. To glance through these pages is to be struck by the never-ending nature of it all, the talent and beauty that always seems to be building up, like waves, before, inevitably, far in the distance, crashing back down again. Even Junior Bazaar seemed to shine, literally, with a short belted trench coat of gold lamé on its cover by a firm called Junior Sophisticates, whose founder and designer was a young woman named Anne Klein. And there would be more to come: at one point in this last year Carmel acquired first serial rights to Truman Capote's latest novel, a frivolity entitled *Breakfast at Tiffany's,* scheduled to be published by Random House.

Carmel at last seemed to prepare for retirement in her own mind, at some point deciding that "the only place I could cheerfully retire *to* was Ireland." When she confided her dream to her old acquaintance and hibernophile, the film director John Huston—then the owner of St. Cleran's, a beautiful manor house in County Galway—he sounded a cautionary note: "It's fine if you can get away from it." As Carmel wrote, "I realized this was true, at least in the winter."

She traveled to Dublin, no doubt relishing the escape from the fraught atmosphere at 572 Madison. Ever connected, she met with the well-known architect Michael Scott, whom she recruited to help find a house. She had always loved Ireland's Atlantic coast, "even though during the Famine the inhabitants would say, 'We're from Mayo, God help us,'" she quipped, and it wasn't long before she found her "castle in the air" there, a nine-bedroom, eighteenth-century residence called Rockfleet, located a few miles from the town of Newport on a dramatically beautiful, very private seeming body of water called Raigh Bay, an inlet on the north side of Clew Bay.

Without stopping to consult Palen on the matter, she purchased the house and thirty surrounding acres from an Englishman, Sir Owen O'Malley, and his wife, Mary, a novelist who wrote under the pseudonym Ann Bridge, in the spring of 1957 for the sum of £9,000. She promptly renamed it Rossyvera, its original, Gaelic name. "It's the kind of place that makes you think, 'It can't get more beautiful than this.'" its current owner, Ambassador Walter Curley, says. It's not just the matchless setting, with its ever-changing sky and water, but the Adam-style house itself—almost unbelievably solid, with double thick masonry walls. The house was vast, containing, "besides hall, landings and offices, four sitting rooms, nine bedrooms, and three bathrooms," as the *Irish Tatler and Sketch* described it in the early 1950s. Its more striking features manifested themselves at the front door: a skylit, elliptical-shaped entrance hall led into an octagonal drawing room with enormous windows overlooking the water. Like so many old houses, it had been "built a bit higgledy-piggledy over generations," Curley says.

The property included Carrigahowley Castle, a fifteenth-century ruin just

Rossyvera, County Mayo, Ireland

adjacent to the house, a national monument that was once the home of another forceful Irishwoman: Grainne Uaile, aka Grace O'Malley, the famous pirate queen, who moved there after the death of her second husband in 1583, establishing it as her prime keep. (Very incidentally, the castle was "ranked number one in a book of the world's unusual toilets," says Sean Chambers, who now manages the property, referring to one room just over the bay with a hole in its floor. "It's a straight shot down and the tide comes in twice a day.") Another nearby structure, Roigh House, half a mile away, was owned by a New York friend of the Snows, James Johnson Sweeney, the first director of the Guggenheim Museum, from whom Carmel had commissioned articles on twentieth-century artists for *Bazaar*.

Knowing that Rossyvera—her future haven—was there must have helped in the difficult months ahead. Back in New York, Carmel returned to an impasse. She continued trying to do her job as if her statuesque, blond niece hadn't moved into an office down the hall. It wasn't easy. The fact that others on the staff shared Carmel's dismissive opinion of Nancy only made the atmosphere more fraught.

Many thought, as D. D. Ryan did, that she "was never, ever, ever meant to be an editor. She was meant to sell ad space which is why Carmel never trained her to take her place. She was a Hearstling, one of the boys." Still, she was in, while Carmel was on the way out. There were distractions, occasionally even a wonderful one, such as the impending arrival of yet another grandchild (Brigid was pregnant again). But, mainly, her well-ordered life was coming apart.

Carmel headed back to Europe for the couture that summer on her last trip as editor in chief. Gwen Randolph Franklin, the editor she'd fired during the war to free up a job for Louise Macy, had returned as fashion editor, working closely with Vreeland, and she accompanied Carmel to Paris, as did Avedon, traveling with model Suzy Parker. "Paris is a blaze of color," Carmel reported. Hemlines, once again, were on the up and up. There were slender dresses of "discreet perfection" at Dior and "bouffantly feminine" ones at Lanvin- Castillo. Balmain came up with a standout in the form of an ermine evening blouse. One Jacques Fath dress with an inverted pleat in back gave women a "faintly bustled Seurat look," while Balenciaga's suits, by contrast, made them look noodle thin.

Avedon created some of his more famous Paris fashion images on this trip, among them the one of Suzy Parker, bundled in a sumptuous mohair "kill coat" by Lanvin-Castillo and dashing through the Tuileries with a man in a kilt at her side, their faces lit with joy. In another photo, a model posing next to a ladder-climbing, seminude dancer at the Moulin Rouge seems to float in a Griffe columnar evening dress, "twisted to fall like a great, gossamer scarf." The photographer was on a roll, moving from strength to strength. On the last day of the showings, he came up with the idea of photographing models in front of narrow wooden planks, then did some shots with this theme in the *Bazaar* studio. "I was building the surprising use of these planks," he says. The background pleased him; the models leaning against it, to his mind, set the clothes off to advantage. He left his contact sheets at the San Régis for Carmel's approval, then, with the trip over and his work done, headed off with some friends to celebrate. "The last picture was this beautiful Dior dress. I left it in her box."

When he returned, there was a note in his hotel mailbox, asking him to stop by her suite.

> *I walked into that little salon where I'd been a million times before to see Carmel. She was alone, sitting bolt upright in a chair facing the door. I didn't have time to say a single word. Looking straight ahead of her she said.* "Not in my magazine! *I* will not *have a distinguished dress photographed on a plank. . . ."*
>
> *I was established by then, remember. For no one else in the world would I have taken that picture over—not for her, six months before. But I suddenly thought, "For a woman to care that much at this moment! To sit up for hours waiting to let me have it because this is her last appearance as the editor of her magazine!" I said, "I'll take the picture over with pleasure."*
>
> *She said, "Thank you," and walked into her bedroom.*

He adds: "It was like the last thing between us. She knew she'd been fired. I wouldn't have dreamed of not obeying her to the letter at that moment."

There was a new protocol to expediting photos to New York, Franklin recalls.

> *The fashion editor would leave with the last batch of pictures for the deadline. The maid would pack the photos in with their clothes. Carmel . . . [would] say to me, "Don't let the captions people mix up the photos and, by the way, could you take a couple of hats over for me?"*

The latter presented a problem since Franklin, like a true Vreeland acolyte, imitated her mentor by wearing snoods, not hats. "Gwen, just put it on on top of your head," Carmel snapped impatiently. "They won't know anything about your not wearing hats." Franklin obeyed. "You couldn't resist, you wanted to help her out."

It was Carmel's last trip to Paris as the head of *Harper's Bazaar.* It was an inescapable fact. She knew she'd return to that city as a consultant for the magazine, but she must also have known that it would never be the same. It was over. She didn't leave the spotlight gracefully. She couldn't. She became "very demanding and very insulting," Avedon recalled. And her drinking was worse than ever. Learning that a huge party was to be given at one of the Rothschild mansions, Carmel asked Bousquet to wangle an invitation on her behalf. Avedon tells the story tersely, without embellishment. (None is needed.)

> *Carmel heard about it and said she wanted to go. She drank. There was a large stairway. She peed on the stairway and Marie-Louise had to take her home. End of story.*

Some who witnessed this moment, even those who had loved her for so long, found it unforgivable. In Paris, appearances trump everything, and Carmel hadn't kept up her end. It doesn't matter that she was "beautifully turned out," as one buyer describes her, always, to the last. Or that she'd been decorated by the government for the work she'd done for France. Chic or not, devoted or not, she'd lost her composure, and that, in this milieu, was fatal. "Life in general, and Parisian life in particular," as Edith Wharton once wrote, "is the cause of many such effacements." Wharton was writing of Cocteau, but the phenomenon remains the same. Carmel's reputation was compromised to such a degree that it was indeed an effacement, and in the place that mattered most. The news preceded Carmel to New York, arriving well before she did. "The word came back that there had been a catastrophe," recalls Perényi, who was by then a features editor working under Charles Rolo. "She'd gotten drunk and embarrassed herself. It was noticed very much in Paris. It didn't go over well there." The fashion capital is tough, its verdicts irreversible. It was an ignoble end to a triumphant career in that city.

Carmel probably never knew how fast, and how far, that story traveled. She took her time returning from France, spending the rest of August 1957 at Rossyvera, readying it for her retirement. Palen, Carmel, and Brigid came to visit, returning to New York with amusing stories about their mother on her native soil. She shopped for antiques in Dublin with Charles Rolo, putting "everything I have of taste into the furnishings. . . ." Her efforts paid off, according to Walter Curley. "You'd have walked in and said, 'Oop, it's Carmel.' It was fresh. It was flowery. It was cheerful. It was in keeping with the dignity of the house." She had the dining room painted a chartreusey-yellow, furnishing it with a ten-foot dining table for the dinner parties she envisioned taking place there, full of Paris friends and American colleagues who had stopped off at Shannon Airport on the way to and from the collections.

She went back to work, as if nothing had taken place, and as if nothing were about to. What else could she do? Some around her took heart from the fact that, in New York, "she didn't have that much of a chance to make a public fool of herself," in Perényi's harsh words, as she had so disastrously in Paris. But a short time later, she headed back to France after receiving shocking news from across the Atlantic—Christian Dior, then only fifty-two, had died of a heart attack on October 24 while in Italy on a course of treatment. The talented couturier had scarcely been in business for a decade, but was the head of a vast international empire. His creativity seemed inexhaustible. He'd only just finished writing his charmingly modest memoir, *Christian Dior et Moi.* And he'd found love, after years of frustration in his romantic life. To please his new young lover, a North African named Jacques Benita, he'd headed to Montecatini on a thinning cure, ignoring, for the first and only time, the advice of Madame Delahaye who, seeing disaster in his cards, had insisted that he not make the trip. He died on the tenth day of the regimen, just after finishing a game of canasta.

Dior's death was treated as a national tragedy in the French media—a famous photograph in *Paris Match* captured the mood by depicting his house models, dressed in mourning (by Dior, of course), leaving his funeral, trooping through the city's gray, autumnal streets, looking both ravishing and ravaged.

Carmel attended the funeral, then penned an affecting reminiscence of him for the magazine—"Triumph became a habit with him," she wrote—with contributions by both Flanner and Cocteau.

Back in the mid-1950s, Dior had hired a brilliant young Frenchman named Yves Saint Laurent, raised in Algeria and still in his teens, as a designer. St. Laurent took over the line on Dior's death, when he was only twenty-one, presenting a stellar first collection in the winter of 1958, including his famous trapeze dress, a flared A-line dress with a nonexistent waist, a daring repudiation of Dior's own New Look. It was a triumph, as were other styles. In the course of this one fashion show, the House of Dior, its future so recently in doubt, was saved. The national mood turned jubilant and another famous photograph was flashed around the world—of the almost morbidly sensitive-looking young man, wearing black-rimmed glasses and a somber mien, standing pensively on a balcony over the avenue Montaigne, as media from all over the world gathered in the street below (shades of the New Look). Another promising Dior assistant, Marc Bohan, who had just been hired that year, went off to head up Dior's enterprise in London.

Back in New York, life at *Bazaar* was more grim than ever. One of the few bright spots came in September 1957, in the form of a letter from John Appleton, an editor at Harper and Brothers, with

> *a sneaky inquiry about whether you had thought of taking any time to write about yourself. . . . Although we probably cannot claim to have been the first to approach you, I hope you will accept this note as evidence of our continuing interest in a book by Carmel Snow. . . .*

Carmel replied, saying, "I could not possibly be more flattered by your letter," on October 1, but then—not surprisingly, given the increasing tension in her working days—the correspondence between them seemed to stop.

"In the last few weeks, when Nancy had already started to work [at *Bazaar*] and before Carmel left she was one step before a basket case," Trotta recalls. "It was a really sad ending. They overlapped. . . . Carmel was such a brilliant woman and she had made such a difference in publishing. . . . It's terrible to end like that. It's so sad. You have to know when the party is over." And it was indeed over—the lights had dimmed, the music fallen silent. The clock struck midnight, but she didn't quite leave. "They practically had to take her out under duress," adds Gwen Randolph Franklin. "She'd hardly quit than fly. You can hardly blame her." Her boss's firing was particularly painful for Franklin because, only a few years earlier, Carmel had faced down Fifty-seventh Street on her behalf, pushing to get her a decent salary and equal billing to Vreeland as fashion editor. "She was there backing me up all the way. A year or two went by and they really wanted her to get out. They don't do anything correctly."

It was only fitting, for such a devout Catholic, that Carmel's last issue was a Christmas one. She'd always done something special for December, usually a page or two with a religious theme, a reminder that the holiday had to do with more than just the ringing of retailers' cash registers. This year it was particularly Christmasy, with a gift list from a six-year-old with expensive taste named Eloise, who was clamoring for baubles from Van Cleef & Arpels or a little something to wear from Givenchy. And there was a gilt Christmas tree by Warhol that was all ornaments, no pine. The accompanying story, entitled "Merry Christmas—with Love," cheerfully opined that "any woman, giving from the heart, can have a merry Christmas." A sentiment that, from Carmel's point of view, must have seemed bitterly untrue.

"Dick Berlin was the one that got her out . . . eventually," according to her son-in-law, Thornton Wilson. He gave her the verbal shove, presumably, that finally got her to empty her desk and leave. And she did, taking boxes of office files with her. Her resignation was a euphemism. She was given a grand title—chairman of the editorial board—some limited power, and cash. "They asked her to resign and paid her a great sum," Kate White recalls.

And so it happened that, one Monday morning in the late fall of 1957, Carmel did not take a cab to 572 Madison Avenue, stopping in to say a quick rosary at one or another church on the way. She didn't step into the elevator—resplendent in Balenciaga, emanating Joy—and call out her orders, suggestions, stray thoughts, or funny stories to whichever of her staffers happened to be on board. Instead, she stayed home, as the clock ticked, minute after minute, hour after hour. *Harper's Bazaar* had been her life, and it was over. "She always said she *was* the magazine," Dorothy Edson says. All through her career, "she was in command every living minute," Dick Deems adds. And now she was not. Nancy White was listed in the magazine as editor in chief for the first time in January 1958. Carmel's name was still there, just above it, but with a new, completely meaningless title. It offered no consolation. It's no wonder that, as Edson says, "after she left she shrank."

She wasn't alone. "We were all just so depressed," Allen recalls. *Time* magazine reported that "high fashion's highest priestess" had resigned. Office morale plummeted. The triumvirate disbanded. Brodovitch lost his job at about the same time, "partly due to management changes," according to Andy Grundberg, "and partly to his increasing inability to control his drinking." Vreeland stayed on for a few years more, but everything shifted around her. And some others in the Old Guard were dispatched at the same time. Even Edson, who'd stuck with Carmel through years of ups and downs. "One day she got a pink slip with two weeks' salary," Avedon reports with outrage. "Not even. It was over."

Another victim was fictional. Holly Golightly, Capote's famously spirited protagonist, had been scheduled to make her debut in *Breakfast at Tiffany's* in the May 1958 issue.

> *Mrs. Snow had been the protector of editorial integrity, the abbess of the convent, and while she was there, the men from the publisher's office rarely had the nerve to ask questions about her fiction. Now they did, objecting to Truman's use of a few four-letter words and the relaxed lifestyle of his heroine: Holly Golightly was not exactly a call girl, but she did make her living from sex.*

To make things worse, when Nancy heard of the upcoming title, she ran it by a friend at another New York retailer, Bergdorf Goodman, to see what he thought of the idea. The idea was absurd—Tiffany's is hardly the subject of the book, whose deeper themes involve death, identity, love, and more. But, fatally, White's friend canvassed others in the retail community and relayed back to her what he'd heard. "She came back with the news that Tiffany's would be deeply offended if you published anything called *Breakfast at Tiffany's,*" an editor reports. The clamor on Fifty-seventh Street grew louder and louder. As fiction editor Alice Morris recalled:

> *They all were reading as they had never read before, word for word. I kept saying to Nancy, "This is a slightly raffish society Truman's talking about. There's nothing ugly or pornographic about it. He's only used words where they would be absolutely natural, never simply for effect. Tiffany's will someday display it in their window." Finally I got all the objections boiled down and showed the list to Truman.*
>
> *"I'm not going to change a word," he said. But finally he agreed he would. I think he said yes partly because I showed him the layouts. We had about six pages with beautiful, atmospheric photographs. Then when all the changes had been made and we were just about to send the whole thing to the printer, Nancy called me into her office and said, "I've just had a call from Dick Deems, and we're not going to be able to run* Breakfast at Tiffany's." *Without much ado,* Harper's Bazaar *had ended its long and distinguished history of printing quality fiction.*

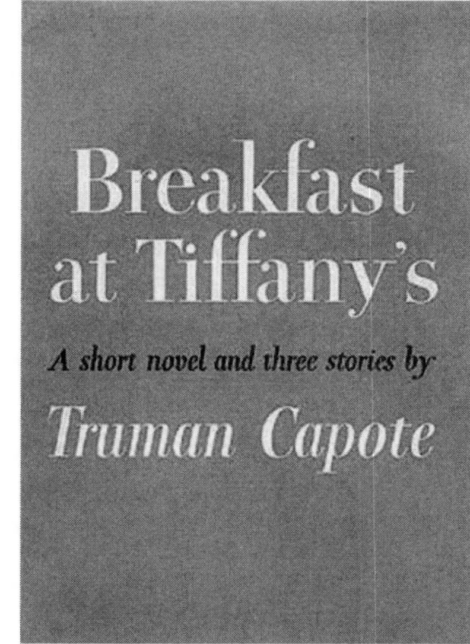

First edition cover of Capote's disputed novel, *Breakfast at Tiffany's*

Truman "never forgave the new, Snow-less *Bazaar*," his biographer Gerald Clarke wrote. Interviewed for *Newsweek*, the author said: "I'm not angry, I'm outraged—that's an entirely different thing. Publish with *them* again? Why, I wouldn't spit on their street." And Alice Morris was right. When the book came out, "the famed jeweler even devoted a window of its Fifth Avenue store to it," Clarke writes. They were, in fact, ecstatic to have the free publicity, even more so after Audrey Hepburn, then just about the most elegant person alive, starred in the movie of the same (unchallenged) name. But it was too late.

Good fiction, by the way, still turned up here and there in *Bazaar*, although much less frequently than before. But it would never again *dare* the reader, the way the fiction published under Carmel so often did. And there was no one left to do the same to the Hearst organization itself, as she had done, instinctively and often. "Nancy was more aware of the commercial aspects of the magazine," as Kate White puts it. "Perhaps she didn't have the clout" to fight back. Instead, she *was* management, almost as much as her father had been.

Nancy's tenure at *Bazaar* is beyond the scope of this story. Suffice it to say that there are two views. One, as summed up by dell'Orefice, "I don't think she wanted the post she got, but she lived up to it." The other by Polly Mellen, who says that after Carmel and, later, Vreeland, left, "I stayed on and learned mediocrity" at *Bazaar*. (She didn't last for long.) The truth, no doubt, lies somewhere between the two.

For a long time, every effort the new editor made seemed to fall short. "It was a tough thing," Gloria Moncur says, putting it mildly, "to follow in Mrs. Snow's shoes." Some staffers didn't bother to conceal their contempt. Vreeland made her famous comment—"We needed an artist and they sent us a house painter." It's easy to image how quickly *that* one traveled up and down *Bazaar*'s halls. Others joined in, their hostility palpable, fifty years after the fact. Eleanor Perényi recalled,

> *When Nancy was brought in, everyone who worked for Carmel just despised her. Let's face it, she was a totally commercially minded girl. She was a Philistine and a boob and we all pretty well formed a wall of*

hostility against her, we old-timers who had worked for Carmel for a number of years. Nancy was a disaster, and we all made her feel that she was a disaster.

And it wasn't just the "old-timers." Geri Trotta returned to the magazine, hired by White as a features editor. "She gave me this bunch of photos of basset hounds dressed as people. I refused to run it. I did something I've never done before or since. I hid the photos. I purposely lost them." Trotta's respect for White, never enormous in the first place, dwindled even further. "She didn't have the perspicacity for the job. She was as bland as oatmeal and had no capacity. She had none of Carmel's flair at all. She was square and dull."

One thing Trotta does concede is that White "was smart enough to know that she was out of her depth." Which must have made it that much more awful. Given the atmosphere, it's no surprise that she seemed to careen from one mistake to another. And, poignantly enough, there's every indication that White held her aunt in as high esteem as her own critics did. Her humility was such that she didn't move into Carmel's corner office right away. Instead, it stayed for a long while much as Bossy herself had left it, a kind of shrine suspended over Madison Avenue. But now its door was closed.

In February 1958, a month after she'd left, Carmel accompanied White to the collections. "In some ways it was all the same," Avedon recalled. But in so many ways it was not. "She came back to Paris, but she was no longer the queen," says Kate White. "Carmel realized she'd fallen from the pedestal." She still assumed the seat of honor at the couture houses, with White perching behind. But it was clear to all that, before too long, their positions would be reversed. And Carmel's friends, her undying friends, seemed less available than they had once been. "She used to go to mass with Marie-Louise Bousquet," White adds, "but as soon as Carmel was no longer the editor in chief, she never heard from Marie-Louise again." Actually, they remained in touch, although Bousquet was definitely skittish from this point on about Carmel, a condition Janet Flanner diagnosed as "some nervous feeling of a new loyalty to Nancy White. . . ." (Like everyone she was scared for her job.) According to Flanner, she also had

> *sometimes distressing memories of the weekends she spent with Carmel at [Balenciaga's] country house wherever it is in France, when Carmel was really daft on him there is no other expression & when darling Carmel was drinking too much. . . . M-L adored Carmel before the cocktail period began which carrie [sic] such occasionally [sic] costly experiences so far as the bankruptcy of the affections were concerned, in public, that her devotion underwent deviations before Nancy became her boss, which gave them an official shape. This is confidential of course.*

Paris had become joyless for her, perhaps for the first time. It may even have felt demoralizing to be traveling with Avedon—the perpetually ever-rising star ("I was so lucky to be the young person I was at that moment")—while she had entered the twilight. Still, she kept working as always, covering the collections, supervising photo shoots, editing the final results, while White tried unobtrusively to learn the ropes—with the most reluctant teacher imaginable. Everything was as normal, only nothing was.

Before heading to France, Carmel had been approached by her old friend Blanche Knopf, cofounder, with her husband, Alfred, of the publishing firm of the same name, asking whether "she might have the time and inclination to write her memoirs of the world of fashion." An internal Knopf memorandum described Carmel as "even more than Edna Woolman Chase [whose own memoir had been published in 1954], *the* fashion dictator of America." In early February, Knopf refined her vision for the project in a letter to Carmel at the San Régis, proposing that she do a book "combining two themes: 1) what fashion means and how it is created; and 2) your own life and career in the world of fashion." Knopf also mentioned that she was just back from Stockholm, where one of her authors, Albert Camus, had been awarded the Nobel Prize for Literature.

"I have had several offers such as yours," Carmel replied on February 8, adding that she was flattered by the overture and suggesting that they meet to discuss it further upon her return to New York the following month. Back in Manhattan in March 1958, she informed John Appleton, the Harper's editor, that she was in discussions with Knopf, news he described as "quite a disappointment." But by the end of the month she'd accepted another offer altogether, writing to Knopf on March 25 that she would be putting together her memoirs for an unnamed publisher, "who I explained to you had spoken to me quite a long time before you did," with Frances McFadden as her collaborator.

After Carmel left, and before too long, *Bazaar* became "a whole different entity," according to Allen. "Nancy was so different in her taste." The change was "kind of a symbol of a changing of the times," Kate White said, "from a time of perfection and style to a *Good Housekeeping* approach to life where there's suddenly frozen food and no servants." For those who'd known the old *Bazaar,* it wasn't an improvement. "The magazine was deteriorating," says the writer Marianne Hauser, who had contributed to it since the 1930s. "They took more and more advertising. It became a glorified fashion catalogue—a little more like *Vogue.*" Which would have been, of course, anathema to Carmel. As that magazine's former editor, Grace Mirabella, has written: "*Vogue* in the 1950s, in the McCarthy era, was notably silent on all that was political, or problematic, or complicated, or unpleasant. It was a picture book." It was not for a minute Carmel Snow's *Harper's Bazaar.*

She continued to try to dictate the course of events. In June 1958, after Allen gave birth to a son, "Carmel came to the hospital with my husband and said she didn't want me to go back to work at *Bazaar.* Now that she was out, she didn't want anyone she cared for staying on." The young woman acquiesced.

I was a fine assistant but I could not have been the art director. I really just knew how to work in the Brodovitch mode. They needed a change. I think Dick [Avedon] found the right person. The look was changed and

should have changed. . . . Within six months I had another job. I did it for her. She wanted me to leave and I left.

Carmel returned to Paris with White that August and into the coming years. For a time, she still had the last word about Paris fashion, only the art director who determined how to present her pages was Henry Wolf, an Austrian whom Avedon had recommended, and the editor who oversaw them was her niece. Carmel rode White just as Edna Chase had ridden her successor, firing off memos and second-guessing more or less everything she was trying to do. But Carmel was becoming rapidly obsolete; before long, her Paris pages "shriveled to nothing," in Edson's words. And while she kept up with the Fashion Group, chairing the fashion show at its September 1958 meeting, that connection, too, began to loosen. Mainly, like Dahl-Wolfe, she gradually and painfully moved on. As the photographer wrote:

> *The* Bazaar *was heaven for twenty-two years. But in 1958 Carmel Snow and Alexey Brodovitch resigned. [sic] The new art director put in a surprise visit to my studio and had the presumption to look through my ground glass at what I was photographing. This had never happened in all my years. Suddenly my enthusiasm vanished. Enthusiasm for me was half the battle. The great era of my magazine was finished . . . and so I retired to the country.*

16 into the irish mist

For a woman of my temperament, retirement is a strange experience.
—Carmel Snow

There's a madness in Ireland.
—Henri Cartier-Bresson

CARMEL, TOO, WITHDREW TO THE COUNTRY, or at least she tried to. In the summer of 1958, she decamped to County Mayo with her sister, Christine, now retired and a widow. "I wanted her to share this Irish adventure with me." She kept her apartment in New York for future visits home and for Palen, who, immersed in his American life, didn't seem likely to spend much time across the Atlantic. Rural Ireland would be hers, not his: for all its beauty and proximity to the outdoor pursuits he adored, his life was not there.

At Rossyvera, Carmel took "the ghost room," an enormous, six-sided bedroom on the third floor with three large windows overlooking the bay, so called because the house's staff believed it to be supernaturally inhabited. It was all part of their "eternal tales of ghosts and fairies which they wouldn't let us hear because they thought we wouldn't believe them," Carmel wrote. Her sister settled into a bedroom off the back staircase on the second floor, which was "warmer and quieter even in the more bitter weather," according to Walter Curley.

They hired servants, including a cook, chambermaid, and a young girl whose job it was to keep all thirteen of the house's fireplaces burning to counteract the Atlantic coast's notorious damp. The house's "steward"—caretaker, really—was a handsome man named Michael Chambers, known as "Mick," who lived in a farmhouse on the property with his wife and their brood of sixteen children; his job included more or less everything, including carpentry and chauffeuring the two women around in their "little English car." Most of their food was locally produced. The house included a dairy, just off the kitchen, where butter was churned. (Three cows were kept on the property.) There were chickens, too, and an apparently limitless supply of fruit and vegetables from its kitchen garden. Rossyvera was nothing if not open to nature: birds flew in and out, and once "Michael's enormous sow" actually took a stroll through the ground floor, "walking through the ever-open front door."

In Carmel's account, "We settled happily into the familiar round of Irish hospitality, receiving calls from all our neighbors." It wasn't a question of telephoning—the phone (number: Carrowbed 2) was cut off at seven every evening and all day Sunday—but of stopping by in person. In this and so many other ways, nothing in this part of Ireland had changed for millennia. "The past was almost tangible" at Rossyvera then, Curley says. "You could feel the past, you could touch the past. It was almost a time warp. It went back centuries. There was definitely a little worldly feeling."

The trouble is, the past wasn't really where Carmel wanted to be. Mainly, she was interested in the here and now, and she very much wanted her new home to function as a pit stop for friends crisscrossing the Atlantic. To this end, she got the house's staff in order, enlisting the help of the fireplace girl on weekends to be "put in uniform to help serve in the dining room and unpack for guests." She devised a menu that took full advantage of local produce and wildlife. "As usual my dinner-party menus were uniform: clear soup, salmon, our own vegetables (including potatoes), and a deep-dish fruit tart or some of our marvelous raspberries with thick cream." And then, mainly, she waited.

There was one big weekend party in August 1958, not long after she and Christine moved in, when Marie-Louise Bousquet, the photographer Brassai (by now well known for his imitations of his deep-voiced hostess), and his wife came from Paris, along with, at least nominally, some Irish friends from Dublin. "The

Irishmen," Christine remembers, "being thoroughly unconscious of time, arrived at midnight, so they only breakfasted with us, as the others had to return to Paris on Saturday." Carmel would occasionally head east to Dublin, usually by train, for parties at Sybil Connolly's and other entertainments. Her children came at various points, too, as well as the occasional friend or former colleague, including editor Mary Phillips, who later told friends back at the magazine that when a rat jumped onto the bottom of Carmel's bed while both women chatted in the bedroom, it hadn't bothered the steely former editor a bit. (Her visitor was less sanguine.) Rodents or not, such visits were rare.

It was as if she'd planned for a huge, festive party, and nobody turned up. It's no wonder that Dorothy Edson, who kept up with Carmel long after both had been fired, described her sojourn in Mayo as "the disaster of all time. She thought people would stop by on the way to Paris but nobody came, really. Her husband didn't like it—she bought it without consulting him. . . . As far as I know he just went once." Carmel hadn't lived in Ireland since the 1890s and she was no longer used to its ways. Its slow pace of life was charming: every encounter, whether with a dentist or fishmonger, was preceded by a long, meandering chat in which both parties appeared to have no intention of doing business with each other at all. But it had a backward side, too, that was very much not Carmel. Once, when she was sick with pneumonia, the local doctor who came to examine her was so appalled by the lacy, daring Paris nightgown she was wearing that he ordered her to put on something more modest instead. And, as for visits with her neighbors, goodwill between her and the Sweeneys, just down the road, evaporated early on in a protracted battle over water rights. "There was no love lost," in one local's words.

Ever since she'd bought the place, all through the dark, final days at *Bazaar,* Carmel had "luxuriated in the thought of being there," Curley says. She had thought it would be an ideal place to begin working on her memoirs. But the reality of life on the Irish coast proved to be daunting. "In September high tides began lapping the retaining sea wall and fierce winds began sweeping in from the Atlantic. . . . It could be lonely then. . . ." The dark tower of Carrigahowley Castle was picturesque but sinister, too. And the isolation was deadening. Carmel tried her best to beat it by, among other things, "imperiously telling Michael to take her to these outposts of civilization like Castlebar and Galway, major expeditions," according to Curley, but such diversions offered only temporary relief. Mainly, she was falling apart.

"She was notorious for drink," says McGarry Fergus, who worked on the property at the time. "You'd never see her. She was a very frail woman. She looked to be a woman of eighty." She was too fragile, even, to drive; finally, Christine, who had somehow lived for decades in the vast expanses of the American Midwest without learning how, assumed the task of transporting the pair of them around. "She learned to drive in the field in the castle side to the road," Fergus recalls. "She was out in the car in maybe six or eight days." In contrast to her sister, Christine thrived in Mayo. She painted daily, setting up her easel in the fields, and altogether seemed to enjoy her retirement. "She was the manager. She'd go to town and do the shopping. She was as nice a woman as you'll meet," says Fergus. But for Carmel such tranquillity proved elusive.

> *I think Mrs. Snow was drunk the weight of the time, or in bed. Once she rolled down the staircase and broke her arm. She came out with a glass in her hand, took three or four steps and, next thing we knew, she was down the stairs.*

When her oldest daughter, Carmel Wilson, visited, the older woman got into a bath at one point with her clothes on, leaving her daughter to fear that her mother might be losing her mind.

Clearly, Rossyvera was a fantasy that had to end. Carmel later claimed to have given it up because of Palen, saying, variously, that his throat was "gravely affected" by the weather or that he was "elderly and in failing health." She said that it was too much for him "to make this relatively rigorous, bumpy long ride on a narrow road from Shannon," according to Curley, but, in reality, he scarcely factored in. "The irony of it was that she was quite fragile herself." Carmel returned to New York, while her sister stayed on for a time. "Christine spent more time at Rossyvera than I did during the three happy years I owned it, and she was really the chatelaine," she wrote with deceptive cheer in her memoir. (She actually owned the property for only half that period.) She added that Christine claimed that 'life was quiet there, except when you came!'"

Having bought the house and land from one ambassador, she sold it to another: Walter Curley, a future envoy to both France and Ireland, who, by coincidence, lived with his wife, Mary, and children in the same building as the Snows on East Eighty-sixth Street in Manhattan. In the Irish tradition, the sale was a charmingly protracted process, involving repeated meetings over cocktails at Carmel's apartment, which Curley teasingly referred to as their "trysts." They laughed together and talked seemingly about everything else. "Let's not rush to a conclusion," Carmel told him at one point. "Don't you think we should negotiate more on subsequent occasions?" She later told Curley that she'd sold him Rossyvera only because she knew he would take care of it. The Curleys bought some of her furnishings, too, including the long dining table and some deep velvet living room draperies. Ever observant, Carmel also offered them some valuable lowdown on the locals: "She had some very interesting takes on the neighbors that I found very accurate, given the short amount of time she'd been there."

The dream was over. And, strangely enough, another one—her longstanding nightmare of drowning—went at about this time, too. No matter how untenable her sojourn in Ireland had proven to be, that country always loomed large in her mind. As she wrote a few years later: "Now that I no longer dream my recurrent dream of being inundated by the ocean, I dream sometimes of Rossyvera, of just quietly disappearing into the Irish mist."

17

lighter than air

She always said when she didn't have that job anymore she'd just fade away. . . .
—Dorothy Wheelock Edson

I have no fear of death whatsoever.
—Carmel Snow

PALEN'S SORE THROAT turned out to be esophageal cancer. "For ten weeks or more [he] has been at death's door," Carmel wrote to her friend Blanche Knopf in June 1959. "He was convinced it was going to be curtains," says the couple's daughter Brigid, who recalls being woken up in the middle of the night during a visit to Rolling Hill Farm in this period. Convinced that his death was imminent, her father was up and making a series of requests. "He said, 'Here's a list of my pallbearers. I want to resign from my quail shooting club, I want to resign from the Piping Rock. I don't want my golf clubs to be part of my estate.'" It was all so Palen. But unnecessary, as it turned out: rather than dying, he recovered after surgery.

Palen in later life

As the years went on, the couple seemed further and further apart. "They lived totally separate lives. Totally," in the words of one relative. "And they only got together for the major holidays." By now, both seemed dramatically older. They had false teeth. (Carmel had had her teeth removed, more or less impulsively, at about the time her finger was amputated—another decision she would come to regret.) Palen kept his in a glass of water by the bed and would be disoriented if he didn't see them when he woke. "I remember my father calling out 'Nellie, please, where are my teeth?'" Flanigan recalls. "He never did anything for himself."

Carmel never returned to the mists of County Mayo; instead, she was drawn back into the asphalt landscape of Manhattan, spending part of her time in East Norwich, with side trips to Paris. Gradually, she took up the life of any other woman of her age and station. Unlikely as it sounds, she began playing the staid old game of bridge, according to her son-in-law Thornton Wilson, and was always after her daughters to do the same. She played the game with "Social Register types," whom she scarcely resembled at all, Wilson added. And she volunteered for her favorite charity, the Lighthouse for the Blind, persuading her friends on Seventh Avenue to design for this organization that helps the seeing-impaired remain independent. She'd long supported the organization in *Bazaar,* at one point featuring a yellow apron in dotted swiss, designed by Claire McCardell and made by the blind, in its pages, one of many such handicrafts to be found at the Lighthouse's boutique on East Fifty-ninth Street. In her retirement, she worked on revamping this shop altogether. "Now, especially at Christmas time, they do a roaring business in babies' clothes, toys, aprons, really delightful things that I am happy to persuade my friends to buy, as of course I do myself."

With more time on her hands, Carmel could throw herself into grandmotherhood. (Brigid's latest, Timothy Palen Flanigan, had been born in December 1957.) "She was game to the end," as Walter Curley puts it, and particularly when it came to her young relatives, whom she loved to gather together en masse in her apartment "The whole point of my children's parties is that I always let my young guests do what they can't do at home." Antic games of "sardines," a more raucous version of hide-and-seek, were de rigueur. At one party, attended by twelve children, among them some of her grandchildren and the offspring of both Avedon and Allen, each of whom by then had a small son, Carmel—dressed in a pumpkin-colored Balenciaga suit and hat—took refuge behind the shower curtain in Palen's bathroom. What happened next was breathlessly recounted to Avedon by his son, John, then seven or eight. "When they found her she deliber-

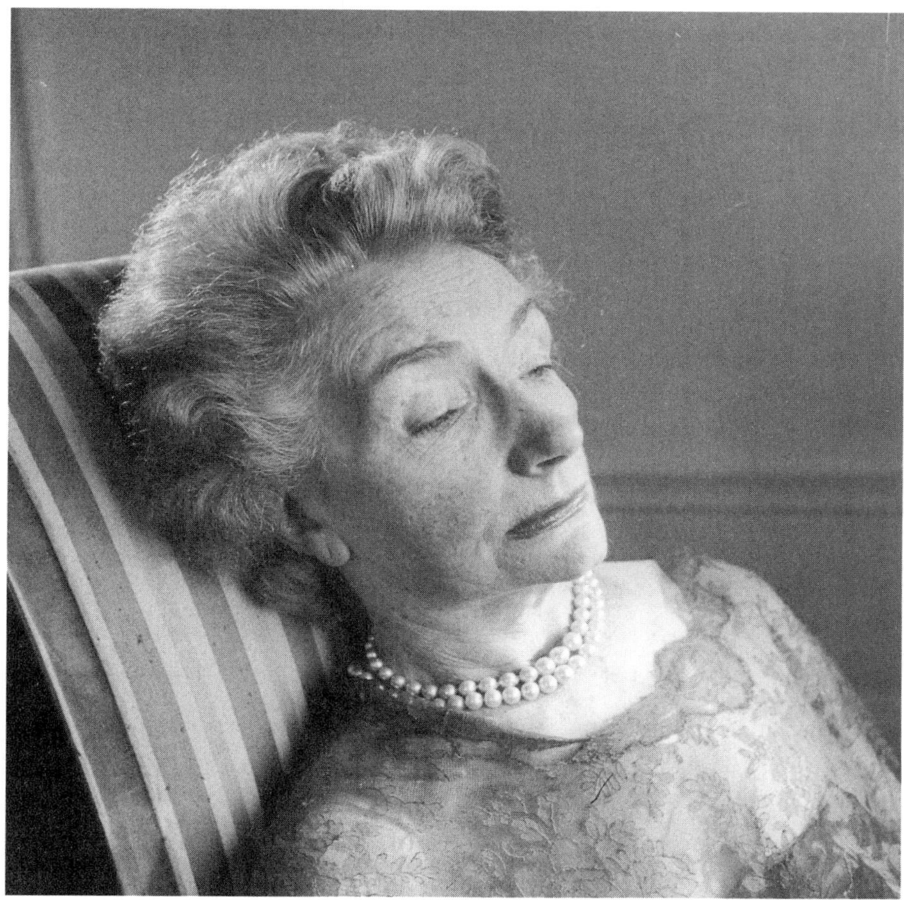

Carmel Snow toward the end of her career

ately turned on the shower. The children were screaming with laughter." Her hair, then in a purplish phase, was drenched, her suit, everything. . . . Later, recounting the story, Carmel wrote: "I hope it's the way the children will always remember me." (It is.)

In her new life, Carmel also had time for more leisurely, and perhaps even more liquid, meals than before. "I lunch with my friends of the fashion world, but no longer at the best table in Le Pavillon or the Côte Basque," she wrote serenely, but Truman Capote painted a much bleaker picture. "No longer was she seated at the best table in Le Pavillon, a restaurant she'd done a lot to create," he wrote seethingly, after sharing a meal with her there. "Oh no, she was shoved into an obscure little corner by the cash-register." Widely considered to be the best French restaurant in New York, Carmel had championed Le Pavillon since it was opened by Henri Soule in 1941, roping the chic and famous in, patronizing it with unswerving loyalty. But all, apparently, had been forgotten, both there and at other haunts she'd frequented for so long. Not surprisingly, when her son-in-law Thornton Wilson opened his Ermitage Restaurant at the basement level of 45 East Fifty-eight Street, she frequented it in earnest. "There, at least, I can entertain as I used to do," she wrote.

Perényi recalls one lunch (at Pavillon, as it happened) with Carmel at about this time. As usual, she pushed her plate of food away, Perényi reports, but not her glass. It became clear, at the end of the meal, that her former boss couldn't stand up. As she was steering her awkwardly toward the door they passed a table at which sat the suave, silver-haired Iva Patcevitch, then the head of Condé Nast Publications. "She stopped to say hello. Patcevitch didn't stand, didn't say hello, he just stared at her as if to say, 'Who is this drunken old woman?' " Perényi recalls. "I never forgave him—or her for putting herself in that position." It was a humiliation she didn't deserve. There were others that aren't worth enumerating. The most benign were theater dates that she slept through; others were worse. When they could, those around her learned to take preventive measures: Thornton Wilson always had his staff make her weak Bloody Marys when she came to Ermitage.

In short, Carmel didn't do well on the sidelines. It's not surprising, really; for her it was uncharted territory, a place she'd never known. Bassman recalls a moment when, forgotten but still present in Paris, the editor was approached by the impresario Sol Hurok, when she and the photographer were dining in a restaurant full of fashion people, few of whom seemed to notice the slight, lavender-haired woman in their midst. Hurok, who had represented Marian Anderson at the time Carmel published her photo in *Bazaar* twenty years earlier, came over to pay homage to the woman who had single-handedly broken the color barrier at Hearst. "He walked over and kissed her hand and everyone turned," Bassman says. "It really gave her a big lift. It was the kind of moment that happened ten times an hour just a few years before."

There was fashion news, some of it explosive, such as when, in September 1960, the young prodigy Yves Saint Laurent was drafted into the French army after only half a dozen collections, ranging from his brilliant debut to his most recent one, by all accounts a disappointment. "Many observers have felt that he never matched his first showing," the *New York Times* reported. Marc Bohan, then thirty-five, took over as chief designer, while the fragile Saint Laurent, who had been previously deferred from the draft, went off to do his military service. Tormented by his fellow recruits in basic training, he boomeranged almost instantly into a hospital, the victim of a quite predictable "nervous collapse." After recuperating, Saint Laurent sued to be reinstated in his former job, without success. By then, Bohan, whom Carmel called "the brilliant young successor to Dior," had presented his first in a long series of collections for that fashion house. But such dramas must have seemed, to Carmel, to take place at one remove. They weren't hers anymore, no matter how well she knew each and every member of the cast.

Even after her promised Paris pages had proven to be ephemeral, she still made the ritual trip to the collections twice a year. She got there to discover that "the seat of honor isn't reserved for me," she wrote. Which was an understatement. By this time, "No one was paying attention to her in Paris," according to Bassman, who was there during the couture season to shoot a Chanel campaign one year. Like Carmel, she stayed at the San Régis, which was "sort of like the office of the *Bazaar* in Paris at that point," in Bassman's words, but Carmel was only tangentially involved. "I had a lot of sad moments with her," recalls Gloria Moncur, a former assistant fashion editor who accompanied her to some of the collections in her last years. Carmel seemed to be unwell, Moncur says, and on prescription medication. At some showings, she was so ill that she'd leave before the end, something she never would have countenanced before.

Bassman and she kept company. "I'd come in at twelve or one in the morning and knock on her door and sit up with her for a while." Carmel had guided Bassman for years, as she had done with so many young people of talent; now, it was as if their roles had been reversed, with Bassman helping her former boss along. "I used to confront her," the photographer recalled, I'd say, 'Why are you bothering your niece at the *Bazaar*?' I'd say, 'For Christ's sake, you need a job.' And she got one." Carmel's friend Elizabeth Arden hired her as a consultant to handpick Paris couture models to be featured in the Arden collection. It may not have been all consuming, but it gave her a raison d'être, at least a part-time one, in Paris.

The job was short-lived. Even after it fell away, Carmel still kept going to France. As Aswell wrote:

> *When she no longer had any official connection with the couture, she continued to go to Paris twice a year for the collections. Alone. When she got there she went to every showing, she took down the numbers of the clothes she liked in her little red book, she went back the next day to look at the clothes again, she did everything she had always done except issue orders. She was still editing her magazine. For nobody. For no one. Except herself.*

But you could also say that she was also doing it for *Bazaar.* Long after she left the magazine, she still saw each issue before it went to press. And while she could be deeply critical of the pages before her, Nancy White, to her immense credit, resolved to learn from what her aunt had to say.

> *Everything she ever said to me and every criticism that she made, for the most part was very constructive. . . . And I remember a lot of it today. Some of those days weren't all that happy as she complained bitterly about something I'd done.*
>
> *She once said to me "Where is the surprise in the magazine, Nancy?" and she was right. There was no surprise.*

Back in New York, people paid homage. She received the Gimbel Order of Merit for her volunteer work at the Lighthouse, and a Philadelphia fashion group put on an event they called a "Love Letter to Carmel Snow" in her honor. It was "a moving experience for me." She broke her usual rule by dressing American for the occasion, wearing a raspberry pink suit from Ben Zuckerman with, inevitably, a Balenciaga hat. A gang of friends and family, including her sister, Christine, A. G. Allen, and Leo Lerman, who'd arranged the event, journeyed to Pennsylvania with her, joining her on the stage of the Bellevue-Stratford ballroom while people read out testimonials and pictures from her life were flashed on the screen.

Honors are by nature bittersweet; they imply that one has peaked. And Carmel, clearly, had. Her health was deteriorating. Some relatives thought she'd suffered from a stroke; her memory became sketchy. "I went up to New York and went to dinner with her and she didn't know who I was," her niece Julie Groupp recalls. Three young sisters, Irish relatives visiting the United States, were left with an eerie impression after they visited her on Eighty-sixth Street in 1960. "She seemed like she was much older than seventy," recalls Ann Hanlon Reilly. "It was a very dark apartment. Everything was dark. There was a big dark old piano with masses of photos on it in silver frames. She was incapable of getting up to show us the photos." Dinner, to the sisters' horror, involved jellied consommé: "It was inedible from my point of view," Reilly says. "I was petrified that she'd insist on my finishing my soup." The girls, who were in America doing charity work regarding Irish orphans, found that Carmel "wasn't at all interested in us or what we were doing." This apathetic reaction, from someone known to be "deeply interested in people, all kinds of people," as Geri Trotta describes it, was perhaps most distressing of all.

With Carmel's health declining, Christine came from Louisiana, where she was then living, to spend more and more time with her sister in New York. Against increasing odds, Carmel traveled to Paris in January 1961 to attend the spring collections. Mary Louise Aswell recounted her departure.

> *The day she left New York . . . she was seventy-three years old and alarmingly frail. When it was time for her to leave for the airport, she got up out of bed, stepped into her suit, called to her husband, "Good-*

bye, Snowie," and turned herself to the door on her tottering little stork legs. Following that celebrated, infallible, tip-tilted nose, she started alone for Paris.

There, she "covered" the collections for herself, shutting her eyes, presumably, to the fact that, with each visit, she became an increasingly peripheral figure in the world of haute couture.

Once back in Manhattan, she set to work on her book in earnest, looking for a new collaborator since McFadden, by then retired and living in Boston, had been either unwilling or unable to take on the task. Carmel approached a novelist

Carmel Snow and her sister, Christine. Photograph by Louise Dahl-Wolfe

friend, Nancy Wilson Ross, but she was immersed in another project and didn't have the time. She also asked Eleanor Perényi, who demurred more directly. "I told her there was a lot I would have to write that she might not want to read," the latter recalls, so that collaboration ended before it began.

By March 1961, Aswell, then living in Santa Fe, had agreed to work with Carmel. Whatever publishing agreement Carmel had entered into earlier was apparently now moot. She went fishing once more, approaching Blanche Knopf through Aswell's literary agent in New York, Diarmuid Russell of Russell & Volkening. "I guess Mrs. Snow will actually be deciding where the book will go. She seems to know so many people," Russell wrote. Knopf grabbed the bait—yet again—responding that she and Carmel had "talked about the possibility of this biography for a long, long time" and reiterating her interest. But by May, Carmel had been "offered a fat contract for the book sight unseen," according to a Knopf internal memo, and had signed a deal with the McGraw-Hill Book Company.

Truman Capote, who had been close to Aswell since she'd published him in *Bazaar* in the 1940s, wrote a cautioning letter from Switzerland just as she was heading to New York.

> *My advice is: enjoy this little junket to N.Y.—and then quietly return to Canyon Rd. At any rate, my love, how can I help:* much *as I would like. If you were going to write the true story of Carmel and how she was pushed out of the* Bazaar *(and was no longer allowed to sit at the best table in the Pavillon)—ah, that is high drama!*
>
> *Seriously, though, my entire knowledge of Carmel consists of a few dinner parties, and a half-dozen Pavillon lunches (during which I couldn't understand half of what she said—the fault, on both sides, of the many martinis).*
>
> *Of course the book could be really very, very interesting, if Carmel would tell the truth about advertising, and Hearst, and the whole fashion racket . . .*

Lord I wish you luck. But if you don't really find it working out—don't be a fool, say so, and quit.

But Aswell, by her own account, couldn't refuse. "From Steichen in his eighties to a grandchild of four, from her sister in Louisiana to myself in New Mexico, when Carmel summoned us, we came." She headed to New York for three months to work with her former boss, taking notes and taping her reminiscences on a reel-to-reel tape recorder. "It was a very difficult time for my mother," Aswell's daughter, Mary Doll, recalls. Aswell was far from her life and her home, staying with friends, and Carmel could be impossible. But she stayed. On April 13, when their work together was done, she packed up and headed back out west, her luggage full of tapes and eleven notebooks of notes, to write the text.

During the first weekend in May, Christine and Carmel "were together every waking moment," Christine said. That Saturday, Carmel went to the movies with A. G. Allen, who recalled, "She hadn't been wonderfully well, but she was fine. She had wonderful tenacity. She wouldn't give up." In the course of the evening, Carmel talked about the difficulty of the last few years, the inelegant end to her career at *Bazaar,* her abortive retirement to Ireland. It was a rare vulnerable moment—"Carmel was the sort of person who never dropped the mask," as Gwen Randolph Franklin once said—and it drew the two friends even closer. "We had a nice time and we made plans to get together a couple of weeks later."

Carmel spent the next evening, May 7, at a birthday party for her son-in-law Thornton Wilson, who was turning thirty-eight. "She was in good spirits and well," her daughter Carmel Wilson reported. On the next morning, a Monday, Nellie went in to wake Carmel at eight-thirty, as always. "She thought Carmel was still sleeping," Holbrook recalled, "then realized her color was different. I went in to see her, and I have never seen anything so peaceful. I fell on my knees to thank God He had taken her that way." The night before, Carmel had apparently taken off her glasses, put down her book, and turned out the light. She died in the night of a heart attack in her sleep.

The news took everyone by surprise. "Cathy Dives, her secretary, called me up that Monday morning," Allen recalled. "I was just devastated, especially since I had just seen her and nothing seemed unusual." In a letter to Carmel Wilson, Janet Flanner wrote,

> *I feel a mixture of awe and relief that your mother had the greatest good fortune in that last experience with life, which is leaving it. She was able to depart with the elegance of manner she had in living. And the timing of her death seems almost a part of that dated schedule on which she punctiliously ran her life.*

The timing was perfect, as Aswell wrote. "It was the way she wanted to go. Her daughters were settled, her work was done, her story was told, and she went."

At the *New York Times,* which did not write obituaries in advance in those days, the task of writing Carmel's story should have gone to Carrie Donovan, then a young fashion journalist, but she was out with the flu that Monday, so it fell to Marylin Bender, a reporter on what was then known as "the women's pages" instead. Even so, it was a collaboration of sorts: the two women conferred frequently over the telephone that day and Donovan "had a lot of input into the piece."

In its first paragraphs, the obituary moved to establish Carmel's importance to a nonfashion audience:

> *Mrs. Snow, who was chairman of the editorial board of* Harper's Bazaar, *was renowned on both sides of the Atlantic for her memory and her uncanny ability to spot a talent or a trend as it was being born. The presence of the blue-haired, blue-eyed editor at a fashion show, usually attired in a costume made by a French couturier, conferred recognition on the designer or manufacturer.*
>
> *A woman of wit and intelligence who counted many of the most famous artists and writers of the twentieth century as her friends, she*

> *was regarded as a strong executive who softened her occasional exercises in professional ruthlessness with charm and persuasiveness.*

It was obvious to Donovan where the piece should run. "I felt it should lead [off the front page], and I urged that. Mrs. Snow was such a towering figure in the world of fashion journalism.... In those days very rarely did obituaries go on the front page. But I felt she deserved it." But her editor at the time, Elizabeth Penrose Howkins, was a former Condé Nast staffer, at both *Glamour* and British *Vogue,* who had been "one of Condé's protégées," Donovan recalled. "Maybe she had even been a former mistress." In any case, Howkins impressed upon the higher-ups at the *Times* that "Mrs. Snow was a very important figure, but it did not have to go off the front page." In this way, Nast, who never got over Carmel's departure from *Vogue,* ended up with the last word. The obituary ran on page 39, a fact that still rankled Donovan three decades later. "In my mind, there was no question that she deserved [the front page]. It was a real injustice. It still makes me angry."

Wherever it ended up, Carmel's story spoke for itself, recalling all the raw talent—from Colette to Eudora Welty to Balenciaga to Lauren Bacall—that the editor had distilled over the years, decanting it into the pages of the magazine she had made into the most distinguished one in America, if not the world. Of all the tributes quoted in the *Times,* perhaps the loveliest came from Avedon, then in his early thirties, who said: "She wasn't just an editor, she was the only editor. Most of the rest are just business departments with legs on them. She was a teacher and friend to everyone that worked for her." (And to nobody more than he.) As he would later say, "It was a life devoted to quality, where everything mattered."

Diana Vreeland was quoted in another paper, the *New York Journal-American,* on the same day:

> *She had a sense of literature, of art, of photography, of the whole range of editing, Mrs. Vreeland said.*

Her life was between Paris, London, Rome, New York. She had the greatest personal style, a woman who accepted only the tops. She could not compromise. It was always either the best or nothing for her.

According to the same paper, Cathy Dives, Carmel's secretary, had accompanied Carmel to a fashion show in New York on Thursday, May 4, at which Dior's Bohan was also in attendance. He "just seemed to pay court to her," Dives told the paper. "Everyone who knew her felt that way about her. The people at the magazine—the photographers, the artists, everyone. She had a way about her that drew the best from everyone. She inspired them." One photographer, who had been contributing to *Bazaar* for a quarter century, ended his career upon hearing the news. "After the death of Carmel Snow. . . . Brassai gave up photography altogether."

For Aswell, Carmel's death wasn't yet final. For days after she returned, letters from Carmel arrived in New Mexico, following up on things she'd promised, checking facts, making suggestions, and on and on. The last came just before her funeral with the following postscript: "I say a prayer each day for the book and from now on I will say a special prayer for you yourself." Aswell added: "The intense concentration with which I myself have worked since then almost persuades me that a very potent spirit is operating somewhere still."

On the day of the funeral, Eugenia Sheppard published "They Remember Carmel," a compilation of comments from members of the fashion world, in the *New York Herald Tribune.* "Carmel Snow was a bit of a witch," she wrote, adding that she was "almost superstitiously respected for her uncanny insight into unhatched fashion trends. ('She knows,' they used to say as they studied her poker face at fashion shows.)" Sheppard focused not on *Bazaar,* or Carmel's accomplishments there, but on the personal style of this "enchanting little woman who lived with the elegance she preached." Everyone mentioned Balenciaga, of course, and her love of pastels; "She wore pink coats and suits before anyone did," one pointed out. John Fairchild, of *Women's Wear Daily* recalled a Balenciaga hat of hers that he particularly favored, bright white, with a red rose.

A High Requiem Mass was scheduled to be held at eleven in the morning on Wednesday, May 10, in Carmel's honor at the Lady Chapel of St. Patrick's Cathedral, where services for both her mother and her brother Tom had been held. It was the perfect location, this soaring edifice set in the thronging streets of midtown Manhattan, one of so many places Carmel would dash into for a quick prayer in the course of her working day. When thousands of people showed up, the service was moved at the last moment from the chapel to the main part of the cathedral instead. "Her funeral was most impressive of all the funerals I've ever seen. It was crowded and crowded," Edson recalls. "Every cloak and suiter from New York was there." Most moving of all was the sight of "old Pa going down the aisle with the girls behind him. By then, he was quite an old man." The crowd included "the last of her mother's old seamstresses, the aging model, the great jeweler, the fashionable Long Islander, Seventh Avenue en masse," Frances McFadden added. And, needless to say, there were armies of well-dressed females: "I never saw so many chic women in my life," Jane Strong says. "It was really extraordinary."

The Snow family had requested that, instead of flowers, donations be made to the Lighthouse instead, but some chose to ignore this, notably the designer Tom Brigance, who contributed a floral arrangement in the shape of a white Balenciaga hat with a red rose—Fairchild wasn't its only admirer—instead. It was the talk of this very chatty crowd, as was Elsa Schiaparelli's overheard remark that "everyone in the trade was wondering which Balenciaga Carmel was wearing." And she was, of course, wearing a suit by this designer, whose work she had so admired, when she was buried shortly afterward in a family plot in Cold Spring Harbor, Long Island, in a grave next to the one containing her long-dead infant son. In her will, which she had executed in June 1958, she left nothing to Palen, at his own request, but allowed him to use all her possessions until his own death, when they were to pass to Brigid and Carmel. She created a trust fund for Mary Palen, the only one still unmarried, to provide income for the rest of her life.

Later, in Paris, another ceremony was held, one very different from that held in New York—but no less representative of who she was—in that it was simple, unshowy, and deeply, even profoundly Catholic. Carmel's niece Kate White organized a mass to be said in her honor in a small chapel near the Invalides. It was the kind of out-of-the-way place of worship that her aunt had loved to find and then, ritually, to return to again and again. "You think you know Paris and all of a sudden you see a gem like this," Carmel had said the first time her niece led her there. It was a place she loved.

Word of the mass spread quietly among the devout and, in the end, about a dozen people from the fashion world came, most of them ones White didn't recognize. They weren't the grander people of the couture—many of those had flown to New York to see her off—but the smaller ones, the quieter talents, whom she'd loved equally well, some of them the same people who had been so startled, and so moved, to see her appear in their midst so many winters earlier, when Paris was in the depths of war. Together, they stopped and prayed, as Carmel had done, at least once a day, for more than seventy years. They contemplated this diminutive Irish American editor and her crowded, victorious, professional life, saying a rosary or two in her name. And then, revivified, they dispersed.

Portrait of Carmel Snow by Louise Dahl-Wolfe

18 *carmel snow lives*

People who are spirited never leave you.
—D. D. RYAN

AT CARMEL'S DEATH, one chapter ended and another began. Aswell continued working on the book, approaching numerous people for their memories of Carmel, among them Capote, who answered from Switzerland on June 6.

> *What I'd like to write about is the last time I saw her, crammed into an obscure corner of Le Pavillon, after so many years at a center table. It's such a good little study in the meaness [sic] of New York. . . . I'd like to write about all that, this marvelous little woman and what happened to her after she was kicked off the* Bazaar. *Naming names. But I don't suppose you want anything like that. I suppose the book will end on a note of continuing fame and success. But if you want the other, believe me I'd love to do it. . . .*

As he suspected, Aswell didn't want "the other," although it was the true story of Carmel's last years.

The tributes continued, and also the strange parallels with earlier lives. Letters and cables poured into the family homes, as they had upon the death of Peter White in Dalkey seventy years before. Nancy White asked Janet Flanner to commemorate *Bazaar*'s former editor for the magazine. "It would be a reflective pleasure," Flanner replied. Carmel Wilson also asked her to do the same, telling the journalist that her mother often spoke of her and that, in Flanner's words, "she was sure she would have wished me to write about her & I think this is true." The fact that Carmel kept a photo of her on her table, which Flanner learned from Wilson, "touches me more than you can know."

Flanner's tribute to Carmel ran in the July 1961 issue, a long appreciation of her friend and editor, accompanied by a rash of family photographs, including ones showing Carmel seated among her three small daughters; wearing a straw boater in a joyous, colorful Vertès portrait; sitting side by side with a very irritated-looking Balenciaga; in a double portrait with Palen—both smiling, Europe bound. "She was first and foremost an editor," Flanner wrote. "That was her profession. She was an extraordinary editor, creative, concrete, facile to work with because she knew what she wanted, difficult because she wanted only the best." She added, "All the legends about her were true," including Carmel's "ocular total recall," the way, once she glimpsed a fashion, it was embedded in her memory for good. It was a vivid portrait, but in Flanner's view, not vivid enough. "I was quite disappointed in what I wrote about Carmel in the *Bazaar,*" she later told Aswell. "It failed to give her magic or her contact with reality, both." It hardly reads like a failure. Unless, perhaps, Flanner was reading it with the eyes of the woman who was its subject—the ultimate editor, exacting and severe.

One can only speculate how Nancy White felt, beyond her grief at losing a favorite relative. It must have been a relief to, at last, be able to move out from under her aunt's shadow, to create, for better or for worse, her own version of the magazine. As she later said, "Carmel Snow was Carmel Snow. End of story." And those words capture the yin and the yang of it, both her aunt's personal warmth as well as her professional antipathy. A new *Bazaar* was born, no doubt one that would have caused pain to Carmel, Brodovitch, and the team that worked so closely on the old one. But their voices no longer mattered. Carmel once wrote that "there will always be successors, to Dior, to me, even to Balenciaga . . ."; with her aunt gone, White could at last become one.

Six months after Carmel's death, on January 24, 1962, Palen married Carol Kobbé Morgan, a widow, in an Episcopal ceremony at the house of Brigid and Peter Flanigan and their family on East Ninety-first Street. Carmel's secretary,

Cathy Dives, gave a party to welcome Palen's new bride, who duly moved into the family residence at 530 East Eighty-sixth Street. Needless to say, Carmel's former staffers were intensely curious to meet the new Mrs. Snow. On doing so, "I thought, 'Quite a change!'" Edson recalls.

> *She was so different. She was a beefy woman. She was rather square looking, really nothing like Mrs. Snow. She had dyed black hair and she liked to go down and hunt with the men. Palen liked the hunting sort of woman, you know, the ones that go shooting with you down in South Carolina.*

Christine Holbrook was taken aback by the timing, Edson recalls. "Mrs. Snow's sister said, 'I do think Palen might have waited a year!'" But his daughters, worried about their father, greeted his new bride—so different from GanGan!—with relief. "She welcomed us and made Daddy so happy," Brigid recalls.

That fall, on September 27, the Snow family and the editors of *Harper's Bazaar* hosted a cocktail party at the Flanigans' to celebrate the publication of *The World of Carmel Snow.* The book was entertaining and well written, but it offered a distinctly sanitized version of Carmel's life. And the design of it, by Brodovitch, was a disappointment. When Edson asked Aswell why she hadn't included anything controversial or difficult or just plain unflattering in the book, the author said, "Carmel wouldn't permit me to."

But others blame others. The book was drastically edited between Aswell's first draft and the final, published version. With Carmel gone, the family, as a letter from Carmel Wilson to a friend indicates, was heavily involved in the process. Wilson also called Janet Flanner, asking her for reminiscences for the book, and to suggest other people who might come through. One no-show was Balenciaga, something that didn't surprise Flanner one bit. ("Marie-Louise [Bousquet] thinks Balenciaga will most certainly *not* contribute anything because of his own evasive private Spanish character.") Flanner delicately suggested to Aswell that, given Carmel's general deterioration in her last years, testimonials from friends might not be as plentiful as they might once have been, apparently encouraging her to make them up, if necessary ("It will have to be supplied almost editorially by you, to be frank . . .").

Inevitably, some of the book's more controversial passages disappeared. "Christine told me that she took the part about Palen and the scandal with his mistress out of the book," one relative says. "I know it was Carmel's intention to put that all in." Carmel had enjoyed the brouhaha about it hugely, at least in later life, the same relative adds. Never mind—Marion Hurley and her perfect shape were neatly, permanently excised. In this way, the book Carmel had wanted to write metamorphosed into something else, a process that some who were involved, Flanner among them, found discouraging. "Bless you for all you are doing. Your heart & pen & touch are the authentic instruments in all this," the journalist wrote to Aswell. "My mother finished the book," says Christine Holbrook's son, Jack. Flanner, too, took a pass at the manuscript. With so many hands at work, it's no wonder that many who knew Carmel think that it didn't reflect her irrepressible sense of humor and fun. "It lacks Mummy's Irish way of talking," Brigid Flanigan says. Her sister Carmel also thought "the book didn't have the right tone," her daughter, Carmel Fromson recalled. "It's because Mary Louise Aswell took the tapes and wrote it herself."

A month after *The World of Carmel Snow* was published, far away in Ireland, a couple entered their bedroom—Carmel's bedroom, aka the "ghost room"—at Rossyvera on the night of October 24 to find "a ball of light with the intensity of a strong radium-dial watch" hovering above the bed. As one of them wrote,

> *I checked the drawn curtains and peered out of the windows into a moonless night. There were no cars or bicycles with headlights, no lighthouse beams, no stars, no lights that could have pierced the drawn and lined curtains; there was no fire in the grate. The sphere of light,*

about the size of a tennis ball, and completely round, was there. It quivered while stationary and seemed to drift a few inches each way.

The ball dissipated soon enough, becoming a Rossyvera legend, but this time one recounted by people who don't for a minute believe in those little people and other fanciful creatures of which the Irish are so fond. It became an abiding mystery of the kind Carmel adored, and it's tempting to see her hand in it.

As for the living, and accounted for, at the time of Carmel's death, Carmel and Brigid—who went on to have a total of seven children—remained in New York City for their early married lives while Mary Palen moved to the suburbs, where she carried "on the Mayne tradition of needlework," as Carmel wrote, designing needlepoint rugs. Years later, after her marriage to Victor Rossi, she gave birth to a daughter, Martha. She remained fragile. "Her husband looked after her," her sister Brigid recalls.

Of the triumvirate, Brodovitch checked into Wards Island for treatment of alcoholism and depression after the death of his wife in 1959; there, an artist to the last, he took an affecting series of photographs of his fellow inmates with a hidden camera. A few years later, he retired to France. As for Vreeland—the one who would become the most famous, although not until long after she left *Bazaar*—she began putting out feelers for new employment soon after Carmel departed, entering into correspondence with the advertising agency J. Walter Thompson for the job of fashion coordinator. Nothing came of it. A few years later, in March 1962, she followed Carmel's long-ago trajectory, moving from one rival magazine to another, but in reverse, heading to *Vogue* as associate editor before assuming the role of editor in chief the following year. Polly Mellen later joined her there, becoming another one of the great names in fashion. Many of the *Bazaar* editors who worked together during the Snow years remained in New York City, forming an ad hoc "admiration society we all belong to for Carmel Snow and Diana," according to Gwen Randolph Franklin, a charter member.

As to why Vreeland's reputation has grown so dramatically over the years, gathering force and momentum, whereas Carmel's, mainly, has not, the answer lies in longevity and changing times, according to Avedon. "It's because Vreeland lasted," he said. "[Carmel] was older, right? Much older, and she faded before stardom became the thing. There weren't stars in her day. Fashion people weren't stars. Carmel was the only star there was." At the end of it all, she was just an editor, and *Bazaar* was just a magazine.

Although she died decades ago, the fashion world today is largely as Carmel Snow left it. Only more so. It's a killing ground, a high-stakes business where incomprehensible amounts of money are in play. Originality is prized—sometimes to a lunatic degree. Even at fashion houses like Givenchy and Christian Dior, places where gentility and elegance were once worshipped, a canny, commercially minded madness now reigns. In one perverse homage to the homeless, models dressed in newspaper took their turns down the runway; other designers have featured third sleeves, trailing tampon strings, unfurled condoms, just about anything else, in their designs.

What would Carmel have made of all of this? Who would have stood to applaud this time—she, or the rest of the pack? Clare Booth Luce once said that "Condé would have been, as Frank Crowninshield would have been, as Mrs. Snow would have been, shocked by the modern so-called fashion." But I don't agree. Carmel, who once said that "all good fashion is young," moved effortlessly forward, turning, unflinchingly, from the new to the next. A daring new style wouldn't faze her, as long as it was combined with the "top quality" that was her credo. In common with many designers working today, she "understood that fashion was much more than a hemline," Dick Deems says. "She understood that it existed in fiction, travel, movies, theater. She understood that influences come from everywhere, from skateboarding or Harlem." Only, she knew it long ago, while they're only learning it now. "She bought modernity to the things she touched and the life she lived," in Nancy White's words. It was never forced.

And that's why I'll end this book with an image of Carmel Snow in motion—tearing along, at full velocity, into the future. It's easy to picture her hurtling forward on a subway somewhere, heading to the latest off-beat runway show—in a circus tent in the bois de Boulogne, perhaps, or a parking garage in Queens—on her way to witness the debut of a young designer who just may, or more likely may not, still be in business next season. The idea of this demure-looking Irishwoman, in pearls and a pillbox hat, sitting on the L train or on Paris's Ligne 10, hardly feels like a stretch. Once she arrives at the fashion show, she will doubtless take her seat, once again, in the place of honor. Whether she'll rise to her feet clapping at the end of it, though, is anybody's guess. Only one thing is certain: she wouldn't miss it for the world.

acknowledgments

The idea for this book germinated before the wedding twenty years ago of my mother, the former Arden Kip Du Bois James, to Paul Desmond White. Their engagement party was given by Nancy White Thompson, the chic, ageless former editor in chief of *Harper's Bazaar,* at her apartment off Fifth Avenue. It was a convivial evening, with lots of high-speed chatter by various members of the spirited White clan. And a name kept recurring—that of Paul's aunt, Carmel Snow.

That name, as it happened, often came up when the Whites assembled, and I began to notice that it recurred beyond their circle as well. Reading Calvin Tomkins's elegantly accomplished article in *The New Yorker* about Carmel Snow, which I did while living in Paris in the mid-1990s, further fueled my interest. Later, my brother, Eliot W. Rowlands, told me that Carmel Snow had written a memoir; it was that curiously charming tome, *The World of Carmel Snow*, which Snow wrote with Mary Louise Aswell, that set me on the track that led here. I owe Eliot a debt of gratitude for that introduction, as well as for his conviction that Carmel Snow was someone who deserved to be brought back on the scene.

Another key early support was my agent, Fred Hill, whose encouragement, editorial help with the initial proposal, and expert navigation of the marketplace quite simply allowed this book to happen. I'm enormously grateful, too, to my friend Roxane Farmanfarmaian who, early on, when I explained why this project couldn't go forward, contradicted me deftly and in detail. Her elegantly simple road map for how it could be accomplished—not to mention her sustaining friendship—has served me ever since. Thanks, too, to another friend, Jamie Bowles, who lit candles on this project's behalf for several years, starting back when it was only a faintly flickering idea, and who turned up to help, fairy godmother–like, at key moments along the way. For their early encouragement and ideas, I also wish to thank Katharine Andres, Marisa Bartolucci, Judy Fayard, Sandra Gary, Lucy Gray, Jane Hewes, Diana Ketcham, Rita Laven, Jack Leggett, Peter Minichiello, Cathy Nolan, Barbara Plumb, Pamela Street, David Thomson, and Véronique Vienne.

It was my phenomenal luck that my proposal for *A Dash of Daring* was bought by Atria Books. My appreciation to everyone on their awesomely efficient team, starting with Atria's publisher, Judith Curr. I'm especially grateful to my editor, Malaika Adero, for overseeing things with such aplomb, for her perspective, and for her calm confidence that things would turn out all right—even when all evidence indicated otherwise. And to her assistant, Krishan Trotman, for so ably keeping things on track.

A huge thank-you to Lisa Keim, Atria's director of subsidiary rights, for being such a wonderful ambassador for this book and to publicist Angela Stamnes for helping it into the world. Thanks, too, to Martha Schwartz and Nancy Inglis, for their care with words on the page, to Nora Reichard for inspired copyediting and fact checking, and to Lynn Anderson. Also, to designer John Vairo, Jr., and illustrator Mona Mark for such a perfect jacket, and to Linda Dingler in the design department.

As a first-time biographer, I was unprepared for the generosity of my fellow biographers, some of whom approached me unbidden, knowing that their research had intersected with mine and offering to share it with me. My thanks, first of all, to my friend Caroline Seebohm, whose kindness, experience, and joie de vivre informed this book on so many levels. Besides lending material, she offered invaluable counsel—not to mention the pleasing ritual of Wednesday night glasses of wine on the Delaware River. David Thomson was an astute—and much appreciated—guide to the nuances of biographical research. My thanks, also, to Alexandra Anderson-Spivy, Eleanor Dwight, Natasha Fraser-Cavassoni, Diane Johnson, Robert O'Byrne, Mitchell Owens, Roxana Robinson, Sherill Tippins, Hugo Vickers, and Nicholas Fox Weber for their advice and help.

I'm particularly grateful to another writer Michael Patrick Hearn for sagely suggesting, over dinner in Manhattan, that I "write the book that needs to be written," rather than worrying unduly over length or tone. His words had a liberating effect.

Calvin Tomkins, of *The New Yorker,* did me the enormous service of allowing me to read his notes and research material on Carmel Snow before they were cataloged at the Museum of Modern Art, New York, where his papers are now housed. In doing so, he afforded me access to interviews with key figures who had died before I began my work—an inestimable gift. Thanks to Michelle Elligott of the MoMA archives for her help with this material. And to both for giving me permission to publish what I found.

I'm grateful, too, to members of Carmel Snow's immediate family, including, especially, Brigid Flanigan, her only surviving daughter, for hosting lunches at her home and talking to me about her family. And to Martha McDermott and Carmel Fromson for their support and assistance and for the combined passion they bring to the subject of their remarkable grandmother. Also, for lending me the tape of their interview with Polly Mellen—a wonderful supplement to my own brief conversation with that key fashion figure. I can scarcely convey the extent to which Lucy White, one of Carmel Snow's grandnieces, took pains on my behalf, supplying a steady stream of contacts and material, including nineteenth-century family scrapbooks, ancient photographs, family deeds, and on and on. Not to mention dinner parties at which extraordinary people turned up, among them John Esten, a former art director at the post-Snow *Bazaar* and the author of books on Man Ray, Diana Vreeland, and more. John turned out to be an inexhaustible source, supplying people to interview and corners of research to explore, as well as material from his own archives. No one knows the *Bazaar* era more intimately than John, and I benefited hugely from his perspective, insight, and friendship. Thanks also to Katie Delahaye Paine, another grandniece of Carmel Snow's, who gave me access to a miraculously surviving trunk of family papers that once belonged to her grandfather Thomas Justin White—a veritable treasure trove.

Other members of the White family who shared their memories of Carmel Snow include Nancy White Thompson, her successor at *Harper's Bazaar*. Kate White spoke to me of her aunt Carmel back when this book was only a hint of an idea; as a former, longtime resident of France, she provided a rare, insightful glimpse into Carmel's biannual visits to Paris, the city she so adored. My thanks to Kate also for drawing—both literally and figuratively—a map of the artists Carmel encouraged along the way. A big thank-you, too, to John Michael White, Julie Groupp, and Father Jack Holbrook. Carmel White Eitt was a delightful source both in an interview and on the page: I'm grateful to her, too, for providing me with some of the charming letters she wrote home from her sojourn in France during World War II. It's my abiding regret that my stepfather, Paul Desmond White, didn't live to see this volume published; I take solace from having told him of my plans to undertake it before he died. Thanks to his surviving siblings, Christine White Man and V. Gerald White, Jr., for their reminiscences.

I couldn't have imagined, when I first chose Carmel Snow as my subject, the kind of reverence she inspired among those who worked with her. The photographer Richard Avedon set the tone when he greeted me from the top of the stairs leading up to his apartment with the words "I will do anything to help anyone writing about Carmel Snow." His support for this project was unstinting, as is my gratitude for it. Happily, he was not alone. My encounter with Henri Cartier-Bresson, and his mystical evocation of a woman he revered, will burn in my memory forever. Other *Bazaar* photographers who spoke to me include Gleb Derujinsky, who walked me through the experience of receiving much-coveted photographic assignments for the magazine, and Lillian Bassman, who not only talked candidly of her *Bazaar* years but also helped to identify long-ago former colleagues at *Junior Bazaar*. My thanks to Hiro, Irving Penn, and Kathryn "Fuffy" Abbe, too.

I would especially like to single out the team of editors and other former employees of *Harper's Bazaar* who, in conversations with me, brought its atmosphere so vividly to life. Dorothy Wheelock Edson's recollections of her *Bazaar* years left me helpless with laughter; her friendship has been a gift. And *merci mille fois* to all the rest, among them: Adrian Gilbert Allen, Jo Jeanne Millon Barton, Luc Bouchage, Laura Pyzel Clark, Ray Crespin, Mary Fullerton Faulconer, Gwen Franklin, Polly Mellen, Anne Hopkins Miller, Melanie Witt Miller, Gloria Moncur, Catherine di Montezemolo, Eleanor Perényi, D. D. Ryan, Babs Simpson, Barbara Slifka, Geri Trotta, and Ann Murphy Vose. One former *Bazaar* editor, the novelist Mary Lee Settle, was, by coincidence, my first college writing teacher and an early mentor; it was a special pleasure to hear again anecdotes that I dimly recalled her telling back when I was twenty.

There was a time when all roads seemed to lead to Carmel Snow, so it hardly seemed surprising when I came across two people I'd planned to approach on the subject at the same party in Paris. I'm grateful to Lee Radziwill and Marisa Berenson for so gracefully talking with me about *Bazaar*-related matters at such an unexpected time and place.

Others who who shared their time and comments include: Susan Mary Alsop, Mary Aswell Doll, Geoffrey Beene, Rosamond Bernier, Marc Bohan, Mary Butler, Jan Cowles, Walter Curley, Peter H. Brown, Marion "Oatsie" Charles, Fleur Cowles, Mary Stair Dempwolf Crane, Richard Deems, Jeanne Eddy, Marilyn Evins, McGarry Fergus, Denise Bouché Fitch, Eileen Ford, James Galanos, Toni Gardner, Hubert de Givenchy, Jeremiah Goodman, Francine du Plessix Gray, Bettina Graziani, Andy Grundberg, Marianne Hauser, Carmen dell'Orefice Kaplan, Nan Kempner, Barbara Kerr, Eleanor Lambert, Dorian Leigh, Isabelle LaMotte, Kenneth Jay Lane, Beth Levine, Anthony Mazzola, Dr. Jay Meltzer, Grace Mirabella, Joan Munkacsi, Johnny Nicholson, Ned Rorem, Helen O'Hagan, William "Tish" Rand, Mary Jane Russell, Carmel Semmes, Sidney Stafford, Martha Lou Stohlman, Jane Bouché Strong, Geraldine Stutz, Sean Sweeney, Susan Train, Frederick Vreeland, Nicholas Vreeland, Margot Wilkie, and Frank

Zachary. Thanks to all of the above and also to Art Buchwald, who afforded me the shortest, punchiest telephone conversation of all on the subject of Carmel Snow: ten words, no more, no less.

For providing leads, material, advice, and other help, my thanks to J. Winthrop Aldrich, Mindy Aloff, Elizabeth Ballantine, X. Theodore Barber, William Ballard, Thomas Barton, Lenore Benson, Dilys Blum, Mary Blume, Frances Bowes, Frish Brandt, Laurent de Brunhoff, Bill Buchman, Priscilla Caldwell, Stephanie Cassidy, Marcelle Clements, John Corins, Sue Daly, Cécile Schall d'Aram, Francine Deroudille, Diana Edkins, Pamela Eldridge, Gray Foy, Martine Franck, Myrna Frommer, Diana Fuller, Jon Fox, Toni Gardner, Mike Gallagher, Denise Gosé, Liz Groves, Carol Hasko, Horace Havemeyer III, Penny Hayes, Maris Heller, Nancy Holmes, Judy Hynes, Brian Jones, Will Kingsland, Susan Kismaric, Phillipe LeMoult, Eva Maréchal, Lara Marlowe, Ved Mehta, Joan Middleton, Margot Mifflin, Arvia Morris, Roland Mouron, Jutta Neimann, Maggie Nolan, Cormac O'Malley, Iris Ory, Bill Patten, Gladys Perint Palmer, Anthony Petrillose, Sarah Plimpton, Roger Prigant, Thomas Quinn, John Remsen, Michael Ravnitzky, Sally Robbins, Mollie Rogan, Phyllis Rose, Amy Rule, Jean-Frédéric Schall, Jennifer L. Santo, Joanna Seddon, Rosalie Segal, Lee Silver, Susan Silver, Melvin Sokolsky, Walter Sohier, Irving Solero, Jay and Diana Stege, Michael Steier, Karen Stone, Robert Thurman, Susanna Van Langenberg, Hélène Véret, Anne Wencélius, Joshua Waller, Pamela Wilson, Taki Wise, Helen Wright, Alexandra Yu.

I'm especially grateful to Norma Stevens and Jennifer Rizzuto Congregane of the Richard Avedon Foundation for the use of Avedon's portrait of Carmel Snow and for all their other assistance. Also to Denise Bouché Fitch for allowing the publication, for the first time, of the beautiful sketches of the Paris collections by her late husband, the fashion illustrator René Bouché, which serve as endpapers to this book. And to Gillette Piper for the Marcel Vertés watercolor.

To friends who hosted me during research trips for this project, many thanks: Katharine and Clay Andres in Connecticut; Jamie and Philip Bowles in San Francisco; Joanna Seddon and Howard Weinberg in New York City; Katie Delahaye Paine in New Hampshire; and, recurrently, Rita and Michael Laven in London.

Drowning in data and short of time, I was helped—you might say saved—by two friends who happen to be accomplished editors and journalists. My thanks to Sandra Gary for superb research in California and New York and to Colleen Daly for the same in Texas.

I was lucky enough to work on this book in some of the world's great research libraries—a heartening experience. I owe a particular debt to Beverly Brannan, curator of photography at the Library of Congress, who helped me find my way through the Toni Frissell archive and to Ruth Alvarez of the University of Maryland who did the same with the Katherine Anne Porter papers. Valerie Wingfield, manuscripts librarian at the manuscript and archives division of the New York Public Library, not only steered me through the Fashion Group Papers and the Diana Vreeland Archives at that facility but suggested avenues to explore at other institutions. And Fredric Woodbridge Wilson, curator of the Harvard Theatre Collection at Houghton Library of the Harvard College Library, Harvard University, and Tara Wanger and Paul Johnson of the Harry Ransom Humanities Research Center of the University of Texas at Austin, offered valuable comments regarding fair use and copyright.

Other libraries I consulted include: the Rare Book & Manuscript Library at Butler Library, Columbia University; the Archives at Drexel University; the University Library of Georgetown University; the Recorded Sound Reference Center at the Library of Congress; the

Archives of the Museum of Modern Art, New York; Firestone Library, Princeton University; the Princeton Public Library, the Archives of American Art, Smithsonian Institution, Washington, D.C.; Bancroft Library at the University of California, Berkeley; the Rare Books and Manuscripts Library of the University of Southern California; and the Beinecke Library at Yale University.

I spent many days over the course of two years at the New York Society Library, and, most of all, at the periodicals room of the Gladys Marcus Library of the Fashion Institute of Technology in New York, as well as in its Special Collections area, poring over early issues of both *Vogue* and *Harper's Bazaar*. My thanks to the staffs at both institutions. Also to the amazingly multicultural students of FIT for providing continuous visual entertainment in the form of miniskirts, pierced navals, spiky hair, multiple earrings, clunky boots, and other accoutrements, not to mention great dialogue ("I'm definitely the dumbest Asian in the class"). I also benefited from the resources of the New York Genealogical and Biographical Society, both its library and its Web site.

In Europe, I had the good fortune to work at: the National Library of Ireland in Dublin; in London, at the Kensington Central Library and the National Art Library at the Victoria and Albert Museum; and, in Paris, at the Centre de Documentation of the Musée de la mode et du textile of the Musée des arts décoratifs, the library of the Musée Galliera, Musée de la mode de la ville de Paris, the American Library in Paris, and the Faidherbe and Trocadéro branches of the Bibliothèque de la ville de Paris. Hoping to spare its staff some grief, I won't name the French museum in which, after a day of research, Tom Coradetti and I found ourselves locked in after closing time—suffice it to say that it was a bonding experience. Many thanks to the security guard who finally let us out.

In Ireland, Ambassador Walter Curley opened up his beautiful corner of County Mayo to me, generously arranging for Sean Chambers to give me a tour of Rossyvera and environs. Thanks to both of them and to Ann Hanlon Reilly and Joan Regan, stateside relatives of Carmel Snow's, for putting me in touch with their very helpful counterparts in the Emerald Isle, Veronica Freeman and Helen and David Sheehy, who then passed me on to Paul McQuaid and Mary Meade. (Helen also helped with last-minute transatlantic fact checking.) In Dalkey, I'm grateful to Father John McDonagh of the Church of the Assumption of the Blessed Virgin Mary for access to White family baptismal records and to the head nun at Loretto Abbey, whose name I never learned.

Closer to home, I'm grateful to my mother, Arden White, for—among so much else—bringing me into Carmel Snow's orbit in the first place, and by way of romance, something Carmel would have adored. And to the two people with whom I share my daily life: Thomas Coradetti, and my son, Julian Rowlands, both of whom listened to my endless stories about Carmel Snow, if not exactly tirelessly, then, for the most part, with grace and humor. Besides offering moral support, Tom, who trained in physics and something mysterious known as "double E," turned out to be a wonderful researcher, excavating the depths of the Internet and even, at one point, successfully combing through books written in a language he doesn't speak. And Julian—surely the world's most knowledgeable teenager, however unwittingly, on the subject of a certain editor in a pillbox hat?—offered his own unique perspective, leavening the whole process with fencing and Jon Stewart and rap music and Steinbeck and Arabic and electric bass and the whole wide, wonderful arc of his interests. My thanks, and love, to all three.

notes

a note on sources

A Dash of Daring is based on more than a hundred interviews that I held with friends, family, and former colleagues of Carmel Snow's over a span of several years, beginning in about 2001. Unless otherwise indicated, all quotations in this book were taken from these interviews, which I conducted in either English or French, both in the United States and in Europe. Quite a few of the people I met with have also been quoted elsewhere; I've made a distinction between remarks that I elicited and those recorded by others, acknowledging sources of the latter in either the notes or text. (All unattributed interviews referred to in these notes were conducted by the author.)

Equally important for this book were the actual issues of the magazines where Carmel Snow once worked: *Vogue* in the 1920s and, of course, *Harper's Bazaar,* where she was employed from 1932 through 1957. To peruse twenty-five years of periodicals, published at least a dozen times a year (and, in the case of *Vogue* in its early years, twice as often as that), was truly to enter the world of Carmel Snow; these magazines provided a clear view of what life was like at this time both for their readers and for those who toiled within their halls. In particular, the "Editor's Guest Book," a contributors' page that Carmel instituted at *Bazaar* in the 1930s and that ran each month for the length of her employment there, offered a smart, and often very amusing, contemporaneous commentary on key figures in the cultural life of this country and beyond.

Many of the voices that sound out through this volume are of people who worked in and around the fashion industry generations ago. I was surprised, as I hope *A Dash of Daring*'s readers will be, by how vivid these first-person accounts remain, even in cases where the events they describe were played out in the first half of the last century.

I've quoted liberally from the memoirs of seven editors, so much so that it seemed a distraction to give the origin of this material each time it appeared on the page. Unless otherwise indicated, all quotes from Carmel Snow are from *The World of Carmel Snow,* written with Mary Louise Aswell and published posthumously in 1962. Diana Vreeland's are from *DV,* Edna Chase's from *Always in Vogue,* cowritten with her daughter Ilka Chase; Bettina Ballard's from *In My Fashion;* Jessica Daves's from *A Ready-made Miracle;* and Harry Yoxall's from *A Fashion of Life.* A more recent voice, that of Grace Mirabella, was drawn from *In and Out of Vogue,* written with Judith Warner and published in 1995.

The sources of all other written material are supplied in the notes. Unless stated otherwise, all translations are mine.

1. chippendale and cottage

5 "Irish goods were not": "Dressmaker Now in Exclusive Block," *The New York Times,* Oct. 5, 1911, p. 7.

8 Ishbel wrote to Annie White: Letter from I. Aberdeen to A. White, April 11, 1993. Thomas Justin White Papers, collection of Katie Delahaye Paine.

9 "a feminist before feminism": interview with Kate White.

12 "with Irish rich bog turf": "From the Ould Sod," *Chicago Evening Post,* Dec. 30, 1893.

16 "How glad he must be": Telegram from I. Aberdeen to A. White, April 7, 1894. Thomas Justin White Papers.

16 on the *Luconia* this date and that of other White family Atlantic crossings come from Ellis Island records, the Statue of Liberty/Ellis Island Foundation, Inc.

16 a well-worn trajectory: R. F. Foster, *Modern Ireland, 1600–1972* (London: Penguin, 1988), pp. 345–55.

18 "Descendants of the McGuillicuddy": Also spelled MacGillycuddy and described in an as-yet-unpublished text on the ancient families of Ireland, written by Ambassador Walter Curley.

19 He arrived in the Midwest: *The New York Times'* obituary dates Tom White's arrival as 1898; Ellis Island records and other sources differ on both the year of this voyage and on White's age upon his arrival in the United States. The one offered here seems the most likely of several alternatives.

2. the steamer trunk

24 After he married White: The date of the arrival of the younger White siblings is based on family accounts and Ellis Island records.

24 "She just greeted him": Told to Kate White by her father, Jim White.

25 "He had the priceless": *Vogue,* Nov. 9, 1929.

29 "After Paris explains the mode": *Vogue,* April 15, 1926.

29 "You all know how quickly": Lecture by Edna Chase to the Fashion Group, New York, N.Y. Oct. 22, 1931.

29 Douglass's youngest child: As recalled by Kate White.

30 "Year in, year out": Janet Flanner, *Paris Was Yesterday* (New York: Viking Press, 1972), p. 15.

31 And for a brief: Anne Rittenhouse, "What the Well-Dressed Women Are Wearing," *The New York Times,* Jan. 16, 1910.

32 "The atmosphere of a great": Christopher Gray, "Streetscapes/57th Street and Fifth Avenue. An 1870 Marble Row, Built in an Age of Brownstones," *The New York Times,* April 7, 2002.

34 "White—Surely your mother": Note from RPH or RTH to Tom White; undated but clipped to an Oct. 5, 1911, *New York Times* story on Annie Douglass. Thomas Justin White Papers.

34 In December 1912; "How to Beat Paris at Her Own Game," *The New York Times,* Dec. 19, 1912.

35 Peter White's trusts: Letter from George Collins of the Dublin firm Casey, Clay & Collins, acknowledging Deed of Appointment by Mrs. Douglas [*sic*], June 17, 1914. Thomas Justin White Papers.

36 In the summer of 1914: The date of this trip is based on correspondence of Walter Pach from the Archives of American Art, Smithsonian Institution, Washington, D.C., and Ellis Island records.

38 within the walls of T. M. and J. M. Fox: Lenore Benson of the Fashion Group provided a rare eyewitness account of Carmel's working life at T. M. Fox, albeit a secondhand one: her father, a New York retailer, used to visit Fox and spoke of being impressed there by Mrs. Douglass's bright young daughter.

38 Sitting on the top level: Edna Chase told the story of her Fashion Fête in a talk to the Fashion Group on June 26, 1940, as well as in her memoir.

39 They knew each other: This meeting was described in a May 22, 1962, letter from Virginia Gillette White's sister, Mrs. Prentiss Bassett, to one of W. R. Hearst's biographers, W. A. Swanberg. Swanberg Papers, Rare Book & Manuscript Library, Butler Library, Columbia University, New York.

39 In a letter she wrote: Undated letter from Carmel

White to Thomas White. Thomas Justin White Papers.

40 In marrying Tom: Letter from A. Douglass to V. Gillette, June 15, 1915. Thomas Justin White Papers.

40 "acute business depression": Letter from T. White to "Aunt Suie" Mayne, March 1915. Thomas Justin White Papers.

41 Victor, who had been: The story of Victor White's service in the AFSAC is told in an undated letter written from the Somme by William R. Berry of the same service. Thomas Justin White Papers. Victor White's tenure in the American Field Service was discussed in his obituary, "Victor G. White Painted Murals," *The New York Times,* April 23, 1954, p. 17. The AFS Web site chronicles the tenure of both Victor and James White, in the service.

42 Madeleine Vionnet's had shut down: Ilka Chase, *Past Imperfect* (Garden City, N.Y.: Doubleday, Doran, 1942), p. 117.

42 "France, in her time": Letter to the editor by Anne Rittenhouse, *The New York Times,* March 23, 1917.

42 "Women must have clothes": Georgina O'Hara, *The Encyclopedia of Fashion* (New York: Abrams, 1986), p. 72; Edna Woolman Chase and Ilka Chase, *Always in Vogue* (Garden City, N.Y.: Doubleday, 1954), p. 117.

43 "In 1919, I woke up famous": Valerie Steele, *Women of Fashion* (New York: Rizzoli, 1991), p. 246.

44 "With a black pullover": Christian Dior, *Talking About Fashion,* trans. Eugenia Sheppard (New York: G. P. Putnam's Sons, 1954), p. 9.

45 "It was no bed of roses": "It Was All So Different in 1917," *Harper's Bazaar,* July 1940.

46 The Red Cross girls: Anne Rittenhouse, "How Paris Dropped Gayety as War Shadows Deepened," *The New York Times,* Sept. 20, 1914.

47 "But wait till you hear the news": Letter from C. White to A. Douglass, April 2, 1919. Thomas Justin White Papers.

48 They were later published: Penelope Niven, *Steichen: A Biography* (New York: Clarkson N. Potter, 1997), p. 414.

51 She didn't keep a diary: Excerpts of the Ruby Ross Goodnow diaries were provided to the author by Mitchell Owens.

3. miss white of vogue

55 "Never has the art of the dress": Christian Dior, *Talking About Fashion,* trans. Eugenia Sheppard (New York: G. P. Putnam's Sons, 1954), p. 21.

56 Even so, Carmel's: Caroline Seebohm, *The Man Who Was Vogue, The Life and Times of Condé Nast* (New York: Viking Press, 1982), p. 132.

56 Founded in December 1892: Ibid., p. 42.

57 "Where do you date intellectually?": *Vanity Fair* advertisement in *Vogue,* Oct. 1, 1927.

58 Nast was a solid midwesterner: Seebohm, *The Man Who Was Vogue,* p. 5.

59 "Even at his busiest": Bettina Ballard, *In My Fashion* (New York: David McKay, 1960).

60 "extra instinctive feeling": interview with A. G. Allen

60 "She was deeply interested": interview with Dorothy Wheelock Edson.

60 "he had great simplicity": Ballard, *In My Fashion,* p. 92.

61 "They were a perfect team": Transcript of interview with Alexander Liberman, Dec. 3, 1980. Caroline Seebohm Papers.

63 "He developed a technique": Jessica Daves, *Ready-made Miracle* (New York: G. P. Putnam's Sons, 1967), p. 16.

63 "Women had to pose": George Hoyningen-Huene, oral history (unpublished) (Los Angeles: Oral History Program, University of California at Los Angeles, 1967), pp. 15, 42.

64 Baron de Meyer's baronetcy: According to Alexandra Anderson-Spivy, who's working on a biography of Adolph de Meyer.

66 "Vogue, the Ancient Mariner": *Vogue,* Aug. 1, 1925.

67 Their relationship was by all accounts: From part 2 of Geoffrey T. Hellman, "Last of a Species," a two-part profile of Crowninshield, *The New Yorker,* Sept. 26, 1942.

67 "the most glamorous parties": Ballard, *In My Fashion,* p. 92.

67 "from the stockroom, the messengers": Letter from Rosalie

Zimmerman to Caroline Seebohm, Aug. 9, 1979. Caroline Seebohm Papers.

67 "a dozen or so": Transcript of interview with Ewart "Red" Newsom, Aug. 29, 1979. Caroline Seebohm Papers.

67 There were buckets: Seebohm, *The Man Who Was Vogue,* p. 6.

68 "terribly close": Letter from Carmel Snow to John Brown, April 23, 1959. Houghton Library, Harvard University.

68 "deep inferiority complex": Transcript of interview with Alexander Liberman, Dec. 3, 1980. Caroline Seebohm Papers.

70 At a dinner afterward: Ruby Ross Goodnow diary, April 14, 1921.

70 Later in the same month: *The New York Times,* April 19, 1921.

70 "Women entered the second": Alison Lurie, *The Language of Clothes* (New York: Random House, 1981), p. 74.

70 "cooked asparagus": Cecil Beaton, *The Glass of Fashion* (New York: Clarkson N. Potter, 1997), p. 360.

70 Carmel also favored: As described in the "Editor's Guest Book," *Harper's Bazaar,* June 1956.

73 Or they might dine at: Dilys E. Blum, *Shocking! The Art and Fashion of Elsa Schiaparelli* (Philadelphia: Philadelphia Museum of Art, 2003), p. 10.

73 "Harpie's Bazaar": Ilka Chase, *Past Imperfect* (Garden City, N.Y.: Doubleday, Doran, 1942), p. 112.

74 "Romantic young women": Ibid., p. 57.

74 "keen as mustard": Edna Woolman Chase and Ilka Chase, *Always in Vogue* (Garden City, N.Y.: Doubleday, 1954), p. 221.

75 One of these was Edward Steichen: The story of Steichen's hiring is told by Caroline Seebohm in *Always in Vogue,* Penelope Niven in *Steichen: A Biography* (New York: Clarkson N. Potter, 1997), and in Steichen's own memoir, *A Life in Photography* (Garden City, N.Y.: Doubleday, 1963).

75 Rather than seeking: Steichen, *A Life in Photography,* p. 7.

76 The latter had jumped ship: Dodie Kazanjian and Calvin Tomkins, *Alex: The Life of Alexander Liberman* (New York: Knopf, 1993), p. 112.

76 Steichen's decision to work: Seebohm, *The Man Who Was Vogue,* p. 200

76 who had championed Steichen: Steichen, *A Life in Photography,* p. 6.

76 Stieglitz had been unstinting: Niven, *Steichen* p. 383.

76 "From then on, Stieglitz": Richard Whelan, *Alfred Stieglitz: A Biography* (Boston: Little, Brown, 1995), p. 441.

77 "amazingly knowing": Robert Gorland, *New York World Telegram,* no date and title on newspaper clipping.

77 The photographer had planned: As recounted by Carmel Snow with Mary Louise Aswell in *The World of Carmel Snow* (New York: McGraw-Hill, 1962) and by Steichen in *A Life in Photography*

78 "When I started making photographs": Steichen, *A Life in Photography,* p. 8.

79 "She said that she learned": interview with Richard Avedon.

79 An editor who lived: interview with Dorothy Edson.

80 Still, Luce, in her two-faced way: Erwin Blumenfeld, *Eye to I,* trans. Mike Mitchell and Brian Murdoch (London: Thames & Hudson, 1999), p. 276.

81 Carmel was a very hands-on: Transcript of interview with Dorothy Googins, Nov. 14, 1979. Caroline Seebohm Papers.

82 "She went around with a ribbon": Recalled by Mary Lee Settle.

82 Colored nail polish: Charlotte Seeling, *Fashion: The Century of the Designer* (Cologne: Konemann, 2000), p. 123.

86 "was a daring in combining": "The Fine Art of Dressing. *Paris in the Twenties* by Alice-Leone Moats," *Town & Country,* Oct. 1978, p. B24.

87 and former sculptor: "Finds Bobbed Hair Not Old-Fashioned," *The New York Times,* Nov. 26, 1927, p. 3.

87 an unforgettable shade of blue: Georgina O'Hara, *The Encyclopaedia of Fashion* (New York: Abrams, 1986), p. 20.

87 And she always shopped: Transcript of interview with Nancy White. Calvin Tomkins

Papers, The Museum of Modern Art Archives, New York.

90 This semicommunal living arrangement: Described in James Thurber, *The Years with Ross* (Boston: Little, Brown, 1959), as well as in Carmel Snow with Mary Louise Aswell, *The World of Carmel Snow* (New York: McGraw-Hill, 1962).

91 She was certainly showy: "Through a Glass Lightly," *Harper's Bazaar,* July 1941.

91 Wood was increasingly: Ruby Wood's career is described by Billy Baldwin in an undated manuscript (Caroline Seebohm Papers), in Wood's own diaries (courtesy of Mitchell Owens), and in Snow with Aswell, *The World of Carmel Snow.*

93 "enormous, big, gorgeous emerald": Interview with Eleanor Perényi.

94 a foxhunting mecca: *Harper's Bazaar,* May 1931.

95 The guest list was worthy: "Miss White Bride of George P. Snow," *The New York Times,* Nov. 12, 1926, p. 19.

98 A brothel on the Left Bank: Blumenfeld, *Eye to I,* p. 281.

98 And a wildly fashionable: Snow with Aswell, *The World of Carmel Snow,* p. 63.

4. an elegant life

99 "I didn't get it": Interview with Eleanor Perényi.

102 "one-story Malmaison sort": *Harper's Bazaar,* July 1941.

102 "MFH of Meadowbrook": *Vogue,* Jan. 18, 1930.

102 large and very country clubby: Interview with Dorothy Edson.

102 the new towering Graybar Building: *Vogue,* December 1927.

105 "where all the smart world": *Vogue,* Jan. 1, 1926.

106 That same year: Facsimile edition of the 1887 *Social Register* (New York: Social Register Association, 1986).

107 "It looked comfortable": Interview with Dorothy Edson.

107 "There may not have been": Transcript of interview with Thornton Wilson. Calvin Tomkins Papers, The Museum of Modern Art Archives, New York.

108 notable neighbors: Letter from C. Snow to C. Roosevelt Robinson, undated. Houghton Library, Harvard University.

108 "the turnout of the field": Carmel Snow with Mary Louise Aswell, *The World of Carmel Snow* (New York: McGraw-Hill, 1962), p. 68.

110 "she then took": Letter from Victoria Sackville-West to Harold Nicholson, Sept. 24, 1926, quoted in Caroline Seebohm, *The Man Who Was Vogue: The Life and Times of Condé Nast* (New York: Viking Press, 1982), p. 127.

112 "with some very fine lemons": Ilka Chase, *Past Imperfect* (Garden City, N.Y.: Doubleday, Doran, 1942), p. 117.

112 "not to molest": Cable from C. Nast to W. R. Hearst, March 28, 1931. Bancroft Library, University of California, Berkeley.

112 "an unbeatable combination": Designer Jacques Worth, quoted in Edna Woolman Chase and Ilka Chase, *Always in Vogue* (Garden City, N.Y.: Doubleday, 1954), p. 221.

114 Agha removed: Polly Devlin, quoted in Kerry William Purcell, *Alexey Brodovitch* (London: Phaidon Press, 2002), p. 63.

115 "Nast said the only thing": Transcript of interviews with Ewart "Red" Newsom, Aug. 29, 1979. Caroline Seebohm Papers.

116 "small, unpolished, and ill at ease": "Reporting Paris Styles Is a Business," *Life,* Sept. 6, 1937, p. 34.

116 "I would have to go to dance places": George Hoyningen-Huene, oral history (unpublished) (Los Angeles: Oral History Program, University of California at Los Angeles, 1967), p. 13.

117 lived in dread; Francine du Plessix Gray, *Them: A Memoir of Parents* (New York: Penguin Press, 2005), p. 256.

118 "The French didn't believe": "The Fine Art of Dressing. *Paris in the Twenties* by Alice-Leone Moats," *Town & Country,* Oct. 1978, p. B24.

118 "To Age Gracefully": *Vogue,* Aug. 1931.

119 "She is the sort": Hugo Vickers, *Cecil Beaton: The Authorized Biography* (London: Weidenfeld and Nicolson, 1985), p. 111.

119 "a good-looking, goatishly-fawnish": Ibid., p. 110.

119 "Wise, kind, witty": Ibid., p. 111.

120 "I had no idea": Cecil Beaton, *The Wandering Years: Diaries: 1922–1939* (Boston: Little, Brown, 1962), p. 8; Beaton seems to have misdated this entry in his diary. The date used here is from Vickers, *Cecil Beaton.*

120 "looking like a fox terrier": The story of this meeting is told in Beaton, *The Wandering Years.*

121 "Young Palen died": "Deaths," *The New York Times,* June 27, 1929.

121 "You could talk about": John Brooks, *Once in Golconda. A True Drama of Wall Street, 1920–1930* (New York: Wiley, 1999), p. 82.

121 On Black Tuesday: David Nasaw: *The Chief: The Life of William Randolph Hearst* (Boston: Houghton Mifflin, 2000), p. 423.

122 "Groups of men": *The New York Times,* Oct. 30, 1929.

122 "Actually they saw little enough": *The New York Times,* Oct. 30, 1929.

123 At *Vanity Fair,* Crowninshield: This story is recounted in H. W. Yoxall, *A Fashion of Life* (New York: Taplinger, 1966), p. 84.

124 "With the generality of her": "Evangeline Adams, Astrologer, Dead," *The New York Times,* Nov. 11, 1932.

124 "One is still grand": Cecil Beaton, "Goodby New York," *Vogue,* June 8, 1929.

124 "Now you know, Beaton": Vickers, *Cecil Beaton,* p. 136.

124 "Can you see them": Quoted in Chase and Chase, *Always in Vogue,* p. 70.

125 "Galoshes Attain Smart Standing": *Vogue,* Jan. 1, 1928.

125 Schiaparelli was still: *Vogue,* Jan. 18, 1930.

124 "Most of Hearst's": W. A. Swanberg, *Citizen Hearst: A Biography of William Randolph Hearst* (New York, Galahad Books, 1996), p. 439.

126 a former mistress: "$250,000 Suit on Trial. Former Show Girl Says G. P. Snow Broke Promise to Wed Her," *The New York Times,* May 20, 1930, p. 7.

127 "MISS MARION HURLEY": Best & Co. ad, "A Corset Demonstration on Living Models," *The New York Times,* May 18, 1924, p. 7.

127 A court document: Untitled one-page document, New York Supreme Court, May 20, 1930.

128 "not merely a close": Letter from C. Nast to C. Snow, Dec. 20, 1932. Archives of the Condé Nast Publications, New York.

128 Their mutual devotion was: Seebohm, *The Man Who Was Vogue,* p. 263.

129 "At first it became": Steichen, *A Life in Photography.*

129 "Sorry to bother you": Telegram from C. Nast to W. R. Hearst, March 28, 1931. William Randolph Hearst Archive, Bancroft Library, University of California at Berkeley.

130 "Carmel is the daughter": *Vogue,* March 8, 1932.

133 "She was fully aware": Chase and Chase, *Always in Vogue,* p. 255.

134 "Mrs. Chase thought": Seebohm, *The Man Who Was Vogue,* p. 263.

5. changing sides

135 "prestige and thirty-five dollars": Interview with Dorothy Wheelock Edson.

136 Yoxall put him to bed: This episode is recounted by Caroline Seebohm in *The Man Who Was Vogue: The Life and Times of Condé Nast* (New York: Viking Press, 1982), p. 264, and by H. W. Yoxall, *A Fashion of Life* (New York: Taplinger, 1966).

136 "I have cleared my desk": Letter from C. Nast to C. Snow, Dec. 20, 1932. Archives of the Condé Nast Publications, New York.

139 "He is more familiar": Cable from W. R. Hearst to W. M. Johnston, March 9, 1929. Bancroft Library, University of California, Berkeley.

141 Carmel answered Nast's letter: Letter from C. Snow to C. Nast, Dec. 23, 1932. Archives of the Condé Nast Publications, New York.

6. reinventing harper's bazaar

143 Like its rival: The story of the founding of *Harper's Bazaar* is recounted in Jessica Daves, *Ready-made Miracle: The American Story of Fashion for the Millions* (New York: G. P. Putnam's Sons, 1967), p. 118, and in "Inside America's Most Luxurious Magazine, *Harper's Bazaar," The Circulator,* Dec. 1948, p. 6.

144 "the nation's most powerful": David Nasaw, *The Chief: The Life of William Randolph Hearst* (Boston: Houghton Mifflin, 2000), p. xiii.

144 "By 1930, he owned twenty-six": Ibid., p. 405.

144 Hearst's magazine holdings: Ibid., p. 227.

144 "power of the media": Ibid., p. xiv.

146 Hearst cut salaries: Ibid., p. 462.

146 "Flipped a coin": Introduction to *Designs by Erté: Fashion Drawings and Illustrations from "Harper's Bazar,"* (New York: Dover, 1976).

148 "The editorial pencil": K. Howard, talk to the Fashion Group, New York, June 4, 1931.

149 Its editor, Chase Harindean: As recounted to the author by Geri Trotta.

149 "The day before yesterday": *Fashion Group Bulletin,* October 1940.

150 "Fifty million ermine": *Harper's Bazaar,* September 1933.

151 "lend the weight": *Harper's Bazaar,* June 1933.

151 "Women who wouldn't": *Harper's Bazaar,* April 1933.

152 "A Molyneux *ensemble":* Caroline Rennolds Millbank, *Couture: The Great Designers* (New York: Stewart, Tabori & Chang, 1985), p. 149.

152 She had hers custom fitted: According to her daughter, Brigid Flanigan.

152 "Every morning she looked": Interview with Dorothy Wheelock Edson.

153 "She wore a hat": Interview with Annie Hopkins Miller.

153 "I think she probably took": Transcript of interview with Nancy White. Calvin Tomkins Papers, The Museum of Modern Art Archives, New York.

154 Carmel approached: Carmel Snow with Mary Louise Aswell, *The World of Carmel Snow* (New York: McGraw-Hill, 1962), p. 116.

155 even writing to Charles Hanson Towne: Letter from W. R. Hearst to C. H. Towne, Feb. 1, 1929. William Randolph Hearst Papers, Bancroft Library, University of California at Berkeley.

156 regaling her relatives: As recounted to the author by Kate White.

156 "the most indestructible": Janet Flanner, *Paris Journal, 1944–1965* (New York: Atheneum, 1965), pp. 61–62.

156 red apartment: Cocteau's famous apartment is described in Ned Rorem, *Setting the Tone: Essays and a Diary* (New York: Coward-McCann, 1983), p. 177, among other sources.

157 "They stride like giantesses": Marcel Vertès, "The Skyscrapers," *Harper's Bazaar,* July 1937, p. 70.

157 "superb, fresh and vital": George Hoyningen-Huene, oral history (unpublished) (Los Angeles: Oral History Program, University of California at Los Angeles, 1967), p. 26.

157 "In Paris it was considered": Cecil Beaton, *The Glass of Fashion* (Garden City, N.Y.: Doubleday, 1954), p. 263.

157 His detailed suggestions: Boris Kochno with Jean Clair, *Christian Bérard* (Paris: Herscher, 1987), p. 54.

157 "Bébé was so heavily on drugs": Transcript of interview with Thornton Wilson. Calvin Tomkins Papers, The Museum of Modern Art Archives, New York.

158 once almost silenced the teeming restaurant: "Editor's Guest Book," *Harper's Bazaar,* July 1948.

158 "the century's tycoons": Richard Avedon and Truman Capote, *Observations* (New York: Simon & Schuster, 1959), p. 7.

158 "Almost all the work was done": "Bérard," by George Davis, *Harper's Bazaar,* May 1949, p. 116.

158 It's no wonder: "Reporting Paris Styles Is a Business," *Life,* Sept. 6, 1937, p. 33.

160 wall panels he created: *Vogue,* July 1, 1931.

160 "that strange 1930 Paris": Flanner, *Paris Journal,* p. 570.

161 who always stayed: as recounted to the author by Gwen Randolph Franklin.

161 a model leaps: *Harper's Bazaar,* Jan. 1934.

165 "immediately grasped the potential": Nancy White and John Esten, *Style in Motion* (New York: Clarkson N. Potter, 1973), p. 2.

167 "If any writer writes": Letter from W. R. Hearst to J. A. Moore,

editor of *Good Housekeeping,* April 5, 1916. William Randolph Hearst Papers, Bancroft Library, University of California, Berkeley.

167 "it was made known to her": Ann Thomas, *Lisette Model* (Ottawa: National Gallery of Canada, 1990), p. 100.

169 "Hearst Organizations has no": Dorothy Wheelock Edson, quoted in Myrna Katz Frommer and Harvey Frommer, eds., *It Happened in Manhattan: An Oral History of Life in the City During the Mid–Twentieth Century* (New York: Berkley Books, 2001), p. 98

167 "Nothing got into": Nasaw, *The Chief,* p. 551.

167 Publications that weren't: W. A. Swanberg, *Citizen Hearst: A Biography of William Randolph Hearst* (New York: Galahad Books, 1996), p. 384.

167 "He placed tremendous faith": Letter from Lee Ettelson, editor at the *News-Call Bulletin,* to W. R. Hearst, Dec. 30, 1959. Rare Book and Ms. Division, Butler Library, Columbia University, New York.

168 Arriving at Los Angeles's: The trip guests took to San Simeon is described in D. Nasaw, *The Chief,* p. 369.

168 "of decorative schemes and arrangements": Swanberg, *Citizen Hearst,* p. 415. I also relied on David Nasaw, *The Chief,* for this description of San Simeon; on "San Simeon," *Harper's Bazaar,* July 1955, p. 39; and other published and first-person accounts.

169 "sometime in the spring": Nasaw, *The Chief,* p. 369.

169 Carmel's brother Tom: As recounted to the author by Tom White's son, John Michael White.

170 "These were high-salaried men": Swanberg, *Citizen Hearst,* p. 473.

172 "by making it a smashing success": Nasaw, *The Chief,* p. 450.

172 but the Chief himself never complained: Swanberg, *Citizen Hearst,* p. 451.

173 "We fought editorial battles": From speech given by C. Snow at the College of Home Economics, Drexel Institute of Technology, Philadelphia, May 5, 1955; text reproduced in Snow with Aswell, *The World of Carmel Snow,* pp. 192–95.

173 the first nude to be shown: Interview with Joan Munkasci.

174 "I'm on the street": Valentine Lawford, *Horst: His Work and His World* (New York: Knopf, 1984), p. 112.

174 "I was just a little German boy": Transcript of interview with H. Horst by C. Seebohm, Dec 4, 1979. Caroline Seebohm papers.

176 "Agha was the wrong person": G. Hoyningen-Huene, quoted in a letter from *Vogue* editor Margaret Case to Edna Chase, quoted in Caroline Seebohm, *The Man Who Was Vogue, The Life and Times of Condé Nast* (New York: Viking Press, 1982), p. 215.

176 "He posed me like a statue": Lauren Bacall, *Lauren Bacall: By Myself* (New York: Knopf, 1978), p. 67.

7. assembling the team

178 Like Hoyningen-Huene: George Hoyningen-Huene, oral history (unpublished) (Los Angeles: Oral History Program, University of California at Los Angeles, 1967), p. 12.

178 "beautiful, technically flawless pictures": Virginia Smith in "Launching Brodovitch," quoted in Kerry William Purcell, *Alexey Brodovitch* (London: Phaidon Press, 2002), p. 41.

179 "the repetitive presentation": Ibid., p. 57.

180 "the most perfect Norman building": "Hearst has Tilting Field," *The New York Times,* Sept. 16, 1925, p. 16.

180 A scandal had erupted: David Nasaw, *The Chief: The Life of William Randolph Hearst* (Boston: Houghton Mifflin, 2000), p. 403.

180 "a wraith in flowing robes": "Hearst Castle Haunted," *The New York Times,* Nov. 25, 1928, p. 11.

182 giving a radio address: On Aug. 17, 1934, as advertised in *Harper's Bazaar.*

182 Brodovitch, who'd agreed: Purcell, *Alexey Brodovitch,* p. 58.

182 His Paris connections: Neil Baldwin, *Man Ray, American Artist* (New York: Clarkson N. Potter, 1988), p. 188.

183 "I looked like an angel": Antony Penrose, *The Lives of Lee Miller* (New York: Holt, Rinehart and Winston, 1985), p. 16.

183 "the stranglehold of reality": Phyllis Lee Levin, *The Wheels of*

Fashion, 1965, quoted in Baldwin, *Man Ray,* p. 189.

184 a surprisingly figurative drawing: *Harper's Bazaar,* June 1937.

185 "dozens of photostats": Lillian Bassman, quoted by Andy Grunwald, in *Brodovitch* (New York Abrams, 1989) p. 98.

185 He signed a lease: "Apartment Rentals," *The New York Times,* Oct. 10, 1934.

185 "was the son Brodovitch never had": As described by Geri Trotta.

186 "Sometimes she appeared drunk": Transcript of interview with Richard Avedon. Calvin Tomkins Papers, The Museum of Modern Art Archives, New York.

187 "He loved white paper": from the catalogue *Alexei Brodovitch and His Influence,* Philadelphia College of Art in collaboration with the Smithsonian Institution, pp. 32–33.

188 "It was the magazine editor": Calvin Tomkins, "The World of Carmel Snow," *The New Yorker,* Nov. 7, 1994, p. 148.

190 "Largely owing": Caroline Seebohm, *The Man Who Was Vogue: The Life and Times of Condé Nast* (New York: Viking Press, 1982), p. 241.

190 "You'd do anything": Interview with Dorothy Edson.

190 "She would use people": Transcript of interview with Babs Simpson. Calvin Tomkins Papers, The Museum of Modern Art Archives, New York.

190 "tall, cool Vassar graduates": S. J. Perelman, "Scrub Me, Daddy, Eight to the Bar," *The New Yorker,* June 28, 1941, p. 17.

192 signed a lease: "Apartment Rentals," *The New York Times,* Feb. 20, 1937, p. 30.

192 "She always liked the girls": Transcript of interview with Thornton Wilson. Calvin Tomkins Papers, The Museum of Modern Art Archives, New York.

192 At one point: Mary Louise Aswell in Carmel Snow with Mary Louise Aswell, *The World of Carmel Snow* (New York: McGraw-Hill, 1962), p. 207.

193 "The door swung open": Ibid., p. 107.

194 "Miss Diana Dalziel": *Vogue,* Jan. 15, 1922.

194 "For her fashion is of the essence": "Editor's Guest Book," *Harper's Bazaar,* May 1941.

194 At the time of her encounter: Eleanor Dwight, *Diana Vreeland* (New York: William Morrow, 2002), p. 49.

194 "Money. Why does anyone": quoted in Philippa Toomey's obituary of Diana Vreeland, *The Times* (London), May 1989; Ernestine Carter, *Magic Names of Fashion* (London: Weidenfeld and Nicolson, 1980), p. 169.

195 According to Mildred Morton Gilbert: Mildred Morton Gilbert, "When Truth Was in Fashion," unpublished manuscript, unpaginated. Caroline Seebohm Papers.

195 "She used to come in": Ibid.

196 "like a blond": "Editor's Guest Book," *Harper's Bazaar,* May 1941.

196 She, too, had a signature scent: Interview with Geri Trotta.

197 Like other editors: Grace Mirabella with Judith Warner, *In and Out of Vogue* (New York: Doubleday, 1995), p. 100.

198 "It was like going into fresh fields": Snow with Aswell, *The World of Carmel Snow,* p. 103.

198 "Lady editors in those days": Tina Fredericks in Jesse Kornbluth, *Pre-Pop Warhol* (New York: Panache Press at Random House, 1988), p. 10.

199 "You'd be given a dress": Louise Dahl-Wolfe, *A Photographer's Scrapbook* (New York: St. Martin's/Marek, 1984), p. 39.

200 "She'd say a geisha girl": Interview with Lillian Bassman.

200 "a great comic figure": Interview with Eleanor Perényi.

200 "These little fetishes": Interview with Melanie Witt Miller.

200 "a poetical quality": Cecil Beaton, *The Glass of Fashion* (Garden City, N.Y.: Doubleday, 1954), p. 316.

201 "One of her talents": Dahl-Wolfe, *A Photographer's Scrapbook,* p. 22.

201 So attuned is Carmel Snow: Beaton, *The Glass of Fashion,* p. 316.

201 "Half Irish . . . and half Inca": quoted in Calvin Tomkins, "The World of Carmel Snow," *The New Yorker,* Nov. 7, 1994, p. 148.

202 "Diana Vreeland had been

right": Mirabella with Warner, *In and Out of Vogue,* p. 152.

202 "The sharpest fashion journalist": Erwin Blumenfeld, *Eye to I: The Autobiography of a Photographer,* trans. Mike Mitchell and Brian Murdoch (London: Thames & Hudson, 1999), p. 276.

203 "The day didn't begin": Mary Louise Aswell in Snow with Aswell, *The World of Carmel Snow,* p. 209.

203 "you knew the world had changed": Interview with Mary Faulconer.

203 "as old as Kate Carney's cat": Eugenia Sheppard, "They Remember Carmel," *New York Herald Tribune,* May 9, 1961.

203 "Wrath, or real RAGE": Snow with Aswell, *The World of Carmel Snow,* p. 106.

204 "It can be seen that": Beaton, *The Glass of Fashion,* p. 363.

205 "If a perfectly strange lady": S. J. Perelman, "Frou-Frou or the Future of Vertigo," *The New Yorker,* April 16, 1938, p. 15.

205 "it was very upsetting": Diana Vreeland, *DV,* edited by George Plimpton and Christopher Hemphill (New York: Da Capo Press, 1997), p. 93.

205 a touching, handwritten note: Ibid.

206 "Thank you for your kind invitation": Seebohm, *The Man Who Was Vogue,* p. 264.

207 "I'm of an independent mind": As recounted by Nan Richardson in Vicki Goldberg and Nan Richardson, *Louise Dahl-Wolfe* (New York: Abrams/Umbrage Editions, 2000), unpaginated.

207 "This is the work of": Dahl-Wolfe, *A Photographer's Scrapbook,* p. 14.

207 "criticism was merciless": John Duka, "A Chronicler of Fashion, at 88, Reflects on Change," *The New York Times,* Sept. 28, 1984, p. B6.

208 "when not faced with a deadline": From the preface by Frances McFadden, in Dahl-Wolfe, *A Photographer's Scrapbook,* p. xii.

208 who contributed fashion: Kertesz's fashion photographs ran in *Harper's Bazaar,* Dec. 1944.

208 "She understood that my genius": told to Kate White by André Kertesz, interview with Kate White.

208 "The Eastman Kodak company": Edward Steichen, *A Life in Photography* (Garden City, N.Y.: Doubleday, 1963)

209 "it was reported that she drove": Goldberg and Richardson, *Louise Dahl-Wolfe,* unpaginated.

209 one of the first to use color: Ibid.

209 "There was an extraordinary": quoted in *Harper's Bazaar,* Jan. 1939.

209 "Now we're going to see": Interview with Roxana Robinson.

209 She was very temperamental: Interview with Dorothy Wheelock Edson.

210 "That's perfectly ghastly": Dwight, *Diana Vreeland,* p. 86.

210 "Sometimes, when commissioned": Dahl-Wolfe, *A Photographer's Scrapbook,* p. 43.

212 "As a chunk of life": Letter from W. H. Auden to George Davis, Dec. 21, 1938. George Davis Papers, Weill-Lenya Research Center, Kurt Weill Foundation, New York.

212 Carmel sent him twice to Europe: Interview with Sherill Tippins, author of *February House.*

212 "She would always say": Polly Meller, interview with Martha McDermott and Carmel Fromson, June 10, 2002.

213 she knocked down his barricade: "Marian Anderson Sings," *Harper's Bazaar*, Sept. 1937, p. 98.

213 "I won't have that nigger": Quoted in Calvin Tomkins, "The World of Carmel Snow," *The New Yorker,* Nov. 7, 1994.

213 "eight pages of Openings": "Reporting Paris Styles Is a Business," *Life,* June 6, 1937, p. 33.

213 All three *Vogue* editions: Ibid, p. 33.

214 "Carmel Snow, our editor-in-chief": Ad in *Harper's Bazaar,* Sept. 1, 1937.

215 "I think the Cassandre covers": Letter from W. R. Hearst to C. Snow, Dec. 7, 1936. William Randolph Hearst Papers, Bancroft Library, University of California, Berkeley.

216 Erté saves face: "Things I remember," quoted in Purcell, *Alexey Brodovitch,* p. 61.

216 Chase would have no mercy: Seebohm, *The Man Who Was Vogue,* p. 269.

217 "I do not believe in wasting": Letter from W. R. Hearst to C. Snow, Dec. 15, 1936. William Randolph Hearst Papers, Bancroft Library, University of California, Berkeley.

8. parallel lives

219 their mother's absence: Calvin Tomkins, "The World of Carmel Snow," *The New Yorker,* Nov. 7, 1994.

220 when she'd cancel evenings: Ibid.

220 "It was a sink-or-swim atmosphere": Transcript of interview with Carmel Fromson, Calvin Tomkins Papers, The Museum of Modern Art Archives, New York.

220 "out of kilter with life": Bernadine Morris, oral history, June 6–7, 1990. Oral History Project, Special Collections, Gladys Marcus Library at the Fashion Institute of Technology, New York.

221 "They lived separate lives": Transcript of interview with Brigid Flanigan. Calvin Tomkins Papers, The Museum of Modern Art Archives, New York.

222 "It was White's job": David Nasaw, *The Chief: The Life of William Randolph Hearst,* (Boston: Houghton Mifflin, 2002), p. 462.

222 "Would you be thinking": Letter from T. White to N. White, April 18, 1936, Thomas Justin White Papers.

222 Vreeland's father: Diana Vreeland, *DV,* edited by George Plimpton and Christopher Hemphill (New York: Da Capo Press, 1997), p. 90.

223 Unable to sell it at $6 million: *New York Herald Tribune,* April 1, 1938; quoted in W. A. Swanberg, *Citizen Hearst: A Biography of William Randolph Hearst* (New York: Galahad Books, 1996), p. 487.

223 "a white elephant": Swanberg, *Citizen Hearst,* p. 462.

234 "I still have a little comb": Transcript of interview with Nancy White. Calvin Tomkins Papers, The Museum of Modern Art Archives, New York.

225 "Carmel, who is almost as busy": Letter from T. White to Nancy White and Carmel White, Jan. 10, 1936. Thomas Justin White Papers.

226 "The grave couldn't be lovelier": Letter from C. Snow to T. White, Nov. 9, 1936. Thomas Justin White Papers.

227 "Brisbane reminded Cissy": Ralph G. Martin, *Cissy: The Extraordinary Life of Eleanor Medill Patterson* (New York: Simon & Schuster, 1979).

227 "Although White had": Ibid., p. 368.

227 "Patterson toyed with both": Ibid., p. 371.

230 White moved on: Alfred Allan Lewis and Constance Woodworth, *Miss Elizabeth Arden: An Unretouched Portrait* (New York: Coward, McCann & Geoghegan, 1972), p. 200.

230 "she mistrusted the lines": Lindy Woodhead, *War Paint: Madame Helena Rubenstein and Miss Elizabeth Arden: Their Lives, Their Times, Their Rivalries* (Hoboken, N.J.: John Wiley 2003), p. 241.

232 "The architects Sacchetti & Siegel": Christopher Gray, "A Tenement Complex Rebuilt for the Social Register," *The New York Times,* Dec. 14, 1997.

233 perhaps inspired by another: *Harper's Bazaar,* Jan. 1941.

234 "After the years spent": Carmel Snow with Mary Louise Aswell, *The World of Carmel Snow* (New York: McGraw-Hill, 1962), p. 123.

235 "light, bright": Interview with Mary Jane Russell.

234 "quite simple": Interview with Dorothy Wheelock Edson.

234 "She had this God-given talent": Transcript of interview with Thornton Wilson. Calvin Tomkins Papers, The Museum of Modern Art Archives, New York.

234 "lesson in coziness": Transcript of interview with Richard Avedon. Calvin Tomkins Papers, The Museum of Modern Art Archives, New York.

235 "alone at the end of the world": Christopher Gray, "A Tenement Complex Rebuilt for the Social Register," *The New York Times,* Dec. 14, 1997.

235 he'd seemed at loose ends: letter from T. White to A. Douglass, undated. Thomas Justin White Papers.

236 as Gleb Derujinsky: Recounted in a conversation with the author.

236 Dorothy insisted: Snow with Aswell, *The World of Carmel Snow,* p. 160.

236 "Do you think I could bear": Interview with Dorothy Wheelock Edson.

237 "He had nice lady friends": Transcript of interview with Thornton Wilson. Calvin Tomkins Papers. The Museum of Modern Art Archives, New York.

238 "Our mother never pushed us": Transcript of interview with Carmel Fromson. Calvin Tomkins Papers, The Museum of Modern Art Archives, New York.

238 who became president: Nasaw, *The Chief,* p. 588.

238 "a close family friend": Transcript of interview with Thornton Wilson. Calvin Tomkins Papers, The Museum of Modern Art Archives, New York.

238 the Berlins lived extremely well: Bob Colacello, *Holy Terror: Andy Warhol Close Up* (New York: HarperCollins, 1990), p. 64.

239 "Some day—more than anything": Letter from C. Snow to K. A. Porter, Jan. 6, 1941. Papers of Katherine Anne Porter, Special Collections, University of Maryland Libraries.

239 "Old Snowy was stretched": Interview with Dorothy Wheelock Edson.

239 "She was just incredibly special": Transcript of interview with Nancy White. Calvin Tomkins Papers. The Museum of Modern Art Archives, New York.

240 "I remember the joy": Ruth Lynam, *Couture: An Illustrated History of the Great Paris Designers and Their Creations* (Garden City, N.Y.: Doubleday, 1972), introduction.

240 in May 1939, she accompanied: Cable from T. White to V. White, May 20, 1939. Thomas Justin White Papers.

9. descending into war

243 "It is really a commonplace": Janet Flanner, *Paris Was Yesterday, 1925–1939* (New York: Viking Press, 1972), p. 224.

243 The late 1930s: *Harper's Bazaar* circulation figures were supplied by the archives department, *Harper's Bazaar.*

243 "On a spring Monday": Preface by Frances McFadden in Louise Dahl-Wolfe, *A Photographer's Scrapbook* (New York: St. Martin's/Marek, 1984), p. xiii.

243 "more men read *Harper's Bazaar*": *Harper's Bazaar,* Nov. 1939.

244 "an extremely intelligent": Lisette Model interview, *Interview,* Jan. 1980, p. 36.

244 "laying down the magazine": Interview with Eleanor Perényi.

244 might convey with a gesture: Eleanor Dwight, *Diana Vreeland* (New York: William Morrow, 2002), p. 85.

245 "Look at the flow": This sequence was described by Polly Mellen in an interview with Martha McDermott and Carmel Fromson, June 10, 2002.

247 "Mrs. Snow . . . really helped": Eleanor Lambert oral history, Dec. 8, 1977, Oral History Project, Special Collections, Gladys Marcus Library at the Fashion Institute of Technology, New York.

248 "in the early summer": Charlotte Seeling, *Fashion: The Century of the Designer* (Cologne: Konemann, 2000), p. 140.

249 a time of shoulder pads: Ibid., p. 140.

249 a radio broadcast: "Fashion Report from Paris, France," Feb. 10, 1938, Blue Network, shortwave NBC. Library of Congress.

250 "the most spectacular poet alive": "Editor's Guest Book," *Harper's Bazaar,* April 1940.

250 "Two years ago Miss Porter": "Editor's Guest Book," *Harper's Bazaar,* Dec. 1939.

250 "a revolutionary intellectual act": *Ballad of the Sad Café* ran in *Harper's Bazaar* in Oct. 1940; Flanner described the events leading up to its publication in "Carmel Snow," *Harper's Bazaar,* July 1961, p. 45.

251 "During my years": Mary Louise Aswell, in Carmel Snow with Mary Louise Aswell, *The World of Carmel Snow* (New York: McGraw-Hill, 1962), p. 206.

251 "It was a terrible, terrible life": Mae Morrissy, "Your Obedient Servent," *Harper's Bazaar,* Jan. 1944, p. 56.

252 "*Vogue* published two issues": Letter and questionnaire from Diana Vreeland to Caroline Seebohm, April 22, 1980. Caroline Seebohm Papers.

252 "It so happens": Caroline Seebohm, *The Man Who Was Vogue: The Life and Times of*

Condé Nast (New York: Viking Press, 1982), p. 271.

253 Someone tipped off Walter Winchell: Ibid, p. 211.

253 "the most famous gossip columnist": Philip Roth, "The Story Behind *The Plot Against America*," *The New York Times Book Review*, Sept. 19, 2004.

253 It only took a quick mention: described in Hugo Vickers, *Cecil Beaton: The Authorized Biography* (London: Weidenfeld and Nicolson, 1985), p. 210, as well as in Seebohm, Snow, and other sources.

253 I felt anti-semitism: Transcript of interview with Richard Avedon. Calvin Tomkins Papers, The Museum of Modern Art Archives, New York.

254 "The Scalpers": As told to the author by Jo Jeanne Barton.

254 exclusionary comments . . . "Diana . . . antisemitic": Transcript of interview with Richard Avedon, ibid., and other sources.

254 "He filched every idea": Erwin Blumenfeld, *Eye to I: The Autobiography of a Photographer*, trans. by Mike Mitchell and Brian Murdoch (London: Thames and Hudson, 1999), p. 279.

254 "It has been my experience": Seebohm, *The Man Who Was Vogue*, p. 269.

255 "debutante wages": Grace Mirabella with Judith Warner, *In and Out of Vogue* (New York: Doubleday, 1995), p. 206.

255 Carmel wrote to Vreeland: Memo from Carmel Snow to Diana Vreeland, April 12, 1939. Diana Vreeland Papers, Manuscripts and Archives Division, New York Public Library, Astor, Lenox and Tilden Foundations.

256 "Louie explained to me": Snow with Aswell, *The World of Carmel Snow*, p. 117.

258 "It sailed out of the car": As recounted to the author by Dorothy Wheelock Edson.

258 "Isn't Carmel a sketch?": described by Frances McFadden in preface to Louise Dahl-Wolfe, *A Photographer's Scrapbook*, p. xii.

258 "You parked your car": Snow with Aswell, *The World of Carmel Snow*, p. 135.

259 "Nothing is more mysterious": From Marie-Andrée Jouve, *Cristóbal Balenciaga* (Paris: Éditions du Regard, 1988), p. 12.

261 "Immediately after the photography": William Ewing, *Eye for Elegance: George Hoyningen-Huene* (New York: International Center for Photography/Congreve Publishing, 1980).

262 "Like every female fashion editor": Blumenfeld, *Eye to I*, p. 276

264 "When I told him": Ibid., p. 281.

266 at one dinner party: Louise Macy, "Letters from Paris," *Harper's Bazaar*, Dec. 1939.

268 "joined Man Ray": Neil Baldwin, *Man Ray, American Artist* (New York: Clarkson N. Potter, 1988), p. 223; *Harper's Bazaar*, March 15, 1940.

269 "a cacophanous din": Francine du Plessix Gray, *Them: A Memoir of Parents* (New York: Penguin Press, 2005), p. 194

269 Among the refugee-packed: Willis Thornton, *The Liberation of Paris* (New York: Harcourt, Brace & World, 1962), p. 4.

10. bazaar *ascendant*

271 "Every issue . . . is full": *Harper's Bazaar*, Nov. 1939.

272 would make his way: "Editor's Guest Book," *Harper's Bazaar*, Oct. 1941.

272 "Carmel Snow dominated": Erwin Blumenfeld, *Eye to I: The Autobiography of a Photographer*, trans. by Mike Mitchell and Brian Murdoch (London: Thames and Hudson, 1999), p. 320.

274 "Have you any": Carmel Snow with Mary Louise Aswell, *The World of Carmel Snow* (New York: McGraw-Hill, 1962), p. 95.

274 "Keep right on": "Dress as the War Production Board Wants You To," *Harper's Bazaar*, March 15, 1942, p. 60.

274 "We are starting late": *Fashion Group Bulletin*, Oct. 1940, p. 2.

275 "On the whole": Ibid.,

276 "bed hopping was standard": Stephen McGinty, "Bohemian Rhapsody," *The Scotsman*, June 7, 2002.

276 "George had the nastiest": Gerald Clarke, *Capote: A Biography* (New York: Simon & Schuster, 1988), p. 88.

277 Actually, he stormed out: Davis's frequent departures from *Bazaar* were described by Sherill Tippins, both in her book *February House* (Boston: Houghton Mifflin, 2005) and in correspondence with the author.

277 "I'm not awfully conceited": Letter from G. Westcott to K. A. Porter, Aug. 20, 1940. Papers of Katherine Anne Porter, Special Collections, University of Maryland Libraries.

277 "Our bizarre friend": Letter from K. A. Porter to G. Westcott, Jan. 21, 1941. Papers of Katherine Anne Porter, Special Collections, University of Maryland Libraries.

278 "the story, in its edited form": Ibid.

278 "Mrs. S. . . . said": Ibid.

278 "Caramel Fudge is really": Letter from K. A. Porter to G. Westcott, Aug. 23, 1940. Ibid.

279 "Darling, the real point": Letter from K. A. Porter to G. Westcott, Jan. 21, 1941. Ibid.

279 But Porter was in a rage: Joan Givner, *Katherine Anne Porter: A Life* (New York: Simon & Schuster, 1982), p. 322.

279 "not at the price of": Letter from K. A. Porter to G. Westcott, Jan. 23, 1941. Papers of Katherine Anne Porter, Special Collections, University of Maryland Libraries.

280 "I made an exception": Katherine Anne Porter, *Letters of Katherine Anne Porter.* Ed. by Isabel Bayley (New York: Atlantic Monthly Press, 1990), p. 189; letter from K. A. Porter to G. Westcott, Jan. 23, 1941. Papers of Katherine Anne Porter, Special Collections, University of Maryland Libraries.

280 "C.S., so far as concerns": Ibid.

280 "He's gone back to Snow": Letter from G. Westcott to K. A. Porter, Jan. 24, 1941. Ibid.

281 "turned out to be": Ibid.

281 "I need not be ashamed": Porter, *Letters of Katherine Anne Porter,* p. 189.

281 "It has been a long time": Letter from C. Snow to K. A. Porter, Feb. 4, 1943. Papers of Katherine Anne Porter, Special Collections, University of Maryland Libraries.

282 "Although she's asked me": Porter, *Letters of Katherine Anne Porter,* p. 494; Letter from K. A. Porter to C. Snow, Jan. 7, 1956. Ibid.

282 "I have to confess": Letter from C. Snow to K. A. Porter, April 30, 1942. Ibid.

282 She even wrote to Gypsy: Letter from C. Snow to Gypsy Rose Lee, Oct. 1940. Billy Rose Collection, New York Public Library for the Performing Arts.

282 a congratulatory telegram: Letter from C. Snow to G. Davis. George Davis Papers, Weill-Lenya Research Center, Kurt Weill Foundation for Music, New York.

283 "remarkable, but little-remembered": Clarke, *Capote,* p. 81.

283 "I know how truly": Letter from C. Snow to M. Faulconer, May 2, 1941. Private collection.

283 "Dear, dear Harry": Letter from Carmel Snow to Harry L. Hopkins, Feb. 14, 1944. Harry L. Hopkins Papers, Georgetown University Library, Special Collections, Washington, D.C.

284 "The literary department": Clarke, *Capote,* p. 93.

284 "I can't hold my head up": Ibid., p. 83.

284 "Now, Mary Louise": Ibid.

285 "To tell the truth": Snow with Aswell, *The World of Carmel Snow,* p. 163.

286 No less a continental: Caroline Rennolds Millbank, *New York Fashion: The Evolution of American Style* (New York: Abrams, 1989), p. 149.

289 She in turn called him: Interview with Eleanor Perényi.

289 "Mr. Nast's magazines are": "Conde Nast Dead, Publisher, was 68," *The New York Times,* Sept. 20, 1942 p. 39.

290 What it didn't describe: Nast's decline is described in Caroline Seebohm, *The Man Who Was Vogue: The Life and Times of Condé Nast* (New York: Viking Press, 1982), Chapter 18.

290 About eight hundred people attended: "Associates Attend Condé Nast Rites," *The New York Times,* Sept. 23, 1942.

291 In August 1941: Letter from T. White to V. White, Aug. 29, 1941. Thomas Justin White Papers.

293 "a party that lasted a year": As described to the author by Richard Avedon.

293 Bacall was then eighteen: Lauren Bacall tells the story of her experiences at *Harper's Bazaar* in her memoir, *Lauren Bacall: By Myself* (New York: Knopf, 1978), beginning on p. 64.

293 "very direct in manner": Ibid., pp. 65–66.

294 "Mother had no sense": "In memoriam: Diana Vreeland

1903–1989," *Vanity Fair,* Jan. 1990, p. 17.

295 Carmel had already pounced: Slim Keith with Annette Tapert, *Slim: Memories of a Rich and Imperfect Life* (New York: Simon & Schuster, 1990), p. 124.

295 "Slim had no affiliations": Bill Blass, *Bare Blass,* edited by Cathy Horyn (New York: HarperCollins, 2002), p. 89.

298 where she worked as an inspector: According to Snow in *The World of Carmel Snow.*

298 a New Jersey munitions factory: As told to the author by Roxana Robinson.

11. "seeing and feeling everything"

299 "Every visit was crammed": Bettina Ballard, *In My Fashion* (New York: David McKay, 1960), p. 128.

299 "all lovely and saved": Gertrude Stein, "Raoul Dufy," *Harper's Bazaar,* Dec. 1949, p. 93.

300 "They are anxious to have me go": Letter from Carmel Snow to L. M. Hopkins, Aug. 30, 1944. Harry L. Hopkins Papers, Georgetown University Library, Special Collections, Washington, D.C.

300 "What I am terribly worried": Ibid.

300 "a speech of mud-slinging": "Text of Dewey's 'Point-by-Point' Denunciation of the Speech Made by the President," *The New York Times,* Sept. 26, 1944, p. 15.

302 "Paris, to anyone in": Dorian Leigh with Laura Hobe, *The Girl Who Had Everything: The Story of the "Fire and Ice" Girl* (Garden City, N.Y.: Doubleday, 1980), p. 74.

302 "The Whites are not quitters": Letter from Carmel White to Virginia White, Nov. 27, 1944. White Family Papers.

303 She checked into the Ritz: Carmel Snow described this trip in both her memoir and a talk to the Fashion Group on April 18, 1945. Fashion Group International Records, Manuscripts and Archives Division, New York Public Library, Astor, Lenox and Tilden Foundations.

303 "My Darling Palen and Children": Carmel Snow with Mary Louise Aswell, *The World of Carmel Snow* (New York: McGraw-Hill, 1962), p. 146.

303 "Mr. Balenciaga called": Ibid., p. 146.

304 "Darling children and Palen": Ibid., p. 147.

304 "I thought a fly": Carmel Snow, talk to the Fashion Group, April 18, 1945.

305 "They'd take in a piano": Ibid.

306 "at the hotel she once": Letter from Carmel White to Tom White, Jan. 4, 1945. White Family Papers.

306 Carmel woke to the call: Larry Collins and Dominique Lapierre, *Is Paris Burning?* (New York: Simon & Schuster, 1965), p. 16.

306 "The population of Paris": Janet Flanner, *Paris Journal, 1944–1965* (New York: Atheneum, 1965), p. 3.

307 At most Parisian hotels: Talk by Mrs. Cookman, fabric buyer, to the Fashion Group, 1944.

307 "No Parisian": Flanner, *Paris Journal,* p. 4.

307 "We fell all over each other": Letter from C. White to V. White, Dec. 27, 1944. White Family Papers.

308 He had been married: "Cartier-Bresson, Artist Who Used Lens, Dies at 95," *The New York Times,* Aug. 5, 2004.

308 Yet he had already packed: "Editor's Guest Book," *Harper's Bazaar,* August 1946; ibid. *The New York Times,* Aug. 5, ibid.

308 "I had a copy of *Ulysses*": Told to the author by H. Cartier-Bresson.

308 "a great general contemporary record": Flanner, *Paris Journal,* p. 298.

309 Carmel was repulsed: Told to the author by Carmel White Eitt.

310 And Carmel's support for him: Pierre Assouline, *Henri Cartier-Bresson: L'oeil du siècle* (Paris: Plon, 1999), p. 245.

310 "She is invited out plenty": Letter from Carmel White to Virginia White, Jan. 8, 1945. White Family Papers.

311 Bousquet was at the very heart: Described in Ned Rorem, *The Paris Diary and the New York Diary, 1951–1961* (New York: Da Capo Press, 1998), and in memoirs by Ballard, Carter, and Snow. N. Rorem spoke with the author about meeting Carmel at Bousquet's salon. Bousquet was described in *Harper's Bazaar* in "Editor's

Guest Book" entries in April 1951 and Oct. 1956.

311 On the night Carmel dined: Janet Flanner, "Carmel Snow," *Harper's Bazaar,* July 1961, p. 45.

311 "the mirror of Paris": Christian Dior, *Christian Dior et moi,* (Paris: Bibliothèque Amiot Dumont, 1956), p. 201.

312 Paris life functioned: Snow, talk to the Fashion Group, April 18, 1945.

312 "The poor lamb": Letter from Carmel White to Virginia White, Jan. 8, 1945. White Family Papers.

312 the editor found: Snow, talk to the Fashion Group, April 18, 1945.

313 When the Germans first: Marie-Andrée Jouve, *Christóbal Balenciaga* (Paris: Editions du Regard, 1988), p. 45.

314 In the midst of the coiled: British *Vogue,* 1952.

314 a former diplomat and spy: Francine du Plessix Gray, *Them: A Memoir of Parents* (New York: Penguin Press, 2005), p. 170.

315 "Perfume is the cheapest thing": Comments by C. Snow. Transcript of luncheon meeting held by the Fashion Group on April 18, 1945. Fashion Group International Records, Manuscripts and Archives Division, New York Public Library, Astor, Lenox and Tilden Foundations.

315 They were continually harassed: Valerie Steele, *Paris Fashion: A Cultural History* (New York: Oxford University Press, 1988), p. 266.

317 "She is the most wonderful": Carmel Snow, talk to the Fashion Group, April 18, 1945.

317 "beautiful, lavish, plush": Letter from Carmel White to Virginia White, Jan. 8, 1945. White Family Papers.

317 Katharine Cornell turned up: "Editors Guest Book," *Harper's Bazaar,* Oct. 1945.

318 "perfect, my dear, simply perfect": Letter from Carmel White to T. White, Jan. 4, 1945. Courtesy of Carmel White Eitt.

318 "We realize, Mrs. Snow": C. Snow, talk to the Fashion Group, April 18, 1945.

318 a character of a man: "Editor's Guest Book," *Harper's Bazaar,* May 1947.

319 "When the Gestapo came": Snow, talk to the Fashion Group, April 18, 1945.

319 a sound Flanner likened: Flanner, *Paris Journal,* p. 15.

320 "The first winter": Snow, talk to the Fashion Group, April 18, 1945.

321 Some women had gone so far: Comments by Mrs. Cookman, fabric buyer. Transcript of luncheon meeting held by the Fashion Group on April 18, 1945.

321 Others soared a foot into the air: Flanner, *Paris Journal,* p. 16.

321 "You should see the hats!": Carmel White to Nancy White, Nov. 5, 1944. Thomas Justin White Papers.

322 "His hats are charming": Snow, talk to the Fashion Group, April 18, 1945.

322 The look was jive: Steele, *Paris Fashion,* p. 271.

322 "the strange chic of the female Zazous": Flanner, *Paris Journal,* p. 16.

322 "Perhaps on some semiconscious level": Steele, *Paris Fashion,* p. 267.

322 "the first sizable collection": *Life,* Aug. 16, 1943, quoted in Caroline Rennolds Millbank, *Couture: The Great Designers* (New York: Stewart, Tabori & Chang, 1985), p. 143.

323 "She is the most dreadful-looking": Snow, talk to the Fashion Group, April 18, 1945.

325 "It was a totally bewildering exercise": Letter from C. White to V. White, Jan. 8, 1945. Thomas Justin White Papers.

12. new faces, new names

327 "Carmel was a rascal": Stephanie Mansfield, *The Richest Girl in the World: The Extravagant Life and Fast Times of Doris Duke* (New York: G. P. Putnam's Sons, 1992), p. 190.

328 "They streamed out": Janet Flanner, *Paris Journal, 1944–1965* (New York: Atheneum, 1965), p. 26.

328 "During all those war years": Dorian Leigh with Laura Hobe, *The Girl Who Had Everything: The Story of the "Fire and Ice" Girl.* (Garden City, N.Y.: Doubleday, 1980) p. 74.

328 "American designers really": E. Sheppard, "They Remember Carmel," *New York Herald Tribune,* May 10, 1961.

329 "Being given specific": Caroline Rennolds Millbank, *New York Fashion: The Evolution of American Style* (New York: Abrams, 1989), p. 133.

329 "the minute Paris opened up": Transcript of interview with Babs Simpson. Calvin Tomkins Papers, The Museum of Modern Art Archives, New York.

329 "It was modern": Millbank, *New York Fashion,* p. 143.

329 nation's top-of-the-line: Ibid., p. 132.

329 "the first designer to take": Ibid., p. 158.

329 "to look all of thirteen": "Editor's Guest Book," *Harper's Bazaar,* Nov. 1946.

330 "agile, unconventional eye": "Editor's Guest Book," *Harper's Bazaar,* Dec. 1947.

330 He became a frequent presence: Gerald Clarke, *Capote: A Biography* (New York: Simon & Schuster, 1988), p. 93.

331 "I posed him against the fire hydrant": "The Avedon Look," cover story, *Newsweek,* Oct. 16, 1978.

331 "one of the most fervently admired": Dodie Kazanjian and Calvin Tomkins, *Alex: The Life of Alexander Liberman* (New York: Knopf, 1993), p. 114.

331 on a par with its rival: Jane Trahey (ed.), *Harper's Bazaar: 100 years of the American Female* (New York: Random House, 1967), p. 94.

332 "They demanded": Richard Avedon, interview with the author.

332 "They were older": Transcript of interview with Richard Avedon. Calvin Tomkins Papers, The Museum of Modern Art Archives, New York.

332 "Her reply was": Letter from Carmel Snow to Toni Frissell, July 6, 1945. Business correspondence—*Harper's Bazaar.* Toni Frissell Personal Papers, Library of Congress.

332 "so upset by the whole matter": Ibid.

332 "Dahl-Wolfe was a horrible": Dorothy Wheelock Edson, quoted in Myrna Katz Frommer and Harvey Frommer, *It Happened in Manhattan: An Oral History of Life in the City During the Mid-Twentieth Century* (New York: Berkley Books, 2001), p. 97.

334 "Mrs. Vreeland never looked": Avedon eulogy for Diana Vreeland. Given at the Metropolitan Museum of Art, New York, Nov. 6, 1989, and reproduced in Richard Martin and Harold Koda, *Diana Vreeland: Immoderate Style* (New York: Metropolitan Museum of Art, 1993).

335 "There was a dedication": Transcript of interview with Richard Avedon. Calvin Tomkins Papers, The Museum of Modern Art Archives, New York.

335 "What have you seen?": Ibid.

335 "He was a little spot": Frommer and Frommer, *It Happened,* p. 97.

336 "very different—cold, removed": Calvin Tomkins, "The World of Carmel Snow," *The New Yorker,* Nov. 7, 1994, p. 148.

336 "You never have to call": Transcript of interview with Richard Avedon. Calvin Tomkins Papers, The Museum of Modern Art Archives, New York.

336 "The day she can't use you": Ibid.

337 "She wasn't dictatorial": A. G. Allen, quoted in Tomkins, "The World of Carmel Snow," *The New Yorker,* p. 148.

337 a fresh-faced Jacqueline Bouvier: *Harper's Bazaar,* Dec. 1947.

338 "Away with those skinny models": Cholly Knickerboeker, *New York Journal-American,* May 12, 1949.

338 "I have been passing photographs": Memo From Carmel Snow to Louise Dahl-Wolfe et al., Business correspondence—*Harper's Bazaar.* Toni Frissell Personal Papers, Library of Congress.

338 "very much better than her": Frommer and Frommer, *It Happened,* p. 97.

339 "What Brodovitch knew": Transcript of interview with A.G. Allen. Calvin Tomkins Papers, The Museum of Modern Art Archives, New York.

339 "Too late": Transcript of interview with Richard Avedon. Ibid.

339 "Dick wanted his models": Leigh with Hobe, *The Girl Who Had Everything,* p. 75.

340 one of the shyest men: "Editor's Guest Book," *Harper's Bazaar,* May 1947.

340 "Brandt spliced together": Liz Jobey., "Dreams of the

Decades," *London Review of Books,* July 8, 2004.

340 He came early: Pierre Assouline, *Henri Cartier-Bresson: L'oeil du siècle* (Paris: Plon, 1999), p. 232.

341 "I like Cartier-Bresson": Letter from Truman Capote to Mary Louise Aswell, July 31, 1946, *Too Brief a Treat: The Letters of Truman Capote,* ed. Gerald Clarke (New York: Random House, 2004), p. 22.

341 "I've never worked so hard": Letter from T. Capote to Mary Louise Aswell, Aug. 4, 1946, in *Too Brief,* p. 23.

341 "Yes, Cartier has done": Letter from T. Capote to John Malcolm Brinnin, Aug. 1946, in *Too Brief,* p. 27.

341 "The Hearst Corporation": *Too Brief,* p. 24.

344 cabled her congratulations: Telegram from M. L. Aswell to T. Capote, Aug. 10, 1946, in *Too Brief,* p. 34.

344 "I think the folks": Letter from T. Capote to M. L. Aswell, June 19, 1953, in *Too Brief,* p. 27.

344 Models who traveled: As described to the author by Mary Jane Russell.

344 "the most exciting event": Leigh, with Hobe, *The Girl who had Everything,* p. 74.

345 "we have no contracts": Memo from C. Snow to T. Frissell, July 14, 1949. Business correspondence—*Harper's Bazaar,* Toni Frissell Personal Papers, Library of Congress.

346 "two strong silhouettes": "Cable from Paris," *Harper's Bazaar,* Oct. 1945.

346 "a magazine covering the world": *Harper's Bazaar,* Oct. 1945.

346 "My heart's soul": Letter from C. Snow to T. Frissell, July 6, 1945. Business correspondence—*Harper's Bazaar,* Toni Frissell Personal Papers, Library of Congress.

346 *Seventeen* had been founded: The history of *Seventeen* was supplied to the author by Elizabeth Dye, *Seventeen.*

346 *Teen Vogue*: David Carr, "Coming Late, Fashionably, Teen Vogue Joins a Crowd," *The New York Times,* Jan. 13, 2003, p. C1.

346 The new magazine: Letter from C. Snow to T. Frissell, July 6, 1945. Business correspondence—*Harper's Bazaar,* Toni Frissell Personal Papers, Library of Congress.

348 The ponytailed Brennan: Brennan's story is told in Angela Bourke, *Maeve Brennan: Homesick at the* New Yorker (New York: Basic Books, 2004).

349 first photo of a bikini: In May 1947. John Esten, *Diana Vreeland: The Bazaar Years* (New York: Universe, 2001), p. 39.

349 "One's relationship": Mary Louise Aswell in Carmel Snow with Mary Louise Aswell, *The World of Carmel Snow* (New York: McGraw-Hill, 1962), p. 205.

350 The photographer remembers: Told to the author by Richard Avedon.

350 "The thing was defeated": Transcript of interview with Richard Avedon. Calvin Tomkins Papers, The Museum of Modern Art Archives, New York.

351 Cars could be seen again: "Letter from Paris," *Harper's Bazaar,* May 1946.

351 when photographer Maurice Tabard: "Editor's Guest Book," *Harper's Bazaar,* May 1947.

351 "Paris Working Girl 1946": *Harper's Bazaar,* June 1946.

351 appearance on the masthead: "Editor's Guest Book," *Harper's Bazaar,* March 1959.

352 "to be everywhere, posing": Cecil Beaton, *The Glass of Fashion* (Garden City, N.Y.: Doubleday, 1954), p. 317.

352 "They earn nothing": Lindy Woodhead, *War Paint: Madame Helena Rubinstein and Miss Elizabeth Arden: Their Lives, Their Times, Their Rivalry* (Hoboken, N.J.: John Wiley, 2003), p. 321.

352 "wacky looking, with her": Transcript of interview with Richard Avedon. Calvin Tomkins Papers, The Museum of Modern Art Archives, New York.

352 "a sprightly little monkey": As recounted by Susan Train.

352 "an ugly woman with": As described by Geri Trotta.

353 "The drinks are bad": Richard Avedon and Truman Capote, *Observations* (New York: Simon & Schuster, 1959), p. 7.

353 "The drink, served in": Ernestine Carter, *With Tongue in Chic* (London: Michael Joseph, 1974), p. 76.

354 "the most completely alive person": Bettina Ballard, *In My Fashion* (New York: David McKay, 1960), p. 128.

354 "was a great personality": Diana Vreeland, *DV*, edited by George Plimpton and Christopher Hemphill (New York: Da Capo Press, 1997), p. 15.

354 "In 1946, she was a distant": Carter, *With Tongue in Chic*, p. 72.

355 "She had been pictured": Ibid., p. 135.

355 "impassive, absent-eyed, with her": Celia Bertin, *Haute couture, terre inconnue* (Paris: Hachette, 1956), p. 29.

358 "mannerisms and her low voice": Transcript of interview with Babs Simpson. Calvin Tomkins Papers, The Museum of Modern Art Archives, New York.

358 "style-snitching espionage agents": "Paris Style Rooms Cloaked in Secrecy to Thwart Spies," *The New York Times*, Jan. 18, 1955, p. 15.

359 "Finding out which designs": Leigh, *The Girl Who had Everything*. p. 79.

359 "a bunch of old laundry": Described by Mary Lee Settle.

359 "she looked like a cook": Described by Geri Trotta.

360 "Mrs. Chase began": Caroline Seebohm, *The Man Who Was Vogue: The Life and Times of Condé Nast* (New York: Viking Press, 1982), p. 265.

361 buyers found themselves stranded: Lucie Noel, "U.S. Buyers Flocking to Paris for Showings of Spring Styles," *New York Herald Tribune*, Paris Edition, Feb. 2, 1947.

361 "a waterfall of pink tulle": *Harper's Bazaar*, Nov. 1947.

361 "The most important principle": Christian Dior, *Talking About Fashion*, trans. by Eugenia Sheppard (New York: G. P. Putnam's Sons, 1954), p. 26.

362 "you will make your living": Recounted in Chapter 1, ibid, p. 30

362 "like a bland country curate": Beaton, *The Glass of Fashion*, p. 292.

362 "Marie-Louise [Bousquet] introduced me": Christian Dior, *Christian Dior et Moi* (Paris: Bibliothèque Amiot-Dumont, 1956), p. 232.

362 Working first for Piguet: Pierre Provoyeur in *Hommage a Christian Dior, 1947–1957* (Paris: Musée des arts de la Mode et du Textile, 1987).

362 Forty American buyers: Lucie Noel, "U.S. Buyers Flocking to Paris For Showing of Spring Styles," *New York Herald Tribune*, Paris Edition, Feb. 5, 1947.

363 *"Harper's Bazaar* was the sofa": Dior, *Christian Dior et Moi*, p. 77.

363 "There was a world": Carter, *With Tongue in Chic*, p. 75.

363 "No show ever began": Dior, *Christian Dior et Moi*, p. 77.

363 "absurd puff of a dog": George Davis, "Bérard," *Harper's Bazaar*, May 1949, p. 116.

364 an extravagantly full skirt: Francine du Plessix Gray, "Prophets of Seducton," *The New Yorker*, Nov. 4, 1996.

364 Dior had a genius: Françoise Giroud, *Dior: Christian Dior, 1905–1957*, trans. by Stewart Spencer (New York: Rizzoli, 1987), p. 88.

364 "a brilliant nostalgia": Beaton, *The Glass of Fashion*, p. 293.

364 "all his dresses have": *Harper's Bazaar*, April 1947.

365 "My God what have I done?": "Dictator by Demand," cover story on C. Dior, *Time*, March 4, 1957.

365 most likely explanation: Giroud, *Dior*, p. 9; Demornex in Marie-Andrée Jouve, *Balenciaga* (Paris: Éditions du Regard, 1988).

365 a Reuters reporter: Marie-France Pochna, *Christian Dior: The Man Who Made the World Look New*, trans. by Joanna Savill. (New York: Arcade Publishing, 1996), p. 135.

365 Yet another theorized: Elisabeth Flory in *Hommage à Christian Dior, 1947–1957*. Marylène Delbourg-Delphis in ibid.

365 "From one day to the next": Françoise Giroud, *Les Années* Elle, *1945–2000* (Paris: Filipacchi, 2000), unpaginated.

365 returning to France: Giroud, *Dior*.

366 "On the night before": Dior, *Talking About Fashion*, p. 30.

366 "Success was too new": Dior, *Christian Dior et Moi*.

366 Dior took a critical step: Teri Agins, *The End of Fashion: The*

Mass Marketing of the Clothing Business (New York: Morrow, 1999), p. 28.

366 "Seventh Avenue joyfully discovered": "Dictator by Demand," *Time*, March 4, 1957.

367 "Every day and in every place": Undated letter from C. Snow to L. Dahl-Wolfe. Center for Creative Photography, University of Arizona.

367 "Carmel Snow was there": In Pochna, *Christian Dior: The Man Who Made the World*, p. 167.

368 Given such enthusiasm: According to Ballard, *In My Fashion*, p. 241.

368 "the dumbest misnomer": Francine du Plessix Gray, "Prophets of Seduction," *The New Yorker*, March 19, 2004.

369 "was a success only": Dior, *Talking About Fashion*, p. 110.

369 Its ecstatic reception: Dior, *Christian Dior et Moi*, Chapter 3.

369 "There was a letdown": M. L. Aswell in Snow with Aswell, *The World of Carmel Snow*, p. 209.

369 "Carmel, it's divine": Beaton, *The Glass of Fashion*, p. 362

369 American men wanted: Pochna, *Christian Dior: The Man Who Made the World*, p. 202.

369 all that material: Giroud, *Dior*, p. 15.

370 publishing a survey: Pochna, *Christian Dior: The Man Who Made the World*, p. 180.

370 "She wore it with aplomb": Preface by Frances McFadden, Dahl-Wolfe, *A Photographer's Scrapbook*, (New York: St. Martin's/Marck, 1984) p. xii.

370 "saw them acting lovey-dovey": Recounted by John Michael White.

371 Carmel had originally hired: Mansfield, *The Richest Girl in the World*, p. 190.

372 the wedding had been: "Doris Duke to be Wed to Dominican Official," *The New York Times*, Aug. 30, 1947, p. 38.

373 "But Rubi's mood changed": Mansfield, *The Richest Girl in the World*, p. 192.

373 "During the ritual": "Doris Duke Is Wed to Envoy in Paris," *The New York Times*, Sept. 2, 1947, p. 23.

374 "the *Bazaar* thing": Letter from T. White to N. White, April 2, 1948. Thomas Justin White Papers.

375 approached by Rose Kennedy: Transcript of interview with Carmel Fromson. Calvin Tomkins Papers, The Museum of Modern Art Archives, New York.

375 The first to go was Carmel: "Nuptials Are Held for Carmel Snow," *The New York Times*, June 11, 1947, p. 34.

377 another brother, Peter Desmond: "Peter D. White, 59, An Industrialist," *The New York Times*, May 7, 1948, p. 23.

377 among the mourners: As told to the author by Carmel White Eitt.

13. triumphing over all

379 "Carmel recognized Dick's threat": Mary Louise Aswell in Carmel Snow with Mary Louise Aswell, *The World of Carmel Snow* (New York: McGraw-Hill, 1962), p. 203.

379 "little guy in a black suit": Transcript of interview with Richard Avedon. Calvin Tomkins Papers, The Museum of Modern Art Archives, New York.

380 "She talked through the night": Richard Avedon in Snow with Aswell, *The World of Carmel Snow*, p. 207.

380 "known only to those": Dorian Leigh with Laura Hobe, *The Girl Who Had Everything: The Story of the "Fire and Ice" Girl* (Garden City, N.Y.: Doubleday, 1980), p. 78.

380 "while she was barefoot": Transcript of interview with Richard Avedon. Calvin Tomkins Papers, The Museum of Modern Art Archives, New York.

381 "You know the first act of *Rosenkavalier?*": Snow with Aswell, *The World of Carmel Snow*, p. 178.

382 "to help revive the French": Richard Avedon and Judith Thurman, *Richard Avedon: Made in France* (San Francisco: Fraenkel Gallery, 2001), unpaginated.

383 "A model couldn't": Leigh, *The Girl Who Had Everything*, p. 62.

384 years to master: Avedon and Thurman, *Richard Avedon: Made in France*, unpaginated.

384 The Paris staff knew: As described by Gleb Derujinsky.

385 "It took all of Carmel's genius": Mary Louise Aswell, in

Snow with Aswell, *The World of Carmel Snow,* p. 204.

386 "Now, Karen, we've had": Ibid., p. 180.

386 Holly Golightly Sweepstakes: Gerald Clarke, *Capote: A Biography* (New York: Simon & Schuster, 1988), p. 314.

386 *Bazaar* had rented: Leigh, *The Girl Who Had Everything,* p. 77.

387 "She wanted me to be exposed": Transcript of interview with Richard Avedon. Calvin Tomkins Papers, The Museum of Modern Art Archives, New York.

388 "fashion bible": Teri Agins, *The End of Fashion: The Mass Marketing of the Clothing Business* (New York: Morrow, 1999), p. 26.

388 "Even taxi drivers": Louise Dahl-Wolfe, *A Photographer's Scrapbook* (New York: St. Martin's/Marek, 1984), p. 73.

389 "perfect artisan": Avedon and Thurman, *Richard Avedon: Made in France,* unpaginated.

389 "There was hardly enough room": Ibid.

389 "The pictures Dick had taken": Leigh, *The Girl Who Had Everything,* p. 81.

389 impossible to obtain: Ibid.

390 "I was interested in the challenge": Avedon and Thurman, *Richard Avedon: Made in France,* unpaginated.

392 "too inexperienced": Bettina Ballard, *In My Fashion* (New York: David McKay, 1960), p. 110.

392 "Balenciaga, as usual, was not": *Harper's Bazaar,* Sept. 15, 1940.

392 "an absolute master": François Baudot, *La Mode du siècle* (Paris: Assouline, 1999), p. 154.

392 the precision of a surgeon: Eleanor Dwight, *Diana Vreeland* (New York: William Morrow, 2002), p. 203.

392 "He was the architect": *Hommage à Balenciaga* (Lyon: Musée Historique des Tissus, 1985).

394 "Dior, he doesn't dress": Francine du Plessix Gray, "Prophets of Seduction," *The New Yorker,* March 19, 2004.

394 "the master of us all": Ballard, *In My Fashion,* p. 117.

395 "This year's suit has": *Fashion Group Bulletin,* Sept. 19, 1950.

395 "Why has this great dressmaker": Ibid.

395 "tense performances": Snow with Aswell, *The World of Carmel Snow,* p. 116.

395 Dior collections had: Ernestine Carter, *With Tongue in Chic* (London: Michael Joseph, 1974), p. 77.

396 "a total break": Jacqueline Demornex in Marie-Andrée Jouve, *Cristóbal Balenciaga* (Paris: Éditions du Regard, 1988), p. 59.

396 "badly adjusted": Ibid., p. 59.

396 "Madame Snow Applaudit": Ibid., p. 46.

397 "You can't keep an exciting": From Carmel Snow's speech, "The Mysterious Ways of Fashion," given at the College of Home Economics, Drexel Institute of Technology, Philadelphia, May 5, 1955; Snow with Aswell, *The World of Carmel Snow,* pp. 192–95; *Alumnae News,* Drexel Institute of Technology, vol. 7, no. 3, May 7, 1955.

397 "Balenciaga was Carmel's": Mary Louise Aswell in Snow with Aswell, *The World of Carmel Snow,* p. 203.

398 "the new name to know": *Harper's Bazaar,* March 1952.

399 "because I have no neck": Carter, *With Tongue in Chic,* p. 78.

399 "The stand away collars": Jacqueline Demornex in Jouve, *Cristóbal Balenciaga,* p. 60.

399 Carmel showed her niece: As recounted to the author by Geoffrey Beene.

399 "She was in love": Transcript of an interview with Richard Avedon. Calvin Tomkins Papers, The Museum of Modern Art Archives, New York.

400 "The dresses were so unusual": Agins, *The End of Fashion,* p. 175.

401 "to prevent leakages": "Balenciaga: Top Creator Still Enigma," *The New York Times,* Jan. 31, 1958, p. 12.

401 "she scornfully declined": Ernestine Carter, obituary of Carmel Snow, *The Times* (London), May 1961.

403 long transatlantic conversation: Carmel recounted this story to the Fashion Group, Sept. 14, 1951. Fashion Group International Records, Manuscripts and Archives Division, New York Public Library, Astor, Lenox and Tilden Foundations.

403 "Please do come": Letter from Carmel Snow to Nancy White, April 6, 1949. Thomas Justin White Papers.

404 The award was presented: "Carmel Snow Receives the Legion of Honor," *Harper's Bazaar,* June 1949, p. 50.

404 "with rare little flames": George Davis, *"Bérard," Harper's Bazaar*, May 1949, p. 116.

404 "while working, after midnight": Janet Flanner, *Paris Journal, 1944–1965* (New York: Atheneum, 1965).

404 "Bébé was our blood donor": *Harper's Bazaar,* May 1949.

404 "We used to think": Ilka Chase, *Past Imperfect* (Garden City, N.Y.: Doubleday, Doran, 1942), p. 265.

405 San Régis bathrobe: According to Richard Avedon.

407 "When first asked to model": Dwight, *Diana Vreeland,* p. 90.

407 "India pink": *Harper's Bazaar,* Jan. 1950.

407 well-connected, if unruly: Davis's tenure at *Flair* is discussed in Truman Capote, *Too Brief a Treat: The Letters of Truman Capote,* edited by Gerald Clarke (New York: Random House, 2004), pp. 91, 96.

407 so chaotically imaginative: *The New York Times,* June 22, 2003, p. 8.

408 "I never crossed her path": According to Mary Lee Settle.

409 "Knowing Frances as I do": Letter from Carmel Snow to George Davis, Oct. 4, 1950. George Davis Papers. Weill-Lenya Research Center, Kurt Weill Foundation for Music, New York.

411 "It was love at first": Interview with Polly Mellen by M. McDermott and C. Fromson, June 10, 2002.

413 "When Richard was born": Transcript of interview with Thornton Wilson. Calvin Tomkins Papers, The Museum of Modern Art Archives, New York.

414 Thornton was surprised: Ibid.

414 published in a limited edition: By J. J. Augustin, 1945.

414 "It was probably the inherent": Kerry William Purcell, *Alexey Brodovitch* (London: Phaidon Press, 2002), p. 196.

414 Anything might be found: *Portfolio,* Summer 1950 issue.

415 injuring his hip: Andy Grundberg, *Brodovitch* (New York: Abrams, 1989), p. 153.

415 "at ungodly hours": *Time,* March 23, 1942, p. 40, in David Nasaw, *The Chief: The Life of William Randolph Hearst* (Boston: Houghton Mifflin, 2000), p. 595.

416 "On thinking back": Dahl-Wolfe, *A Photographer's Scrapbook,* p. 145.

417 tool with a design: Dwight, *Diana Vreeland,* p. 86.

14. ideal daughters

423 "Years later, Andy loved": Bob Colacello, *Holy Terror: Andy Warhol Close Up* (New York: HarperCollins, 1990), p. 21.

424 *"Harper's Bazaar* was essential": Jesse Kornbluth, *Pre-Pop Warhol* (New York: Panache Press at Random House, 1988).

424 a very different look: See, e.g., the 1949 photo of Warhol published in Michel Nuridsany, *Andy Warhol* (Paris: Flammarion, 2001).

424 "faint expletives": Tina S. Fredericks in Kornbluth, *Pre-Pop Warhol.*

424 "He was always at": Nuridsany, *Andy Warhol.*

424 "From the beginning": Colacello, *Holy Terror,* p. 22.

424 In 1954: As recounted by John Esten.

425 "had every agency in town": T. Fredericks in Kornbluth, *Pre-Pop Warhol,* p. 16.

425 "by 1970, Andy Warhol": Colacello, *Holy Terror,* p. 10.

427 he sent copies: Diana Vreeland Papers, Manuscripts and Archives Division, New York Public Library, Astor, Lenox and Tilden Foundations.

428 "They were at *Bazaar* then": "Blass: At Home on Park Ave. and 7th Ave," *The New York Times,* Dec. 28, 1980.

428 "buttons that button": "The American Look," *Time,* May 2, 1955.

428 shocked the fashion world: Ernestine Carter, *With Tongue in Chic* (London: Michael Joseph, 1974), p. 77.

428 "I have seldom seen": Carmel Snow, talk to the Fashion Group, Sept. 14, 1951. Fashion Group International Records, Manuscripts and Archives Division, New York Public Library, Astor, Lenox and Tilden Foundations.

428 "As the most powerful": Carter, *With Tongue in Chic,* p. 108.

429 the shows had expanded: The growth of Italian couture is charted in Valerie Steele, *Fashion Italian Style* (New Haven, Conn.: Yale University Press, 2003).

429 Carmel chose Irene Brin: "Editor's Guest Book," *Harper's Bazaar,* Nov. 1951.

430 the willful Miss Arden: Alfred Allan Lewis and Constance Woodworth, *Miss Elizabeth Arden: An Unretouched Portrait* (New York: Coward, McCann & Geoghegan, 1972), p. 270.

430 "I am the first member": Amy Fine Collins, "Pucci's Jet-Set Revolution," *Vanity Fair,* Oct. 2000, p. 378.

431 he'd drop to his knees: Mariuccia Casadio, *Emilio Pucci: Mémoire de la mode* (Paris: Assouline, 1998).

431 Emilio of Capri and Florence: *Harper's Bazaar,* July 1952.

431 "Because we Americans were so": Collins, "Pucci's Jet-Set Revolution."

432 "a certain nervousness": Ibid.

432 His technique could be startling: Dorian Leigh with Laura Hobe, *The Girl Who Had Everything: The Story of the "Fire and Ice" Girl* (Garden City, N.Y.: Doubleday, 1980), pp. 2–3.

432 "near rape": Michael Gross, *Model: The Ugly Business of Beautiful Women* (New York, William Morrow, 1995), p. 109.

432 "Dorian, don't you know": Leigh, *The Girl Who Had Everything,* p. 4.

432 "was a ruthless man": Transcript of interview with Babs Simpson. Calvin Tomkins Papers, The Museum of Modern Art Archives, New York.

432 "ruling passion with American": From a speech given by Carmel Snow at the School of Home Economics, Drexel Institute of Technology, Philadelphia, May 5, 1955; Carmel Snow with Mary Louise Aswell, *The World of Carmel Snow* (New York: McGraw-Hill, 1962), pp. 192–95.

433 Pucci to Cristina Nannini: Collins, "Pucci's Jet-Set Revolution."

434 "fearfully île on the Île": Letter from Kenneth Tynan to Carmel Snow, Jan. 24, 1952. Private collection.

434 "a green iridescent suit": Kathleen Tynan, *The Life of Kenneth Tynan* (London: Weidenfeld and Nicolson, 1987), p. 140.

434 rivetingly peculiar pair of: Described by Dorothy Wheelock Edson.

435 "ensnared the legendary": Kathleen Tynan, *The Life of Kenneth Tynan,* p. 140.

435 "I'm told you think": Letter from Kathleen Tynan to Carmel Snow, Jan. 24, 1952. Private collection.

435 The extended caption: *Harper's Bazaar,* Sept. 1952.

436 "She bristled and barked": Letter from Kenneth Tynan to Cecil Beaton, March 22, 1952. Kenneth Tynan, *Kenneth Tynan Letters,* edited by Kathleen Tynan (New York: Random House, 1998), p. 186.

436 "To be given virtual carte blanche": Kenneth Tynan in Snow with Aswell, *The World of Carmel Snow,* p. 208.

436 "It's wonderful when it isn't you": *Harper's Bazaar,* April 1954.

436 "Ms. Monroe's entourage": Letter from Cecil Beaton to Dorothy Wheelock Edson, Nov. 5, 1956.

437 "the word of thanks": Jean Chiesa in Snow with Aswell, *The World of Carmel Snow,* p. 210.

437 "You are a wonder!": Letter from Carmel Snow to Toni Frissell, March 24, 1947. Business correspondence—*Harper's Bazaar,* Toni Frissell Personal Papers, Library of Congress.

437 "wonderful, terribly hard work": Letter from Carmel Snow to Diana Vreeland, April 6, 1954. Diana Vreeland Papers, Manuscripts and Archives Division, New York Public Library, Astor, Lenox and Tilden Foundations.

437 "I was heartbroken": Carmel Snow to Melanie Witt Miller, April 6, 1954. Private collection.

439 "The day after unsatisfactory": Mary Louise Aswell in Snow with Aswell, *The World of Carmel Snow,* p. 210.

439 "Towards the end": Mary Louise Aswell, ibid., p. 203.

439 "She showed me what was good": Richard Avedon, ibid., p. 210.

440 "Without casting more than a glance": Cecil Beaton, ibid., p. 208.

440 "At the time when Garbo": Diana Vreeland, ibid., p. 202.

440 "She was extremely fond": Mary Louise Aswell, ibid., p. 202.

442 "In twenty-four hours": Preface by Frances McFadden, Louise Dahl-Wolfe, *A Photographer's Scrapbook* (New York: St. Martin's/Marek, 1984), p. 22.

442 "So Carmel came": Truman Capote in Snow with Aswell, *The World of Carmel Snow,* p. 183.

443 "Ireland's first fashion show": Carmel Snow, talk to the Fashion Group, Sept. 17, 1953. Fashion Group International Records, Manuscripts and Archives Division, New York Public Library, Astor, Lenox and Tilden Foundations.

444 "It's a shame": Robert O'Byrne, "Sybil Connolly," *Irish Arts Review* (Dublin), vol 16, 2000, p. 109.

444 "Ireland's grand man of letters": *Harper's Bazaar,* Sept. 1953.

445 "I'm a freak in Ireland": *Saturday Evening Post,* Nov. 1957, quoted in Robert O'Byrne, "Sybil Connolly," *Irish Arts Review,* p. 107.

446 the news wasn't huge: Carmel Snow, talk to the Fashion Group, Sept. 17, 1953, Fashion Group International Records, Manuscripts and Archives Division, New York Public Library, Astor, Lenox and Tilden Foundations.

446 She decided to finance: Axel Madsen, *Chanel: A Woman of Her Own* (New York: Holt, 1990), pp. 283–84.

447 Chanel was made: François Baudot, *La Mode de siècle* (Paris: Assouline, 1999), p. 74.

447 "wallowing in extravagance": Charlotte Seeling, *Fashion: The Century of the Designer* (Cologne: Konemann, 2000), p. 99.

447 "The Marshall Plan": Snow with Aswell, *The World of Carmel Snow,* p. 177.

448 another sibling's death: "Victor G. White, Painted Murals," *The New York Times,* April 24, 1954, p. 17.

448 Brigid Snow, then twenty-one: "Peter M. Flanigan weds Brigid Snow," *The New York Times,* Nov. 28, 1954.

15. being eclipsed

451 "When she was sixty-eight": Transcript of interview with Richard Avedon. Calvin Tomkins Papers, The Museum of Modern Art Archives, New York.

452 "A stout man and quite": Letter from Dorothy Wheelock Edson to Kenneth Tynan, Jan. 16, 1956. Private collection.

453 a Viennese knitware manufacturer: "In Vienna: The Dressmaker Sweaters," *Harper's Bazaar,* Jan. 1956, p. 120.

454 For Cartier-Bresson, who hated opera: Pierre Assouline, *Henri Cartier-Bresson: L'oeil du siècle* (Paris: Plon, 1999), p. 384.

454 "The new building is": "The Reborn Opera House," *Harper's Bazaar,* Jan. 1956, p. 91.

455 the summing up of a philosophy: The text of this speech is given in Carmel Snow with Mary Louise Aswell, *The World of Carmel Snow* (New York: McGraw-Hill, 1962), p. 197.

456 Carmel brought charges: Ibid., p. 174.

456 color-shot painting by Raoul Dufy: As recalled by A. G. Allen.

456 "Dufy is pleasure": *Harper's Bazaar,* Dec. 1949.

456 solitary splendor: As described in E. Sheppard, "They Remember Carmel," *New York Herald Tribune,* May 10, 1961.

457 Charles Rolo replaced West: "Editor's Guest Book," *Harper's Bazaar,* Nov. 1956.

459 "Despite all her years": Cecil Beaton, *Self-portrait with Friends: The Selected Diaries of Cecil Beaton, 1926–1974,* edited by Richard Buckle (London: Weidenfeld and Nicolson, 1979), p. 299.

462 a farmhouse that went up in flames: Described in Kerry William Purcell, *Alexey Brodovitch* (London: Phaidon Press, 2002), p. 149.

464 "As long as I am alive": E. Sheppard, "They Remember Carmel," *New York Herald Tribune,* May 10, 1961.

465 Vreeland "was a brilliant": A. G. Allen, quoted in Eleanor Dwight, *Diana Vreeland* (New York: William Morrow, 2002), p. 100.

465 "Carmel was much better": Transcript of interview with Nancy White. Calvin Tomkins Papers. The Museum of Modern Art Archives, New York.

465 Vreeland's subsequent claims: Diana Vreeland, *DV*, edited by George Plimpton and Christopher Hemphill (New York: Da Capo Press, 1997), p. 144.

466 "thrilled to death": Memo from Nancy White to Carmel Snow, Jan. 16, 1948, Thomas Justin White Papers.

467 "a make-believe siren": *Harper's Bazaar,* June 1956.

467 Carmel acquired first serial rights: According to Gerald Clarke, *Capote: A Biography* (New York: Simon & Schuster, 1988), p. 307.

468 Without stopping to consult: According to Dorothy Wheelock Edson.

468 "besides hall, landings and offices": "Rockfleet," *Irish Tatler & Sketch,* May 1954.

471 "I walked into that little salon": Richard Avedon in Snow with Aswell, *The World of Carmel Snow,* p. 212.

472 "Life in general, and Parisian": Francis Steegmuller, *Cocteau: A Biography* (Boston: Little, Brown, 1970), p. 419.

473 "Palen, Carmel, and Brigid came": Letter from J. Appleton to C. Snow, Sept. 25, 1957. *Harper's* Collection. Harry Ransom Humanities Research Center, University of Texas at Austin.

473 And he'd found love: As described by Francine du Plessix Gray, "Prophets of Seduction," *The New Yorker,* Nov. 4, 1996.

473 a game of canasta: Charlotte Seeling, *Fashion: The Century of the Designer* (Cologne: Konemann, 2000), p. 264.

474 Carmel attended the funeral: As described in Marie-France Pochna, *Christian Dior: The Man Who Made the World Look New,* trans. Joanna Savill (New York: Arcade Publishing, 1996).

474 "Triumph became a habit": "Homage to Dior," *Harper's Bazaar,* Dec. 1957, p. 130.

474 "a sneaky inquiry": Letter from J. Appleton to Carmel Snow, Sept. 25, 1957. *Harper's* Collection. Harry Ransom Humanities Research Center, University of Texas at Austin.

474 "I could not possibly": Letter from Carmel Snow to J. Appleton, Oct. 1, 1957. *Harper's* Collection. Harry Ransom Humanities Research Center, University of Texas at Austin.

475 "Dick Berlin was the one": Transcript of interview with Thornton Wilson. Calvin Tomkins Papers. Museum of Modern Art Archives, New York.

476 "high fashion's highest priestess": "The Press. White for Snow," *Time,* Dec. 16, 1957.

476 "partly due to management changes": Andy Grundberg, *Brodovitch* (New York: Abrams, 1989), p. 138.

476 "Mrs. Snow had been the protector": Clarke, *Capote: A Biography,* p. 308.

477 "She came back with the news": According to Eleanor Perényi.

477 "They all were reading": Clarke, *Capote: A Biography,* p. 308.

478 "I'm not angry, I'm outraged": "Newsmakers," *Newsweek,* June 2, 1958, p. 44.

478 "the famed jeweler even": Clarke, *Capote: A Biography,* p. 313.

478 "We needed an artist": Dwight, *Diana Vreeland,* p. 100.

480 "some nervous feeling:" Letter from Janet Flanner to Mary Louise Aswell, June 27, 1961. Private collection.

480 "sometimes distressing memories": Ibid.

480 "even more than Edna Woolman Chase": Memo from "HR" to "BWK" (Blanche Knopf), Jan. 28, 1958. Alfred A. Knopf Collection, Harry Ransom Humanities Research Center, University of Texas in Austin.

480 Knopf refined her vision: Letter from Blanche Knopf to Carmel Snow, Jan. 31, 1958. Alfred A. Knopf Collection. Harry Ransom Humanities Research Center, University of Texas at Austin.

481 she informed John Appleton: Letter from C. Snow to J. Appleton, March 27, 1958. *Harper's* Collection. Harry Ransom Humanities Research Center, University of Texas at Austin.

481 she'd accepted another offer: Letter from C. Snow to B. Knopf, March 25, 1958. Alfred A. Knopf

Collection. Harry Ransom Humanities Research Center, University of Texas at Austin.

481 "a whole different entity": Transcript of interview with A.G. Allen. Calvin Tomkins Papers. The Museum of Modern Art Archives, New York.

482 firing off memos: As described by Lillian Bassman.

482 "The Bazaar was heaven": Louise Dahl-Wolfe, *A Photographer's Scrapbook* (New York: St. Martin's/Marek, 1984), p. 145.

16. into the irish mist

483 thirteen of the house's fireplaces: According to Rossyvera's owner, Ambassador Walter Curley; Carmel Snow, in her memoir, gives the number as 14 (p. 190).

485 parties at Sybil Connolly's: According to W. Curley.

485 a rat jumped: Recounted by Gwen Franklin.

486 leaving her daughter to fear: Transcript of interview with Carmel Fromson. Calvin Tomkins Papers. Museum of Modern Art Archives, New York.

17. lighter than air

489 "For ten weeks or more": Letter from Carmel Snow to Blanche Knopf, June 29, 1959. Alfred A. Knopf Collection. Harry Ransom Humanities Research Center, University of Texas at Austin.

490 "Social Register types": Transcript of interview with Thornton Wilson. Calvin Tomkins Papers. Museum of Modern Art Archives, New York.

491 "No longer was she seated": Letter from Truman Capote to Mary Louise Aswell, in Truman Capote, *Too Brief a Treat: The Letters of Truman Capote,* edited by Gerald Clarke (New York: Random House, 2004), p. 319.

492 Hurok, who had represented: "Editor's Guest Book," *Harper's Bazaar,* Nov. 1956.

493 "Many observers have felt": "St. Laurent Brings Suit Against Dior," *The New York Times,* May 10, 1961, p. 51.

494 Elizabeth Arden hired her: Lindy Woodhead, *War Paint: Madame Helena Rubinstein and Miss Elizabeth Arden: Their Lives, Their Times, Their Rivalry* (Hobooken, N.J.: John Wiley, 2003), p. 389; E. Sheppard, "They Remember Carmel," *New York Herald Tribune,* May 9, 1961, p. 31.

494 "When she no longer": Mary Louise Aswell, in Carmel Snow with Mary Louise Aswell, *The World of Carmel Snow* (New York: McGraw-Hill, 1962), p. 212.

494 "Everything she ever said": Transcript of interview with Nancy White. Calvin Tomkins Papers. Museum of Modern Art Archives, New York.

494 people paid homage: As described in Snow with Aswell, *The World of Carmel Snow,* pp. 192–95.

495 Christine came from Louisiana: According to her niece, Julie Groupp.

495 "The day she left New York": Mary Louise Aswell in Snow with Aswell, *The World of Carmel Snow,* p. 212.

496 Carmel approached a novelist friend: Letter from Nancy Wilson-Ross to Carmel Wilson, May 20, 1961. The Nancy Wilson-Ross Collection. Harry Ransom Humanities Research Center, University of Texas at Austin.

497 "I guess Mrs. Snow will actually": D. Russell to B. Knopf, Feb. 7, 1961. Alfred A. Knopf Collection, Harry Ransom Humanities Research Center, University of Texas at Austin.

497 "offered a fat contract": Memo from J. B. Jones to B. Knopf, May 9, 1961. Alfred A. Knopf Collection, Harry Ransom Humanities Research Center, University of Texas at Austin.

497 "My advice is: enjoy this little junket": Letter from T. Capote to Mary Louise Aswell, March 2, 1961, in Capote, *Too Brief a Treat,* p. 312.

498 "when Carmel summoned us": Mary Louise Aswell in Snow with Aswell, *The World of Carmel Snow,* p. 206.

498 "She was in good spirits": C. Wilson in Snow with Aswell, *The World of Carmel Snow,* p. 199.

498 "She thought Carmel was still sleeping": C. Holbrook in Snow with Aswell, *The World of Carmel Snow,* p. 199.

499 "I feel a mixture of awe and relief": Undated letter from Janet Flanner to C. Wilson, in Snow

with Aswell, *The World of Carmel Snow,* p. 199.

499 "had a lot of input": Transcript of interview with Carrie Donovan. Calvin Tomkins Papers. Museum of Modern Art Archives, New York.

499 "Mrs. Snow, who was chairman": "Carmel Snow, Editor, Dies at 73; Headed Harper's Bazaar Board," *The New York Times,* May 9, 1961, p. 39.

500 "I felt it should lead": Transcript of interview with Carrie Donovan. Calvin Tomkins Papers. Museum of Modern Art Archives, New York.

500 "It was a life devoted to quality": Transcript of interview with Richard Avedon. Calvin Tomkins Papers. Museum of Modern Art Archives, New York.

500 "She had a sense of literature": *New York Journal American,* May 9, 1961.

501 "After the death of Carmel Snow": Museum Ludwig Cologne, *Photography of the 20th Century* (Cologne: Taschen, 2001), p. 35.

501 "I say a prayer": Carmel Snow in Snow with Aswell, *The World of Carmel Snow,* p. 200.

501 "They Remember Carmel": E. Sheppard, "They Remember Carmel," *New York Herald Tribune,* May 10, 1961.

502 The Snow family had requested: Mary Louise Aswell in Snow with Aswell, *The World of Carmel Snow,* p. 201.

502 In her will: Will of Carmel Snow, Surrogate's Court, County of New York, June 3, 1958.

503 Later, in Paris, another ceremony: described to the author by Kate White.

18. carmel lives

505 "What I'd like to write": Letter from Truman Capote to Mary Louise Aswell, June 6, 1961, in Capote, *Too Brief a Treat: The Letters of Truman Capote,* edited by Gerald Clarke (New York: Random House, 2004), p. 319.

505 "It would be a reflective pleasure": As told by Nancy White to J. Esten.

505 "she was sure she would have": Recounted by Janet Flanner in her letter to Mary Louise Aswell of June 27, 1961. Private collection.

506 "I was quite disappointed": Ibid.

506 Palen married: "George P. Snow Weds Mrs. Carol K. Morgan," *The New York Times,* Jan. 25, 1962.

507 was heavily involved: Letter from C. Wilson to Mrs. Stanley Young (Nancy Wilson-Ross), Oct. 22, 1961. Nancy Wilson-Ross Collection, Harry Ransom Humanities Research Center, University of Texas at Austin.

507 "Mary-Louise [Bousquet] thinks Balenciaga": Letter from Janet Flanner to Mary Louise Aswell, June 27, 1961. Private collection.

508 "Bless you for all you": Ibid.

508 "the book didn't have": Transcript of interview with Carmel Fromson. Calvin Tomkins Papers, Museum of Modern Art Archives, New York.

509 checked into Wards Island: Kerry William Purcell, *Alexey Brodovitch* (London: Phaidon Press, 2002), p. 248.

509 feelers for new employment: According to correspondence in the Diana Vreeland Papers, Manuscripts and Archives Division, New York Public Library, Astor, Lenox and Tilden Foundations.

510 "It's because Vreeland lasted": Transcript of interview with Richard Avedon. Calvin Tomkins Papers, Museum of Modern Art Archives, New York

510 "Condé would have been": Clare Boothe Luce, interview with Caroline Seebohm, Jan. 1980. Caroline Seebohm Papers.

bibliography

Agins, Teri. *The End of Fashion: The Mass Marketing of the Clothing Business.* New York: Morrow, 1999.

Alexey Brodovitch and His Influence. Washington, D.C.: Philadelphia College of Art/Smithsonian Institution, 1972.

Amory, Cleveland, and Frederic Bradlee, eds. *Vanity Fair: Selections from America's Most Memorable Magazine.* New York: Viking Press, 1960.

Arnaud, Claude. *Jean Cocteau.* Paris: Gallimard, 2003.

Assouline, Pierre. *Henri Cartier-Bresson: L'oeil du siècle.* Paris: Plon, 1999.

Avedon, Richard. *An Autobiography.* New York: Random House, 1993.

———. *Evidence, 1944–1994.* Edited by Mary Shanahan. New York: Random House, Eastman Kodak Professional Imaging in association with the Whitney Museum of American Art, 1994.

———. *Avedon—Photographs 1947–1977.* New York: Farrar, Straus and Giroux, 1978.

———. *Richard Avedon Portraits.* New York: Abrams/Metropolitan Museum of Art, 2002.

———, and Truman Capote. *Observations.* New York: Simon & Schuster, 1959.

———, and Judith Thurman. *Richard Avedon: Made in France.* San Francisco: Fraenkel Gallery, 2001.

Bacall, Lauren. *Lauren Bacall: By Myself.* New York: Knopf, 1978.

Baldwin, Neil. *Man Ray, American Artist.* New York: Clarkson N. Potter, 1988.

Ballard, Bettina. *In My Fashion.* New York: David McKay, 1960.

Balmain, Pierre. *My Years and Seasons.* London: Cassell, 1964.

Bancroft, Hubert Howe. *The Book of the Fair: An Historical and descriptive Presentation of the World's Science, Art, & Industry as Viewed Through the Columbian Exposition at Chicago in 1893.* Chicago and San Francisco: The Bancroft Company, 1893.

Baudot, François. *La Mode du siècle.* Paris: Assóuline, 1999.

Barillé, Elisabeth. *Lanvin: Mémoire de la mode.* Paris: Assouline, 1997.

Bassman, Lillian. *Photographs by Lillian Bassman.* Boston: Little, Brown, 1997.

Beaton, Cecil. *Cecil Beaton: Memoirs of the 40s.* New York: McGraw-Hill, 1972.

———. *The Glass of Fashion.* Garden City, N.Y.: Doubleday, 1954.

———. *Self-portrait with Friends: The Selected Diaries of Cecil Beaton, 1926–1974.* Edited by Richard Buckle. London: Weidenfeld and Nicolson, 1979.

———. *The Wandering Years: Diaries: 1922–1939.* Boston: Little, Brown, 1962.

Benaïm, Laurence. *Yves Saint Laurent.* Paris: Bernard Grasset, 1993.

Bertin, Celia. *Haute couture, terre inconnue.* Paris: Hachette, 1956.

Bettina. *Bettina par Bettina.* Paris: Flammarion, 1964.

Blass, Bill. *Bare Blass.* Edited by Cathy Horyn. New York: HarperCollins, 2002.

Blum, Dilys E. *Shocking! The Art and Fashion of Elsa Schiaparelli.* Philadelphia: Philadelphia Museum of Art, 2003.

Blum, Stella, ed. *Designs by Erté, Fashion Drawings and Illustrations from Harper's Bazar.* New York: Dover, 1976.

Blumenfeld, Erwin. *Eye to I: The Autobiography of a Photographer.* Translated by Mike Mitchell and Brian Murdoch. London: Thames & Hudson, 1999.

Bockris, Victor. *Warhol: The Biography.* New York: Da Capo Press, 2003.

Bony, Anne. *Les Années 50 d'Anne Bony.* Paris: Editions du Regard, 1982.

Bourke, Angela. *Maeve Brennan: Homesick at The New Yorker.* New York: Basic Books, 2004.

Brandau, Robert, ed. *De Meyer.* New York: Knopf, 1976.

Brooks, John. *Once in Golconda: A True Drama of Wall Street, 1920–1938.* New York: Wiley, 1999.

Brubach, Holly. *A Dedicated Follower of Fashion.* London: Phaidon, 1999.

Bunker, George R. *Alexey Brodovitch and His Influence.* Washington, D.C: Philadelphia College of Art/Smithsonian Institution, 1972.

Capote, Truman. *Breakfast at Tiffany's: A Short Novel and Three Stories.* New York: Random House, 1958.

———. *The Complete Stories of Truman Capote.* New York: Random House, 2004.

———. *Too Brief a Treat: The Letters of Truman Capote.* Edited by Gerald Clarke. New York: Random House, 2004.

Carter, Ernestine. *Magic Names of Fashion.* London: Weidenfeld and Nicolson, 1980.

———. *With Tongue in Chic.* London: Michael Joseph, 1974.

Casadio, Mariuccia. *Emilio Pucci: Mémoire de la Mode.* Paris: Assouline, 1998.

Charles-Roux, Edmonde. *Chanel and Her World.* New York: Vendome Press, 1981.

Chase, Edna Woolman, and Ilka Chase. *Always in Vogue.* Garden City, N.Y.: Doubleday, 1954.

Chase, Ilka. *Past Imperfect.* Garden City, N.Y.: Doubleday, Doran, 1942.

Clarke, Gerald. *Capote: A Biography.* New York: Simon & Schuster, 1988.

Cocteau, Jean. *Portraits-Souvenir, 1900–1914.* Paris: Bernard Grasset, 1935.

Colacello, Bob. *Holy Terror: Andy Warhol Close Up.* New York: HarperCollins, 1990.

Collins, Larry, and Dominique Lapierre. *Is Paris Burning?* New York: Simon & Schuster, 1965.

Corbett, Patricia. *Verdura: The Life and Work of a Master Jeweler.* New York: Abrams, 2002.

Dahl-Wolfe, Louise. *A Photographer's Scrapbook.* New York: St. Martin's/Marek, 1984.

Daves, Jessica. *Ready-made Miracle: The American Story of Fashion for the Millions.* New York: G. P. Putnam Sons, 1967.

Dear, I.C.B., ed. *The Oxford Companion to World War II.* Oxford and New York: Oxford University Press, 1995.

Delay, Claude. *Chanel Solitaire.* Paris: Gallimard, 1983.

Derrick, Robin, and Robin Muir, eds. *Unseen Vogue: The Secret History of Fashion Photography.* London: Little, Brown, 2002.

Dictionnaire de la mode au XXème siècle. Paris: Editions du Regard, 1994.

Dior, Christian. *Christian Dior et Moi.* Paris: Bibliothèque Amiot-Dumont, 1956.

———. *Talking About Fashion* Translated by Eugenia Sheppard. New York: G. P. Putnam's Sons, 1954.

Dwight, Eleanor. *Diana Vreeland.* New York: William Morrow, 2002.

de l'Ecotais, Emmanuelle. *Man Ray, 1890–1976.* Cologne: Taschen, 2001.

Epstein, Beryl Williams. *Fashion Is Our Business.* Philadelphia: Lippincott, 1945.

Erté. *Designs by Erté: Fashion Drawings and Illustrations from Harper's Bazar.* New York: Dover, 1976.

———. *Oeuvre Graphique Complète.* Paris: Albin Michel, 1992.

———. *Things I Remember: An Autobiography.* New York: Quadrangle, 1975.

Esten, John. *Diana Vreeland: Bazaar Years.* New York: Universe, 2001.

———. *Man Ray: Bazaar Years.* New York: Rizzoli, 1988.

Ewing, Elizabeth. *History of 20th Century Fashion.* New York: Scribner's, 1974.

Ewing, William. *Eye for Elegance: George Hoyningen-Huene.* New York: International Center of Photography/Congreve Publishing, 1980.

Fairchild, John. *Chic Savages.* New York: Simon & Schuster, 1989.

Flanner, Janet. *Paris Journal, 1944–1965*. New York: Atheneum, 1965.

———. *Paris Was Yesterday, 1925–1939*. New York: Viking Press, 1972.

Fraser, Kennedy. *The Fashionable Mind: Reflections on Fashion, 1970–1981*. New York: Knopf, 1981.

Frissell, Toni. *Toni Frissell Photographs 1933–1967*. New York: Doubleday, 1994.

Foster, R.F. *Modern Ireland, 1600–1972*. London: Penguin, 1988.

Frommer, Myrna Katz, and Harvey Frommer, eds. *It Happened in Manhattan: An Oral History of Life in the City During the Mid-Twentieth Century*. New York: Berkley Books, 2001.

Giroud, Françoise. *Les Années Elle, 1945–2000*. Paris: Filipacchi, 2000.

———. *Dior: Christian Dior, 1905–1957*. Translated by Stewart Spencer. New York: Rizzoli, 1987.

Givner, Joan. *Katherine Anne Porter: A Life*. New York: Simon & Schuster, 1982.

Goldberg, Vicki, and Nan Richardson. *Louise Dahl-Wolfe*. New York: Abrams, 2000.

Gray, Francine du Plessix. *Them: A Memoir of Parents*. New York: Penguin Press, 2005.

Gross, Michael. *Model: The Ugly Business of Beautiful Women*. New York: William Morrow, 1995.

Grundberg, Andy. *Brodovitch*. New York: Abrams, 1989.

Hackett, Pat, ed. *Andy Warhol Diaries*. New York: Warner Books, 1989.

Hall, Carolyn. *The Thirties in Vogue*. New York: Harmony Books, 1985.

———. *The Twenties in Vogue*. New York: Harmony Books. 1983.

Hartshorn, Willis, and Merry Foresta. *Man Ray: In Fashion*. New York: International Center of Photography, 1990.

Hawes, Elizabeth. *Fashion Is Spinach*. New York: Grossett & Dunlap, 1940.

———. *It's Still Spinach*. Boston: Little, Brown, 1954.

———. *Why Is a Dress?* New York: Viking Press, 1942.

Hommage à Balenciaga. Lyon: Musée historique des tissus, 1985.

Hommage à Christian Dior, 1947–1957. Paris: Musée des arts et du Textile de la mode, 1987.

Hoyningen-Huene, George. Oral history (unpublished). Los Angeles: Oral History Program, University of California at Los Angeles, 1967.

Jenkins, Roy. *Gladstone*. London: Macmillan, 1995.

Jouve, Marie-Andrée. *Cristóbal Balenciaga*. Paris: Editions du Regard, 1988.

———. *Balenciaga*. New York: Vendome Universe, 1997.

Kazanjian, Dodie, and Calvin Tomkins. *Alex: The Life of Alexander Liberman*. New York: Knopf, 1993.

Kazmaier, Martin. *Horst: Sixty Years of Photography*. New York: Rizzoli, 1991.

Keith, Slim, with Annette Tapert. *Slim: Memories of a Rich and Imperfect Life*. New York: Simon & Schuster, 1990.

Kirke, Betty. *Madeleine Vionnet*. San Francisco: Chronicle Books, 1998.

Kochno, Boris, with Jean Clair. *Christian Bérard*. Paris: Herscher, 1987.

Kornbluth, Jesse. *Pre-pop Warhol*. New York: Panache Press at Random House, 1988.

Lahr, John, ed. *The Diaries of Kenneth Tynan*. London: Bloomsbury, 2001.

Lambert, Eleanor. *World of Fashion: People, Places, Resources*. New York: R. R. Bowker Company, 1976.

Lawford, Valentine. *Horst: His Work and His World*. New York: Knopf, 1984.

Leigh, Dorian, with Laura Hobe. *The Girl Who Had Everything: The Story of the "Fire and Ice" Girl*. Garden City, N.Y.: Doubleday, 1980.

Lewis, Alfred Allan, and Constance Woodworth. *Miss Elizabeth Arden: An Unretouched Portrait*. New York: Coward, McCann & Geoghegan, 1972.

Liaut, Jean-Noël. *Hubert de Givenchy: Entre vies et légendes*. Paris: Bernard Grasset, 2000.

Liddell Hart, B. H. *History of the Second World War*. New York: G. P. Putnam's Sons, 1971.

Lurie, Alison. *The Language of Clothes.* New York: Random House, 1981.

Lynam, Ruth, ed. *Couture: An Illustrated History of the Great Paris Designers and Their Creations.* Garden City, NY.: Doubleday, 1972.

Madsen, Axel. *Chanel: A Woman of Her Own.* New York: Holt, 1990.

Magnus, Philip. *Gladstone.* New York: Dutton, 1945.

Mansfield, Stephanie. *The Richest Girl in the World: The Extravagant Life and Fast Times of Doris Duke.* New York: Putnam, 1992.

de Marly, Diana. *Worth: Father of Haute Couture.* London: Elm Tree Books, 1980.

Marquand, Lilou. *Chanel m'a dit.* Paris: Editions Jean-Claude Lattès, 1990.

Martin, Ralph G. *Cissy: The Extraordinary Life of Eleanor Medill Patterson.* New York: Simon & Schuster, 1979.

Martin, Richard, and Harold Koda. *Christian Dior.* New York: Metropolitan Museum of Art, 1996.

———. *Diana Vreeland: Immoderate Style.* New York: Metropolitan Museum of Art, 1993.

McCardell, Claire. *What Shall I Wear? The What, Where, When and How Much of Fashion.* New York: Simon & Schuster, 1956.

Mellen, Joan. *Kay Boyle: Author of Herself.* New York: Farrar, Straus & Giroux, 1994.

de Meyer, Adolph. *A Singular Elegance: The Photographs of Baron Adolph de Meyer.* San Francisco: Chronicle Books/ International Center of Photography, 1994.

Millbank, Caroline Rennolds. *Couture: The Great Designers.* New York: Stewart, Tabori & Chang, 1985.

———. *New York Fashion: The Evolution of American Style.* New York: Abrams, 1989.

Mirabella, Grace, with Judith Warner. *In and Out of Vogue.* New York: Doubleday, 1995.

Mona Bismarck, Cristóbal Balenciaga, Cecil Beaton. Paris: Mona Bismarck Foundation, 1995.

El Mundo de Balenciaga. Catalogue of the Exposition in the Palaceo de Bibliotecas y Museos in Madrid: Producatoras Nacionales de fibras artificiales y sintéticas y la cámara de la moda Española, 1974.

La Musée Christian Dior. Paris: Gallimard-L'Oeil Magazine, 1997.

Museum Ludwig Cologne. *Photography of the 20th Century.* Cologne: Taschen, 2001.

Nasaw, David. *The Chief: The Life of William Randolph Hearst.* Boston: Houghton Mifflin, 2000.

New York Graphic Society. *Henri Cartier-Bresson, Photographer.* Boston: New York Graphic Society, 1979.

Niven, Penelope. *Steichen: A Biography.* New York: Clarkson N. Potter, 1997.

Nuridsany, Michel. *Andy Warhol.* Paris: Flammarion, 2001.

O'Brien, Flann. *The Dalkey Archive.* London: Flamingo, 1993.

O'Hara, Georgina. *The Encyclopedia of Fashion.* New York: Abrams, 1986.

Penrose, Antony. *The Lives of Lee Miller.* New York: Holt, Rinehart and Winston, 1985.

Pentland, Marjorie. *A Bonnie Fechter: The Life of Ishbel Marjoribanks, Marchioness of Aberdeen and Temair.* London: Batsford, 1952.

Plimpton, George. *Truman Capote.* New York: Doubleday, Nan A. Talese, 1997.

Pochna, Marie-France. *Christian Dior: The Man Who Made the World Look New.* Translated by Joanna Savill. New York: Arcade Publishing, 1996.

———. *Dior: Mémoires de la Mode.* Paris: Assouline, 1996.

Poiret, Paul. *En habillant l'époque.* Paris: Bernard Grasset, 1930.

Porter, Katherine Anne. *Letters of Katherine Anne Porter.* Edited by Isabel Bayley. New York: Atlantic Monthly Press, 1990.

Purcell, Kerry William. *Alexey Brodovitch.* London: Phaidon Press, 2002.

Rawsthorn, Alice. *Yves Saint Laurent.* London: HarperCollins, 1996.

Rorem, Ned. *Knowing When to Stop: A Memoir.* New York: Simon & Schuster, 1994.

———. *The Paris Diary and The New York Diary 1951–1961.* New York: Da Capo Press, 1998.

———. *Setting the Tone: Essays and a Diary.* New York: Coward-McCann, 1983.

Rosenblum, Naomi. *A History of Women Photographers.* New York: Abbeville Press, 1994.

Schiaparelli, Elsa. *Shocking Life.* New York: Dutton, 1954.

Seebohm, Caroline. *The Man Who Was Vogue: The Life and Times of Condé Nast.* New York: Viking Press, 1982.

Seeling, Charlotte. *Fashion: The Century of the Designer.* Cologne: Konemann, 2000.

Shellard, Dominic. *Kenneth Tynan: A Life.* New Haven, Conn.: Yale University Press, 2003.

Snow, Carmel, with Mary Louise Aswell. *The World of Carmel Snow.* New York: McGraw-Hill, 1962.

Steegmuller, Francis. *Cocteau: A Biography.* Boston: Little, Brown, 1970.

Steele, Valerie. *Fashion, Italian Style.* New Haven, Conn.: Yale University Press, 2003.

———. *Paris Fashion: A Cultural History.* New York: Oxford University Press, 1988.

———. *Women of Fashion: Twentieth Century Designers.* New York: Rizzoli, 1991.

Stegemeyer, Anne. *Who's Who in Fashion.* 3rd ed. New York: Fairchild, 1996.

Steichen, Edward. *A Life in Photography.* Garden City, N.Y.: Doubleday, 1963.

Stokesbury, James L. *A Short History of World War II.* New York: Morrow, 1980.

Swanberg, W. A. *Citizen Hearst: A Biography of William Randolph Hearst.* New York: Galahad Books, 1996.

Szarkowski, John. *Irving Penn.* New York: Museum of Modern Art, 1984.

Thomas, Ann. *Lisette Model.* Ottawa: National Gallery of Canada, 1990.

Thornton, Willis. *The Liberation of Paris.* New York: Harcourt, Brace & World, 1962.

Thurber, James. *The Years with Ross.* Boston: Little, Brown, 1959.

Tippins, Sherill. *February House.* Boston: Houghton Mifflin, 2005.

Trahey, Jane, ed. *Harper's Bazaar: 100 Years of the American Female.* New York: Random House, 1967.

Tynan, Kenneth. *Kenneth Tynan Letters*, edited by Kathleen Tynan. New York: Random House, 1998.

Tynan, Kathleen. *The Life of Kenneth Tynan.* London: Weidenfeld and Nicolson, 1987.

Vickers, Hugo. *Cecil Beaton: The Authorized Biography.* London: Weidenfeld and Nicolson, 1985.

Vreeland, Diana. *DV.* Edited by George Plimpton and Christopher Hemphill. New York: Da Capo, 1997.

Weitzenhoffer, Frances. *The Havemeyers: Impressionism Comes to America.* New York: Abrams, 1986.

Whelan, Richard. *Alfred Stieglitz: A Biography.* Boston: Little, Brown, 1995.

White, Nancy, and John Esten. *Style in Motion: Munkacsi Photographs of the '20s, '30s, and '40s.* New York: Clarkson N. Potter, 1979.

White, Palmer. *Elsa Schiaparelli: Empress of Paris Fashion.* New York: Rizzoli, 1986.

———. *Poiret.* New York: Clarkson N. Potter, 1973.

Woodhead, Lindy. *War Paint: Madame Helena Rubinstein and Miss Elizabeth Arden: Their Lives, Their Times, Their Rivalry.* Hoboken, N.J.: John Wiley 2003.

The World in Vogue. Compiled by the Viking Press and *Vogue.* New York: Viking Press, 1963.

Yoxall, H. W. *A Fashion of Life.* New York: Taplinger, 1966.

index

Photo Credits

Endpapers by René Bouché, 1957, courtesy of Denise Bouché Fitch; page xii: Courtesy of *Harper's Bazaar;* page 2: Courtesy of the White family; page 3: Courtesy of the White family; page 4: Courtesy of the White family; page 11: Courtesy of the White family; page 23: Courtesy of the White family; page 24: Courtesy of the White family; page 27 (top): Mabel Meeker Edsall/Archives of the Arts Students League; page 27 (bottom) : Courtesy of the James Graham gallery; page 37: Courtesy of the White family; page 41: Courtesy of the White family; page 43: Courtesy of the White family; page 46: Courtesy of the White family; page 57: Leonard McCombe/Time & Life Pictures/Getty Images; page 65: Cecil Beaton Studio Archive, Sotheby's; page 70: Leonard McCombe/Time & Life Pictures/Getty Images; page 81: Louise Dahl-Wolfe © 1989 Center for Creative Photography, Arizona Board of Regents. Collection Center for Creative Photography, the University of Arizona; page 90: Courtesy of the White family; page 92: Carl Klein; page 97: Louise Dahl-Wolfe © 1989 Center for Creative Photography, Arizona Board of Regents. Collection Center for Creative Photography, the University of Arizona; page 109: Edward Steichen. Reprinted with permission of Joanna Steichen; page 112: George Karger/Time & Life Pictures/Getty Images; pages 113 and 125: photographer unknown; pages 158 and 159: Roger Schall; pages 171 and 173: © Joan Munkasci, courtesy Howard Greenberg Gallery; page 175: Roger Schall; pages 185 and 199: George Karger/Time & Life Pictures/Getty Images; page 203: Roger Schall; page 211: © Bettman/Corbis. George Hoynigen-Huene; page 215: Courtesy of *Harper's Bazaar;* page 233: Courtesy of Carmel Eitt; page 241: Paul Radkai; pages 246 and 247: Walter Sanders/Time & Life Pictures/Getty Images; page 249: Courtesy of *Harper's Bazaar;* page 261: Robert Doisneau; page 289: Courtesy of Dorothy Wheelock Edson; page 297: Courtesy of *Harper's Bazaar;* page 313: Roger Schall; page 327: Associated Press/Wide World Photos; pages 342-343: Philippe Halsman/Magnum Photos; page 347: Courtesy of Melanie Witt Miller; page 351: Toni Frissell/Library of Congress; page 357: Photograph by H. Erskine. Courtesy of Dorothy Wheelock Edson; page 367: © Association Willy Maywald/ADAGP, Paris/ARS, New York; page 372: The Anna-Maria and Stephen Kellen Archives Center of Parsons School of Design, New School University; pages 372 and 378: photographer unknown; page 381: Robert Doisneau; page 385: Henri Cartier-Bresson/Magnum Photos; pages 386–387, 388: Robert Doisneau; page 389: Louise Dahl-Wolfe/Courtesy of Staley-Wise Gallery; page 391: Toni Frissell/Library of Congress; page 393: Richard Avedon; page 400: Walter Sanders/Time & Life Pictures/Getty Images; page 402: Photograph by R. Falcke. Courtesy of Katie Delahaye Paine; page 403: Courtesy of *Harper's Bazaar;* page 406: Gleb Derujinsky; page 413: Toni Frissell/Library of Congress; pages 418 and 419: Courtesy of *Harper's Bazaar* © Sevenarts Ltd.; page 426: David Lees/Time & Life Pictures/Getty Images; page 437: Courtesy of Melanie Witt Miller; page 449: Walter Sanders/Time & Life Pictures/Getty Images; page 450: Toni Frissell/Library of Congress; page 452 Feliks Topolski; page 453: © Association Willy Maywald/ADAGP, Paris/ARS, New York; page 455: Courtesy of Ann Murphy Vose; page: 458 (left and center): photographer unknown. Courtesy of Dorothy Wheelock Edson, page 458 (right): Cecil Beaton Studio Archive, Sotheby's; page 459: David Seymour / Magnum Photos; page 466: Margaret Bourke-White/Time & Life Pictures/Getty Images; page 469: Penelope Rowlands; page 477: Random House; pages 489 and 491: Toni Frissell/Library of Congress; page 496: Louise Dahl-Wolfe © 1989 Center for Creative Photography, Arizona Board of Regents. Collection Center for Creative Photography, the University of Arizona; page 503: Louise Dahl-Wolfe / Courtesy of Staley-Wise Gallery.

Permissions

Every effort has been made to trace the ownership of all copyrighted material. Please notify the publisher of any inadvertent omissions, which will be corrected in a subsequent edition.

The author gratefully acknowledges the following for generously giving permission to quote from copyrighted material.

Lauren Bacall for *Lauren Bacall: By Myself.*

The Condé Nast Corporation for the December, 1932, correspondence between Condé Nast and Carmel Snow. Nast and Snow Letters © The Condé Nast Publications Inc.

Dr. Mary Aswell Doll for *The World of Carmel Snow* by Carmel Snow with Mary Louise Aswell.

Doubleday, a division of Random House, Inc., for *Always in Vogue* by Ilka Chase and Edna Woolman Chase ©1954 by Edna Woolman Chase and Ilka Chase; *A Life in Photography* by Edward Steichen ©1963 by Edward Steichen; *In and Out of Vogue* by Grace Mirabella with Judith Warner © 1995 by Grace Mirabella; and *The Girl Who Had Everything: The Story of the "Fire and Ice" Girl* by Dorian Leigh, with Laura Hobe © 1980 by Dorian Parker.

Special Collections department of the Gladys Marcus Library of the Fashion Institute of Technology, New York, for the oral histories of Eleanor Lambert and Bernardine Morris.

Brigid S. Flanigan for the correspondence of Carmel Snow.

Harold Ober Associates, Inc. for S. J. Perelman's "Frou-Frou, or the Future of Vertigo," *The New Yorker,* April 16, 1938, and "Scrub Me, Daddy, Eight to the Bar," *The New Yorker* June 28, 1941.

HarperCollins Publishers Inc. for *Diana Vreeland* by Eleanor Dwight, copyright © 2002 by Eleanor Dwight.

The Houghton Mifflin Company for *The Chief: The Life of William Randolph Hearst* by David Nasaw. Copyright © 2000 by David Nasaw. All rights reserved.

Mrs. William Murray, Trustee of the estate of Janet Flanner, for Flanner's *Paris Journal* and *Paris Was Yesterday.*

The New York Times for Carmel Snow's obituary. Copyright © 1961 by The New York Times Co. Reprinted with Permission.

Seton O'Reilly for Bettina Ballard's *In My Fashion.*

Phaidon Press for *Alexey Brodovitch,* copyright © 2002 Phaidon Press.

Anatole Pohorilenko for correspondence of Glenway Westcott.

The Estate of Katherine Anne Porter, Barbara Davis, Trustee, for the letters of Katherine Anne Porter.

Caroline Seebohm for *The Man Who Was Vogue,* Viking Press © 1982 Caroline Seebohm.

Simon & Schuster Adult Publishing Group for *Capote: A Biography* by Gerald Clarke. Copyright © 1988 by Gerald Clarke.

Sll/Sterling Lord Literistic, Inc., for *Cissy*, by Ralph G. Martin. Copyright © 1979 by Ralph G. Martin.

Thames & Hudson Ltd and Yorick Blumenfeld for *Eye to I: The Autobiography of a Photographer* by Erwin Blumenfeld, Translated by Mike Mitchell and Brian Murdoch. © 1999 Thames & Hudson Ltd, London.

Calvin Tomkins for "The World of Carmel Snow," by Calvin Tomkins, *The New Yorker,* November 7, 1994.

The Truman Capote Literary Trust, Alan Schwartz, Trustee, for the letters of Truman Capote.

Hugo Vickers for the works of Cecil Beaton: © The Literary Executors of the late Sir Cecil Beaton, 2005.

Jonathan Warburg for the March 28, 1937, telegram from C. Nast to W. R. Hearst.

John Michael White for Thomas White's letters.